*An Ecological Perspective on
Human Communication Theory*

An Ecological Perspective on Human Communication Theory

Jo Liska
University of Colorado, Denver

Gary Cronkhite
Indiana University, Bloomington

Harcourt Brace College Publishers

Fort Worth   Philadelphia   San Diego   New York   Orlando   Austin   San Antonio
Toronto   London   Sydney   Tokyo

Publisher: Ted Buchholz
Acquisitions Editor: Carol Wada
Developmental Editor: Laurie Runion
Production Manager: Debra A. Jenkin
Cover Designer: Peggy Young
Editorial & Production Services: Michael Bass & Associates
Text Designer: Nancy Benedict
Cover Image: © Telegraph Colour Library/FPG International

Copyright © 1995 by Harcourt Brace & Company

All rights reserved. No part of this publication may be reproduced or transmitted in any form or by any means, electronic or mechanical, including photocopy, recording, or any information storage and retrieval system, without permission in writing from the publisher.

Requests for permission to make copies of any part of the work should be mailed to: Permissions Department, Harcourt Brace & Company, 6277 Sea Harbor Drive, Orlando, Florida 32887-6777

Copyrights and Acknowledgments appear on page 443, and constitutes a continuation of the copyright page.

Photo Credits: Dedication: © Anne Whitfield; Unit 1: © George Holton/Photo Researchers; Chapter 1: © David Ryan/D. Donne Bryant Stock; Chapter 2: © Margot Granitsas/The Image Works, Inc.; Chapter 3: © Will McIntyre/Photo Researchers; Unit 2: © Jo Liska; Chapter 4: © Gary Cronkhite; Chapter 5: © Roberto Soncin Gerometta/Impact Images; Unit 3: © UPI/Bettmann; Chapter 6: © Jo Liska; Chapter 7: © Jo Liska; Chapter 8: © Cathie Archbould; Chapter 9: © Jerry Schad/Photo Researchers; Unit 4: © Megan Biesele/Anthro-Photo; Chapter 10: © Jo Liska; Chapter 11: © Jo Liska; Chapter 12: © Jo Liska; Chapter 13: © Jo Liska; Chapter 14: © Jo Liska; Chapter 15: © Jo Liska.

Printed in the United States of America

Library of Congress Catalog Card Number: 94-18914

ISBN: 0-15-500271-6

4 5 6 7 8 9 0 1 2 3   016   9 8 7 6 5 4 3 2 1

*There is no knowing ourselves individually
until we know ourselves as a species.*

—Paul Shepard

I awakened with the realization that my time in the "wild" was too soon to end. In two days I would go, via bush plane, to Nairobi, and then by jet into the noise, clutter, and overly crowded classrooms I inhabited in the States. I sat up in my netted cocoon and listened for the calls of the lion that echoed in the silence of the dawn. I recalled my manic chase after the chattering vervet monkey who stole my only pair of shorts (I got them back), and listened for the sounds of their awakening. Then I remembered the vervets, and Tom and Jerry, the ravens, with whom I wrestled for my breakfast. They would be there to joust for the jams and sugar. Eagerly I dressed and rushed to breakfast.

That day I lingered in the haunts of the elephant's daily routine, listening and watching. With dusk approaching, I returned to my hut, and then wandered to the river to once again watch the evening ritual of the crocs harrassing the storks.

Lost in thought, the crack of a twig snapped me back to attention. I turned to see elephants and baboons moving through the brush by the river. Quietly watching me, the elephants wound their way into the edge of darkness. Several baboons ascended the low stone wall on which I sat, a big male closest to me. For several moments we sat gazing into the distance, and then they too moved on. I watched as their dark forms became distant shadows, and then, swallowed by the night, all that remained were their ghostly forms etched forever in my memory—shadows of a distant ancestor we shared.

It is to those who went before—those distant shadows—that we dedicate this book. Gone but not forgotten.

Contents

Preface xxi

To the Student xxv

UNIT 1   *Ecology of Communication: Past, Present, and Future*   1

The first human being who hurled an insult instead of a stone was the founder of civilization.
                —attributed to Sigmund Freud

Chapter 1   *A Rationale for an Ecological Perspective on Communication*   3

COMMUNICATION AND ECOLOGY 4

     Physical Ecologies 4
     Sociocultural Ecologies 6
     Cognitive Ecologies 8
     The Interface between Cognition and Communication 10
     Human Effect on Ecologies 12

CONCLUSION 15

KEY TERMS 17

NOTES 17

REFERENCES 17

Chapter 2 *Communication and Survival* 21

WHAT IS COMMUNICATION? 21

    Signs: Symptoms, Semblances, and Symbols 22
    Intention vs. Nonintention 25
    Stages of Communication 26

WHAT ARE SOME FUNCTIONS OF COMMUNICATION? 27

    Information Gathering 27
    Facilitating Cooperation 29
    Enhancing or Reducing Competition and Conflict 30
    Self-Actualization 31
    Entertainment 33

WHAT IS THE ROLE OF COMMUNICATION IN HUMAN SURVIVAL? 33

HOW DO IDEAS EVOLVE? 35

    Communication and Survival 35
    Ideological Evolution 35

WHAT IS THE ROLE OF COMMUNICATION IN THE EVOLUTION OF IDEAS? 37

CONCLUSION 38

KEY TERMS 38

NOTES 38

REFERENCES 39

Chapter 3 *The Ghosts of Our Ancestors: The Development of Communication, from Tools to Television* 43

INTRODUCTION 43

IN THE BEGINNING 44

    From Dinosaurs to Primates 44
    Role of Sociality 45
    Primate Advantages 49

THE DAWN OF HUMANS 49

    Relation of Human and Nonhuman Primates 49

ROCK AND CAVE IMAGES 52

    Meanings and Significance of Rock and Cave Images 53
    Origins of Writing 54
    African vs. European Rock Art 54

THE DEVELOPMENT OF WRITING 55

    Early Forms of Writing 55
    Development of the Alphabet 57
    Development of Paper 58
    Mass Production of Print 58

THE COMPUTER AGE 61

EXTENSIONS OF OUR EYES AND EARS 63

    Radio 64
    Telephone 65
    Photography 65
    Television 66

CONCLUSION 69

KEY TERMS 70

NOTES 70

REFERENCES 71

Chapter 4   *Origins of Contemporary Communication Theory: A History*   75

MAPS, MODELS, AND THEORIES 76

    Maps 77
    Models 77
    Theories 77

THE CLASSICAL ERA 78

    Plato 79
    Aristotle 80
    Cicero 81
    Isocrates 82
    Sophists 82
    St. Augustine 83

THE MIDDLE AGES AND THE RENAISSANCE 4

    The Middle Ages 84
    The Renaissance 85

MODERN THEORY 85

CONTEMPORARY THEORY 87

    Rhetoric as Meaning 88
    Rhetoric as Value 88
    Rhetoric as Motive 89
    Rhetoric as a Way of Knowing 90

DEVELOPMENT OF COMMUNICATION THEORY 91

    Yale Studies 92
    Information Theory 92

DEVELOPMENT OF PERSPECTIVES ON COMMUNICATION THEORY 93

    Mechanistic Perspective 94
    Human Interaction Perspective 94
    Systems Perspective 95
    Semiotic Perspective 95

DEVELOPMENT OF APPROACHES TO STUDYING COMMUNICATION 95

CONCLUSION 97

KEY TERMS 97

NOTES 98

REFERENCES 98

UNIT 2   Social, Mental, and Ideological Ecologies   103

We both know what a successful relationship is built on: communication. Whatever the conflicts between two lovers (or for that matter, two neighbors or two nations), those tensions can be resolved with communication—open and honest sharing of opinions, experiences, and credit cards.

—Roger L. Welsh

Chapter 5   Communication and the Social Environment   105

SOCIAL PERCEPTION 106

Deriving Perceptual Criteria from Situations   106
Inferring Attributes from Observations of People   108

PERSONAL DIFFERENCES, EMPATHY, AND PROJECTION   116

An Analysis of *The Breakfast Club*   117
Empathy vs. Projection   117

PERSONALITY CHARACTERISTICS   119

Dogmatism   119
Machiavellianism   123
Self-Esteem and Communication Anxiety   124
Locus of Control   126
Androgyny and Sex-Role Stereotyping   127

CREDIBILITY AND REFERENCE GROUPS   132

Factor-Analytic Approach to Credibility   132
Functional Approach to Credibility   134
Reference Groups vs. Membership Groups   136

CONCLUSION   138

KEY TERMS   138

REFERENCES   139

Chapter 6   *The Ecology of Ideas: Opinion Formation and Change*   143

SOCIAL LEARNING   144

Classical Conditioning   144
Operant Conditioning   145
Conditioning of Opinions   146

EGO-MAINTENANCE   148

Value-Expression   149
Ego-Defense   151
Ego-Involvement   154

CONSISTENCY   158

Balancing Opinions of Others with Other Opinions   159
Let's Make the Best of It   160
Logical Thinking and Wishful Thinking   165
The Relationship of Beliefs and Attitudes   167

CONCLUSION   168

KEY TERMS 169

REFERENCES 169

Chapter 7   *The Ecology of Ideas: Cognitive Processing, Critical Thinking, and Social Influence*   175

A NETWORK OF ENTITIES AND RELATIONSHIPS: THE AESOP MODEL   177
     Entities and Relationships   178
     Relationships   178

TYPES OF RELATIONSHIPS   179

IMPORTANCE OF PLANS AND CONSEQUENCES OF AESOP   180
     Making Critical Choices   181

TYPES OF CONSEQUENCES,   182
     Decisional Balance Sheet   182

DECIDING WHAT PLANS WILL PRODUCE WHAT CONSEQUENCES   185
     Toulmin's Model of Argument   186
     Modified Toulmin Model: The AESOP Model   186
     Implications of the Decision-Making Model   187

BARRIERS TO CRITICAL DECISIONS   187
     Noncausal Reasoning   187
     Elaboration Likelihood: Central vs. Peripheral Processing   189
     Credibility   189
     Personality Characteristics   190
     Drama and Comedy   190

SOME SUGGESTIONS FOR THINKING CRITICALLY   194
     Some Common Fallacies   196

PERSUASION   199

COMPLIANCE STRATEGIES   203

CONCLUSION   207

KEY TERMS   207

REFERENCES   208

UNIT 3 Ecological Role of Messages   173

To have a mind is to have the capacity to acquire the ability to operate with symbols in such a way that it is one's own activity that makes them symbols and confers meaning upon them.

—A. J. P. Kenny and others,
The Development of Mind

Chapter 8   Theories of Language Meaning   213

LANGUAGE OPERATES BY RULES, NORMS, AND PRINCIPLES   213

　Language as a Game   213
　Rules   214
　Norms   214
　Principles   215
　Is It a Principle, or Is It a Rule?   216

LANGUAGE IS STUDIED AT FOUR LEVELS: PHONEMIC, SYNTACTIC, SEMANTIC, AND PRAGMATIC   217

　Phonemic Rules   217
　Syntactic Rules   218
　The Semantic and Pragmatic Levels   219

WHAT IS THE MEANING OF *MEANING*?   220

　Referential Theories   220
　Rule-Governed Theories   222
　Behavioral Theories   226
　Ideational and Cognitive Theories   227

CONCLUSION   231

KEY TERMS   231

REFERENCES   232

Chapter 9 Research on Language Effects 235

HOW DO DOUBLESPEAK, SEMANTIC REDEPLOYMENT, AND EUPHEMISMS POLLUTE OUR LANGUAGE? 236

Doublespeak 236
Semantic Redeployment 236
Euphemisms 238

SEXISM AND OTHER TYPES OF LINGUISTIC DISCRIMINATION 239

Generic Pronoun *He* 239
The Word *Man* 240
"Oh Stewardess—May I Have Another Cup of Coffee?" 240
Other Examples 241
Six Types of Linguistic Bias 241

DOMINANT LANGUAGE IS NOT JUST FOR MEN ANYMORE IS IT? 242

Women's Language 242
"Eat the Floor, Dogbreath" 243
Research Evidence on Women's Language 243

YOU TALK FUNNY: YOU MUST THINK FUNNY 244

Dialects 244
Effects of Dialect 245

HOW CAN LANGUAGE REGULATION BE POLITICAL REPRESSION? 249

English as Official Language 249
The Case of Quebec 250
English in Africa 250

HOW DOES LANGUAGE AFFECT PERCEPTION AND THOUGHT? 250

General Semantics 253

WHAT MAKES LANGUAGE PLEASING, INTENSE, OR OBSCENE? 255

Language Clarity 255
Figurative Language 256
Metaphors 256
Language that Pleases 257
Language Intensity 259
Obscenity 259

CONCLUSION 261

KEY TERMS 262

REFERENCES 262

Chapter 10 Functions of Nonverbal Communication in Social Relationships 265

ECOLOGICAL ANALYSIS 266

TYPES OF NONVERBAL SIGNS 267

OUR PRIMATE LINK: SENSORY AND NEURAL 268

　The Human Brain 269

FUNCTIONS AND OUTCOMES OF NONVERBAL BEHAVIOR 270

HOW DO ENVIRONMENTAL CHARACTERISTICS AFFECT OUR PERCEPTIONS? 272

　Early vs. Contemporary Human Environment 272
　The Modern Environment and Its Effects 274
　Time and Communication Behavior 276

WHAT DO OUR BODIES, FACES, AND EYES SAY ABOUT US? 278

　Body Type 278
　Clothing and Personal Effects 281
　Body Position, Posture, and Orientation 284
　Gestures 285
　Faces and Facial Expressions 286
　Eye Behavior and Gaze 290

WHAT DO OUR VOICES REVEAL ABOUT US? 293

　Judging Emotions for the Voice 293
　Voice Preferences 294
　Interpreting Vocal Characteristics 294
　How Voice Signals Status 295
　Meaning of Silence 295

WHAT IS THE SIGNIFICANCE OF TOUCH IN OUR SOCIAL RELATIONSHIPS? 295

　Harlow's Studies 295
　Lack of Touching and Early Development 296
　Functions of Touch 296
　When Are We Likely to Touch? 297
　Differences in Amount and Type of Touch 297

HOW DOES OUR USE OF SPACE AND TERRITORY AFFECT OUR SOCIAL RELATIONSHIPS? 298

　Territoriality 298
　Personal Space 299

CONCLUSION 300

KEY TERMS 300

REFERENCES 301

UNIT 4 Types of Communication Ecologies 309

The easiest kind of relationship for me is with ten thousand people. The hardest is with one.

—Joan Baez

Chapter 11 Interpersonal Relationships 311

FIRST IMPRESSIONS AND INITIAL INTERACTION 312
  Self-Perception 312
  Perception of Potential Partners 313
  Social Exchange, Predicted Outcome Value, and Reinforcement 315

RELATIONSHIP DEVELOPMENT 319
  Perception of the Relationship 319
  Content and Relational Dimensions of Conversation 320
  Equity Negotiation 320
  Reciprocal Self-Concept Support 321
  Stages of Developing and Stable Relationships 322

RELATIONAL EQUILIBRIUM 323
  Relational Intricacies 324

RELATIONAL DISSOLUTION 325
  Phases of Relational Dissolution 325

KEY TERMS 326

REFERENCES 327

Chapter 12 Groups and Organizations 329

GROUPS 330
  What Constitutes a Group? 330
  Why Do People Join Groups? 331
  How Do Groups Stay Together? 333
  How Are Groups Structured? 336

Contents xvii

What Influences Group Interaction? 338
What Is the Best Way to Resolve Group Conflict? 340

HOW DO GROUPS AND ORGANIZATIONS DIFFER? 342

HOW IS COMMUNICATION IN ORGANIZATIONS STRUCTURED? 343

Theory X vs. Theory Y 343
Networks 344
Formal Networks 344
Informal Networks 346
External Networks 347

CONCLUSION 347

KEY TERMS 348

REFERENCES 349

Chapter 13 Mediated Communication 353

FUNCTIONS OF MEDIA 354

Surveillance 354
Selection and Interpretation of Information 354
Cultural Transmission 355
Social Roles 356
Establishment of Personal Identity 356
Entertainment 357
Interpersonal Interaction 357
Uses and Gratifications 358

MEDIA EFFECTS 358

Diffusion of Innovations 359
Media-Effects Models 360
Televised Sex and Violence 361

MEDIA, REALITY, AND CENSORSHIP 363

Media Construction of Reality 363
Media as an Economic Force 364
Effects of Advertising 364
News as Entertainment 366

CONCLUSION 367

KEY TERMS 367

REFERENCES 367

Chapter 14 Communication and Culture 373

WHAT ARE SOME DIMENSIONS ON WHICH CULTURES DIFFER? 375
Individualism vs. Collectivism 376
High vs. Low Context 377

WHAT IS THE RELATIONSHIP BETWEEN CULTURE AND LANGUAGE? 379
Language and Perception 379
Honorifics, Titles, and Status 380

HOW DO LANGUAGE STYLES DIFFER ACROSS CULTURES? 381
Restricted vs. Elaborated Codes 381
Direct vs. Indirect Communication Styles 382
Elaborate, Exacting, and Succinct Communication Styles 384
Personal vs. Contextual Communication Styles 385
Instrumental and Affective Styles 386

WHAT ARE SOME CULTURAL DIFFERENCES IN NONVERBAL BEHAVIOR? 387
Ritual Behaviors 388
Posture 389
Vocal Characteristics 389
Back-Channeling 389
Personal Space 389
Subgroup Differences 390

WHAT BELIEFS AND VALUES DEFINE AMERICAN CULTURE? 392
Beliefs About the Physical World 392
Beliefs About Human Nature 393
Beliefs About the Supernatural 393
Values: Family, Friends, and Money 394

WHAT PROBLEMS MIGHT WE ENCOUNTER IN CROSS-CULTURAL EXCHANGES? 394
Conflicting Beliefs or Values 394
Ethnocentrism 395
Conflicting Priorities 395
Conflicting Cultural Assumptions 396
Conflicting Behavioral Expectations 397

CONCLUSION 397

KEY TERMS 398

NOTES 398

REFERENCES 398

Chapter 15   *Some Final Thoughts 403*

        ROLE OF COMMUNICATION IN FORGING HUMAN COMMUNITIES   403

        THE NATURAL WORLD VS. THE WORLD OF SYMBOLS   403

        CROSS-CULTURAL DIFFERENCES   404

        INTRACULTURAL DIFFERENCES   405

        PROBLEMS AND SOLUTIONS   405

        ETHICS   407

        KEY TERMS   409

        REFERENCES   409

Student Activities and Discussion Topics   *410*

Copyrights and Acknowledgments   *443*

Index   *444*

Preface

> *The use of nature as measure proposes an atonement between ourselves and our world, between economy and ecology, between domestic and the wild. Or it proposes a conscious and careful recognition of the interdependence between ourselves and nature that in fact has always existed and, if we are to live, must always exist.*
> —Wendell Berry, What Are People For?

ABOUT THE ECOLOGICAL PERSPECTIVE

The word "interdependence" provides a key concept that is a foundation to the perspective on communication adopted in this book. We believe that communication in the form of natural, iconic, and symbolic signs is the substance that binds humans together, creating an interdependent system of communities whose very survival depends upon the quality of their communication. It is also clear that humans are not merely interdependent with other humans, but also with the various ecologies they inhabit and with the other species with whom they share those ecologies. The nature and substance of these interdependencies, and the role of communication in weaving the fabric of human experience, constitutes the overall theme of this book.

The perspective we have taken expands the boundaries of the study of communication by providing insights into the biological foundations of communication. This is an area beginning to take hold in the discipline, but as yet largely unrepresented in available textbooks. We believe that awareness of the biological influences on communication will serve to enhance a more complete understanding of communication processes in general. More specifically, since humans, when compared to other species, appear to be unusual in their creation of and dependence upon symbolic communication, it is important to come to grips with the forces that laid the foundation for the emergence of such an unusual ability.

Because we believe that we cannot know where we are until we know where we have been, we have included considerable discussion of the development of symbolic communication, the history of communication technologies, and the history of the study of human communication. These areas receive only cursory attention in most available textbooks; yet, we consider this information essential to providing a broad perspective on communication and in facilitating understanding of the complex web of information that constitutes human experiences.

We have not limited discussion or definition of "ecology" to its more common usage meaning natural environments. In addition to nature humans also reside in sociocultural ecologies, cognitive ecologies, and symbolic ecologies, which ecologies are described in terms of their impact on human interaction. This approach emphasizes the interrelationships among these types of ecologies, the types of information of which those ecologies are constituted, and the role of messages in negotiating within and among those ecologies. We explain that ecologies are in a perpetual state of flux and that communication serves as a primary means by which we adapt to these changes.

We believe that the perspective adopted in this book reflects growing concern with the relationship of humans to their environment, exploration of the ways in which humans are unique, and examination of the role of communication in meeting the challenges of a changing world. We leave it to succeeding generations to meet those challenges using the adaptive device most characteristic of our species—communication. If they are to be successful, they need to be aware of the role of communication in creating, sustaining, and altering their physical, sociocultural, and mental environments. We hope the content of this book will facilitate such awareness.

ABOUT THE BOOK

We have aimed this book at students enrolled in their first course on communication theory. We do not presume any extensive methodological training. Because we presume that undergraduate students will be the primary audience, we attempted to write in a style that would grab and hold their attention, while providing a comprehensive description of theories and supporting data. The style is thus informal and personal, one which, in using drafts of the manuscript in our own courses, turned out to be successful. Our students reported considerable enthusiasm for the style. Reviewers of the manuscript concurred.

The book is divided into four units. Unit 1 begins with a general discussion of the ecology of communication, an overview of the development of communication and communication technologies, and ends with a historical analysis of the study of communication. Unit 2 focuses on communication and the social environment, the role of communication in the development of opinions and policies, and the role of communication in cognitive processing and critical thinking. Unit 3 examines the ecological role of messages as they are developed via language and nonverbal behavior. Unit 4 explores various type of communication ecologies including interpersonal relationships, groups and organizations, mediated communication, and culture. The ecological theme is used to tie together these various aspects of communication behavior.

To facilitate the development of students' ideas and understanding of concepts, we have provided a student manual at the end of the text. In that manual we provide ideas for papers and projects, questions for them to reflect upon, and problems for them to solve. We have also included suggested formats for various types of papers they might write to fulfill course requirements. To our knowledge, no other communication theory textbook includes a similar manual.

To further facilitate preparation for exams and integration of material, we have offered lists of key terms for each chapter. Our students report those as especially useful.

Finally, we have provided an instructor's manual containing an example syllabus, "objective" and essay exam items, annotated descriptions of videotapes and films illustrating various communication concepts, and suggestions for types of assignments students might complete. We have found that using videos and films provides common stimuli for discussion, facilitates discussion, and allows students to apply the communication principles they are learning. Some of the films and videos suggested provide information further elaborating content offered in the text. An instructor's manual can be obtained by contacting your local Harcourt Brace representative.

ACKNOWLEDGMENTS

While a number of people have been invaluable in offering thoughtful and useful suggestions for the book, we first thank our students for their candid assessments of this and other books. They were equally as ready to offer praise as criticism, and we appreciate their efforts and sensitivity. We thank Isabelle Bauman, University of Washington; Buford Crites, College of the Desert; William Cupach, Illinois State University; Vincent Hazleton, Radford University; Peter Marston, California State University–Northridge; C. David Mortensen, University of Wisconsin; and Shawn Spano, San Jose State University, who participated in reviewing the original idea and/or subsequent versions of the manuscript. We are grateful for their patience, thoughtful analysis, gentle criticism, and worthy suggestions for improvement. We extend a special note of thanks to our editor, Laurie Runion, and to Debbie Frank, project editor, for their support, gentle nudges, and careful attention to detail.

To The Student

It's not what we don't know that hurts, it's what we know that ain't so.
Will Rogers

An intellectual is a person whose mind watches itself.
Albert Camus

Because we think it is important for you to have some sense of the people who write the books that you read, we will briefly describe our academic interests and approaches to the study of communication. We believe that the study of communication is inherently and necessarily interdisciplinary—that understanding communication requires integrating information from a variety of arenas including, but not limited to, anthropology, biology, linguistics, psychology, and sociology. And because it would be extremely difficult to understand communication from all of these perspectives, communication scholars tend to adopt one or another of these perspectives as their focus. For example, those who study the role of communication in social or task groups are likely to adopt a sociological perspective. Those interested in how communication differs across cultures are probably going to take an anthropological approach. Furthermore communication is not studied only by those who reside in departments variously labeled communication, speech communication, or mass communication. Communication processes are of interest to those who call themselves anthropologists, linguists, psychologists, or zoologists, to name only a few. Consequently, you will find that we have included information from a variety of academic fields and sources.

Because of the limitations of our own interests and areas of expertise, you will also note that we have emphasized some perspectives over others. One of us, Jo Liska, focuses on communication from a biological and anthropological vantage point. Her research and teaching interests include evolutionary foundations of communication, cross-species comparisons of communication systems, cross-cultural communication, and the role of media in developing attitudes toward animals, wildlife conservation, and biodiversity. She claims her primary research interest in communication is identifying the fundamental principles on which all communication systems are built.

Co-author, Gary Cronkhite, is primarily interested in psychological or cognitive aspects of communication. He is concerned with how communication mediates thought. His current focus is on how persuasive messages are processed, and he has developed a cognitive model of that activity. Corollary to that interest is his research on the effects of persuasive messages on the attitudes, beliefs, and behaviors of listeners/readers. His other interest is in how symbolic meaning is constructed, derived, and perceived.

Both of us believe that human communication is the consequence of evolutionary processes, and that the roots of human communication can be identified in other species, especially species closely related to humans. Thus, we have included examination of the communication systems of other species as a means for identifying the possible evolutionary path that led to human language. In that discussion we have identified the ways in which human and nonhuman animal communication systems are similar, as well as the ways in which they differ.

We believe that understanding communication is facilitated by discussion of how communication has developed across the course of human history. Consequently, we have described the development of communication in ancient cultures, as well as contemporary ones. We hope the result is recognition of how culture molds and is molded by communication processes.

We believe that like the behavior of all species, human behavior is subject to ecological forces and constraints. The structure and content of communication reflects the impact of particular physical, social, and ideological ecologies on the people who inhabit them. Thus, for example, environmental problems such as habitat destruction, overpopulation, and famine are reflected in the ways we communicate and in the content of those messages. Those who are hungry are unlikely to engage in philosophical discussions; their conversations will probably center on the ways to obtain food. Indeed, some may be so weak that any conversation is too energy intensive and thus avoided.

We believe that symbolic communication is an essential and inescapable part of being human. Indeed, we appear to be genetically programmed to use and respond to symbols. Consequently, we have included some discussion of the acquisition of language by human children, in part as evidence for the claim that humans are largely so defined. As far as we know, no other species matches our symbolic dependence.

We believe that communication patterns influence and are influenced by the contexts in which communication occurs. Therefore we have examined communication behavior in interpersonal relationships, in groups, and in organizations. Further, we have explored the ways in which media influence the content and structure of interaction patterns and our perceptions of ourselves and of our world.

We believe that communication can be used for good, for evil, or for various points in between. The approach we take is to forewarn and forearm by providing the means for analyzing the communication to which we are exposed. We seek to provide an arsenal of critical weapons with which to defend ourselves from the army of messages that assault us.

Finally, we believe that self-awareness is as important as awareness of others. We all participate in this process we call communication, and we need to be concerned with the substance and quality of the messages we send, as well as with the messages sent by others. Our survival may depend upon it.

The first human being who hurled an insult instead of a stone was the founder of civilization.

　　　　—attributed to Sigmund Freud

UNIT 1
Ecology of Communication: Past, Present, and Future

This unit is devoted to explaining the ecology of communication, the evolutionary prehistory of communication, the history of communication technologies, and the history of the study of communication processes and patterns. In Chapters 1 and 2 our concern is with placing communication within ecological boundaries, highlighting the role of communication in our survival as a species, and discussing the role of communication in our everyday lives. Further, we define communication and describe its functions in meeting the needs and goals of those who use it. Chapter 3 describes the relationship of human communication to that of nonhuman animals, postulates the possible course of the evolutionary development of human communication, identifies the basic components and principles on which human communication rests, and overviews the development of communication technologies. In Chapter 4 we survey the changing role of communication throughout human history (with special emphasis on the cultures and the people who influenced the study of communication behavior), describe approaches to the study of communication as they have developed and expanded since the writings of the ancient Greeks and Romans, and examine contemporary scientific approaches to the study of communication.

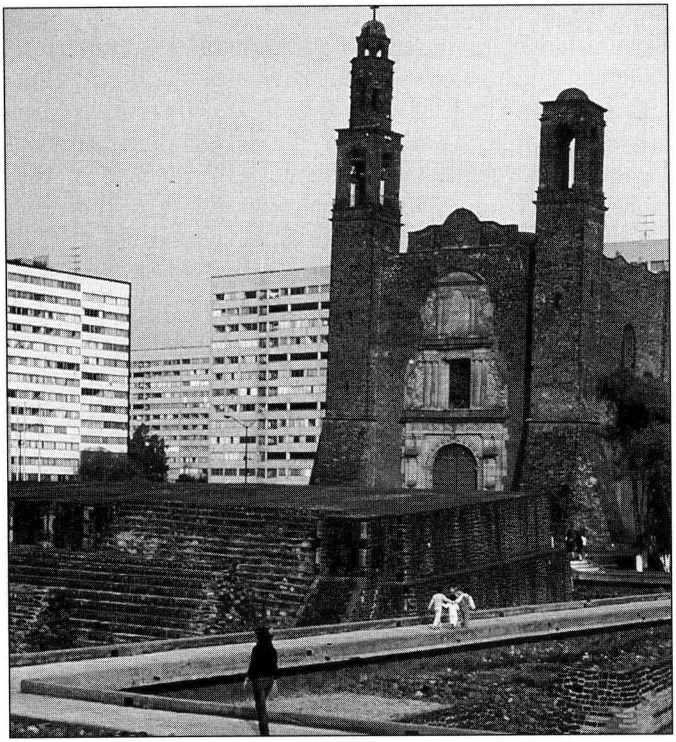

A Rationale for an Ecological Perspective on Communication

1

CHAPTER OUTLINE

Communication and Ecology
Physical Ecologies
Sociocultural Ecologies
Cognitive Ecologies

The Interface Between Cognition and Communication
Human Effect on Ecologies

> *Without context, there is no communication [p. 402].*
> *Let me start from the natural ecosystems around [humans]. An English oak wood, or a tropical forest, or a piece of desert, is a community of creatures. In the oak wood, perhaps 1000 species, perhaps more; in the tropical forest perhaps ten times that number of species live together. I may say that very few of you here have ever seen such an undisturbed system; there are not many of them left; they've mostly been messed up by Homo sapiens who either exterminated some species or introduced others which became weeds and pests, or altered the water supply, etc., etc. We are rapidly, of course, destroying all the natural systems in the world, the balanced natural systems. . . . What is true of the species that live together in a wood is also true of the groupings and sorts of people in a society, who are similarly in an uneasy balance of dependency and competition [pp. 430–431; emphasis added].*
> *Lack of systemic wisdom is always punished. We may say that the biological systems—the individual, the culture, the ecology—are partly living sustainers of their component cells or organisms. But the systems are nonetheless punishing of any species unwise enough to quarrel with its ecology [p. 434].*
>
> —Gregory Bateson, *Steps to an Ecology of Mind*

COMMUNICATION AND ECOLOGY

The study of **ecology,** the science of the relationship between organisms and their environment, or sometimes known as the science of communities, is generally focused on the structure and function of nature. More specific to our purposes, it is the examination of the relationships between organisms and their environments, as well as the interdependencies among and within species.[1] Ecologies are not just collections of species, but are constituted of interrelationships among species in such a way that removing one species has an impact on the entire ecology (Wilson, 1992).

All species are influenced by physical aspects of their ecology and by the behavior of other species with whom they share that ecology. Further, many species live in social ecologies (e.g., communities or groups such as families) and are therefore influenced by others in their group. And changes in the community structure have the potential to affect every aspect of life. Consider the changes wrought in family relationships when a new sibling is added, when a divorce occurs, and/or when a stepparent moves in. We humans also live in an ecology of ideas, which we will describe in some detail in Chapter 2, that shape the way we view our relationships with one another, other species, the world, and the universe. Consider the impact of the discovery that the earth was not the center of the universe.

> That moral center had allowed people to believe that the Earth was the stable center of the universe and therefore that humankind was of special interest to God. After Copernicus, Kepler, and especially Galileo, the Earth became a lonely wanderer in an obscure galaxy in some hidden corner of the universe, and this left the Western world to wonder if God had any interest in us at all. (Postman, 1993, p. 29)

Physical Ecologies

When ecologists describe **environments,** they are typically interested in characteristics such as land formations, availability and type of food resources, water sources, seasonal variations in temperature and moisture, and the various species that inhabit those areas. These characteristics have an important influence on the design, behavior, and social organization of all species. But environments are constantly changing; and in order to survive, all species must change in response. They do so in four fundamental ways: "morphological adaptations, physiological adjustments, behavior patterns, and community relations" (Kendeigh, 1961, p. 6).

Our own history as a species is the result of environmental forces and our persistent attempt to adapt:

> Earth's crust and atmosphere change constantly, and wedged in between them like a sandwich filling, life evolves as well. To what extent are extinction and speciation—the evolution of new species out of ancestral populations—tied to geophysical changes? Did humans origi-

nate in response to some identifiable cosmic or climatic event? (Vrba, 1993, p. 47)

Vrba goes on to provide data suggestive of morphological changes in early humans that coincide with two major climatic changes. One of those climatic changes occurred about 2.5 million years ago and along with it the fossil record indicates "an explosive radiation among hominids" (p. 49). Accompanying that radiation is the development of stone tools, the earliest yet found (Ethiopia). "Using tools to obtain and prepare food was an important innovation for hominids and indicates increased brain size and function" (p. 50). Note that a climatic change may have accounted for dramatic changes in the morphology, number, and behavior of those early hominids—a complex pattern of changes to meet the needs of a changing environment. Indeed, it may be that we can attribute our journey down the road to "dominance" to alterations in climate. (According to Kendeigh, 1961, organisms that are predominant make up the greatest mass of living material, and modify and exert influence over the environment.)

In our species, as among all long-lived animals, morphological adaptations occur slowly. And whereas bacteria and insects reproduce prodigiously and frequently, leading to rapid species morphological modification, humans reproduce slowly and cannot count on morphological adaptations to ensure their survival. The key to our adaptability rests on our ability to change our behavior, and this is an important focus of ecological research.

The question is: How do particular environmental conditions affect the evolution of species, their adaptation to changes in their environment, and the particular behavioral strategies that facilitated adaptation? Along with physical characteristics of particular species, behavioral characteristics are the result of constraints imposed by the environment on the organisms that inhabit that environment. Since communication is one form of behavior, it too is studied in terms of the environments in which it emerged. So, for example, whales and dolphins probably acquired sonar as their primary means of communication because it is more efficient and effective than other forms of communication for the particular environment in which they live. Communication that depends upon visual transmission would be far less effective in the darkness of the ocean depths. Similarly, most bats use echolocation as a means for negotiating the darkness of caves. Their environment restricts the potential for visual interaction. Indeed, some species of bats are blind or have poor vision. Their environment also inhibits the kind of auditory interaction used by humans, because caves do not afford good sound transmission. Thus, echolocation and sonar are likely the result of constraints imposed by those environments.

Krebs and Davies (1987, p. 326) illustrate the relationship further:

In four parts of the world, Andorra, Turkey, Mexico, and the Canary Islands, local peasants have developed extraordinary whistling languages with elaborate vocabularies. Although the details of the language and the methods of sound production vary from place to place, all are designed for long-distance communication. The four places are all mountainous with steep-sided, rocky valleys; distances are not very great as the crow flies but are large in terms of the effort needed to cross from one side of the valley to the other. The whistling languages are used for communicating across the steep valleys. They have all their sound energy concentrated into a narrow band of frequencies and are therefore well designed, like forest bird songs, to be detected and interpreted over relatively large distances.

Elephants are social animals who live in small family groups, and they interact with one another via touch, visual signs, and a series of calls and bellows that are quite audible to humans (e.g., Moss, 1988; Payne, 1986; Chevalier-Skolnikoff and Liska, 1993). However, elephants also frequently form large herds of related individuals. And since they are frequently dispersed over large areas of land, it was somewhat of a puzzle as to how they could communicate over such long distances. That they could so communicate was apparent because widely dispersed family groups came together into herds quite quickly. As it turns out, they use a series of infrasound calls at a frequency so low as to be inaudible to humans. Low-frequency sounds can travel over great distances; in the case of elephant calls, they travel up to five miles, which is well beyond the range of technically unassisted human speech. Elephants, the largest of land mammals, need to range widely in order to find sufficient food and to avoid competition with others of their kind. However, since they are also intensely social animals, they, like all social animals, depend upon interaction with other members of their group. Consequently, the development of infrasound enabled them to range widely in search of food while still maintaining contact with other members of their group.

Sociocultural Ecologies

Environmental characteristics set the stage for the sensory apparatus most efficient for communication signs for each particular species. Furthermore, as we have seen by cursory examination of elephants, the social system further influences communication behavior. Of course, the social system is also constrained by environmental forces and by the sensory system used for communication. It is a complex web of forces that work together to bring about the behavior of any given species.

Social systems are the result of the interaction between species characteristics and environmental forces. Crook, Ellis, and Goss-Custard (1979, p. 543) write:

> A major objective in the study of mammalian societies is to develop an understanding of the way in which, through evolution, species characteristics and environmental forces have interacted to shape the structure and dynamics of these diverse and complex systems. Such an understanding should make it possible to state how a society operates and to predict how changes in intrinsic (species) or extrinsic (environmental) characteristics may affect social organizations and the relations between individuals.

Social Structure The ecology of any particular species has broad influence on the social structure and patterns of interaction maintained by that species. The impact of ecological constraints may affect family structure, optimal number of offspring, division of labor (female-male, young-old), attendance to cultural conventions such as marriage, and so forth. In extreme cases, such as when population densities strain the carrying capacity of the environment, conflict within or between communities of species may occur. Goodall (1986) describes a territorial dispute between two chimpanzee groups at Gombe that resulted in the annihilation of one of the groups. The dispute was over territorial dominion and may have been motivated by limited resources due to an extended drought. Such disputes are, of course, not uncommon among humans.

Access to limited resources such as jobs and money, which are peculiar to human civilizations, can alter a social structure in profound ways. As the timber industry shrinks in response to decreasing timber resources and to pressure from environmental groups, human workers are left without jobs and without the skills necessary to fit other types of work. Moreover, jobs in timber areas such as the Pacific Northwest are not generally plentiful. The impact of these employment deficits will be felt not just by the individuals affected but by the entire community. Those most profoundly affected are older loggers, who have less opportunity to retrain. Their age works against them.[2] In fact, our aging population is offered as one of the most important concerns for public policy. As Olshansky, Carnes, and Cassel (1993, p. 46) note: "Our species has modified the evolutionary forces that have always limited life expectancy. Policymakers must consequently prepare to meet the needs of a population that will soon be much older."

Studies of the effects of environmental forces on human behavior are ongoing. Some of the concern focuses on how crowding due to increases in population density affects our social relationships and social structure. What effects (immediate and long-term) did disasters such as Hurricane Andrew in 1992 and the Los Angeles earthquake of January 1994 have on local social structure and relationships? What differences in social relationships and structure does one observe between rural and urban locales? How can we explain the increase in single-parent families in the United States, especially those in which an individual has consciously elected to establish a single-parent home? Of course, the impact of changes wrought by such forces will be evident in communication patterns.

Living in groups or societies has a number of advantages, not least among them the ability to bring the group to bear to modify the environment (Bonner, 1980). Bonner cites beavers and bees as examples and then goes on to say: "The initial advantages of togetherness could conceivably be achieved by making the self-made environment a buffer against the vagaries of the conditions of the outside world; and this, in turn, could have led to more elaborate social interactions" (p. 97). "It is essentially true by definition that one cannot have culture without social interaction" (p. 25).

Culture Culture is one of the primary ways in which humans (and other animals to varying degrees) respond to environmental changes. Bonner (1980, p. 5) defines **culture** as "the transfer of information by behavioral means, most particularly by the process of teaching and learning." Culture afforded a way to bypass the constraints of genetic modification via evolution because cultural evolution has the potential to be very rapid. And rapid it is, because we can learn and teach others the fruits of our discoveries, enhanced by the development of permanent forms of communication (e.g., writing). Indeed, we may soon be able to take a hand in genetic evolution by medically modifying dysfunctional genes to ensure the survival of individuals and their offspring. We already modify the genetic environment through selective breeding and planting of particular foods, through use of hormones to facilitate plant and animal growth, and by changing old-growth forests into more manageable and humanly desirable plots of trees. In the long run, we may have changed our ecology in ways ultimately deleterious to our well-being, the survival of other species notwithstanding.

Cognitive Ecologies

All of this—social interaction and culture—is orchestrated by the brain, an information-processing structure that we only feebly understand. Yet its size and complexity are what afford us the ability to go beyond merely adapting to our environment, as we did early in our evolutionary history, to exploiting new ecological niches, and finally to creating environments that suit our changing needs. Yet our lives are affected as much by the environments that we create as by those created by nature. If we are to survive natural forces such as earthquakes, homes must be built that are flexible enough to withstand violent movement of the earth. If we are to survive urban life, a human creation, we must somehow adjust to the noise, pollution, and crowded conditions characteristic of the megalopolis. This requires new ideas and new ways of thinking that guide adaptations in behavior.

The consequences of our evolutionary history provided humans with **cognition,** that is, generalized thinking abilities supported by an elaborated communication code for transmitting the fruits of our cognitive labors. Via communication we can coordinate our ideas and, in the process, construct complex societies governed by those ideas. Societies that survive do so by adapting their ideas, their cooperative cognitive efforts, to confront better the challenges they face. And the ideas they adopt will reflect changing environmental challenges. Consider, for example, that in the not-so-distant past humans, in the industrialized world at least, believed that the earth would live forever and that her resources would sustain generations reaching to infinity. And we lived as though there were no tomorrow. Well, tomorrow has arrived, and with it have come demands to alter not just our lifestyles but our thoughts and ideas. Resist as we may, the environment will alter our ways of thinking, or we won't survive to finish the story begun so long ago.

Impact of TV on Human Cognition   Let's consider one of the prominent features of our daily environment—television—on our ideas, thoughts, sense of well-being, and social relations. TV has been the subject of considerable research and controversy, some of which will be discussed at various points in this book. For now, I want to suggest the ideas offered in a book that I found thought-provoking. McKibben (1992) compares the information available to us from the media, specifically television, to that found in nature. He is especially interested in how the two information sources influence our perceptions of the world and our place in it. He argues that, among other things, television isolates us from community, which is a strong human need. At the same time it rewards us for watching it by providing us with programs that stress a sense of community, albeit vicariously. He writes (p. 173):

> Still, TV clearly understands that at least the *idea* of community ties attracts us. What is "Cheers" but an enclosed neighborhood where people depend on one another when the chips are down? "Where everybody knows your name, and they're glad you came." No one moves away, no one can break up the kind of love that constantly makes jokes to keep from acknowledging that it is a kind of love. "You want to go where everybody knows your name." That's right—we do. That's why we loved "M*A*S*H," another great TV community. But on TV, of course, while *you* know everybody's name, they've never heard of yours.

Television, this wonder of human communication ingenuity, has altered our perceptions in other ways. Television has become an antidote to information overload in a complex world where there appear to be very few "sure things." It is a world marked by rapid changes that make entire professions obsolete in a matter of a generation, where fear of one's neighbors appears only too rational, where long commutes on tangled freeways packed bumper-to-bumper with poison-spewing vehicles jangle one's nerves and add to an already stressful existence, where some people don't even know their neighbor's name—television provides something familiar, predictable, and filled with families, friends, and entire towns (e.g., "Northern Exposure," "Evening Shade," and "Hearts Afire") happily, for the most part, relating to one another.

Television programs and commercials provide us with images on which we can model our thoughts, feelings, and behavior. Good times can't be had without beer. Respect, love, and friendship come in bottles filled with goo and glop. Youth can be found in a bottle of Pepsi or a package of hair dye. And we can save our job by using an overnight shipping service, uphold our family's unity with a fifteen-minute dinner of macaroni and cheese, and maintain our sanity by using the right long-distance phone service. We can get "a whole day's news every half hour" on CNN, which is probably good, since we'd hate to waste the entire day catching up on world, national, and local events. Television goads us into believing that more is better, more is available, more will ensure happiness.

Nature, on the other hand, challenges these entrenched ways of thinking. McKibben (1992, p. 108) suggests:

> A shift in a different direction [which] would require a certain amount of sacrifice—a sacrifice at least of the idea that we should forever expect more and better. It would also demand a willingness to share what we have, both in wealth and technology, with people like Cambodians so their path to a decent life doesn't require cutting down all their forests and sending them to Japan.

It's worth thinking about.

The Interface Between Cognition and Communication

The types of communication signs available to a species provide a window into their cognitive characteristics and abilities (Griffin, 1978, 1991, 1992). I will discuss types of communication signs in detail in Chapter 2, but for the moment I want to describe the underlying cognitive abilities these types of signs suggest.

Symptoms Symptoms, which form the foundation for all animal communication systems, are genetically determined and can be modified only by genetic means, and are dependent upon predictable ecological influences over time. These signs are typically outside the voluntary control of the user and are the consequence of the physical or physiological conditions of the organism. Symptoms are reflex signs that express emotional states such as fear, surprise, and pleasure. Cognitive responses to them tend to be automatic, involuntary, and primary.

Semblances Semblances are signs that have come under increasing voluntary control of the organism and that are exaggerated to serve social interaction functions. Semblances resemble their referents, that is, the conditions on which they are based. Thus, feigning an expression of fear, putting on a happy face, or raising a fist as a sign of fake aggression constitute semblances, as do drawings that resemble the referent (e.g., a stick figure drawing of a human). Several hypotheses relevant to cognitive effort involved in producing and recognizing these signs have been offered, including reduction of ambiguity, social manipulation of others, cooperative and noncooperative functions, and honesty, which has to do with the reliability of signs (Krebs and Davies, 1987). It is likely that all of these explanations are relevant. Further, I have suggested that

> Semblances expanded the data base on which predictions about the behavior of others could be made, resulting in more sensitivity in interpreting those data. Thus, one could potentially change an antagonistic encounter into a session of play by manipulating the relevant signs. Manipulating, and especially, modifying objects to serve a variety of purposes important to survival probably enhanced sensory integration and elaboration and may have helped to provide a more consistent and substantial diet for an energy-consuming, developing brain (Liska, in press).

Symbols Symbols—arbitrary, conventionalized signs—provide the opportunity to construct and discuss abstract concepts, to create and manipulate a *symbolic* reality that may or may not conform to natural reality. Symbols "are both the substance of and consequence of internal representations of other possible worlds" (Liska, in press). Symbols allow us to represent such abstractions as "justice," "freedom," and "equality," which are human-made linguistic constructions that have no counterpart in the natural world. With symbols we have created a variety of conceptualizations of "gods." With symbols we can change our perceptions of a war by calling it a "police action." We can alter our perceptions of firing employees by saying that they have been "selected out," "placed out," or "nonretained," or that we have "eliminated the redundancies in the human resources area" (Lutz, 1993). Deaths of civilians in time of war become "collateral damage." With symbols we can lie, that is, manipulate reality to attempt to save our skin.

> Symbols made it possible to . . . misrepresent "real events" so as to manipulate others, save face, and/or defend one's ego, learn vicariously, construct and choose possible courses of action based on predictive and cause-effect reasoning, perceive and construct contingency relationships (if-then), daydream, maintain the illusion of choice, and so on. (Liska, in press)

Symbols free us from the constraints of direct, immediate experience—the here and now—and allow us to reflect on the past and dream about the future. These cognitive abilities are the impetus for and consequence of symbolic behavior.

Humans orchestrate all of these types of signs into a complex symphony. Other species may also engage in such songs, but—at least as far as we know now—to a lesser degree than do humans. What is important is that we have become dependent upon the symbols we use and create. They constitute the substance of our thoughts, express our ideas and emotions, guide our self-conceptions, and have even been the foundation for some of our most serious interpersonal, social, and international conflicts. They are the substance of our social relationships, and provide the foundation for culture and civilization. With the advent of the use of symbols we became no longer entirely dependent upon the resources of the natural world; we could create resources. Symbols distanced us from the natural world and launched us into a world of our own creation. In this we are a most unusual species.

Human Effects on Ecologies

All species are subject to constraints imposed by the environment. Additionally, all species are subject to the limitations imposed by the lifestyles of other species.

Territoriality Since most species are territorial, for instance, a species can only grow in number relative to the carrying capacity (resources such as food and water) of its territory. When the carrying capacity of a particular ecology is exceeded, some members of the group must find a new territory or risk death by starvation or death inflicted by members of its own group. Acquiring new territory may pose enormous obstacles. For example, if the seas become too polluted to sustain life, dolphins and whales, who are simply not equipped to move onto land, may have no place to go. If ozone depletion increases the earth's temperature by a significant amount, species adapted to cold conditions may have no new territory to access, and thus no alternative but to die out. And acquiring a new territory may require conflict with other species already occupying that territory. This problem may be illustrated by the ecological crisis we are now facing.

Humans, without doubt one of the most adaptable species on the planet, have systematically overrun the territories of other species and human groups, and in the process have displaced or eliminated those other species and humans. When the early immigrant settlers arrived in what is now the United States, they displaced the indigenous populations of Native Americans already living here. As they marched further and further west, these new populations drove out or exterminated most of the flora and fauna in their path. The grasslands of the plains fell to the plow. The buffalo, antelope, deer, bear, and wolves were felled by guns, or fled to remote regions then inaccessible to the advancing humans. The trees were the victims of axes wielded by the pioneers. And the Native Americans, whose territories obstructed the route west, were killed by disease, guns, and/or alcohol, or were rounded up and moved onto undesirable tracts of land. Our ancestors are not alone in their quest for new territories and power attained through increasing numbers; this story has been repeated many times in the history of humanity. And it is a story still unfolding, especially in Africa and in the rain forests of Indonesia, Southeast Asia, and South America.

But to return to our forefathers: the movement west was a struggle to overcome the obstacles laid down by geologic time. Whereas the railroads, the pony express, and the telegraph facilitated settlement of the west, it was water, or the lack thereof, that was the critical factor in western expansion. Water is scarce in the plains, and food was also not easily found by a population used to growing it in their backyards and therefore largely unaccustomed to foraging for it. Indeed, access to water was the single most important obstacle to development of much of the western plains area.[3] Additionally, the Rocky Mountains posed enormous difficulties for people without benefit of flight to carry them over the mountains. As a result, many people stopped their trek west and colonized the plains, while those who set their sights further skirted the mountains on the Oregon and Sante Fe Trails. And, the people and other animals of the area did not give up without a fight.

The Forces of Nature Nor have we succeeded in mastering nature. In 1992, Hurricane Andrew bore down on Florida to the tune of billions of dollars in damage, not to mention the trauma of death, injury, and homelessness. A massive blizzard in March of 1993 left over 100 dead in the eastern United States, many more injured, and a bill totaling millions of dollars. In January,

1994 an earthquake shook southern California, resulting in the loss of lives, livelihoods, and homes, with the cost to rebuild placed at over $30 billion, and bringing an immeasurable psychological cost to those involved. Simultaneously, a glacial blast hit the eastern half of the United States leaving in its wake death, destruction, and another high price tag.

The relentless march of the desert in Ethiopia and Somalia has brought starvation to millions, in spite of the efforts of relief agencies. The late Sam Kinison once joked that the people of those areas should move because they could not now or ever grow food in their desert homeland. While his point was well taken, imagine your reaction to being told that several million Somalis were going to move to the United States. I expect you might argue that we simply have neither the room nor the resources to accommodate them.

In fact, immigration limits and restrictions are one way to prevent others from moving into a nation's territory. I heard on CNN that local citizen groups were forming in Los Angeles to try to thwart the movement of people from Mexico into southern California. They are worried that these migrating aliens will take jobs away from U.S. citizens, who are already having a difficult time due to the shaky economy in that area. Furthermore, it was reported that health care is provided free to these immigrants, many of whom are financially comfortable; and some students cross the border daily to attend schools in southern California, only to return to their homes in Mexico after school. Apparently this scene is played out with U.S. government sanction.

And the future looks grim:

> Within the next 50 years, the human population is likely to exceed nine billion, and global economic output may quintuple. Largely as a result of these two trends, scarcities of renewable resources may increase sharply. The total area of highly productive agricultural land will drop, as will the extent of forests and the number of species they sustain. Future generations will also experience the on-going depletion and degradation of aquifers, rivers and other bodies of water, the decline of fisheries, further stratospheric ozone loss, and, perhaps, significant climatic change.
>
> As such environmental problems become more severe, they may precipitate civil or international strife. (Homer-Dixon, Boutwell, and Rathjens, 1993, p. 38)[4]

Yet, regardless of the consequences, the fact still remains that humans have colonized almost every available ecological niche on the planet. How has this been possible? Undoubtedly the reasons are numerous, but one that comes immediately to mind is our ability to communicate, and especially our ability to learn from previous generations, who about 8,000 years ago began to permanently record their experiences, to the potential benefit of subsequent generations. Though we are not the only species to have developed advanced forms of **communication,** and though we are not the only species to pass down information from generation to generation, we appear to be the only species to be able to access information from times long past and from remote places. Diamond (1992) writes: "While our language and art and agriculture aren't quite unique, we really are unique among animals in our capacity to learn from the experience of others of our species living in distant places or in the distant past."

Cultural Evolution Although the early period in human evolution was not especially distinctive, the development of language, speech, writing, and technology such as the printing press, radio, television, and computers propelled our species into a position of prominence and power. Some may find it a dubious distinction, however, given the havoc we have wreaked on world ecology and the other species with whom we share that ecology. The communication weapons we wield may have been the resource for our rise to power; they equally well might result in our fall from grace. The truly cynical among us may see little hope for the situation and merely live out their lives scowling in disgust. Some, I hope, believe that the very means that brought us to the precipice may also save us from falling off the edge. In offering an approach to meet the ecological crisis that faces us, Homer-Dixon, Boutwell, and Rathjens suggest that "social ingenuity as a precursor to technical ingenuity is often overlooked" (1993, p. 45). And social ingenuity is fueled and shared via the most fundamental of human technologies—communication.

CONCLUSION

As is the case with all species, we humans compete for access to limited resources: food, territory, mates, friendships and alliances, social standing, information, and so forth. Additionally, we compete for money, jobs, access to the best schools and universities, and so on. Each level or type of ecology (i.e., physical, sociocultural, or cognitive) has limited resources available for our consumption. Consequently, all species must adopt strategies that maintain the delicate balance among survival of self, offspring, and kin and survival of the group or community and species, and at the same time preserve the ecology on which all depend. While competition may to some extent accurately describe our efforts to obtain our share of the available resources, some argue that "nature is not at war, one organism with another. Nature is an alliance founded on cooperation" (Augros and Stanciu, 1987, p. 129). They go on to write (p. 99):

The elimination of competition by division of the habitat into niches is so universal in the plant and animal kingdoms that it has become a principle of prediction and discovery for field studies. Colinvaux writes: "Whenever we find rather similar animals living together in the wild, we do not think of competition by tooth and claw, we ask ourselves instead, how competition is avoided. When we find many animals apparently sharing a food supply, we do not talk of struggle for survival; we watch to see by what trick the animals manage to be peaceful in their coexistence [*Why Big Fierce Animals Are Rare: An Ecologist's Perspective* (Princeton, N.J.: Princeton University Press, 1978), p. 145].

Further, different features of the ecology are significant to different species. "Though all share one world, all may be said to live in different worlds, since each perceives best only that part of the environment essential to its success" (Tinbergen, 1965, p. 45). The key word here is *best*. Each species is undoubtedly largely egocentric, selfish, and generally unconcerned with the welfare of other species. Indeed, most species lack the cognitive abilities necessary to be aware of their own needs and how those needs impact the other species with whom they share their ecology. They respond to times of hardship using strategies largely dictated by their genetic constitution—instructions for behavior written in their genes. Humans too are largely egocentric and selfish, but we have the capacity to comprehend our place in the world's ecologies, to study our relationships with and impact on other residents, and to modify our behavior accordingly. That is, we do if we so choose.

It is clear that our needs have come into conflict with the needs of other species. For example, jobs and money are not significant to spotted owls, who want only stands of old-growth forest in which they can feed, mate, and raise their young. Indeed, given their environmental history, old-growth forests are necessary to their survival. Yet humans too want to use the old-growth forests to provide lumber for homes in which to mate and raise their young, and for buildings that house their economic ventures, which in turn are necessary to support their families. We could pose the question: Whose needs are more important? This question assumes a competitive stance. And the outcome is likely to be that one species will win and the other will lose. Of course, even the winner may lose in the long haul, since destroying old-growth forests may have negative consequences on quality of life. Instead we could ask: What alternatives are available for a compromise that might serve the interests of both species? The answers won't come easily, but come they must, because these are the kinds of questions that persistently face us, and our answers may irrevocably change the future.

This discussion of the ecology of communication is intended to provide a foundation for the importance of communication at a rather global level. Since communication appears to be the tool by which we humans have come to be so pervasive, understanding how it functions may be the key to using it to improve the quality of our daily lives, and to ensure our very survival and the survival of other species on whose existence we depend. With this thought in mind, we turn to a more detailed discussion of the nature and substance of communication.

KEY TERMS AND CONCEPTS

ecology
environments
culture
cognition

symptoms
semblances
symbols
communication

societies
social interaction
human-ecology relationship
 and resources

NOTES

1. For discussions of ecological issues, see: P. Ehrlich and A. Ehrlich, *The Population Explosion* (New York: Simon and Schuster, 1990); W. V. Reid and K. R. Miller, *Keeping Options Alive: The Scientific Basis for Conserving Biodiversity* (Washington, D.C.: World Resources Institute, 1990); M. E. Soule (ed.), *Conservation Biology: The Science of Scarcity and Diversity* (Sunderland, Mass: Sinauer, 1986); and E. O. Wilson (ed.), *Biodiversity* (Washington, D.C.: National Academy Press, 1988).
2. For a detailed discussion of this situation, see William Dietrich, *The Final Forest* (New York: Penguin Books, 1992).
3. Water remains a national and international problem. For discussions see: Water: The power, promise, and turmoil of North America's fresh water, *National Geographic* (special edition, 1993); P. J. Vesilind, Middle East water—critical resource, *National Geographic* (May 1993), pp. 38–71.
4. For philosophical discussions of conservation see: P. Singer, *The Expanding Circle: Ethics and Sociobiology* (New York: Farrar, Straus, and Giroux, 1981); H. Rolston III, *Philosophy Gone Wild: Essays in Environmental Ethics* (Buffalo: Prometheus Books, 1986); H. Rolston III, *Environmental Ethics: Duties to and Values in the Natural World* (Philadelphia: Temple University Press, 1988).

REFERENCES

Augros, R., and Stanciu, G. (1987). *The New Biology: Discovering the Wisdom in Nature.* Boston: New Science Library.

Bonner, J. T. (1980). *The Evolution of Culture in Animals.* Princeton N.J.: Princeton University Press.

Chevalier-Skolnikoff, S., and Liska, J. (1993). Tool use by wild and captive elephants. *Animal Behavior* 46: 209–219.

Crook, J. H., Ellis, J. E., and Goss-Custard, J. D. (1979). Mammalian social systems: Structure and function. In *Primate Ecology: Problem-Oriented Field Studies,* edited by R. W. Sussman, pp. 543–567. New York: Wiley.

Diamond, J. (1992). *The Third Chimpanzee.* New York: HarperCollins, p. 366.

Goodall, J. (1986). *The Chimpanzees of Gombe: Patterns of Behavior.* Cambridge, Mass: Harvard University Press.

Griffin, D. R. (1978). Prospects for a cognitive ethology. *Behavioral and Brain Sciences* 1: 527–538.

———. (1991). Progress toward a cognitive ethology. In *Cognitive Ethology: The Minds of Other Animals,* edited by C. A. Ristau, pp. 3–17. Hillsdale, N.J.: Erlbaum.

———. (1992). *Animal Minds.* Chicago: University of Chicago Press.

Homer-Dixon, T. F., Boutwell, J. H., and Rathjens, G. W. (1993). Environmental change and violent conflict. *Scientific American* (February), 38–45.

Kendeigh, S. C. (1961). *Animal Ecology.* Englewood Cliffs, NJ: Pentice-Hall.

Krebs, J. R., and Davies, N. B. (1987). *An Introduction to Behavioural Ecology.* Sunderland, Mass: Sinauer.

Liska, J. (in press). Sign arbitrariness as an index of semiogenesis. *Studies in Language Origins.* The Hague, Netherlands: Benjamins.

Lutz, W. D. (1993). Language, appearance, and reality: Doublespeak in 1984. In *Anthropology 93/94,* edited by E. Angeloni, pp. 43–47. Guilford, Conn.: Dushkin.

McKibben, B. (1992). *The Age of Missing Information.* New York: Plume.

Moss, C. (1988). *Elephant Memories.* New York: Ivy Books.

Olshansky, S. J., Carnes, B. A., and Cassel, C. K. (1993). The aging of the human species. *Scientific American* (April), 46–52.

Payne, K. (1986). Elephant calls that humans can't hear. *Science News* (February 22), p. 129.

Postman, N. (1993). *Technopoly.* New York: Vintage.

Tinbergen, N. (1965). *Animal Behavior.* New York: Time-Life.

Vrba, E. S. (1993). The pulse that produced us. *Natural History* (May), pp. 47–51.

Wilson, E. O. (1992). *The Diversity of Life.* Cambridge, Mass: Belknap of Harvard University Press.

Communication is simply the perception of meaning.

—Gary Cronkhite

Communication and Survival

2

CHAPTER OUTLINE

What Is Communication?
   Signs: Symptoms, Semblances, and Symbols
   Intention vs. Nonintention
   Stages of Communication

What Are Some Functions of Communication?
   Information Gathering
   Facilitating Cooperation
   Enhancing or Reducing Competition and Conflict

   Self-Actualization
   Entertainment

What Is the Role of Communication in Human Survival?

How Do Ideas Evolve?
   Communication and Survival
   Ideological Evolution

What Is the Role of Communication in the Evolution of Ideas?

WHAT IS COMMUNICATION?

We can examine **communication** at many different levels and from different points of view. My own focus is on the evolutionary/biological foundations of communication; my coauthor adopts a more cognitive or psychological perspective. Many scholars of communication study the effects of the contexts, or physical and social ecologies, in which communication occurs. That is, they may study how organizational structure influences communication behavior, or how mediated communication influences decision making. Some people study how people communicate in various types of relationships, for example, friendships and marriages. Still others investigate communication differences as they emerge in various cultures, an area currently receiving considerable attention as we move further into a global economy.

    We encounter the word *communication* frequently in our daily interaction. The term has a variety of meanings. It (or a variant) frequently substitutes for the word *talk*, as in "He's not very communicative." *Communication* sometimes stands for lack of "agreement" between people, as in the now-famous line from the movie *Cool Hand Luke*: "What we have here is a failure to communicate." A parent who finally feels he or she has made progress with a difficult offspring may exclaim, "I think we're finally beginning to communicate," implying steps toward mutual understanding. And former President Ronald Reagan was frequently called the "Great Communicator" by the press, referring to his ability to present himself well in scripted public presentations. (Some may have used the term sarcastically.) These commonplace uses of the word *communication* suggest conceptions based on the effectiveness or success of the interaction.

Some definitions of *communication* are so broad as to include *all* behavior. The bumpersticker slogan "One cannot not communicate," adapted from Watzlawick, Beavin, and Jackson (1967), illustrates this type of definition. Others are more specific and suggest that only "intentional," "planned," and/or "other-directed" messages are communication.[1]

When you think of communication you may visualize recent developments in communication technologies, such as television and computers. Those are extensions of our ability to communicate, and they influence our behavior in important ways. They are not, however, the "stuff" of communication. Nor are speech and writing the substance of communication; they are channels for transmitting communication.

Given all of these various perspectives on and uses of the term, you may be wondering: "So, what is communication?" For our part, communication is the exchange of certain types of signs. Let me explain first what I mean by *signs*.

Signs: Symptoms, Semblances, and Symbols

A **sign** is anything that stands for something else. Thunder is a sign of rain. A black hat is a sign of the villain. The hand gesture meaning "OK" in the United States is a sign. The words I am typing are signs. And when I hear the signs "Uh, Huh!," I think of Pepsi . . . or is it Coke?

Signs may take the form of words and sentences (language), images or pictures, odors, gestures, artifacts such as dress and jewelry, environmental characteristics such as seating arrangements, use of color and light, and background noise such as music, and/or a host of body positions and movements, eye contact, tone and rhythm of voice. As you can see, these signs seem to be of different types.

We send three types of messages: symptoms, semblances, and symbols.[2] Let's begin with the most fundamental type of sign/message, the symptom.

Symptoms **Symptoms** are signs that are innate, such as blushing, pupil dilation, a trembling voice or shaking hands (reflecting that we are stressed or nervous), and the grimace we make when we are angry. Physicians look to our symptoms as clues for identifying disease. Communicators look to symptoms as clues to the emotional states and intentions of others.

Think back over the feelings you experienced in the moments prior to giving a public presentation such as a speech. You may have experienced dry mouth, tightness in your throat, hand or vocal tremors, a feeling of having "butterflies" in your stomach, and so on. These are symptomatic signs, and they are manifestations of your feelings of nervousness and anxiety. They are difficult to control, even with practice, and I still experience such symptoms in mild form before presenting a paper at a conference, even though I have given such presentations many times. I understand these symptoms to be the result of nervousness associated with putting myself on public display; and when I see them in others who are in a similar situation, I assume they too are nervous. I have an empathic understanding of others' experiences with feelings such as anxiety when performing in public because I have such experiences myself.

If taken by surprise, we tend to jump and possibly even scream. These symptoms are natural and predictable; they are part of the "startle reaction." Many of our facial expressions are symptoms, as in a look of fear, pain, or ecstasy in response to certain events. Body movements and orientation, such as covering the face to protect it from a moving object, running from danger, or slumping in a mood of dejection, are examples of symptoms. The reactions you would have in response to learning that you had won millions in the state lottery would undoubtedly be the symptoms of shock.

Symptomatic signs are not under our direct control, except under extraordinary circumstances. Women in the 1800s used belladonna drops in their eyes to cause pupil dilation, which was considered very attractive. And Hollywood stars provide visible testimony to the miracles a cosmetic surgeon can create. Generally, however, our size, shape, and physical characteristics are inherited rather than created by modern medicine. We blush when we are embarrassed, with little hope of controlling it. And tears of grief are difficult to hold back. Hungry stomachs growl for attention at the most inappropriate times, and our voices quaver in situations, such as job interviews and oral presentations, when we most want to appear confident.

All animals, including humans, display symptomatic signs, and therefore we consider them the foundation on which communication is built. From a communication point of view, symptoms yield important information in that they reveal when we are angry, sad, feeling ill, and so forth. Communication that occurs within the context of anger will be undoubtedly less satisfying and effective, and we may want to put off trying to "reason" with anyone who is angry. Symptoms also provide clues to deceptive attempts in that most people who are trying to deceive will subtly and inadvertently leave clues to their intent. Word repetition, foot shuffling, fidgeting with objects, and a dramatic increase or decrease in the amount of talk may signal deception.

Semblances Semblances are exaggerated symptoms. They are signs that mimic symptoms but can be manipulated at will by the user. While symptoms are not typically under our voluntary sensory control, we have gained some degree of voluntary control over our faces, bodies, and hands. For example, we can control our faces to indicate anger even if we aren't really angry, attempt to appear relaxed when we aren't, "put on a happy face," and throw a fake punch. Greetings such as kissing and hugging are examples of ritual semblances. Bluffs, which mimic the symptoms of anger during bouts of pretend or play fighting, are semblances. The begging hand gesture, which may have evolved from the symptomatic behavior of reaching to grab something, is a semblance.

This ability to mimic symptomatic signs, to modify and exaggerate them for use in other contexts, is a learned behavior that enhances our ability to communicate by enabling us to create ways of sharing experiences independent of our immediate experiences. Surprise parties are sometimes not a surprise to the person for whom they are intended, yet most feign surprise at the appropriate moment. Some students get very good at feigning interest in lectures when actually they are a million light years away. People who wish to appear of high status may adopt such trappings of dominance and status as expensive clothes, cars, and home furnishings. The nonverbal signs used to create these impressions are semblances. A semblance sign is one that mimics or looks like the act or referent for which it stands, and many nonverbal signs are semblances. Some of the signs of American Sign Language are based on pantomime and resemble the meanings for which they stand. Mimes act out entire stories using a series of semblamatic signs, and the game of charades tests our skills at finding nonverbal signs that look like the words to movie and song titles.

We can see one of the clearest examples of semblances at the end of a class session when students begin to close books and notebooks, move about in their chairs, and stuff their belongings into backpacks. These semblances are especially exaggerated if the class has gone over its allotted time limit. These semblances are the exaggerated symptoms of leave-taking behaviors.

Some semblances are signs that resemble their referents. Examples include realistic paintings and sculptures, photographs, line drawings, and onomatopoeic words, which are words that sound like their referent, as in the *buzz* of an insect or the *bark* of a dog. In the movie *Dances With Wolves*, Lt. John Dunbar mimicked the look and behavior of a buffalo in order to get the idea across to a group of Sioux with whom he didn't share a language. He used a series of semblances—pawing the ground, and using his fingers to suggest horns—to produce a visual imitation of a buffalo.

Some semblances vary in how realistically they represent their referents. Maps and blueprints are probably the best examples of extreme realism, for they are designed to be two-dimensional reproductions of a territory. Maps that were stylized abstractions would be useless to the traveler. Imagine trying to find your way around a new metropolis with some cartographer's impressionistic version of the layout. Some of the rock art in northern Europe, which dates back about 20,000 years, portrays the animals of the era so realistically that scientists can see what those now-extinct animals looked like.

Symbols Some signs become so completely unrelated to symptoms that the relationship is arbitrary. We call such signs **symbols.** Symbolic signs are totally arbitrary, and their meaning is the result of agreement among the users of those signs. With the exception of onomatopoeic words, all words are symbols, and their meanings do not depend upon an apparent relationship between the words and their referents. For example, the communication device variously called the "television," the "boob-tube," or the "idiot box" could have equally well been called a "blindey," a "plino," or a "tovelle." The book you are currently reading could have been called a "wano," a "selvin," or a "plobo." The point is that the names we attach to various objects and ideas are done so by convention, that is, by agreement among the users of a particular language. The relationship between the word and the object or idea is not natural; it is arbitrary. Arbitrariness means that the words we use bear no necessary relationship to their referents or concepts. Thus, we could construct our own language as long as we agreed to the meanings specified by the words we created. As far as we know, humans created symbols, and we are still doing so. New words are created daily, frequently by public relations or advertising firms pushing a new product. In fact, there are now companies in the business of creating names for new products and testing the impact of those names on consumers. A commercial for a salad dressing serves as illustration. The salad dressing is called Healthy Sensation, and in the commercial an interviewer asks a consumer if she likes the name. The consumer says yes and talks on about how wonderful the name is and how well it suits the product. The interviewer ends by asking if it is a better name for the product than "say, Ed." Both laugh heartily.

With symbols,

> we can conjure up the sight, sound, smell, or feeling of a skunk, where no real skunk exists. We can give him wings! We can dress him in blue denims, name him Jimmy, and have him play out a whole series of adventures with his friend Peter Rabbit. (Smith, 1985, p. 144)

Intention vs. Nonintention

You may be thinking that the distinction among these types of signs/messages is based on **intention.** We believe in *un*intentional symbolic behavior. It is very difficult for us to determine when we intend to behave from when we don't. Certainly, some of our symbolic behavior is strategically planned, such as when we compose a speech or visualize an important conversation we plan to initiate with a friend or co-worker at some later date. However, a great deal of our behavior operates at a subconscious level, that is, out of our range of awareness. So-called Freudian slips are one example of unintentional symbolic behavior. Consequently, we can never be sure, as either actors or observers, when our behavior is intentional.[3]

It is important to note that we are not trying to define communication for all people and for all time. Definitions are not right or wrong; they are only more or less useful to one's purposes and to particular circumstances. We said earlier that we consider communication to be the exchange of certain types of signs/messages. We are most interested in semblances and symbols, but symptoms provide important clues in interactions with others.

Stages of Communication

These communication stages are like the layers of an onion: Symptomatic signs form the core of the onion, followed in order by semblances and symbols. Thus, semblances didn't replace symptoms, but expanded on our communication potential. Symbols certainly didn't replace symptoms and semblances, and our daily communication is an elegant orchestration of all these communication stages. That is, simultaneously we produce facial expressions symptomatic of our feelings, employ gestures to indicate direction, emphasis, and so on, and use words to convey ideas and opinions.

The inner layers of the onion must form before the outer layers can emerge. That is, the ability to create and use symbols is dependent upon the ability to use semblances. And we must have acquired voluntary control over some sensory systems in order to create semblances based on symptoms. This seems to be true for children and seems to have been true in the evolution of humans.

These communication stages reflect the order in which children learn language. Infants are capable only of symptomatic behaviors until they are about six months old. Until that time their behavior is dictated largely by internal states, such as hunger, pain, and pleasure. At about six months we begin to see their sign behavior expand as they obtain increasing control over their faces, bodies, and hands. They begin to use **ritual** semblances to indicate their wishes and needs. They are also entering the "babbling" phase, during which time they practice the sounds of their language. By the time they speak their first word, which is likely to be the proper symbol "mama," at about a year, they are pointing and using the begging, or "gimme," gesture regularly. These gestures are ritual semblances. Two-word phrases begin to occur at about two years of age; by three, children are beginning to use conceptual and syntactic symbols. By the age of five a child has learned to use and understand almost a thousand rules of grammar. Of course, children can't explain those rules; they just *know* them. It is important to note that each stage builds on the foundation laid by the preceding stage. Further, old stages are not supplanted by the new; rather, new stages incorporate the old ones, thereby expanding the communication potential of the individual and the species.[4]

These stages are significant in that they appear to parallel the evolution of communication (Bonner, 1980; Reynolds, 1981; Liska, 1993a, 1993b). If we look to other animals for insights into the stages of evolution of communication behaviors, we find a distinct trend toward increasingly symbolic behavior as we move from simple to complex species. For example, although ants use scent signs to coordinate a complex, highly organized society, their behaviors are genetically determined symptoms, which can only be modified through genetic means. Chimpanzees, our closest living relative, use tools, an instance of semblamatic behavior, and use semblances to initiate bouts of play or to coordinate hunting activities (Goodall, 1986). Captive chimps are known to be able to learn to use symbolic signs to communicate with other chimps and with their human companions (Gardner, Gardner, and Van Cantfort, 1989; Savage-Rumbaugh, 1986). Clearly, chimpanzees have the potential to acquire and use symbols. To our knowledge, however, they have not created a set of symbols in the wild. Their communication does allow them considerable flexibility in adapting to their environment, an ability well beyond that of the social insects.

WHAT ARE SOME FUNCTIONS OF COMMUNICATION?

Information-gathering, facilitating cooperation, enhancing or reducing competition and conflict, self-actualization, and entertainment are major functions of communication. Communication may serve a variety of other goals, depending upon the situation. We may use communication to defend our egos, reinforce our self-image, or simply as a release of emotions. Those are rather specific goals for communication. The goals we will discuss here cut across situations, people, and time, and appear fundamental to communication messages.

Information Gathering

One of the fundamental properties of any ecology is that it is information rich. In order to survive, individuals of all species must be able to process, respond to, act upon, and control the information to which they have access. We live in a complex world in which communication technologies have dramatically increased the amount of information available for our consumption. Not only has the amount of information increased, but the responsibility for sorting through it and determining its worth has increased proportionately.

Shortcuts to Gathering Information This vast array of knowledge may appear overwhelming given the time we have available to digest it. We cannot know about everything, so we take shortcuts in gathering information. Sometimes those shortcuts produce less than a reasoned decision, as when we vote along party lines rather than find the time to sift through all the candidates' positions on the issues. At other times we may make decisions strictly on the basis of who someone is, who they associate with, their occupation, and/or their opinions on other issues. Again, this may result in a flawed decision. We might make a decision based on the opinion of only one "expert," which is not a solid foundation on which to decide.

Unequal Access to Information One of the resources we compete for is information. This may sound strange given the apparent wealth of information available to us, but we do not have equal access to information. Nor do we have equal opportunity to participate in decisions that affect our lives. The practice of insider trading, which is illegal but nevertheless practiced, serves as one example. Our relationship with the medical community is another example: Because most of us are unfamiliar with medical terminology, which requires expert interpretation and translation, we probably accept whatever explanation is provided by our physicians and rarely attempt to sort through the information ourselves. How many of you ask to see your x-rays, lab test results, or MRI reports? And if you did, could you make sense of what you saw/read? How many of you look up a report on a prescribed drug to check its chemical compound or possible side effects?

The Importance of Critical Thinking Gathering information requires critical assessment and thinking about the source and content of the information. Early in life we learn that we cannot believe everything we hear, see, and read. For example, Loftus' (1979, 1980) research on the fallibility of eyewitness testimony is clear evidence that we see through a filter of beliefs, values, and expectations that profoundly influence our perceptions and subsequent reporting of events. Loftus found that varying key words in questions about an event could bias the observers' reports. Specifically, she asked observers for the assessment of damages in a car wreck they witnessed. Their damage estimates went up when they were asked about the two cars that "smashed" into one another, as compared to lower estimates when asked about the two cars that "hit" one another. Clearly, the difference between "hit" and "smash" is costly. People with racial prejudices are more likely to report erroneously that a criminal is a person of color than are those without prejudice. Knowing that these predispositions can affect the accuracy of eyewitness testimony can be very helpful to lawyers, judges, and juries faced with the task of determining the accuracy of eyewitness reports.

Criteria for Critical Decisions   We have emphasized the importance of "reasoned" **critical decisions** in response to communication. You may wonder just what criteria we are advocating for making such decisions. We are suggesting that: (1) decisions should be based on the best, most current information available; (2) information sources should be reliable and unbiased; (3) the needs of all parties should be carefully considered; (4) long-term as well as short-term consequences should be considered; and (5) the decision maker(s) should be as free from bias as possible. This is a pretty tall order, and it is unlikely than any of us will ever be able to apply all of these standards to all of the decisions we make.

Thoroughly unbiased decisions are especially difficult (if not impossible) to make, because we all have blind spots that impede our ability to be objective. We are, for example, most likely to react negatively to characteristics of others that we dislike in ourselves. We are less likely to make objective decisions when we are ego-involved in a topic or issue. And we are less likely to make unbiased decisions when we only have access to limited information. Sometimes we avoid information that conflicts with what we already believe, a process called **selective exposure.** At other times we may only hear and read what we want to, and filter out the rest. As Simon and Garfunkel put it: "A man hears what he wants to hear and disregards the rest." This is called **selective perception.**

Of course, it is of considerable advantage to an individual to learn to detect unreliable information. It is also advantageous for a democratic society to take care that its populace learns to detect biased information. That members of a society are adept at critical thinking and listening helps to prevent single groups from exercising control over all others. An open market requires that consumers be able to evaluate advertising and make decisions about what products to purchase. The implementation of democratic principles mandates that voters be able to examine political propaganda critically and then decide how to vote.

Facilitating Cooperation

Communication also serves as the glue that holds societies together. We are an intensely social species whose lives are thoroughly interdependent. Therefore, we are constantly trying to balance selfish needs with the needs of others. Sometimes those needs come into conflict and we need to negotiate solutions that account for the best interests of all involved. This is no easy task, as any of you with a spouse, siblings, or roommates will immediately understand.

The strain on our ability to cooperate has undoubtedly increased as the world's population has grown. That is, as population density increases, so too does our need to find creative solutions through communication increase. For example, all over the world, human population growth has forced other native species into smaller and smaller territories. Many scientists are concerned with how to balance the land and economic needs of people with those of wildlife. Various solutions have been tried. In some places, such as South Africa, "culling" of herds of elephant has been one way to keep the elephant population stable for the land available, and out of the way of human development. In Rwanda, Uganda, and Zaire, the only home of the mountain gorilla, brief, guided gorilla treks are providing much needed jobs and income for locals used to living at a subsistence level. In the process, the natives have come to understand better the gorillas and their significance to the ecology. Armed with information rather than guns, the local people are working out a system of mutual benefit to themselves and the gorillas.

Enhancing or Reducing Competition and Conflict

Interaction within and across species is frequently founded on competition for limited resources, and this struggle has been characterized as nature "red in tooth and claw" (Alfred, Lord Tennyson). That competition is a fact of life would be disputed by few, and the use of communication in the quest for a share of the available resources is evident in the massive numbers of advertisements for products and services. In fact, the prevailing theme in the capitalist West is of an economy and social structure based on a "dog-eat-dog" world. And, while the real message from nature appears to be one emphasizing mutualism and symbiosis, individual, social, and economic competition is still a reality with which we all must contend.

The resources for which we compete may take the form of natural resources (such as food, land, and water), money, things, status, and/or friends. My 10-year-old niece, Courtney, has two close friends, one of whom recently decided that she didn't like the third friend in the trio. She set about pointing out to Courtney all the shortcomings of the third girl, apparently in order to convince Courtney to exclude the girl from their activities. When this did not work, she told Courtney that she would have to choose between them. I interpreted this as competition for Courtney's time and friendship, a situation that is not particularly unusual. There are tales of law students trying to stay at the top of their class by tearing out articles from law books or stealing the books in order to prevent others from having access to them. And it is not uncommon for football and basketball players to attempt to psych-out members of the other team by whispering demeaning comments to them while on the field or court. Using strategies of ingratiation with teachers and bosses is another way to attempt to gain an advantage over others.

Even an apparently cooperative stance can result in a competitive edge. Prior to publishing his treatise on the evolution of species, Darwin learned that a younger scholar named Wallace had written a paper that presented the same theory Darwin had developed. Darwin "appealed to his friends to find some honorable way that would recognize both his priority and Wallace's discovery. His friends proposed a joint presentation of Wallace's paper with some of Darwin's earlier, unpublished writings" (Gould, 1993, p. 21). Their papers were jointly presented in London and later published in 1858 in the *Proceedings of the Linnean Society of London.* It is interesting to note that Darwin's name is a household word, while Wallace is relatively unknown outside the halls of academia.

As a final illustration of the use of communication as an instrument of competition, I turn to the U.S. legal system, which by definition is an adversarial one in which only one side can prevail, even in the case of plea bargaining. And do not let television courtroom dramas such as "Matlock," "Perry Mason," or "L.A. Law" suggest otherwise: The object of this communication game is not to discover the truth, but to win.

We may reduce competition by seeking cooperative solutions that benefit all parties, as in the case of the mountain gorillas I referred to earlier. Or we may choose to exit from interactions with those seeking competition and choose others who appear more cooperative. Karl Marx offered socialism as an alternative to the competitiveness of capitalism; but in practice, competition prevailed and the ruling party took most of the profits and left the masses with little. We may eliminate competitors by emphasizing their weaknesses, by buying them out, by voting them out, or via more violent means.

Self-Actualization

Effects of Social Isolation Humans are so dependent upon social interaction that communication deprivation is known to result in temporary perceptual disturbances, mental disability, and emotional disruption. If you have ever had the experience of being isolated from other humans and communication media for some length of time, you know that the drive to interact is so great that you may talk to yourself or to other objects in your environment. Infants deprived of touch early in life may evidence slower physical and mental development. As a form of communication, touch is considered to be so important to development and bonding with other humans that babies born prematurely must be stroked and touched frequently by their parents and caregivers.

Research on the effects of social isolation on rhesus macaques (monkeys) offers a dramatic illustration of how dependent primates are on interaction with others. In a series of studies conducted at the Yerkes Primate Center,

Harlow and his colleagues separated newborn monkeys from their mothers and from any interaction with others (Harlow and Harlow, 1965). After several weeks or months these isolates were introduced to other monkeys. The isolates ran from their conspecifics, screaming with fear. Even with time, the isolates never integrated into the group. Moreover, they demonstrated severely aberrant behaviors, such as self-mutilation. Given the similarities across all species of primate, it is probably safe to assume that were such research conducted with humans, the results would be similar.

The self-actualization function has to do with the effects of communication upon the self. We self-actualize by using communication to serve the following subfunctions: regulating uncertainty, developing empathy, and sharing subjective experience.

Regulating Uncertainty We try to make our lives a balance between uncertainty and predictability by regulating the amount and complexity of information we take in. Communication can be used to reduce uncertainty when we are experiencing information overload. Thus, we may avoid communication sources for a while in order to reduce uncertainty. Or we may fall back on a trusted source. Rather than gather all the available information about new models of cars, for instance, we may depend upon a single, trusted source such as *Road and Track* or *Consumer Reports*. We also use communication to overcome an environment that is uncomfortably predictable. When we are feeling information deprived (bored), we may seek out the company of others, turn on TV, read a new book, or go to a movie.

A stressful physical or social ecology may inhibit our ability to self-actualize. A work environment marked by intense competition or personality conflicts, or one in which information is restricted and thus rumors run rampant, may result in feelings of distrust and alienation. Such feelings are counterproductive to our sense of self-worth, and thwart our ability to self-actualize. Of course, we are unlikely to be able to self-actualize if basic physical needs such as food, water, and safety are not met.

Developing Empathy Communication may improve our feelings of empathy with others. The ability to empathize with others, to "walk a mile in their moccasins," helps us get along with others more effectively. It may also bring about greater self-understanding. My coauthor once described the highest level of empathy thusly: When you cry, I taste salt.

Sharing Subjective Experience Via communication we share our subjective feelings with others in order to confirm our feelings and thus to gain confidence. Sharing our subjective experiences helps us sort out our biases and blind spots. For example, in sharing our feelings with a friend, we discover that our suspicions that she was ignoring us due to something we unwittingly did or said were not accurate. Actually, she was simply so swamped with work that she didn't have time to call or stop by. Thus, sharing experiences helps to keep our emotions anchored and in check. Sharing feelings and experiences is also one of the most important ways in which we develop empathy for others. In sharing different experiences we gain knowledge about one another, and that knowledge is essential to the quality of our relationships. Finally, sharing experiences may act as an outlet for ventilation of emotions before they fester or reach an explosive level.

Entertainment

People engage in conversation because they like to converse and find it a pleasurable experience (Rubin, Perse, & Babato, 1988). In fact, a great deal of our social interaction may occur primarily for the purpose of entertainment. We may have friends who engage in friendly debates on almost any topic just for the fun of it. We frequently go to movies and watch television simply for entertainment; and while some programs may have a deep message, many are just lighthearted and fun. Finally, we may choose to watch or interact with certain people just because we find them entertaining.

Interactions frequently serve multiple functions. Thus, for example, in the course of a casual conversation we may simultaneously be informed, further a budding friendship, and be entertained. Beyond providing the means for acquiring knowledge, facilitating cooperation, enhancing or reducing competition and conflict, and serving as entertainment, social interaction is fundamental to our mental health and essential to our survival.

WHAT IS THE ROLE OF COMMUNICATION IN HUMAN SURVIVAL?

All animals communicate, but humans have made it their single most distinguishing characteristic. Our exaggerated need for and fascination with using signs is probably not matched by any other living species. Although apes such as the chimpanzee, gorilla, and orangatun have learned to manipulate symbolic signs via some form of manual language, that is, sign language, it was our early hominid ancestors who first *created* symbols, and, ultimately, language. This is not to suggest that other species don't possess advanced communication systems, because they do. Wild-living apes engage in a wide range of symptomatic and semblamatic signs, such as gestures and calls (Goodall, 1986). Whales sing an intricate song that changes over time and that varies from group to group (Payne, 1991). Orca (killer whales) use calls that have specific meanings and that vary from group to group, much as different human groups have different dialects (Gormley, 1990). And wolves use an elaborate set of postures for coordinating the pack. But humans seem especially driven to engage in inventing and manipulating symbolic signs. Indeed, humans seem to communicate because they *have to*. As Thomas (1974) has written:

> It begins to look, more and more disturbingly, as if the gift of language is the single human trait that marks us genetically, setting us apart from the rest of life. Language is, like nest-building or hive-making, the universal and biologically specific activity of human beings. We engage in it communally, compulsively, and automatically. We cannot be human without it; if we were to be separated from it our minds would die, as surely as bees lost from the hive. (p. 89)

It appears that our very existence is bound up in communication signs. We use communication signs to reveal our likes and dislikes, to negotiate relationships with family, friends, and co-workers, and, thanks to television, to peek in on the lives of famous people across the world. Signs tell us when to stop, when to go, and when to yield. Signs used by advertisers tell us what products we should own and what labels to look for, as well as showing us how we should live and dress. Libraries and computer data banks are storehouses for the knowledge generated through the ages. Books offer advice on how to manage, store, and retrieve information, and suggest strategies for how we can manage the stress associated with the information-laden world in which we live. Computer software programs are available to help us manage, store, and retrieve vast amounts of information generated in our homes, businesses, and offices. I spend about two hours a day using electronic mail to keep in touch with my colleagues at institutions around the world, and to gather data via "networks" that provide information about new books, jobs, and ideas in various academic disciplines. According to Miller (1967):

> In order to survive in a fluctuating environment, an organism must have some capacity to collect, process, and use information. This capacity is greatest in man, so that he is able to learn elaborate coding systems and to organize his social behavior by communicating with his fellow men. (p. 46)

(These ideas apply equally well to women, of course.)

John Lilly, who is famous for his research on the communication between humans and dolphins, has suggested that "for the mental health of each one of us, for the national and international peace of all of us, communication is a paramount and pressing issue" (1967, p. 22).

HOW DO IDEAS EVOLVE?

Communication and Survival

Clearly, communication is essential to our survival. However, this is not to suggest that communication will ensure our survival. We have wielded word weapons that have caused serious wounds to our environment. We have used symbols to represent the processes of nuclear fission, thereby creating a weapon of immense destructive powers—the nuclear bomb. Communication was used to build the Iron Curtain, and communication ultimately tore it down. Leaders such as Napolean, Hitler, and Stalin used communication to destroy governments and cultures. We are bombarded with diverse information from various sources, and asked to decide who, and what information, is correct. How are we to decide which side of a controversy we are on when so many different opinions are bombarding us? How can we sift through the frequently conflicting information provided us by various individuals, groups, and organizations?

Ideological Evolution

The answer to this question rests on our individual and collective ability to generate and critically evaluate the opinions to which we are exposed. This process has been called **ideological evolution,** and, like biological evolution, the process depends upon three necessary conditions: **variety, selection,** and **retention** (Cronkhite, 1976). In biological evolution, genetic variety is essential to the survival of species. Animals that are too inbred, that is, genetically similar, will be more susceptible to the ravages of and changes in the environment. For instance, the wild cheetah population is now so genetically similar that scientists have real concern that a feline virus could wipe out the entire remaining population. In nature, selection is the weeding out of those individuals who are unfit; they will either die out or fail to reproduce. The removal of unfit members of the species facilitates the strengthening of the species as a whole. Retention has to do with the fact that some structures and behaviors are passed on by those who produce more offspring, who in turn live to produce offspring of their own. The elaboration of communication found in "higher" mammals, and especially humans, is the result of retention. Indeed, humans appear to be genetically wired for language with what Chomsky (1957, 1965) refers to as an innate Language Acquisition Device (LAD).

Ideological evolution also requires variety, selection, and retention, but of ideas rather than genes. "If we don't have a variety of ideas and plans available to us, we may suddenly find ourselves facing a time whose idea has not yet come" (Cronkhite, 1976, p. 9). What this means is that we need to encourage free and creative thinking in order to generate a great variety of ideas from which to select. Thus, the right to free expression of ideas is fundamental to our very survival.

Variety Recent history attests to the importance of a variety of ideas. Hitler, Lenin, and Stalin each severely restricted the right to free and open exchange of ideas. In all cases, people who didn't abide by those restrictions were incarcerated; many were killed. Even though people suffered severe social and economic inequities, they were not free to criticize the governments and people responsible for those inequities.

Attempts at censorship are not unknown in the United States either. Some groups support banning books containing "questionable," "radical," or "obscene" material. Movies and television programs are targets for these groups also. And our government frequently withholds information from the public on the grounds that to reveal such information would threaten "national security." Remember that at one time slaves were not allowed to learn to read or write, and whites were not allowed to teach them. Keeping blacks illiterate was one way to prevent them from integrating into white society. Moreover, people who are not literate cannot compete for good jobs. Nor are they as able to participate in the political decision-making process, thereby limiting their influence on social and economic policies. Sometimes we avoid offering new ideas because the environment is inhibiting and/or we feel uncomfortable. We may not offer a new idea for fear of sounding foolish or ignorant. Or we may feel hesitant to offer ideas because others in the group are not open to new ideas and tend to reject them out of hand.

Selection Along with freedom comes the responsibility of selecting ideas worth keeping. We are not suggesting that we accept all ideas equally. Clearly, some ideas are better than others, more appropriate to the problem or issue, more efficient, more ethical, and/or more practical than others. These and other criteria will be important in helping us sort the better ideas from the total population of ideas. We are not advocating some version of censorship either. We are not suggesting killing ideas outright. Rather we suggest adopting some ideas over others because they are the most reasonable at the time. An idea has been selected when it is accepted by those who are capable of retaining and propagating it.

Retention Retained ideas become "institutionalized" and find their expression in the form of laws, customs, and conventions. These institutionalized ideas become the fabric from which a culture is woven. As ideas change, so do cultures. Ideas may outlive their utility, change as a result of changing information and conditions, and/or die a natural death. It now seems strange to contemplate a time when people believed that the world was flat and that the earth was the center of the universe. So-called "blue laws" are laws that are on the books but no longer enforced because cultural ideas have changed. The idea that women are best suited to playing the role of homemaker has changed rather rapidly in the past thirty years, in the United States at least. And more Americans are advocating political isolationism, meaning they want more attention and money directed at domestic rather than international problems. This same view was popular between World War I and World War II, indicating that old ideas frequently remain dormant until conditions warrant their revival.

WHAT IS THE ROLE OF COMMUNICATION IN THE EVOLUTION OF IDEAS?

Communication is clearly central in the evolution of ideas. Free, uncensored communication produces a variety of ideas; critical individual and public deliberation constitutes the means by which ideas are selected; and the selected ideas are then publicized, institutionalized, and retained using the various communication media:

> The functioning of this selector mechanism depends upon the use of communication. . . . Of course, communication is involved in all three processes: mutant ideas are carried like seeds on the winds of communication; the retention-propagation system uses communication as a selective herbicide to destroy the ideological mutations and as a fertilizer to maintain the health of the ideological strains that have been chosen for preservation. But at the heart of the entire process is the selector mechanism and the discipline which ministers to its health: . . . communication. (Cronkhite, 1974, p. 268)

We play a major role in this process of ideological evolution. We discuss ideas with our friends, family, and co-workers, thereby testing our ideas against the opinions of others. As parents we teach our children not only the ideas of their culture, but the standards by which those ideas are or should be judged. As teachers of communication we try to make students aware of a variety of ideas, the data on which those ideas are based, and the standards by which they should be judged. Equally as important, we attempt to make students aware of the influences that may prevent them from making reasoned decisions. We discuss the ways in which verbal and nonverbal signs influence their perceptions, as well as how their views of themselves and others may direct their decisions in response to communication messages. We discuss how communication contexts influence communication behavior, and how media may be used to manipulate our thoughts and expectations. Finally, we offer an ecological view of communication in order to illuminate how communication has evolved across species, cultures, and time, in the hopes that such a perspective will enable this and succeeding generations to understand better the power of the tools at their disposal.

CONCLUSION

The overriding goal of this book is to facilitate your understanding of your own and others' communication, thus enabling you to recognize the forces at work that may facilitate or constrain communication. That is, we hope to help you become *critical* consumers of communication messages. Postman and Weingartner (1969) argued that the function of education is to facilitate the development of "crap-detection devices" in students' minds. We couldn't agree more.

KEY TERMS AND CONCEPTS

communication	symbol	selective exposure
sign	intention	selective perception
symptom	ritual	ideological evolution:
semblances	critical decisions	variety, selection, retention

NOTES

1. For a discussion of these issues, see References for complete citations for Infante, Rancer, and Womack, 1993; Andersen, 1991; Motley, 1986, 1990, 1991; Cronkhite, 1986.
2. For an elaborated discussion of these types of signs see: J. Liska, Variations in the arbitrariness of ASL: An assessment of the symbolicity of simian signs, *Human Evolution* 2 (1987): 205–212; and Liska, 1993a, 1993b.
3. See References for complete citations for Andersen, 1991; Cronkhite, 1986; Motley, 1990, 1991.
4. For further discussion of language development in children see: P. S. Dale, *Language Development*, 2nd. ed. (New York: Holt, Rinehart, and Winston, 1976); V. Fromkin and R. Rodman, *An Introduction to Language* (New York: Holt, Rinehart, and Winston, 1983); E. H. Lenneberg and E. Lenneberg (eds.), *Foundations of Language Development*, I & II (New York: Academic Press, 1975); M. Bowerman, Language development, in H. Triandis and

A. Heron (eds.), *Handbook of Cross-Cultural Psychology: Developmental Psychology* (Boston: Allyn and Bacon, 1981); E. Wanner and L. Gleitman, *Language Acquisition: The State of the Art* (Cambridge, England: Cambridge University Press, 1982); F. S. Kessel, *The Development of Language and Language Researchers: Essays in Honor of Roger Brown* (Hillsdale, N.J.: Lawrence Erlbaum, 1988).

REFERENCES

Andersen, P. A. (1991). When one cannot not communicate: A challenge to Motley's traditional communication postulates. *Communication Studies* 42: 309–325.

Bonner, J. T. (1980). *The Evolution of Culture in Animals.* Princeton, N.J.: Princeton University Press.

Cheney, D. L., and Seyfarth, R. M. (1990). *How Monkeys See the World.* Chicago: University of Chicago Press.

Chomsky, N. (1957). *Syntactic Structures.* The Hague: Mouton.

———. (1965). *Aspects of the Theory of Syntax.* Cambridge, Mass.: MIT Press.

Cronkhite, G. (1974). Rhetoric, communication, and psychoepistemology. In W. Fisher (ed.), *Rhetoric: A Tradition in Transition,* pp. 261–278,. East Lansing: Michigan State University Press.

———. (1976). *Communication and Awareness.* Menlo Park, Calif.: Benjamin/Cummings.

———. (1986). On the focus, scope, and coherence of the study of human symbolic activity. *Quarterly Journal of Speech* 72: 231–246.

Diamond, J. (1992). *The Third Chimpanzee.* New York: HarperCollins.

Gardner, R. A., Gardner, B. T., and Van Cantfort, T. E. (1989). *Teaching Sign Language to Chimpanzees.* New York: State University of New York Press.

Goodall, J. (1986). *The Chimpanzees of Gombe: Patterns of Behavior.* Cambridge, Mass.: Harvard University Press.

Gormley, G. (1990). *Orcas of the Gulf: A Natural History.* San Francisco, Calif: Sierra Club Books.

Gould, S. J. (1993). The first unmasking of nature. *Natural History* 4: 14–21.

Harlow, H. F., and Harlow, M. K. (1965). The affectional systems. In *Behavior of Non-Human Primates,* edited by A. M. Schrier, H. F. Harlow, and F. Stollnitz, pp. 287–334. New York: Academic Press.

Infante, D. A., Rancer, A. S., and Womack, D. F. (1993). *Building Communication Theory,* 2nd ed. Prospect Heights, Ill.: Waveland Press.

Lilly, J. C. (1967). *The Mind of the Dolphin: A Nonhuman Intelligence.* New York: Discus-Avon.

Liska, J. (1988). Ritual/representation as the semiogenetic precursor of hominid symbol use. Paper presented at the International Conference on the Biology of Language: Essentialist vs. Evolutionist in the Nature of Language. Czerniejewo, Poland.

———. (1993a). Bee dances, bird songs, monkey calls, and cetecean sonar: Is speech unique? *Western Journal of Communication* 57: 1–26.

———. (1993b). Signs of the apes, songs of the whales: Comparing signs across species. *European Journal of Cognitive Systems* 3–4: 381–397.

———. (in press). Sign arbitrariness as an index of semiogenesis. *Studies in Language Origins.* Amsterdam/Philadelphia: John Benjamins.

Loftus, E. F. (1979). *Eyewitness Testimony.* Cambridge, Mass.: Harvard University Press.

———. (1980). *Memory.* Reading, Mass.: Addison-Wesley.

Miller, G. A. (1967). *Psychology of Communication.* Baltimore: Penguin Books.

Motley, M. T. (1986). Consciousness and intentionality in communication: A preliminary model and methodological approaches. *Western Journal of Speech Communication* 50: 3–23.

———. (1990). On whether one can(not) communicate: An examination via traditional communication postulates. *Western Journal of Speech Communication* 54: 1–20.

———. (1991). How one may not communicate: A reply to Andersen. *Communication Studies* 42: 326–339.

Payne, K. (1991). A change of tune. *Natural History* 3: 45–46.

Postman, N., and Weingartner, C. (1969). *Teaching as a Subversive Activity.* New York: Delacorte Press.

Reynolds, P. C. (1981). *On the Evolution of Human Behavior.* Berkeley, Calif.: University of California Press.

Rubin, R. B., Perse, E. M., and Babato, C. A. (1988). Conceptualization and measurement of interpersonal communication motives. *Human Communication Research* 14 (4): 602–628.

Savage-Rumbaugh, S. (1986). *Ape Language: From Conditioned Response to Symbol.* New York: Columbia University Press.

Smith, C. G. (1985). *Ancestral Voices.* Englewood Cliffs, N. J.: Prentice-Hall.

Thomas, L. (1974). *Lives of a Cell: Notes of a Biology Watcher.* New York: Viking-Penguin.

Watzlawick, P., Beavin, J. M., and Jackson, D. D. (1967). *Pragmatics of Human Communication.* New York: Norton.

To remain ignorant of things that happened before you were born is to remain a child.
—Cicero

The future isn't what it used to be.
—variously ascribed

The Ghosts of Our Ancestors: The Development of Communication, from Tools to Television

3

CHAPTER OUTLINE

Introduction

In the Beginning
> *From Dinosaurs to Primates*
> *Role of Sociality*
> *Primate Advantages*

The Dawn of Humans
> *Relation of Human and Nonhuman Primates*

Rock and Cave Images
> *Meanings and Significance of Rock and Cave Images*
> *Origins of Writing*
> *African vs. European Rock Art*

The Development of Writing
> *Early Forms of Writing*
> *Development of the Alphabet*
> *Development of Paper*
> *Mass Production of Print*

The Computer Age

Extensions of Our Eyes and Ears
> *Radio*
> *Telephone*
> *Photography*
> *Television*

INTRODUCTION

It is a common belief that humans are unique in their ability to engage in such advanced forms of communication as language, speech, reading, and writing. And certainly, communication seems to be a defining characteristic of our lives. We talk to one another not just to share information, but apparently for the sheer pleasure of it (Rubin, Perse, and Babato, 1988). In the course of our history, especially our more recent history, we have invented tools and technologies for expanding our abilities to communicate with those who inhabit territories far removed from our own. At one time in our not-so-distant past, we knew little of the activities, beliefs, traditions, and ceremonies of tribes living relatively close to us. The use of animals such as Asian elephants, camels, and horses to broaden our range of travel, water-going vessels, and then motorized vehicles of various sorts were initial steps in promoting cross-tribal interaction. As humans from various cultures came into contact they fought, intermarried, and, most importantly, interacted, thus forever altering their view of themselves and their world. The blending of cultural beliefs, traditions, and languages has been facilitated further by communication technologies such as the printing press, the telegraph, the telephone, television, the computer, the fax machine, and satellites. The "military action" in Vietnam was the first war to be projected via television into our homes. The famines of Ethiopia and Somalia, the racial wars of South Africa, the ethnic conflicts of the former Yugoslavia, the Persian Gulf War, the demise of the Berlin Wall, and the spreading wave of democracy in a once-totalitarian part of the world are points of debate and discussion for those of us who observe those events from a distance of thousands of miles. As Schramm (1988) puts it:

> We now stand at a point in time that historians and scientists think may be the beginning of an Age of Communication, or, as some prefer to call it, an Age of Information, in which communication of information may be the chief source of human productivity in the same way as practical science and industry were chief sources during the Industrial Revolution. This provocative theory gives us cause to think that some examination of and reflection on the remarkable history of communication is timely and worthwhile. (p. xv)

Yet these technologies, these tools of communication, find their source in our distant past. The Age of Communication began long ago, and the foundations were built by our now-long-extinct ancestors, distant shadows lurking in the equatorial forests we once called home. It is to them we must pay homage, for they were the ones who set the stage on which we currently play out our lives. It is to these ghosts of our ancestors, to those who went before, that this chapter, and indeed this book, is dedicated.

IN THE BEGINNING

From Dinosaurs to Primates

With a resounding asteroidal bang the age of dinosaurs came to an end, and the age of mammals began, an age in which we currently live.[1] The dinosaurs had ruled the earth for well over 100 million years, their legacy modern-day birds and reptiles.

But the dinosaurs were not alone on earth. Among other species, the mammals, probably comparatively few in number, took this opportunity to invade niches otherwise inhabited by the more dominant and prolific aristocracy, the dinosaurs. Among those mammals was a small, probably nocturnal animal, a prosimian, to which we owe our ancestry. This animal, similar to the modern-day lemur of Madagascar, was the foundation stock out of which all primates radiated, including monkeys, apes, and humans, who still roam the earth. The evidence for this first ancestor suggests it was alive some 60–65 million years ago. In the course of those many years since, numerous branches grew from the main stem, with subsequent branches shooting off those secondary stalks.

By approximately 40 million years ago appeared the Old World monkeys of what is now Africa. Their cousins of the New World (the continents of what are now North, Central, and South America) split from the ancestral stock about 30 million years ago. This branch is subsequently unrelated to humans, who evolved in the Old World. The first apes appeared about 25–30 million years ago, the first hominids approximately 5–7 million years ago, the time at which the ancestors of present-day chimpanzees went their separate way from our ancestors, the Australopithecines.[2]

Primate Characteristics All primates share certain anatomical, neurophysiological, and behavioral characteristics: grasping hands, with nails (instead of claws) and an opposable thumb; overlapping fields of vision (stereoscopy) and sensitivity to color; reduction of the size and sensitivity of olfactory apparatus; a large and complex brain, particularly in the regions controlling vision, touch, and the coordination of the two; and long life spans characterized by long childhoods, dependency upon the mother, and a low rate of reproduction (Jolly, 1985). Of particular significance to our discussion is that primates generally are highly social animals whose very survival as individuals depends upon the coordinated efforts of the group. The claim that "no [hu]man is an island" can be generalized to include most primates. And this intense sociality is thought to have played an important role in the development of communication (Humphrey, 1976).

Role of Sociality

All social species evidence elaborate forms of communication. Social insects such as ants use a chemical code that organizes a complex organization based on division of labor, differentiation of roles, and a hierarchy of dominance (Wilson, 1971, 1992). Indeed, the complexity and efficiency of their social coordination may be unmatched by any other species of "higher" intelligence. So too the bees, whose dances are legendary in their ability to communicate essential information to other members of the hive. Bees perform a variety of dances for the benefit of other worker bees as to the direction, type, and readiness of pollinating plants they use to make honey (von Frisch, 1967). However, their roles and functions within the hive, and the various steps incorporated into their dances, are largely **genetically fixed,** not learned.

While this suggests the enormous power of the genes to code for highly specific behavior, it is a situation quite different from the "languages" used by other social species such as dogs, wolves, elephants, and primates. Whereas the signs used by bees and ants are symptoms, many of the signs used by dogs, wolves, and so on are learned and modified by experience. These signs are rituals, and they expanded markedly the ability to communicate.

Of particular importance is that these signs are more under the voluntary control of individuals and can therefore be used for a wide variety of purposes and in a variety of conditions or situations. For example, with signs such as rituals, animals can misrepresent their feelings and deceive others. Thus, a young male chimpanzee may use signs of submission to placate the pack leader, all the while planning a takeover of leadership, an idea best kept secret until the actual time of the attempted coup. Vervet monkeys, a species widely distributed in east Africa, have arbitrary names for predators—eagle, snake, and leopard—and such naming is a fundamental characteristic of language (Cheney and Seyfarth, 1990). Moreover, a vervet under attack by another member of his group may use an alarm call to distract his attacker, a clear instance of using communication to save one's skin (Cheney and Seyfarth, 1991). I well remember that as a youth I used a similar strategy with my little brother when I wanted to get something he had but was unwilling to give up. I would shout, "Look out!" point, and adopt a fearful expression. And when he followed my cue, I would grab from him whatever it was I wanted. This was successful as long as I didn't overdo it. Had I not been able to feign a look of fear, the ploy wouldn't have been possible. Thus, while symptoms always tell the truth because they are immutable, signs such as rituals offer the individual capable of using them a greater flexibility in communication.

Chimpanzees use a wide variety of postures, gestures, facial expressions, and vocalizations for engaging in social interaction, many similar to those used by humans. Chimps maintain friendships and alliances, hold grudges, attempt revenge on those who have slighted them, deceive one another, use and make tools, hunt, and teach one another the ways of their culture using a series of ritual signs learned by observation and imitation. They further evidence the capacity for human forms of language, a capacity that clearly must be much older than the 7 million years since the split of the human-chimp lineage.[3]

But two questions remain: (1) Why might sociality be so important in promoting advanced forms of communication? (2) What is unusual about primates that they developed forms of communication well beyond those of other social species such as insects and bees? The answers to each question are clearly interrelated, but for the sake of clarity I will deal with them separately.

Why Might Sociality Be So Important in Promoting Advanced Forms of Communication?   Consider what is required of a social animal: At the very least, you must be able to distinguish self from others, to identify as individuals parents, siblings, and other kin, as well as others who comprise the group. You must be able to predict the behavior of others relative to your own behavior, and must know the norms or expectations for behavior considered appropriate (and inappropriate) by the group. Thus, for example, you need to recognize who the leaders are and how to show them the proper respect.

Let's take dominance hierarchies as one illustration since they are fundamental to all social groups. **Dominance** may be determined by heritage, as in the case of the monarchies of Europe. That is, you have status and dominance by virtue of being born into a family already possessing a high level of social status. On the other hand, you may achieve status and dominance via strength; that is you may fight your way to the top using physical force. This strategy carries a big risk, for you may not live long enough to pass on your genes.

Now, consider instead using a series of threats and bluffs (rituals) to obtain a leadership position. This has the advantage of physical force without the potential risks of injury and possibly death. Think of the advantages of developing friendships and alliances with those of higher rank: You can move up the hierarchy with minimal risk to self and enjoy the pleasure of the company of others. You may have a special skill that is sought out by other members of the group, thus elevating your status as a result of that particular expertise. Those early humans who were especially skilled at making stone tools, at identifying medicinal plants, at treating the illnesses of others, or at tracking game may have enjoyed leadership positions in the group. Those particularly skilled at social interaction may have been called upon to mediate conflicts and thus been much sought after and held in high esteem. Note that these latter strategies require increasingly sophisticated modes of communication.

> While some degree of dominance may result from one's birth order, kinship, or physical attributes, social and expert skills are also important. One's birth order may no longer be remembered by most members of the group, one's family may have died off, and one's age and physical condition may no longer reflect strength and vigor; yet, if one is socially skilled and wise, and if strong alliances and friendships have been maintained, one may continue to exert a strong influence over the lives of others in the group. (Liska, 1990, p. 77)

Group living requires sensitivity to the needs of others, a sense of community or "groupness," and an ability to negotiate your own needs, feelings, and concerns with those of others. You must know the personalities of others: who to trust and who to avoid, who is congenial and who is moody and unpredictable, and who is knowledgeable and who isn't. Since it is a fundamental truth that individuals attempt to gain for self at the expense of others, it is valuable to know how to detect deception and the strategies of ingratiation and false friendship. Just as these strategies depend upon communication for their enactment, you must be skilled at reading the communication of others and adjust accordingly. Thus:

> Social understanding and foresight—a social intelligence—developed in the context of coping with family or band problems of interpersonal relationships, of gaining a personal advantage without tearing the social fabric upon which one's continuing existence depends. The development of such an intellect has been seen to be the result of one or another "arms race," a gradual ratcheting up of the ability to influence one's band mates, and this same process has been seen to exist in other social animals, in particular primates where something like deception (and the vigilance against deception) or reciprocal altruism (and the vigilance against welshing on a "deal") may be present. (Morton and Page, 1992, p. 239)

What Is Unusual About Primates That They Developed Forms of Communication Well Beyond Those of Other Social Species Such as Ants and Bees? The most obvious answer is that these other social species simply do not live long enough to depend upon learning social interaction strategies and must instead enter life with a **hard-wired** set of behaviors for negotiating with other members of their species. Their amazing adaptability lies in the rapidity with which they reproduce.

The Case of the Honeybee A honeybee lives about six weeks, and within a few hours of her birth begins performing a set of tasks prescribed by her genes. Her first job is to remove wax from the partitions of the honeycomb into which the queen will lay eggs. She then plays nurse to those eggs until they are sealed into the comb to develop. Her next job is to guard the entrance to the hive. Her last venture is nectar collection, and it is then that her inborn skills at dance will be evident. She attends to the dances of other workers and follows their direction to specific plants at the height of flowering. Upon her return she provides instructions for the workers awaiting their turn at collection. When her wings are so frayed that she can no longer carry her load of nectar, she leaves the hive and dies, frequently in the mandibles of a carnivorous insect or spider. Should she die in the hive, her body sends off a particular chemical message signaling the others to remove her. Even a live bee, tainted with this chemical by a human scientist, will be carried wriggling and buzzing out of the hive by her companions. Her companions have no choice; they are simply acting on the instructions written in their genes.

Primate Advantages

But primates, and other longer-lived species, enjoy a long period of childhood in which they learn, by observation and imitation, how to identify and interact with other members of their group, the behavior expected of them, and the skills necessary to survive (e.g., food gathering, tool use, and the social strategies involved in affiliation, play, dominance, and deception, to name only a few). Their brains are far larger and more complex than those of the social insects. Combined with long periods of development, this affords them the opportunity of forging new connections, learning new behaviors, and therefore adjusting their behavior to changing conditions. Bees, on the other hand, show no preferences for some bees over others, do not dance so as to withhold information about especially rare or desirable flowers and thus keep them for themselves; instead, they cooperate fully with their colleagues and report truthfully the whereabouts of the plants on which their lives depend. Bees are born fully equipped to carry out their roles and obligations; primates are born quite incapable of surviving on their own and must learn their places in the group via their interaction with others.

This discussion could continue by examining in more detail the specifics of social interaction relative to the particular characteristics that define primates, but we discuss some of these specifics in other chapters. My point in considering sociality here is to illustrate its importance in the story of the development of communication, and how it may have influenced the elaboration of communication skills, tools, and technologies evident in contemporary humans.

THE DAWN OF HUMANS

Relation of Human and Nonhuman Primates

We can gain some insight into the communication behavior of humans by examining that found among living nonhuman primates such as monkeys and apes, because their behavior points up the capacities and abilities likely to be found in our common ancestor(s). Thus, by the time chimps and humans went their separate ways some 5–7 million years ago, it is likely that a wide range of ritual signs were in use, and the foundations for language, such as naming, were already in place.

That living chimpanzees can learn the rudiments of language strongly suggests that our common ancestor also had some form of language, or at least the capacity for it. And that language was probably a mix of gestures and vocalizations. It is unlikely that it was "speech" as we know it today, because the primates of that era did not have the vocal anatomy necessary to construct the phonemes of modern-day languages (e.g., Wind, 1983; Lieberman, 1984). Indeed, some believe that speech did not appear until *Homo sapiens* dispersed out of Africa some 200,000 or so years ago (e.g., Lieberman, 1984). Thus, it is unlikely that we would understand the vocalizations of *Homo habilis* or *Homo erectus* beyond such symptomatic vocalizations as cries of pain, fear, and joy. We would probably understand many of their facial expressions, body positions, and gestures, however, and especially those reflecting a common set of emotions, attempts at deception, and signs of dominance or submissiveness. We recognize many of these in our primate relatives; yet we encountered great difficulty in identifying the predator names used by vervet, since those signs are arbitrary, conventionalized, and thus symbolic. It is a difficulty similar to what we encounter when attempting to identify the sound patterns, words, and meanings of those humans who speak a language different from our own.

Of course, we can never know what form of communication, beyond that just described, our early ancestors used, because gestures and vocalizations do not fossilize and thus do not leave evidence of their presence. Therefore, we can only offer educated guesses as to those early communication systems. In addition to examination of the communication systems of other related species, those interested in the evolutionary foundations of communication and language depend upon the fossil and archaeological record for speculating about early communication. Let's now turn to considering some of that data as it is suggestive of the ways in which communication developed.

Upright Walking Australopithecus, the first in the hominid line, by 3.7 million years ago had developed into fully bipedal (upright) beings (Leakey, 1978). These early hominids who ventured out of the forests onto the savannahs would have been preyed upon by a number of carnivorous animals. They probably threw stones to defend themselves from those predators, and may have used other objects as tools in food gathering, much as modern chimpanzees use tools as weapons, to dig up termites, and for cracking nuts. Moreover, they were probably scavenging meat and may have been opportunistic hunters, much as chimpanzees are now. The use of tools to supplement their diet with insects, nuts, and animal flesh provided a diet enriched in protein, which probably facilitated brain growth. Moreover, **upright**

walking further freed the hands for activities such as tool use and gesture, which increasingly facilitated precision of motor control over hand movements, which in turn facilitated the ability to create tools.

Toolmaking *Homo habilis,* "handy man," entered the scene about 2–3 million years ago. The name was chosen because *Homo habilis* appears to be the first **toolmaker,** although tool use was undoubtedly common, for we find it among chimpanzees with whom we shared a common ancestor before the appearance of Australopithecus and *Homo habilis.* And toolmaking suggests important cognitive developments unusual to, although, as is now known, not unique to, hominids. Acheulean technology developed by *Homo erectus* ("upright man") about 1.7 million years ago was the primary form of tools up until the time of archaic *Homo sapiens* of some 200,000 years ago. In fact, stone tools similar to those of this era were still manufactured by all human cultures only 10,000 years ago (Toth, Clark, and Ligabue, 1992).

Toolmaking is important because it reflects an organized group structure dependent upon learning important skills and the ability to plan for the future. Tools may have been the first valued possessions of early humans, in that they were carried from place to place and may have been traded among bands. Thus, tools may have had economic value and toolmakers may have enjoyed high status positions in their groups.

Tool use and manufacture may not require much direct communication in that you can learn such skills via observation, imitation, and molding. Certainly, speech would not have been necessary to the teaching or learning of such a task. But drawing diagrams of the tools in the dirt or molding the hands of the student may have been very useful in tool manufacture.

Also important to our purposes, toolmaking is associated with hunting, a task that requires considerable organization of the hunters. The division of the spoils back at camp may well have been an important social gathering, which may have included considerable communication among those present. Again, hunting does not necessarily require a great deal of communication during the hunt; however, hunting parties may have attempted to plan strategies in advance, which would require communication.

Finally, tool use and manufacture was probably important in refined motor control of the hands, which is essential to the later development of writing. Goody writes: "It [writing] depends ultimately on man's ability to manipulate tools by means of his unique hand with its opposable thumb" (1981, p. 106).

Tanner (1981) has argued that elaborated systems of communication found among contemporary humans have their roots in mother–infant interactions and in food gathering, both being tasks undertaken by females. She too uses the data from chimpanzee society as her guide, and notes that it is females who make and use termite fishing poles and use rocks to crack open nuts. Those skills are passed from mothers to their offspring. Further, she draws on observations of hunter-gatherer societies and suggests that they provide a model for the behavior of our early hominid ancestors. Women in those societies gather food in groups, use tools in extracting tubers from the ground (a dietary mainstay especially of savannah-dwelling societies), and share with their children their knowledge of medicinal plants and of the location of and seasons for various plant food sources. Of course, since they are primarily responsible for the care of children, the children are members of food-gathering groups. Passing on this knowledge requires considerable communication. And, while women rarely participate in a hunt, they share in the task of skinning, butchering, and preparing the meat, all of which require considerable agility with tools. Again, the opportunity for social interaction surrounding these tasks may have been important in furthering the need for communication.

By about 1 million or so years ago, humans (*Homo erectus*) had learned to use and control fire, had established camps used as home bases, were becoming increasingly expert at tool manufacture, and increasingly supplemented their diet of plants and fruits with meat. Moreover, some groups of *Homo erectus* had traveled out of their native Africa into Asia, the Middle East, and northern Europe. Out of that stock arose *Homo sapiens*, who built permanent dwellings, buried their dead, developed bone wind instruments, made jewelry and other artifacts, and drew **pictographs,** signs on cliff faces and walls of caves.

Use of Fire The use of fire is significant because it probably provided protection from predators, could be used to cook meat (thus destroying many bacteria injurious to humans), extended the hours of the day (thereby providing an opportunity for continuing tasks such as tool manufacture, working bone into jewelry, and food preparation), and, importantly, further extended the opportunity for social interaction. Based on archaeological evidence, hearths appear to occupy a central location in dwellings and may have been the focus for group activities, ceremonies, and so on. Bone wind instruments suggest an ability to control air flow, which may mean that these people used some form of speech (Hewes, 1991). But it is the drawings they left behind that constitute the first hard evidence for their ability to use symbols.

ROCK AND CAVE IMAGES

Drawings on rock are located in South Africa, but it is the cave images of northern Europe, some of them dating back 18,000–20,000 years, that have received the most attention from scholars. Among the more famous are the paintings found in Altamira, now Spain, and in Lascaux in what is now France (Ruspoli, 1986). The paintings at both of these sites are located deep in the recesses of underground caves. Many of the paintings are of the animals of the area (e.g., horses, bison, wild cattle, woolly mammoths, woolly rhinoceroses, lions, and bears), and some are so realistically represented that contemporary scholars have used them to identify now-long-extinct animals (Begley, 1989). Some of the panels include both human and nonhuman animal figures and appear to picture hunting expeditions. Others portray single figures of animals and/or humans, some of them highly stylized and abstract, patterns of dots, and the outlines of human hands. In fact, the outline of human hands, apparently made by blowing paint through a reed around a hand, are found at most sites up through the rock images made by the Anasazi peoples of the southwestern United States.

The paints were made from iron minerals that produced various shades of brown, yellow, red, and black. The minerals were probably mixed with animal fat and/or blood, and brushes may have been made from animal hair. Lumps of pigments may have been used like crayons, and engravings were made using sharply edged, flaked stone tools or specialized tools called *burins* (Robbins, 1990).

Meanings and Significance of Rock and Cave Images

The meanings and significance of these drawings and their locations are not known, but many have speculated that they reflect "group planning or social purpose" (Schramm, 1988, p. 3). The hunting scenes, for example, may have been drawn as a means for planning a hunt, for visualizing its outcome, as a ceremonial reenactment of the hunt, or as a means for casting a magical spell over the hunters and their prey. The figures of humans may represent important people in the group, such as the shaman or the chief, or they may represent some concept of the gods that ruled over the affairs of humans. The patterns of dots may stand for the number of young males initiated into manhood, the number of animals killed in a given hunt or over time, the number of births and/or deaths in the band, or the number of other human competitors slain in battle. The outlines of hands are especially difficult to interpret, since they typically occur in isolation from other figures, but their repeated occurrence across sites and time suggest that they are important. Possibly, hands were considered a most important part of the human body because they are critical in our ability to produce tools, weapons, carvings, and drawings. Maybe they were the artists' signatures or the hands of shamans and chiefs, people of revered status in the band.

That many of these paintings are located deep in the bowels of caves, and in locations that required considerable climbing agility on the part of artists and viewers, and therefore are hidden from all except those familiar with their location, suggests that they may have been important in religious, magic, or initiation ceremonies. Of course, any paintings and etchings that may have been drawn in more open and accessible locations may not have survived the ravages of time and geological change. The drawings and etchings on cliff faces and rock walls in the southwestern United States, although far more recent, show considerable wear due to the effects of wind and water and, more recently, as a result of human destruction.[4]

Origins of Writing

Some of the locations have hundreds of abstract markings and scratches that may be early **hieroglyphics** and may represent the earliest attempts at writing. The next attempt at writing for which there is archaeological evidence occurred 8,000–9,000 years ago in the Middle East with the development of what Schmandt-Besserat (1978) calls counting tokens, used to record transactions such as the trading and storage of sheep and grain. And the first alphabet was developed about 4,000 years ago (Harris, 1986).

Carvings of human figures made of bone and antler also appear in the archaeological record of this period. These figures are largely of what appear to be pregnant females, and they are thought to be fertility charms. They are stylized and do not have the variability and details one would expect if they were models of particular individuals.

African vs. European Rock Images

The rock images of Africa differ from those of Europe. The images of Africa are more widespread than those of Europe, are easier to see because they were done on rock overhangs located out in the open, and depict animals indigenous to the area, such as zebra, antelope, baboons, and ostriches. These collections of rock images also include more symbols than do the panels thus far found in Europe, although the symbols used by both peoples are similar—dots, circles, lines, and so forth. Another interesting contrast is that African rock artists pictured humans far more frequently than did Europeans. And rather than being pictured singly, the human figures are shown in groups. Further, radiocarbon dating suggests that African rock images are older than those of Europe, with some panels dating back about 28,000 years (Robbins, 1990). And some African rock images depict the first contact of Europeans with Africans and portray such European introductions as horses, wagons, and white people. These images are only a few hundred years old.

As with the drawings found in Europe, the meaning and significance of African images cannot be understood fully by modern humans. Some of the images are thought to tell stories; other scenes appear to picture hunts, funerals, dances, and honey gathering. The artists who pictured the coming of the Europeans may have been able to shed light on the meanings and significance of the ancient paintings, but because their numbers were decimated and the tradition of rock drawings had ceased, there is no way of obtaining that information directly.

However, a German linguist, Wilhelm Bleek, collected information about the traditions, myths, stories, and language of the San people, whose ancestors created many of the images, and subsequent analyses have helped us understand some of the meanings of those images. For example, the eland, the largest antelope, is an important symbol in San culture. The San spiritual leaders take their healing powers from the eland. They also engage in a trance dance in which they touch the eland in order to receive the animal's power. These dances, with the eland as a central figure, are depicted frequently in their renderings. And some of the zigzag lines included in the scenes apparently represent the first stages of hallucination experienced by those involved in the trance dance.

These early renderings are important not only because they provide a picture of the beliefs, traditions, and lifestyles of the ghosts of our past, but also because they reflect a move from dependence on the oral transmission of information to a more permanent form (Donald, 1991). Thus, the knowledge, stories, beliefs, traditions, and ceremonies important to the people could be recorded for the benefit of succeeding generations. Permanent records of information were a major revolution in the transmission of information, and they set the stage for later developments in communication technology with which you and I are familiar, such as books, magazines, and computer-generated hard copy.

THE DEVELOPMENT OF WRITING

Early Forms of Writing

A recurring theme in history is that inventions often appear independently in widely separated areas but in the same general cultural milieu. This is certainly true for writing, which was probably invented at least four times in the Old World (Egypt, Mesopotamia, the Indus Valley, and China) and also in the New World among the Mayas and Zapotecs of Mesoamerica. (Robbins, 1990, p. 194)

Robbins goes on to say:

The use of abstract symbols and primitive notation can be traced back to at least the Upper Paleolithic, as evidenced by the abstract signs in cave art. . . . I do not feel, however, that these Stone Age efforts were systematic attempts to codify a language. Most available evidence suggests that the impetus for writing occurred during the development of the first bureaucracies, when there was a need to keep records of economic transactions, to codify the rules that kept the state functioning, and to document religious ideas and records. (1990, p. 194)

Cuneiform The cuneiform writing on clay tablets developed by the scribes of Mesopotamia apparently finds its source in the clay "tokens" identified by Schmandt-Besserat (1986a, 1986b, 1986c). These tokens, distributed from Turkey to the Nile Valley of the Sudan, are in the shapes of disks, triangles, and cones, and were in use from about 9,000 years ago until about 3500 B.C. These tokens have marks on them in the forms of goats, sheep, and grain, and probably were used to record the amount of grain harvested and stored, and the number of sheep and goats traded among a number of economically interdependent communities. As time went on, the inscriptions on the tokens took on the form found in later cuneiform tablets. The sign for sheep, for example, was a circle divided by a cross. While the tokens themselves were probably significant at first and the number of them indicative of the number of sheep or goats traded, later the marks on the tokens took the place of the tokens, and a single token could be inscribed to indicate the number of items traded, harvested, or stored. As Robbins notes, "It is remarkable to see how seemingly insignificant, simple clay disks, cones, triangles, and other tokens were, in reality, the seeds of a complex system of writing" (1990, p. 197).

Cuneiform systems were widely spread throughout the Middle East, and in their earliest stages were pictographic; that is, the written signs bore some degree of resemblance to the objects for which they stood. As cuneiform developed, however, the signs became increasingly abstract, until the relationships between the sign and the thing for which it stood were unrecognizable. Writing was then used largely to record transactions of agricultural goods and property. Relatively little poetry, religious beliefs or traditions, and so forth were recorded.

Egyptian Hieroglyphics More familiar and famous are the **hieroglyphics** of Egypt, which were first produced about 3000 B.C. Hieroglyphics appear on the walls of tombs and on monuments. The Egyptians also used a cursive form of writing known as *hieratic* on paper made from papyrus plants. With the collapse of the Egyptian empire, the use of hieroglyphics faded. Our ability to decipher them might have been lost were it not for the efforts of an unknown scribe in the time of King Ptolemy V, who in 196 B.C. wrote a message on a piece of basalt, four feet high and a foot thick, known as the Rosetta Stone. The scribe wrote his message in both Egyptian hieroglyphics and Greek, which facilitated later decoding of the writings of the ancient Egyptians. A Frenchman, Jean Francois Champollion, and an Englishman, Thomas Young, are credited with major contributions in deciphering Egyptian hieroglyphics.

Other Early Forms Other scripts that were based on or included large numbers of pictorial signs were developed by Proto-Indians in the Indus Basin on the Indian subcontinent about 2200 B.C. Also emerging were other scripts such as Cretan in Crete and Greece in about 2000 B.C., and Chinese in about 1500 B.C.

Development of the Alphabet

The use of single abstract signs (letters) to represent the sounds of a particular language was a major step in simplifying writing. Imagine the difficulty in representing each word in a language with a different sign. One of the obvious problems is that the same word may have many different meanings; thus each different meaning would require a different sign. The later cuneiform and Egyptian scripts attempted to solve this problem by developing a class of signs called "determinatives" to clarify the ambiguity. *Assur* is a cuneiform word meaning both "city" and "patron god." A determinative was used to indicate the correct meaning for a particular sentence. This was followed by **syllabic writing,** which allowed sound combinations rather than the meanings of individual words to be specified. The Cherokee of the United States had a syllabic system of writing developed by a half-Cherokee named Sequoyah in the early 1800s. Syllabic systems generally replaced pictographic systems, and were used in Arabia, Europe, West Africa, and the Mediterranean.

Who Invented the Alphabet? There is some controversy surrounding who is responsible for inventing the alphabet, with some suggesting it was invented in Greece about 750 B.C., while others believe its origin to be by Western Semites about 1500 B.C. (Goody, 1981). And it appears that both views are correct, in that each group provided something different to the construction of the early alphabets. Consonant signs were apparently of early origin in Western Asia by the speakers of Canaanite, a Semitic language, while the Greeks added specific vowel signs. The Canaanite script was adopted by the Hebrews, and it is the script of the Dead Sea Scrolls. The Greeks also adopted Canaanite. Sometime during the 8th century B.C. the Canaanite alphabet diverged into three types: Phoenician, Hebrew, and Aramaic. The Phoenician alphabet was adopted by the the Greeks, the Etruscans of central Italy, and the Romans, and subsequently spread throughout Europe. In the time of Cicero (106–43 B.C.), the Latin alphabet consisted of twenty-one letters: ABCDEFGHIKLMNOPQRSTVX. Y and Z were added later to correspond to the Greek "upsilon" and "zeta."

Importance of Alphabetic Writing The development of writing is marked by increasing simplification from the representation of entire words with pictures, through a combination of pictographic signs and signs that represent the sound syllables of a language, up to the use of signs to represent the individual sounds (phonemes) of a language. Now, rather than trying to remember thousands of signs, you only had to remember a few signs, which could be combined in ways so that all the words of a language could be recorded and new ones invented. This "democratized" language in that it made reading and writing available to many rather than to just a few scribes who spent their entire lives learning the signs of their written language and who, by the way, enjoyed elite status in their societies because of their unusual knowledge and skill. Of course, illiteracy is still a problem in many cultures, including our own. But the development of the alphabet at least made it possible for all people to learn to read and write, to share their ideas with others beyond the constraints of face-to-face interaction, and to benefit from the ideas of those who lived long ago.

Development of Paper

Early writings were painted onto or etched into cave walls and rock cliffs. These people may have also used hides, wood, bone, and antler as writing surfaces. Clay tablets were commonly used in the Middle East, and the earlier tokens used in that area were also made of clay. The Egytians, the Maya, and others inscribed their genealogies, economic transactions, and significant ideas on the walls of their cities, in tombs, and on rock slabs called *stelae*.

The Egyptians are credited with the development of an early form of paper from the papyrus plant; the Dead Sea Scrolls written by Hebrews were also made from papyrus. Native Americans of the United States used animal hides to record the passing seasons. Paper was first invented in A.D. 105, and the first printing was in the form of reliefs cut out of blocks of wood, which were then inked and set to paper. By the 10th century, the Chinese were making individual characters and setting them side by side to form continuous texts. The Turks of the 13th century used wooden letters, and letters made from copper were used in Korea in the 15th century. The writing of ancient cultures was largely done by hand and by a group of scribes who worked in the royal courts, in convents, or in monasteries. These scribes produced and copied religious works, legal documents, and literature, collections of which were held in palaces, churches, and ultimately libraries and universities. Paper was introduced to Europe by the Arabs. This eliminated the use of parchment made from animal hides.

Mass Production of Print

By the 14th century, woodcuts were being used to imprint paper as well as to make designs on cloth. Mechanical reproduction of the Latin alphabet was first done using a set of metal letter punches to make a mold. Then lead or tin was poured into the mold to make the letters, which were inked and then pressed onto paper. Using this process, many letters of identical quality could be produced. In 1457, **Gutenberg,** financed by Fust, published the first printed book, and by 1500 more than 200 printing establishments had sprung up across Europe.

The printing press developed by Gutenberg remained largely unchanged for 300 years. The publishing business soon developed. Martin (1981) estimates that some 20 million volumes, assuming about 500 copies per book, were published by 1501. Additionally, publishing houses were producing pamphlets announcing festivals, funerals, military victories, and so forth. And in the 18th century, English publishing houses began producing tickets, posters, and the texts of political candidates' speeches. Thus began the age of "public opinion" (Martin, 1981).

Newspapers and Magazines Monthly news sheets were evident in the late 1500s, and the era of the Sunday paper began in England in 1779 with the *Sunday Monitor*. The rise of the newspaper coincided with the Industrial Revolution in Europe, "reminding us that this was essentially a revolution in communication" (Martin, 1981, p. 140). In 1835, de Girardin instituted the *Presse*, which was largely supported by advertisements, thus minimizing the cost to individual subscribers. It quickly generated 20,000 subscribers and set the stage for other papers across Europe to follow suit. The era of the daily paper had begun. Access to information was no longer monopolized by the powerful elite but was available to the masses, at least to the extent that they could read or knew others who could read for them.

Political Effect of the Free Press   By the time of the Industrial Revolution, the vast monarchies of Europe were collapsing, in part due to the free presses that had been established. The French Revolution had freed the presses from the political control of the elite. And with the decline of serfdom, the rising proletariat began to leave rural areas and move into cities, where manufacturing was gaining in importance. The era of manufacturing was made possible by such inventions as the railroad, the steamship, metal hulls, and the optical and then electric telegraph. Writers and publishing houses turned their attention from book production for the "literary salons" to the general public, and the "best seller" was born.

Advances in Typesetting   The refining of papermaking was facilitated by the steam engine. *The Times* of London was the first to print using Konig's steam-powered press. Large-diameter cylinders were introduced for feeding paper, and these new presses could print, fold, and trim tens of thousands of newspapers every hour (Martin, 1981). The first linotype machine, on which type could be cast, was perfected by a German immigrant to America by the name of Ottmar Mergenthalers. Only recently (late 1960s) was the linotype replaced by computerized typesetting. Piece by piece the mass production of the printed word developed, and with it the character of politics, economics, and lifestyle changed dramatically.

Developments in America Separated by an ocean from their ancestors in Europe, a group of people was establishing a new country on a vast continent.

> Nowhere could match the explosive growth of the press in the United States, however. Here an aggressive style of popular journalism emerged, with arresting headlines and plentiful illustration, making much use of comic strips like the famous "Yellow Kid" (started in 1894), skillfully addressing itself to the very basic culture of the millions of new immigrants. (Martin, 1981, p. 144)

Newspapers printed in urban areas in states with high ethnic concentrations published in the native languages of those ethnic groups. My grandparents, who immigrated from central Europe (Hungary and Bohemia), read papers produced in their area (Chicago) in their native languages. My grandfather, who was literate in English, also read newspapers and magazines printed in English.

The News Goes West Newspaper publishers such as Joseph Pulitzer (1847–1911) and William Randolph Hearst (1863–1951) held powerful positions in this developing nation. For those seeking to expand the boundaries of the nation by traveling west along the Santa Fe and Oregon Trails, the Pony Express—a group of young, single men—delivered, along with letters from family back east, the newspapers and journals published in the east, thus distributing the news to those isolated from the politics of their nation. Along with saloons and the general store, newpapers were among the first businesses to spring up in towns and mining camps. America was also at the forefront in producing illustrated magazines, publicity materials, and advertisements for public consumption.

The Advertising Industry Arrives Attributed to the Postal Act of 1879, which afforded cheap postage for magazines, the advertising industry came of age (Postman, 1993). Postman writes: "As a consequence, magazines emerged as the best available conduits for national advertising, and merchants used the opportunity to make the names of their companies important symbols of commercial excellence" (p. 168).

The Telegraph Like newspapers, the telegraph expanded access to information beyond the local level. Postman (1993, pp. 67–68) wrote that:

The telegraph removed space as an inevitable constraint on the movement of information, and, for the first time, transportation and communication were disengaged from each other. In the United States, the telegraph erased state lines, collapsed regions, and, by wrapping the continent in an information grid, created the possibility of a unified nation-state. But more than this, telegraphy created the idea of context-free information—that is, the idea that the value of information need not be tied to any function it might serve in social and political decision-making and action. The telegraph made information into a commodity, a "thing" that could be bought and sold irrespective of its uses or meaning.

As you are undoubtedly aware, the development of the computer in the late 1950s was soon to revolutionize the publishing industry, not to mention expanding the ease with which large amounts of information could be processed, analyzed, stored, and disseminated.

THE COMPUTER AGE

The printing press, moveable type, and linotype machines made possible the transmission of large amounts of information on a massive scale. The computer made this process even more efficient. Computer technology also provided individuals with more efficient means of information transfer. The manual typewriter, constructed by an American inventor named Christopher Latham Sholes in 1867, had numerous advantages over handwriting in that it standardized typefaces, offered speed and clarity, and afforded the production of special symbols. Electronic typewriters, word processors, and finally the personal computer made the production of documents easy for individuals.

In 1946 John von Nuemann published an article on the theory of the modern computer; every computer built is based on his design. In 1947 Bardeen, Brattain, and Shockley, inventors at Bell Telephone Laboratories, developed the first transistor. But the idea for computer technology did not necessarily begin with these people. For example, a small electronic computer designed by Atanassoff was operating at Iowa State University in 1939. Generally, the first computers were very large, their size reduced first by the invention of the transistor, and again with the development of the microchip in the 1970s. One of the early "portable" computers was typically about the size of a piece of carry-on luggage and weighed about 30 pounds. The computer I am working on now weighs about 9 pounds and fits in a briefcase. My coauthor has a "notebook" computer, which weighs about

4 pounds and would fit in my purse. Even smaller full-screen computers are now available.

The computer made possible mathematical computations of enormous complexity. The dissertation I did for my Ph.D. would have been close to impossible to produce without the data-crunching capabilities of computers. Just as the microscope made it possible to examine the inner workings of our bodies, computers have spawned the development of medical technology such as MRI (magnetic resonance imaging), with which we can examine directly the activity of the brain and central nervous system. The computer made possible moon walks, satellite transmission of images of other planets, direct communication with people of other nations via electronic mail, and the testing of the effects of various substances without the need for animals previously used in such testing. We can explore the holdings of libraries across the country without ever stepping foot into those buildings because of a national system of computer networks accessible from the home. By forging computer links with television and telephone, we are instantly privy to political upheavals, wars, famines, catastrophes, and celebrations as they occur in countries far away from our own.

Those links are the foundation for Al Gore's "information superhighways," which are touted as vast information networks allowing us to access "everything from airline schedules to esoteric scientific journals to video versions of off-off-off Broadway" (*Newsweek*, 1993, p. 42). In theory these networks will be readily available to all, will allow equal access to information of all types, will make our lives easier, and will even allow us to participate in creating our own versions of reality, called virtual reality. That is *in theory*. However,

> even the truest believers have a hard time when it comes to nailing down specifics about how it will actually work. Will we control the data via the telephone, the TV, the personal computer or a combination of all of the above? When will it be available? Will it be cheap enough for everyone? How will we negotiate such a mass of images, facts, and figures and still find time to sleep? Will government regulate messages sent out on this vast data highway? And, frankly, what do we need all this stuff for anyway? (*Newsweek*, 1993, p. 42)

The impact of these superhighways on our ecology, our personal lives, our relationships, and so forth is the source of much discussion and debate. Postman (1993) argues that we are putting technology into place without knowing its impact on our ecology, ourselves, and our society. Postman cautions that, like television, superhighways and virtual reality will operate largely to benefit profit-oriented corporate America and will create "knowledge monopolies" by which further social control can be exercised. It may result in the further exacerbation of economic and social inequities by allowing information access and control only to a new ruling class. He fears that the outcome may be the development of a totalitarian state.

Computer technology has forged entire new academic disciplines, such as AI (artificial intelligence), in which scientists endeavor to model and understand human thought processes via the computer. Indeed, the computer has become the overarching analogy for explanations of how the brain works. Computers clearly assist and expand the potential of human thought and decision making: They help fighter pilots fly planes and hit targets, they can simplify and perform mathematical operations that would challenge even the most astute of mathematicians, they can compose music, play a game of chess that challenges the expertise of world-class human chess players, learn from their mistakes, revise their circuits to adapt to new information and changing conditions. And some computers have even been programmed to talk. Computer "brains" allow robots to perform fairly complex tasks on an automobile assembly line, and these robots can be fitted with sensory apparatus that allows them to "see" and "hear" beyond the limits of their human creators. Impressed with the potential of computers, "Marvin Minsky has been quoted as saying that the thinking power of silicon 'brains' will be so formidable that 'if we are lucky, they will keep us as pets'" (Postman, 1993, p. 111).

But questions remain: Have we built a machine in our own image? Does the computer actually reflect or model the processes by which our lives are guided? Have we, as Clarke (1976) puts it, invented our successor? The answers remain to be seen.

EXTENSIONS OF OUR EYES AND EARS

Humans were undoubtedly capable of sharing their thoughts and feelings via talk, gesture, body position, and so forth well before they began drawing on cliff faces and the walls of caves. The lives of early humans centered around the members of their group with whom they engaged in face-to-face interactions. The beliefs and traditions of the group were largely oral histories and thus relatively impermanent. The ability to represent those histories in writing was a major transition in human culture, one that was not evident in all societies. Of some 10,000 oral languages, only a small fraction was ever represented by a visual notation system. Yet, "for several centuries, the written language held a preeminent place" (Crystal, 1987, p. 178).

This view has met with considerable criticism in this century, and proponents of this view argue that (1) speech develops naturally in children whereas writing and reading have to be taught systematically, (2) writing is really nothing more than the transcription of speech sounds, and (3) speech is the primary means of communication among all people of the world. Thus, the stress in this century has been on orality.

This view actually finds its roots in the concerns of ancient Greece and Rome, where oratory was highly valued and where the study of rhetoric emerged as the first academic discipline. Corax, in 466 B.C., produced the first known text on the strategies of rhetorical discourse. However, an earlier written description of the status and function of public speakers in Greece in the 5th century B.C. exists in the form of a slab of white marble erected in the Acropolis at some point between 446 and 442 B.C. Dieter (1965) named this slab the "Rhetor Stone." In modern times, a number of technologies were developed to facilitate the mass dissemination of oral discourse: the radio, the telephone, and the recording machine.

Radio

Even more than the newspapers of the 19th century, radio broadcasting was truly a mass medium. "It was a one-way medium that gave a few producers in the capitals a means to address the whole nation. It was an instrument listened to in the home alone or with one's family. It was the companion of the lonely hour, the addiction of those without other friends" (Pool, 1981, p. 170). It brought news to those living in rural areas far removed from the political and business centers of the country. It provided entertainment in the form of variety shows and soap operas, passed along news, and informed the public of the latest products and inventions in a world increasingly dependent upon the consumption of manufactured goods. It provided a center for family activities, especially for those in isolated areas who had little other social life beyond the church supper. "In countries like Great Britain, where radio from the start was noncommercial but national in origination, it was a channel by which an approved culture was disseminated to all regardless of the subculture to which they belonged" (Pool, 1981, p. 171). But for Americans, the radio was largely supported by advertising, aimed at the general public who went about humming the words of advertising tunes, and abhored by elite intellectuals. The standards set by radio as a vehicle for commercialism were later adopted by the television industry.

The invention of short-wave radio in the 1930s made radio a main source of information, especially important during World War II. Radio networks used this technology to transmit live broadcasts from war-torn Europe, and many Americans alive today recall listening to Hitler's speeches. By 1950, when television began to overtake radio broadcasting, there were 2,829 radio stations in the United States.

Telephone

Although the telephone was not a new idea, its invention is attributed to Alexander Graham Bell in the 1870s. The telephone was first marketed to businesses and rich individuals with interests at various locations. Along with streetcars and trolleys, the telephone allowed businesses to move out of the city to take advantage of cheaper rents, enabled management to move their offices away from their manufacturing plants, which were generally located on the outskirts of cities, and allowed people to negotiate business deals with others located in distant places. Thus the telephone's first impact was on furthering the development of commercial businesses. Suburban development resulted from the fact that, via telephone, people could stay in contact with friends, family, and business while enjoying life removed from the noise and pollution of the city. Ultimately, the telephone linked residents of rural communities to the goods and services offered in distant cities, and afforded communication across continents and oceans. Like so many inventions, what began as a handmaiden for the rich became an indispensible tool of the masses (Pool, 1981).

While the telephone forged links from home to home and business to business, it still initially tied us to specific physical places. All of that changed when cordless phones arrived, though their range was limited. That changed again with the advent of cellular phones that allowed us to talk to one another from any place at all. Clinton's threat in early 1994 to impose trade sanctions on Japan raised considerable concern over access to cellular technology, at which Japan excels. CNN ran a story on the issue illustrating the impact of cellular technology on the lifestyle of many Americans. The video footage accompanying the story showed people in Los Angeles conducting their personal and business affairs by cellular phone while wandering the streets and roaming the freeways. The image was that of a people as dependent on cellular technology as a fetus is dependent on the nourishment provided via the umbilical cord.

Photography

The old adage "A picture is worth a thousand words" may date back to the first human who doodled on the face of a cliff. And the production of images has a long history, beginning with those first doodlings and culminating in the production of moving images that you and I are exposed to daily on our televisions. Postman (1993, p. 68) wrote:

> The new imagery, with photography at its forefront, did not merely function as a supplement to language but tended to replace it as our dominant means for construing, understanding, and testing reality. By

the end of the nineteenth century, advertisers and newspapermen had discovered that a picture was worth not only a thousand words but, in terms of sales, many thousands of dollars.

Still images were created using lithographic techniques dating back to the woodcuts made by the Chinese. Newspapers made use of woodcut images until the invention of the camera in the early 1700s. The Eastman Company, using the trade name Kodak, made the camera commercially available in the late 1800s, and marketed their camera with the slogan "You press the button, we do the rest" (Jowett, 1981). "By 1914, on the eve of World War I, the motion picture had become the largest form of commercial amusement in the history of the world, and 'going to the movies' was accepted as a normal part of 20th-century life" (p. 193). Fears about the influence of movies, especially on the youth of America and Europe, led the League of Nations in the period between 1928 and 1937 to establish a series of commissions to assess those effects. "Like radio and television at a later date, cinema bypassed the existing channels of social communication and authority structures in the sphere of politics, religion, education, kinship and economics, and established direct contact with the individual" (p. 195). The effects of these media, but especially film and television, are still of concern among parents, scholars, and educators.

Television

History Television, which merges our two most important channels of communication, vision and sound, actually dates back to the early 1800s, during which time experiments with electricity indicated the potential for transmitting pictures over a wire. And the advances in moving pictures used in early films further contributed to the development of television. Scientists in England were the first to demonstrate television, in London in 1926, and it was the BBC that first initiated regularly scheduled programming. By 1939 a Russian immigrant to the States, Vladimir Zworykin, who worked for RCA (Radio Corporation of America), patented the iconoscope (sending) tube and the kinescope (receiving) tube that did away with mechanical scanning.

At the 1939 World's Fair held in New York City and aptly named "The World of Tomorrow," electronic television was seen publicly for the first time. By July 1, 1939, two commercial television stations were broadcasting in New York City. And by the time America entered World War II, between 10,000 and 20,000 television sets were in use in New York City, Philadelphia, Chicago, and Los Angeles. After a temporary freeze on licensing of new stations from 1948 to 1952, a more regulated system allowed expansion of television across the United States. By 1962, 90 percent of American homes had at least one television set.

Tied to technological advancements in the portability and sophistication of cameras, on-the-spot broadcasting from across the world became possible. Television quickly became the major source of news, bypassing radio and newspapers. No other industry has enjoyed such rapid growth and power.

> Never before had there been a form of cultural activity quite like television, with its enormous worldwide audiences, its increasing absorption of available leisure hours, and its ability to create instant celebrities or to focus attention on important or unimportant events with equal emphasis. Television, already the most prolific disseminator of images, has become the most widely shared general culture in the history of mankind. (Jowett, 1981, p. 197).

Dangers of TV Today While we get very little in the way of programming from cultures other than England, America has been a consistent exporter of its programming, which, as you can imagine, provides other cultures with a rather incomplete and frequently warped view of the way we live. Imagine having American lifestyles represented by such shows as "I Love Lucy," "Three's Company," "All in the Family," "Family Ties," "Married With Children," "Dallas," "Falcon Crest," and "Knots Landing," "Beverly Hills 90210," and "Melrose Place," not to mention the soap operas and other dramatic programs that litter our viewing day. A well-educated Austrian friend of mine, who watches a number of the American programs available in Austria, once asked me in all seriousness how many of us in the States live like the people portrayed on "Dallas."

While these programs may not reflect the reality of life in the United States, their impact at home and abroad is cause for some reflection and even concern. Television is a powerful tool that can be used to exploit our insecurities, sway our opinions, dictate what is important and significant, keep our attention on some issues and distract us from others, provide us with prototypes of how we should look, feel, and live, and suggest ways in which we can relieve ourselves of our hard-earned dollars.

Our susceptibility to the power of television is well illustrated in an early episode of "Northern Exposure": Holling put up a satellite dish so Shelly could watch television, which was unavailable in Cecily without a dish. It had apparently been some time since Shelly had seen TV, and she became obsessed with it. She watched programs in languages she didn't even understand, and spent her days and nights "glued to the tube." Her obsession bordered on the pathological when she spent the $4,000 she and Holling had saved for their honeymoon on products offered on the shopping channel. And so ended her days as a TV fanatic.

Postman (1985) describes the impact of television viewing on the ways we process information and make decisions in response to that information. Postman argues that the metaphor for our national character is Las Vegas,

> a city entirely devoted to the idea of entertainment, and as such proclaims the spirit of a culture in which all public discourse increasingly takes the form of entertainment. Our politics, religion, news, athletics, education and commerce have been transformed into congenial adjuncts of show business, largely without protest or even much popular notice. The result is that we are a people on the verge of amusing ourselves to death. (pp. 3–4)

He notes that the emphasis on image and entertainment has changed forever the face of American politics, education, and economics. "Even the Japanese, who are said to make better cars than the Americans, know that economics is less a science than a performing art, as Toyota's yearly advertising budget confirms" (p. 5). Advertising, of course, has been an integral factor in the development of communication technologies since the Industrial Revolution began, and this is especially true of the United States.

Postman goes on to argue that print media produced the Age of Exposition, which depended upon a particular mode of thought: "a sophisticated ability to think conceptually, deductively and sequentially; a high valuation of reason and order; an abhorrence of contradiction; a large capacity for detachment and objectivity; and a tolerance for delayed response" (p. 63). With the advent of television, the Age of Entertainment replaced the Age of Exposition, and along with it came a new way of thinking, one dependent upon seeing, not reading. "Americans no longer talk to each other, they entertain each other. They do not exchange ideas; they exchange images. They do not argue with propositions; they argue with good looks, celebrities and commercials" (p. 93). Fundamentally, Postman argues that the question of how television affects culture is no longer relevant; television has *become* our culture.

The impact of television on our daily lives, on the decisions we make, on the opinions and values we hold, and on cultural change has spawned a field of study in which scholars attempt to identify its effects on child development, voting behavior, and so forth. You are probably familiar with such issues as the effects of televised violence, and especially sexual violence, on behavior. Questions as to the role of advertising in influencing consumer practices, especially those of children, are of considerable concern to corporations trying to hawk their wares, to educators attempting to teach critical thinking to their pupils, and to parents attempting to hang on to their money. The economic recession of the early 1990s was explained by some as a crisis in consumer confidence fed by the constant barrage of economic indicators presented by the media. A colleague of mine who is a physician in Holland did a cross-cultural analysis of the incidence of anorexia nervosa, a debilitating and sometimes fatal eating disorder that typically plagues young women (Wind, personal communication, 1992). He found it almost nonexistent outside of the United States. He argues that U.S. advertisers' emphasis on thinness as the ideal for women is responsible for the disorder's predominance in America. I don't know whether he is right, but it is something worth thinking about. A movie called *Looker* is a frightening statement about the lengths to which advertisers will go in creating the "perfect" woman. Again, I don't know if it portrays accurately what corporations will do in the fight to sell their products, but it too is worth thinking about.

> The amount of time that is spent watching television, again especially by children, has raised the question of "media influence" to a minor social science of its own. The role of television in shaping our ideas and subsequently our values has always been acknowledged, but the behavioural and cultural mechanisms by which this is accomplished, and their relative importance in comparison with the other socializing influences in our lives (such as the school, the family, the church, and peer groups), is still a matter for considerable speculation. What is known is that television can, under certain conditions, become a very important source of information and therefore contribute to the formation of our ideas; and that so-called "entertainment" programmes have built-in "message systems" which act as potent devices for communicating those values about which such shows are structured. These values are reinforced by constant repetition, in every episode, week after week. (Jowett, 1981, p. 198)

The real and potential influences of mass media on our behavior will be discussed in some detail in a chapter on that subject, so I will not repeat that discussion here. The point is to stress the ways in which the media have altered the ways in which we perceive ourselves, others, and our world.

CONCLUSION

> Since the progress of human technology is a continuum, to pick a particular milestone—the domestication of fire, say, or the invention of the bow and arrow, agriculture, canals, metallurgy, cities, books, steam, electricity, nuclear weapons, or spaceflight—as the criterion of our humanity would be not just arbitrary, but would exclude from humanity every one of our ancestors who lived before the selected invention or discovery was made. There is no *particular* technology that makes us human; at best it could only be technology in general, or a propensity for technology. But that we share with others [species]. (Sagan and Druyan, 1992, p. 398)

The dawn of the Age of Information began with the first symbol, and the explosion of symbols that followed allowed the development of communication systems such as language to flourish. Refinements in tool technology, the creation of economic systems, trade, and centers of production, the development of agriculture, and the domestication of animals to serve human needs all resulted in and required expansion of oral/gestural language to include more permanent records of the transactions of these developing cultures. And the development of writing facilitated the creation of civilizations whose members could ensure their immortality by leaving records of their beliefs, traditions, and accomplishments for those who followed. Subsequent advances in communication technologies have knitted cultures together via a vast network of sounds and images. And despite the problems associated with those technologies, they are here to stay. We can never return to the days when the distant hoots of our ancestors signaled their presence in the forest. But the echoes of their voices are still with us.

KEY TERMS AND CONCEPTS

role of sociality
genetically fixed communication
dominance
hard-wired
primate advantages
relation of human and nonhuman primates
voluntary control
upright walking

toolmaker
pictographs
rock and cave art
origins of writing
hieroglyphics
syllablic writing
importance of alphabetic writing
invention of paper
Gutenberg

importance of the Communication Revolution
computers and communication
function(s) of radio
function(s) of the telephone
functions of TV
dangers of TV

NOTES

1. There is considerable debate over the cause(s) of the fate of the dinosaurs, who roamed the earth for some 165 million years. Among others (e.g., a virus or a gradual climate change), a dramatic cooling of the earth resulting from the impact of a comet or asteroid has received some support [see: R. Gore, Dinosaurs, *National Geographic* 183(1) (1993): 2–53; C. Sagan and A. Druyan, *Shadows of Forgotten Ancestors* (New York: Random House, 1992); J. M. Florentin, R. Maurrasse, and G. Sen, 1991, Impacts, Tsunamies, and the Haitian cretaceous-tertiary boundary layer, *Science* 252 (1991): 1690–1693; W. Glen, What killed the dinosaurs? *American Scientist* 78(4) (1990): 354–370; S. M. Stanley, *Extinctions* (New York: Scientific

American Books, 1987). A more recent theory is that dinosaurs succumbed to a "greenhouse" effect and slowly suffocated to death (*Earthwatch,* 1993 (Nov/Dec).
2. For elaboration on this sequence see: B. M. Fagan, *People of the Earth* (New York: HarperCollins, 1992); B. Fagan, *The Journey from Eden* (New York: Thames and Hudson, 1990); P. Mellars and C. Stringer, *The Human Revolution: Behavioural and Biological Perspectives on the Origins of Modern Humans* (Edinburgh: Edinburgh University Press, 1989); R. Lewin, *In the Age of Mankind* (Washington, D.C.: Smithsonian Books, 1988); B. Campbell, *Humankind Emerging,* 5th ed. (Glenview, Ill.: Scott, Foresman, 1988). For discussion of post-hominid radiation and cultural diversification see: J. Reader, *Man on Earth* (New York: Harper & Row, 1988); B. M. Fagan, *The Great Journey* (London: Thames and Hudson, 1987); P. Farb, *Humankind* (New York: Bantam, 1987).
3. See: D. Peterson and J. Goodall, *Visions of Caliban* (Boston: Houghton-Mifflin, 1993); E. S. Morton and J. Page, *Animal Talk* (New York: Random House, 1992); J. Goodall, *Through a Window* (Boston: Houghton-Mifflin, 1990); M. P. Ghiglieri, *East of the Mountains of the Moon* (New York: Free Press, 1988); J. Goodall, *The Chimpanzees of Gombe* (Cambridge, Mass.: Harvard University Press, 1986); S. Savage-Rumbaugh, *Ape Language* (New York: Columbia University Press, 1986); D. Premack and A. J. Premack, *The Mind of an Ape* (New York: Norton, 1983).

   Chimpanzees are not the only tool-using species. Among others, elephants use tools and engage in painting. For discussion of elephant tool use see: S. Chevalier-Skolnikoff and J. Liska, Tool use by wild and captive elephants, *Animal Behaviour* 46 (1993): 209–219. For discussion and illustration of art work produced by elephants see: D. Gucwa and J. Ehmann, *To Whom It May Concern: An Investigation of the Art of Elephants* (New York: Norton, 1985).
4. For a detailed discussion and analysis of these Anasazi drawings and etchings see: Mallery, 1972; Schaafsma, 1980; Grant, 1981.

REFERENCES

Begley, S. (1989). The first wildlife artists. *International Wildlife* (March/April): 22–27.

Cheney D. L., and Seyfarth, R. M. (1990). *How Monkeys See the World.* Chicago: University of Chicago Press.

———. (1991). Truth and deception in animal communication. In *Cognitive Ethology: The Minds of Other Animals,* edited by C. Ristau. Hillsdale, N.J.: Lawrence Erlbaum.

Clarke, A. C. (1976). *Profiles of the Future,* 2nd ed. London: Richard Clay.

Crystal, D. (1987). *The Cambridge Encyclopedia of Language.* Cambridge, England: Cambridge University Press.

Donald, M. (1991). *Origins of the Modern Mind.* Cambridge, Mass.: Harvard University Press.

Dieter, O. A. (1965). The rhetor stone. *The Quarterly Journal of Speech,* December, pp. 426–432.

Goody, J. (1981). Alphabets and writing. In *Contact: Human Communication and Its History,* edited by R. Williams, pp. 105–126. New York: Thames and Hudson.

Grant, C. (1981). *Rock Art of the American Indian.* Golden, Colo.: Outbooks.

Harris, R. (1986). *The Origin of Writing.* London: Duckworth.

Hewes, G. W. (1991). Problems of the Ursprache: A possible gestural template? Paper presented at the annual meeting of the Language Origins Society, DeKalb, Ill.

Humphrey, N. K. (1976). The social function of intellect. In *Growing Points in Ethology,* edited by P. P. G. Bateson and R. A. Hinde, pp. 303–317. Cambridge, England: Cambridge University Press.

Jolly, A. (1985). *The Evolution of Primate Behavior,* 2nd ed. New York: Macmillan.

Jowett, G. S. (1981). Extended images. In *Contact: Human Communication and Its History,* edited by R. Williams, pp. 183–198. New York: Thames and Hudson.

Kantrowitz, B., and Ramo, J. C. (1993). An interactive life. *Newsweek* pp. 42–44.

Leakey, M. D. (1978). Pliocene footprints at Laetoli, Tanzania. *Antiquity* 52: 133.

Leiberman, P. (1984). *The Biology and Evolution of Language.* Cambridge, Mass.: Harvard University Press.

Liska, J. (1990). Dominance-seeking strategies in primates: An evolutionary perspective. *Human Evolution* 5(1): 75–90.

Mallery, G. (1972). *Picture-Writing of the American Indians,* Vols. I & II. New York: Dover.

Martin, H. J. (1981). Printing. In *Contact: Human Communication and Its History,* edited by R. Williams, pp. 127–150. New York: Thames and Hudson.

Morton, E. S., and Page, J. (1992). *Animal Talk.* New York: Random House.

Pool, I. (1981). Extended speech and sounds. In *Contact: Human Communication and Its History,* edited by R. Williams, pp. 169–182. New York: Thames and Hudson.

Postman, N. (1985). *Amusing Ourselves to Death.* New York: Penguin.

Postman, N. (1993). *Technopoly.* New York: Vintage.

Robbins, L. H. (1990). *Stones, Bones, and Ancient Cities.* New York: St. Martin's Press.

Rubin, R. B, Perse, E. M., and Babato, C. A. (1988). Conceptualization and measurement of interpersonal communication motives. *Human Communication Research* 14(4): 602–628.

Ruspoli, M. (1986). *The Cave of Lascaux.* New York: Harry N. Abrams.

Sagan, C., and Druyan, A. (1992). *Shadows of Forgotten Ancestors.* New York: Random House.

Schaafsma, P. (1980). *Indian Rock Art of the Southwest.* Albuquerque: University of New Mexico Press.

Schmandt-Besserat, D. (1978). The earliest precursor of writing. *Scientific American* 238: 38–47.

———. (1986a). An ancient token system: The precursor to numerals and writing. *Archaeology* 39(6): 32–39.

———. (1986b). The origins of writing: An anthropologist's perspective. *Written Communication* 3(1): 31–45.

———. (1986c). Tokens: Facts and interpretation. *Visible Language* XX3: 250–272.

Schramm, W. (1988). *The Story of Human Communication: Cave Painting to Microchip.* New York: Harper & Row.

Tanner, N. M. (1981). *On Becoming Human.* Cambridge, England: Cambridge University Press.

Toth, N., Clark, D., and Ligabue, G. (1992). The last stone ax makers. *Scientific American* (July): 88–93.

von Frish, K. (1967). *The Dance Language of the Bees.* Cambridge, Mass.: Belknap of Harvard University Press.

Wilson, E. O. (1971). *The Insect Societies.* Cambridge, Mass.: Belknap of Harvard University Press.

———. (1992). *The Diversity of Life.* Cambridge, Mass.: Belknap of Harvard University Press.

Wind, J. (1992). Personal communication.

Wind, J. (1983). Primate evolution and the emergence of speech. In: Glossogenetics: *The Origin and Evolution of Language,* edited by E. de Grolier, pp. 15–35. Paris: Harwood Academic Publishers.

It is better to know some of the questions than all of the answers.

—James Thurber

Origins of Contemporary Communication Theory: A History

4

CHAPTER OUTLINE

Maps, Models, and Theories
  Maps
  Models
  Theories

The Classical Era
  Plato
  Aristotle
  Cicero
  Isocrates
  Sophists
  St. Augustine

The Middle Ages and the Renaissance
  The Middle Ages
  The Renaissance

Modern Theory

Contemporary Theory
  Rhetoric as Meaning
  Rhetoric as Value
  Rhetoric as Motive
  Rhetoric as a Way of Knowing

Development of Communication Theory
  Yale Studies
  Information Theory

Development of Perspectives on Communication Theory
  Mechanistic Perspective
  Human Interaction Perspective
  Systems Perspective
  Semiotic Perspective

Development of Approaches to Studying Communication

Wilson (1992, p. 93) wrote that "the major remaining questions of evolutionary biology are ecological rather than genetic in content. They have to do with selection pressures from the environment as revealed by the histories of particular lineages, not with genetic mechanisms of the most general nature." What he is saying is that the history of any given species has important implications for the current state of that species. That any species can engage in communication behavior is partly the result of carrying the genetic program necessary for their particular form of communication. However, that behavior is further constrained by the ecological circumstances in which that species finds itself, and those circumstances change over time.

All species have a history. But humans have developed the means for recording and preserving their history, so the ideas, knowledge, achievements, and mistakes of those who came before are accessible to those living now, as well as to future generations. Our elaborated communication system has enabled us to record and preserve our accumulated knowledge. And the role of communication in the saga of human history became a focal point of study. That history is the substance of this chapter.

The game of communication is played by all species, yet it is humans who have made it a focal point of life. In addition to playing the game of communication, humans have developed rules, norms, and technologies for its enactment. In the process, maps, models, and theories have been constructed to describe and explain the nature and functions of communication in everyday life. As far as we know, no other species has attempted specifically to describe and explain how communication works, what makes some communication strategies more effective than others, or how communication technologies influence the lives of the organisms who use them.

In the previous chapter I discussed the evolution of communication processes and technologies. This chapter is devoted to a survey of the study of communication as far back as the written record allows. This chapter will focus on major perspectives on the process of communication rather than on a detailed examination of all of the people who offered their opinions on the subject. Some ideas have withstood the test of time, while others have not. It is with the former that I will be concerned here.

MAPS, MODELS, AND THEORIES

All animals probably build maps, models, and theories (in the form of mental representations) about their world and about the behavior of other species who share their territory. A cheetah may have a "theory" about the behavior of her prey, who in turn may have a "theory" about the cheetah's behavior. Some animals may even construct theories about their own behavior relative to the behavior of other members of their group. The intricacies of functioning in complex societies undoubtedly require developing complex representations for negotiating in those social relationships.

Humans have become especially expert at constructing maps, models, and theories. Chimpanzees may have mental representations in the form of maps, models, and theories about their immediate territory and about the relatives, friends, and enemies in their group, but humans have endeavored to map, model, and theorize about all life forms on the planet. Using maps, models, and theories as a guide we have genetically altered wild species into forms that better serve our needs, tamed rivers and irrigated deserts into productivity to suit our whims, and broken the constraints of gravity to explore other parts of our solar system.

Maps

Maps are semblamatic representations of a territory (e.g., a globe, a map of the world, or a map of prehistoric human migrations). A map may also be used to describe the areas of the face that best reveal a variety of emotions. A map may be used to represent how languages and cultures diversified over time. Medicine's PET scanner provides a map of brain activity, which is being used to understand where in the brain language is processed. Maps are spatial descriptions, and they are judged by how accurately they represent the territory.

Models

A **model** is typically a description of a process. The Goals/Grasp model, which we will describe in detail in a later chapter, is a description of how people come to evaluate and choose other people as communicators. It describes the types of information used for evaluating others (e.g., physical appearance and interaction style), criteria for evaluating others, and the motivational and situational constraints that affect judgments of others.

The quality of a model is assessed by the extent to which the model accurately represents the process. To do this, a model must specify all the necessary elements. Early models of communication were overly simplified and thus not very accurate representations. The Source-Message-Receiver model of communication was a considerable improvement over the Source-Receiver view, but it has undergone serious revision in the past thirty or so years. The model has been expanded to include as a central element the influence of situation or context on interaction.

Maps and models are ways of representing—describing—physical, social, and/or cognitive relationships. Maps and models provide the descriptions of the essential elements, and a theory is developed to explain the relationships among the elements—in the form of hypotheses—and to test the accuracy of those relationships. Theories depend upon but go beyond description and are attempts to explain, predict, and control events and processes.

Theories

A **theory** is a set of statements explaining a particular phenomenon. Put another way: A theory involves generalizations about the way the world works. The theory of evolution is an attempt to explain how species have arisen and developed over the course of time. The theory of gravity specifies how objects respond to the gravitational pull of the earth. Both theories describe the important elements of the event and specify the relationships among those elements. Further, both theories explain how the process works and with what effects. Finally, based on this information, predictions about future effects will serve to test the utility of the theory.

G. A. Kelly, a well-known psychologist, "pictures an individual as a sort of lay scientist [theory builder and tester] who forms perceptual hypotheses, tests them, and attempts to construct theories regarding what people [and other animals] are like and how they will act" (Cronkhite, 1984, p. 106). As a simple example: I believe that a threatening dog generally will back down if stones are thrown at it. I hypothesize that dogs who have previously had stones thrown at them are likely to back down if I bend down and merely pretend to pick up stones. I have tested this hypothesis on several occasions with a variety of dogs. I have not, however, tested a random sampling of all possible dogs; nor have I tested the hypothesis in all possible situations in which a dog might threaten. Consequently, I qualify my generalization by saying that, *so far,* pretend stone-throwing has been a good strategy with dogs displaying hostile behavior. I further speculate that to act similarly with a police dog might provoke attack, for it may have been trained to perceive even pretend stone-throwing as an attack. My generalization is qualified thusly: Pretend to throw stones, but not at police dogs. They are a possible exception. Someday we might encounter a group of dogs no longer frightened of humans who pretend to throw stones. Any such new findings would further qualify the generalization.

Thus, theories change over time as they become replaced, revised, or extended. New data, new technologies, new ways of thinking, and so forth demand revisions and extensions of theory. The brief history of the development of communication theory that follows illustrates the progression of theory as it has been modified and extended over generations and cultures.

THE CLASSICAL ERA

The disciplines of law and communication find their roots in the writings of the ancient Greeks and Romans, and especially in the writings of a Greek named **Corax,** who, in about 466 B.C., outlined a system for organizing and arguing a legal case, which, for a fee, he made available to others. Legal disputes were common in Greek society. And while typically all free citizens spoke for themselves, those who could afford it frequently enlisted the assistance of a speech writer. Since juries were constituted of a large number of citizens, sometimes 500 of them, the ability to produce well-crafted and moving orations was frequently more important than the actual facts of the case

(Golden, Berquist, and Coleman, 1983). Thus, ghost writers, then known as logographers, "amassed considerable fortunes" writing speeches for those of means (Golden, Berquist, and Coleman 1983, p. 38). Greece was a democracy governed by its free citizens, who might be called upon at any moment to present their opinions publicly; therefore the ability to speak effectively was an important and highly valued skill.

The Greeks valued the spoken word and engaged in oratory in a variety of settings: legal, or forensic; political, or deliberative; ceremonial, or epideictic; and dramatic, or poetic. The competent or effective speaker was conceived as one who was intelligent, honest, socially responsible, and capable of moving the minds and emotions of others. This emphasis on oratory as a political, social, and legal force profoundly influenced the development of their culture and subsequently that of the Romans, who borrowed generously from the Greeks. Indeed, Greek views on government, education, art, law, and oratory provided the foundation for our own system of government and law, and influenced our emphasis on the power of the spoken word.

Although Plato and Aristotle are probably the best known of the early Greek theorists, their views of oratory, or rhetoric, were influenced by Greek poets, such as Homer, and the philosophical orientation of Socrates, a teacher of oratory known for his question-and-answer (dialectical) approach to teaching. Socrates never committed his views to writing. But one of his followers, Plato, revealed the dialectic methods of Socrates in his writings on rhetoric. Plato, born about 429 B.C., founded a school called the Academy in which he taught wealthy young men mathematics and philosophy. Plato wrote two books, the *Gorgias* and the *Phaedrus,* in which he essentially argued that rhetoric did not provide "truth" but instead facilitated making good appear evil and evil appear good. For Plato, Absolute Truth could only emerge through dialectic in which the participants would recall knowledge granted them long before they were born. Rhetoric, on the other hand, grew out of our experience via trial and error and therefore did not constitute true knowledge. Thus, Plato had a general disdain for rhetoric and his book *Gorgias* is really an attack on rhetoric as an "artifice of persuasion," the "shadow of politics" (Cronkhite, 1969). In the *Phaedrus,* Plato outlines how rhetoric may be used to produce the greatest good by speakers who are a combination of philosopher, logician, psychologist, and statesman. He does not, however, offer much in the way of explaining how or why persuasion is constituted or functions.

Plato

Plato's views of rhetoric appear consistent with popular contemporary views of rhetoric as a means for undermining truth rather than facilitating it. The term *mere rhetoric,* now frequently used to describe the speeches of politicians, suggests that such words are empty and cannot be trusted to be an accurate reflection of the current state of affairs. Most of us realize that words can be used to describe conditions contrary to fact, that politicians might say anything to appease us and thus ensure our support, that attorneys will portray their clients in the best light possible regardless of the facts. We, like Plato, are suspicious of the words used by those who have something to gain by manipulating our perceptions and opinions. Of course, rhetoric can also be used to enlighten and expand our base of knowledge; and the best antidote to the disease of "mere rhetoric" is to understand the means by which persuasion is effected. This is the approach advocated by Aristotle, a student of Plato's. Thus rhetoric can be a tool for good or for evil in the ecology of ideas.

Aristotle

Aristotle, born in 384 B.C., opened his own school, called the Peripatetic School, in Athens. His compilation of lectures, called the *Rhetoric,* was essentially a practical handbook of public speaking. Aristotle was an early empiricist, which means that he believed that our experiences constitute knowledge and that those experiences could be shared with others via rhetorical discourse. Aristotle adopted a more scientific approach to the study of rhetoric in that he attempted to describe it as we would describe a material or physical object. He outlined the elements involved in persuasion and attempted to specify how persuasion could be used effectively. Unlike Plato, Aristotle believed that rhetoric was amoral and therefore could be used either to the detriment or to the good of society, depending upon the morality of the speaker. Rhetoric, he argued, could be used to get at the truth, could be used to guide audiences otherwise ignorant of relevant facts to an informed opinion, could train speakers to argue both sides of an issue so as to better prepare speakers to refute contrary opinions, and should be studied as a means to prepare speakers to be critical thinkers.

Aristotle described rhetoric as consisting of three aspects: (1) *ethos,* or the character of speakers, which is now referred to as "credibility"; (2) *pathos,* or the ability of speakers to move the emotions of their audiences; and (3) *logos,* or the logical truth of speakers' arguments. In describing these qualities of rhetoric, Aristotle emphasized the importance of analyzing the beliefs, values, and opinions of the audience. He noted that speakers were most effective when they used those lines of reasoning typically accepted by the types of persons represented in the audience "to appeal to those motives which characteristically move those persons" (Cronkhite, 1969, p. 21).

This emphasis on audience analysis is at the heart of contemporary theories of persuasion; it also provides a practical guide for those seeking to sell their ideas and products. Politicians take great care to craft their speeches so as to address the values, needs, and concerns of particular audiences. Companies spend considerable fortunes analyzing the buying habits of consumers, and those engaged in public relations, advertising, and marketing attempt to match product images with the values, hopes, and dreams of the public. Postman (1993, pp. 169–170) noted that "the television commercial, for example, is rarely about the character of the products. It is about the character of the consumers of products." The life of a television show depends not upon its quality but upon ratings, in the form of the number of people willing to watch it. The 1976 movie *Network* is an inspired look at the ratings game that drives television. Thus, Aristotle's influence is still at work in contemporary approaches to persuasion.

Cicero

Unlike Plato, but similar to Aristotle, **Cicero**, a Roman living from 106–143 B.C., was largely concerned with the practical application of rhetoric. Like the Greeks, the Romans idolized the spoken word, and Cicero epitomized the ideal citizen. "A brilliant speaker, a lifelong student of philosophy and liberal studies, a clever politician, ambitious, expedient, marvelously literate and articulate, Cicero epitomized the Roman Republic a half century before Christ" (Golden, Berquist, and Coleman, 1983, p. 42). Cicero described the methods of persuasion in several books: *De Inventione; De Oratore; Orator, Brutus;* and *De Partitione Oratoria*. Cicero described five canons of rhetoric: (1) invention, or creating of ideas and arguments for a speech; (2) arrangement, or organization of ideas; (3) style, or the manner in which a speech is worded; (4) memory, or the art of recalling ideas vividly; and (5) delivery, or the manner in which speakers used their voices and bodies in presenting speeches. For Cicero, and for Romans generally, rhetoric was a form of art, along with drama, literature, and sculpture.

Cicero's contribution to law is found in his discussion of *stasis,* which is the "point at which the argument initially (and temporarily) comes to rest, the initial point of clash. Out of this initial confrontation, a new line of argument may develop, and a new crucial issue or point of 'stasis' will develop" (Cronkhite, 1969, p. 24). Consider the issue of animal rights as an example of stasis, or the point of clash in an argument. Suppose a research lab is charged with violating the rights of their chimpanzee subjects by performing tests on them without benefit of anesthesia, and that when performed on humans the same tests are always done using anesthesia. The prosecution argues that chimpanzees are "just like humans." The stasis of the argument rests on deciding whether or not chimps and humans are alike. Now suppose the defense argues that chimpanzees are not like humans, because they do not talk. The argument then comes to rest on the issue of whether or not chimpanzees can talk. Thus "stasis" is the crucial issue on which any argument is built.

Isocrates

Both Cicero and another Roman, named **Quintillian,** were profoundly influenced by Isocrates. Isocrates developed a philosophy of rhetoric based on four principles: (1) Speakers should have a broad understanding of nature and society; (2) speakers must present ideas with concern for their morality; (3) speakers must be thorough and well structured in developing and presenting their ideas; and (4) speakers should develop ideas with an eye for their longevity.

Isocrates believed that effective speakers were people of culture, in the sense that they were well educated in the arts, the humanities, and the social sciences; were concerned with scholarship; and were of high moral character. Cicero was particularly concerned with establishing standards of style for speeches and for written documents. He also suggested that the strongest arguments should be placed both first and last and that the speaker's character was vital in influencing listeners. Quintillian, like Cicero, believed that a good orator was born rather than made and that nature provided the raw materials, such as a quick mind and a clear voice. However, education, a strong moral character, and facility in the arts of reading and writing could be provided by culture and experience. Thus, following Isocrates' lead, Cicero and Quintillian placed considerable emphasis on the relationship among scholarship, education, and morality in providing the basic material for the speaker or writer. They emphasized the content of oratory, its moral grounding, and its stylistic eloquence.

Sophists

The Sophistic movement (A.D. 50–400) in the Roman Empire emphasized ornate expression and powerful delivery. During this period, freedom of speech was restricted and rhetoric was reduced to the art of delivery. This is a marked departure from the preceding ideals, which considered the orator an exemplar of the learned and moral person. Orators of the time were frequently subjected to political pressures, their freedom of expression restricted; thus they had left only their ability to express accepted ideas with power and eloquence. The emphasis was not on *what* was said but *how* it was presented. Golden, Berquist, and Coleman (1983) write that the "sophistic tradition has been influential during certain periods in the history of rhetoric" (p. 93), and that influence is still evident. "Image-makers" are modern-day sophists in that they focus largely on presentation rather than on substance. Advertising campaigns are especially likely to portray this position. Since many products are quite similar in quality and function (e.g., laundry soaps, cosmetics, and even automobiles), the marketing of those products is only successful if an image can be devised that is particularly appealing to consumers. A Bank One commercial serves as one illustration of this point.

Bank One is a multinational bank with offices across the world. Yet one of their most frequent commercials shows a man in a rural setting leaving his house with a dog at his side. He heads for the barn, gets into his pickup, and drives out. Just outside the barn, his truck begins chugging, smoke seeps out from under the hood, and the engine dies. The announcer says: "We're there to help the day Fred's truck decides to die. We're your hometown bank." Now I'd bet a lot of money that when Fred goes in to his "hometown" bank that he is not known by name and that he doesn't just get money handed to him to buy a new truck. Yet that is the assumption we are supposed to make.

Other examples abound: Advertisers lead us to believe that automobiles come equipped with beautiful women, that laundry detergents will improve our home life, and that cosmetics will prevent aging. Note, however, that the ads present little in the way of *data* or *evidence* in support of their claims. Instead they provide us with a contrived image they hope we will associate with their product. I haven't yet purchased a car that came with a sexy man. Possibly this was one of those options they failed to tell me about.

Politicians, attorneys, and businesspeople are all concerned with their image, and they pay a lot of money to people skilled at manipulating those images. It is my understanding from national news reports that Anita Hill was tutored by professional speakers before she presented her testimony at the Hill-Thomas hearings. Her tutor emphasized style of presentation. Nixon lost to Kennedy in their 1961 debate largely because he didn't present himself as well, although most analysts have agreed that Nixon provided more informational substance. And Ronald Reagan, frequently referred to as the "Great Communicator," earned that label because he was expert at delivery and at reading a teleprompter.

I could cite numerous other examples, but I will leave you with just one: I regularly taught a course in advanced public speaking in which I had students critique not only the speeches of others, but videotaped presentations of their own speeches, as well. Even when I instructed them to focus on content—that is, the quality of information, sources, and arguments—they inevitably focused most of their comments on delivery. It was a battle I pursued but rarely won.

St. Augustine

The era of **St. Augustine** (A.D. 354–430) was marked by religious strife. In A.D. 313 Emperor Constantine ended the persecution of the Christians and gave them equal status with adherents of Roman pagan religions. Augustine, of mixed Christian and pagan parentage, turned from religion to more secular ideas, only later to convert to Christianity. He became a Bishop in Hippo and, as a follower of Cicero, wrote his treatise of rhetoric, entitled *On Christian Doctrine*. In that book he rejected the beliefs of the Sophists and adapted rhetoric to the needs and goals of the Christian movement.

Christianity had grown out of an oral tradition for the dissemination of the teachings of the gospels via two particular forms: apologia, or speeches in defense of the Christian faith, and sermons, which were aimed at converting heretics and at strengthening the beliefs of orthodox Christians. Some Christians, however, considered rhetoric as pagan and saw no need for it, since "truth" would automatically be revealed without concern for the ways in which oratory was structured. Augustine's contribution was in providing a rationale for the use and study of rhetorical principles in service of the Christian mission. He focused especially on the methods for motivating action and commitment to Christian ideals via the rhetoric of sermons and apologia (Corbett, 1965; Kennedy, 1980). His *On Christian Doctrine* stands as the first manual on the art of preaching.

On Christian Doctrine is one of the most significant works of the era in its description of rhetoric as the process of understanding the meanings of signs. "All instruction is either about things or about signs; but things are learnt by means of signs" (Augustine, I. 2). This concern with how we come to understand the meanings of signs is evident in contemporary theories of communication.

THE MIDDLE AGES AND THE RENAISSANCE

The Middle Ages

The Middle Ages saw little in the way of development in rhetorical theory. By comparison to the scholarly advances made in the preceding and subsequent times, the Middle Ages pales. This is perhaps why the period is sometimes referred to as the Dark Ages or the Eclipse. Of note is the fact that rhetoric increasingly became associated with religion, and Christianity turned from an emphasis on evangelism, or conversion of pagans, to education. This was an era in which monastic schools grew in number, their mission being to educate students in finding a deeper, more personal experience with their faith. Rhetoric at this time was taught not as a practical endeavor but as a scholastic and religious exercise. "Many contemporary scholars have characterized the period as being essentially 'scholastic,' in the worst sense of that term" (Harper, 1979, p. 69).

During this era the Christian clergy became a powerful political force. The Roman Empire was replaced by "Monolithic Christian Feudalism." It was "monolithic" in that by the end of the fourth century A.D., the Christian

Church was established as the most pervasive and powerful institution in the Western World" (Harper, 1979, p. 70). Further, "Christian leaders saw the rhetorical tradition as a threat to their most fundamental beliefs. . . . Thus, Christian leaders condemned the study of the 'pagan' art of rhetoric" (p. 70).

The focus was on two major types of rhetoric: letter writing, and preaching. The skills of letter writing were taught in schools, and practical guides became available. Preaching, the primary form of oratory, was also taught in school. Both types were taught with an emphasis on skills and practices.

"Political leaders came to view rhetoric, not as a form of oratory, but as an administrative tool which provided rules for the composition of formal letters and official documents directed toward the passage and administration of laws" (Golden, Berquist, and Coleman, 1983, p. 98). It was during this period that rhetoric became one of the cornerstones of a liberal arts education. Rhetoric, or public speaking, is still considered fundamental to a liberal arts education.

The Renaissance

In the **Renaissance** (A.D. 1400–1600), **rhetorical theory** focused on the means for the discovery of truth, as revealed in the words of God via scripture readings and sermons. Forms of speeches and their component parts were described in great detail. The focus was on "interpretation" of meaning, which meant understanding and reciting scripture.

Another view saw rhetoric as the art of flattery, or ingratiation. Teachers of rhetoric were concerned with teaching the socially proper or acceptable forms of expression, a focus reminiscent of the Sophists. Rhetoric was then considered a branch of etiquette (Ehninger, 1967). The development of the printing press late in this era changed the nature of rhetoric from an immediacy between speaker and audience to a more remote relationship mediated by the printed word. Harper wrote: "The oral tradition began to take a back seat to print" (1979, p. 136). This shift necessarily led to less concern with delivery and more emphasis on language style. Further, the concept of "interpretation" of the meaning of signs that emerged in the Medieval and Renaissance eras set the stage for the emphasis on human psychological processes that emerged in the modern era.

MODERN THEORY

Francis Bacon was among the first to adopt the scientific stance on human nature formulated in the early 1700s. Bacon described humans as possessing a number of "**faculties**," including understanding, reason, imagination, memory and appetite (passion). In a way, Bacon was an early psychologist in that he attempted to describe the motivations of human behavior and the role of rhetoric in innovating and/or altering behavior. Bacon was an important force in the increasing interest in human cognition; that is, how people come to understand, interpret, and even create symbolic meaning.

George **Campbell,** a professor of divinity in Scotland, followed the trend toward scientific explanation, or empiricism, and advocated the description of the general principles of rhetorical effectiveness. Campbell described two forms of knowledge: **intuitive knowledge,** and **deductive knowledge.** His concern with intuitive knowledge illustrates the influence of the scientific revolution on his thinking, in that he expresses concern with the number of examples observed and the uniformity of those observed examples. These two requirements are fundamental to scientific observation. In addition to the number and uniformity of observations, Campbell suggested the following requirements of rhetorical argument: probability, plausibility, importance, proximity of time, connection of place, relation to the persons addressed, and interest in the consequences (Golden, Berquist, and Coleman, 1983). These conditions provide critical criteria for evaluating the arguments advanced by scientists and rhetoricians alike.

Richard **Whately's** *Elements of Rhetoric,* published in 1828, is especially noted for its description of two types of argument: **a priori argument,** and **argument from sign.** For Whately, a priori argument is arguing from cause to effect, while arguments from sign move from an effect to a condition. Included in the latter category is testimony or opinion, and he illustrates the importance of testimony in persuasive effectiveness. He carefully distinguishes this type of argument from argument based on factual accounts of events. Thus, Whately emphasizes the role of perception in both the interpretation of facts and the persuasive potential of such interpretations. The study of *credibility,* that is, the character and believability of an observer, is derived in part from Whately's stance. Of course, it is important to remember that Aristotle, too, wrote about the character of speakers, and his conceptualization of ethos is evident in contemporary studies of credibility. The role of perception in the observation of events is an important issue and has received considerable attention from social scientists. Elizabeth Loftus (1979), for example, investigates the role of personal characteristics and resulting perceptual biases in eyewitness accounts of crimes. Her research has important implications for weighing eyewitness testimony presented in courtroom trials and hearings.

In the 1800s, Thomas Sheridan revived the focus of the Sophists, which emphasized aspects of delivery, such as pronunciation and voice. Sheridan sought to revive the long-lost art of oratory. Gilbert Austin, also an elocutionist, argued for the standardization of dialect. And William Henry Bulwer emphasized the importance of gestures, which he considered to be natural signs and prior to speech.

In describing the overall thrust of this period in rhetorical theory, Harper wrote:

> In general, modern theorists agree, there are four generic functions of communication—conviction, pleasure, passion, and persuasion. Campbell says that a communicative act may work to "enlighten the understanding, to please the imagination, to move the passions, or to influence the will." (1979, p. 173)

CONTEMPORARY THEORY

Though up to this point the postclassical theorists were largely concerned with the written rather than the spoken word, the elocutionists are a notable exception. Theorists of this period were largely from the disciplines of grammar and literature. This trend shifted by the late 1800s, when we find at least fifty-two colleges with departments of speech. In 1914 a national organization of speech teachers was formed by seventeen men. That organization, first called the National Association of Academic Teachers of Public Speaking, then the Speech Association of America, is now called the Speech Communication Association (see Delia, 1987).

While scientific methodology influenced the writings of British theorists such as Campbell, the major impact would not be felt until the mid-1900s, when new scholars joining departments of speech and rhetoric began calling themselves scholars of communication.

By the 1960s, the discipline was suffering an identity crisis, and the issue "Rhetoric and communication: One world or two?" was hotly debated. The debate centered on methodological differences between the two camps, with communication theorists largely adopting the methods of science, and the rhetorical theorists defining their methods as critical and humanistic. In 1969 a group of scholars, among them one of the authors of this book, gathered in New Orleans to set forth a description of the discipline and its mission. The results of that meeting appear in a book titled *Conceptual Frontiers in Speech Communication*. Also in the 1960s, a group of scholars interested in a broader view of communication processes, and especially including study of mass communication technologies and their influence on communication, formed a new organization called the International Communication Association.

These scholarly upheavals notwithstanding, rhetorical and communication theorists became increasingly interdisciplinary in their view of communication, and borrowed liberally from such areas as psychology, sociology, and the natural sciences. This trend still marks theory development in the discipline of communication.

Contemporary rhetorical scholars developed theory with the following four themes: (1) rhetoric as meaning, (2) rhetoric as value, (3) rhetoric as motive, and (4) rhetoric as a way of knowing (Golden, Berquist, and Coleman, 1983). I. A. Richards and Marshall McLuhan are especially noted for their focus on meaning, although behaviorists such as B. F. Skinner also influenced conceptions of meaning.

Rhetoric as Meaning

I. A. Richards (1936) described language as an instrument, like the microscope or telescope, of our sense organs. Richards' theory of meaning has been called the Referential Theory (see Chapter 8 of this book). Marshall McLuhan (1965) broadened this view to include meaning as it is produced by all forms of media. (His views are described in detail in Chapter 13 of this book.) B. F. Skinner (1957), a psychologist and behaviorist, defined meaning as the response produced by a stimulus, such as a word, a sentence, or an extended message. Unlike Richards and McLuhan, who believed that humans play an active role in the creation of meaning, Skinner argued that responses to stimuli were learned via reinforcement. Indeed, like all behaviorists, Skinner believed that since mental operations could not be directly observed, and since humans like all animals learned as a result of rewards and punishments, mental operations occurring in the "black box" were not of interest. This view, though once profoundly influential, has more recently been displaced by another view, one specifically focused on the role of thought, experience, imagination, memory, and so on in the creation of meaning. Noam Chomsky (1959), a linguist, is well known for his insightful and incisive attack on Skinner's approach. Charles Osgood (1963), a psychologist interested in mind, defined meaning as a "mediating response," and his research clearly demonstrated that meaning was not simply a response to a stimulus, but was mediated by perceptions, beliefs, and experience. What is sometimes referred to as the "cognitive revolution" pervades theory in all of the social sciences.

Rhetoric as Value

Many of the classical theorists were interested in the relationship between rhetoric and ethics. Issues of morality and character were considered fundamental to effective rhetorical practice. Golden, Berquist, and Coleman (1983, p. 270) write that "ethics is concerned with the values of the communicator as revealed in his rhetorical behavior. In other words, are the rhetor's choices 'good,' 'right,' or 'moral'?" Rhetoricians should have in mind the best interests of their audiences, should honor the opinions of their audiences, take responsibility for their choices, and speak with "good intent." Thus, the rhetorician must take responsibility for advocating not just opinions that are factual or "true," but also for what is right and just for others. Rhetoric, then, is only as moral as the people who use it.

Rhetoric as Motive

Kenneth Burke   Kenneth Burke (1950, 1957, 1962, 1966, 1969) is undoubtedly the most important and influential communication theorist of this century. His contributions to the study of communication are numerous and far-reaching, and reflect considerable knowledge of a wide range of disciplines. I have heard Burke speak, and his lectures touched on many topics including psychology, sociology, linguistics, philosophy, anthropology, and biology, yet always with relevance to communication. His command of those topics was awesome, and at times thoroughly incomprehensible. Even so, I walked away from those lectures with some important ideas about communication.

For Burke, communication is the bridge that spans troubled waters and has the potential to calm the angry seas of human misunderstanding. He is particularly well known for his discussions of *identification* and *consubstantiality*. He begins with a clear concern for human relationships and for the problems that result in divisiveness and estrangement. He argues that the first step toward bringing people together centers on their ability to identify with one another's needs, goals, experiences, beliefs, values, and so forth. Through the process of identification, one can achieve a state of consubstantiality, or oneness with others. Additionally, Burke focused his discussion of communication on the notion of *motive*. He wrote that "the basic function of rhetoric" is the "use of words by human agents to form attitudes or to induce actions in other human agents" (1950, p. 41). Language is a "symbolic means for inducing cooperation in beings that by nature respond to symbols" (1950, p. 43). Therefore, we can deduce that language motivates people to behave and is the means by which we can identify with one another in an attempt to become consubstantial.

Burke was apparently influenced by theories espoused by anthropologists, sociologists, and psychologists, especially by Sigmund Freud. Thus, Burke talks about universal rhetorical situations that guide the behavior of all humans. His notions of identification, consubstantiality, and motive are embedded in his ideas about rhetorical situations. Burke's ideas, and especially his analytic paradigm called the *pentad*, have been applied to the study and criticism of speeches, books, plays, poetry, advertising, and even architecture. Thus, his influence has been felt in arenas other than communication.

Bowers and Ochs   The question of how language is used to motivate people is central to the study of social movements and social protest. John Waite Bowers and Donovan Ochs (1971) wrote an influential book on the rhetoric of protest, and focused their discussion on the role of rhetoric in producing social change, or movement away from the status quo. They focus on two important concepts: *agitation* and *control.* Agitation occurs when people outside or on the fringes of the establishment attempt social change, which is met with resistance by the establishment (the dominant or ruling force). While those seeking change attempt to "agitate" the system, those who seek to enforce the status quo attempt to exert "control." This tension is both facilitated by and, ultimately, resolved through rhetoric/communication. The rhetoric of agitation generally operates outside normal communication channels. Bowers and Ochs present detailed analyses of the civil rights and antiwar movements of the 1960s.

Rhetoric as a Way of Knowing

That we acquire knowledge from rhetoric/communication may seem rather obvious to you, and certainly early theorists such as Socrates noted the importance of rhetoric in the formulation and revision of knowledge. While we may depend upon our personal sensory experiences to obtain a goodly amount of knowledge, we also learn vicariously, that is, based on the reports and opinions of others. The role of rhetoric, and especially argument, in forming a foundation for knowledge has been systematically examined by people such as Stephen Toulmin (1959) and Chaim Perelman (1969). Overall, they view rhetoric or debate as a "critical and cooperative instrument of investigation" (Golden, Berquist, and Coleman, 1983, p. 373). Theoretically, by engaging in the critical interaction of argument and debate, all sides of an issue can be openly examined, which provides both a broader understanding of the issue and a means for deciding which of a number of alternative courses of action are best suited to the people and their particular circumstances.

Ernest Bormann (1972) described the importance of **fantasy themes** in structuring and influencing group and individual knowledge. These "rhetorical visions," or fantasy themes, are either based on past events that happened to the group or reveal a dream of what the group might do in the future. These myths are replete with villains and heroes who address issues and situations of relevance to a particular group or culture. Each culture and group has a set of myths that define it, and these myths are applied to a variety of issues and situations in order to reinforce and preserve dominant cultural and group beliefs and values. Advertisers are adept at manipulating such myths in service of selling their products, by providing us with brief dramas that suggest ways in which their products can help us achieve our fantasies.

This perspective of communication as a way of knowing has broadly influenced communication theory, and especially those theorists who consider communication as the means by which we construct our social reality. Borrowing heavily from P. L. Berger and T. Luckman's *The Social Construction of Reality* (1967) and from the philosophical writings of those interested in *phenomonology* (the study of personal experience), communication theorists have noted that communication is an important source for social, group, and self-definition. That is, communication is used not just as a means for describing others but also as a source of our own special knowledge and perspectives. The Theory of Linguistic Relativity, which describes how the language one learns structures the perceptions of its users, is grounded in the presumption that communication produces a certain way of looking at the world that differentiates among cultures and groups.

At the individual level, we know that the labels applied to us can profoundly influence our views of ourselves. Children who are repeatedly told they are stupid may well not only see themselves as such but also behave in ways consistent with the label. As another example: People who watch a lot of television frequently describe the world as a more dangerous place than it actually is (Gerbner and Gross, 1976). Such perceptions may result from the fact that violence is a regular feature of news programs, as well as programs described as entertainment. It is important to remember, however, that rhetoric as a way of knowing originally referred to argument and debate, which is a more restricted view than that advocated by constructivists.

Thus far I have largely focused on rhetorical theorists and theories, since they provided the foundation, at least historically, for contemporary views of communication processes and behavior. Most of these theorists adopted critical analysis as their tool or method for understanding rhetoric and its role in structuring societies and cultures. By midcentury a new breed of scholars armed with the tools of science broke away from the mainstream of rhetorical scholarship and began an investigation of communication that took its impetus from the natural and behavioral sciences. It is to their influence we turn next.[1]

DEVELOPMENT OF COMMUNICATION THEORY

The general trend in the early part of this century was marked by interest in speech, rhetoric, argumentation and debate, and print media. By the 1940s researchers in anthropology, political science, economics, and psychology had turned their attention to a systematic study of persuasion and propaganda, some of which was fueled by the two world wars. With the advent of radio in the 1920s and then television in the 1940s, the study of mediated communication and its influence on attitudes, beliefs, and values expanded earlier conceptions of communication: Paul Lazarsfeld (1940), a sociologist, explored the influence of mass media on society; Erving Goffman (1967), also a sociologist, examined relational development and social communication; and anthropologists such as E. T. Hall (1977) concerned themselves with the role of nonverbal communication in social interaction and the creation of meaning. Simultaneously, political scientists explored the role of mass media in structuring world opinion. By the 1950s linguists and psychologists interested in language had developed the area of psycholinguistics. Along with these trends, interest in the production and processing of speech and impairments of the process developed into the science of speech pathology and audiology.

Yale Studies

The Yale Studies, conducted by Carl Hovland, Irving Janis, and Harold Kelley (1953) shortly after World War II, focused on attitude change as a function of persuasion. In contrast to the behaviorists of the era, these scholars adopted a cognitive approach to learning. They are generally credited with moving the discipline of communication to adopt a social scientific approach to research. Prior to this body of literature, communication research was conducted in a number of disciplines and lacked a coherent focus. Delia (1987, p. 56) noted:

> The years following World War II were witness to the emergence of consolidation of communication research as a distinct domain of investigation. Our examination of research up to 1940 has shown the enormous range of interests and approaches to communication across developing disciplines of the social sciences. The war years saw an intensification of these research interests; and after the war, publications literally burst forth across the range of disciplines and topics.

Information Theory

In 1949 Claude Shannon, an engineer at Bell Telephone Laboratories, and Warren Weaver, a mathematician, developed a mathematical approach to the study of communication that became known as **information theory** (Shannon and Weaver, 1949). Their concern was with the efficiency of information transmission via electronic signals across a telephone wire, but their formulation became broadly applied to the study of human communication. They suggested that *information,* defined as the freedom of choice in selecting a message from a set of possible messages, is central to any communication process. Related to the concept of information are *uncertainty* and *predictability.* Uncertainty is the lack of predictability of a message choice. If a message is perfectly predictable, it has little information value. To the extent that a message is unpredictable, one is uncertain, and the message will have considerable information value, at least in the way those terms are defined. Let's consider an example that is frequently used to explain these terms.

In English, the letter *q* is almost always followed by the letter *u*, as in the word *quickly*. Thus, the choice of *u* to follow *q* is perfectly predictable, uncertainty is 0, and the information value of *u* is also 0. Now suppose I ask you what letter is likely to follow *u*. Since in English a number of letters can follow *u*, your uncertainty as to what to choose is high, predictability is low, and the information value of the next letter is high.

The concepts of *entropy* and *redundancy* are also important to information theory. Entropy is the extent of randomness or disorganization in a situation, and redundancy, the opposite of information, is the degree of regularity in a message. All languages are to some extent redundant; if they weren't, we would have incredible difficulty understanding one another. Redundancy, or repetition, is critical to understanding, especially if we are in a noisy environment, if we are unfamiliar with the information, or if we are inattentive. If you have had a course in public speaking, your professor probably told you to overview your main points in the introduction and review them in the conclusion so that your audience has plenty of opportunity to understand and remember what you said. This is redundancy designed to facilitate comprehension and retention of the message. A rock concert is a noisy environment and therefore difficult for conversation. We find ourselves repeating or asking for repetition in such an environment. It was these issues that information theory was designed to address.

Information theory has been heavily criticized because it doesn't tell us very much about meaning. But then, Shannon and Weaver were concerned with the transmission of electronic signals; it was others who attempted to apply it to *human* communication.

DEVELOPMENT OF PERSPECTIVES ON COMMUNICATION THEORY

A *perspective* (sometimes called a *paradigm* or an *epistemology*) is a set of assumptions (knowledge or beliefs) about the nature of the world. A perspective helps us make sense out of what we observe and experience. A perspective guides observations, influences the types of questions posed, and influences the answers. Whereas theories are designed to explain specific events, perspectives tie theories together into a single, global explanation. Theories inconsistent with the perspective are modified or rejected. Perspectives are not static, however. In fact, they vary over time, cultures, and groups. Communication scholars appear to be divided among at least four perspectives: mechanistic, human action (symbolic interactionism), systems, and semiotic.

Mechanistic Perspective

A fundamental premise of the mechanistic perspective is that the world behaves in a perfectly predictable fashion; all we need to do is figure it out. Nature obeys a set of determined laws that we will discover through empirical observation. The goal is to find the ultimate causes of the behavior of inanimate and animate objects. Devised first in the natural sciences, the mechanistic perspective was adopted by scholars in the social and behavioral sciences. In its strictest form, the mechanistic perspective assumes human behavior to be determined and thus predictable.

B. F. Skinner, a well-known behaviorist, applied the mechanistic perspective to human behavior. Skinner and his followers believed that since human behavior was determined by external events, and since human actions, thoughts, and emotions had no bearing on outcomes, there was no need to examine "the black box," the seat of awareness, thought, emotions, and so forth.

This mechanistic (and overly simplistic) perspective retains few followers in communication. In fact, Skinner and his followers notwithstanding, few scholars since Einstein have subscribed to the assumptions of a mechanistic perspective or to the strict tenets of behaviorism. Many do, however, continue to advocate and use the experimental methods developed within the mechanistic perspective.

Further, many of the scholars who reject mechanistic and behavioristic perspectives on human communication behavior still attempt to identify "laws," though the meaning of "laws" has changed considerably. More typically they are referred to as "generalizations" based on probabilities, not certainties. Further, such scholars are less concerned with finding ultimate causes of behavior; instead, concern is with the regular patterns of behavior within certain described boundaries.

Nevertheless, the trend has been toward interactionist and systems perspectives, which emphasize the ways in which people participate in the creation of meaning, or put another way, how people participate in the creation of social realities.

Human Interaction Perspective

In the strictest interpretation of the mechanistic perspective, reality conforms to a set of regular patterns found in nature. Those who adopt a human interaction perspective believe that we experience reality subjectively; that is, we interpret reality and assign it meaning. The interpretation we construct is probably partly shared by others who come from a common sociocultural background, and partly idiosyncratic because some of our experiences are unique. The process of how we construct and share meanings is of central concern to those who adopt this perspective. Kelly's (1955) Personal Construct Theory of human behavior, Coordinated Management of Meaning (Cronen, Pearce, & Harris, 1982), and constructivism (Berger and Luckman, 1967; Delia, O'Keefe, and O'Keefe, 1982) are examples of the application of the human interaction perspective. It is worth mentioning that a perspective similar to the human interaction perspective was advanced several hundred years ago by Augustine.

Systems Perspective

A *system* is a set of interrelated and hierarchically organized parts that work together to adapt to environmental constraints and changes. This view, advocated by von Bertalanffy (1968), a biologist, is consistent with the ecological perspective adopted in this book. We have suggested that all organisms are a part of a massive system of interdependencies. A change in one part of the system may have substantial ramifications throughout the system. This global system is constituted of a number of interacting subsystems, but all work together for survival. It is the nature of the relationships among units of any given system that we seek to explain.

Semiotic Perspective

Semiotics is generally defined as the study of signs and sign relationships. Those who advocate a semiotic perspective attempt to specify how signs are interpreted and acted upon by those who use them. Fundamental to this perspective is the idea that meanings are created by groups (societies and cultures) rather than by individuals. This notion of socioculturally shared meaning is similar to that expressed in the human interaction perspective. Further, this perspective is consistent with a systems perspective in that both attempt to identify how sign and sign relationships function within and across systems of interaction. Finally, the semiotic perspective is also consistent with the ecological view we have offered. In our conceptualization, the ecologies organisms inhabit are constituted of various types of signs (e.g., symptoms, semblances, and symbols) to which they attribute meaning.

DEVELOPMENT OF APPROACHES TO STUDYING COMMUNICATION

Approaches (methodologies) to studying behavior have changed to accommodate changes in perspective. Mechanistic views of communication behavior led to an emphasis on laboratory research and statistical manipulation of data. Surveys and questionnaires that afforded mass testing and ready analysis by statistical means grew in popularity. Experimentation became the norm. American scholars of communication typically revered a quantitative approach to the study of communication, a trend apparent in all the social sciences as they are studied and practiced in this country (e.g., Postman, 1993). As you will discover in Chapter 14, on intercultural communication, Americans generally have looked to science and technology as the ways to address pressing social and environmental issues.

But these methods were inconsistent with interactionist, systems, and semiotic perspectives. Devotees of these views charged that experimental methods could not account for all of human behavior because their approach lacked grounding in the "real" world. Further, they argued, human behavior is far too complex to be explained by responses to a questionnaire. Experiments, they argued, could not illuminate the richness and diversity of human behavior.

Among those to challenge the utility of strict experimentalism were members of the Frankfurt school of critical theory, who have had considerable influence on American scholars, especially in mass communication. An issue of the *Journal of Communication* titled "Ferment in the Field" (1983) is devoted to an examination of the status and importance of approaches to the study of communication. Several of the authors, who call themselves critical theorists, advocate an alternative approach to the study of communication. They claim the focus should be on the role of communication in expressing and revising cultural values using critical and historical approaches.

Naturalistic approaches to the study of communication are increasing in popularity (see the special issue of *Western Journal of Communication*, 1994). Those who do naturalistic research tend to focus on detailed descriptions and interpretations of interactions as they occur within a variety of contexts. For communication scholars the emphasis may be on description of conversational exchanges (including nonverbal behavior) as they occur in everyday life (see: Saville-Troike, 1982; Bernard, 1988; Fetterman, 1989). I have adopted this approach for studying the social interaction and tool-using behavior of elephants, and to study the communication behavior of nonhuman primates. Unlike more traditional approaches to doing science, which emphasize prediction and control, naturalistic approaches emphasize ongoing observation and detailed description and analysis of behavior as it occurs in daily life.

Naturalistic approaches are consistent with an ecological perspective. Gibbs (1979, p. 127) wrote:

> The general claim of the ecological reformers is that empirical psychologists have become so enamored of laboratory precision that they have lost their sense of the human problem, that generalization to the authentic significance of the person in the real environment has been sacrificed to the quest for certainty in our knowledge.

Our view on the choice of methodology is (Liska and Cronkhite, 1994, p. 58): "Whatever research method you use, use it well to answer a theoretically important question to which it is ideally suited."

CONCLUSION

The emphasis on orality has shifted dramatically over the years, and while many departments still retain the title "Speech Communication," the study of communication clearly entails the analysis of oral and visual messages, either separately or as they are conjoined in conversation and in television. Recognition of this fact is evident in the recent proposal to change the name of the Speech Communication Association to the American Communication Association. While a majority (about 63 percent) favor the change, the bylaws of the organization require a two-thirds majority, and a recent vote fell short of that requirement.

Further, the study of communication has included focus on oratory and the conduct of the orator, the structural characteristics of speeches and language, psychological influences, social context and cultural differences, and more recently, the biological and evolutionary foundations of communication. Many media theorists have expanded their views of media effects on public opinion and cultural development to include the role of media in everyday interpersonal communication.

The dominance of experimental approaches has been supplemented by historical, critical, semiotic, and naturalistic methodologies. The trend is toward a more holistic, global, and integrated view of communication behavior. Further, the integration of theory and method from related disciplines such as anthropology, biology, psychology, and sociology is surely the sign of a healthy concern with scholarship rather than academic politics and the protection of territory. The process and study of communication are inherently and necessarily interdisciplinary, which calls for cooperation among scholars who share the goal of understanding communication behavior. We owe our legacy to a variety of voices; our future lies not in a single voice but in a chorus.

KEY TERMS AND CONCEPTS

Maps
Model
Theory
Corax
Plato

Aristotle
Cicero
Isocrates
Quintillian
Sophists

St. Augustine
Rhetorical theory in
    the Renaissance
Francis Bacon "faculties"
Campbell intuitive and

deductive knowledge
Whately a priori argument
and argument from sign
rhetoric as meaning
rhetoric as value
rhetoric as motive
rhetoric as a way of knowing
fantasy themes
Yale studies
information theory
cognition
organization of the field of communication

NOTES

1. Both of the authors are trained in the scientific approach to the study of communication, which will be evident in the information presented in this book. Consequently, in this chapter we will only highlight the development of scientific methods as applied to the study of communication. Further, those methods are relatively new when cast against the history of the discipline as a whole. Therefore, attention to rhetorical methods is necessarily extended.

REFERENCES

Augustine, Saint. *De Doctrina Christiana.* Translated by Sister Therese. Originally written about 426 A.D.

Benson, T. W. (ed.). (1985). *Speech Communication in the 20th Century.* Carbondale, Ill: Southern Illinois University Press.

Berger, P., and Luckman, T. (1967). *The Social Construction of Reality.* New York: Doubleday.

Bernard, H. R. (1988). *Research Methods in Cultural Anthropology.* Newbury Park, Calif.: Sage.

Bormann, E. G. (1972). Fantasy and rhetorical vision: The rhetorical criticism of social reality. *Quarterly Journal of Speech* 58: 396–407.

Bowers, J. W., & Ochs, D. J. (1971). *The Rhetoric of Agitation and Control.* Reading, Mass.: Addison-Wesley.

Burke, K. (1950). *A Rhetoric of Motives.* Englewood Cliffs, N.J.: Prentice-Hall.

———. (1957). *The Philosophy of Literary Form: Studies in Symbolic Action.* New York: Vintage Books.

———. (1962). *A Grammar of Motives and a Rhetoric of Motives.* Cleveland: World.

———. (1966). *Language as Symbolic Action: Essays on Life, Literature, and Method.* Berkeley: University of California Press.

———. (1969). *A Grammar of Motives.* Berkeley: University of California Press.

Chomsky, N. (1959). Review of B. F. Skinner's *Verbal Behavior. Language* 35: 26–58.

Corbett, E. P. J. (1965). *Classical Rhetoric for the Modern Student.* New York: Oxford University Press.

Cronen, V. E., Pearce, W. B., and Harris, L. M. (1982). The coordinated management of meaning: A theory of communication. In *Human Communication Theory,* edited by F. E. X. Dance, pp. 61–89. New York: Harper & Row.

Cronkhite, G. (1969). *Persuasion: Speech and Behavioral Change.* Indianapolis, Ind.: Bobbs-Merrill.

———. (1984). Perception and meaning. In *Handbook of Rhetorical and Communication Theory,* edited by C. C. Arnold and J. W. Bowers, pp. 51–229. Boston: Allyn and Bacon.

Delia, J. G. (1987). Communication research: A history. In *Handbook of Communication Science,* edited by C. H. Berger and S. H. Chaffe, pp. 20–98. Newbury Park, Calif.: Sage.

Delia, J., O'Keefe, B. J., and O'Keefe, D. J. (1982). The constructivist approach to communication. In *Human Communication Theory,* edited by F. E. X. Dance, pp. 147–191. New York: Harper & Row.

Ehninger, D. (1967). On rhetoric and rhetorics. *Western Speech,* 31.

Fetterman, D. M. (1989). *Ethnography: Step by Step.* Newbury Park, Calif.: Sage.

Gerbner, G., and Gross, L. (1976). The scary world of TV's heavy viewer. *Psychology Today* (April), 41–45.

Gibbs, J. C. (1979). The meaning of ecologically oriented inquiry in contemporary psychology. *American Psychologist* 34 (2);127–140.

Goffman, E. (1967). *Interaction Ritual.* New York: Pantheon Books.

Golden, J. L., Berquist, G. F., and Coleman, W. E. (1983). *The Rhetoric of Western Thought,* 3rd ed. Dubuque, Iowa: Kendall/Hunt.

Hall, E. T. (1977). *Beyond Culture.* Garden City, N.Y.: Anchor Books.

Harper, N. (1979). *Human Communication Theory: The History of a Paradigm.* Rochelle Park, N.J.: Hayden.

Hovland, C. I., Janis, I. L., and Kelley, H. H. (1953). *Communication and Persuasion.* New Haven, Conn.: Yale University Press.

Kelly, G. A. (1955). *The Psychology of Personal Constructs.* New York: Norton.

Kennedy, G. A. (1980). *Classical Rhetoric and Its Christian and Secular Tradition from Ancient to Modern Times.* Chapel Hill: University of North Carolina Press.

Kibler, R. J., and Barker, L. L. (eds.). (1969). *Conceptual Frontiers in Speech Communication.* New York: Speech Communication Association of America.

Lazarsfeld, P. F. (1940). *Radio and the Printed Page.* New York: Dvell, Sloan and Pearce.

Liska, J., and Cronkhite, G. (1994). On the death, dismemberment, or disestablishment of the dominant paradigm. *Western Journal of Communication* 58 (winter): 58–65.

Loftus, E. F. (1979). *Eyewitness Testimony.* Cambridge, Mass.: Harvard University Press.

McLuhan, M. (1965). *Understanding Media: The Extensions of Man.* New York: McGraw-Hill.

Osgood, C. E. (1963). On understanding and creating sentences. *American Psychologist* 18: 735–751.

Perelman, C., and Olbrechts-Tyteca, L. (1969). *The New Rhetoric: A Treatise on Argumentation.* Translated by John Wilkinson and Purcell Weaver. Notre Dame, Ind.: Notre Dame University Press.

Petronio, S. (ed.). (1994). The dialogue of evidence. *Western Journal of Communication,* 58(1).

Postman, N. (1993). *Technopoly.* New York: Vintage Books.

Richards, I. A. (1936). *The Philosophy of Rhetoric.* New York: Oxford University Press.

Saville-Troike, M. (1982). *The Ethnography of Communication.* Oxford, England: Basil Blackwell.

Shannon, C. E., and Weaver, W. (1949). *The Mathematical Theory of Communication.* Urbana, Ill.: University of Illinois Press.

Skinner, B. F. (1957). *Verbal Behavior.* New York: Appleton-Century-Crofts.

Toulmin, S. (1959). *The Uses of Argument.* Cambridge, England: Cambridge University Press.

von Bertalanffy, L. (1968). *General Systems Theory.* New York: Braziller.

Wilson, E. O. (1992). *The Diversity of Life.* Cambridge, Mass.: Belknap of Harvard University Press.

AUDREY COHEN COLLEGE LIBRARY
75 Varick St. 12th Floor
New York, NY 10013

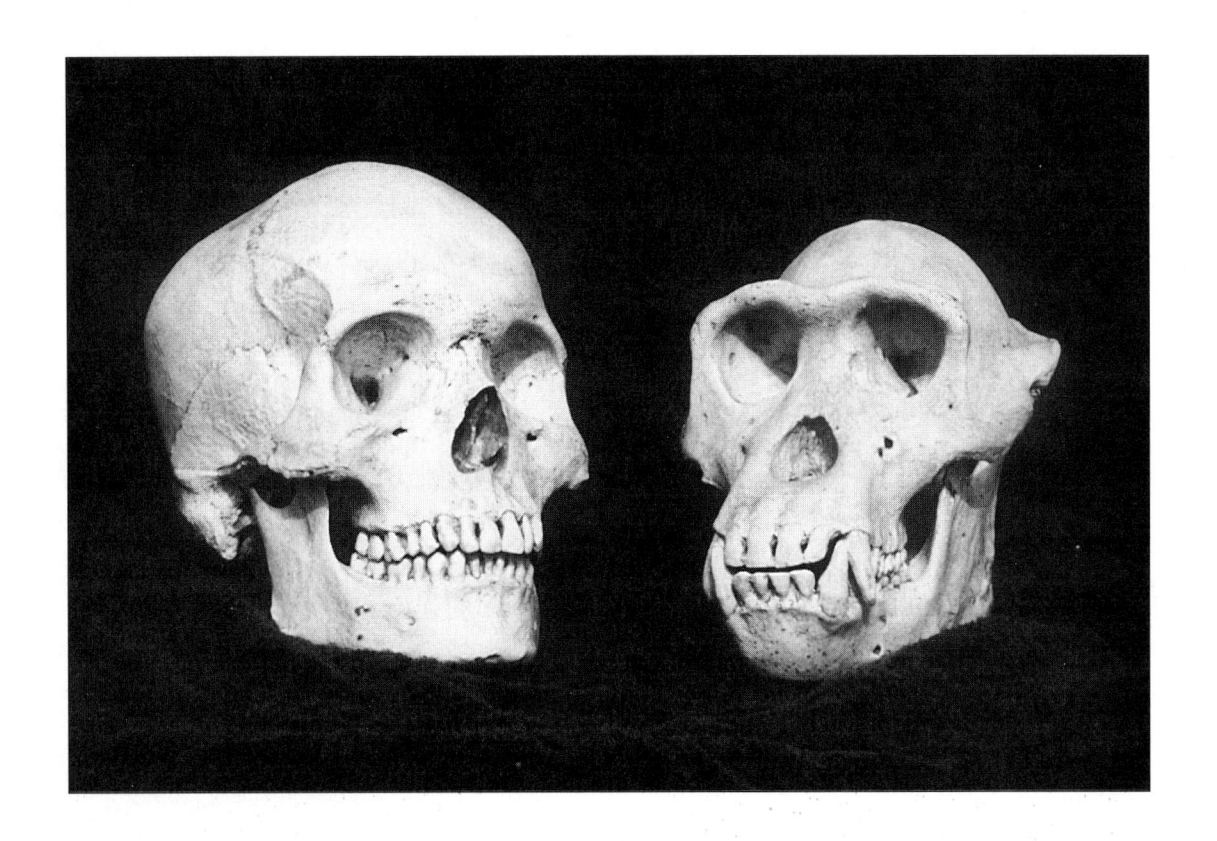

We both know what a successful relationship is built on: communication. Whatever the conflicts between two lovers (or for that matter, two neighbors or two nations), those tensions can be resolved with communication—open and honest sharing of opinions, experiences, and credit cards.

—*Roger L. Welsh*

UNIT 2
Social, Mental, and Ideological Ecologies

Ecology is not only the study of the relation of humans to their physical environments but also the study of social environments, mental organization and function, and ideological evolution. In this unit we discuss these other ecologies and how they relate to communication. In Chapter 5 we discuss how people perceive one another, depending on their GOALS in situations and their GRASP of those situations in which they interact. We discuss how personal characteristics are formed in interpersonal interaction and how several of these modify communication. Then we turn to the processes of credibility and reference group formation and influence, with some commentary regarding the ways in which personal characteristics, credibility, and reference groups may interfere with critical decision making. In Chapter 6 we discuss the core principles we have used so often they have become the principles by which our more peripheral opinions are organized—those of social reinforcement, ego-maintenance, and cognitive consistency. We discuss the mechanisms of classical and operant conditioning by which opinions are learned, and mechanisms of ego-defense and the consistency of our opinions with our attitudes toward sources, past choices, logical and wishful thinking, and prior beliefs and attitudes. In each case we discuss how these mechanisms and processes can be prevented from causing us to make uncritical decisions.

In Chapter 7 we confront critical listening more directly. We describe a model of critical decision, barriers to critical listening, and some of the ways others attempt to persuade us and gain our compliance.

Basically, Unit 2 deals with the means by which we can keep our social and mental environments free from pollution.

In many ways the saying "know thyself" is lacking. Better to know other people.
   —*Melander (342?-292? B.C.)*

There are more of them than us.
   —*Herb Caen*

Communication and the Social Environment

5

CHAPTER OUTLINE

Social Perception
Deriving Perceptual Criteria from Situations
Inferring Attributes from Observations of People

Personal Differences, Empathy, and Projection
An Analysis of "The Breakfast Club"
Empathy vs. Projection

Personal Characteristics
Dogmatism
Machiavellianism
Self-Esteem and Communication Anxiety
Locus of Control
Androgyny and Sex-Role Stereotyping

Credibility and Reference Groups
Factor-Analytic Approach to Credibility
Functional Approach to Credibility
Reference Groups vs. Membership Groups

> Learning the contexts of life *is a matter that has to be discussed, not internally, but as a matter of the relationship between creatures. . . . It is correct (and a great improvement) to think of the two parties to the interaction as two eyes, each giving a monocular view of what goes on and, together, giving a binocular view in depth. This view is the relationship. (p. 142) . . . The old Greek advice "know thyself" may carry many levels of mystic insight, but in addition to these aspects of the matter, there is a very universal and, indeed, pragmatic aspect. It is surely so that all outside knowledge whatsoever must derive in part from what is called* self-knowledge. *(p. 145)*
> —Gregory Bateson, Mind and Nature: A Necessary Unity

Ecology is the science of the relationship between organisms and their environment, sometimes known as the science of communities. In everyday use, people tend to think of ecology as the study of the relation of humans to their physical environment(s). However, it is also the study of the relationships of humans to one another in their social environments. That is the focus of this chapter.

SOCIAL PERCEPTION

We do not perceive another person in a vacuum, or without preconceived ideas of what to look for. On your campus you probably walk past hundreds of people every day without really noticing them, perhaps registering their existence, but not really attending to them until something attracts your attention. Definitions of perception are plentiful, and differ drastically. But the perception in which I am interested here is purposeful, attentive perception in which one evaluates another in terms of some preconceived purpose, imposing a framework on that perception, although the process may operate at a low level of awareness. Here I am going to focus on the issue of how one "decides" to which of a number of available people one will attend and thus perceive. This is not the momentary glance some would define, probably correctly, as perception. That is probably best described in the chapters dealing with nonverbal communication. What I am going to describe here is a process of attentive perceptual exploration.

The framework I believe best describes the process of such person perception is the **GOALS/GRASP Model**. The central assumption on which this model rests is that we perceive people differently in different situations, depending on our *GOALS* in a given situation and on our understanding, or *GRASP,* of the characteristics of the situation that impede or assist us in achieving those goals. It may seem strange to begin a discussion of the perception of *people* by discussing perception of *situations,* but if you bear with us I think you will see why we are doing that.

The GOALS/GRASP Model is diagrammed in Figure 5.1. The left side of the model is a diagram of the characteristics of people, and the right side is a diagram of the relevant characteristics of situations. I will begin my description by focusing on the right side, the situation-perception side.

Deriving Perceptual Criteria from Situations

Actually, *GOALS* is an acronym for Goals Operant and Achievable in Light of the Situation. You have many goals in your life, I am sure. You want to understand this book, you want to pass this course, you want to maintain a good GPA, you want to graduate from your college, you want to get a good job, you want to marry someone you love, . . . and on and on. But you don't have all these goals in mind at any given time. In a specific situation you keep in mind smaller goals that you think you may be able to achieve in that situation. This smaller set of goals are the GOALS important in the perception of a situation.

Now, there are some aspects of that situation that will make it easier for you to achieve those GOALS and some that will make it more difficult. Not all aspects of the situation are related to your GOALS. It may be that the size

Sources of Data	Attributed Characteristics		Derived Criteria	GOALS/GRASP
Reputed Nonverbal Verbal Social Interaction Self-Reported	Honesty Power Similarity Intentions Intelligence Opinions Age Needs/Goals Self-Esteem Socioeconomic Status Etc.	Attribute-Criteria Matching	Honesty Objectivity Similarity Intelligence Responsibility Warmth Creativity Persuadibility Security Empathy Etc.	Goal-Relevant Aspects of the Situation in Persuasion (GRASP)

Tentative Judgements of Degree of Acceptability

Goals Operant and Achievable in Light of the Situation (GOALS)

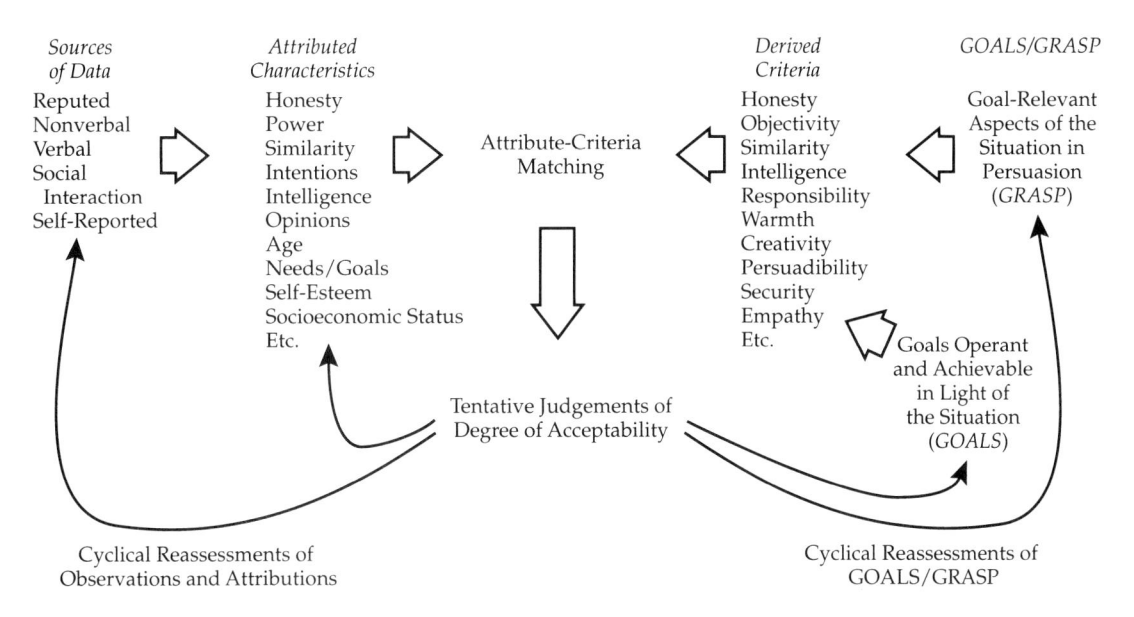

Cyclical Reassessments of Observations and Attributions

Cyclical Reassessments of GOALS/GRASP

FIGURE 5.1
Diagram of the process by which an individual judges the acceptability of another individual

of the room is irrelevant, or the number of people nearby, or the fact that it is raining outside. On the other hand, those matters may be very relevant in that they facilitate or hinder your GOALS-achievement in some way. If you have a GRASP of the situation, you understand which are relevant and which are not. *GRASP* is an acronym for Goal-Relevant Aspects of the Situation Perceived.

The intersection of your GOALS and your GRASP of the situation gives rise to the criteria by which you evaluate the people around you. This is especially true if the people around you are potential communicators. If your class meets in a large lecture hall with no public address system, your goal to hear what the professor is saying and your GRASP of the acoustic problems of the room make it very likely that the volume of the professor's voice will be an important criterion by which you evaluate that professor. In contrast, in a small seminar room vocal volume may not be an important criterion, and might be an aspect of the professor you would never notice.

Airport Example Let me give another example, rather easy and obvious. Imagine a couple waiting in an airport terminal for their plane to leave. The man goes into the restroom and fails to return after twenty minutes. Their flight time is approaching, and the woman begins to worry that he may have become ill or that something else has happened. Her goal is to find out if something is wrong, but she doesn't want to go into the men's restroom. She begins looking at passing strangers for someone she might ask to check on him. She GRASPs the situation in that she understands it is inappropriate in our culture for a woman to enter a men's restroom, so she narrows her search to men. But she also GRASPs the fact she is a woman alone in a public place, so approaching a man might be misunderstood. Thus another criterion that guides her perception is that the man must exhibit some characteristic or behavior that suggests he would not misunderstand. Consequently she is especially interested in men dressed as priests or men accompanied by other women. Her GOALS and her GRASP of the situation dictate the criteria that guide her perceptions.

Friendship vs. Romance Example The considerations that guide your search for friends and romantic partners are much more complicated and longer-lasting, but they can be viewed as a coincidence of GOALS and GRASP. The GOALS have to do with what you expect from a relationship, and the GRASP relates to your long-term situation. But together they yield criteria for a person who will constitute a satisfactory—and the best—friend or Significant Other. Of course, analyzing friendship and romance this way may seem to take the friendship and romance out of the search. But that is because we are directing conscious, rational attention to a process that may be somewhat unconscious and may appear irrational. Still, the process is susceptible to analysis.

For example, it appears totally irrational that some men persistently carry on affairs with married women, so they are almost doomed to unhappiness. But if we analyze such people in terms of this model, we are led to the conclusion they must be satisfying certain—perhaps perverse—GOALS by their behavior that they believe they could not otherwise satisfy because of a GRASP of which observers may not be aware. They may want to avoid long-term entanglements, or they may fear rejection. If they are rejected by someone who is married, they have a ready-made reason for the rejection that is not ego-threatening. "Of course she rejected me, because she didn't want to give up her home and family. It probably hurt her as much as it hurt me." Thus the man attains the GOALS of avoiding a long-term commitment or ego-damaging rejection. But we see his behavior as irrational and even pathological.

Roommate Example Suppose we consider an example less trivial than the airport one but less emotion-laden than romance. Most of you probably have roommates; most college students do, unless they are attending commuter schools. Do you remember how you chose your present roommate? The GRASP were imposed by financial considerations, probably. The university makes arrangements for students to live together because it is cheaper that way, and they usually provide individual rooms rather than suites for the same reason.

Your GOALS probably were to maintain an atmosphere conducive to studying and yet provide for some social activity, and to retain insofar as possible the freedom to study when you want and socialize when you want. The criteria for a satisfactory roommate are bound to spring out of the GRASP of living in close quarters in which both parties have to be engaged in the same activity at any given time, or at least engaged in compatible activities. Your GOALS of study and socializing—given the situation—dictate that your roommate have similar goals, a similar time schedule, and enough consideration for you that the two of you can work cooperatively to eliminate differences that may arise. Frequently the person who becomes your best friend does not make the best roommate, and your roommate may not become your best friend, because the criteria for friends and roommates are not necessarily the same; that is, the GOALS and GRASP are not necessarily the same.

Inferring Attributes from Observations of People

Now suppose we consider the left-hand side of the model, the person-perception side. Here our attention is directed to those *sources of data* about people, and the ways we convert those raw data to **inferred attributes** that we then try to match with the perceptual criteria derived from the situation. Two of the sources of data are verbal and nonverbal behavior of others. In Chapters 8 through 10 we discuss verbal and nonverbal behavior at considerable length, so there's no compelling need to discuss them much here. Suffice it to say we observe how well others use language and for what apparent purposes, we observe their nonverbal behavior, especially that which we assume is less under the conscious control of the actors, and we observe the extent to which their verbal behavior and their nonverbal behavior seem to be consistent.

Other people also tell us about themselves. This self-disclosure may or may not be believable on its face, since people sometimes do not really know themselves, and even when they do know themselves they usually try to describe themselves in the most favorable terms. However, even when it is not accurate, what they say about themselves may still be very informative, for it does tell us what they would *like* to be like, at the very least. But we can learn about others from what they tell us about their past experiences and how they feel about those experiences, their opinions on important issues, their opinions of others, especially mutual acquaintances, and their opinions of ourselves.

There is also a category of especially revealing and intimate opinions and experiences that are very private that are not revealed to most people. Those are really the opinions and experiences that are most informative. Perhaps you have seen the movie *The Breakfast Club*, which contains a good scene to illustrate very personal self-disclosure. When the students really begin to relate with one another is when they begin to describe their family lives: The Criminal tells how his father abuses him, tells him he is no good, burned him with a cigar as a punishment, and bought him a carton of cigarettes for a present last Christmas. The Princess tells how unhappy she is that her parents expect her to succeed in everything social. The Brain has the same complaint about his parents' academic expectations, and tells how he contemplated committing suicide with a flare gun because he is going to get an F in shop. And the Athlete registers the same complaint about his father's high expectations for his athletic success. The Basket Case reveals that she is contemplating running away from home because her parents pay no attention to her. That is really the point at which personal differences begin to recede and the students begin to band together.

The reports of others about the person in question are important sources of data, of course, although we must consider the source to decide whether the reports are to be believed.

Finally, the interactions of the target person with others are available for observation. The nature of such interactions can be very informative, including the people with whom they interact and the styles of interaction. Do they interact openly with many people, or with a select few they seem to consider their equals or superiors? And do they seem to condescend to those of lower status and be obviously ingratiating to those of higher status?

Inferred Attributes Now, as we gather these data, we draw inferences regarding the other, what are represented in the model as inferred attributes. We wrote in our original description of the model:

> Our list of inferred attributes includes the following, some of which overlap others: honesty, power, physical attractiveness, similarity to the perceiver (especially opinion and goal similarity), reward potential, intentions, needs/goals, intelligence, sex, sexual preference, sexuality, age, warmth, politeness, compliance/persuasibility, responsibility, potential for reciprocity, dogmatism, self-esteem, tendency to manipulate others, opinions on important issues, liking for the perceiver, empathic ability, need for affiliation, need for intimacy, extroversion/introversion, bias, security, aggressiveness, state of stress/activation/anxiety, educational level, and socioeconomic status. Obviously, the list does not exhaust the possibilities of even general attributes, not to mention those which are situation specific. (Cronkhite and Liska, 1980, pp. 118–119)

It is especially important to note that none of these inferred attributes can be observed directly. They are all attributes we infer from the data we gather. You may question some attributes on the list.

Is Sex an Inferred Attribute? My students frequently argue that sex can be observed directly, for example. These tend to be midwestern students from rural areas or small towns, however. No one who has spent any time in the Castro District or Ghirardelli Square in San Francisco, in the French Quarter in New Orleans, or in the West Village in New York City would argue that sex is anything but an inferred attribute under ordinary circumstances. I have a videotape of a striptease performance by Miss Gay U.S.A. that I sometimes show to drive that point home. Students are flabbergasted when I tell them the performer is actually a man. (I always adequately forewarn students they are going to view an R-rated performance the class period before the showing, and tell them they can come to class a few minutes late if they believe that will be objectionable. A few come late, but most come early and some bring their friends.)

Educational level and socioeconomic status are to some extent matters of public record and thus in part available as data, but we seldom resort to investigating transcripts and financial reports before drawing conclusions about those attributes.

But how do we move from our observations of others to inferences about them? George Kelly (1955) described people as amateur scientists, in this case amateur social scientists, who form perceptual hypotheses on the basis of their observations, test them, and form their own theories about what people are like and how they will act. These theories intervene between the observed characteristics and the inferred attributes we have described. Kelly calls these **personal constructs.** They include ideas about the combinations of observed characteristics from which one can infer attributes of others, and the inferred attributes that go together. Some believe that direct eye contact and a steady voice, both observable characteristics, are signs of honesty, an inferred attribute. That is a part of a personal construct. Some believe a high forehead, widely spaced eyes, and a perpetually serious expression, more observable characteristics, are signs of intelligence, another inferred attribute. That is another part of a personal construct. We all have an inventory of these beliefs too numerous to count.

Other parts of our personal constructs relate two or more inferred attributes to one another. Do honest people tend to be more intelligent or less intelligent than dishonest people? What about those who are athletic? Do you believe in the "stupid jock" stereotype? What about the "studious nerd"? the "prostitute with a heart of gold"? Whatever you believe about these and other stereotypes, whether you accept or reject them, and whatever personal stereotypes you maintain, they form parts of your personal constructs.

Others have asked and attempted to explain how we combine these characteristics and inferred attributes to form an impression of a whole person. **Asch** (1946) asked whether we sum the individual traits to construct a view of an entire person, or do essentially the opposite: form an overall impression and use it to organize the individual traits. He favored the second explanation. **Gestalt theorists** hold a closely related view, that the whole is greater than the sum of its parts, or at least the whole person is *different* from the sum of the traits.

There has not been a final answer to this question, but at least the question seems fairly clear. Suppose you first encounter a person in the exercise room lifting weights and assume they are a student, although they seem a little older than the average. You encounter the person there on several occasions. And when you see them in the cafeteria later, the two of you have lunch together. Then the next semester you walk into your American History class and discover, to your surprise, that the professor is the person you originally met in the weight room and have had lunch with. Now, do you incorporate this new information into the overall impression you have already formed, meaning you would describe the person as a friendly, young, athletic type who also happens to be a professor, integrating the new "professor" information into the impression you have already formed? But what if you know the person is a professor *before* the encounter in the weight room? If your overall view would be the same regardless of which information came first, the summation explanation would be confirmed. But if the later information were integrated into the original impression and modified by it, then the Asch/Gestalt explanation would hold. The process probably differs depending on the strength of the initial impression and the timing of the items of information. (By the way, the use of "they" as the third-person singular pronoun when the sex of the person is undetermined is deliberate. See the discussion of this issue in Chapter 9.

Self-Presentation Goffman (1956) based his explanation on a combination of **self-presentation** and empathy. He said we all present public selves. Then when we observe the behavior of others, we ask ourselves what it would represent or imply if we were performing it. (This really sounds more like projection than empathy, a distinction I will make shortly.)

Prototypes Cantor and Mischel (1979) theorize we form categories, or sets, within which we place people we meet. Many of these are "fuzzy sets"; they have no distinct boundaries. Instead of actually placing new acquaintances "within" the boundaries of the sets, we compare them with prototypical personalities that represent each set, and place them at various distances from the **prototypes** and thus more or less representative of the sets. Madonna is probably my prototype of a set of "female sexual opportunists." It should then be possible to place other attractive female rock stars at various distances from Madonna, depending on the extent to which I believe they use their sexuality for economic gain. You can do this for yourself.

Some female rock stars will be completely out of the set. For example, my impression is that Mariah Carey has such an impressive voice she has no need to trade on her sexuality, although it is not a handicap that she is attractive. She would be entirely out of the set for me. Others would be rather close to the Madonna prototype.

Attribution Theories   Howard Kelley (1972) is one of several theorists who have labeled as "schemata" what we carry around in our heads and use to judge those we meet. Actually, his term is **causal schemata,** on the assumption that each schema relates two or more mental elements causally. Kelley was one of the early advocates of *attribution theory.*

Attribution theories have been designed to explain how we decide where to place the praise or blame for actions we observe. We can attribute the "cause" of the action either as internal to the individual or as external, in the environment. Let me describe two of the theories that apply to cases in which we observe single instances of behavior.

Correspondence Inference   Jones and Davis (1965) have proposed what has been termed the **Correspondence Inference** theory. It applies when we have observed someone making a choice between alternatives. We make stable attributions of which we are certain if the alternatives differ considerably in their consequences, so by choosing one alternative over the others, the actors make their priorities clear. Imagine a person who nicks another car while driving out of a parking lot. The question is: Should the person leave a note on the windshield of the damaged car, or just drive away (assuming there has been no traceable damage to the driver's own car)? The consequences are very different, and we would make very different attributions depending on which alternative is chosen. However, Jones and Davis complicate the picture by adding the issue of the social acceptability of the alternatives: Leaving a note on the windshield is socially acceptable, so if there are witnesses to the accident, the fact that the driver leaves a note really doesn't tell us much about internal ethical beliefs. However, if the driver leaves a note that reads, "The witnesses to this accident think I'm writing a note with my name and phone number, but I'm not, so better luck next time," the owner of the damaged car will know the offending driver had some concern with social appearance, but a lack of ethics that outweighed that concern.

Discounting and Augmentation   One of Kelley's (1973) attribution theories also applies to observations of single choices, but he referred to two different principles: **discounting and augmentation.** A single choice is *discounted* if there is more than one possible explanation for it. In the auto accident example, though the driver drove away without leaving a note, it is possible that they did not realize they had hit the other car. On the other hand, if the driver got out and left a note in a powerful rainstorm, the fact that the action was difficult would *augment* the extent to which we would attribute the action to internal ethical beliefs.

Covariation   Another of Kelley's (1967) attribution principles, **covariation,** applies to cases in which we have opportunities to observe another in many different activities and situations. In these cases, Kelley said, three principles apply: **consistency, differentiation,** and **deviation from consensus.** The first principle seems almost self-evident. Over a period of time, one forms a stable attribution of behavior if that behavior seems to be governed by consistent motives. However, consistency must be balanced by differentiation. A person who consistently chooses to watch movies on the American Movie Classics channel or the Nostalgia channel might be suspected of preferring old movies to recent movies. But to be sure of that, we would have to see if they also choose to watch "Mystery Science Theater 3000" on the Comedy Central Channel, which also shows old movies but deliberately airs the worst of that genre, with the worst plots, acting, and visual effects. If they choose not to watch "Mystery Science Theater 3000," we may conclude their preference is for *classic* movies, not for those that are merely old. It is by our observation of consistency and differentiation that we are able to identify the principle governing such people's choices.

Now, if a person persists in watching classic movies even though their friends all prefer the most recent releases, and if the person would rather stay home alone to watch *Casablanca* for the thirtieth time even though a group of friends is going to the theater to watch the latest release, we have to add the third consideration, deviation from consensus, to our attribution. What we are trying to do is to attribute behavior to either (1) some motivation internal to the individual, (2) some characteristic of the stimulus, or (3) some characteristic of the situation. In this example, we would attribute the behavior of staying home to watch *Casablanca* primarily to internal motivation that is consistent but differentiating, and perhaps secondarily to characteristics of the stimulus, the movie. Certainly the attribution could not be to the situation, since there is nothing about the chosen situation—staying home alone—that is particularly compelling.

Attribute–Criteria Matching   If those available for your observation are strangers, then the processes just described will have to occur in a very brief time, perhaps simultaneously with analysis of the situation. In this case the process will occupy a mere fraction of the time it has taken to describe it or read about it. On the other hand, if you are among acquaintances, the inferred attributes may have been derived from extensive past experience. In either case, the person who is interesting enough to attract attentive perception will be the one whose inferred attributes best match the criteria derived from the GOALS and GRASP of the situation.

What is being described here is a process that requires some expenditure of energy, not casual glancing around a room. When you *choose* a person to whom to attend and explore perceptually, you may have to invest some time and energy. At a party, for example, you can only choose to invest perceptual energy in one or at most a small number of people. Thus what we're talking about is a perceptual screening process. At this point the perceptual process begins to blend imperceptibly into the acquaintance process, if the person chosen is unknown to you. (The acquaintance process will be discussed in Chapter 11 on interpersonal communication, so I will not pursue it here.) On the other hand, the person you need may be someone known to you for some time but who now fits the criteria derived specifically from the GOALS and GRASP of this present situation.

Cyclical Reassessment Once you have made a tentative choice, the process is not ended. Notice in Figure 5.1 that there is provision for cycling back through the GOALS and GRASP, the sources of data, and the inferred attributes. You check to be sure your initial choice was correct. If there are minor discrepancies, you may revise your observation of characteristics, the inferences you draw from those characteristics, the GOALS you maintain, and your GRASP of the situation, in order to achieve a better attribute–criteria match. However, if it turns out there is too great a mismatch you may make another choice.

Let me bring this closer to home: Imagine you are trying to decide on someone with whom to study for a midterm exam. Your GOALS initially are to understand and remember the material, and the GRASP are the requirements of a review to be conducted shortly before the exam. Thus the criteria for a satisfactory study partner are intelligence, attentiveness, studiousness, and ability to explain. You look around the class trying to remember which of the students have attended class consistently and have participated well in class discussion. Your attention and further perceptual exploration are focused on a subset of other students, some of whom you may not have previously favored with a second glance, because your perceptual criteria have been different. Some of your best friends may be in the class, and though you may like to spend time with them, you may also know from past experience that their attributes do not match your criteria for good study partners. You make an initial choice and fall into conversation with that person after class. In your perceptual exploration you may discover the person is studious and intelligent but seems to be somewhat short on motivation and ability to communicate clearly, so you must either take pains to become better acquainted to see if the person is just shy, reduce the importance of explanatory ability in your hierarchy of criteria, or choose another person on whom you will expend your perceptual attention.

Once again I want to emphasize that this attentive perception is a process that may occupy a longer period of time than other textbooks accord to perception. It may apply to some extent to the sort of perception that is fleeting, depending on momentary shifts of attention, as when we enter a room filled with strangers and try to choose someone to talk to. But it applies even better to perceptual exploration over a period of time, which may begin to become indistinguishable from the acquaintance process described in Chapter 11. It must also be obvious that this process involves a great deal of communication on the part of both the perceiver and the perceived.

Thus one does not perceive another as one might perceive a rock. Social perception is generally a cooperative process among people exchanging information about themselves. The information may be "accurate" or "inaccurate." It may consist of mutual attempts at self-presentation, as Goffman argues. It is certainly facilitated by mutual self-disclosure. Above all else it is a *process,* not an *act.*

PERSONAL DIFFERENCES, EMPATHY, AND PROJECTION

> Dear Mr. Byrd: We accept the fact we had to sacrifice a whole Saturday in detention for whatever it was we did wrong. But we think you're crazy to make us write an essay telling you who we think we are. You see us as you want to see us, in the simplest terms, the most convenient definitions. But what we found out is that each one of us is a Brain, an Athlete, a Basket Case, a Princess, and a Criminal. Does that answer your question? (*The Breakfast Club*)

The five people who spent the day together in detention in the high school library to atone for their sins in *The Breakfast Club* represented drastic differences in personal characteristics, lifestyles, home lives, motivations, and socioeconomic status. Yet by the end of the day they came together in important understandings of one another through the operation of empathy facilitated by **self-disclosure.** Earlier, I described the self-disclosure scene in which they really began to relate to one another. By the end of the movie, The Athlete and the Basket Case have paired off as a couple, as have the Criminal and the Princess. They have all come to realize they share more important similarities than differences.

Self-disclosure is an important contributor to empathy, and empathy is a bridge over interpersonal differences. **Empathy** is the ability to put oneself in another's place, to experience what the other is experiencing. It can bridge differences such as those experienced by the characters in *The Breakfast Club* as well as others. You can rent that movie if you have not already seen it; it is certainly worthwhile and entertaining. Perhaps your professor will devote some time to showing it. Because it is movie length, that may have to be done outside class time.

An Analysis of *The Breakfast Club*

The five main characters are high school students who, for one reason or another, have been assigned to spend a Saturday together in detention in the high school library. They are probably as different as high school students can be. The Athlete is clean-cut and handsome, and apparently comes from a middle-class family with a macho father, judging from his conversation and from the fact that he is delivered to school by a man in a four-wheel-drive utility vehicle. The Brain is also neatly dressed, and apparently middle-class. The Princess, played by Molly Ringwold, is attractive, very well dressed, and apparently from an upper-class family; she is delivered to school in a BMW. The Basket Case, a girl, looks as if someone had thrown clothes at her, and her hair is completely unkempt, falling over her eyes. She is delivered in a Cadillac. The Criminal is dressed as a derelict, and he is not delivered to school. It appears his family is lower-class.

At first there is a great deal of conflict; insults fly among them. The first signs of group formation occur in scenes in which they band together against their warden, a hard-nosed and even cruel teacher who reveals he really does not like teaching and resents having to be there on a Saturday, although he revels in the authority it gives him. The first half of the film is devoted to acquainting the viewer with each of the five characters, and in the process revealing each of their vulnerabilities. Then comes the scene presented earlier in which they each describe their home life.

After the self-disclosure, the Princess takes the Basket Case into the restroom and transforms her, by hairdo and makeup, into a really attractive girl who, in fact, attracts the Athlete; the transformed Basket Case and the Athlete leave together. The Princess and the Criminal also leave together. He says to her at one point that, since her parents use her against one another, he would probably make an excellent weapon for retaliation. The Brain stays in the library and writes the letter that began this section.

It is clear that, once the five came to understand one another, they realized they had one thing in common: They were all being victimized by their parents in one way or another. And they came to realize that their underlying similarity was more important than the surface differences.

Empathy vs. Projection

There are many differences to be bridged by empathic communication: differences in age, sex, race, educational level, socioeconomic status, and place of residence, to name a few—all the characteristics the U.S. Census Bureau uses to classify people, as well as a few others such as intelligence, height, and weight. Those the Census Bureau uses are technically termed *demographic* characteristics. They are also the variables advertisers and television programmers use to identify their target populations.

What is important here is that people who differ in these ways are likely to have had different experiences that affect their personalities, opinions, policies, reference groups, and motives. They may have *real* differences that cannot be bridged, only compromised, but empathic communication is capable of determining which differences are real and which only perceived.

> Empathy, the ability to feel and understand what another person is feeling and thinking, is probably the most valuable asset a communicator can acquire. Empathy is both a cause and an effect of successful communication; in fact, cause and effect in this case blend so completely that in a broad sense we can say that empathy is communication. If one is able to empathize with another, they are better able to communicate; if they are better able to communicate, they are better able to empathize. (Cronkhite, 1976, p. 80)

Kenneth Burke (1950) refers to "**identification** through consubstantiality"—becoming of the same substance—which seems to be ultimately indistinguishable in Burke's system from communication, rhetoric, and persuasion. This identification and communication help bridge the "natural divisiveness" among people that is caused in large part by these interpersonal differences. Martin Buber (1958) writes of "dialogic" as the study of relationships between "I" and "Thou." On the other hand, there are a number of ways people act so as to prevent their true selves from being revealed, and this, of course, hinders the development of empathy. Goffman (1956) explains how people present themselves in everyday life, choosing their clothes, the books they read, their friends, their expressed opinions, the interests they claim, their behaviors, and the ways they communicate so as to create a coherent image of themselves. It seems that, for Goffman, life is one constant resume and interview. Goffman's **interaction rituals** are a barrier to the development of empathy. So are Berne's (1964) "games people play," in which communicators adopt the personae of Child, Parent, or Adult in games such as "Man Talk," "Ain't It Awful," "Morning After," and "Rapo." These games are strategies for concealing our true selves, sometimes quite deliberately and sometimes at a low level of awareness.

The Brain, the Athlete, the Princess, the Basket Case, and the Criminal in *The Breakfast Club* began their Saturday detention engaging in interaction rituals and playing games to present themselves as they wanted to be seen, and in each case concealing their vulnerabilities. But over the course of the day their interaction rituals, their self-presentations, their dramatic personae, and their games began to slip and their true selves and vulnerabilities began to show through. Eventually they came to engage in mutual trust and self-disclosure so that they discovered their deep similarities were more important than their surface differences. *The Breakfast Club* is a metaphor, an allegory, for the process by which we can bridge interpersonal differences.

Unfortunately, many people in communication theory, and many textbooks for that matter, confuse *empathy* with *projection,* when in fact the two are mortal enemies. Empathy, as I have said, is the ability to feel and understand what another person is feeling and thinking. To do that, one must really know the other person and really listen to them. Too often, instead of really experiencing what the other person is experiencing, we ask ourselves what we would be feeling *if we were in that situation.* That is something quite different. That is projection, not empathy. We are projecting our own feelings, opinions, needs, wants, securities, and insecurities onto the other person, and by doing that we may in fact reduce empathic understanding. Other people are not all like you. You cannot project your own feelings onto them in their situation and then believe you understand them. One must *listen* to others, and come to understand not only their situations but their feelings about them.

Someone has described empathy thusly: When you cry, I taste salt. Such empathy cannot be achieved by mere projection. Projection is too easy. To develop empathy requires cooperation among people. It is an *ecological* enterprise, whereas projection is the act of individuals in touch only with themselves, not with one another.

PERSONALITY CHARACTERISTICS

You know you and your friends react differently to the same event in the same situation. You know to some extent you can predict how your friends will react given certain circumstances. These tendencies for a person to act in a predictable manner in a variety of circumstances is what I mean by *personality.*

Personalities are interactive. Your personality develops in interaction with others. Of course, it is in part genetically determined, but it also develops in social contexts.

There are certainly too many personality characteristics for me to discuss in these few pages. But there are some characteristics that are especially related to communication, because they affect the ways we process communication or to some extent determine the kind of communication we produce.

Dogmatism

Dogmatism is one of the personality characteristics closely related to communication. Rokeach (1960) originally described dogmatism and built a test to measure it. Dogmatism is also called *closed-mindedness.* Open-mindedness, its opposite, was described by Rokeach as "the extent to which the person can receive, evaluate, and act on relevant information received from outside on the basis of its own intrinsic merits, unencumbered by irrelevant factors in the situation arising from within the person or from outside". In clearer English: Open-minded people can react to communication objectively, without being biased by previous opinions. Open-minded people may not agree with a communication, but their reasons for disagreeing will be objective.

Characteristics of Dogmatic People The clearest characteristic of dogmatic people is that they tend to agree with communication from people they believe are authorities and reject communication from those they dislike or distrust. "Oh, I never listen to anything they say" is a dogmatic response, as is "If they said it, I believe it." One of the items on the Dogmatism Scale with which a dogmatic person will agree is "In this complicated world of ours the only way we can know what's going on is to rely on leaders or experts who can be trusted." The other side of this is that dogmatic people are quick to reject people with whom they disagree. They will agree strongly with another item from the Dogmatism Scale: "My blood boils whenever a person stubbornly refuses to admit he's wrong." Dogmatism is the equivalent of *authoritarianism,* people's tendency to agree with those presumed to be authorities and to do what they are told to do by those in positions of authority. Of course, we all do this to some extent; but with highly dogmatic people, being slaves to "authorities" is a way of life.

Another characteristic of dogmatic people is that they tend to maintain very strong central beliefs that are difficult to change. These central beliefs generally have to do with the nature of authority, what constitutes "personal worth," and what is our purpose on earth. Dogmatics agree with statements such as "It is better to be a dead hero than a live coward," and "The main thing in life is for a person to want to do something important." Thus, when dogmatics encounter communication, they accept or reject it, not on the basis of its merits but depending on whether it challenges or reinforces their central beliefs.

Example: The Abortion Issue I think the controversy over abortion is so heated and so unlikely to be resolved because it is closely related to the central beliefs of two groups. One group firmly believes all human life is sacred, including the lives of those yet unborn. Some people in this group believe the lives of the unborn are sacred because God has ordained those lives, has set those lives in motion, and to end them, even before birth, is to thwart God's will. These are very central beliefs for some people, and to give them up would require abandoning their beliefs about authority and the meaning of life. The other group believes just as strongly in the supremacy of the individual and in the right of individuals to make their own decisions in matters that most directly affect them. Thus they are "pro-choice"; they believe a woman has the right to decide matters that affect her body in the most personal and private ways. They are not going to change their opinions either, because to do that would require them to give up their central beliefs in the authority of the individual and individual freedom as the meaning of life. Dogmatics on both sides are willing to go to jail and even to give up their lives for these central beliefs. After all, it is better to be a dead hero than a live coward.

I do not mean that everyone on either side of the abortion issue is dogmatic, only that the abortion issue is going to bring out the dogmatism in those who believe themselves to be most open-minded.

Famous Dogmatics   In fact, some of the most noted people in history are remembered because they held extremely central beliefs for which they were willing to die. Patrick Henry's well-known cry "I know not what course others may take, but as for me, give me liberty or give me death!" was about as dogmatic as can be. Joan of Arc dogmatically refused to recant her central beliefs and was burned for them. Malcom X knew his central beliefs and his open statement of them endangered his life, and he died for them. I am not saying that we should *never* stand up for our central beliefs, only that dogmatic people are especially likely to do so and to have central beliefs that surface on an unusual number of issues that others consider trivial. The difference between cheesecake and pecan pie is probably not worth dying for.

Dogmatism and Compromise   Dogmatics also tend to divide ideas and the people who advocate them into two categories: those they accept and those they reject, those that are true and those that are false, those that are good and those that are evil, those that are right and those that are wrong. They are unwilling to see that people can be right about some things and wrong about others, or that ideas can have some good aspects and some bad. There is no room for compromise. In fact, two of the items on the Dogmatism Scale with which they tend to agree are: "There are two kinds of people in this world—those who are for the truth and those who are against it," and "To compromise with our political opponents is dangerous because it usually leads to betrayal of our own side."

Dogmatism and Contradiction   Finally, dogmatic people can comfortably maintain contradictory beliefs simultaneously and not recognize that one is relevant to the other. They agree with the statements that "The highest form of government is a democracy, and the highest form of democracy is a government run by those who are most intelligent," and "Even though freedom of speech is a worthwhile goal, it is unfortunately necessary to restrict the freedom of speech of certain political groups." They do not recognize that these statements are internally contradictory, that one does not truly believe in freedom of speech if one is willing to grant it only to those with whom one agrees. Everyone agrees with that.

Dogmatism and Intelligence Although this description of dogmatic people may make them sound stupid, in fact there have been many studies of the relationship between dogmatism and standard intelligence tests, and none of those studies have found evidence that people who are highly dogmatic are less intelligent. As college students and professors we tend to believe we are more intelligent than average, and let's hope that is true. But being intelligent is apparently no guard against being dogmatic. There are intelligent dogmatics and dogmatics who are not intelligent. None of us is safe.

Dogmatism and Agreeableness Another temptation is to believe that those who agree with us are open-minded. Actually, the opposite may be true. Open-minded friends can be very difficult, because they tend to question us rather than agree automatically just because they are our friends. On the average, dogmatic friends are probably more agreeable than are those who are open-minded.

Dogmatism and Persuasiability One final caution is this: It seems reasonable to expect that dogmatic, closed-minded people are difficult to persuade. That has not generally been found to be the case. It is difficult to persuade dogmatic people *to change their central beliefs*, but we do not ordinarily argue about central beliefs. The abortion issue is unusual because it brings into conflict opposing central beliefs. Dogmatic people change their peripheral beliefs more easily than do open-minded people, because they are willing to sacrifice their peripheral beliefs to keep their central beliefs intact. All you have to do to persuade dogmatic people on a peripheral issue, such as which stereo system is better, is to find someone they respect who agrees with you. The respected person does not have to be an authority on stereo systems; they can be an authority on anything, so long as the dogmatic respects them. That will not work with an open-minded person.

    Example: "All in the Family" Archie Bunker, the central character of TV's "All in the Family," was certainly dogmatic. Archie had his own set of "experts" whose opinions he trusted regardless of the issue, and people whose opinions he rejected regardless of the issue. He had a set of central beliefs from which he could not be shaken, and peripheral beliefs he would give up in an instant if his "experts" contradicted them. He believed firmly there were two types of people: those who were for his patriotic, conservative "truths," and the pinko, Commie liberals who were against those "truths." And Archie was perfectly capable of maintaining contradictory beliefs. He professed his belief in God, but in one episode he said "Faith is what you believe that no one in their right mind would believe."

But there are problems with using Archie Bunker as an example of someone who is dogmatic. Though we were never sure watching that program just how intelligent Archie was, he was certainly ignorant, which is not a necessary characteristic of the dogmatic. And while Archie was decidedly right-wing politically, and racist besides, some dogmatic people are liberal, not conservative. "Meathead," Gloria's boyfriend and later her husband, may well have been as dogmatic as Archie at the opposite end of the political spectrum.

I have spent so much space discussing dogmatism because it is a personality characteristic that so clearly affects the ways we process and use communication, and that is so clearly a threat to the ecology of ideas. Now let me turn to another personality characteristic that is directly and obviously related to communication: Machiavellianism.

Machiavellianism

Some people seem to have a strong urge to influence others. This urge has been termed **Machiavellianism** by Christie and Geis (1968), and they have devised various tests to measure it. Some of the test items indicate what they believed the Machiavellian personality to be like. In one version of the test, the Mach IV, the people taking the test are supposed to indicate on a scale from +3 to −3 how strongly they agree or disagree with a series of statements. One item is "Never tell anyone the real reason you did something unless it is useful to do so," and another is "The best way to handle people is to tell them what they want to hear." In both cases agreement with the item indicates a tendency to manipulate others. Other items are "reversed," in that the highly Machiavellian person would *disagree* with the statement. Examples are: "Honesty is the best policy in all cases," and "There is no excuse for lying to someone else."

Machiavellianism is directly related to communication, since communication is almost always the means of manipulation. As you can see, communication is involved in all the items just presented.

The problem with the Mach IV test is that it seems to measure only a need to manipulate others *unethically*. That is not the only sort of Machiavellianism. Maurice, the rich ex-astronaut in TV's "Northern Exposure," is persistently trying to manipulate others on that show, and seems to have no qualms about violating ethics in doing so. TV's Bart Simpson also seems to be a clear example of a Machiavellian who has no more ethics than absolutely necessary.

But do you remember the classic film *Twelve Angry Men*? The character played by Henry Fonda in that film manipulated the other men on the jury to vote "not guilty," and by doing so saved the life of the young boy accused of murder, which the viewer is led to believe was a heroic achievement. It is clear the Fonda character has a strong desire to manipulate: He bought a switchblade knife and concealed it in his pocket until just the right moment to pull it out and stab it into the table beside the murder weapon to demonstrate that the knife alleged to be the murder weapon was not unique. He goaded the character played by Lee J. Cobb into shouting "I'll kill you!" to illustrate that such words shouted in anger are sometimes meaningless. These are symptoms of a need—and an ability—to manipulate others, but not a need to do so unethically. You may be more familiar with TV's "Murphy Brown," who certainly manipulates others, or TV's Hawkeye on "M*A*S*H," who does the same, but neither of those characters seems to be unethical (or at least when they recognize it in themselves, they move to correct it).

Thus we need a test of Machiavellianism that does not assume a lack of ethics on the part of the respondent. Christie and Geis do not provide such a test, but you might be able to. Try to think of some statements with which characters such as Murphy Brown, Hawkeye, and the one played by Henry Fonda would agree, but statements that are *not* unethical. You might want to try your test items on some other students (in another class, of course).

Self-Esteem and Communication Anxiety

Low **self-esteem** is not the same as communication anxiety, but they may be related. It has been shown that people low in self-esteem are easier to persuade than those high in self-esteem.

Janis-Field Feelings of Inadequacy Scale There are many measures of self-esteem, but the Janis-Field Feelings of Inadequacy Scale (Hovland and Janis, 1959), revised by Eagly in 1967 but never published in that form, is a rather straightforward illustration of the characteristic. Respondents are supposed to indicate how often they have certain feelings by responding on a five-point scale to questions such as: "How often do you have the feeling there is nothing you can do well?" "How often do you feel self-conscious?" and "How often do you dislike yourself?" If they indicate they have those feelings frequently, they are judged to be low in self-esteem. Half the items are worded in the opposite direction: "How often do you feel that you are a successful person?" "How sure of yourself do you feel when among strangers (e.g., very sure)?" and "In general, how confident do you feel of your abilities (e.g., very confident)?" People who respond "very . . . " on these items are judged to be high in self-esteem.

What is not clear is that people low in self-esteem are necessarily anxious when called on to communicate. But this does seem reasonable, and at least six of the twenty items on the Janis-Field test seem to tap feelings of adequacy-inadequacy in communication situations: "When you have to talk in front of a class or a group of people your own age, how afraid or worried do you usually feel?" "How much do you worry about how well you get along with other people?" "How often do you feel you have handled yourself well at a social gathering?" "When you talk in front of a class or a group of people your own age, how pleased are you with your performance?" "How comfortable are you when starting a conversation with people whom you don't know?" and "When you speak in a class discussion, how sure of yourself do you feel?"

Measuring Communication Anxiety James McCroskey has advanced a construct and test of what he terms **communication anxiety** (CA) that is probably the most researched area in human communication theory. The Personal Report of Communication Anxiety (PRCA) has been developed as a measure of that characteristic. When McCroskey originally proposed the construct in 1970, he held that communication anxiety is a *trait* that distinguishes it from the *state* of stage fright. Communication anxiety, he argued, is a personality condition in which people feel unusual anxiety in many situations in which they are expected to communicate orally, whereas stage fright is a state experienced by many people in a specific situation, and is not indicative of any unusual characteristic. CA is "a trait of an individual which has many implications for the person's everyday life" (McCroskey, 1977, p. 79). To make another distinction, CA is a *chronic* anxiety, whereas stage fright is an *acute* situational anxiety.

However, there has been much discussion in research reports since that time of the relationship CA and the PRCA bear to other constructs and measures of anxiety, including "reticence," "unwillingness to communicate," "shyness," and "manifest anxiety." We probably need not concern ourselves with all these fine distinctions. For our purposes, we need to remember that it is quite natural to feel anxious in a public-speaking situation, for example. In fact, people who do not feel some anxiety in such a situation probably will not do well. Even the most experienced speakers report they need to "get up" for a public appearance if they are to seem interested and interesting. But about 20 percent of college students, in particular, seem to be afflicted with a level of anxiety that is to some extent disabling and also generalized across many types of communication situations.

What Causes CA? There is some disagreement about the answer to this question. Some argue it may be hereditary, of course; others believe it is primarily a matter of learning that occurs during our early years—the ancient nature-nurture controversy that recurs persistently in discussions of human characteristics. McCroskey leans toward the learning explanation. I am inclined to say both.

What Can Be Done About CA?   Proposed treatments have included hypnosis, biofeedback relaxation, group counseling, reality therapy, conditioned relaxation, false heart-rate feedback, cognitive modification, skills training, and systematic desensitization. These last three have received the most recent attention. Cognitive modification is based on the assumption that people high in CA simply have false beliefs about the consequences of communication. Skills training is based on the assumption that high-CAs have simply learned maladaptive behaviors. Systematic desensitization is a type of treatment in which high-CAs are put into a relaxing environment and then exposed to a series of descriptions of potentially anxiety-producing communication situations. The situations are arranged so they increase in order of likely anxiety production. The clients are told to indicate whenever they feel anxiety, at which time the therapist returns to one of the earlier descriptions and attempts to move back toward the description that created the earlier anxiety. Systematic desensitization seems to be the method of McCroskey's choice, although cognitive modification and skills training have also been shown to be effective.

The PRCA is a self-report measure, which may be somewhat of a problem since the people being measured are asked to agree or disagree to some extent with statements of the following sort:

> "I like to get involved in group discussions." "I'm afraid to speak up in conversations." "I feel relaxed while giving a speech." (McCroskey, 1982)

Probably the most complete description of communication anxiety appears in McCroskey, 1984.

Locus of Control

Some people believe they are at the mercy of fate and other people and nothing they do can make much difference in their lives and the events that happen to them. Such people are said to be highly *external* in their **locus of control.** Others believe they are in control of their own destinies, so that they are rewarded or punished for what they do; both achievement and failure are their own doing. They are said to be highly *internal* in their locus of control. Of course, most of us can be located between those two extremes, sometimes believing more of the one and sometimes the opposite.

Rotter's (1966) Internal-External Locus of Control Scale was designed to measure these tendencies. The respondent is asked to choose one of two paired statements such as these:

2. a. Many of the unhappy things in people's lives are partly due to bad luck.
    b. People's misfortunes result from the mistakes they make.
5. a. The idea that teachers are unfair to students is nonsense.
    b. Most students don't realize the extent to which their grades are influenced by accidental happenings.
10. a. In the case of the well-prepared student there is rarely if ever such a thing as an unfair test.
    b. Many times exam questions tend to be so unrelated to course work that studying is really useless.
15. a. In my case getting what I want has little or nothing to do with luck.
    b. Many times we might just as well decide what to do by flipping a coin.
22. a. With enough effort we can wipe out political corruption.
    b. It is difficult for people to have much control over the things politicians do in office.

So what does this have to do with communication? If someone is trying to get you to take some action they say will affect your future, and you are inclined to believe your future depends on fate and the actions of others, not on your own actions, you are likely to reject their appeals without really giving them careful consideration. On the other hand, if you are trying to persuade someone else to take some action, and the other person is high in external locus of control, you will have a difficult time.

Locus of control, self-esteem, and communication anxiety are all developed in interactions with others. Others reward or discourage us for relying on ourselves, and our experiences with others influence what we think of ourselves—whether we are confident, uncertain, or anxious. And our actions influence others in similar ways.

Androgyny and Sex-Role Stereotyping

Androgyny is the ability of an individual of either sex to take action that is appropriate and effective in a given situation without being bound by sex-role expectations. Thus an androgynous man is capable of being sensitive and caring when that is appropriate, and an androgynous woman is capable of being decisive and assertive when that is called for.

TV's "Saturday Night Live" frequently does a skit allegedly dealing with androgyny that features a character named "Pat," a person of indeterminate sex. The action in the skits is an attempt to determine Pat's sex, at different times by a hairdresser/barber, a nurse, or an exercise instructor. It is a funny bit, but Pat is a poor representative of the androgynous person. An androgen is not a cross-dresser, a hermaphrodite, or AC/DC. Androgyny as we are discussing it has nothing to do with uncertainty about a person's biological sex or sexual preference.

Examples of Sex-Role Stereotyping and Androgyny Suppose we consider some examples of people you know who represent different degrees of sex-role stereotyping and androgyny. Andrew Dice Clay may be the all-time champion of male chauvinism—not to mention rudeness and obscenity. TV's "Major Dad" is represented as a highly chauvinistic male character. Suzanne, played by Delta Burke on TV's "Designing Women," seems clearly a sex-role stereotyped female, while her sister Julia, played by Dixie Carter is probably a good representation of female androgyny. Hawkeye, the character played by Alan Alda on "M*A*S*H," seems generally androgynous, although his sexual exploits seem exploitive, which is not an androgynous characteristic. (Alan Alda as a person, however, and in other roles he has played, is generally considered to be a good role model for the androgynous male.) But I really would nominate Ted Danson and Farrah Fawcett as the best illustrations of male and female androgyny, respectively.

Ted Danson Ted Danson plays Sam, the bartender on TV's "Cheers." In that role he is clearly sex-role stereotyped: He is a retired professional athlete, vain, and exploitive of women. But in other roles, as in the film *Three Men and a Baby*, he has abandoned the hairpiece he wears in "Cheers" and has definitely shown a sensitivity that is uncharacteristic of Sam. In the film *Something About Amelia* he played a father who sexually abuses his child, a role that could—and would—only be played by a person sensitive to such problems. Danson has become a spokesperson against sexual molestation of children and a spokesperson for women's rights. He is also caring for a wife who has been seriously handicapped by a stroke. As the character on "Cheers," he is sex-role stereotyped; as a person and in other roles he is androgynous.

Farrah Fawcett played the epitome of a sex-role stereotyped female as one of "Charlie's Angels" on the old television show. Most observers believed that was the range of her acting capabilities. But she has since played the lead roles in films clearly devoted to women's rights, among them *The Burning Bed* and *Extremities*. Whereas a few years ago she would never have been indicted and certainly not convicted of either acting ability or androgyny, she is now guilty of both.

Other Examples Segue to late-night television: Rhonda, who introduces movies on "USA: Up All Night," before introducing a highly forgettable movie titled *Assault of the Killer Bimbos,* traced the history of bimbos, a tribe in South America captured and brought to Southern California, from where they spread across the entire nation. Later she announced she was forming a radical feminist group called H.E.R.: Hyper-Estrogen Revolutionaries. Androgynous women are far from being either bimbos or Hyper-Estrogen Revolutionaries.

Cannibal Women in the Avocado Jungle But while we are on the subject of late-night television, let me describe a movie titled *Cannibal Women in the Avocado Jungle of Death,* not because I recommend it as an intellectual experience, but because it is an interesting parody of the misunderstandings between the sexes. Shannon Tweed plays an unlikely anthropologist who is recruited by the government to lead an expedition into the Avocado Jungle, located just south of San Bernardino, to investigate why there is a serious avocado shortage. The jungle is under the control of two sects of Cannibal Women, the Women and the Barracuda Women, all of whom eat men but who prefer them with different kinds of sauce. The anthropologist expresses surprise that that is the only difference between them, and says, "No wonder we weren't able to pass the Equal Rights Amendment. Men can agree on football, but we can't agree on anything." Of course, she is eventually able to persuade the man-eating women to become more tolerant.

But the most precious scene in *Cannibal Women* comes when the character played by Bill Maher, whom you may know as a stand-up comedian and host of "Politically Incorrect," tries to retrain a group of effeminate men whom the Cannibal Women spare so long as the men bring them hot chocolate and knit them warmers and scarves. He shows them how to drink beer and crush the cans while watching sports on television, and how to cruise the boulevard palming the steering wheel with one hand while shouting at "dames, broads, and wenches" such things as "Hey sexy mama, hey love machine, want to ride in my Corvette?"

Measuring Sex-Role Stereotyping

Bem's Sex-Role Inventory In a less humorous and more scholarly vein, Sandra Bem (1981) has devised a measure of androgyny and sex-role stereotyping, the **Bem Sex-Role Inventory**. Respondents are asked to rate themselves on a scale from 1 to 7 on each of a number of characteristics. The "masculine" characteristics are: self-reliant, defends own beliefs, independent, athletic, assertive, strong personality, forceful, analytical, has leadership abilities, willing to take risks, makes decisions easily, self-sufficient, dominant, masculine, willing to take a stand, aggressive, acts as a leader, individualistic, competitive, and ambitious. Every respondent receives a "masculinity" score on these characteristics. The "feminine" characteristics are: yielding, cheerful, shy, affectionate, flatterable, loyal, feminine, sympathetic, sensitive to the needs of others, understanding, compassionate, eager to soothe hurt feelings, soft-spoken, warm, tender, gullible, childlike, does not use harsh language, loves children, and gentle. Each respondent also receives a "femininity" score.

The determination of whether a respondent is sex-role stereotyped or androgynous depends on the *difference* between the two scores. Men who have high masculinity scores and low femininity scores are male sex-role stereotyped, and women who have high feminity scores and low masculinity scores are female sex-role stereotyped. Respondents who score high on both masculinity and femininity are androgynous. Those who score low on both are "undifferentiated." Men who score high on femininity and low on masculinity, and women who score high on masculinity and low on femininity, are cross-typed.

It must seem apparent to even the untrained observer that there are confusing aspects of this test, and indeed the research has been mixed. One problem is that there are six categories. Another problem is that the scores reflect the respondents' perceptions of their own characteristics and behaviors.

The S.E.X. Test   Another, and perhaps better, test would be one based on respondents' *beliefs.* My undergraduate students in a course in measurement and statistics devised a test we called the S.E.X. test, an acronym for Sexual Equality eXam. I am not aware of any published test that asks respondents to tell their beliefs about sexual equality, so I am going to reproduce that one here. I think beliefs about sexual equality are an important aspect of androgyny and sex-role stereotyping, and Bem's test does not reflect that.

Sexual Equality eXam

Please respond to the items that follow by deciding the extent to which you agree or disagree with the statement. If you strongly agree, please fill in the bubble marked (a) on the accompanying answer sheet. Similarly, if you somewhat agree, mark (b); if you neither agree nor disagree, mark (c); if you somewhat disagree, mark (d); and if you strongly disagree, mark (e). There are no right or wrong answers. We simply want to know your opinions.

1. It is O.K. for a man to cry.
2. It is acceptable for boys to play with dolls.
3. It is acceptable for girls to play with toy trucks.
4. In a marriage, it is better for the husband to make more money than the wife.
5. It is acceptable for the husband to stay home and take care of the children while the wife works.

6. It is good for a marriage for the husband to help with the housework.
7. It is acceptable for women to work as laborers such as construction workers.
8. It is acceptable for men to work as nurses.
9. Women can be just as good drivers as men.
10. A woman should know about the mechanical aspects of cars.
11. Girls should be encouraged to participate in sports.
12. It is perfectly acceptable for boys to take dancing lessons if they wish.
13. A wife's responsibility is to stay home with the children.
14. It is a wife's responsibility to have dinner ready when the husband comes home from work.
15. Birth control should be the responsibility of the man.
16. It is more important for parents to send their sons to college rather than their daughters if a choice must be made.
17. Backyard barbequeing is the husband's responsibility.
18. Taking out the trash is the husband's responsibility.
19. The husband should be the principal driver on trips.
20. Men should pay on dates.
21. It is the responsibility of the wife to get up when the baby cries.
22. The wife should do most of the grocery shopping.
23. The husband should control the family finances.
24. The wife should generally do the laundry.
25. It is the husband's responsibility to discipline the children.
26. It is the wife's responsibility to comfort the children.
27. The wife should be responsible for the social obligations of the family.
28. Men are generally better at math than are women.
29. Women generally have better language skills.
30. Women are generally more compassionate than are men.
31. Women are generally more emotional than are men.
32. Men have a greater capacity for critical thinking than do women.
33. Women should be virgins at marriage.
34. It is generally good for a man to be sexually experienced before marriage.
35. Women who ask men out on dates are probably easy.
36. Women should let men win at competitive games.

37. It is usually less harmful to a marriage for the husband to have an extramarital affair than for the woman to have one.
38. In a business meeting, it is more appropriate for a woman to serve as the secretary.
39. In general, the husband should be responsible for maintenance of the house.
40. If there is a garden, it is more appropriate for the wife to tend it.

To score yourself on this test, give yourself the following points on items 1–12: A = 5, B = 4, C = 3, D = 2, E = 1. Give yourself the following points on the remaining items: A = 1, B = 2, C = 3, D = 4, E = 5. The highest possible score is 200, which represents the strongest possible favorable attitude toward sexual equality. The lowest possible score is 40, which represents the strongest possible negative attitude toward sexual equality.

I do not believe this is the best possible test. For one thing, there are too many negative items. Another problem is that the items are too obvious, so those who want to fake their responses can easily do so. Nevertheless, I believe this approach to testing sex-role stereotyping and androgyny will prove to be more useful than Bem's approach.

By the way, items 28–32 may be questions of empirical fact. While there is no doubt sex roles are in part the result of cultural biases and childhood training, there is also good evidence that some differences are due to differences in the brains of the two sexes, caused by the influences of the sex hormones estrogen and testosterone. [If you are interested in this issue, a good book to consult is *Brain Sex . . .* by Moir and Jessel (1991).]

So what does this have to do with communication? Of course, if listeners are sex-role stereotyped, they will be difficult to persuade regarding issues of sexual equality. Both men and women who are sex-role stereotyped will probably be less likely to be persuaded by women, at least on stereotypically male-oriented issues, but more susceptible to persuasion consistent with traditional sex roles.

As with all these personality characteristics, it is important to consider how our own characteristics may cause us to misperceive incoming communication.

CREDIBILITY AND REFERENCE GROUPS

Factor-Analytic Approach to Credibility

Actually, we developed the GOALS/GRASP Model described earlier in this chapter as an alternative to the type of credibility research that had occupied much of the previous two decades. In 1959, Berlo, Lemert, and Mertz (1969) conducted a study in which they asked students to rate prospective speakers on a number of semantic differential scales, that is, seven-point rating scales that have adjectives opposite in meaning at their opposite ends. Thus an abbreviated set of such scales might look like this:

Edward Kennedy

competent __:__:__:__:__:__:__ incompetent

untrustworthy __:__:__:__:__:__:__ trustworthy

active __:__:__:__:__:__:__ passive

Of course, Berlo, Lemert, and Mertz used many more scales than this, but their factor analysis indicated that their subjects were actually using all the scales to respond as if they represented only three dimensions, which they labeled "trustworthiness," "competence," and "dynamism." Although their study was conducted in 1959, and reported in a convention paper at that time, it was not published in a scholarly journal until 1969. In the meantime, however, it was widely publicized, and influenced much credibility research. One of the rash of studies of this sort, for example, was reported by McCroskey in 1966. McCroskey found dimensions of "character" and "authoritativeness," which seemed similar to the credibility dimensions of "trustworthiness" and "competence" reported by Berlo, Lemert, and Mertz. McCroskey included no "activity" scales that could have loaded on the "dynamism" dimension.

Gerald Miller, in 1969, wrote of this sort of research:

> Acquaintance with the research suggests only two generalizations about credibility which one can make with much confidence: First, if a communicator has a lot of it, he [sic] is somewhat better off than if he [sic] has a little of it; second, given the operational procedures typically used in factor analytic research, credibility appears to be a multidimensional construct. (The 'operational procedures' hedge stems from the fact that there is little convincing evidence that these dimensions will hold up in a communication situation. . . .) In spite of all the hustle and bustle of research activity, these generalizations reflect little knowledge about credibility. (p. 57)

Despite this skepticism and other published reservations, there were more than two dozen such studies reported in print between 1959 and 1976. The dimensions reported differed both in their names and in the scales that composed them. But as serious were the apparent attempts to make the dimensions reported seem comparable to one another when in fact they were not.

In 1976, we published a critique of such studies (Cronkhite and Liska, 1976). We criticized them on some technical grounds, but our simplest and probably most important criticism was that researchers had abandoned *thinking* about the process by which credibility developed and had let computers do their thinking for them, trying to find a set of scales that would measure credibility regardless of the source, the listeners, or the situation. We did not feel that the studies were any great improvement over Aristotle's statement in the fourth century B.C. that *ethos* (his word for credibility) consists of "character," "wisdom," and "good will."

Our critique was well-received; it received the Speech Communication Golden Anniversary Award for Outstanding Scholarship for 1976. Moreover, factor-analytic studies of credibility have essentially disappeared from the communication literature since 1976. We do not harbor any fantasy that our critique put an end to that type of study. It is much more likely that other scholars in our field had simply grown weary of the factor-analytic approach, and our critique summed up their reservations.

Functional Approach to Credibility

But others soon began to suggest that if we were criticizing current credibility research for being short on thought about the credibility process, perhaps it would behoove us to publish some thinking of our own. It took us until 1980 to publish such theorizing. Cronkhite and Liska (1980) presented the GOALS/GRASP Model as our notion of how the process of credibility operates. We argued that one communicator's conception of what constitutes a desirable other communicator changes from one situation to another, as described earlier in this chapter in the section dealing with social perception.

Of course, if we are dealing with listeners in a persuasive situation in which information is being presented that they cannot verify for themselves, such matters as the competence, trustworthiness, character, wisdom, and good will of other potential communicators are likely to be important. But sometimes one of those characteristics will be much more important than the others, and in some situations people who would not ordinarily be considered believable at all become quite believable because of other considerations. For example, if an accused criminal agrees to turn state's evidence and testify against former cronies, the credibility of that witness will be decided by very different criteria from those produced by the factor-analytic studies. Moreover, if you are trying to choose another person in whom to confide personal problems in the hope of receiving sound advice, most of the usual dimensions of credibility will go out the window, or at least have considerably different meaning. Put very simply, while you may consider your dentist to be competent and trustworthy in a specific situation, you probably would not ask your dentist for financial advice, simply because the situations, especially including your goals, are different.

On the other hand, there are some general questions that would be reasonable to ask about potential communicators you are choosing to testify to matters that you cannot verify personally:

These are traditional **tests of testimony:**

1. Are they or were they in a position to observe the facts?
2. Are they or were they capable of observing; that is:
   a. Are they or were they physically capable?
   b. Are they or were they mentally capable?
   c. Are they or were they psychologically or emotionally capable?
   d. Are they or were they sensitive to the facts in question?
   e. Have they had experience making such observations?
3. Are they motivated to perceive and report accurately?
   a. Have they anything to gain by deceiving?
   b. Are their goals similar to or compatible with yours?
4. Have they reported accurately in the past on this and other topics?
5. Are they responsible, in the sense of being in positions to be held accountable for their testimony?

Reference People But there are others in the communication process who are not immediately present who also exert an influence on our opinions because of their opinions. These "others" are those with whom we have previously communicated. Two students who meet to discuss doing a cooperative term paper on a controversial topic are haunted by the ghosts of opinions they have encountered in the past and expect to encounter again, just as they are constrained by their previous commitments. The opinions they express to each other will be determined in part by people they have met in the past, whose opinions have become influential for one reason or another. Sometimes these "others" will have been respected and their opinions adopted. Sometimes the "others" will have been highly disliked or distrusted, so that their opinions have been rejected. In either case, we will refer to such others as *reference persons*. Reference persons are those not directly involved in the present communication event who nevertheless, for one reason or another, influence the opinions we bring to that event. They may be close friends or they may be respected authorities we have never met; they may be enemies or public figures we distrust so intensely that we will believe the opposite of whatever they say. We should be aware of the means by which our opinions are being influenced. Suppose we consider the ways in which the opinions of reference persons operate to influence our own opinions.

A reference person is, in fact, a past source. Thus the credibility of a reference person consists of the same factors as does the credibility of a present source, and the GOALS/GRASP Model can be used to describe the process by which reference people are chosen. The reference person, however, has one characteristic beyond that of a present source: We know his or her opinions have remained influential and salient over a period of time. What we are really dealing with, then, is this question: What are the characteristics that perpetuate the influence of a source, transforming that source from a presently influential communicator into a reference person having lasting influence?

The answer to that question seems to lie in the concept of *groupness*, or *cohesiveness*. Previous writers have referred almost exclusively to *reference groups*. I agree with that approach as long as it is allowed that such "groups" may contain only two people.

Reference Groups vs. Membership Groups

The first step in dealing with the question seems to be to distinguish between **reference groups** and **membership groups.** A reference group is simply a group that influences one's opinions and policies. A membership group, on the other hand is, probably not surprisingly, a group to which you perceive you belong. The two are not necessarily the same. A group can serve as a reference even though it is not a membership group. However, membership groups are especially likely to become positive reference groups; people tend to be unusually persuaded by those within their membership groups and tend to reject "out-group" influence attempts. There are negative reference groups, too; these are groups that negatively influence our opinions, so that we tend to react against them rather than toward them.

When a Membership Group Is Not a Reference Group If you belong to a fraternity or sorority, that is certainly a membership group. The students at your college or university constitute a membership group—a group to which you belong. The people at the place where you work constitute a membership group for you. However, none of these groups may be a *reference* group for you. You may belong to your sorority or fraternity as a matter of social convenience, but the members may not influence your opinions, although they will probably try. The students at your university constitute a membership group more or less by accident, until some common issue such as a threatened tuition increase brings them together and the school newspaper begins to influence everyone's opinions. Your co-workers, similarly, were probably thrust upon you, and they are not a reference group for you until as a group you decide to pressure management for a raise or better working conditions.

When a Reference Group Is Not a Membership Group On the other hand, there are groups to which you do not belong that influence your opinions. These are reference groups but not membership groups. I do not belong to the Sierra Club or Greenpeace, but they are positive reference groups for me. I also do not belong to the Ku Klux Klan or the National Rifle Association, but those groups influence my opinions. Most of what they favor I oppose. They are negative reference groups for me.

Functions Groups Serve   What is it about the perception of "groupness"—a relationship vis-à-vis one other or a number of others—that causes the other or others to maintain influence over a period of time?

Social Support   For one thing, groups provide social support, especially when judgments to be made are ambiguous. We come to depend upon the perceptions of others we consider similar to ourselves in various ways to provide social reinforcement for our opinions. To some extent this may be due to liking or trusting the members of such a group, but not entirely. Being liked by the group seems to be a very important incentive in this case.

Defining Social Reality   Groups may also serve to define social reality. They impose their perceptions on social reality probably to a greater extent than upon physical reality, because social reality is more ambiguous. Thus we build expectations regarding various groups and are threatened if those expectations are not fulfilled. Left-leaning radicals who find their own opinions on a specific issue supported by the Young Americans for Freedom and opposed by Americans for Democratic Action may begin to feel they are losing their grip on social reality.

Opinion Conformity   If you value membership in a group or value some relationship to a group, you may use your opinions to maintain that membership or relationship. Some groups demand greater opinion conformity than do others as the price of continued membership, and some groups demand opinion conformity in only certain areas. The group may not demand anything of you. You may not be a member of the group and it may be that no one in the group has ever heard of you, yet you may arrange your opinions so as to maintain a self-satsifying relationship to that group. This effect is especially pronounced if you occupy a low-power position within or relative to the group and expect to continue to be associated with the group in the future.

GOALS and GRASP and Reference Groups   In any case, your choice of a reference group in a given situation depends on your GOALS in that situation and your GRASP of the elements of the situation that constrain or facilitate the achievement of those GOALS. Thus the right side, or situation-perception side, of Figure 5.1 remains the same whether we are dealing with a potential communicator or a group of people not present in the situation but with whom we have had previous contact—a reference group.

However, the data available for inferring the characteristics of reference groups will not be the same as those available from individuals. Mostly, observations of nonverbal and verbal characteristics will probably be less important, so we must depend more heavily on the reputations and self-reports of such a group. The characteristics of social interaction become the types of people who belong to the group, even though you may not belong to it yourself. On the basis of those sources of data you infer certain characteristics of the group that more or less conform to the criteria derived from your observation of the situation, and you choose a reference group based on the extent of that conformity.

CONCLUSION

The GOALS/GRASP Model, the basis for this chapter, is a model of the ways in which people interact with one another in different situations. We choose the others with whom we want to communicate, and at the same time those others are choosing the others with whom they want to communicate. Sometimes there is a happy intersection of those choices, and a relationship develops. Sometimes there is no such intersection. We may choose but not be chosen, and no relationship develops. Still, in the process we learn about ourselves.

In any case, the choices are made on the basis of attributes we infer from our observations of others, and their choices are made on their inferences from observations of us. In a sense, it is a persistent, mutual audition. We observe personal and personality differences, and try to empathize with those from whom we differ. We bridge those differences by communication. We evaluate others as individuals in terms of their credibility, and we evaluate groups in terms of their suitability as reference groups.

All of this forms both the social environment within which communication operates and the social ecology to which it contributes.

KEY TERMS AND CONCEPTS

GOALS/GRASP Model
observed and inferred attribution
personal constructs

Asch and Gestalt theorists
self-presentation
prototypes
attribution theories

casual schemata
Correspondence Inference
discounting and augmentation

Covariation:
  consistency,
  differentiation,
  deviation
  from consensus
attribute—criteria
  matching
self-disclosure
empathy
identification (inter-
  action rituals

empathy versus
  projection
Dogmatism
Machiavellianism
self-esteem/com-
  munication anxiety/
  locus of control
androgyny
sex-role stereotyping
Bem Sex-Role
  Inventory

factor-analytic
  approach to
  credibility
functional approach
  approach to
  credibility
reference people
reference groups
  vs. membership
  groups

REFERENCES

Asch, S. (1946). Forming impressions of personality. *Journal of Abnormal and Social Psychology* 41: 258–290.

Bateson, G. (1979). *Mind and Nature: A Necessary Unity.* New York: Bantam.

Bem, S. (1981). Gender schema theory: A cognitive account of sex typing. *Psychological Review* 88: 354–364.

Berlo, D. K., Lemert, J. B., and Mertz, R. J. (1969). Dimensions for evaluating the acceptability of message sources. *Public Opinion Quarterly* 33: 563–576.

Berne, E. (1964). *Games People Play: The Psychology of Human Relationships.* New York: Grove Press.

Brehm, J. W., and Cohen, A. R. (1962). *Explorations in Cognitive Dissonance.* New York: Wiley.

Buber, M. (1958). *I and Thou.* Translated by Ronald Gregor Smith. New York: Scribner.

Burke, K. (1962). *A Rhetoric of Motives.* New York: Meridian, World.

Cantor, N., and Mischel, W. (1979). Prototypes in person perception. In *Advances in Experimental Social Psychology,* Vol. 12, edited by L. Berkowitz. New York: Academic Press.

Christie, R., and Geis, F. (1968). Some consequences of taking Machiavelli seriously. In *Handbook of Personality Theory and Research,* edited by E. F. Borgatta and W. W. Lambert. Chicago: Rand-McNally.

Cronkhite, G. (1976). *Communication and Awareness.* Menlo Park, Calif: Benjamin-Cummings.

Cronkhite, G., and Liska, J. (1976). A critique of factor analytic approaches to the study of credibility. *Communication Monographs* 43: 91–107.

———. (1980). The judgment of communicator acceptability. In *Persuasion: New Directions in Theory and Research,* edited by M. Roloff & G. Miller, pp. 101–139. Beverly Hills, Calif.: Sage.

Goffman, E. (1956). *The Presentation of Self in Everyday Life.* Edinburgh, U.K.: Social Sciences Research Centre.

Hovland, C. I., and Janis, I. L. (1959). *Personality and Persuasibility.* New Haven, Conn.: Yale University Press.

Jones, E., and Davis, K. (1965). From acts to dispositions: The attribution process in person perception. In *Advances in Experimental Social Psychology,* Vol. 2, edited by L. Berkowitz. New York: Academic Press.

Kelley, H. (1967). Attribution theory in social psychology. *Nebraska Symposium on Motivation.* Lincoln: University of Nebraska Press.

———. (1972). Causal schemata and the attribution process. In *Attribution: Perceiving the Causes of Behavior,* edited by E. E. Jones et al. Morristown, N.J.: General Learning Press.

———. (1973). The process of causal attribution. *American Psychologist* 28: 107–128.

Kelly, G. (1955). *The Psychology of Personal Constructs.* New York: Norton.

McCroskey, J. (1966). Scales for the measurement of ethos. *Speech Monographs* 33: 65–72.

———. (1970). Measures of communication-bound anxiety. *Speech Monographs* 37: 269–277.

———. (1977). Oral communication apprehension: A summary of recent theory and research. *Human Communication Research* 4: 78–96.

———. (1982). Oral communication: A reconceptualization. In *Communication Yearbook 6,* edited by M. Burgoon. Beverly Hills, Calif.: Sage.

———. (1984). The communication apprehension perspective. In *Avoiding Communication,* edited by J. A. Daly and J. McCroskey, pp. 13–38. Beverly Hills, Calif.: Sage.

McGuire, W. (1964). Inducing resistance to persuasion. In *Advances in Experimental Social Psychology,* Vol. I, edited by L. Berkowitz. New York: Academic Press.

Miller, G. R. (1969). Human information processing: Some research guidelines. In *Conceptual Frontiers in Speech-Communication,* edited by R. J. Kibler, pp. 51–68. New York: Speech Association of America.

Moir, A., and Jessel, D. (1991). *Brain Sex: The Real Difference Between Men and Women.* New York: Dell.

Rokeach, M. (1960). *The Open and Closed Mind.* New York: Basic Books.

Rotter, J. B. (1966). Generalized expectancies for internal versus external control of reinforcement. *Psychological Monographs* 80(1, 609).

The human mind resists a new idea the way the body treats a strange protein; it rejects it.
    —Biologist P.B. Medawar

Some things have to be believed to be seen.
    —Ralph Hodgson

The Ecology of Ideas: Opinion Formation and Change

6

CHAPTER OUTLINE

Social Learning
    Classical Conditioning
    Operant Conditioning
    Conditioning of Opinions

Ego-Maintenance
    Value-Expression
    Ego-Defense
    Ego-Involvement

Consistency
    Balancing Opinions of Others with Other Opinions
    Let's Make the Best of It
    Logical Thinking and Wishful hinking
    The Relationship of Beliefs and Attitudes

> *Ideas which survive repeated use are actually hand-led in a special way which is different from the way in which the mind handles new ideas. The phenomenon of* **habit formation** *sorts out the ideas which survive repeated use and puts them in a more or less separate category. These trusted ideas then become available for immediate use without thoughtful inspection, while the more flexible parts of the mind can be saved for use on newer matters.*
>
> *In other words, the* **frequency** *of use of a given idea becomes a determinant of its survival in that* **ecology of ideas** *[emphasis added] which we call Mind; and beyond that the survival of a frequently used idea is further promoted by the fact that habit formation tends to remove the idea from the field of critical inspection.*
>
> *But the survival of an idea is also certainly determined by its relation with other ideas. Ideas may support or contradict each other; they may combine more or less readily. They may influence each other in complex unknown ways in polarized systems.*
>
> *It is commonly the more generalized and abstract ideas that survive repeated use. The more generalized ideas thus tend to become* **premises** *upon which other ideas depend. These premises become relatively inflexible.*
>
> —Gregory Bateson, Steps to an Ecology of Mind

The most frequently used and enduring of the premises spoken of in the preceding Bateson quote are the principles by which people form and change their opinions, because such principles are adopted early in life, used constantly, and almost never evaluated critically. Some, such as the principles of social reinforcement, seem to be innate. Indeed, we probably are born with the principle of responding to reinforcement, but what constitutes reinforcement, especially social reinforcement, is certainly acquired. The principle of self-defense is probably innate, but defense of the psychological *ego*-self, and the means by which that is to be achieved, is probably learned. The predisposition to maintain cognitive consistency is so universal in humans as to be a strong candidate for innateness, but the types of cognitive consistency are probably the premises Bateson would consider to be used frequently, to be enduring, and thus seldom evaluated critically.

Opinions are formed and changed by learning, in order to maintain and defend our egos, and to maintain cognitive consistency. (The term *opinions* here includes both beliefs and attitudes, a distinction that will be clarified later.) Suppose we consider those principles in turn, and observe why they may be so frequently used and enduring and why they need to be examined critically, at least on occasion.

SOCIAL LEARNING

> You've got to be taught to be afraid
> Of those whose skin is a different shade
> Of people whose eyes are oddly made.
> You've got to be carefully taught.
> —From the musical South Pacific

Actually, the teaching need not be all that careful. Learning can occur without the teacher's or the student's being aware of it. The mother who draws her child close when a person of different dress, skin color, facial features, or a handicap passes by is teaching quite subtly that there is something in that person to fear. Sometimes the "teacher" is quite aware, but the learner is oblivious to the teaching, as when viewers are conditioned to respond favorably to a product advertised on television by the simple matter of showing the product in a favorable context.

It seems useful to distinguish between two major types of learning, or conditioning, and then to illustrate how they may participate in the formation of our opinions: *classical conditioning* and *operant conditioning*.

Classical Conditioning

You have probably heard of Pavlov's experiments in conditioning dogs, if not elsewhere, at least in a course in general psychology. This type of conditioning is **classical conditioning,** and many of our opinions develop this way. Pavlov exposed his dogs to a bell or a tone and followed that immediately by blowing meat powder into the dogs' mouths. The dogs salivated without previous training in response to the meat powder, but at first had no response to the prior bell or tone, beyond possibly pricking up their ears. After several hundred repetitions, however, they came to salivate in response to the bell alone, even without the meat powder.

Television Advertising as Classical Conditioning You can probably remember many TV commercials in which a product is similarly paired with something to which you already respond favorably. Sex is used in many ways in advertising, but one way it is frequently used exemplifies classical conditioning. A product being advertised for men will be paired with the presence of an attractive woman; a product for women will be paired with an attractive man. In classical conditioning the men or women need not participate in any interaction with the product; their mere presence is enough. An automobile intended for sale to the affluent will be shown in country club settings or in the wide, sweeping driveways of mansions. There was a commercial being aired for a game in which children build a little wall with miniature plastic blocks and then use a tiny replica of a jackhammer to knock out as many blocks as possible without destroying the wall. The name of the game is "Knockout." Only little boys are shown playing the game. In another game, "Mall Madness," little girls are shown using a replica of a mall and their own toy credit cards to "shop till they drop." No sonorous voice announces " 'Knockout' is suitable for boys, and 'Mall Madness' is suitable for play by girls," but the message is clear, and it is communicated via classical conditioning. Did someone say sexism is dead?

What is so insidious about classical conditioning is that the viewer—or learner—need do nothing except experience the pairing in order for the conditioning to take place. Indeed, the viewer/learner *cannot* do anything to avoid the conditioning except use the remote control to change the channel—only to be exposed to more conditioning.

Operant Conditioning

On the other hand, **operant conditioning** requires the learner to *do* something, which is then rewarded or punished or not reinforced. B. F. Skinner is the person best known for developing operant conditioning. In his arrangement a pigeon was placed in a box in which there was only a lever, which, if pressed, would produce a grain of corn. Left in the box long enough, the pigeon would learn to press the lever, sometimes feverishly. The same general arrangement could be used to teach pigeons and rats to treat themselves to drugs, for brain stimulation, and to avoid electric shock. Notice that in operant conditioning the subjects are responsible for their receiving the reinforcement, since reinforcement is given only when they perform the desired behavior. There is no automatic pairing, as in classical conditioning.

Television Advertising and Vicarious Operant Conditioning Operant conditioning is more difficult to use on television (or in advertising in general). A commercial may urge viewers to *do* something, but there is no way for the advertiser to be sure viewers are doing what they are urged to do and then to administer or withhold reinforcement. That may be possible as television becomes more interactive, but we are not there yet. Instead, advertisers use *vicarious* operant conditioning that consists of little scenarios in which viewers observe others learning to perform the desired behaviors and then being rewarded for it. The poor wife is forced to endure the taunt "Ring around the collar" as an attractive other woman examines her husband's shirt. In a happy coincidence most of us never experience, however, after she learns to use the "right" laundry product, examination at another party by the same woman reveals no ring around the collar. Vicarious operant conditioning has just occurred. In another scenario, the husband drives the new neighbors away with his bad breath. When they leave, he runs upstairs and uses a mouthwash. But when he returns, his wife tells him he now has "medicine breath." He then goes back upstairs, uses the "right" fresh-tasting minty mouthwash. Now when he comes back down, the neighbors return and his social life is saved—by vicarious operant conditioning.

Of course one's friends and significant others have no such difficulty performing operant conditioning: They can shape your behavior until it is acceptable to them, and then administer immediate reinforcement in the form of approval or sexual reward or whatever they perceive to be likely to motivate you. (Of course, your friends and significant others would never do that. Of course not—no more than you would do it to them.)

Conditioning of Opinions

Neither Pavlov nor Skinner would speak of internal concepts such as "opinions." For scientific purposes, dogs and pigeons and rats—and people—do not have "opinions." Skinner's First Commandment to his disciples seems to have been "Thou shalt have no internal responses, nor shalt thou look upon those of others, nor shalt thou contemplate them in thy most secret heart. Selah." What they conditioned was *behavior*, not *opinions*.

Osgood's Internal Mediating Response But other theorists, most notably Charles Osgood (1963), in the field of communication, have demonstrated that classical and operant conditioning *do* work to form and to change internal states such as opinions. The **internal mediating response**, which Osgood considers to be meaning, is discussed at some length in Chapter 9, language effects, because Osgood's theory is a theory of meaning in general, not a theory of opinion formation and change specifically. However, the evaluative part of his notion of internal mediating response is in fact an opinion, formed by classical conditioning. Here I will be brief, since the theory is covered in some detail elsewhere.

Basically, according to Osgood, what happens is that a novel stimulus, which produces either no internal response or a weak one, is paired with a stimulus to which the "learner" has a strong internal response. By a process of classical conditioning, the novel stimulus comes to share the internal response that was formerly the "property" of the familiar stimulus.

Example: Selling Perfume A young man's response to Brut aftershave may have been neutral at one time, although even the pairing of that name with that fragrance must have produced an internal response to the fragrance, since we all associate "Brut" with the word *brute,* which is clearly masculine. Thus the previously neutral fragrance, or at least its bottle, acquired an internal "meaning" that was strongly masculine. But subsequent pairings of the word and the bottle with photos of adoring and attractive women looking over the shoulder of a muscular man, usually with his shirt off because he had just finished shaving, left no doubt about what one's internal opinion of Brut ought to be. Then when the learner encountered that bottle on a drug store shelf, it activated the new internal response, and predisposed him to buy it. The fragrance itself became the "reward" for the purchasing behavior. And if some attractive woman later asked him the name of the fragrance and told him she liked it, the operant conditioning step was complete. He had learned to peck the lever for a different kind of reward.

The only difference between this analysis and those of Pavlov and Skinner is that here there are internal responses and stimuli as well as external ones that are subject to conditioning.

Example: Learned Attitudes Toward African Americans When I was about four years old my parents moved into a racially mixed neighborhood in a small college town in southern Illinois. The earliest friend I can remember knowing was black. No one ever told me to like blacks. But my mother made it obvious she liked my friend. She says now it was because he never fought; he would always go home when an argument started. I was encouraged to play with him. And when I did, nice things such as cookies and milk happened. Besides, there was not much fighting when I was with him, and fighting hurt. Thus my friend's dark skin color and particular facial characteristics were paired with pleasant stimuli in a process of classical conditioning, and my spending time with him was rewarded by my mother's approval and food in a process of operant conditioning. I learned that blackness in another person meant friendship and safety, and that treating blacks as friends would be rewarded, a process of operant conditioning. I have carried those opinions and behaviors with me ever since.

However, as a young adult I enrolled at the same college my father had attended. I learned that other children in that neighborhood had not learned the same lesson, because there was great fear in the town that blacks from East St. Louis were moving east and would bring with them the poverty and high crime rate of the urban environment they were trying to escape. Young white children in the town more frequently encountered pairing of dark skin with anxiety and fear, and were rewarded for avoiding black children rather than choosing them as friends. There were numerous blacks who attended the college, a few from the United States but many more from other countries where black skin is the norm. The lessons of prejudice and discrimination had been so thoroughly learned that blacks could not get their hair cut in the barbershops in town. During holidays and spring break, when the college diningroom was closed, they were not allowed to eat in the restaurants in town. The faculty of the college organized to provide them meals in their own homes during such times.

Thus toxic mental waste is taught so effectively that the sins of the fathers are visited on the sons, from generation to generation, not to mention the mothers and daughters.

EGO-MAINTENANCE

One major function opinions may serve for an individual is ego-development and ego-maintenance. When I refer to *ego* I am not using the term in the almost mythical, highly speculative sense in which Freud and his followers have used it. Actually, the terms *self-concept* and *identity* will serve equally well, and I will use them frequently and interchangeably. I am really referring to people's images of themselves and their places in the world. For most people, this self-image seems to be the center of the image of the world in general. Thus the image of the world is *egocentric*. I don't mean that in a bad sense, even though *egocentric* in popular use usually has negative connotations. I mean only that people's perceptions of the world are necessarily from their own points of view. After all, that is the only vantage point one has.

The functional approach I am taking in this chapter is generally derived from an approach described by Katz (1960), who wrote of four functions: adjustment, ego-defense, value-expression, and knowledge. (Katz wrote of four functions of *attitudes,* but I don't think I am doing too much violence to his analysis to substitute the term *opinions*.) I treated Katz's "adjustment" function in the first section of this chapter, since he was actually writing of social learning when he described "adjustment." Katz believed people use their opinions to maximize social reward and minimize social punishment. There are other sorts of reinforcement—reward and punishment—of course, but for humans most reinforcement is social.

In this section I have described a general function of ego-maintenance, and I am going to deal with Katz' "value-expression" and "ego-defense" functions as subfunctions under the general category of ego-maintenance. To these two subfunctions I will add a third, ego-involvement, which I believe belongs in the same category.

Value-Expression

Katz says opinions serving the **value-expressive** function are developed for the purpose of "maintaining self-identity, enhancing favorable self-image, self-expression, and self-determination"; they are aroused by cues associated with the individual's values, by "appeals to the individual to reassert the self-image," or when the individual faces "ambiguities which threaten his or her self-concept"; and they are likely to change when the individual changes the self-concept or discovers new attitudes consistent with this existing self-concept.

Thus people who perceive themselves to be politically liberal subscribe to those magazines, buy those books, and watch those TV programs that tell them what opinions and policies political liberals are supposed to maintain. The man who wants to be a sophisticated, urbane playboy is likely to buy *Playboy* or *Penthouse* if he believes those magazines will tell him what sophisticated, urbane playboys are supposed to believe and how they are supposed to act. The woman who has just become conscious of her potential as a liberated woman may consult *MS* or, if she is a little more sophisticated, *Working Woman,* to find out what this potential self-image is like.

Perceived vs. Ideal Self-Image   Now you may have noticed that I seem to be writing about two self-images here and in fact I am. There is the image one *perceives* actually represents oneself at a given time, and the *ideal* self-image one would like to become. These two self-images are more similar for some people than for others. For some people the perceived self-image may coincide with the ideal self-image, and for others they may be very different. Of course, the people whose self-images coincide may advertise the fact, in which case they are likely to be seen as very smug and egotistical, or they may simply go about their business confidently and unobtrusively. Similarly, a person whose self-images differ drastically may respond by working hard to make them coincide.

Communication and Self-Image   Communication enters the picture because one's perceived self-image can become quite unrealistic if it is never tested against the perceptions of others. It is important to know how others perceive us. It would be absurd, of course, to revise one's perceived self-image whenever it fails to conform to one or two others' perceptions. But if it does not match the consensus of others, and especially of others who might be expected to know one well, there may be cause for concern. It may be that one is misperceiving oneself, or it may be that they are communicating false images. In either case there may be a problem.

Similarly, communication with others can help one maintain a realistic ideal self-image. Without knowing how others perceive one's abilities, it is easy to set one's aspirations too low or too high. "Self-actualization" requires one to adopt an ideal self-image that is attainable, but not too easily attainable, and then work toward that self-image. This process of self-actualization depends heavily upon socially meaningful communication. We have all known people who seem to have no clear anchors for their self-images, who go from day to day trying on new personalities as they might try on new costumes. We all go through phases when we are dissatisfied with ourselves but are not quite sure just what we want to be. That is perfectly natural, so long as it doesn't last too long.

At such times it is important to have others capable of understanding us, with whom it is possible to communicate at a fairly intimate level. Such understanding and capacity for intimate communication is not likely to be developed on command at a moment's notice. It has to be developed and practiced *before* it is needed. There is always someone around to tell us what we ought to be and how to achieve it at a very superficial level, and this is frequently to their advantage rather than ours. Advertisers, for example, probably use this device more than any other.

I said earlier that sex is used in a variety of ways, and mentioned conditioning as one process in which it is used. Of course, sex is frequently used in ads simply to get attention. Sometimes, however, it may be used as a ploy in advertising intended to take advantage of this function of value-expression. At first it may appear that the sexy nude or seminude woman in the ad is offering herself to any man who buys whatever product is being hawked. (Now, some men are gullible, but I don't know many who are *that* gullible, and most of those I do know are locked up.) Instead, what such ads are usually portraying the woman as saying seems to be something like: "The kind of man who can have a woman like me is the kind of man who (uses Satyr deodorant, wears Bodyform clothes, drives a Studmobile, . . . your product name here). If you want to be the kind of man who can make it with a woman like me, (use Satyr deodorant, wear Bodyform clothes, drive a Studmobile, . . .)." That is talking directly to the self-image and, I might add, bypassing the brain. Which helps explain why sexy nude women appear so frequently in *women's* magazines. They are saying, in essence, "If you want to be the kind of woman who can compete with me, you'd better (use Mink perfume, wear Next-to-Nothing swimwear,...). Self-images have to be carefully tailored, and they cost more than money. Buy one off the rack, and you may find it looks ridiculous.

Ego-Defense

Opinions and policies serving the function of **ego-defense** develop to protect oneself against internal conflicts and external threats to the ego. Threat and frustration, appeals to "hatred and repressed impulses," and "authoritarian suggestion" lead to arousal of those opinions. Change occurs when the threat is removed, after successful aggression or "catharsis," or after recognition and acknowledgment of the defense mechanisms.

Ego-Defense Mechanisms It is important to remember that ego-defense mechanisms are those of which the individual is not consciously aware, *by definition.* The mechanisms, in fact, serve to eliminate threat and fear from conscious awareness, though general anxiety level remains high without being related to any specific threat the individual can verbalize. Obviously, these threats are not those we encounter every day; they are threats that tend to produce fear so strong that the individual will not or cannot deal with them. Katz distinguishes between anxiety and guilt, and deals only with anxiety. Guilt, however, also can be so strong that the individual banishes it from awareness. Although behaviors that are ego-defensive in the strict sense may be unusual, many of them sound a great deal like behaviors we encounter in ourselves and others every day, although not at a pathological level. Consider some of the following ego-defense mechanisms, how they relate to communication, and the effects they have on one's opinions.

Denial   People deny (even to themselves) that any threat exists. The overt verbal denial may be recognizable in that it may be stronger and more frequent than seems appropriate.

Repression   People simply fail to recognize the existence of any threat, or at least they may fail to deal with or talk about an obvious threat.

Reaction Formation   The individual professes attraction to the threatening agent.

Identification with the Aggressor   People model their own behavior and appearance, as well as the content or style of their communication, after the threatening agent.

Projection   People attribute to others the fear or motives they refuse to recognize in themselves.

Scapegoating People blame others for conditions the others have not caused and that they themselves may have caused. The blame is especially likely to be placed on stereotyped social groups with little power or on persons perceived to be weak.

Paranoid Reactions Paranoia is a complex syndrome of emotional disturbance. People may exhibit paranoid reactions, however, without suffering from the general syndrome. This involves perceiving other persons and agencies to be conspiring to harm them, thus avoiding blame for their own failures and at the same time providing a "rational" explanation for the generalized anxiety they feel but cannot otherwise explain.

Displacement People express fear in situations in which it is not appropriate or at such intensity that it is not appropriate. It is assumed this allows them to express fear without acknowledging the threatening agent. This is one possible explanation for some instances of phobia. They may also exhibit aggression toward someone who hasn't harmed them, because they have been frustrated by someone too powerful to attack or by someone they can't attack because of the social consequences.

Masochistic Reactions People communicate and otherwise behave in ways that are bound to result in their being punished (by compulsive gambling or stealing, for example, or by communicating aggressively with others, especially with people who are important to them). It is assumed this allows them to receive punishment for inconsequential acts and thus assuage guilt without acknowledging the unacceptable motives that are creating the guilt.

Katz's Theory as a Psychoanalytic Theory I said at the beginning of this section that I am not using the term *ego* the way Freud and the psychoanalysts use it. However, Katz does use the term that way, and his *is* a psychoanalytic theory. Still, despite my concern about the vague, speculative nature of psychoanalytic concepts in general, I feel this approach can be very useful in analyzing communication. It can lead to identification of some motives underlying expressed opinions and other communication that might otherwise go unrecognized. It has an obvious drawback in that ego-defense functions are difficult to identify. We can't very well ask others if certain opinions and policies are ego-defensive, since the others don't know. If they knew, by definition they would not be ego-defensive. These mechanisms have to be inferred from behavior that is, in fact, designed—although not consciously—to be misleading.

But Freud's notion of *the unconscious* bothers me a great deal. I agree that people deceive themselves with these ego-defense devices, but to say that they are always completely unaware of what they are doing is pushing the notion a bit far. I would rather assume that though people are sometimes totally unaware of deceiving themselves, sometimes, if they think about it and if someone has explained ego-defensive motives to them, they can come to recognize that they are using such devices.

As a matter of fact, Katz (1960) and Sarnoff (1960) have reported some success in reducing racial prejudice by explaining ego-defensive motives and mechanisms to those who are prejudiced, which suggests that they must be able to achieve some awareness of what they are doing. Further, most of these ego-defense devices look very much like some techniques people use to fool others when they themselves are fully aware they are deceiving. In short, it appears that people range from being totally unaware to being totally aware of using techniques such as these. To the extent that people are unaware, it is simply more difficult to deal with their ego-defense, and it is more likely that they need professional help.

Ego-Defense and Attitude Formation I mentioned that Katz and Sarnoff reduced racial prejudice by instructing prejudiced people about the dynamics of ego-defense. Actually, racial prejudice is very frequently a result of people's feeling insecure and using a particular racial group as a means of reducing their insecurity. Thus people may feel threatened by blacks or guilty about their treatment, but deny it, repress it, and profess to like them ("Some of my best friends . . ."). Or they may model their own behavior and appearance after them. They may feel socially unacceptable motives, such as high sexual desire, and project that sexual motive, attributing sexual promiscuity to blacks or other racial, cultural, or social groups. People who are especially concerned that they may be homosexual are those most likely to refer to others as "fairies," "queers," "butch," and the like. People may feel guilty about their own affluence when there is so much poverty and so may accuse those on welfare of being lazy; or may feel threatened by high taxes and inflation and again blame "lazy niggers," unwed mothers on Aid to Dependent Children, or any other available scapegoat.

People may feel highly anxious, incapable of coping with the world, and guilty about their own failures, so that one convenient escape is to blame it all on a conspiracy of liberals, the devil, "rednecks," Catholics, or the "establishment." They may feel frustrated by their bosses, by the success of their competitors, or by rivals for their girlfriends or boyfriends, but may not be willing to take the consequences of aggression against that boss, competitor, or rival, so they take it out on someone similar to the frustrating person—a person or group safer to attack. They may feel so guilty about something they have done that they feel the need to be punished. But the thing they have done may be so unacceptable to themselves or to others that they are unwilling to admit it and accept the punishment. Instead, they act in self-destructive ways that are at least socially acceptable but will still bring the punishment they feel they deserve. Such analyses explain a great deal of behavior, both in ourselves and in others, that otherwise seems unexplainable. A friend reading this section reacted by saying, "Sometimes I wonder just how much of me I really am." I can't top that.

Knowledge of ego-defense mechanisms is very useful to people who want to analyze their own communication motives, to determine how they may be using their opinions irrationally to defend their own egos, and to guard against communicators who might take advantage of ego-defenses. Such knowledge is less useful in analyzing others.

Ego-Involvement

To say one is **ego-involved** in an opinion generally suggests that the opinion is closely related to one's own self-image and necessary to the maintenance of a satisfactory self-image. Defined that broadly, *value-expression* and *ego-defense* could be considered subfunctions of ego-involvement. I want to use the term more narrowly to apply to opinions that are not merely used to *express* one's self-image or to *defend* it, but rather are so closely related to the self-image as to actually *define* it. These are opinions so closely related to one's self-image that without them one would be essentially a different person.

Rokeach's Theory The previous chapter described Rokeach's theory of the dogmatic personality. More recently, Rokeach (1968) has expanded what began as a personality theory into a comprehensive theory of opinions. A *belief* is the most basic unit of Rokeach's system. It is defined as "any simple proposition, conscious or unconscious, capable of being preceded by the phrase 'I believe that . . .'." Further: "The content of a belief may describe the object of a belief as true or false, correct or incorrect; evaluate it as good or bad; or advocate a certain course of action or a certain state of existence as desirable or undesirable."

An *attitude*, on the other hand, is an organized collection of beliefs: "An attitude is a relatively enduring organization of beliefs around an object or situation predisposing one to respond in some preferential manner." A *value* in Rokeach's system is a special type of "belief" that is "centrally located within one's total belief system, about how one ought or ought not to behave, or about some end-state of existence worth or not worth attaining." At another point, he wrote that a value is "a single belief that transcendentally guides actions and judgments across specific objects and situations, and beyond immediate goals to more ultimate end-states of existence."

Beliefs Since beliefs are the building blocks of Rokeach's system, suppose we consider them more carefully. Rokeach assumes that all beliefs are not equally important to the individual; rather, more central beliefs are more resistant to change and, if changed, produce more reorganization of the rest of the system. Beliefs are more "central" to the extent that they are functionally connected with other beliefs. Rokeach proposes four dimensions that may serve as criteria for connectedness. To the extent that beliefs are *existential*, they deal with physical and social existence and identity, and have many functional connections. To the extent that they are *shared*, they have social connections and are affirmed by social consensus. To the extent that they are *derived* from other beliefs, they have functional connections with other beliefs. Finally, to the extent that they are matters of *taste*, they have few and relatively unimportant functional connections.

Now when Rokeach uses these criteria to arrange beliefs on a dimension of centrality-peripherality, he distinguishes among five general classes of beliefs, which, of course, are not clearly and discretely distinguishable: (1) primitive beliefs that are learned by direct experience with the object and reinforced by unanimous social consensus; (2) primitive beliefs learned through direct experience but not socially reinforced; (3) authority beliefs that are supported by negative or positive authority; (4) derived beliefs that result from identification with authority; and (5) inconsequential beliefs.

Values   The conclusion of this analysis seems to be that the only important type of change that is at all likely to occur is change among *values*, the central beliefs that really define a person's self-concept. This is especially true of change introduced by communication. One's primitive beliefs are seldom changed by communication, because social consensus is either unanimous or irrelevant (because the experience is private), and inconsequential beliefs are just that—inconsequential. Thus it appears that beliefs regarding the nature of authority and beliefs derived from authority are most likely to be changed by communication, although this is never made explicit. That particular class of consequential beliefs that Rokeach calls "values" seems to be of this type.

These values, then, are very important in ego-maintenance, since they essentially *define* the ego or self-image. They are those beliefs a person holds most strongly about what is ultimately good or bad, right or wrong, worth attaining or not worth attaining. People make decisions about how they are going to act—what they will and will not do—on the basis of these general principles. When people talk about choice situations, they are usually talking about situations in which two or more of these central values are brought into conflict, so they must decide which of the conflicting values are more essential to their own self-images. That is no mere *expression* of perceived or ideal self-image, nor is it a *defense* of that self-image against some sort of threat. Rather, it is a decision as to what people consider to be their *essential* self-images, without which they would be different people.

Conversion Rokeach's theory can be used to explain gradual shifts of opinion over time, but I believe it is more useful in explaining the *conversion* phenomenon. *Conversion* is opinion change that involves a large number of opinions and occurs suddenly. Most frequently we think of conversion as a religious occurrence, as happens when Billy Graham invites people in his audience to come forward, confess their sins, and lead a new life.

Example 1: Conversion   In the tiny Mississippi River town where I was born and spent most of my early summers, there lived a man by the name of Shine Nolan, renowned for his drinking prowess and his fighting ability. One hot summer night Shine came to a revival meeting in a tent in a vacant lot near the bar, for a reason I never knew. At the conclusion of a hell-fire-and-damnation sermon, an "altar call" was given, of course, and Shine came forward to confess his sins and "give his life to Christ." Very few ever expected this conversion to last any longer than it took Shine to sober up. But in fact he gave up drinking and fighting, took up religious studies, and became an evangelist. To the best of my knowledge that is still his calling. His conversion "changed his life," in the sense that it changed most of his opinions and behaviors, and it did so in an instant.

Example 2: Conversion   When I was a ministerial student in the evangelical Christian college of which I wrote earlier in this chapter, I preached frequently in the Harbor Lights Mission in St. Louis. The place was always filled with derelicts and winos, most of whom were clearly attending the service because it was required if they were to obtain a meal and a place to spend the night. When I gave the call to come forward to the altar, there were always a good many who did so, but it was also clear a large proportion of them were too drunk to know what they were doing. Still, each night there would be a few who seemed sincere, and some of those in fact "went straight." The mission workers reported their progress to me on later visits. I am no longer of an evangelical Christian persuasion, but I have never given up my belief that radical conversion does take place. I have also seen it in other contexts—and so have you: Students who study so seldom and come to class so seldom that to call them students is itself an act of faith suddenly become serious scholars, to the delight of their professors and the amazement of their classmates. It is not unusual for this to occur in their senior years, when they suddenly come to understand that they face the cold world of a job search or graduate school. A friend takes a summer trip to a foreign country, perhaps a Third World country, and returns with a completely different perspective. Or someone you know as a sexual profligate suddenly meets their one true love and drastically changes opinions and behaviors.

I believe this happens because some event occurs that causes the converts to change their central beliefs, the values of which Rokeach writes, the values by which they define their central selves, and suddenly they become different people. They look the same, but they do not talk or act the same; they have been invaded by the Body Snatchers, who have changed their central values and changed their lives.

Notice that my term *opinion* really includes Rokeach's concepts of attitudes, beliefs, and values. I find the more general term preferable in this chapter, because we will soon consider other theorists who use the terms *attitudes* and *beliefs* in other ways.

Sherif's Theory Rokeach does not apply the term *ego-involvement* to his own theory; that is my doing. Another theorist, Muzafer Sherif (Sherif, Sherif, and Nebergall, 1965), does use the term ego-involvement to describe his theory. In fact, this is the key term in Sherif's theory. But as used by Sherif that term does not mean exactly what it means in common usage, nor is it used in quite the same sense as intended by other theorists.

Latitudes of Acceptance, Noncommitment and Rejection   Taking note of his own research and that of others, Sherif concluded that there is a *latitude of acceptance* around an individual's own opinion. This latitude of acceptance is a range of opinion such that any opinions of others falling within the range will be not only accepted but perceived as lying closer to the individual's own opinion than they really are. It is the width of this range of acceptable opinion that Sherif used to define *ego-involvement:* the narrower the range, the greater the involvement. On either side of the latitude of acceptance lies a *latitude of noncommitment,* within which opinions are perceived relatively objectively and are neither consistently accepted nor consistently rejected. Still further out on either side lies a *latitude of rejection,* within which opinions are not only rejected but also perceived as being more divergent from the individual's own opinion than they really are.

Relation of Sherif's Latitudes to Ego-Involvement   Beyond the identification of these latitudes, Sherif's most important contribution seems to be the conclusion that the latitude of acceptance is smaller and the latitude of rejection is greater when the individual's own opinion is near the extreme on either end of the scale. Thus, while ego-involvement is defined as the narrowness of the latitude of acceptance, it is also presumed, with considerable research support, that ego-involvement is greater if an individual's own opinion is extreme. I see this conclusion as an indication that people are very discriminating about opinions that are ego-involving. They make fine distinctions among opinions close to their own, but they are very intolerant of opinions that are very different from their own.

I am discussing this theory in relation to Rokeach's because I suspect that opinions that are extreme, that have narrow latitudes of acceptance and wide latitudes of rejection, are either the central values to which Rokeach refers or closely related to those central values. That is only a suspicion; I do not have any conclusive research evidence for it.

But if true, it certainly has some implications for communication, especially for critical listening. Notice that the things Sherif says people do with opinions in which they are highly ego-involved are very similar to the things Rokeach says closed-minded people do most of the time. In other words, all of us are closed-minded or dogmatic about opinions in which we are ego-involved.

We can see that happening constantly. Extreme left-wing political groups make fine distinctions among left-wing opinions, and extreme right-wing groups can distinguish carefully and sometimes emotionally among right-wing opinions. Those on the extreme right may make careful distinctions among Senator Jesse Helms, Rush Limbaugh, and Jerry Falwell, distinctions those on the extreme left can neither see nor appreciate. Then anyone to the left of any of those three is considered to be a "bleeding-heart liberal" and unworthy of any serious attention. On the other hand, the radical left may make equally fine distinctions between Senator Ted Kennedy and Jane Fonda, who are both considered part of the same category by those on the right. I saw two bumper stickers on the same pickup in Nebraska last summer. One said "Ted Kennedy's car has killed more people than my gun has," and the other said "I'll forgive Jane Fonda when the Jews forgive Hitler."

Are you exempt from that sort of thinking? I'm sure I'm not, on opinions that are really ego-involving, that serve to define the essences of my self-image. Yet that kind of thinking would be hard to defend as rational. And the disturbing point about this analysis is that it suggests we are least rational about those opinions that are most important to us. (Save us from important opinions.)

CONSISTENCY

People act not only as if they need to acquire knowledge and form opinions about their environments, but also as if they need to see and maintain consistency in their knowledge and opinions. In many respects and in many cases consistency is a good thing. Consistency is the basis for logical reasoning. People who are consistent can be depended upon. To the extent that we find consistent, dependable relationships in the world, we can make plans to deal with the world.

But Ralph Waldo Emerson was so brash as to say in his essay on "Self-Reliance":

> A foolish consistency is the hobgoblin of little minds, adored by little statesmen and philosophers and divines.... Speak what you think today in words as hard as cannon-balls, and tomorrow speak what tomorrow thinks in hard words again, though it contradict everything you think today.

What on earth was he thinking? We're accustomed, since Einstein, to hearing about how parallel lines do eventually meet, about space-time warps, and the like. We've learned to live without knowing whether the universe is exploding or contracting. We've all heard the story of physicists who one day treat light as if it were composed of particles and the next day as if it were composed of waves. And we've managed to maintain some semblance of sanity. Probably because it doesn't really matter if a sidewalk is a whirling mass of electrons, so long as we can still walk on it. But Emerson wasn't talking about that sort of inconsistency, which is largely irrelevant to our daily lives. He was arguing that relying too heavily on consistency in everyday reasoning can be irrational. How can consistency ever be irrational? Well, a variety of types of "consistency" that have been identified by opinion theorists are certainly potentially irrational. Suppose we consider a few examples, most of which have been identified as "psycho-logic."

Balancing Opinions of Others with Other Opinions

People try to maintain a certain type of consistency between their opinions of other people and their opinions of what those other people say. Heider's (1946) **Balance Theory** described this most clearly, but also most simplistically: Figure 6.1 indicates that Person One ($P1$) likes ($+$) Person Two ($P2$) and also likes ($+$) an object, concept, idea, or event (X). However, Person Two does not like ($-$) the same object, concept, idea, or event. Consequently, according to Heider, the situation is unbalanced. It is not consistent to like things one's friends dislike. Person One will try to bring the situation into balance by changing his own opinion of Person Two, by changing his own opinion of X, or by trying to change Person Two's opinion of X.

If he succeeds, the new situation can then be diagrammed in one of the four ways shown in Figure 6.2. These situations will remain balanced until some new "inconsistency" is introduced. There are other possible unbalanced situations, as shown in Figure 6.3. The general rule is that it is "inconsistent" (my term, not Heider's) to disagree with a friend's opinion or to agree with the opinion of an enemy.

Obviously, this is very simplistic; most opinions cannot be diagrammed as simple triangles. But it does illustrate the basic principle. Now, consider this basic question: Is this type of "consistency" rational, or irrational? Does it pollute or purify the mental environment? Even the most likable people are

FIGURE 6.1
Diagram of an unbalanced situation in Heider's model

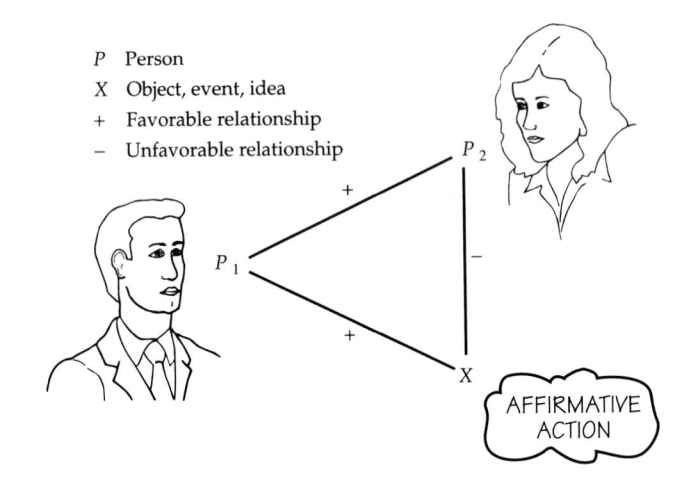

P   Person
X   Object, event, idea
+   Favorable relationship
−   Unfavorable relationship

*P*₁ *P*₂ X AFFIRMATIVE ACTION

wrong sometimes. When one is trying to reach a reliable decision, the opinions of those one strongly likes or dislikes can interfere, because of the temptation to agree with friends and disagree with enemies. Friends are not always right, and enemies are not always wrong. Consequently, their advice and opinions must be evaluated objectively, with special attention to the reasons they are offering the advice or holding the opinions. Trying too hard to maintain consistency between one's opinions of a source and one's opinions of what that source says can destroy that objectivity. Further, one need not come to like other people less just because they are wrong occasionally. Everyone is. And people who are always right are not necessarily the most enjoyable people to be around. Needless to say, it might be best for one's own mental health to avoid people who are wrong all the time or who give bad advice maliciously and intentionally.

Let's Make the Best of It

Another sort of consistency happens after people make conscious choices and irrevocably commit themselves to the chosen alternatives. When people make conscious choices, they frequently try to maintain a curious sort of consistency between the consequences of their choices and the fact that they are responsible for those consequences.

At least since Aesop expounded his fable of the sour grapes, if not before, it has been widely recognized that people attempt to justify their behavior by overvaluing its consequences and derogating the consequences of the alternative courses of action that they rejected. That is not to deny the equally potent "grass-is-greener" theory that people want whatever they don't have. The "sour grapes" theory seems to apply especially well if people perceive

FIGURE 6.2
The four possible balanced situations in Heider's model

that they made conscious choices that are now irrevocable, so that the alternatives are now totally unavailable. If they do not perceive they had a choice, or if there remains any possibility of reversing the choice, the "grass-is-greener" theory may apply. Neither is it to deny the "once-burned" theory: If people have made irrevocable decisions with bad consequences, they will

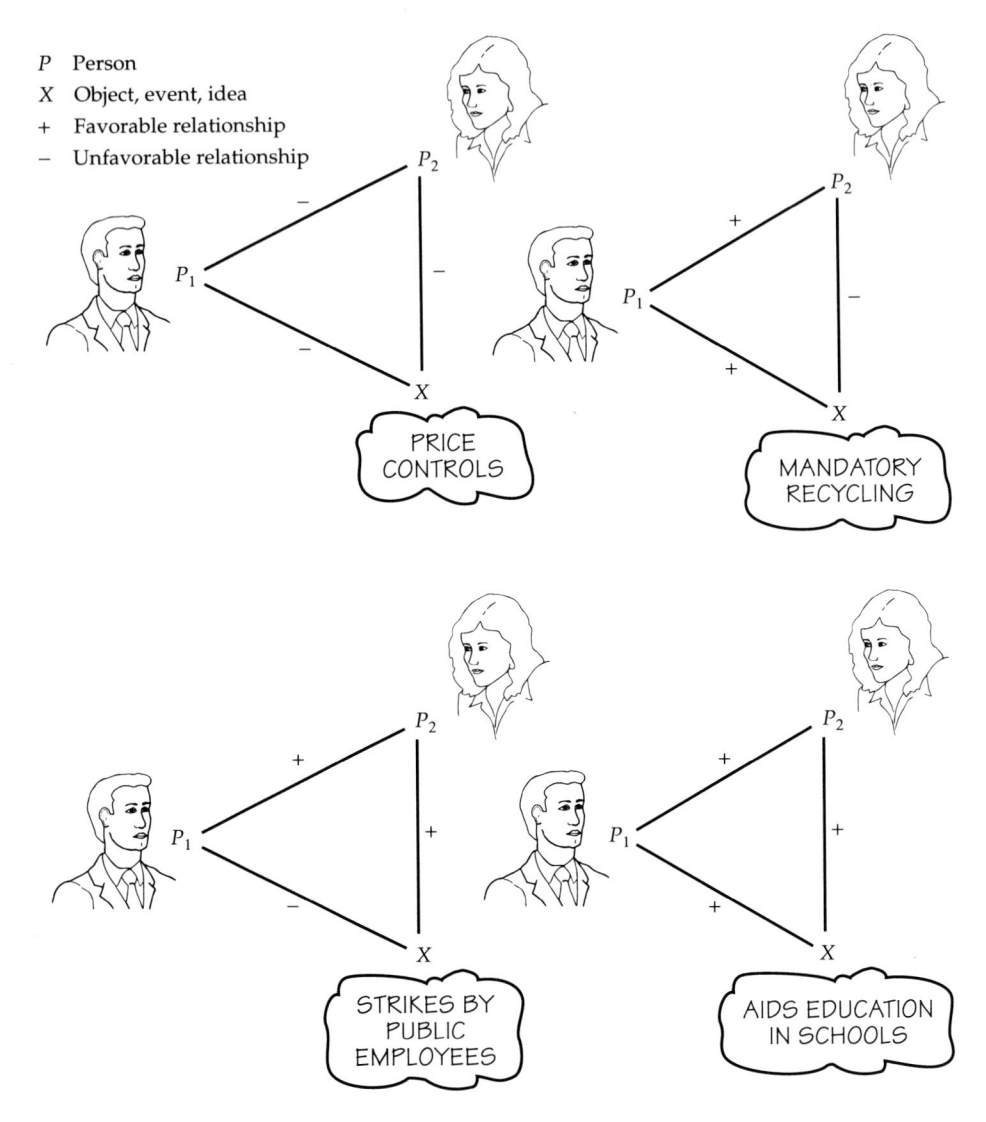

P   Person
X   Object, event, idea
+   Favorable relationship
−   Unfavorable relationship

FIGURE 6.3
The four possible unbalanced situations in Heider's model

probably try to justify them, but if they are ever faced with similar decisions later, they will probably choose different alternatives.

Festinger's Theory of Cognitive Dissonance This is Festinger's **theory of cognitive dissonance,** as it has been modified by Brehm and Cohen (1962).

Festinger (1957) refers to *cognition,* including beliefs, attitudes, opinions, values, and apparently anything else that can be internally experienced. He defines *cognitive dissonance* as the situation in which, considering two cognitive elements alone, the opposite of one follows from the other.

Dissonance theory applies best to situations *after* choice has occurred, although the feeling that occurs while one is considering choosing between two alternatives is sometimes incorrectly termed "dissonance." Greater dissonance is created in the choice situation to the extent that the choice is important; and it is maximum when the alternatives are nearly equal in desirability and so dissimilar as to make compromise impossible. People must perceive that they alone were responsible for making the choice, and must perceive that the choice is irrevocable.

Speakers attempting to analyze an audience will try to determine whether they have made choices of this sort that might freeze their opinions. People under the influence of choice-produced dissonance will try to reduce that dissonance by perceiving the choice to be less important, the alternatives to be more similar, the choice less voluntary and irrevocable, by seeking information and social support for the decision and, most importantly, by becoming more favorable toward the chosen and less favorable toward the unchosen alternative. If speakers' arguments are bucking any of those attempts to reduce dissonance, they will have to provide listeners with alternative means of dissonance reduction or see the proposal rejected. Listeners, on the other hand, should be aware that they are especially susceptible to irrational attempts to justify choices when those conditions are satisfied, and should be alert to the possibility they may be misled into making additional unfortunate decisions in order to justify the original ones.

Example: Your Summer Job   Obviously, you have chosen to attend college after high school instead of other alternatives available to you. Probably some of your high school friends made other choices. Let's imagine that you go back to your hometown in the summer after your sophomore year. For spending money and to help pay your tuition, you take a job at a fast-food restaurant where the primary qualifications are that your IQ be not too far below your body temperature and you be able to say "Would you like fries with that?" You see old friends drive by who chose to attend vocational training programs to prepare them for careers in medical technology, electronics repair, and computer programming. Some of them have already completed their programs and have taken jobs paying considerably more than the $4.50/hour you are making. They drive by in new or near-new cars, and you see them at night spots you can only occasionally afford. Because your decision to attend college has not yet begun to pay off, you have a lot of dissonance to reduce.

You may try to reduce that dissonance by telling yourself your parents really coerced you into choosing college; it was not entirely your choice. You speculate about the possibility that your choice may not be completely irrevocable; you wonder about the consequences of dropping out of college. There is no real hope of convincing yourself the choice is unimportant, which is one means of reducing dissonance that people sometimes use.

One night you and your friends meet at a diner for a reunion. You listen to their stories about their jobs and their new cars, their new apartments, their new CD players, their new TV setups, their new computers, and the trips they are going to take during their vacations. You feel uncomfortable with these people who used to be your best friends, and it comes to you that you *envy* them. You realize that you really can't go home again.

When they ask you about college life, you try to make it sound exciting, but you fear it may be sounding defensive. Certainly, courses in English literature, general psychology, art appreciation, and human communication theory don't sound as exciting as their lives, nor does studying for those courses. Even the Spring Fling and football games sound vaguely juvenile in comparison to their adult activities.

At the end of the evening you make arrangements to meet again, but you know it won't happen. Instead you seek out others from your old circle of friends who also chose to go away to college, and feel much more comfortable with them, even some you used to think were nerds, because they understand, they offer social support for the decision you made.

You are in the throes of dissonance reduction. Never fear, your turn will come. In the meantime, just try to avoid doing anything too foolish to try to reduce that dissonance, because there will be such temptations. Bad decisions are sometimes made to try to reduce the discomfort one feels when one discovers there is a downside to a decision to which one is committed. Once again we have a type of consistency likely to contribute to unreliable decisions in response to communication.

Example: Communication, Sexism, and Dissonance   Very frequently, acts of communication we perform, which are to some extent inconsistent with opinions we hold, create dissonance; and we try to reduce that dissonance later in a variety of ways.

"Hooters" is a chain of hot-wings and beer restaurants that began in Clearwater, Florida and now has over 120 franchises across the country. Certainly much of the popularity of these restaurants can be attributed to the attire—micro-gym shorts and short, tight t-shirts—worn by the waitresses. By the time you read this they may be called "McHooters," and I hesitate to predict what will have been done with the "Golden Arches." In March, 1994, Jane Pauly interviewed a half-dozen former waitresses who are suing the chain on grounds of sexual harassment. Naturally, much of the coverage in the interview was in fact uncoverage, provocative views of the waitresses at work. After all, even "investigative reporting" is supported by ratings.

Now imagine a man—I'll call him George—who considers himself antisexist and generally opposed to the exploitation of women for their physical attributes. He goes next door to watch TV with his neighbor and a group of male friends. One of the former waitresses being interviewed, blonde and attractive, says she was told before she was hired the place was a family restaurant. One of the other men says, "Sure, she probably thought with a name like 'Hooters' it was a comedy club." The conversation turns into a competitive exercise in sexist and dumb-blonde jokes. George is drawn in, and, in fact, does rather well.

Back home George thinks about what he has done. He is a little disturbed by it; he feels dissonant. He realizes it was not consistent with his self-concept. To reduce his dissonance, he tells himself that, in fact, he did not make a totally conscious choice, and he was to some extent coerced into it by the spirit of amaraderie, male-bonding, and the desire to support his buddies. Further, he begins to change his opinions to be more consistent with the communicative acts in which he has engaged; he tells himself *some* women do actually take advantage of their physical rather than their mental attributes. He tells himself that to be truly antisexist he must recognize when women are participating in and benefiting from their own sexual exploitation. He rationalizes his behavior—that is, reduces his dissonance—by changing his opinions to be more consistent with the communicative acts he has performed.

Dissonance theory can be used to explain an opinion change, but so can learning theory. If George's friends thought his sexist jokes and remarks were creative and imaginative; laughed at them; and, generally, gave him social reward, it might have been simply social learning that took place, and he will be expected to repeat the behavior. However, if the social reward was less than he really expected, so his behavior was not really justified by the consequences, then he will feel even more dissonance and will try even harder to justify what he did. When the person feels the behavior was *inadequately justified*, dissonance theory is a better explanation than learning theory. In fact, dissonance theory has been referred to more recently as the "theory of inadequate justification," because its explanations and predictions apply best under such conditions.

Logical Thinking and Wishful Thinking

McGuire (1960) has described a type of thinking he characterizes as **logical thinking,** which involves estimating the probabilities of conclusions from the probabilities of the beliefs on which those conclusions are based.

Example: Coin Tossing We know, for example, that the probability of a coin's coming up heads once is 50 percent, with another 50 percent chance it will turn up tails. Now suppose someone proposes a bet that the coin will not come up heads twice in a row. If you took that bet you would be likely to lose, because the chances are 50 percent it will not turn up heads the first time and, among the 50 percent of the times it does so the first time, there is still only a 50 percent chance it will be heads the second time. Thus you would be betting on something that will only happen 25 percent (.50 × .50) of the time. You can even the odds if your friend is willing to put up $3 each time you bet while you bet only $1. Over a series of such bets, you would win $3 once in four times but lose $3 (3 × $1) on the other three flips of the coin.

The other factor McGuire identifies as operating here is something he terms **wishful thinking.** This is the tendency of people to attach higher probabilities to conclusions they hope are true and lower probabilities to those they hope are false, even though the probabilities are not logically warranted. Drawing to an inside straight in poker is a classic example of wishful thinking, which is simply overestimating the odds in your favor. The moral is simple: "Wishing don't make it so." But there are a good many speakers, politicians, ad writers, and even some of your best friends who will take advantage of your tendency to believe it does. Wishful thinking is also contributing to state finances all over the country as people play state lotteries. They see new millionaires, happy winners of lottery jackpots, on television and rush down to their local Stop-and-Rob convenience stores to buy tickets to try to beat the odds *simply because they want it to happen.*

Example: CD Player Take the example of a person who is trying to decide whether to buy a fairly expensive imported CD player now or later. Let's assume the person has the money to buy now but is trying to decide whether they might get a better deal later. The reasoning could be arranged in a syllogism (although the person probably doesn't reason in a syllogism unless they are as organized as they are rich):

Further dollar devaluation will increase the price of imported CD players.

Further dollar devaluation will occur.

Therefore the price of imported CD players will increase.

Obviously, the person would conclude from such a chain of reasoning that they ought to buy now. Notice, however, that the conclusion that prices are going to increase depends on the first two beliefs. McGuire has tried to describe how these dependencies work. He has used the notion of *dependent probabilities* in his explanation, which is the theory I was using in the coin-tossing example.

In the CD player example: If your friend believes it is .90 (90 percent) probable that further dollar devaluation will increase the price of imported CD players and .50 (50 percent) probable that dollar devaluation will occur, then it would be "logically consistent" to believe there is a .90 × .50 = .45 (45 percent) probability that the price of imported CD players is going to increase. Thus the chance of a price increase, given these beliefs alone, seems to be a little less than 50-50. Of course, there may be other reasons to believe the price of imported CD players will increase or decrease, so this analysis is incomplete as it stands.

Further, those familiar with the Aristotelian syllogism will protest that it does not operate in the area of probability. That is certainly true; McGuire is modifying (or corrupting, if you wish) the Aristotelian syllogism. Probably more important is the objection that people don't think in syllogisms. However, McGuire does not argue that they do, only that they tend to maintain this kind of logical consistency insofar as they perceive propositions to be logically related.

To return to the example of the CD player, suppose our friend really isn't all that rich, but wants that CD player *now*. One way to justify buying it now is to conclude that the price is going to rise, making it a "good investment." The friend will be very tempted to conclude that there is a greater than .45 probability of a price increase, so they can justify rushing down to put it on an already maxed-out credit card. That is wishful thinking in action.

Thus *logical consistency* as described by McGuire seems to be a rational and objective type of consistency, but not wishful thinking. Wishful thinking—the tendency to maintain consistency between what one perceives to be and what one wishes were the case—appears to be irrational in anyone's book. Unfortunately, McGuire's research seems to indicate that his subjects, at least, operated more on the basis of wishful thinking than logical consistency. And that was in the laboratory. Imagine what must happen in the world outside.

The Relationship of Beliefs and Attitudes

Martin Fishbein (1967) is the psychologist probably most responsible for clearly and operationally distinguishing between *attitudes* and *beliefs*. Fishbein believes that people maintain a specific sort of consistency between their attitudes and beliefs. He speculates, and has demonstrated repeatedly, that people keep their attitudes about an object (or concept, event, or idea) consistent with their attitudes toward the attributes they believe that object possesses. For instance, if people believe Kodak cameras have undesirable attributes, they will have unfavorable attitudes toward Kodak cameras; if they believe Nikon cameras have desirable characteristics, they will like them.

Needless to say, neither the theory nor the reality is that simple. People generally believe that objects possess both desirable and undesirable attributes. The problem is to predict just how favorable people will be toward an object, knowing what attributes they believe the object possesses, knowing how strongly they believe each attribute is related to the object, and knowing their attitudes toward each of those attributes. Fishbein uses a formula to describe the relationships involved. I won't go into the computations involved, but will note the ways this theory suggests that a communication can change people's attitudes.

Example: Buying a Camera   Consider a hypothetical individual who believes that Nikon cameras (1) have many useful features, (2) are expensive, (3) are not easy to use, and (4) do not require frequent repairs. If you want to persuade the person to buy a Nikon, you can deal with the *beliefs* by offering evidence to strengthen the first (Nikon cameras have many useful features), weaken the second (Nikons are expensive), weaken the third (Nikons are not easy to use), and strengthen the fourth (Nikons do not require frequent repairs). Or you can deal with the *attitudes toward the attributes* by making that person's attitudes more favorable toward "useful features" and "expense" in cameras, and less favorable toward "ease of use" and "frequency of repair." You can also suggest other favorable attributes of the Nikon that the prospective buyer has not considered. In fact, if you go to one of your local camera stores and indicate you might be interested in buying a Nikon but have some reservations about it, the salesperson will probably do all those things.

Originally, Fishbein presented his theory as a description of how people *do* maintain relationships between their attitudes and beliefs. But more recently he has characterized his more complicated description as a "Theory of Reasoned Action," that is, a description of how people would think if they were to reason their way to a conclusion. The next chapter will describe his more complicated theory, my own related theory (the AESOP model), and the Elaboration Likelihood Model of Petty and Caccioppo. That chapter will also describe in more detail how decisions are made in response to communication. In the meantime, advanced and adventurous students might want to consult a recent and rather technical book on this topic, *The Psychology of Attitudes* by Eagly and Chaiken (1993).

CONCLUSION

I have tried in this chapter to illustrate how we use our opinions to serve the major functions of social reward, ego-maintenance, and consistency. The survey has not been very heartening, since I have discussed a vast number of ways in which people can be misled as they try to make rational decisions in response to communication. But once again this awareness, uncomfortable as it may be, is absolutely essential to communication in a society in which consumers and the electorate are free to decide what they will buy and who will govern them. Without such awareness, advertisers and politicians could indeed become evil "insects preying on the people," and *freedom* "just another word for nothin' left to lose." This awareness is at the very center of our ecology.

KEY TERMS AND CONCEPTS

classical conditioning
operant conditioning
internal (implicit)
   mediating response
value-expression

ego-defense
ego-involvement
   per Rokeach
ego-involvement
   per Sherif

Balance Theory
Cognitive Dissonance
   Theory
logical thinking
wishful thinking
Fishbein's belief-
   attitude model

REFERENCES

Brehm, J. W., and Cohen, A. R. (1962). *Explorations in Cognitive Dissonance.* New York: Wiley.

Bateson, G. (1972). *Steps to an Ecology of Mind.* New York: Ballantine Books.

Eagly, A. H., and Chaiken, S. (1993). *The Psychology of Attitudes.* Forth Worth, Tex.: Harcourt Brace Jovanovich.

Festinger, L. (1957). *A Theory of Cognitive Dissonance.* Evanston, Ill.: Row, Peterson.

Fishbein, M. (1967). A behavior theory approach to the relations between beliefs about an object and the attitude toward the object. In *Readings in Attitude Theory and Measurement,* edited by M. Fishbein, pp. 389–400. New York: Wiley.

Heider, F. (1946). Attitudes and cognitive organization. *Journal of Psychology* 21: 107–112.

Katz, D. (1960). The functional approach to the study of attitudes. *Public Opinion Quarterly* 24: 163–204.

McGuire, W. J. (1960). A syllogistic analysis of cognitive relationships. In *Attitude Organization and Change: An Analysis of Consistency Among Attitude*

Components, edited by C. I. Hovland and M. I. Rosenberg, pp. 65–111. New Haven, Conn.: Yale University Press.

Osgood, C. E. (1963). On understanding and creating sentences. *American Psychologist* 18: 735–751.

Petty, R. E., and Cacioppo, J. T. (1986). The elaboration likelihood model of persuasion. In *Advances in Experimental Social Psychology,* Vol. 19, edited by L. Berkowitz, pp. 123–205. San Diego: Academic Press.

Rokeach, M. (1968). *Beliefs, Attitudes and Values: A Theory of Organization and Change.* San Francisco: Jossey-Bass.

Sarnoff, I. (1960). Psychoanalytic theory and social attitudes. *Public Opinion Quarterly* 24: 251–279.

Sherif, C. W., Sherif, M., and Nebergall, R. E. (1965). *Attitude and Attitude Change: The Social Judgment-Involvement Approach.* Philadelphia: Saunders.

Skinner, B. F. (1953). *Science and Human Behavior.* New York: Macmillan.

No matter how cynical you get, it's never enough.
>—Lily Tomlin

What luck for rulers that men [sic] do not think.
>—Adolph Hitler

7
The Ecology of Ideas: Cognitive Processing, Critical Thinking, and Social Influence

CHAPTER OUTLINE

A Network of Entities and Relationships: The AESOP Model
Entities and Relationships
Relationships

Types of Relationships

Importance of Plans and Consequences in AESOP
Making Critical Choices

Types of Consequences
Decisional Balance Sheet

Deciding What Plans Will Produce What Consequences
Toulmin's Model of Argument
Modified Toulmin Model: The AESOP Model

Implications of the Decision-Making Model

Barriers to Critical Decisions
Noncausal Reasoning
Elaboration Likelihood: Central vs. Peripheral Processing
Credibility
Personality Characteristics
Drama and Comedy

Some Suggestions for Thinking Critically
Cultural Literacy
Some Common Fallacies

Persuasion
Does Organization Matter?

Compliance Strategies

> *Ernest Hemingway once said, In order to be a great writer, a person must have a built-in, shock-proof crap detector.... It seems to us that Hemingway identified an essential survival strategy and the central function of the schools in today's world. We have in mind a new education that sets out to cultivate just such people—experts at crap detecting.*
> —N. Postman and C. Weingartner, Teaching as a Subversive Activity

Donald Campbell (1965), a psychologist-philosopher from Northwestern University, has described the process of ideological evolution. Evolution, in general, requires three things: variety, selection, and retention. To see why these three are necessary, suppose we imagine what might happen if atmospheric pollution were to continue to increase gradually over the next three centuries. First, if there is too little variety among human respiratory systems, the human race will soon become extinct because it cannot adapt. There must be enough human beings with large lung capacities, less need for oxygen, and high tolerance for pollutants for the species to survive. If everyone were the same in all these characteristics, they would all die off before evolution had a chance to save the species.

Second, there will have to be a selection mechanism. In biological evolution that selection mechanism is very harsh. Unfit organisms either die or fail to reproduce. In my example, as atmospheric pollution increases we will expect more of those with small lung capacities to die at an early age or to be less capable of reproduction. But variety and selection, by themselves, would not save the species—people would just die off slowly. Although those with large lung capacities would disappear last, the number of human beings would still slowly dwindle.

But that does not take into account what Campbell called the "retention or propagation mechanism." Notice that in each succeeding generation a greater proportion of those with large lung capacity will be reproducing and thus transmitting large lung capacity as a genetic characteristic to their offspring. In effect, by continuing to pollute the atmosphere, we will be selectively breeding a new type of human being with large lungs, a reduced need for oxygen, and an increased tolerance for pollutants. It is all a race, of course. Atmospheric pollution may increase so rapidly this evolutionary process cannot keep up with it, and we will soon join the dinosaurs, the sabretooth tigers, and the dodo bird in Species Heaven.

This kind of evolution is strictly biological. Fortunately, we also have on our side *ideological evolution—the evolution of ideas.* If we can change public policy fast enough, we can stop pollution before it stops us. The problem is that ideological evolution works very much like biological evolution. Public policy is overrun with ideological dinosaurs, dodos, and sterile cuckoos. The evolution of ideas also requires variety, selection, and retention. If we do not have a variety of ideas and plans available to us, we may find ourselves suddenly facing a time whose idea has not yet come. The evolution of ideas requires that we encourage free thinking. If we allow censorship of ideas by those now in power, we may find ourselves sharing a common tomb later when the ideas that are powerful now are no longer equal to the challenge of a new age. Freedom of speech is not just an academic sacred cow; it is a very practical necessity for survival.

But if we have a variety of ideas, we are also going to need a reliable means of selecting those we need at any particular time. We cannot allow every weird idea that comes along to be put into practice immediately. In biological evolution, many—in fact most—mutations are ill-adapted and do not survive on their own. The same is probably true of ideological evolution. Without some means of selection we would soon be overrun with ideological mutations.

By selection of ideas I do not mean censorship. There is a vast difference between killing an idea and merely refusing to adopt it. An idea that seems to be a wild mutation today may be exactly what we need in the future when conditions have changed. Death is not the selection mechanism in the evolution of ideas. An idea is selected when it is accepted by those who are capable of retaining and propagating it. In ideological evolution, retention is the process of weaving a selected idea into the fabric of society, institutionalizing it by expressing it in laws, customs, and conventions, and defending it against attack.

To return to the pollution example, if this process of ideological evolution progresses rapidly enough, we may never have to face the harsher prospect of biological evolution. At the very worst, we may be able to buy time so humanity can evolve biologically instead of becoming extinct. To do that we need to encourage free-thinking people to produce a variety of ideas—even radical ideas—for dealing with pollution. We need a gigantic, worldwide brainstorming session. At the same time, we must evaluate critically all of the ideas in order to select those that are most likely to assure our survival, and we must institutionalize as public policy those that are selected.

And what is the role of communication in this process?

> Communication is involved in all three processes. Mutant ideas are carried like seeds on the winds of communication. The retention-propagation mechanism uses communication as a selective herbicide to destroy unacceptable ideological mutations and as a fertilizer to maintain the health of the ideological strains that have been chosen for preservation. But at the heart of the entire process is the selector mechanism and the discipline that ministers to its health—communication. (Cronkhite, 1974, p. 268)

In this chapter I want to describe a model of how our minds operate, then extend that model to a description of what constitutes critical decision making, make some recommendations as to how one can think critically, and review relevant research in social influence, all with a view to improving your participation in the process of ideological evolution.

A NETWORK OF ENTITIES AND RELATIONSHIPS: THE AESOP MODEL

What I am about to describe is a way of thinking about thinking. It is not a description of how the brain operates. It is a metaphor, and to some extent speculation. However, it does represent how I believe the mind is organized, and it is consistent with current knowledge of cognitive processing.

Entities and Relationships

People store their conceptions of the universe as something like networks. The networks can be thought of as consisting of entities and relationships among those entities. By an **entity** I mean anything one can perceive or conceive. Thus the **objects** in the universe constitute one class of entities. The house you live in, the car you drive, the objects you carry in your pocket, purse, or backpack, and the merchandise you see in the mall are all entities as I am using the word. In this case it might be clearer to call them "things," which they are, but that would not be nearly as scholarly, and it would only apply to this class of entities.

People It would not apply as well, for example, to the **people** who populate one's mental universe, which people are also among these entities. You yourself are one of these entities, and possibly the most important one. The members of your family, your friends, and your most significant other are all entities in this mental image, as are mere acquaintances, people you have never met but only observed on television or in films, people you have only heard of or read about, and, in fact, people who exist only as characters in fiction.

Ideas There are very abstract entities such as **ideas**, that have no representation in reality. When one hears about abstract ideas, one is inclined to think of truth, virtue, and fairness; but there are ideas that are much more familiar and immediate.

Behaviors Another class of entities consists of behaviors or behavioral **plans** performed or contemplated by yourself or others. These may be simple behaviors, such as brushing your teeth, or complex series of interrelated behaviors, such as completing the requirements for this course.

Relationships

Now these entities are connected, mentally, by **relationships.** An object such as a pen may be used to write a note to your boyfriend telling him you are going to study tonight when in fact you are going to meet someone else at a local bar. Suddenly a whole collection of entities, including objects, people, behaviors, and ideas, become related in complex but concrete ways, in some cases causally, in others by definition or inclusion, and in still other cases by approval.

People have attitudes, feelings of like or dislike, for the entities in their cognitive universe. Since the entities are related, the attitude toward any given entity is likely to be influenced by one's attitude toward those entities

**FIGURE 7.1
Cognitive entities and their relationships**

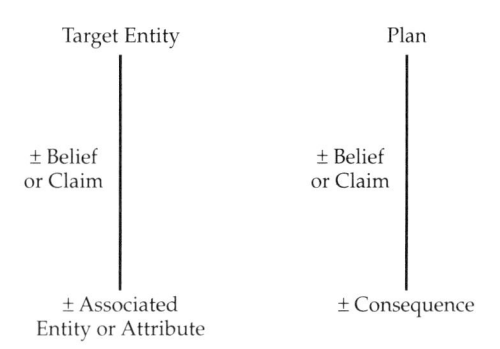

```
        Target Entity              Plan
              |                      |
              |                      |
         ± Belief               ± Belief
         or Claim               or Claim
              |                      |
              |                      |
         ± Associated           ± Consequence
         Entity or Attribute
```

to which it is most closely related. As I pointed out in Chapter 6 on attitude formation and change, it is difficult to like an idea or behavior of which a close friend disapproves, and difficult to dislike a behavior that leads to pleasurable consequences. The relationship between two entities is pictured in the left-hand diagram in Figure 7.1. One of those entities has been labeled a *target entity*, only because it is one in which we are presently interested, and the other has been labeled arbitrarily an *associated entity*. A "target entity" can become an "associated entity" if the focus of interest shifts.

TYPES OF RELATIONSHIPS

Causes/Signs   Entities can be related because one is perceived as a **cause** or a **sign** of the other, in which case we would expect the perceiver to have similar attitudes toward both the cause and its effect or toward the sign and that which it signifies. Thus if you believe your favorite team is having a losing season because the coach refuses to play an outstanding athlete, you are likely to have a negative attitude toward that coach.

Similarity   Entities can be related in that they are **similar** in some way. Thus there was much argument over whether the United States should begin a war with Iraq, because it seemed to some that such an action would be similar to the way we became involved in the Vietnam War, while others perceived no such similarities.

Inclusion   Entities can be related in that one is **included** in the other or in that they are mutually exclusive. The act of writing exam answers on your arm may be included in your concept of cheating or excluded from your concept of fairness; thus, the attitude toward the act depends upon your attitude toward cheating and fairness.

Approval Entities can be related in that one **approves** or disapproves of the other, if one of the entities is a person or an agency capable of approval and disapproval. We know that Nancy Reagan disapproved of drug use, for example, and our attitudes toward drug use are bound to be influenced somewhat by our attitudes toward Nancy Reagan. The campaign to enlist rock stars in the war against drugs was an attempt to take advantage of this type of relationship.

Conditioning Finally, entities can be related coincidentally or by means of **conditioning**, sometimes accidentally, but frequently by design, as is frequently the case in advertising. Advertisers spend a great deal of money to cause consumers to relate their products to pleasant scenes and activities that have no discernible connection to that product.

IMPORTANCE OF PLANS AND CONSEQUENCES IN AESOP

To this point what I have described is a general model of how people organize their mental universes. I have termed it the AESOP Model. **"AESOP"** stands for **"Affective and Epistemological Schema of Perception."** Thus it is a model of a person's *feelings* (or "affect") of liking or disliking for entities, and that person's *knowledge* or *understanding* (or "epistemology") of how those entities are related to one another in a cognitive *schema*. Now I would like to extend that model to describe how critical decisions are made. People do not always make critical decisions. Too frequently they are mislead by relationships of similarity, approval, inclusion, or conditioning introduced by persuaders who have something to gain by misleading them. Sometimes they understand it is important to assess the consequences of alternative plans of action, but fail to evaluate adequately the reasoning and evidence supporting the causal relationship between plans and consequences. The remainder of this discussion describes how decisions *ought to be* made if they are truly critical, not necessarily how they *are* made.

Remember from Chapter 6 that Fishbein has come to describe his somewhat similar model as the Theory of *Reasoned* Action because, I gather, he has come to understand that people also act in ways that are unreasonable. I am going to present my model, the Affective and Epistemological Schema of Persuasion, with a similarly modest claim. I propose that this way of reasoning will help you reach critical decisions.

I believe the entities of importance in decisions can be termed **Plans** and **Consequences**. This is my way of looking at the decision process (others may view it differently). It is my view that whenever someone makes a decision, it is a decision to *do* something—that is, to adopt a Plan—and thus the Consequences of that Plan are the important considerations. To maintain this view,

I have to utilize a particular, and rather broad, definition of *Plans*. Thus, in the right-hand diagram in Figure 7.1 the term *Plan* has been substituted for *target entity*, and the term *Consequence* has been substituted for *associated entity*.

Anytime one makes a decision to take a particular course of action, one is choosing one of some number of alternative plans. I must note at once that the terms *choosing* and *Plan* imply a very conscious process, and I do not intend to limit the discussion to such conscious choices. We choose and enact plans constantly—at very low levels of awareness, of course, and in some cases that is very necessary. You would not make much headway getting ready to go to school in the morning if you spent much time pondering exactly how to conduct toothbrushing and taking a shower. These are Plans that have been rendered automatic as a result of a lifetime of practice. However, I do believe that too many more important decisions are made at too low a level of awareness, and one of our purposes in this book is to try to increase the level of awareness at which you evaluate the Plans you choose to enact.

Making Critical Choices

It seems fairly obvious that choices among overt behavioral alternatives constitute choices among Plans. Moreover, behaviors tend to organize themselves into clusters and hierarchies that I will term *personal policies*. Thus, you do not merely choose to watch one episode of a television program; rather, that choice is probably made largely as a result of a larger policy of watching television on that night of the week and a policy of including that program in your television schedule. Frequently, one policy will conflict with another. For example, the policy of watching television on Thursday night may sometimes conflict with a policy of preparing for exams; that will be so if you have an exam on Friday morning. The policy of generally voting for Republican political candidates may conflict with some other policy in a particular election, and the policy of buying General Motors automobiles may come into conflict, in a particular instance, with a policy of getting the best possible deal. A policy of not dating athletes may be overridden in a particular instance by the attractiveness of a particular individual who happens to be an athlete.

I also want to emphasize that the Plans to which I refer are not necessarily Plans for overt behavior. A Plan may be a decision to change your mind, meaning there is no overt, externally observable behavior at the moment the Plan is enacted, although the implications for later behavior may be considerable.

Now, the immediate importance of this view of the decision process is this: *If decisions always involve choices among alternative Plans, it seems clear decisions ought always to be based on the comparative consequences of the alternatives.*

In fact, they are not. Too frequently a course of action is taken because it feels good as a result of prior conditioning, or because it is recommended by someone who is well liked but not particularly well informed, or because it is superficially similar to some other course of action in some other situation, or because it is a part of some more general category of policies one likes, or because it tends to accompany (be a sign of) things one likes. What I am arguing is that *critical* thinking involves a conscious choice of an alternative Plan because there is evidence that Plan will cause generably favorable Consequences. That is, of the types of relationships I described among entities, only a *causal* relationship between a Plan and its Consequences will yield a critical decision.

TYPES OF CONSEQUENCES

The most obvious Consequences of adopting a Plan are physical pleasure and pain. It almost goes without saying that one adopts one Plan over another because—on balance—it will achieve pleasure better and avoid pain better. Economic Consequences are so closely related to physical Consequences that they may not deserve a separate category. In our culture at least, economic advantages and disadvantages translate fairly directly into physical advantages and disadvantages. We will term these *Utilitarian* Consequences.

Decisional Balance Sheet

The **Decisional Balance Sheet** proposed by Janis and Mann (1977) presents an excellent system for thinking about types of Consequences. That Balance Sheet is reproduced in Table 7.1. From left to right across this sheet are columns in which you can represent alternative courses of action you are considering. From top to bottom are rows intended to represent types of Consequences to be considered in choosing among these alternatives. To fill in the Balance Sheet, you enumerate the consequences, both favorable and unfavorable, of each type for each of the alternative Plans.

Utilitarian Consequences for Self The first row consists of **Utilitarian Consequences for Self**, which I just described. Consider the example of choosing among possible jobs, which is a decision most of you probably hope to be making soon. In this category you would enter such considerations as salary, workload, opportunities for advancement, and location, including such matters as climate, size of the town, and opportunities for entertainment.

Utilitarian Consequences for Others The second row also calls attention to Utilitarian Consequences, in this case for Significant Others. If you are married or emotionally involved with another, this is easy to illustrate. Suppose

TABLE 7.1 A Schematic Balance Sheet Grid for Conceptualizing Decisional Conflict

Types of anticipation (with examples from research on career conflicts of lawyers)	Alternative courses of action					
	Alternative 1 (e.g., job with Department of Justice)		Alternative 2 (e.g., job with a Wall Street firm)		Alternative 3 (e.g., private practice in a small town)	
	+	−	+	−	+	−

A. Utilitarian gains or losses for self
  1. Personal income
  2. Interest value of daily work
  3. Opportunity to live in a preferred city
  ⋮
  n						

B. Utilitarian gains or losses for significant others
  1. Social status for family
  2. Reducing political corruption in community
  3. Advancing civil rights for nation
  ⋮
  n						

C. Self-approval or -disapproval
  1. Moral considerations pertaining to ethical legal practices
  2. "Ego ideal" of being an independent thinker
  3. Self-image as defender of innocent people
  ⋮
  n						

D. Social approval or disapproval
  1. From wife (or husband)
  2. From close friends
  3. From a national professional organization
  ⋮
  n						

The cells in this schematic grid should be visualized as being filled with positive (+) and negative (−) entries of varying magnitude depicting the strength of the incentives to accept or reject each alternative. The purpose of filling out the grid is to predict vulnerability to subsequent setbacks by identifying the main sources of conflict. Ordinarily the grid is set up with the rows representing the alternative courses of action; the rows and columns are reversed in this table in order to list examples of subcategories within each of the four types of anticipations.
Source: Janis and Mann (1977).

your spouse or consort has an attractive job or job offer in the area in which you are presently living, and your best alternatives appear to involve a move. For the spouse or consort to give up an attractive job to move with you may involve seriously negative Utilitarian Consequences that you are going to have to consider. Moreover, it may be that your parents live near the school you are presently attending, so a move on your part might involve seriously negative Utilitarian Consequences for them as well.

Utilitarian Consequences for Significant Others are not always negative, as this example might seem to suggest. In fact, generally they will sometimes, and to some extent, be positive as well as negative. The possible Plans will simply differ in the extent to which they produce Utilitarian Consequences that are good for you and for others who are important to you.

Consequences to Self-Perception The third row calls attention to attitudes toward self, which are Consequences that may differ among the alternative Plans. Assuming you have a particular conception of yourself, as everyone surely does, the choice of one of the job alternatives may conflict with your self-concept while another reinforces it. If you consider the defense of the environment to be an important part of your self-concept, taking a job with a company that does not have a good reputation for conservation may seriously threaten that self-concept, while an alternative position with an organization devoted to the preservation of the environment might reinforce that self-concept. Such considerations might outweigh the Utilitarian Consequences previously described.

Consequences to Perception by Others Finally, the fourth row calls attention to the fact that the attitudes of significant others toward yourself constitute an important type of Consequence. If your relationships with your spouse or consort, your friends, and your parents are built on your being a certain type of person, as in most cases, then the alternative jobs in this example will be very likely to differ in the extent to which they violate or reinforce those expectations. That is not a trivial consideration for anyone. If your spouse or consort has always thought of you as considerate, thoughtful, and caring, and your relationship has been built on that perception, for you to take a job that forces you to be inconsiderate, thoughtless, and uncaring will probably damage your relationship, and that may constitute a serious negative Consequence.

Consequences for Cognitive Consistency I would suggest the addition of a fifth row labeled Consequences for Cognitive Consistency, because I believe people act in order to maintain consistency with their beliefs, attitudes, and previous behaviors, including previous verbal commitments, in ways that are not completely captured by the third and fourth categories in the Balance

FIGURE 7.2
Plan with associated types of consequences

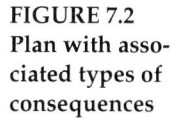

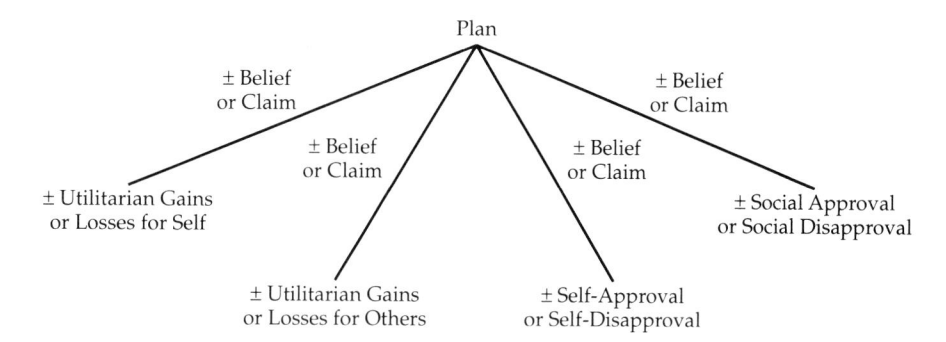

```
                              Plan
          ± Belief      /  |    |  \      ± Belief
          or Claim     /   |    |   \     or Claim
                 ± Belief      ± Belief
                 or Claim      or Claim
± Utilitarian Gains                              ± Social Approval
or Losses for Self                               or Social Disapproval
          ± Utilitarian Gains    ± Self-Approval
          or Losses for Others   or Self-Disapproval
```

Sheet. There is a strong drive to keep our present Plans consistent with those prior beliefs, attitudes, and behavioral/verbal commitments that goes beyond our self-concepts and reputations. (That sort of consistency was described in some detail in Chapter 6 dealing with attitude formation and change.)

The idea behind this Balance Sheet is that you can make your decisions considerably more critical by formally enumerating the Consequences of the alternative Plans. Of course, you are not going to take out a sheet of paper and construct a Balance Sheet every time you decide whether to go to a movie or study on a given night, but it might not be a bad plan when you are faced with more consequential decisions. And there is nothing to prevent you from carrying this sort of organizational scheme in your mind for use even when you do not commit your analyses to paper.

The considerations described in the Balance Sheet are diagrammed in Figure 7.2 so as to show how they relate to the Plan-Consequence model. Obviously there are many Consequences of any given Plan, so a complete diagram would be much more complicated than this. Moreover, this is a diagram of only one Plan and its associated Consequences. To diagram all the possible Consequences of all the alternative Plans would not be possible. That is why I consider the Decision Balance Sheet to be more useful when comparing Plans and their Consequences. Figure 7.2, however, is my attempt to diagram the sort of network in which our cognitions are stored, with the four types of Consequences from the Decisional Balance Sheet entered into the diagram.

DECIDING WHAT PLANS WILL PRODUCE WHAT CONSEQUENCES

So far I have described how you might enumerate the likely Consequences of alternative Plans. But I have not discussed how you might evaluate the probability that a given Plan will in fact lead to a given Consequence.

Toulmin's Model of Argument

A model of argument offered by the English philosopher Stephen Toulmin (1959) seems useful for that purpose. If we view the relationship between a Plan and a Consequence to be a **Belief** if it exists in the mind of a person and a *Claim* if it occurs in a message, we have the first element of Toulmin's model, which he terms the **Claim.** To support a Claim, one must offer or search for an item of Evidence, which is a statement believed by a listener or decision maker that seems relevant to a Claim. The Evidence is generally a statement about a condition that exists or has existed in the world.

Example: Midnight Toxic Waste Disposal Systems Suppose we consider an example in which you are trying to decide whether to accept a position at a fairly high salary with Midnight Toxic Waste Disposal Systems. You suspect that one Consequence of adopting such a Plan would be that you would be working for a firm that pollutes the environment, which would seriously damage your self-concept. But that stands as an unsupported Belief until you analyze it critically. What is the **Evidence** for this Belief?

One sort of statement that might constitute Evidence would be: "This firm has been indicted for illegal dumping by the Environmental Protection Agency on four occasions." It seems apparent that this statement is relevant to the Belief/Claim. But if you are to continue this critical evaluation, you must ask that the relevance be made explicit. The statement that allows you to make the inference from the Evidence to the Claim is what Toulmin calls the **Warrant.** In this case the Warrant would be something such as "Indictment by the E.P.A. is adequate to establish a presumption of guilt." Figure 7.3 is a diagram of the way the major elements of the Toulmin Model are related to this Plan and Consequence.

Modified Toulmin Model: The AESOP Model

But I have suggested some ways the Toulmin Model can be modified to cover some additional aspects of decision making (Cronkhite, 1976). First, more than one line of reasoning can support a single Belief or Claim. In the present example, the decision maker may believe that "This firm leases several dump sites in locations in which local agencies do not conduct adequate inspections." This might constitute Evidence related to the Belief/Claim by the Warrant: "Leasing of uninspected dump sites leads to the suspicion the lessee may be polluting the environment."

Second, an item of Evidence may require further support if it is questioned by a decision maker. Thus the statement "This firm has been indicted four times by the E.P.A." may itself become an Evidence-Claim that will require a further item of Evidence, such as "*Business Week* reported these indictments in its May 14 issue last year." Then the new item of Evidence will

FIGURE 7.3
Modified Toulmin Model attached to the persuasion paradigm

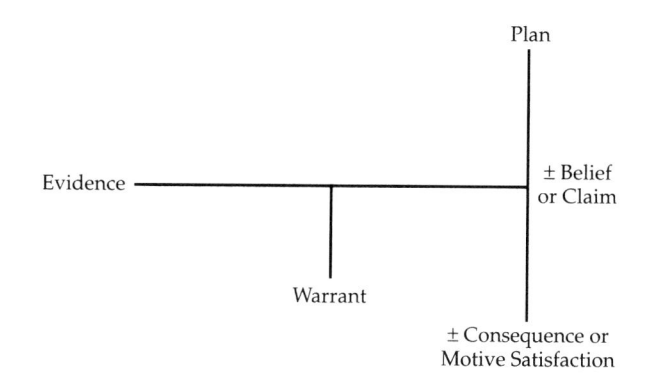

```
                                           Plan
                                            |
                                            |
                                            |± Belief
         Evidence ──────────────────────────  or Claim
                            |
                            |
                          Warrant
                                            ± Consequence or
                                            Motive Satisfaction
```

require a Warrant of its own, such as *Business Week* is a credible source for information such as this."

Third, a decision maker may question the original Warrant, in which case it will require an Evidence-Warrant unit to support it. One such item of Evidence might be "Ninety percent of E.P.A. indictments have resulted in guilty pleas or convictions." The new Warrant would then be "A high conviction rate gives credibility to an agency's indictments." These modifications to the basic Toulmin Model are diagrammed in Figure 7.4.

Implications of the Decision-Making Model

So what does this model of decision suggest? First, it suggests that in making a critical decision, we will analyze that decision as a choice among alternative Plans, which Plans may be for overt behavior or covert opinion change. Second, we will be aware of the possibility that irrelevant relationships of Sign, Similarity, Inclusion-Exclusion, Approval, and Conditioning or Coincidental Association may be influencing the decision. Third, we will evaluate the desirability of alternative Plans by listing their likely Consequences. The Decisional Balance Sheet seems to be a useful tool for this purpose. Finally, we will assess the soundness of our Beliefs or a persuader's Claims of Plan-Consequence relationships. The modified Toulmin Model seems to be a useful tool for this purpose.

BARRIERS TO CRITICAL DECISIONS

Noncausal Reasoning

Persuaders will do their best to cause us to make decisions on bases other than causal relationships between Plans and Consequences. Imagine that

FIGURE 7.4
Fully modified AESOP Model

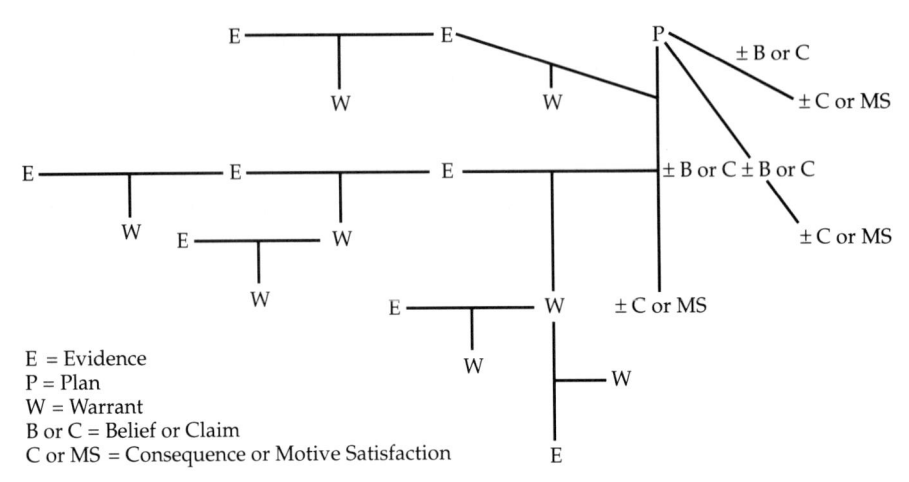

E = Evidence
P = Plan
W = Warrant
B or C = Belief or Claim
C or MS = Consequence or Motive Satisfaction

Types of Relationships (Beliefs or Claims):
- Coincidental association (S – S pairing, no coincidence in advertising)
- Mere approval/endorsement (dependent on liking, not expert qualifications)
- Categorical inclusion and exclusion (the basis of syllogistic reasoning in general, but usually the basis of image incursion in advertising)
- Similarity/dissimilarity
- Contingency (including sign, effect-to-cause, and cause-to-effect)

Types of Consequences or Motives:
- Utilitarian Gains or Losses for Self
- Utilitarian Gains or Losses for Others
- Self-Approval or Disapproval
- Social Approval or Social Disapproval

Midnight Toxic Waste Disposal Systems becomes disturbed by its image and decides to hire a public relations firm to change its image via a series of television commercials. A first step, of course, would be to change the name of the company, to avoid the negative connotations of the name as it stands. Suppose the name is changed to Sunshine Conservation Enterprises. This takes advantage of viewers' favorable associations with the words *conservation* and *enterprise*. Notice, however, that nothing has changed yet except the company's semantic spots. A first commercial might show a beautiful building, with the new name prominently displayed, surrounded by rolling, forested countryside with squirrels and deer gamboling about. This relies simply on *conditioning* and *association*. It constitutes no reason to change one's mind about the company. That would be obvious if one were to attempt to diagram the commercial in terms of Plans, Consequences, Evidence, and Warrants. But corporate enemies of the environment have used these and other tactics so frequently that the general approach has even contributed a new word to our vocabulary: *Greenscam*.

Another approach, perhaps in the same commercial, might be to hire a celebrity to speak favorably about Sunshine Conservation Enterprises, using the relationship of *approval*. The celebrity might compare the company to legitimate agencies, such as the Environmental Protection Agency, charged with cleaning up the environment by disposing of waste at polluted sites, using the relationship of *similarity*. In fact, that celebrity might actually claim that Sunshine Conservation Enterprises is a part of the nation's new awareness of the need for systematic waste disposal, using the relationship of *inclusion*.

Note that such a commercial would not be offering any claims of *causal* relationships between support for the company (the Plan) and any favorable Consequences, so it could not be evaluated—or even described—in terms of Plans, Consequences, Evidence, and Warrants.

Elaboration Likelihood: Central vs. Peripheral Processing

To some extent when people listen to persuasive messages, they evaluate or elaborate what they hear. They have cognitive responses in which they relate what they hear to information they have previously encountered, and assess the extent to which the present message is acceptable or unacceptable in light of the previous information; they test the reasoning and evidence in the message to see if it is internally consistent.

But we do not do this sort of elaboration nearly as often as we would like; I know I do not. Petty and Cacioppo (1986a,b) have described two modes of cognitive response to persuasive messages, the central and the peripheral. **Central processing** is what I have just described, the careful assessment of reasoning and evidence in light of our prior information, and a decision based on the merits of the argument. **Peripheral processing** is quite different. In peripheral processing the listener for one reason or another fails to conduct this careful assessment, and responds quickly, not on the merits of the case, but on the basis of cues that may be irrelevant but short-circuit the reasoning process.

Credibility

Sometimes we switch into this peripheral processing mode because we are confronted with people who are so credible for us that we accept what they say without subjecting it to careful central scrutiny. The opposite is possible: Sometimes people are so disliked or so distrusted that we reject their messages without considering the possibility they may be right in this case. Recall from Chapter 5 that this is the essence of dogmatism.

Sometimes speakers reveal their intent to persuade us of something to which we are so opposed that we turn off the message immediately and spend the time either attending to something else or refuting everything that is said. Conversely, sometimes we are so convinced we are going to agree with the message that we do not bother to assess it critically.

Sometimes we are exposed to messages on topics in which we are so uninvolved and uninterested that our processing is only peripheral, whereas we are much more likely to conduct central processing if the topic is involving. Closely related is the possibility that the message or the situation produces emotional involvement so high we are unable to assess it critically.

Sometimes speakers are arguing in ways that cause us to experience cognitive dissonance, telling us decisions or commitments we have made were unjustified, and such messages are likely to be rejected without being given adequate consideration.

Sometimes the message conflicts with prior conditioning or is so consistent with prior conditioning that we respond with knee-jerk reactions instead of careful processing.

Personality Characteristics

In many cases, our personality characteristics may interfere with central processing. A person low in self-esteem may be too easily persuaded for the wrong reasons. People who have a strong external locus of control, who believe they are controlled by fate and the actions of others, are unlikely to carefully process messages urging them to take control of their own destinies. And those who are highly sex-role stereotyped will be likely to accept or reject messages on the basis of whether the action advocated is consistent with their sex roles rather than on the basis of its merits.

Drama and Comedy

But one of the most pervasive and insidious types of persuasion masquerades as drama or comedy. I do not necessarily mean that writers, producers, directors, and actors always set out to create persuasive messages when they put dramatic productions on the screen. Rather, the dramas they produce are inevitably persuasive in one way or another. And worse, because of their very nature as dramas, they encourage—almost require—peripheral processing.

Willing Suspension of Critical Analysis The most important reason that is so is because of what I am going to call the **willing suspension of critical analysis.** Dramatic theorists persistently refer to the "willing suspension of disbelief" as a necessary contract producers of drama must create and viewers of drama must accept in order for the viewers to enjoy the dramatic experience. And we have learned to accept it almost without question. In a horror movie, viewers seeing the serial killer approach the couple parked in Lovers' Lane enter into the contract to such an extent that they sometimes scream and even faint, not saying to themselves, "Wait—This boy and girl are actors. The serial killer is an actor. All three are just earning their pay. No one is going to be murdered and dismembered. There is a director there, and other actors out of camera range. There are camera operators, and lighting specialists, and script and teleprompter handlers. There are lights and cameras all around. This is not a deserted road. It may not be a road at all; it may just be part of a movie set in a studio. What is all the excitement about?"

We don't draw back from the drama that way because if we did it would prevent us from enjoying it. Only occasionally, when children become so involved and suspend disbelief so completely they become truly frightened, do their parents themselves temporarily suspend their entry into the contract to reassure the children.

No harm done to this point. But what I am saying here is that when we suspend our disbelief, we may also suspend our critical analysis. When listeners are somehow forewarned they are going to be exposed to a persuasive message, either overtly or by virtue of the context (a political rally or debate, or a commercial), especially if the point of view of the persuader is different from their own, they will *counterargue* as they listen, evaluating the reasoning and evidence and thinking of opposing arguments. This is what Petty and Cacioppo (1986a,b) mean by *central processing,* and it is what I mean to describe in the AESOP Model. But when viewers believe they are supposed to enjoy a drama or comedy, they let their critical guards down. The persuasive message then slips in and burglarizes their minds while they are distracted, watching television.

Rhetorical Depiction

We need to understand now a concept Michael Osborn (1986) has termed **rhetorical depiction.** The characters in a drama or comedy are depicted in a certain way; they are depicted by the actors who have been cast in the roles, they are depicted by the ways they are dressed and the makeup they wear, and they are depicted by the way the actors deliver their lines. The events in a drama are also depicted in a certain way, as they contribute to the overall plot. Those events are not real; they are contrived by the writers and interpreted by the directors to serve the depiction that is to be achieved. The camera angles and distances, the lighting, the sound track, and of course the dialogue all contribute to a particular depiction.

We as viewers seldom stop to ask any of the following: "Are police really the way they are depicted here? Are juvenile delinquents really as despicable or vulnerable as they are depicted? Do real women and men fit the stereotypes in which they are cast? Are business*men* really this chauvinistic and secretaries this vulnerable to their advances? Does this plot depict a realistic set of circumstances representative of those in the real world?" Of course, the answer will be, sometimes yes and sometimes no. But the point I am trying to make here is that we seldom ask those questions when we are enjoying a comedy or drama, whereas if similar people or events were described in an overtly persuasive message, we would subject them to careful scrutiny.

Suppose we think back about some of the dramas and comedies we have seen, and ask how they may have affected us. Consider first a TV show that was both drama and comedy, "M*A*S*H." As you think back, it is hard to avoid the realization that both the comedy and the drama in that show were decidedly antiwar and antiauthority. Yet I have seldom heard the show criticized even by the most radical "hawks," even by those who most supported the Vietnam War, for example. It is as if they never fully recognized the message behind the entertainment.

TV's "All In the Family" is another interesting example. Archie Bunker's lines were racist, sexist, and on most occasions worshipful of authority. But the cast and the writers and the director of the show assured us they were written to express racism, sexism, and authoritarianism so stupidly that they would be rejected by the viewers. To their surprise, Archie Bunker became a folk hero to what Spiro Agnew called the "Moral Majority." But did viewers ever stop to analyze the characters—Archie and Edith and Gloria and Meathead—or the events depicted, for their isomorphism with or resemblance to reality? I doubt that many did until the reviewers began calling it to their attention.

"Three's Company" probably persuaded many parents that young people of opposite sex can live together and still maintain a platonic, nonsexual relationship.

What did you learn from "Hill Street Blues" about police officers? What did you learn from "L.A. Law" about attorneys? What did you learn about doctors and other medical workers from "St. Elsewhere" and "General Hospital"? In those cases there were so many characters you probably learned a useful lesson: There is a great deal of variation among police, attorneys, and doctors. What did you learn about family relationships from "Leave It to Beaver," "The Donna Reed Show," "The Waltons," and "The Cosby Show"? Nothing very realistic, I dare say. What did you learn about working women from "The Mary Tyler Moore Show" and currently from "Murphy Brown"? What have you learned about the way Americans live from "Dallas" and "Dynasty"? Asians and Europeans and Russians, among whom those shows are very popular, are learning strange things about our culture. What did you learn about aging women from "Golden Girls," and what are you learning from "Golden Palace"? And what have you learned about California high school students from "Beverly Hills 90210"? What have you learned about parent-child relationships from "Roseanne" and "The Simpsons"? Is Bart your hero?

Has "Picket Fences" persuaded you regarding issues of civil rights? Have the series that deal with long-term intimate relationships, such as "Mad

About You" and "Love and War," taught you anything about acceptable behavior in such relationships?

Among movies, what did *Dances With Wolves* and *Last of the Mohicans* teach you about treatment of Native Americans? One of my students in human communication theory surveyed undergraduates at this university and found those who had seen those two movies were significantly more favorable toward Native Americans than those who had not seen them. (This does not mean seeing the movies *caused* the more favorable attitudes; it may be that students who already had favorable attitudes chose to see the movies.)

Have movies such as *Close Encounters of the Third Kind, E.T.,* and *Starman* predisposed you to treat aliens more favorably if you encounter them? For that matter, *Splash!* and *Harry and the Hendersons* seem to have carried the same message, except with aliens other than the extraterrestrial variety.

The specific answers to these questions are not nearly as important as is the realization that this "learning" was in fact *persuasion,* and that it was accomplished by film and television entertainment, drama and comedy, probably while you were willingly suspending your critical analysis.

Example: Taster's Choice Commercial Moreover, I have begun to notice the dramatic format appearing in commercials, and I suspect the reason is exactly what I am describing. One of the commercials is for Taster's Choice coffee, devised to reinforce the admonition to "Enjoy the *sophisticated* taste of Taster's Choice." As slowly as this drama is unfolding, it will probably still be running when you are reading this, years after I am writing it. An obviously sophisticated man met an obviously sophisticated woman when he knocked at her door to borrow coffee. She warned him it had a very sophisticated taste, and he responded by saying "My guests are very sophisticated." Subsequent episodes always occurred in sophisticated settings, of course. In one scene the man knocked on her door, and was met by a very sophisticated man who told him the woman was in the shower. They dealt with this situation in a very sophisticated way, of course. It developed later that the man in her apartment was her brother. In a later episode they met at the elevator. He was carrying luggage. She asked him if he was leaving, and he said "Just a business trip." Later he called her from Paris. She said "How romantic." He said "It could be." Most recently a young man claiming to be her son appeared at the door. Who knows what may have happened between two such sophisticated people by the time you read this. But has anyone stopped to consider the possibility that Roseanne may serve this very coffee to her family? Certainly there is nothing inherently sophisticated about a cup of coffee.

Example: Saturn Commercial A current commercial for the Saturn automobile uses a similar format. A middle-aged man appears on camera to tell us that he offered to let his son take one of his vehicles to college, and was surprised when the son chose the four-door Saturn instead of a two-door vehicle. Now, this may have been a reenactment of a real event, although there is no statement to that effect. But whether it is a representation of a real event is not the point. I had seen it three times before I even thought that it was just another instance of persuasion masquerading as drama, this time quite intentionally, since it appears in a commercial.

SOME SUGGESTIONS FOR THINKING CRITICALLY

Steve Allen wrote a book titled *Dumbth: And 81 Ways To Make Americans Smarter.* He explained:

> Mountains of evidence—both in the form of statistical studies and personal testimonies—establish that the American people are suffering from a new and perhaps unprecedented form of mental incapacitation for which I have coined the word *Dumbth.* (1989, p. 15)

Cultural Literacy

Very simply, dumbth is the inability to think critically. But Allen's analysis of the causes of *dumbth* adds something to what I have said about critical thinking. He is convinced, as I am, and as are many who teach critical thinking, that one of the absolute foundations of critical thinking is a broad education that leads to what Hirsch (Hirsch, 1987; Hirsch, Kett, and Trefil, 1988; and Hirsch, 1989) has termed cultural literacy. "Cultural literacy," very simply, is "what every American needs to know" in order to function adequately in our culture. Hirsch wrote: "Only by accumulating shared symbols, and the shared information that the symbols represent, can we learn to communicate effectively with one another in our national community" (Hirsch, 1987, p. xvii).

> [Cultural literacy is] the network of information that all competent readers possess. It is the background information, stored in their minds, that enables them to take up a newspaper and read it with an adequate level of comprehension, getting the point, grasping the implications, relating what they read to the unstated context, which alone gives meaning to what is read. (p. 2)

But cultural literacy is especially important in responding critically to persuasive communication, because most arguments assume a great deal of information about our history, our cultural norms, and our expectations of others.

This is easiest to see with respect to humor. I have several graduate students from other countries, many of them Asian, all quite bright and quite fluent in English. But I have the experience frequently of being asked to explain a joke or humorous remark, and at such times I realize just how deeply our humor is embedded in our culture. Watching the TV series "Northern Exposure" with one of these students was especially instructive. Humor I took for granted was simply opaque to the student. And explaining it generally didn't help. You may have had the same experience watching British comedy with a laugh track or a live British audience and wondering what on earth was so funny.

Persuasion is similarly embedded in our culture, and thinking critically about it requires a great deal of cultural literacy. Persuasion is elliptical; that is, most of the reasoning behind it is never stated explicitly. That is especially true in advertising, as it appears in single pages of magazines and thirty-second television commercials. More and more it is true in politics and national affairs in general, for what we hear on television are brief "sound bites" generally as short as fifteen seconds, on the basis of which we are expected to decide which candidates to vote for and which causes to support. What does it mean to say, "Abortion is murder"? One must know a great deal about religion, legal definitions, and biology to decide whether such a statement makes sense. Some of the few times we are exposed to fully developed political arguments are when "debates" are conducted every few years at times of national elections. And then we only infrequently hear a fully developed argument on a single issue in which all the assumptions, evidence, and reasoning are spelled out. Most of the time we are left to our own cultural knowledge to fill the gaps.

Hirsch's three books are titled *Cultural Literacy: What Every American Should Know, The Dictionary of Cultural Literacy,* and *A First Dictionary of Cultural Literacy,* the latter intended for children. An examination of even the children's volume left me with a serious self-esteem problem. That book is divided into twenty-one sections, the titles of which may suggest the sort of knowledge we are discussing: Proverbs, Idioms, English, Literature, Mythology, Music-Art-Architecture, the Bible, Religion-Philosophy, American History to 1865, American History Since 1865, Politics-Economics, World History to 1600, World History Since 1600, United States Geography, World Geography, Mathematics, Physical Sciences, Earth Sciences-Weather, Life Sciences, Medicine-the Human Body, and Technology.

Steve Allen (1989) has constructed an excellent list of rules for making critical decisions and avoiding *Dumbth,* the title of his book. Several of these rules involve improving one's cultural literacy in order to be able to evaluate arguments more critically. The master rule, however, seems to be that one must make a conscious decision to reason critically. Subsequent rules suggest the need to postpone decisions until all the facts are in, to avoid one's own erroneous assumptions, biases, personal prejudices, and superstitions; to beware of "arguments" that consist only of slogans or labels; to avoid being either optimistic or pessimistic in general; to avoid being overly affected by the opinions of one's friends and enemies, and to be humble, so one does not confuse intelligence with the ability to reason critically. Remember, no significant correlation has ever been demonstrated between IQ and open-mindedness.

Some Common Fallacies

Kahane (1988) has divided fallacies into two types: Reasoning that is *fallacious because it is invalid,* and reasoning that would be *fallacious even if it were valid.*

Fallacious Because Invalid   The first type consists of an appeal to authority (under which he included popularity and traditional wisdom), provincialism (including excessive loyalty or patriotism), use of irrelevant reasons, ambiguity, slippery slope (including "Balkinization" and the "domino theory"), ad hominem argument, two wrongs make a right, tokenism, hasty conclusion, questionable classification, questionable cause, and questionable analogy. Suppose we consider examples of each of these in turn.

Appeal to Authority   An appeal to authority is currently exemplified by a number of commercials that use people who are authorities in one area to testify to the worth of products they really know little about, as when Bobby Knight, who may be an excellent basketball coach for Indiana University, is used in commercials for a local automobile dealership, Pizza Hut, and a local furniture store. It is not that Knight does not know anything about autos, pizza, and furniture, but I have no reason to believe he knows any more about them than I do. An appeal to popularity is used currently by a chain of well-known sandwich shops, who are touting the fact they are the second largest fast-food chain in the world. I am always reminded in cases such as these of the sarcastic adage, "Eat garbage. Fifty gazillion flies can't be wrong." (Not that this chain's sandwiches are garbage; I eat them frequently. But this sort of reasoning is garbage.) An appeal to traditional wisdom would likely begin with the words, "Everyone knows. . . ."

Provincialism   Provincialism, excessive patriotism, or devotion to one's own group, was exemplified clearly by the slogan directed at protesters against the Vietnam War, "America: Love It Or Leave It," and more recently by the suggestion that those who did not support Desert Storm were not true Americans, but lovers of "turban-heads." Closer to home, it could be exemplified by the suggestion that one must agree with every belief espoused by one's fraternity or sorority.

Irrelevant Reason   This might be exemplified by the argument that tuition rates must be increased because professors are underpaid or, conversely, they should be decreased because administrators are overpaid, neither of which is necessarily relevant to the cost of tuition.

Ambiguity "Abortion is murder" rests on an ambiguous use of the word "murder," in which that word is undefined. It is not clear whether it is meant that abortion is legally murder, or that it should be, or that it is similar to murder.

Slippery Slope This could be exemplified by the argument that Clinton's plan for government-regulated medical care will lead to socialized medicine, which will lead to our being herded like cattle through giant medical facilities in which the personnel are uncaring and too busy to attend to individual needs.

Argument Ad Hominem This type of argument consists of an attack on the *person* rather than the argument itself. When an alleged rape victim's reputation is attacked rather than the specific facts of her allegation, that is argument ad hominem, and is generally ruled inadmissable in court unless, of course, it is specifically an attack on her credibility. This difference between an attack on a person and a relevant attack on the person's credibility is sometimes a difficult distinction to make. Were the testimonies of Anita Hill's co-workers that she was not well-liked in the office argument ad hominem or an attack on her credibility in the Hill-Thomas confirmation hearings?

Two Wrongs Make a Right Was Lorena Bobbit's mutilation of her husband's penis justified by his previous mistreatment of her? Was the Menendez brothers' killing of their parents justified by their alleged previous sexual molestation by those parents? Would justifying Lorena's husband's mistreatment of her by the fact that such mistreatment is a common practice be an acceptable argument?

Tokenism Since certain corporations have pledged to donate an unspecified proportion of their profits to environmental causes, does that constitute a reason to buy those products, or is it just more "Greenscam"?

Hasty Conclusion Does the finding of the numbers 666 (the "sign of the devil") or the word "Crips" scrawled on a public wall in a small town justify the conclusion that the town is overrun with devil-worshippers and gang activity?

Questionable Classification Can students protesting on the Quad against tuition hikes be classified as general malcontents or antiuniversity demonstrators?

Questionable Cause Can the appearance of such demonstrators be attributed to the contemporary breakdown in morals and the failure of the schools to teach respect for authority?

Questionable Analogy   Can such demonstrations against tuition hikes be compared to the demonstrations in the 1960s against the Vietnam War, either by those hoping for a resurgence of such demonstrations or by those who fear it?

Fallacious Even If Valid   Kahane's second category of fallacy consists of arguments that would be fallacious even if they were valid. He lists as sub-types suppressed evidence, questionable premise (including unknown fact, questionable evaluation, straw man, false dilemma, begging the question, and inconsistency), and the false charge of fallacy. The third, false charge of fallacy, simply consists of a speaker branding another's argument as fallacious when in fact it is not. Suppose we consider the other two types in more detail.

Suppressed Evidence   Generally the suppression of evidence consists simply of the failure to reveal known evidence that might hurt one's case. Suppose a representative of a university administration argues in a public speech there is no evidence that the university has in any way harmed the environment but knows the groundskeepers have been instructed to use a banned herbicide to control weeds on campus. That person is guilty of suppressing evidence.

Questionable Premise   In general, this category includes any use of evidence that is somehow questionable. There are so many ways in which evidence can be faulty that there is not much profit in trying to enumerate all the ways. For example, *evidence* can consist of statements of alleged *fact* that neither the speaker nor the listener actually know to be true, and in some cases alleged facts that could not be known; it can consist of gross evaluations presented as fact when they are actually only opinions; it can consist of the reduction of the possible alternatives to only two, when in fact there are more than two alternatives. A speaker might say, for example, "We are going to have to bomb the aggressors or see innocent cities overrun," when in fact there are other alternatives, including, perhaps, use of U.N. peacekeeping troops or peace negotiations.

Sometimes two items of evidence used by a source will be contradictory. Two especially interesting types of questionable premise are termed *straw man* and *begging the question*. In the straw man type of fallacy a speaker describes an argument that has not been advanced by his opponent, usually because it is easier to refute than arguments that have actually been advanced. "My opponent would favor unisex restrooms" would be such a fallacy if the opponent had not actually made a statement favoring unisex restrooms. "A person who makes such a statement should not be elected to public office" would beg the question if the opponent had never been proven to have made the statement.

Statistical Fallacies Speakers may cite statistics that are based on too small a sample or an unrepresentative sample; ones that are merely relational when the speaker is claiming a cause-to-effect relationship; ones that lead to hasty conclusions because they are in some way incomplete; ones that make faulty comparisons generalized from one time or place to another, or ones based on the use of ambiguous words to lump together in a single category instances that are different in some important way. One of the most-used statistical fallacies is the use of statistics that could not be known or could not be known so precisely to try to give an air of scientific quantification to one's conclusions. One of these is the statistic widely quoted in textbooks in communication theory and nonverbal communication to the effect that verbal channels account for only 7 percent of all social meaning, while the vocal channel accounts for 38 percent, and the facial channel accounts for 55 percent. Such statistics are unknowable because, as explained in Chapters 8 and 9, what constitutes *meaning* is under considerable dispute and certainly is not quantifiable. The calculation of a percentage requires the division of one number (the numerator) by another (the denominator). To reach this present conclusion, one would have to have a number in the numerator representing all the *meaning* transmitted nonverbally and a number in the denominator representing all *possible meaning*. That is obviously impossible. This is simply a useless and unknowable statistic, but communication textbooks repeat it with wild abandon. Its only real use is as an example of fallacious reasoning.

Trenholm (1991) has done a good job of explaining why these statistics as generally cited are useless:

> This research [attributed to Mehrabian (1967)] has been widely quoted and as widely misinterpreted. . . . The figures arose in a highly artificial, experimental context. In actual interaction we can expect the verbal element to play a larger role, and, certainly, when we want to convey abstract, logical information, the verbal code is the most useful. (p. 83).

I could say at this point that "91.3 percent of all statistics are useless," but that would be simply another unknowable statistic used to create the illusion of scientific, mathematical precision, and it would be fallacious.

If you can find it, there is a classic little paperback that treats statistical fallacies with care and humor. *How to Lie With Statistics,* by Darrell Huff, was first copyrighted in 1954 and was in its 31st printing when I acquired a copy in the early 1970s.

PERSUASION

Much of what we have discussed in this book is directly relevant to "persuasion" as discussed in recent textbooks that include that term (or its derivatives) in the title, such as the excellent treatment by Bettinghaus and Cody (1994). Their first unit, for example, deals with theories of attitude change, which are for the most part covered in Chapter 6 of this book and to some extent earlier in this chapter. Their Chapters 5, 6, and 7 deal with topics such as source characteristics, individual characteristics, and reference groups, topics we covered in Chapter 5 of this book. In their Chapters 8 and 9 they deal with language variables and nonverbal communication, which we covered perhaps even more thoroughly, albeit from a different perspective, in our Chapters 8, 9, and 10. They have discussed contexts in which persuasion occurs in their third unit, many of which are the contexts we discuss as those in which communication in general occurs, in our Unit 4.

What we have not yet covered, and what I would now like to deal with, has to do with what they term *structuring message appeals*, mostly having to do with the organization of messages in public speeches.

From the early 1950s until the early 1970s, **research in persuasion** under that name, with special focus on how to construct a message, dominated communication research. My view is that such research declined because it was concentrated on the study of public speeches, and communication researchers came to realize public speaking was declining, being replaced by other forms of social influence. Probably the first major public speech to be broadcast on television was Richard Nixon's "Checkers" speech in 1952. It had a powerful effect on viewers, including the Republican National Committee, who retained him as Eisenhower's vice-presidential nominee largely on the basis of that speech and viewer reaction to it. For a while it appeared public speaking might indeed have found a powerful ally in television. At the same time the Yale School of communication research under the direction of Carl Hovland (see Chapter 4) was beginning to experiment with means of making public speeches more persuasive, varying the characteristics of such speeches and measuring the effectiveness of such variations. There seemed no reason to do otherwise.

In the subsequent twenty years, however, it became clear television was not the great medium for public speaking that it at first appeared to be. Audiences became less and less enthralled with long speeches and attended more to newscasters' reports of such speeches. Eventually, *sound bites*, fifteen-second blips excerpted from public speeches of newsmakers, became the norm and the substitute for extended speeches. Viewers more and more came to expect to be entertained, as Neil Postman has recently explained in his book *Amusing Ourselves to Death*. Stuart Ewen, Chair of the Department of Communication at Hunter College, said on an episode of "The Public Mind" chaired by Bill Moyers titled "Consuming Images," that commercials are the contemporary form of public address.

Certainly there are times when national audiences attend to full-length public speeches, as when Presidential nominees accept the nominations of their parties, occasionally during campaigns when candidates deliver fairly extended speeches, when the eventual winner delivers the inaugural address, later as the President delivers the state of the union messages, and when he—so far *he*—tries to calm the nation at a time of crisis. One can still watch full-length speeches televised on C-Span if one is so inclined, but only a small proportion of the total possible viewing audience seems so inclined. The so-called *debates* among the candidates really hardly deserve the name debate; they certainly are not public speeches. We listen to lectures from celebrities on campus occasionally, and we endure lectures from professors who could use some instruction in public speaking. But public speakers certainly do not achieve the star quality of Lincoln and Douglas in the last century, for example, whose series of debates—really public speeches—fascinated audiences for several hours at a time and were catered by food vendors.

Be that as it may, the fascination of communication researchers with persuasive public speaking has declined drastically. In 1969, I published a book titled *Persuasion: Speech and Behavioral Change* (Cronkhite, 1969). That book was published at what now seems to have been the peak of research into persuasive public speaking, although I certainly did not anticipate that being the case. In that book I wrote an extended section on message organization and interaction. Even though that section is now over 25-years-old, not much has changed since. The topics I discussed then were: (1) Does organization matter? (2) Introductions (3) Conclusions (4) Best foot forward? (5) Problem or solution first? (6) Attack now or later? and (7) When to cite the source? However, remember this was a book that dealt primarily with how *speakers* can most effectively persuade listeners. Since I am concerned in this present chapter with how you can think critically, I will have to translate the findings into admonitions for *listeners* regarding how they can most effectively avoid being exploited by clever speakers.

Does Organization Matter? A number of studies done in the 1960s and 70s raised the question of the extent to which a speech had to be organized in order to achieve a persuasive effect. Random reordering of paragraphs and even sentences sometimes had no noticeable effect on opinion change. However, as I noted in *Persuasion* at the time, some speeches are so bad that random reordering of the *phonemes* might not have made them any worse. Listeners encountering disorganized speeches will probably be well advised to either impose their own organization on the mess or, if that is hopeless, to ignore it.

Introductions Nevertheless, it does appear that what is done in the introduction of a speech does have an effect. Speakers can do certain things in their introductions to make themselves better liked by their listeners, including using humor, mild self-deprecation, and establishing a common background, interests, and goals between themselves and their listeners, especially if they are strangers. Should speakers tell their listeners of their intention to persuade? Speech teachers have been telling students for years they must state their theses and major arguments in their introductions. However, it appears that depends on whether the listeners are hostile—that is, whether they are initially opposed to the point of view that is going to be expressed. If listeners are hostile, knowledge of the speaker's opinion is likely to make them counter-argue, and thus reduce the persuasive effect (see Petty and Cacioppo, 1986a,b). Thus, it may be most effective to suppress not only the thesis but also the statement of major arguments in an introduction when listeners are hostile.

Listeners should remember, first, that likable speakers are not necessarily any more truthful just because they are likable and, second, that evidence and argument presented with no stated intention to persuade needs no less careful evaluation than that advanced in an overt persuasive attempt. In fact, the persuader who disguises his persuasive intent should be subjected to especially careful scrutiny. On the other hand, listeners who reject arguments and evidence simply because they may lead to conclusions with which they initially disagree are simply saying, in effect, "My mind is made up; don't confuse me with the facts."

Conclusions   In conclusions, however, it seems clear effective speakers will summarize what has been argued and appeal for specific action (or at least cognitive acceptance). Such an appeal will not only produce greater opinion change, it will improve listeners' opinions of the speaker as well.

Summaries of the arguments will generally be helpful to listeners trying to evaluate them critically. However, it will usually be to the listeners' advantage to defer action until they have had time to think about the evidence and to consult other sources.

Best Foot Forward?   Reasoning and evidence mentioned either early or late in a speech seems to be better remembered, which seems to lead to the conclusion that the most effective appeals should appear either first or last. If speakers are either strangers or somehow suspect, they can probably create good first impressions by presenting their best arguments first.

For listeners, it will be good to remember that first impressions can be deceiving. Listen critically to *all* the speech, not just the first argument.

Problem or Solution First?   It seems clear that listeners who hear solutions to problems before they are made aware of the problems are likely to become confused. Thus, the organization in which the problems are established first, then the solution to those problems is described, and finally the alleged solution is demonstrated to solve the problems seems most effective.

This is a case in which what seems to be effective for speakers is also advantageous for critical listeners. Certainly it seems reasonable to hear evidence of problems with the status quo before considering proposals for change.

Attack Now or Later?   Should speakers attack opposing arguments before or after presenting their own constructive arguments? That seems to depend on their listeners. If the listeners have recently heard opposing arguments, or if they can be assumed to have those opposing arguments clearly in mind, it is probably more effective to refute the opposing arguments first to make room for one's own arguments. On the other hand, if there is no reason to believe listeners are thinking of opposing arguments, there is no point in reminding them at the outset. Rather, it is probably more effective to give one's own constructive arguments first, then get listeners' commitments, and then forewarn them of opposing arguments they may hear in the future and refute those opposing arguments. The effects of such *forewarning* seem clear: Listeners will be less likely to be influenced by opposing arguments of which they have been forewarned.

Really critical listeners should be able to assess new arguments without being biased by opposing arguments they have encountered in the past. When speakers try to get listeners to commit themselves before they hear opposing arguments, however, critical listeners will resist making such commitments.

When to Cite the Source?   If the source of a quotation or item of information has low credibility with listeners, it appears to be more effective to cite that source after the information, which is better than not mentioning a source at all, but if sources have high credibility it appears to be more effective to name them before the information.

For listeners, if the evidence or reasoning can be evaluated independently of the source, that is the clear route to critical listening. However, it is frequently to listeners' advantage to insist on knowing not only the names of sources but also their qualifications for making their assertions.

COMPLIANCE STRATEGIES

In 1967, Marwell and Schmitt listed sixteen techniques they believed people use to gain the compliance of others. Those sixteen techniques are listed in Table 7.2.

The proposed taxonomy had more of an impact in communication research than it did in other fields, notably sociology, the discipline in which

TABLE 7.2 Sixteen Compliance-Gaining Strategies

1.	Promise	If you comply, I will reward you.
2.	Threat	If you do not comply I will punish you.
3.	Expertise (Positive)	If you comply you will be rewarded because of "the nature of things."
4.	Expertise (Negative)	If you do not comply you will be punished because of "the nature of things."
5.	Liking	Actor is friendly and helpful to get actor in "good frame of mind" so that he will comply with request.
6.	Pre-Giving	Actor rewards target before requesting compliance.
7.	Aversive Stimulation	Actor continuously punishes target making cessation contingent on compliance.
8.	Debt	You owe me compliance because of past favors.
9.	Moral Appeal	You are immoral if you do not comply.
10.	Self-Feeling (Positive)	You will feel better about yourself if you comply.
11.	Self-Feeling (Negative)	You will feel worse about yourself if you do not comply.
12.	Altercasting (Positive)	A person with "good" qualities would comply.
13.	Altercasting (Negative)	Only a person with bad qualities would not comply.
14.	Altruism	I need your compliance very badly, so do it for me.
15.	Esteem (Positive)	People you value will think better of you if you comply.
16.	Esteem (Negative)	People you value will think worse of you if you do not comply.

Source: Marwell and Schmitt (1967)

Marwell and Schmitt did their research and in which they published. They wrote, quite modestly, in 1990:

> Gradually, the thrust of our collaborative work veered toward the determinants of the initiation and disruption of cooperation rather than compliance gaining. In part, this alteration of emphasis resulted from what we perceived as a luke-warm reception of our compliance-gaining

> work within sociology. . . . Only recently have we become aware of the vigorous work on compliance gaining that has been going on in communication. It is a bit like having a long-lost child reappear with a family in tow. (p. 5)

Indeed there has been *vigorous* work in communication dealing with compliance-gaining. Several dozen studies and analytic papers have been published. But before dealing with that burst of energy, I would like to consider how research in persuasion and compliance-gaining relate to one another.

Obviously, compliance-gaining strategies are a subset of persuasive techniques in general. But how can they be distinguished from other techniques? First, the original list was constructed and illustrated within the context of family communication, and subsequent research seems to have operated on the assumption that compliance-gaining phenomena occur in interpersonal relationships. The *persuasion* research was concerned mostly with public communication designed to affect audiences. Second, the announced purpose of the strategies has always been to gain *behavioral compliance,* not to change the minds of listeners and perhaps, subsequently, to gain their compliance. Threats, promises, and enumeration of consequences both physical and to the listeners' reputations and feelings about themselves have been the primary types of compliance-gaining strategies.

Much of this research consisted of describing scenarios in which one person wanted to gain the compliance of another, and asking subjects either to write out the strategies they would use or to indicate the probabilities they would use each of a number of strategies listed for them. Frequently the research appeared to consist of an army of data marching across an unmapped landscape looking for a theory. In 1976, Gerald Miller and a number of his students at Michigan State at last undertook to search for a distinction between strategies chosen in interpersonal and noninterpersonal situations. That paper was presented at a convention of the International Communication Association in 1976. I was assigned to critique that paper. I complimented them on an early attempt to introduce new variables into the research, but bemoaned the continuing lack of theory. Of course, it is the major function of convention critics to bemoan, so I was just doing my job. That paper was subsequently published in *Communication Monographs* (Miller, et. al., 1977). One of the authors of that paper, Frank Boster, wrote fairly recently:

> . . . [W]ithout some principle(s) to organize the facts, or at least some quantitative literature review to tell us what we do and do not know, areas of study are likely to become fallow. I fear that the study of compliance-gaining message behavior is susceptible to such a fate. The

problems of review have been mentioned previously, and in spite of the development of several theories (Baxter, 1984; Chmielewski, 1982; Smith, 1984), none has been able to integrate the baffling set of empirical findings. (Boster, 1990, p.11)

Boster might have been somewhat encouraged had he been able to read the volume of papers in which his own was eventually published (Dillard, 1990b), and I strongly recommend it to the interested reader. For my part, I hold out hope for advances in this area in three respects.

In 1982, the two authors of this textbook presented a paper at the Speech Communication Association convention titled "The GOALS/GRASP procedure for analyzing taxonomies as an alternative to situational taxonomies in the prediction of strategy selection." In that paper we argued, not surprisingly, that people choose different compliance-gaining strategies in different situations depending on their specific goals in those situations (GOALS) and the characteristics of the situations they perceive to be likely to hinder or help in achieving those GOALS (that is, the GRASP). We also presented data from a study we conducted that seemed to confirm that analysis (see Cronkhite and Liska, 1982). The paper did not have much of an effect, in part, at least, because we did not publish it. We are pleased to report that Dillard, Segrin, and Harden (1989) and Dillard (1990a) have done a much more thorough job of analyzing the ways goals operate to influence the selection of strategies.

The second respect in which I expect compliance-gaining research to advance is the study of *effects*. So far the emphasis has been on how people *choose* compliance-gaining strategies, but we have precious little research regarding how effective the various strategies are.

Finally, I anticipate that researchers will soon turn to the question of the *cognitive* aspects of strategy choice and effects.

So what does all this have to do with you as you try to react critically to compliance-gaining attempts? The clearest implication is that critical listeners will ask for *evidence* and *reasoning* to support the threats, promises, and enumeration of likely consequences of which these strategies consist. Look back at the original list of Marwell and Schmitt. We must ask ourselves what evidence we have that physical promises and threats will really be executed, that the expertise is credible, that the gift given in advance really obligates us to comply, that avoiding aversive stimulation is really worth the price and there is no other way of avoiding it, that we really owe the other enough to justify compliance and, finally, that the damage or enhancement of reputation or self-esteem really justifies compliance.

Another concern at this point has to do with the social acceptability of the strategies. Social acceptability has been a frequent explanation of strategy choice, but to my knowledge there has been no independent published test of the comparative social acceptability of these strategies. In a recent paper read at a convention of the Speech Communication Association (Ng, Liska, and Cronkhite, 1992) and submitted for publication, we reported a study in which we asked a sample of college undergraduates to rate each of one hundred strategies as to their social acceptability. (The complete list appears in the Student Activities and Discussion Topics.) We found some of the most acceptable strategies to be "Be straightforward when I ask for compliance," "Explain why they should comply," "Negotiate something agreeable to both of us," "Tell them how important their compliance is," "Reason with them," and "Argue logically." At the opposite end, quite socially unacceptable are, for example, "Tell them if they don't comply I'll never speak to them again," "Act irritated," "Use the silent treatment," "Tell them if they don't comply I'll never do anything for them again," "Pout or cry until I get my way," "Tell them that only bad people would not comply," "Tell the person that if he/she fails to comply he/she would be punished because bad things happen to uncooperative people," "Tell the person I would punish them if they do not comply," "Use verbal threats," "Tell the person I would hate them," "Punish them until they comply," "Threaten to destroy something they value," "Threaten to harm a third person unrelated to the dispute," "Use physical force," and, of course, "Take hostages," which was considered the most antisocial.

One interesting finding was that most of the sixteen strategies listed by Marwell and Schmitt were considered by our subjects to be either moderately or extremely antisocial. Only *altruism* was considered extremely prosocial, and only *promise* and *expertise* were considered to be even moderately prosocial. The first conclusion? Marwell and Schmitt may have been highly Machiavellian, and communication researchers seem to have loved them for it. The second conclusion? You can recognize Machiavellian friends by their use of the Marwell and Schmitt strategies, and it might be helpful to point that out to them.

CONCLUSION

I have described the network of Entities and Relationships, the types of Relationships and Consequences, and the Plans that, persuaders will try to convince you, will produce desirable consequences and avoid those that are undesirable. All this constitutes the AESOP Model, a model for critical thinking. I have also described a variety of barriers to critical thinking, and some rules for thinking critically, some of which are the avoidance of popular fallacies. Finally, I have described methods public speakers and your friends and acquaintances will sometimes use to influence you, methods that will sometimes be in your best interests and sometimes not. I hope that you, armed with this information, can begin to become a critical consumer of communication.

KEY TERMS AND CONCEPTS

entities (objects, people, ideas, behaviors)
relationships (cause, sign, similarity, inclusion, approval, conditioning)
Plans
Consequences (utility for self, utility for others, self-perception, perception by others, cognitive consistency)
Decisional Balance Sheet
beliefs
claims
AESOP (Affective & Epistemological Schema of Persuasion
Toulmin Model
evidence
warrant
multiple lines of reasoning
support for evidence & warrant
barriers to critical decisions
non-causal reasoning
Elaboration Likelihood Model (peripheral & central routes to persuasion)
personality characteristics as barriers
drama and comedy as barriers
credibility as a barrier
willing suspension of critical analysis
rhetorical depiction
Dumbth
cultural literacy
fallacious because invalid
appeal to authority
provincialism
irrelevant reason
ambiguity
slippery slope
argument ad hominem
two wrongs make a right
tokenism
hasty conclusion
questionable classification
questionable cause
questionable analogy
fallacious even if valid
suppressed evidence
questionable premise
statistical fallacies
early persuasion research
Does organization matter?
introductions
conclusions
Best foot forward?
Problem or solution first?
Attack now or later?
When to cite the source?
compliance-gaining strategies
sixteen Marwell & Schmitt strategies
behavioral compliance
cognitive compliance
theories of compliance strategies
goals and situations in compliance strategies
effects of compliance strategies
strategy acceptability

REFERENCES

Allen, S. (1989). *Dumbth: And 81 Ways to Make Americans Smarter*. Buffalo, New York: Prometheus.

Baxter, L. A. (1984). An investigation of compliance-gaining as politeness. *Human Communication Research,* 10: 427–456.

Boster, F. (1990). In Dillard (1990b), pp. 7–17.

Campbell, D. (1965). Ethnocentric and other altruistic motives. In *Nebraska Symposium on Motivation,* edited by D. Levine, pp. 306–307. Lincoln: University of Nebraska.

Chmielewski, T. L. (1982). A test of a model for predicting strategy selection. *Central States Speech Journal,* 33: 505–518.

Cronkhite, G. (1969). *Persuasion: Speech and Behavioral Change.* Indianapolis, Ind.: Bobbs-Merrill.

———. (1974). Rhetoric, communication, and psychoepistemology. In *Rhetoric: A Tradition in Transition,* edited by W. Fisher. East Lansing: Michigan State University.

———. (1976). *Communication and awareness.* Menlo Park, Calif.: Benjamin-Cummings. See especially Chapter Nine.

Cronkhite, G. and Liska, J. (1982). The GOALS/GRASP procedure for analyzing situations as an alternative to situational taxonomies in the prediction of strategy selection. Speech Communication Association Convention, Louisville, Kentucky (November).

Dillard, J. P. (1990a). A goal-driven model of interpersonal influence. In Dillard (1990b).

——— (1990b). *Seeking Compliance: The Production of Interpersonal Influence Messages.* Scottsdale, Ariz.: Gorsuch Scarisbrick.

Dillard, J. P., Segrin, C., and Harden, J. M. (1989). Primary and secondary goals in the production of interpersonal influence messages. *Communication Monographs,* 56: 19–38.

Hirsch, E. D., Jr. (1987). *Cultural Literacy: What Every American Needs to Know.* New York: Vintage.

———. (1989). *A First Dictionary of Cultural Literacy.* Boston: Houghton Mifflin.

Hirsch, E. D., Jr., Kett, J., and Trefil, J. (1988). *The Dictionary of Cultural Literacy.* Boston: Houghton Mifflin.

Huff, D. (1954). *How to Lie with Statistics.* New York: W. W. Norton.

Janis, I. L. and Mann, L. (1977). *Decision Making: A Psychological Analysis of Conflict, Choice, and Commitment.* New York: Free Press.

Kahane, H. (1988). *Logic and Contemporary Rhetoric: The Use of Reason In Everyday Life,* 5th ed. Belmont, Calif.: Wadsworth.

Marwell, G., and Schmitt, D. (1967). Dimensions of compliance-gaining behavior: An empirical analysis. *Sociometry,* 30: 350–364.

———. (1990). An introduction. In Dillard (1990b), pp. 3–5.

Mehrabian, A. (1967). Attitudes inferred from nonimmediacy of verbal communication. *Journal of Verbal Learning and Verbal Behavior,* 6: 294–295.

Miller, G. R., et. al. (1977). Compliance-gaining message strategies: A typology and some findings concerning effects of situational differences. *Communication Monographs,* 44: 37–51.

Ng, R., Liska, J., and Cronkhite, G. (1992). A social acceptability scale for compliance-gaining strategies and its application to competence research. Speech Communication Association Convention, Chicago, Illinois (October).

Osborn, M. (1986). Rhetorical depiction. In *Form, Genre, and the Study of Political Discourse,* edited by H. W. Simons and A. Aghazarian. Columbia: University of South Carolina Press.

Petty, R. E., and Cacioppo, J. T. (1986a). *Communication and Persuasion: Central and Peripheral Routes to Attitude Change.* New York: Springer-Verlag.

——— (1986b). The elaboration likelihood model of persuasion (1986). In *Advances in Experimental Social Psychology,* Vol. 19, edited by L. Berkowitz, pp. 123–205. San Diego, Calif.: Academic Press.

Postman, N., and Weingartner, C. (1969). *Teaching as a Subversive Activity.* New York: Dell.

Smith, M. J. (1984). Contingency rules, theory, context, and compliance behaviors. *Human Communication Research,* 10: 489–512.

Toulmin, S. (1959). *The Uses of Argument.* Cambridge, England: Cambridge University Press.

Trenholm, S. (1989). *Persuasion and Social Influence.* Englewood Cliffs, N.J.: Prentice-Hall.

——— (1991). *Human Communication Theory,* 2nd ed. Englewood Cliffs, N.J.: Prentice Hall.

Silence is argument carried on by other means.
—*Ernesto "Che" Guevara*

UNIT 3

Ecological Role of Messages

The focus of this section is upon language and nonverbal behavior, the means by which communication is enacted and the very core of the discipline of communication. Humans are linked to one another via a complex system of signs that help shape the way we view our social reality, the network of relationships we depend upon for social support, and the means by which we judge the intentions, emotions, and goodwill, and so forth of others. Beyond providing our understanding of social reality, messages enable us to attain knowledge of our environment, allow us to manipulate it and exert control over it, and provide us with the means for transmitting the substance of our knowledge and experience to those generations yet to come.

Language, a system of symbolic representations, has in part enabled humans to break the shackles of the natural ecology and to negotiate a world constructed of ideas, which resulted in a new ecological dimension—a symbolic dimension. Language is a characteristic that appears to set us apart from the rest of the animal world.

Nonverbal communication is a primary and fundamental system that provides important support for language. It carries a wealth of information about our emotional disposition, social position, and temperament, to name only a few such characteristics. Nonverbal signs may be a truer reflection of our nature than is language, because it more clearly ties us to the roots of our evolutionary past. In many respects, nonverbal communication firmly anchors us to our place in a natural ecology.

To have a mind is to have the capacity to acquire the ability to operate with symbols in such a way that it is one's own activity that makes them symbols and confers meaning upon them.

—*A. J. P. Kenny et al.,
The Development of Mind*

Theories of Language Meaning

CHAPTER OUTLINE

Language Operates by Rules, Norms, and Principles
Language as a Game
Rules
Norms
Principles
Is It a Principle, or Is It a Rule?

Language Is Studied at Four Levels: Phonemic, Syntactic, Semantic, and Pragmatic
Phonemic Rules
Syntactic Rules
The Semantic and Pragmatic Levels

What is the Meaning of *Meaning*?
Referential Theories
Rule-Governed Theories
Behavioral Theories
Ideational and Cognitive Theories

Language is probably our primary ecological tool, the primary means by which we relate to our environments. We make sense of our environments by means of language, in that language maps our environments, physical and social, with varying degrees of accuracy. We communicate those senses of our environments to others by means of language, and we try to change our environments by using language. Without language we would have a faulty understanding of our environments, we would be unable to communicate adequately even those faulty understandings, and we would have to accept our environments as we find them, for the most part.

LANGUAGE OPERATES BY RULES, NORMS, AND PRINCIPLES

Language as a Game

Language is easiest to understand if we think of it as a game. However, this is not because it is trivial or inconsequential. Often, it is quite serious, as when a couple at the altar is pronounced husband and wife, corporations enter into contracts, or nations declare war. In other circumstances it may be humorous, as in the quip "I owe, therefore I am." Most of the time it is somewhere between those two extremes, even mundane, as when we "pass the time of day" or engage in "small talk."

Rules

But serious, humorous, or mundane, language is a game because it operates by rules, norms, and principles, as do all games. In learning poker, you must first learn the **rules:** the order of the cards, from the lowly 2 to the powerful ace; the order of hands, from five unrelated cards to a royal flush; the way in which the cards are shuffled and dealt; and the way in which play proceeds. If you violate the rules, you are not playing the game of poker—some other card game, perhaps, but not poker. If you violate the rules, and it doesn't appear you are aware of the violations, are trying to conceal them from other players, or are using them to your advantage, then the other players will think you are a novice, and will only correct you, not reprimand you.

Likewise, language operates by rules, rules we learn at such an early age we are seldom aware we know them. We learn the sounds (*phonemes*) we will use in our native language, how those sounds can be combined into meaningful units (*morphemes*), and then how those units can be combined into coherent sentences. For the most part I am not referring to the rules we learn in school. If children do not know thousands of these rules before they enter school, they will never learn to use language proficiently.

If speakers violate the rules of language, others will think they do not understand the language, probably because it is not their native language and they have not learned it adequately.

Norms

But back to the poker game: Beyond an understanding of the rules, there are other expectations of the players in the group, which we will call **norms,** and violations of the norms have different consequences than do violations of the rules. If players devise ways of looking at the cards of other players, they will be socially sanctioned, or reprimanded. If they violate rules knowingly, with sly concealment and to their own advantage (by stacking the deck and then dealing to themselves off the bottom, for example), they violate a norm in the act of violating a rule.

The game of language, too, has norms—far more so than does the game of poker. Norms specify that certain words, considered to be obscene, should not be used in certain situations with certain people—in church, and in "polite society," for example. To use language to misrepresent fact—that is, to lie—is to violate a norm, under most circumstances. If you say to your roommate, "Please turn your stereo down, O.K.?" you are abiding by language norms; you are inserting the two *politeness markers,* the words *please* and *O.K.* You might say instead, "Would you mind turning your stereo down?" in which case you are using a *wh-imperative.* In either case, you have observed a politeness norm in order to preserve your relationship with your roommate.

On the basis of language rules alone, you could have achieved the same understanding by saying "Turn your stereo down!" We also know we should not interrupt others unless they signal they are ready to be interrupted, and that is a norm. We know our contribution to a conversation should be relevant to what was just said, unless we have requested permission, perhaps subtly and even nonverbally, to change the subject. That is a norm. All these fall under the heading of social norms in general, though many social norms are language norms.

If speakers violate language norms, they may be openly reprimanded; more often, others will come to believe they are socially incompetent or dishonest, and will avoid their company. The speakers will generally receive some sort of social sanction, direct or indirect.

Principles

Finally, when people learn only the rules and norms of a game, they may give the appearance of knowing how to play but do not really know how to *win.* To win, except by accident, they must learn the **principles.**

One of the basic principles of poker is that players will be more successful if they keep their opponents from knowing whether they have strong or weak hands. When novice players are dealt strong hands they may in their innocence openly rejoice, or at least reveal that fact in their facial expressions or conversation. Other players, knowing they have strong hands, will not bet much, and those strong hands will go for naught.

Over a period of time novice players learn to "keep a poker face." Another principle is "Never draw to an inside straight." In the most common variation of poker, players are first dealt five cards and then, after a round of betting, can discard some of those cards in order to have them replaced. Now, suppose I am dealt a hand with an ace, a king, a queen, a 10, and a 7. If I can only draw a jack by trading in the 7, I will have what is called a "straight," and will be very likely to win the hand. But it is highly unlikely that out of the deck of forty-seven cards unknown to me I will be dealt one of the four jacks that I need to fill my straight. Thus the principle of never drawing to an inside straight.

Notice that these are not rules, for one can jump and shout when dealt a good hand and still be playing the game of poker within the rules—not playing well, but not violating the rules. Neither are these norms, because those who violate such principles of effective play will not only not be sanctioned or reprimanded, they will probably become immensely popular at Saturday night poker parties—until their money runs out.

The principles of the language game also determine how the game can be won or lost. But "winning" is not so easily defined in the language game. Sometimes winning consists of persuading another person to buy a product, vote in a particular way, loan money, or go on a date. At other times, as in this book or in your professor's lectures, winning consists of transmitting information clearly so understanding is achieved. As a listener or reader, you are also a participant in this language game, but the professor is not your opponent. You and your professor will both win if you come to understand the material. Sometimes winning the game consists simply of demonstrating your proficiency in using language by engaging in interesting conversation, and sometimes winning consists of presenting yourself as a likable person. In the language game, winning consists of achieving whatever goals you set for yourself, and the principles of language use are the means by which you achieve those goals.

Thus principles are of the form "If A then B"; "If one does A, then listeners will probably do (or think or feel) B." One principle we think we know, for example, is: "If a speaker uses dominant language, listeners will probably consider that person to be more credible and masculine but less warm and caring." That principle requires some qualification, but it seems to be true in general. Other principles are: "If a speaker uses metaphors, listeners may have more difficulty understanding, but will probably find the speech more pleasant," and "Humorous language can disarm hostile listeners." If you have taken a course in public speaking, your professor undoubtedly told you that in order to achieve listener understanding, it is important to state the major point or thesis and to preview the major divisions at the beginning of a speech, thereby letting listeners know what to anticipate. That is a principle.

Is It a Principle, or Is It a Rule?

Notice these are not rules, because speakers and writers may be producing perfectly coherent sentences whether their language is dominant or submissive, filled with or devoid of metaphors, outrageously humorous or totally serious. Neither are these norms, because neither dominance nor its absence, metaphors nor their absence, humor nor its absence are generally considered immoral, unethical, or socially unacceptable.

But now to complicate the picture a little: Sometimes a principle by which a goal can be most effectively achieved involves violating a norm. There is a general social norm against lying, for example, but it would be highly naive to argue that lying is never an effective way of achieving a goal. Although there is a general social norm in favor of politeness, and Clint Eastwood was not very polite when he said "Go ahead, make my day," many would agree that sort of dominant, aggressive, rude language might be an effective means of discouraging violent behavior if you are large enough and/or heavily armed. This is a situation in which politeness is not called for, because observing the norm would interfere with the principle. "Please go ahead, make my day, O.K.?" or "Why don't you go ahead and make my day?" just wouldn't carry the same force or achieve the same effect.

Are you confused? Join the crowd. Just remember, obeying social norms is generally, but not always, a good principle.

LANGUAGE IS STUDIED AT FOUR LEVELS: PHONEMIC, SYNTACTIC, SEMANTIC, AND PRAGMATIC

Phonemic Rules

When scholars study the sounds that are used in a language, they are studying language at the **phonemic** level. That level is not studied very often in departments of communication. Departments that go by names such as "Speech Science," "Communicative Disorders," and "Speech Pathology," however, are vitally concerned with speech sounds. If there is a speech clinic at your university, those who work in that clinic are trying, among other things, to teach clients who have defective speech to produce speech sounds correctly. If there is a TOEFL or TOESL (Teaching of English as a Foreign/Second Language) program at your university, part of that program consists of teaching those whose native language is not English to produce English phonemes. If you are enrolled in a foreign-language course, part of what you will learn is the correct production of the phonemes of that language, many of which are similar to those of English, but some of which are totally foreign, so to speak.

Phonemes A **phoneme** is the smallest unit of speech sound that has "signifi-cance" in a language. There are about forty-four phonemes in English, give or take half a dozen. The phonemes have some correspondence to the letters of our alphabet. But the correspondence is not perfect, obviously, since we have more phonemes than the twenty-six letters of our alphabet. Other languages have closer correspondence between their phonemes and alphabetic characters. In Danish the correspondence is perfect. Languages such as these are called **alphabetic.** In such languages it is possible to "sound out" words to more or less approximate their pronunciation on the basis of their spelling. English, on the other hand, being somewhat irregular, will frequently fool you.

Chinese has no correspondence between its sound system and its written characters. Each of its thousands of characters has a specific meaning, but offers no clue as to how it is to be pronounced. A Chinese typewriter is a massive affair, and even the largest machines contain only some of the most frequently used characters. A language such as Chinese that has no correspondence between its written and spoken forms is called **logographic** or **pictographic.**

The Japanese have three forms of language, one of which consists of borrowed and modified Chinese characters and is thus logographic, and another of which is alphabetic. But the third form, which has one character for each syllable, is called **syllabic.**

Morphemes Now, the phonemic level of language is governed by rules that specify which of the many sounds the human vocal apparatus can produce are going to be used in a given language—that is, which will be *significant*. So what does it mean to say that a sound is significant in a language? Briefly, it means that that particular sound is responsible for the difference between two **morphemes** in that language. And what is a morpheme? A morpheme is the smallest unit of sound that has meaning in the language.

For example, take the sentence "It's better to be dead than Red." (Obviously that sentence has only historical meaning, since there is no more "Red"—that is, Russian Communism—but bear with us.) *Dead* and *Red* are English morphemes. The only difference between them is the *d* and *r* sounds. Because these two sounds are responsible for distinguishing between two morphemes, they have significance in English, and thus they are English phonemes.

The *r* sound is not a phoneme in Japanese, or at least not by itself, because the *r* and *l* sounds are not distinguished in Japanese speech. When American comedians try to imitate Japanese people speaking English, this is one of the surest ways of creating the stereotype. "Better lead than dead" and "Better Red than dead" are indistinguishable to native Japanese speakers, without a great deal of training. They cannot hear the difference, and they cannot produce the difference. That is not because Japanese speech mechanisms or aural mechanisms are different from those of Americans, it is because the difference is not significant in their language.

But Americans should not be smug. I have seen native Japanese dissolve in laughter over Americans' attempts to repeat Japanese words they have just heard. Inflections carry more meaning in Japanese than in English. It is my understanding that the difference between a common kinship term and an obscenity, for example, is carried solely by an inflection to which American ears are not attuned. And such differences are not limited to Asian languages. Pronunciation of the "umlaut" phoneme in German and Greek is a challenge for American students.

Syntactic Rules

Rules that specify how phonemes can be combined into morphemes really lie on the border between phonemics and syntax. The words of English constitute most of its morphemes. Words are *free* morphemes, because they have meaning standing alone. In contrast, *bound* morphemes must be attached to free morphemes in order to have meaning; they modify or clarify the meanings of free morphemes. The difference between *girl* and *girls* is due to the bound morpheme *s*, which has no meaning standing alone but causes some nouns to become plural and some verbs to become singular (e.g., "he runs" versus "they run"). The *s* morpheme happens to consist of only one phoneme. But other bound morphemes, such as *ing* and *ology* are more complex. Again, native speakers of a language learn an amazing number of these rules at a very early age, without formal training. (An interesting issue of some present social significance having to do with morphemes is this: Is *wo* a free morpheme that has no meaning standing alone but is capable of making the difference between the free morphemes *man* and *woman?* I decline to answer.) The rules for English morphemes frequently are also irregular. The plurals of *boy* and *bat* are simply *boy + s* and *bat + s*, but the plural of *man* is a completely different morpheme, *men*, as are the singular and plural forms of *mouse/mice* and *goose/geese*.

Another type of syntactic rule has to do with the formation of sentences. You know far more such rules than you know you know. You may hear a sentence and know there is something wrong with it, but not know exactly what the problem is. That is, you know how to apply rules in many cases in which you cannot state the rule. For instance, one rule of English is that a sentence must have a verb, either a verb of action (e.g., "The boy runs") or a verb of being (e.g., "The boy is calm"). Collections of words that do not have verbs are not complete sentences, unless the verb is "understood" from previous sentences, as, for example, "Not very fast, though." Even then, linguists have generally adopted the term *utterance* to replace *sentence*, to recognize the fact that we do not always—perhaps not even usually—speak in complete sentences.

But native speakers of English are generally able to apply the rules for constructing and recognizing sentences, even though they may not be able to state them. If they do not have those abilities, they are deficient in their knowledge of the language.

Note that these are not the rules of "correct" and "polite" grammar that you learned in the sixth grade—rules such as "It ain't correct to use ain't" and "A preposition is something you shouldn't end a sentence with." As you can see, we can violate such rules and still create sentences that listeners understand. But if we violate the rules of English syntax, the jumble of words that results will be incoherent and incomprehensible. "The green rug on the floor was lying" is a sentence that violates a rule of English most native speakers know at a tacit level, but one that causes problems for nonnative speakers and, when violated, produces incoherent sentences.

The Semantic and Pragmatic Levels

Both the **semantic** and the **pragmatic** levels of language are levels of "meaning" in a sense. Elsewhere I have said we should probably reserve the term *semantics* for meaning determined by rules, and the term *pragmatics* for meaning created by norms and principles. But for our purposes here, *semantic meaning* will refer to the basic *comprehension* of words and sentences, whereas *pragmatic meaning* will refer to the psychological and social *effects* of language.

Since semantic meaning and pragmatic meaning are indispensable aspects of communication, and since they are taught in departments of communication, I am going to explain them in greater detail than I did phonemics and syntax.

WHAT IS THE MEANING OF *MEANING?*

To illustrate the difference between syntax and semantics, Chomsky (1957) used the sentence "Colorless green ideas sleep furiously." His point was that not only does the sentence have syntax, but its syntax its quite acceptable to native speakers of English. The reason it is impossible to comprehend is not that its syntax is defective; the problem is with its semantics. It has some internal contradictions, such as its description of ideas that are both colorless and green, and it has some references that, given the semantic rules of English, are impossible: Ideas cannot be either colorless or green, and certainly cannot sleep, either furiously or calmly. References that are semantically impossible are termed *semantic anomalies.* They may also be said to be logically impos-sible, because semantics is the logic of language. I should mention, by the way, that some students of mine have undertaken—with some success, I must admit—to create scenarios in which "Colorless green ideas sleep furiously" is acceptable, if some of it is taken to be metaphorical. All metaphors are semantic anomalies, in that they violate semantic rules, though they do so for poetic and pragmatic purposes. But not all semantic anomalies are metaphors. Most of them are just mistakes.

There are many theories designed to answer the question "What is the meaning of *meaning?*" Some of them will be familiar to you. The arguments among their advocates have frequently been vicious, and usually the advocates of one theory deny that the others have any merit. But if we had a can of miraculous "Egotrim" with which we could spray these "true believers" and bring them to their senses, they too would recognize that each theory has something to contribute to our knowledge of how people understand words and sentences.

Referential Theories

Referential theories recognize most explicitly the relation between our environments and language meaning, between words and things. Referential theories are those that identify the meaning of a word as consisting of that to which it refers (or, in more sophisticated versions, of the relationship between the word and that to which it refers). The thing to which the word refers is termed its *referent*. The chief advocate of this theory is generally considered to be I. A. Richards (Ogden and Richards, 1923). In a referential theory, the meaning of the word *book*, for example, is the object you are presently reading, and the meaning of the word *reading* is what you are presently doing. A word has the function of pointing to its referent, and its meaning resides in that referent. Notice that the relation between the word and its referent is governed by language rules. Other students would think you strange if you called your professor a *book*, unless, again, you were speaking metaphorically.

Ogden and Richards' Triangle of Meaning Ogden and Richards diagrammed the relation between a symbol and its referent in his famous triangle of meaning, without which no discussion of meaning would be complete. Later versions of this diagram have sometimes replaced the word *reference* with *thought*, but it is not entirely clear that Ogden and Richards would have approved. (See Figure 8.1.) One of the most important elements of the diagram is the dashed line between the symbol and the referent. It is intended to emphasize that this is not a *direct* connection. There is no direct connection between the symbol and the referent, between the word and the thing. The connection is established only *through* the reference. As we first said in Chapter 1, it is this lack of any direct, natural connection that makes some signs symbols instead of symptoms or semblances.

It is hard to deny the truth that lies in this theory. Most of us learned our first words by its application, because most parents teach infants this way. They point to the female parent and say, "Mommy," and to the male parent and say, "Daddy," and, not surprisingly, these are probably the most frequent first words learned by infants. The correct application takes a little longer, and is probably learned by reinforcement, but more of this later. In the meantime, there will be trials and errors in which they call Daddy "Mommy," and embarrassing instances when they identify strange men on the street as "Daddy."

FIGURE 8.1
Ogden and Richards' triangle of meaning

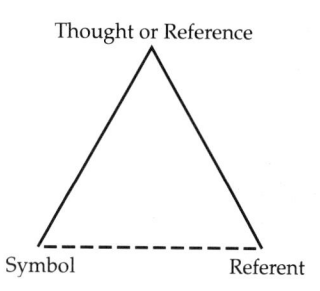

I was born and spent the first two years of my life in my grandmother's house about fifty yards from the main line of the Santa Fe Railroad where it runs along the shore of the Mississippi River in western Illinois. It would not surprise an advocate of the referential theory that my parents report my first word was *train*. Whether it was the sound or the appearance of the train that constituted the referent is not clear, but a sound can be a referent.

What Referential Theories Miss However, though referential theories undoubtedly explain part of meaning, there are other aspects for which they cannot account. First, words such as *if, then,* and *because* have no apparent referents. Second, abstract words such as *eternity, good,* and *intention* have no physical referents. Third, most referents serve as referents for different words, and usually those words have different meanings. *Used car, preowned auto,* and *experienced vehicle* may have the same referent, but they do not seem to have the same meaning.

Fourth, and most damaging to this type of theory, is the fact that a given word can refer to many objects. The book you are reading is not the only referent for that word. You may have others in your bookbag, other students have similar objects, you have others at home, and the library is full of them. Even more of a problem is the fact that the word *book* can refer to objects you have never seen, objects that existed in the past but have been destroyed, objects that have not yet been written or printed, and objects that may never exist because the authors who have listed them in their resumes as "in progress" may never get around to writing them. In fact, as I write this and refer to "the book you are reading" I am assuming that we, the authors, will finish this book, Harcourt will publish it, your professor will adopt it for your class, and you will buy it. Of course, if any of those do not come to pass, you will not be reading this explanation anyway.

What, then, is the referent for the word *book*? No conceivable present, past, future, imaginary, or anticipated object, apparently. And if referential theories cannot account for the meanings of concrete nouns, which seem to be the most obvious referents, those theories are rather severely handicapped.

In my classes, some student will almost always respond by saying "The referent isn't any physical object; the referent is an idea." And that may well be true. But that is a different type of theory, the ideational, not the referential, and we will consider those shortly. In the meantime, suppose we consider another type of theory that, like the referential, has some obvious, but limited, application.

Rule-Governed Theories

Rule-governed theories generally hold that there are certain conditions under which a word or utterance can be properly used, and these conditions are specified by "rules" understood by native speakers of a language. Many of these rules are written, but some are not. The "conditions" generally exist in our physical or social environments, but not always. Sometimes they are imaginary conditions that exist in imaginary environments, in speculation about what was or what could be in the future.

Consider an illustration. Imagine that your professor says, "Please open the door." (Disregard the word *please* for now; it is not relevant to the illustration.) There are certain environmental conditions that must be satisfied in order for this utterance to be used properly.

1. There must be a door. Of course, it would be a strange context in which this would not be the case.
2. There must be a single door, or the door intended must be indicated nonverbally or be clear from the context.
3. The door must be closed. (This is surely obvious to you, but that is because you understand the rules of English so well.)
4. There must be another person in hearing distance who is capable of hearing and understanding the request.
5. It must be possible to open the door. If you were in prison and your cellmates made this request, you would take it as an attempt at humor or conclude they had gone stir-crazy. If the person to whom the request is addressed were seriously physically handicapped, the request would not be appropriate.
6. The people who make such requests must want the door open.
7. There must not be a person already in the act of opening the door.

Thus the utterance *open the door* means (1) there is a door, (2) it is clear what door is intended, (3) the door is closed, (4) there is another person present who is capable of understanding the request, (5) it is possible for the other person to open the door, (6) the speaker wants the door open, and (7) the hearer would not open the door if the request were not made. If any of these environmental conditions does not hold, the speaker must not understand the language, must not understand the conditions, or must be speaking figuratively or humorously.

Rules About When an Utterance Is Appropriate This theory, the "rule-use" theory, and the example come from Alston (1964). These specific conditions are not applicable to every utterance, of course. But there are environmental conditions that must hold for any utterance to be appropriate. Native speakers of a language understand those conditions, and to learn a language is to come to understand the conditions. If someone were to say to you right now, "Please write your score on the final exam in this course," you would recognize at once that that utterance is not appropriate because there is a condition that is not satisfied, namely, that you do not yet know what your final exam score will be. You immediately recognize the utterance as inappropriate because you understand English and how it relates to the environment. You understand the ecology of English.

Rules About When a Word Is Appropriate There are also rules for the use of individual words. Katz and Fodor (1963) use the example of the word *bachelor*. We have to exempt two unusual senses of the word, the sense in which it is applied to a male seal without a mate in the breeding season, and the sense in which it is applied to a young knight in the service of an older knight. Except in those senses, we know that a *bachelor* (1) is an object, (2) is living, (3) is human, (4) is male, (5) has gone through puberty, and (6) is not married. We know that because we understand English. If we hear someone refer to *a bachelor dog, a bachelor woman, a six-year-old bachelor,* or *a happily married bachelor,* we know the person doesn't understand the meaning of the word *bachelor* or is speaking metaphorically. Yes, *bachelor woman* is gaining acceptance, but that is because the rules are changing, not because there is anything wrong with the theory. It is also because the English language historically has had no term for an unmarried woman that is equivalent to *bachelor* in its connotative as well as its denotative meaning. *Spinster, old maid,* and *bachelorette* all have negative connotations of one sort or another. (We will be dealing with issues involving language *connotation* and *effects* in the next chapter.) Because language is closely related to the environment, it changes in response to changes in social (and physical) conditions, and this is one example of a linguistic rule that is changing.

Rules About Speech Acts A third type of rule by which we comprehend language meaning is the sort Austin (1962) and Searle (1976) have described in their theories of the *speech act.* Austin first pointed out that some utterances produce changes *in the act of being uttered,* actually changing conditions in the physical world. For example, "I now pronounce you husband and wife," if uttered by a minister or justice of the peace in accordance with the laws of the state in which it is uttered, accomplishes its purpose as soon as it is uttered, regardless of whether it is comprehended or appreciated by the wedding guests. Certainly it is not necessary for them to be informed or persuaded. The utterance need have no effect on the listeners at all. The couple *is* married once the words are uttered. Other examples are "You're fired" and "I bet you $100 the Broncos will win the game tomorrow." If the first words are uttered by someone authorized to hire and fire, the employee will not show up for work the next day, and will not be paid if he or she does.

Illocutionary Force vs. Perlocutionary Effects Austin goes on to distinguish between two types of speech acts, which he calls *illocutionary* and *perlocutionary.* Illocutionary acts are completed in the act of being uttered, while perlocutionary acts must be evaluated by their effects on others. If you *argue* that the university ought to keep the library open later, that argument is complete as soon as you finish speaking. To argue is to perform an illocutionary act. But if you were to claim you had *persuaded,* that would require that someone *be* persuaded. To persuade is a perlocutionary act, and it is not completed until it achieves an effect. One can lie without successfully misleading anyone, but to deceive requires that someone be deceived.

I would rather refer to **illocutionary force** and **perlocutionary effects,** because a single speech act has both and can be evaluated in terms of both. We can ask whether a speaker has argued in a given message, answer that question, and then ask whether they have persuaded, and the two questions are separable.

Types of Illocutionary Acts Searle (1976) has considerably extended Austin's discussion of illocutionary force, but not his discussion of perlocutionary effects. (I am going to discuss perlocutionary effects in the next chapter.) The part of Searle's discussion that seems most useful here is the description of the types of illocutionary acts (or illocutionary forces). He describes five types: assertives, directives, commissives, expressives, and declarations. Native speakers of any language, and also those who have adequately learned a second language, are capable of recognizing an utterance as creating one of these five types of illocutionary force, and this recognition is a part of understanding the utterance.

A native speaker of English can recognize the utterance "The sky is blue today" as an *assertive.* (I do not mean native speakers can supply the *word* "assertive"; I mean only that they recognize that assertion is the force of the utterance. Like most rules of language, these are understood at a low level of awareness.) The sentence "Please open the door," just discussed at length, is a *directive* to a listener to perform a given behavior, and to be understood it must be recognized as such. The listener may refuse, but the directive has been issued nevertheless. The sentence "I promise to meet you at Nick's at 3:30" will be recognized as a *commissive;* it commits the speaker to a given act. The word *promise* is not necessary to the commitment, by the way. "I believe our government is just too big," is an *expressive;* it expresses an internal state (belief) of the speaker. To understand the utterance, a listener must recognize it as an expressive. Finally, "I quit" is a *declaration,* and it creates a state of affairs in the world, a state of unemployment in this case, unless it is later rescinded and the employer allows the employee to change his or her mind.

A person who speaks and understands a language adequately must understand these three types of rules, rules regarding the conditions under which an utterance is appropriate, rules regarding the conditions under which a single word is appropriate, and rules that specify how types of illocutionary acts can be recognized. In every case the rules specify how the language is understood to relate to the physical, social, or psychological environment in which it occurs, and are thus ecological rules.

Behavioral Theories

If it were possible, I would devote this chapter strictly to the comprehension of language, and the next chapter to language effects. Unfortunately, some of the theories deal with both comprehension and effects. That is true of behavioral theories, for example, because such theories shed some light on how one learns to comprehend and produce language, but they also provide an explanation of how language comes to produce affective or emotional effects.

B. F. Skinner, while not the founder of behaviorism, was probably its best-known advocate. Skinner (1957) explains how behaviorism can be applied to language. To understood how *meaning* might be explained by behaviorists, we must grasp the first law of behaviorism: As behavioral scientists, we cannot consider or discuss anything internal to the individual. We can only consider inputs (stimuli), outputs (responses), and events that depend on the responses (reinforcement).

Then what place does *meaning* have in a behavioral theory of language? The easiest and most obvious answer is "no place." *Meaning* as discussed by most theorists, and certainly by the ideational theorists to follow, is internal to the individual, and thus is off-limits for a behaviorist. We have already discussed behaviorism in Chapter 5 dealing with opinions, attitudes, and beliefs, so what we need to do now is to see if we can find anything in the approach that can help us understand meaning.

In fact, there is a sense in which responses to words constitute their "meanings." As a child, I am sure, I produced orienting responses to the word *train*. That is, I am sure I moved my head in the direction from which the sound had previously originated. When I was able to walk, if an adult said *train* before I noticed the sound, I expect I ran to a window on that side of the house so I could watch it go by. As adults, we have responses to words that can only be explained by conditioning. The initials *IRS* and the words *registration, tuition,* and *Guaranteed Student Loan Financial Statement Evaluation* produce negative verbal and nonverbal responses in many of us, even though the literal, denotative meanings of those terms are not negative. We have been conditioned by prior experiences to respond negatively, to attach negative connotations to the terms. Many have been conditioned to respond favorably to the siren, flashing lights, and clatter of coins that accompany hitting a jackpot at a slot machine, and it is not much of a leap from that to the response to the statement on the official-looking envelope that proclaims, "You may already be a winner." The word *winner* carries favorable connotations, conditioned responses beyond its mere denotative dictionary definition.

But one cannot always determine the "meaning" of an utterance by observing listeners' responses to it. If so, the meaning of your father's admonition to you when you were in high school "Be in by midnight tonight, you hear?" might be thought to have meant "Turn off the car engine and coast the last block to the house, and come sneaking in quietly in your stocking feet at 2:00 A.M.," if we were to judge by the response it produced. Most of us would agree, I am sure, that responses do not always constitute the meanings of the words that stimulated them. Yet we must also agree that responses are a part of, and perhaps a type of, meaning.

Ideational and Cognitive Theories

These theories also relate not only to how language meaning is comprehended, but also to how it comes to have connotations and produce emotional responses.

We have already mentioned the possibility that the meaning of a word, phrase, or sentence may lie in the idea or internal response it produces in the mind of a listener, or in the idea or internal response in the mind of the speaker that causes it to be produced. The 17th century British philosopher/psychologist John Locke produced an early formal statement of this theory. His friend George Berkeley disagreed with him, as friends are allowed to do, arguing instead that words produce and are produced by *images*, not *ideas*, in the mind. I think they were both right, to some extent and at different times.

Example: Shakespeare Suppose we take the well-known speech by Portia in Shakespeare's *Merchant of Venice* for an example. It begins with the line "The quality of mercy is not strained." Now I must confess there are no images flitting through my mind as I ponder that line. However, it does elicit an *idea*, and one I can paraphrase in other words. Neither does the next line, "It is twice blessed," produce an image. But consider the third line: "It droppeth as the gentle rain from heaven." That line does produce an image in my mind, and that immediate image must then be translated more slowly into an idea.

Example: Song Lyrics The lyrics of songs, as well as other poetry, also produce images before they produce ideas. Leonard Cohen wrote "Suzanne," the song that became the Battle Hymn of the 60s Generation, for example. Part of it goes: "And Jesus was a sailor when he walked upon the water, and he spent a long time looking from his lonely wooden tower." Bob Dylan produced similar images in every song he wrote, from his early "Blowing in the Wind" to the later and less metaphorical "Lay, Lady, Lay (Across My Big Brass Bed)." In the present generation, the images of lyrics tend to be made more explicit by the videos that so frequently accompany them, so that the simple lyrics of Michael Jackson's "Man in the Mirror" and Billy Joel's "We Didn't Light the Fire" cannot really be separated from the historical scenes of social injustice and crisis that accompanied them in their respective videos.

Two modern theorists, Begg and Paivio (1969), have argued that we engage in two processes (or phases) as we try to understand language. First, we try to *image* an utterance. That phase occurs very quickly. If it fails because the language is not imageable, we proceed to the slower, second phase, in which we attempt to derive a **proposition** or idea from the utterance. The utterance is then stored, or remembered, as an image or an idea. That explanation seems quite reasonable, and has received some experimental support.

Propositions   The term **proposition** is difficult. How do the propositions we extract and remember differ from the utterances from which they are extracted? That issue still occupies cognitive scientists and computer wizards involved in the study of *artificial intelligence*. We know they are not the same, because people seldom report the exact words of a sentence or passage they have heard or read. Instead, they report the ideas or propositions "in their own words." They paraphrase. Much of cognitive science and the study of artificial intelligence is occupied with the attempt to determine just how these "ideas," "propositions," or "meanings" are extracted and stored.

The concept of *proposition* has been explored at some length by contemporary cognitive psychologists; they have been given various sorts of quasi-algebraic representations. If you are interested in those systems, you might consult the description in Cronkhite (1984, pp. 146–170). But the most concise and useful thing we seem to be able to distill from this research is that listeners do not store propositions merely in the verbatim forms in which they are heard. Rather, they store them as items of information that relate to other information drawn from long-term memory, and recall them in ways that are consistent with their beliefs and opinions.

Presupposition, Topic, Focus, and Inference   Some theorists describe propositions in terms of their **presuppositions, topics,** and **focuses** (e.g., Lakoff, 1971), and they sometimes add **inferences**. Consider an example. The sentence "The University of Nevada at Las Vegas seems to have lost some of its luster as a basketball power since Tarkanian left the coaching position." There are numerous presuppositions here: that UNLV was once a basketball power, that Tarkanian was once a coach there, and that he has left that position. But the sentence seems to assume none of this is news, because it is expressed as presuppositions. The topic—what the sentence is about—is the present status of the UNLV basketball team. And the focus—the "news," as it were—is that the UNLV team is no longer as good as it once was. Moreover, those who follow college basketball may make some inferences from the sentence that go well beyond the information it contains. They might conclude it would no longer be a good idea to bet on UNLV to win the national title, that high school basketball stars might be well advised to enroll at some other university. Or, if they believe that UNLV has in fact had an excellent basketball season since Tarkanian left, they might conclude the speaker doesn't know much about college basketball.

Frequently, listeners will misremember the original utterance, adding elements to it or deleting from it. Certainly they do not store an utterance word-for-word as they heard it. Such a construction assumes that the listeners are already aware of the presuppositions and will not question them. That is the essence of name-dropping. If I were to say, "When I was talking to Jay Leno last night, he said Madonna will never be a guest on his show," the focus is Jay's opinion of Madonna, and that is what the sentence construction offers for listeners' information and, perhaps, for them to question. But in fact, the really new information may be contained in what is presented as a presupposition: that I know Jay personally, which is not true.

Procedures Some scholars in the field of artificial intelligence and cognitive science, because they are interested in devising computer programs capable of mimicking human cognitive activity, have abandoned the attempt to describe the comprehension of sentence meaning in terms of propositions and have turned instead to *procedures*. A computer program can be thought of as a series of instructions or procedures for the computer to follow. The idea here is that a sentence contains instructions to listeners as to procedures they should follow.

Consider this question as an example: "Did Rhonda drive herself to the party?" This question instructs listeners to identify someone named Rhonda, to identify from the context the party in question, to search episodic memory to determine whether Rhonda arrived at the party in the company of someone else, and to determine, if possible, if she arrived in her own car. The listeners are then instructed to plan and then verbalize responses on the basis of their cognitive searches. The responses will probably be "yes," "no," or "I don't know," although they may be more elaborated with explanations and hedges if, for example, the questioner is Rhonda's steady boyfriend and the person with whom she arrived is a competitor for her affections, as we say.

It is easy to see why theorists trying to simulate human language behavior by means of computer programs would turn to procedures rather than propositions. But we need not choose. A computer uses two types of files, those that store data and those that contain programs. Think of what you do when you use a computer word-processing program, perhaps *Word-Perfect*. First you load the word-processing program, which instructs the computer regarding the procedures it is to follow in dealing with the data. Then you call a data file, which in the case of word-processing contains words and sentences. *WordPerfect* knows what to do with words and sentences if you enter commands that activate its procedures. By such commands you can add, delete, and move material in the data file by means of the program. To make this analogous to what humans do, just think of the word-processing program as containing the procedures, and the data file as containing the propositions. What is left is the most difficult: Computer programs only store the propositions verbatim, they will not store them as ideas, and they will not make semantic connections among the stored ideas. Only the human operator can do that.

Associations and Internal Mediating Responses Other theorists, who also believe meaning exists in people's minds, have focused on **associations** and **internal mediating responses.** Of course, our associations are part of the meaning of individual words. But I have found, by looking at lists of word associations in formal studies and by trying it among my own students, that associations do not seem to relate directly to what we think of as word meaning. The most common association students produce to *boy,* for example, is *girl,* to *doctor* is *nurse,* to *love* is *hate,* to *war* is *peace,* and on and on. Some associations make better sense, as *saw* to *hammer,* for example. But in general, associations would not help a foreigner learn the meanings of English words. The associations seem to be words drawn from what is sometimes called the same *semantic domain* as the stimulus word. Again, that sheds some light on word meaning, but is certainly not all of it.

Charles Osgood (1963) said it is an *internal mediating response* that constitutes meaning. He believed when two words are presented about the same time in the same context—perhaps in the same sentence—some of the meaning of the known word transfers to the unknown word. When the previously unknown word is paired with a number of known words, the partial meanings of the known words form an internal mediating response that forms the meaning of the new word.

Example: The Term AIDS Perhaps you can remember when the initials AIDS were either meaningless to you, or were just a misspelling of a popular diet candy, AYDS. But in the early 1980s most of us began to form internal mediating responses to those initials as known words were paired with them. The earliest pairing was probably with homosexuality, and then with certain, if slow, death. The words for which the initials stand, "Aquired Immune-Deficiency Syndrome," became part of the internal mediating response as we came to understand this disease does not itself produce death but, rather, makes us susceptible to diseases that are deadly. Next, drug use, blood transfusions, and heterosexual sex became paired with AIDS, and this developing internal mediating response began to include a worsening sense of personal horror. Then the use of the word *condom* became acceptable, as well as the use of condoms themselves, as the failure to use them became associated with the disease and its horror. Think what a rich—though negative—internal mediating response we have all formed to this set of previously meaningless initials.

CONCLUSION

I have tried in this chapter to explain the meaning of *meaning*. That task is impossible, not because there are no answers, but because there are too many. However, we hope we have made you more sophisticated in this area, in that when you hear someone ask, "What does that mean?" you will know it is a very complicated question.

I have pointed out that language is a game, so understanding meaning is in part to understand the rules, norms, and principles by which it operates. I have noted that language is studied at four levels—phonemic, syntactic, semantic, and pragmatic—and that the issue of meaning is encountered at the semantic and pragmatic levels. This chapter has dealt with semantic, or denotative, meaning. The next chapter will consider language effects, which has sometimes been termed *pragmatic* meaning and which includes connotative meaning.

I have briefly considered the possibilities that the referent of a word constitutes its meaning, that the rules for sentence and word use constitute their meaning, that the response to a word or utterance is its meaning, and that ideas in the minds of speakers and/or listeners constitute meaning. I have focused on the question of what constitutes these ideas: whether they are propositions or images, and how—if they are propositions—they can be described. I have suggested that the meanings of sentences may consist not only of abstract propositions, but also of specific instructions regarding the procedures by which those sentences are to be processed. Finally, I have described theories that consider meaning to consist of associations and internal mediating responses.

You should note that I have not argued that any of these theories are wrong. Each one taken alone seems to be inadequate, but each one contributes something to our overall understanding of the concept of *meaning*. If you want to learn more of the details of these theories, we recommend Cronkhite (1984, pp. 112–170).

KEY TERMS AND CONCEPTS

language as a game норms phonemic
rules principles phonemes

alphabetic	referential theories	proposition
logographic	rule-governed theories	presupposition
(pictographic)	illocutionary forces	topic
morphemes	perlocutionary effects	focus
syllabic	types of	inference
syntactic	illocutionary acts	associations
semantic	ideational and cognitive	internal mediat-
pragmatic	theories	ing response

REFERENCES

Alston, W. P. (1964). *Philosophy of Language.* Englewood Cliffs, N.J.: Prentice-Hall.

Austin, J. L. (1962). *How to Do Things with Words.* London: Oxford University Press.

Begg, I., and Paivio, I. U. (1969). Concreteness and imagery in sentence meaning. *Journal of Verbal Learning and Verbal Behavior* 8: 821–827.

Berkeley, G. (1952). *The Principles of Human Knowledge, 1710.* In *Great Books of the Western World,* Vol. 35: 405–444. Chicago: Encyclopaedia Britannica.

Chomsky, N. (1957). *Syntactic Structures.* The Hague, Netherlands: Mouton.

Cronkhite, G. (1984). Perception and meaning. In *Handbook of Rhetorical and Communication Theory,* edited by C. Arnold and J. Bowers, pp. 51–229. Boston: Allyn & Bacon.

——— (1990). Psychosemiotics. In *The Semiotic Web, 1989,* edited by T. Sebeok and J. Umiker-Sebeok. Berlin: Mouton deGruyter.

Katz, J. J., and Fodor, J. A. (1963). The structure of a semantic theory. *Language* 69: 170–210.

Lakoff, G. (1971). Presupposition and relative grammaticality. In *Semantics: An Interdisciplinary Reader in Philosophy, Linquistics, and Psychology,* edited by D. D. Steinberg and Jakobivits, L. A.

Locke, J. (1690). *Essay Concerning Human Understanding,* Book III. London.

Ogden, C. K., and Richards, I. A. (1923).*The Meaning of Meaning.* London: Kegan Paul, Trench, Trubner.

Osgood, C. E. (1963). On understanding and creating sentences. *American Psychologist* 18: 735–751.

Searle, J. (1976). A classification of illocutionary acts. *Language in Society* 5: 1–23.

Skinner, B. F. (1957). *Verbal Behavior.* New York: Appleton-Century-Crofts.

Sticks and stones can break my bones, but words can do permanent damage.
 —*"Barry Champlain" Talk Radio*

Research on Language Effects

9

CHAPTER OUTLINE

How Do Doublespeak, Semantic Redeployment, and Euphemisms Pollute Our Language?
  Doublespeak
  Semantic Redeployment
  Euphemisms

Sexism and Other Types of Linguistic Discrimination
  Generic Pronoun He
  The Word Man
  "Oh, Stewardess—May I Have Another Cup of Coffee?"
  Other Examples
  Six Types of Linguistic Bias

Dominant Language Is Not Just for Men Anymore, Is It?
  Women's Language
  "Eat the Floor, Dogbreath"
  Research Evidence on Women's Language

You Talk Funny; You Must Think Funny
  Dialects
  Effect of Dialect

How Can Language Regulation Be Political Repression?
  English as Official Language
  The Case of Quebec
  English in Africa

How Does Language Affect Perception and Thought?
  Lingusitic Relativity
  General Semantics

What Makes Language Pleasing, Intense, or Obscene?
  Figurative Language
  Metaphors
  Language That Pleases
  Language Intensity
  Obscenity

When we ask how language affects us, the immediate thought is: How do others affect us by the language they use? In fact, I will deal with that question, but what I will cover in this chapter is broader than that. It is not just the language others use to inform or persuade that affects us. The language we ourselves use, the languages we learn, and the languages of our societies and cultures all have subtle effects of which we need to be aware.

HOW DO DOUBLESPEAK, SEMANTIC REDEPLOYMENT, AND EUPHEMISMS POLLUTE OUR LANGUAGE?

Doublespeak

On October 23, 1983, a terrorist drove a Mercedes truck loaded with explosives into the headquarters building of the U.S. Marine barracks at the Beirut, Lebanon, airport and detonated it, killing himself and 216 Marines.

Ronald Reagan was president at the time. He was caught in a dilemma. It seemed obvious it would be wise to remove our troops from Lebanon since we could not defend them adequately against determined suicidal terrorists. But Reagan had vowed we would never "retreat" from Lebanon. He solved his problem by a simple, if obvious, act of **Doublespeak.** Early the following February he announced we were "redeploying" our troops to ships offshore.

Redeployment does not carry the negative connotations of *retreat*. It suggests a strategic move on a battlefield. Use of the term allowed Reagan to maintain the illusion that our troops had not retreated. Reagan had not even engaged in military planners' older Doublespeak, "strategic withdrawal."

Notice, this is an instance of the violation of the semantic rules discussed in the previous chapter. *Retreat* denotes the movement of troops in response to force or the threat of force, a movement that removes them from the danger of defeat or extreme losses. *Redeployment* denotes only a strategic move, usually for the purpose of putting the enemy in a less desirable position. One might *surround* an enemy, for example, by redeploying troops.

Semantic Redeployment

In fact, Doublespeak is exactly that: a violation of semantic rules for persuasive (political, public relations, rhetorical) purposes. It is, in a sense, a strategic redeployment of words. It is **Semantic Redeployment.**

This strategy was not new to Reagan. Back in his acting days he had hosted a television series titled "Death Valley Days," in which the Colt .45 revolver was referred to as the "Peacemaker." It was not much of a semantic leap for him to name the MX Missile the "Peacekeeper," which he did as president. For weapons of personal and mass destruction to be designated tools of "peace" is a far cry from the semantic rules governing the appropriate use of that word.

It is not surprising that war has spawned so many instances of Doublespeak, because war, which is inevitably ugly, would be less likely to be supported by the people of the warring nations if that ugliness were not camouflaged by deliberate misuse of language. There was never a Korean *War*, for example; Truman insisted on referring to it as a "police action." In the era of the Vietnam War, enemy agents were "neutralized," villages were "pacified," and our own soldiers were killed by our own "friendly fire."

There was never actual loss of life, if the government could prevent it. There were "body counts," which seemed to serve more as scores than as tallies of living human beings who would never return to the mothers, fathers, children, and wives who loved them. The actual bodies were hidden by Semantic Redeployment just as effectively as they were by the body bags used to remove them from the fields and jungles where they had fallen, concealing their ugliness from the prying eyes of the television cameras.

After Kuwait was seized by the Iraqis in 1990, U.S. citizens held by Sadat were described as "detainees" or even "guests" until President Bush finally insisted on calling them "hostages." When the war broke out, Iraqi civilians killed and nonmilitary buildings destroyed in the bombing constituted "collateral damage."

Other examples of the violation of semantic rules have originated outside the context of war. A few years ago public lands in the Southwest were overrun by an infestation of wild burros. The Bureau of Land Management, the federal agency charged with controlling this overpopulation, described the shooting of the burros as the "direct reduction" method.

But it is not only killing and other forms of violence that are warped by Doublespeak. In any highly controversial issue, Semantic Redeployment is bound to be used as a persuasive tool. Abortion is probably the most controversial issue presently on the public agenda. The terms *fetal tissue* and *unborn baby* have the same referent, but are used by those on opposite sides of the issue. Whether or not you agree, the slogan "Abortion is Murder" is a clear attempt at Semantic Redeployment.

I could go on and on, but will spare you. If you are interested in further examples, the Committee on Public Doublespeak of the National Council of Teachers of English publishes the *Quarterly Review of Doublespeak*. Many examples from this publication and other sources have been gathered by William Lutz and published in his 1989 book, *Doublespeak*. His chapter titles will give you an idea of its flavor:

I. Involuntary Conversions, Preemptive Counterattacks, and Incomplete Successes: The World of Doublespeak

II. Therapeutic Misadventures, the Economically Nonaffluent, and Deep-Chilled Chickens: The Doublespeak of Everyday Living

III. Virgin Vinyl, Real Counterfeit Diamonds, and Genuine Imitation Leather: With These Words I Can Sell You Anything

IV. Negative Deficits and the Elimination of Redundancies in the Human Resources Area: Business Communication, Sort Of

V. Protein Spills, Vehicle Appearance Specialists, and Earth Engaging Equipment: Doublespeak Around the World

VI. Predawn Vertical Insertions and Hexiform Rotatable Surface Compression Units: The Pentagon Word Machine Grinds On

VII. Nothing in Life Is Certain Except Negative Patient Care Outcome and Revenue Enhancement: Your Government at Work

VIII. Winnable Nuclear Wars and Energetic Disassemblies: Nuclear Doublespeak

The harms of this strategy are at least two: It pollutes the language with words that do not mean what they seem to mean, and it short-circuits rational deliberation. Words enter the language in disguise, as it were, and become undercover operatives concealing ideologies that should be discussed openly before they are accepted or rejected. Doublespeak is the implacable enemy of the ecology of ideas. It pollutes our language, and through our language, our ideas.

Euphemisms

Not all violations of semantic rules are instances of Doublespeak. Many are **euphemisms,** violations of semantic rules so as to conform to social norms. The semantic domains of sex and death are responsible for many of these. Women are seldom pregnant, for example. They are "pg," "preggies," "with child," or "in the family way," among others. Probably they are seldom pregnant because they seldom engage in intercourse, although they do seem to "have sex" now, even on broadcast television. Couples "sleep together" when in fact they are doing anything but sleeping and may or may not be in bed, they "do it," "make it," or "do the wild thing," "make love," and "have affairs." They do not yet, in "polite company" or on broadcast television, commit the act that goes by the acronym "For Unlawful Carnal Knowledge." Conception, in our "polite" language, seems indeed to be immaculate. People also seem to be immortal. They do not "die"; They are "deceased," they "pass away," "pass on," "are no longer with us," "buy the ranch" and, in the language of political correctness as described by Beard and Cerf (1992), are "terminally inconvenienced."

Generally euphemisms are discussed as a means of sterilizing the language for use in polite society. But exactly the opposite is frequently done in "street talk." Street gangs, for example, engage in "rapping" or "playing the dozens," a game of ritual insult that may substitute for physical violence. The object is to creatively insult the other, and the participants, in fact, devise language that is more explicit and less "socially acceptable" than the original. These frequently begin with something like "Yo Momma is a nice lady—and a high-priced one, too," but go on from there into extremes of vulgarity. The process seems to be the same, in that semantic rules are violated to conform to social norms, but the social norms are different.

SEXISM AND OTHER TYPES OF LINGUISTIC DISCRIMINATION

A movement toward "Political Correctness" is abroad in the land, and in its most extreme instances is simply Semantic Redeployment with more or less good intentions and humorous results. Beard and Cerf (1992) is an interesting, albeit humorous, treatment of these excesses. However, there are many aspects of discriminatory (or exclusionary) language that can benefit from some attention. Sanford Berman, quoted by Rosalie Maggio in her 1991 book *The Dictionary of Bias-free Usage: A Guide to Nondiscriminatory Language*, says:

> [Biased language can also] powerfully harm people, as amply illustrated by bigots' and tyrants' deliberate attempts to linguistically dehumanize and demean groups they intend to exploit, oppress, or exterminate. Calling Asians "gooks" made it easier to kill them. Calling blacks "niggers" made it easier to enslave and brutalize them. Calling Native Americans "primitives" and "savages" made it okay to conquer and despoil them. And to talk of "fishermen," "councilmen," and "longshoremen" is to clearly exclude and discourage women from those pursuits, to diminish and degrade them. (p. 3)

Generic Pronoun *He*

The first example most people think of when called upon to cite instances of gender-biased language is the use of the pronouns *he, him,* and *his* as the generic pronoun to refer to an individual whose sex is for some reason undetermined, as in "The speaker should take care to avoid sexism in his speech." Certainly this is an example of sexism embedded in English, although it is probably not the most serious.

In this book we have struggled to avoid that problem in a variety of ways. Generally we have tried to write sentences in the plural so as to avoid the need for a generic pronoun. In our example, it is easy enough to write, "Speakers should take care to avoid sexism in their speeches." It is amazing how frequently that simple device will avoid the problem. Another device is the use of the second person pronoun, as "In your speech you should take care to avoid sexism." Frequently the offending pronoun can simply be eliminated entirely: "The speaker should take care to avoid sexism in speech (or speeches)." Sometimes we have used *we, us,* or *our* thusly: "We should take care to avoid sexism in our speech (speeches)." By using these and a few other techniques recommended by Maggio, we can avoid the use of any indeterminant pronoun most of the time.

However, in those rare instances when a third-person singular indeterminant pronoun is absolutely required, we have used, and recommend using, *they, their,* and *them* in the singular: "The child using this swing might fall out and hurt themself." Conservative grammarians will cry foul, but we must remember that language changes, and it usually changes for reasons far less compelling than this. In fact, English is already so irregular in its pronouns and in verb conjugation that simply to declare that *they* is not only the third-person plural determinant pronoun but also the third-person singular indeterminant pronoun will not be noticed by most people. The use of the editorial "we" is a case in point. Some writers use "we" to refer to themselves in books and papers of which they are the sole author, and some teachers and editors will recommend that usage. George Rogers (fictitious author) might write "We have argued in this paper . . . ," even though in fact *he* has argued; *he* is the sole author. This is using the first person plural form to substitute for the first person singular. I do not favor such usage. I believe the only people who should use "we" to refer to themselves in the singular are schizophrenics with multiple personalities, the Holy Trinity, and those with tapeworms. Nevertheless it is widely accepted under these specific conditions. Certainly the English language is not going to be destroyed by one more very similar special case, the use of "they" rather than "he" when one is referring to a person of unspecified gender.

The Word *Man*

But I said this use of he as the third-person indeterminant singular pronoun is not the most serious sort of sexism embedded in our language. Suppose we consider some others. One that is closely related is the use of *man, men,* and *mankind*. This use of *man* seems to be one anthropologists are simply not willing to relinquish. That is difficult to understand, since *human, humanity,* and *humankind* are perfectly acceptable grammatically, and easily accessible.

Some may question whether use of either the generic pronoun *he* or the term *man* really matters. However, children are bombarded with those uses long before they comprehend *generic*. And the studies that have been done all seem to indicate that children, not surprisingly, tend to picture "early man" as consisting of men, and overestimate the frequency with which *men* serve in active roles (see Miller and Swift, 1988). Words *do* matter, because they teach us about our world earlier and more effectively than most other educational influences.

"Oh, Stewardess—May I Have Another Cup of Coffee?"

Our language frequently has separate word endings for nouns denoting females who occupy the same roles as men, as in *bachelorette, majorette, waitress,* and *stewardess*. Although this latter has given way to *flight attendant*, it was originally a feminine ending tagged onto *steward*.

That problem is relatively easy to fix. But others are linguistic reflections of attitudes deeply embedded in our culture and difficult to change. "Professors are welcome to bring their wives to the reception" rests on the assumption that all professors are male. The need to use the clarification *lady doctor* or *lady attorney* rests on the assumption that doctors and attorneys are generally male, and the term *male nurse* rests on a similar assumption that nurses are generally women. Among Anglos, both *friend* and *man* appear to be semantically marked for race—specifically, white—since Anglos seem constrained to say things such as "My black friend says... and "A black man stopped to help me." I realize blacks may do the reverse when talking among themselves; I am not privy to such conversations.

Other Examples

I have been heartened to see the appearance of diaper-changing equipment in both men's and women's restrooms in public places. I first noticed that phenomenon in a McDonald's restaurant in southern Indiana, of all places, in the fall of 1991. I walked past the door to the women's restroom and noticed a sign that said, "Changing Table Inside." I was already thinking "How sexist!" when I came to the door to the men's restroom and saw an identical sign. My estimate of the pervasiveness of the sexual revolution took a dramatic leap at that point. I have since noted the appearance of similar signs and equipment in many public restrooms. That represents a considerable cultural change, and one reflected in our language.

Six Types of Linguistic Bias

Maggio (1991) lists six types of linguistic bias:

> Biased language communicates inaccurately about what it means to be male or female; black or white; young or old; straight, gay, or bi; rich or poor; from one ethnic group or another; disabled or temporarily able-bodied; or to hold a particular belief system. It reflects the same bias found in racism, sexism, ageism, handicappism, classism, ethnocentrism, anti-Semitism, homophobia, and other forms of discrimination. Bias occurs in the language in several ways.
>
> 1. Leaving out individuals or groups....
> 2. Making unwarranted assumptions....
> 3. Calling individuals or groups by names they do not choose for themselves (e.g., Gypsy, office girl, Eskimo, pygmy, Bushman, the elderly, colored man) or terms that are derogatory (fairy, libber, savage, bum, old goat).

4. Stereotypical treatment that implies that all lesbians/Chinese/women/people with disabilities/teenagers are alike.
5. Unequal treatment of groups in the same material.
6. Unnecessary mention of membership in a particular group. In a land of supposedly equal opportunity, of what importance is a person's race, sex, age, sexual orientation, disability, or creed? As soon as we mention one of those characteristics—without a good reason for doing so—we enter an area mined by potential linguistic disasters. (p. 6)

Of course there are other types and sources of linguistic discrimination. But if one avoids these six types, it is bound to produce a sensitivity that will help avoid the others. If you are interested in this topic, some sources to consult, in addition to those already cited, are Kramerae (1981), Bosmajian (1983), Frank and Treichler (1989), and Sorrels (1983).

DOMINANT LANGUAGE IS NOT JUST FOR MEN ANYMORE, IS IT?

Women's Language

Robin Lakoff (1975), a Berkeley linguist, set off a storm of controversy and research by describing what she believed to be "women's language." She believed women use a style of language that includes a number of characteristics, most of which contribute to the impression that the speaker is very polite, excessively deferential, trivial, and frilly. For example, she claimed women use more "wh-imperatives" than do men. A *wh-imperative* is a sentence that begins with a "wh" word and sounds like a question but is in fact an order or a request in drag. Thus "Why don't you take out the trash, dear?" may sound like a question, but woe to the husband who takes it to be anything but a request/order. Wh-imperatives don't literally have to begin with "wh." "Doesn't the trash need to be emptied?" is the same sort of request. It's interesting that "wh-imperative" minus the hyphen is "whimperative," and that is what they suggest—a whimper.

A second characteristic is the *tag question*. For example, "We're having fun now, aren't we?" is a question tagged onto what would otherwise be a statement of opinion, but it gives the impression that the speaker has to have that opinion validated by the listener, that the speaker is insecure and feels it necessary to defer to the listener. Lakoff also said women tend to use many qualifiers, as in "If you're into it and don't mind a lot of chit-chat, bridge can sometimes be a lot of fun, if you know and like the other players." An excessive number of apologies is also supposed to mark women's language, as are "empty" adjectives such as *charming, sweet, divine,* and *cute,* and many intensifiers such as *so* and *very* (as in "so divine" and "very sweet"). Rising inflection can also indicate tentativeness. Finally—for our purposes at least—women's language is not coarse or obscene—or wasn't when Robin Lakoff was in college.

"Eat the Floor, Dogbreath!"

One of the authors, Jo Liska, wrote a chapter for the *Communication Yearbook* 15 (1991) that she titled "Dominance-Seeking Language Strategies: Please Eat the Floor, Dogbreath, or I'll Rip Your Lungs Out, O.K.?" Here we have a sentence a linguist might describe as consisting of [politeness marker] [order] [personal insult] [physical threat] [politeness marker/tag question]. The point Liska was making was that the characteristics Lakoff described do not necessarily or automatically make a sentence deferential or polite. We must consider the context, the people involved and their relationships, the culture, and the goals of the people involved. The characteristics of the language constitute only one aspect of deference—dominance.

Let me explain the origin of the title, because it may help clarify the point. You may recognize "Eat the floor, dogbreath, or I'll rip your lungs out" as something Belker was likely to say to criminals he was arresting on the TV series "Hill Street Blues." A friend of ours, a woman, is an undercover narcotics detective in California who buys crack cocaine in biker bars in a California metropolitan area. She was talking about the problems a female officer has in arresting a macho biker/drug dealer: convincing the arrestee she means what she says. She told us she has to use the sort of language Belker used, and worse, and we began talking about how the "women's language" Lakoff described would spoil the effect. Hence the title. In her case the language is a potent persuader, but she does carry a Sig .380 in case words fail her. So far they have not.

Research Evidence on Women's Language

Lakoff's observations were based on intuition, introspection, and informal observations. She did not conduct any survey, systematic observations, or content analyses to be sure that women—all women, some women, a few women—actually speak this way. Research that has been conducted since has indicated that men and women use this sort of language under certain circumstances, usually when they are talking to others they believe are in higher power positions than themselves, for one reason or another. Thus a man speaking to his boss, especially if he feels insecure about his job and he and the boss are not on really friendly terms, will use this language of "ingratiation." It may be that, because prior to Lakoff's observations in 1975 women were usually in lower power positions than were men, women were taught to use this sort of language and they learned the lesson well.

Be that as it may, Liska, Mechling, and Stathas (1981) wrote scripts of small-group discussions in which the fictitious participants used either **deferential language** or **assertive language.** They asked students to read those scripts and give their impressions of the participants. The students were not told the sex of the speakers. Deferential speakers were slightly more likely to be described as feminine, but much more likely to be described as more friendly and warm, while the assertive speakers were more likely to be described as more believable, dominant, and willing to take a stand. Similar results have been reported by many other researchers. You can read about those studies, if you are interested, in Liska (1991).

Thus it appears we use deferential language when we speak to those who have power over us, and we use assertive language with those we consider less powerful or our equals, especially when we are socially close to them. In fact, the language of dominance is frequently used to create a sense of camaraderie among close friends. And it appears that "dominance-seeking" language may be more effective in creating the impression of credibility, but less effective in situations in which the other person needs socioemotional support.

YOU TALK FUNNY; YOU MUST THINK FUNNY

What Robin Lakoff was, in fact, describing is a feminine *dialect,* and we could have treated that dialect in this section, were it not for the fact that the research since Lakoff's original description seems to indicate the characteristics of which she wrote are characteristics of the speech of only some women, at most, and appear to be equally characteristic of the language of men under certain conditions. A subset of a language that seems to appear only in certain situations does *not* constitute a dialect.

Dialects

What, then, is a **dialect?** You have probably become more aware of dialects since you enrolled in college than you were before. If you attend a school in an area of the country other than that in which you were raised, you may have come to realize *you have a dialect,* something you might never have noticed before, because all your family and friends sounded just like you—"normal." When you arrived on campus most everyone else sounded strange. Even if you are attending school in your native region of the country, you have undoubtedly met other students who are from other geographical areas whose speech sounds strange to you.

Somewhat surprisingly, it is not that easy to distinguish between a dialectic difference and a language difference. For our purposes, however, and especially in the United States, the difference is basically—although not always distinctly—that people who speak different dialects can understand one another, but those who speak different languages cannot. The problem is that some dialectic differences even in the United States make speakers virtually unintelligible to one another. If we include English as spoken in Wales, Scotland, and Ireland, the problem with this definition becomes clearer, because forms of English spoken in parts of the British Isles are essentially unintelligible—to many, at least. The best that can be said is probably that two people speaking different dialects *may* have difficulty understanding one another, but two people speaking different languages will seldom understand one another.

It is also important to distinguish between differences in dialect and differences in **accent.** An accent difference is a difference in pronunciation. A dialect involves a system of syntactic (grammar) and semantic (vocabulary) differences as well as differences in pronunciation.

Effect of Dialect

I am going to discuss dialectic differences that depend on geography, race, and socioeconomic class. Remember, I am not concerned here so much about the dialect differences per se as I am about the attitudes of listeners toward speakers of different dialects. People seem fascinated by dialect differences, by speech that sounds different from their own. But we are dealing here with language *effects,* so this is not the place to describe the differences in detail. If you want to explore those differences, an outstanding videotape, titled "American Tongues," is probably available at your school library or public library. Obviously, a videotape can provide examples to which we cannot do justice in print. Perhaps your professor can make time in class to show it, or can arrange a showing outside of class for those who are interested. If you must depend on printed sources, *The Cambridge Encyclopedia of Language* by David Crystal (1987, pp. 24ff) has an excellent treatment. It includes references to numerous other sources. (This book is an outstanding source of information about language in general, by the way; only a small fraction is devoted to dialects.) On the other hand, if you want to do more reading about attitudes toward dialects, *Attitudes Toward Language Variation* by Ryan and Giles (1982) is probably the best reference, although it is a bit dated, having been published over ten years ago.

Attitudes Toward Geographic Dialects Generally we can say that speakers who use a given dialect prefer to hear that dialect, and have negative attitudes toward other dialects. That is true of geographic dialects, although there seem to be two exceptions: Most Americans, regardless of their own dialect, view a person having a Massachusetts or a British dialect as generally better educated and of a higher social class than others. Still, speakers with those dialects are frequently the objects of derisive humor, and the villains in melodramas seem usually to be either British or natives of Boston. Thus it is not entirely clear just how favorable attitudes are toward even those dialects.

Having said this, either there is not much more to be said or there is an entire book to be written. If I were to describe attitudes toward all the dialects in this country, there would be no room for anything else in this book. Anything short of the complete treatment would be just a catalog of stereotypes. Instead, I will briefly cover the relation of dialects to credibility, and will discuss the concept of *accommodation*.

Relation of Dialect to Credibility Speakers are more believable if they speak your own dialect, with the possible exception of British and Bostonian dialects, as mentioned before. This has two implications. First, you as a listener are less likely to believe another who does not speak your dialect, which does not contribute to critical listening. A person who speaks another dialect is not necessarily less informed or trustworthy than one who speaks your own. Jimmy Carter was elected president in 1976 *in spite of* his Southern dialect, not because of it, and there has been much speculation about the extent to which his dialect may have contributed to his eventual downfall. The Southern dialect is so distinctive and so regional it is difficult for a politician from the South to win a national election, in part because most voters do not live in the South.

But there is an additional problem. The stereotype of Bubba, the ignorant white-trash ridge runner, unfair as it is, is invoked for many in the U.S. by the Southern dialect. This stereotype has been so prevalent in the movies and television that it is going to take a long time to rid ourselves of it. The media strike again. There are other dialects that have been mocked by the media, including the stereotype of the airhead California Valley Girl on one coast, and the pushy New Yorker on the other, but no Valley Girl has yet tried to run for president, and the New Yorker stereotype is not as damaging, apparently, as the Bubba stereotype.

It was encouraging that all three of the major presidential candidates in 1992 were allegedly from south of the Mason-Dixon Line, and two of the three, Clinton and Perot, definitely spoke a form of Southern dialect, although they were not Deep South. Both President Clinton and Vice President Gore have distinct Southern dialects, although they are not as thick as that of Carter.

Also, it is tempting as a speaker to try to fake the dialect of the listeners, especially if the response of the listeners is important. This is called *accommodation*, and it is dangerous, because if it fails it will result in the perception of insincerity and deception.

Attitudes Toward Racial Dialects Attitudes toward racial dialects are similar. Black English and Hispanic English are the most frequent racial dialects in the United States.

Black English It has been argued that Black English is a different language, not just a different dialect. But by our definition it is a dialect, because it is generally intelligible to speakers of standard English. In its extreme forms that is not necessarily true.

Perhaps you remember the scene in the movie "Airplane" in which two hip blacks are speaking jive with one another, and the little, old, white-haired white lady sitting next to them breaks into their conversation, obviously understanding and speaking their jive as well as they. I couldn't understand any of it. But I can generally understand the Black English I hear on the street, even with urban slang mixed in.

You can test yourself by viewing a Richard Pryor performance before an all-black audience versus one before a predominantly white audience. Pryor switches codes very adeptly. You can rent videotapes of Pryor's appearances, or perhaps your professor can spring money from the department budget to rent one to show in class. Or you could rent "Airplane," watch the whole thing just to see the bit I have described, and claim you are doing your homework. It is a great comedy. If you have access to cable TV, you can probably experience Black English on the Black Entertainment Network, especially by black comedians before all-black audiences.

Not all blacks speak Black English, by the way. I have had several black students in my classes who simply have not known what I was talking about when I described it.

So what are the attitudes of whites toward Black English? That question is not as easy to answer as might be at first supposed. We cannot simply have blacks speak Black English, either live or on videotape, and measure listeners' attitudes, since those would be attitudes not only toward the dialect but also toward the black speakers. Some studies have used black speakers capable of speaking both standard and Black English, and have found that white listeners: were more favorable toward the black speakers when they spoke standard English; saw those speakers as more similar to themselves; and predicted the speakers would have attitudes more similar to their own.

Apparently, Black English operates in two ways to make white listeners less favorable toward those who speak it: First, for those who are prejudiced against blacks, the dialect emphasizes the speakers' race if they can be seen, and establishes their race if only their voices are heard, calling up the stereotypes. The second effect is that some whites believe Black English is just a substandard form of Anglo English, that those who speak it are trying to speak standard English but are making errors in grammar and vocabulary.

That is *not* the case. Black English has its own rules by which its speakers must abide if they are to speak it correctly. You do not become a fluent speaker of Black English just by making errors in grammar and vocabulary. Whites who do that simply make fools of themselves. Black English has its own rules, especially regarding verb tense, many of which are more sophisticated than those of standard English. For example, "He working," which appears to the speaker of standard English to be a grammatical error, in fact has a very specific meaning in Black English. It means, "He is working *right now*." On the other hand, "He *be* working" means "He has been working for some time" or "He has a job." "He ain't go" means either that he didn't go or that he isn't now on his way, whereas "He ain't goin' " means he isn't likely to go in the future. "Dey ain't like dat" doesn't mean they *aren't* like that, as at first appears; it means they *don't* like that. "He don't know can she go" is the logical application of if-deletion and verb-inversion transformations to the underlying deep-structure sentence "He doesn't know if she can go." (These examples are from Farb, 1974.)

These problems come into focus in the education of black children, especially in inner-city schools. The issue is whether black children whose parents speak Black English in the home should be educated to speak fluent standard English elsewhere. There are arguments on both sides. The major argument for teaching standard English, of course, is that the children are going to grow up to succeed or fail in a world in which standard English is spoken, and their success or failure will depend to a considerable extent on their ability to speak standard English. Given the white prejudice toward Black English, black children's inability to speak another form will at least prejudice their chances for success. This point of view, by the way, is not just that of whites; some black parents insist their children be taught standard English for that very reason.

The major argument for the opposite approach is that black children will come to believe that the dialect their parents speak is an embarrassment because it is substandard, and the cultural heritage of which their dialect is a part will be lost. Farb (1974) lists five sources of Black English: African languages brought to America by the slaves; West African pidgin (a blend of two languages), also spoken by the slaves who had exposure to whites in their homelands before they were captured; Plantation Creole; Anglo English; and urban slang. Thus black children growing up on Chicago's South Side learn to speak a dialect that represents the history and culture of their people, their linguistic roots. Should they be forced to give up that linguistic heritage just to please white employers and customers? The alternative would be to teach them code-switching, to speak standard English when that is appropriate and Black English in other social contexts. But that is a tall order, to teach them to switch codes like a Richard Pryor, yet without leaving the impression that the dialect of their people is inferior, to be spoken only in private.

Hispanic Dialect The problem of Hispanics has similarities and differences to that of blacks. There are many migrant Hispanic families that spend half the year in Mexico and half the year in the United States following the harvest. The problem is especially acute in southern Texas, New Mexico, Arizona, and California. One of the authors encountered the problem when she taught in a Head Start program in the Salinas Valley in California. She did not speak Spanish at the time. Some parents insisted their children be taught in English because they wanted them to succeed in U.S. culture, but others were equally insistent that their children be taught in Spanish so as to retain their Hispanic cultural heritage.

But that is a language problem, not a dialect problem. What Anglos usually hear from Hispanics that makes them sound different is an accent, not a dialect, because it is a matter of pronunciation only, not of syntax and vocabulary. In some cases, however, some Spanish words and sentence structure slip in and create what is essentially a dialect. In the 1981 census, over 13 million Americans identified themselves as Hispanic, and there are surely far more than that now. Within this group there are three major segments represented. Cubans are about 6 percent of the total, Puerto Ricans about 14 percent, and Mexican Americans about 60 percent. Despite their number, these groups suffer from demonstrable prejudice toward their accents. Hispanic-accented English has been shown to make both Anglo and Hispanic listeners less favorable toward its speakers, and even less favorable with the intrusion of Spanish words and sentence construction.

HOW CAN LANGUAGE REGULATION BE POLITICAL REPRESSION?

English as an Official Language

Attitudes toward other languages are so strong on the part of some that they try to declare their own languages "official" and limit the use of other languages. There have been propositions on the ballots in several states recently that have sought to declare English the "official" language of those states, restricting the extent to which other languages, especially Spanish, are taught in the public schools and used in government activities such as the printing of ballots and administration of driver's license tests. It is not that these propositions have been intended to prevent the teaching of other languages in the public schools; rather they have been designed to prevent the teaching of other languages as a substitute for English. In much of the country this would have no real consequences, since English is *the* language in much of the center of the United States, at least outside urban areas. But those are not the states where the Official Language movement has been strongest. In

California and other Southwestern states, New Orleans, Florida, and New York City, and to some extent in Chicago—in short, wherever immigrants arrive from nations where English is not widely spoken—there is friction between those who speak English as a first language and those who do not. Many native speakers of English do not want government money spent "pandering" to those who want to benefit from participation in the U.S. economy but do not want to take the time to learn English.

The Case of Quebec

It is not just in the United States where language is recognized as a powerful tool of politics. One of the best examples is the Canadian province of Quebec and the city of Montreal, which for years has been on the verge of seceding from Canada because the language most spoken there is French rather than the English spoken in the rest of the country. It is the law in Quebec that street signs and business signs must be in French, unless the business has a proper name such as McDonald's. A friend of ours teaches at a university in Montreal, but we could not apply for a teaching position advertised there recently because fluency in French was a legal requirement, and neither of us speaks French. Worse, however, is the fact that most Canadians from the other provinces were also prevented from applying.

English in Africa

All across Africa this battle has been fought in one country after another. In the East African nations, since they were once British colonies, the official language of government and business is English; but as the nationalist movements gain strength in those countries, there are parallel movements to establish Swahili as equally accepted. In West Africa, there is such a variety of tribal languages and dialects that English is "official" only in a metaphorical sense, being used as a sort of common currency when those of different tribes must communicate with one another.

To establish one group's language as "official" is a political triumph. But in a nation such as the United States, described as a "melting pot," (or better as a "stirfry") it is also a blow at the cultural diversity of which we profess to be so proud. The United States should not be a melting pot in the sense that individuals representing diverse cultures are thrown into it, amalgamated, and all poured out into the same mold.

HOW DOES LANGUAGE AFFECT PERCEPTION AND THOUGHT?

The language we learn is important, not only because it affects our ability to communicate and restricts those with whom we can communicate, but also because it affects how we perceive the world. The Sapir-Whorf hypothesis, also termed the *linguistic relativity hypothesis,* holds simply that the language we learn affects our perceptions of the world (Whorf, 1956).

Linguistic Relativity

Of course, those who speak different languages perceive the world differently. But that is not evidence that the different languages *cause* the differences in perception. To some extent the differences are undoubtedly due to differences between the cultures and the environments in which the languages are spoken.

Example: Eskimo words for snow   An example you have probably heard of has to do with the large number of words the Eskimo language has for *snow,* and the ability of Eskimos to distinguish among types of snow. Is the existence of so many words simply the result of the need to make such distinctions—the fact that the culture is so intertwined with the frozen environment—or does the vocabulary teach children to make reliable distinctions as they learn the language? Fortunately, these are not mutually exclusive, alternative explanations. They are probably all correct.

Cronkhite (1976, p. 272) states:

The Eskimo children's language (1) calls [children's] attention to the differences, (2) forces [them] to practice making the distinctions, and (3) prevents [them] from being rewarded by successful communication until [they] get the distinctions correct. Thus one's language is an ever-present teacher, a constant reminder of whatever distinctions are embedded in it. Since the distinctions embedded in one's language are probably those [that] are considered important in one's culture, the language is also a constant reminder of one's culture.

However, it may be that this important learning function of language occurs not just in those areas in which we have large vocabularies, but also in those areas for which we do not have a single, all-purpose word. If the Eskimo language had a single word for snow in general, it would not be so important that it has many words for specific types of snow, because the child could always fall back on the general word.

Example: English words for *car*   Americans learn many words for types of cars, but they have a single word, *car,* on which they can always rely. Consider what that means to us. Suppose we had no word *car,* only the words for specific types of cars, and imagine that you and a friend are preparing to cross the street. The friend steps out, not noticing a car approaching rapidly from one side. You could not say, "Look out for the car!" You would have to say "Look out for the blue 1989 Buick LeSabre sedan!" I venture to say you would learn to make fine distinctions among types of cars, or lose a lot of friends.

One of the characteristics of "women's language," by the way, one that does seem to be sex-specific, is that women on the average have a more extensive color vocabulary than do men. Are women, then, better able to distinguish mauve from beige because they learned to make that distinction when they learned the words, or because they were more carefully taught to make the distinction as well as to use the words? I think I will stay out of this argument, but it might be an interesting question to pursue in class.

The more interesting issue raised by the hypothesis, however, has to do with the effects of syntax, not of semantics. Whorf was especially interested in the Navajo and Hopi languages, so suppose we consider some of those differences.

You were told by your sixth-grade English teacher, no doubt, that a *noun* is "the name of a person, place, or thing," whereas a *verb* names an action. What, then, is a *marathon*—or, for that matter, any *race*? What is a *karate chop*? What are *phase* and *endure*? In fact, a noun is simply a word that can be used in a place in an English sentence in which a noun is called for, and a verb is a word used where a verb is called for. This news may be as traumatic for some as the discovery that Santa Claus was merely your father, who was frequently the tooth fairy as well, and that the Easter Bunny did not really hide those eggs. The decision you must make first when encountering a new word in English is to find out what part of speech it is. When you find a word in a dictionary, that is the first information you will be given. You will find there that *race* can be either a noun or a verb, depending on where it appears in the sentence.

Example: Hopi Language Hopi, too, has two major classes of words, but they are not nouns and verbs. They are "long-term events" and "short-term events." Puffs of smoke and waves are short-term events for the Hopi. True, waves for surfers and sailors are more likely to be long-term events, but the Hopi are not generally acquainted with long-term waves. In fact, a Hopi child first being exposed to the ocean would be linguistically disoriented, having to use the Hopi word for *wave* to apply to a long-term event. Cloud formations and storms are near the border between the two categories; anything longer is a long-term event.

Now we can speculate about the effects this characteristic of the Hopi language must have on children learning Hopi as their first language. First, they learn that *everything* is an event, some long-term and some short-term, but always an event. One's home and school building are events. A pony is an event, as is a ritual dance. Everything is transient, although some things are more transient than others. Second, in a way that appears related, Hopi children learn that time is cyclical, not linear; homes and school buildings and ponies and dances and phases of the moon and winter and summer disappear and reappear. Third, whenever they encounter a new object or phenomenon, Hopi children must decide if it is a short-term or a long-term event.

It is possible to make too much of this, of course. Modern Hopi, even those who live in their traditional villages atop the mesas in northern Arizona, learn English and watch television. Our wedding rings were made by a Hopi silversmith who lives in Shongopavi, Arizona, atop Second Mesa. That village appears extremely primitive, as if it were the next stage of architecture after the cliff dwellings in Mesa Verde—except for an occasional mobile home. After a visit there a few years ago I was just getting my 240Z wound up when I was stopped by a Hopi policeman who had clocked me on his Vascar radar coming from the opposite direction. He was not riding a pony; he was riding about 400 horses. And he led me to understand that my efforts to change a conventionally long-term event, the trip to Window Rock, into a short-term event were not entirely appreciated by the Hopi Tribal Council.

General Semantics

The approach taken by advocates of **General Semantics,** whose founding father was Korzybski (1958), may seem similar at first glance. But whereas Whorf argued that the specific language we learn affects our perceptions, the central idea of General Semantics is that *any* language warps perceptions and thoughts, because *no language adequately maps the territory it is supposed to represent.* That is, there are many ways in which language—any language—does not and cannot adequately represent reality. General Semantics at times seems to be a philosophy, almost a religion, although we have not yet seen their representatives hanging around airports passing out tracts and taking donations. But if we can get past the evangelical fervor, we will find that the ways in which language is said to misrepresent reality can be helpful.

Indexing the Names of Things General Semanticists have developed an indexing system that is probably the easiest way to understand the central point. First, *reality is constantly changing,* whereas language changes much more slowly, and, in some respects, not at all. Have you heard the Rolling Stones cut "Ruby Tuesday" that is played every now and then on Oldies stations? One verse goes:

> Goodbye Ruby Tuesday.
> Who could hang a name on you
> When you change with every new day?
> Still I'm gonna miss you.

It is as if Mick Jagger had been reading in General Semantics at the time he wrote this piece.

To correct the problem that reality changes at a much faster pace than does language, the General Semanticists propose that we place a date-subscript on the name of every person, place, object, and idea. Thus "General Semantics 1952," the title of an article by Irving J. Lee in the *Quarterly Journal of Speech*, is not General Semantics 1992. General Semantics, like everything else, is constantly changing. Ruby, in the Stones' song, must be Ruby Tuesday because she changes with every new day. Thus she must also be a Ruby Wednesday, and certainly a Ruby 1968 and a Ruby 1992, all of which are different. You may not yet have attended your five-year high school reunion, but when you do you no doubt will have the strange experience of talking to people whose *names* you remember but who in various ways do not physically, psychologically, or socially resemble the people to whom those names used to be attached. Thus you will feel the need for a David Jennings 1992 and a David Jennings 1996. Certainly, Russia 1986 was not the same as Russia 1995.

Language Does Not Map Reality Completely Moreover, no two things in reality are identical; but to use language requires us to act as if they are. Democracy 1 is not Democracy 2. Thus we cannot use language without stereotyping, since words represent classes of objects, actions, ideas, and people. This easily leads to overgeneralizing and stereotyping, to the view that "If you've seen one, you've seen them all," when in fact there are many differences among the individuals that compose any class. This leads all too easily to racial and sexual stereotyping, for example. Hispanic #1 is not Hispanic #2, Woman #1 is not Woman #2, and Liberal #1 is not Liberal #2. If we could learn that single lesson from General Semantics, it would be worth the study.

We can never totally describe anything in reality, but language suggests we can. The suggestion here is to add *et cetera* to every description we attempt. The journal of General Semantics is titled *ETC.* for that reason.

> Suppose you have been dating a man for several weeks, and one night you tell him you love him. He asks what you mean by that, and you try to explain. You are bound to be left with a sense of failure, because you can't explain *exactly* what you mean and how your love for him differs from that you feel for your mother, your father, and your best woman friend. A year later, you are engaged to be married, and you are still using the same word. *Now* try to explain. "How do I love thee? Let me count the ways . . . " It isn't possible. Just do the best you can, and then add "etc." at the end of the list. (Cronkhite, 1976, p. 275)

Another problem with language is that language not only allows abstraction but requires it, whereas there are no abstractions in reality. Yet when someone asks you to explain what you mean by a word or concept, the temptation is to explain by becoming *more* abstract, by defining "up the ladder of abstraction," in General Semantics terms, whereas the definition would be clearer if it were less abstract. Someone asks you what you mean by "hard work," and the temptation may be to expand that definition by responding with "physical labor." But if you were to define down the ladder of abstraction, you might not *say* anything; you might just take your friend to a construction area and point to a group of people trying to lift a prefabricated wall into a vertical position. "Now that," you say, "is hard work." Right or wrong, that concrete representation is what some General Semanticists recommend. Of course, that is a generalization. General Semanticist #138 might not recommend that.

There are other ways language fails to match reality, but these should be enough for our purposes. Remember, these are not just ways some languages used by some people do not match reality. These are ways *no* language can *ever* match reality, a fact of which we must constantly remind ourselves.

WHAT MAKES LANGUAGE PLEASING, INTENSE, OR OBSCENE?

Frequently we don't think of ourselves—ordinary people—using "stylistic" language. Perhaps politicians use it in speeches, for example, John Kennedy, Franklin Roosevelt, and Winston Churchill. But in fact, we all use stylistic devices every day in conversation. We use humor, which is a stylistic device, and we use rhetorical questions when we ask questions for effect, not expecting an answer. We use sarcasm and irony. We use exaggeration.

Language Clarity

In trying to be clear, we know enough to avoid unusual words and unusually complex sentences, and if we are really aware of the enemies of clarity, we avoid the passive voice and too many negative constructions. Stuart Chase (1954) gives some examples of how we can *avoid* clarity. He uses the following as an example of what he calls "pedagese":

> Realization has grown that the curriculum or the experiences of learners change and improve only as those who are most directly involved examine their goals, improve their understandings, and increase their skill in performing the tasks necessary to reach newly defined goals. This places the focus upon the teacher, lay citizen, and learner as partners in curricular improvement and as the individuals who must change, if there is to be a curriculum change. (Chase 1954)

We don't ordinarily talk like this in conversation. We are tempted to do it when we are called on to give public speeches, and want to sound scholarly or knowledgeable. But in fact, the straightforward conversational style, perhaps with the omission of slang, obscenities, and colloquialisms, is usually the most impressive style.

Here is what is alleged to be an exchange between an amateur plumber and the National Bureau of Standards:

Plumber: I've found hydrochloric acid is very good for cleaning drains, and thought you'd like to know.

NBS: The efficiency of hydrochloric acid is indisputable, but the corrosive residue is incompatible with metallic permanence.

Plumber: I'm happy to hear I'm right.

NBS: We cannot assume responsibility for the production of toxic and noxious residues from hydrochloric acid, and suggest you utilize an alternative procedure.

Plumber: I'm glad you folks are honest and aren't going to try to take credit for my discovery.

NBS: Don't use hydrochloric acid! It eats the hell out of pipes!

In this example, the unclear sentences use uncommon words. It is not just "big" words that make language unclear; it is unusual words. But the previous example does not really contain unusual words. Its major problem is just that there are too many words. The sentences are too long, too complex, and too repetitive. A simple idea is blown up beyond recognition.

But in fact, clarity is a stylistic device, as are humor, rhetorical questions, sarcasm, and irony, that we use persistently in everyday conversation.

Figurative Language

We also use figurative language, and we are constantly exposed to it on television and in movies. Right now there is a popular song entitled "Walking On Broken Glass." Of course, it is not literally about anyone walking on broken glass; it is about a different sort of pain. And you probably have heard the cut the Doors did in the late '60s called "Light My Fire," which had nothing to do with literal fire. "Heartbreak Hotel" by Elvis Presley had nothing to do with a real hotel. Madonna's recent "Justify My Love" is also figurative although I am afraid I do not really understand its meaning. TV's "As the World Turns" is not literally about the world turning, and the movies *St. Elmo's Fire, The Breakfast Club,* and *The Silence of the Lambs* are not about fire, breakfast, a club, or lambs.

Metaphors

We are bombarded with figurative language, most frequently metaphors. And we use that language not merely every day, but in practically every sentence. The problem is that the metaphors we use are frequently dead or dead-tired, or are cliches. When you ask, "Would you stoop to that?" you are both asking a rhetorical question and using a metaphor, albeit a cliche. Sometimes you have to *bite your tongue* (oops) to avoid using cliches such as *looking for a needle in a haystack,* "One bad apple spoils the bunch," "Leading the good life," "There is no love lost between them," "You can see the writing on the wall," "Let's just lay our cards on the table and be up front about this," "It doesn't amount to a hill of beans," "It isn't engraved in stone yet," "It's snowing to beat the band," "cold as ice," "sharp as a tack," "slow as molasses in January," "hard as nails," or "pretty as a picture," and "He'd give you the shirt off his back." Sometimes it seems people never say anything really original; they just rearrange the same tired cliches in new contexts. The real trick is to invent new, fresh metaphors to replace the easy ones.

Language That Pleases

The language that will keep the attention, interest, and understanding of listeners and readers is language that is *appropriate* to you, to your audience, and to the situation, and that is *strong, active, concrete, specific,* and *personal.* Imagine a newspaper editor looking at a sentence a junior reporter had written, "Voting patterns among Wisconsin's youth are changing rapidly," and deciding it needs to be more lively. Using the principles above, it might be changed to read:

> One day last February, 22-year-old Jan Nordquist of Prairie-du-Chein paused at the top of the ski run, brushed her long blond hair out of her eyes, and told me, "I don't really reject my parents' political views. They were fine for their time. But we have to live in a world that changes every day. I'm not going to commit myself to any one political party today because it might not have the answers tomorrow."

Effective language will also be vivid and sensory; it will appeal to all the senses; it will make readers or listeners see, hear, smell, feel, and taste the experiences being described. Consider this example: There has been much talk lately of providing a minimum level of health care for all Americans. We know the present system of health care forces some people to live in state hospitals and nursing homes, places where they receive only minimal care. We know that, but it is not really brought home to us until we read a vivid, sensory description such as the following, which I originally wrote to describe my experience as a ward attendant at the Colorado State Hospital:

> They were called the "bedpan wards," and for good reason. They were not hospital wards, because there was no expectation that the "patients" would ever recover; instead they were waiting their turns to die. Opening the door was like walking into an animal's cage, and a poorly tended one at that. The stench of human excrement was like a physical force pushing me back; the sharp ammonia-like odor of urine penetrated my sinuses and made my eyes water. The room was oppressively hot and humid. I felt the perspiration start on my forehead, the insides of my arms, the backs of my legs, and knew I would have to live with it for the full eight-hour shift. My clothes clung to me like a wet sheet. The paper on which I wrote stuck to my forearm, and my sweat smeared the ink. The room was dark, but I knew there were people there because I could hear their moans and incoherent mumblings. One old man repeated "Help me, help me . . . " in a low voice for hours, but he couldn't tell me how to help him. Another patient interrupted the endless monotony of her life by waiting until an unsuspecting new attendant came near her bed and then turning loose with a shriek that always made my heart jump in my chest. My lunch usually went only half-eaten on nights I was assigned to those wards, because I could not separate the animal smells from the taste of the sandwich. At the end of the shift I put my clothes in a plastic bag and considered burning them. I felt I never wanted to wear those clothes again. And as I felt the cleansing, refreshing shower wash away the unspeakable micro-organisms I was sure infested every pore of my body, I realized I had been there only eight hours. To the withered, helpless inmates those sounds, those smells, that heat, and that darkness represented home—the last home they would ever know. (Cronkhite, 1978, p. 264)

When vivid, sensory language is made personal, it becomes even more compelling. Here is a passage from the "emotional" speech that was a part of my thesis:

> We of the middle class are self-reliant. We pride ourselves on being able to pay our own way by honest industry. We can meet the normal medical expenses. But what would happen if your next medical checkup revealed the beginnings of multiple sclerosis—you found yourself destined to life as a cripple—could your parents pay for the care you would require? When you're actually [working], what will you do when your child is feverish and in pain, but you can't keep your mind on how best to care for him because you keep thinking what it's going to cost? You may have seen classmates drop out of school to work because of illness in the family. You may have pitied families just like your own that were suddenly stricken by illness and forced into privation and hardship. Or when your brother was ill you may have

seen through your father's strained good humor to realize he was covering worry—worry about how the expense would be met. You and I aren't secure from this threat. Someday we will have children to care for and aged parents who, without us, will face the gray life of a nursing home or public institution. I don't want to pay premiums to a loan shark to conserve my child's health. I don't want my parents to while away their "golden days" of retirement in the crowded solitude of a state hospital, to die on a hard cot in a room full of strangers—and I don't think you want that either. We all want to realize our full capacities, provide ourselves and our children with every opportunity for success—this should be everyone's right—but some of us will never achieve it unless we act to protect ourselves from catastrophic medical expenses.

Language Intensity

Vivid, sensory, personal language is closely related to language intensity. Bowers (1963) did a study in which he found that highly intense language is not as effective in a public speech as is language that is only moderately intense. He also concluded what makes language most intense is its participation in a sex or death metaphor. Thus "Would you *prostitute* yourself to vote for George Bush after he *strangled* the family-leave bill?" is more intense than saying "Would you vote for George Bush after he vetoed the family-leave bill?" *Prostitute* and *strangled* are sex and death metaphors, respectively. Others have continued Bowers' research with language intensity in the years since, and have added other related concepts, such as *opinionated language,* which is a stylistic device in which the speakers say something like "Anyone who believes this is an idiot" or "Any intelligent person would agree with this position," thus expressing not only an opinion on an issue, but also an opinion about the advocates of other positions.

Obscenity

But language intensity can slide, sometimes not so gently, into obscenity. Bowers and Osborn (1966) did a study in which they considered the effects of both literal and intense conclusions in speeches. Osborn wrote a literal conclusion for that study that went like this:

> From what we have learned here today it is obvious that we have listened too long to the voices of those who represent special-interest groups. Too long, we ourselves have stood by and permitted the ruination of our Western economies by those who have proclaimed the doctrine of protective tariff. We have neglected our larger interests for the smaller interests of these special groups, and the result has been—not

a vigorous, protected economy—but rather economic stagnation. I say the time has come to listen no longer in our legislatures to those short-sighted lobbyists. For only when we shut our ears to them, and remove the tariff barriers which stand as so many harmful restrictions on our general welfare, can we achieve the goal of free trade, giving to the entire world new economic hope and a sense of new economic well-being.

Then Osborn wrote a second conclusion based on the first but in which he added an extensive sex metaphor:

> From what we have learned here today it is obvious that we have listened too long to the seductive whisper of special-interest groups. Too long, we have stood by and permitted the rape of Western economies by those who have proclaimed the doctrine of protective tariff. We have prostituted our own interests to satisfy the lust of these special-interest groups, and the result of this impotent union has been—not a vigorous and healthy economy—but economic abortion. I say the time has come to banish from our legislative chambers these economic seducers. For only when we shut our ears to them, and remove the barriers which stand like so many ill-advised parental restrictions, can liberty and economy lie side by side, stimulating each other, giving through free trade a new birth of hope to the world and a new manhood of economic well-being.

This intense sex metaphor could lapse rather easily into obscenity. In fact, some obscenity does consist of sexual metaphors. Sometimes the metaphors are obscene because they are explicit. Just what constitutes obscenity, if we are to judge by what can be said on radio or television, is changing rapidly. *Bitch* is apparently acceptable now, as are *pissed off* and *brown-nose*, all of which are dead metaphors that now appear on television, even in prime time.

Other words are not metaphors; they are just "four-letter words" that may or not have four letters but have for some reason been declared obscene by some unknown power. The word mentioned earlier in the chapter, the acronym for the words "For Unlawful Carnal Knowledge," still cannot be said on broadcast radio or television. (These words, so the story goes, were at one time posted above the stocks where couples were being punished for having committed adultery.) Why this word is obscene and others that have the same meaning, such as *copulate,* are not is a deep mystery.

The use of obscenity is a matter of adaptation. There are circumstances under which it will be effective, and those in which it will be ineffective because it will offend listeners. There have been few studies testing the effects of obscenity. But the conclusion seems to be that it is ineffective in public speeches at least. The two studies with which I am familiar are Mulac (1976) and Bostrom, Basehart, and Rossiter (1973). Yet the use of obscenity clearly depends on the specific speaker, listeners, topic, and situation. Obscenity is expected by some listeners from some speakers in some situations. As Cronkhite (1976, p. 279) said:

> If the foreman of the department in the steel mill where I used to work had ever stopped swearing, the workers (1) couldn't have understood a word he said, (2) would have thought it was quitting time, (3) would have filed a grievance with the union steward (they thought it was Muzak piped in to make their working conditions more pleasant), and/ or (4) would have sent him to the company hospital on the assumption he was having a seizure.

Actually, the word *obscenity* is the general term used to cover three types of "objectionable" language: obscenity, profanity, and scatology. *Obscenity* in its narrower sense refers to sexually explicit language, *profanity* covers religious references used disrespectfully, and *scatology* is language referring to bodily waste and bodily functions. It is a comment on our society that violent terms are not generally considered objectionable.

CONCLUSION

As students of communication, we of all people should become aware of our linguistic environments and work to manage them. If we do not, they will manage us. We must remember Doublespeak conceals meanings so as to prevent us from making informed political and purchasing decisions. Euphemisms, while not so dangerous, do conceal meanings.

Language that discriminates against certain social groups prevents us from using the full potential of those groups even though, counting women and minorities, they constitute most of the population. Added to that use of discriminatory language are negative attitudes toward the dialects of other groups, and attempts to decrease cultural diversity by establishing a single language as legally approved.

We may fail to realize the extent to which our own beliefs and perceptions are embedded in the language we speak, so we may fail to evaluate them critically, and we may fail to realize the extent to which *any* language fails as an adequate representation of reality.

Finally, as students of communication we should understand how language that is pleasing can so fascinate us and intense and obscene language can so offend us that we may make important decisions on the basis of the language used by the advocates of both sides rather than on the basis of the evidence. It is very difficult to avoid being a prisoner of language.

KEY TERMS AND CONCEPTS

Doublespeak
Semantic Redeployment
euphemisms
linguistic bias
deferential language
assertive language
dialects
accents

effect of a dialect
attitudes toward
   geographic and
   racial dialects
language regulation and
   political repression
language and perception
General Semantics

ways language does
   not map reality
language clarity
figurative language
pleasing language
metaphors
language intensity
obscenity

REFERENCES

Beard, H., and Cerf, C. (1992). *The Official Politically Correct Dictionary and Handbook.* New York: Villard Books.

Bosmajian, H. A. (1983). *The Language of Oppression.* New York: University Press of America.

Bostrom, R., Basehart, J. R., and Rossiter, Jr., C. M. (1973). The effects of three types of profane language in persuasive situations. *Journal of Communication* 23: 461–475.

Bowers, J. (1963). Language intensity, social introversion, and attitude change. *Speech Monographs* 30: 345–352.

Bowers, J., and Osborn, M. (1966). Attitudinal effects of selected types of concluding metaphors in persuasive speeches. *Speech Monographs* 33: 147–155.

Chase, S. (1954). *The Power of Words.* New York: Harcourt, Brace.

Cronkhite, G. (1976). *Communication and Awareness.* Menlo Park, Calif.: Benjamin-Cummings.

———. (1978). *Public Speaking and Critical Listening.* Menlo Park, Calif. Benjamin-Cummings.

Crystal, D. (1987). *The Cambridge Encyclopedia of Language.* Cambridge, England: Cambridge University Press.

Farb, P. (1974). *Word Play: What Happens When People Talk.* New York: Knopf.

Frank, F. W., and Treichler, P. A. (1989). *Language, Gender, and Professional Writing.* New York: Modern Language Association.

Korzybski, A. (1958). *Science and Sanity.* Lakeville, Conn.: International Non-Aristotelian Library.

Kramerae, C. (1981). *Women and Men Speaking.* Rowley, Mass.: Newbury House.

Lakoff, R. (1975). *Language and Women's Place.* New York: Harper & Row.

Liska, J. (1991). Dominance-seeking language strategies: Please eat the floor, Dogbreath, or I'll rip your lungs out, O.K.? *Communication Yearbook* 15. Newbury Park, Calif.: Sage.

Liska, J., Mechling, E. and Stathas, S. Calif. (1981). Differences in subjects' perceptions of gender and believability between users of deferential and nondeferential language. *Communication Quarterly* 29: 40–48.

Lutz, W. (1989). *Doublespeak.* New York: Harper & Row.

Maggio, R. (1991). *The Dictionary of Bias-Free Usage: A Guide to Nondiscriminatory Language.* Phoenix: Oryx.

Miller, C. and Swift, K. (1988). *The Handbook of Nonsexist Writing: For Writers, Editors, and Speakers,* 2nd ed. New York: Harper & Row.

Mulac, A. (1976). Effects of obscene language upon three dimensions of listener attitude. *Communication Monographs* 43: 300–307.

Ryan, E. B., and Giles, H. (eds.). (1982). *Attitudes Toward Language Variation: Social and Applied Contexts.* London, England: Edward Arnold.

Sorrels, B. D. (1983). *The Nonsexist Communicator: Solving the Problems of Gender and Awkwardness in Modern English.* Englewood Cliffs, N.J.: Prentice-Hall.

Whorf, B. L. (1956). *Language, Thought, and Reality,* edited by John Carroll. Cambridge, Mass.: MIT Press.

Let me have men about me that are fat,
Sleek-headed men, and such as sleep a-nights.
Yon Cassius has a lean and hungry look;
He thinks too much: such men are dangerous.
—William Shakespeare, Julius Caesar

Functions of Nonverbal Communication in Social Relationships

10

CHAPTER OUTLINE

Ecological Analysis

Types of Nonverbal Signs

Our Primate Link: Sensory and Neural
The Human Brain

Functions and Outcomes of Nonverbal Behavior

How Do Environmental Characteristics Affect Our Perceptions?
Early vs. Contemporary Human Environments
The Modern Environment and Its Effects
Time and Communication Behavior

What Do Our Bodies, Faces, and Eyes Say About Us?
Body Type
Clothing and Personal Effects
Body Position, Posture, and Orientation
Gestures
Faces and Facial Expressions
Eye Behavior and Gaze

What Do Our Voices Reveal About Us?
Judging Emotions from the Voice
Vocal Preferences
Interpreting Vocal Characteristics
How Voice Signals Status
Meanings of Silence

What Is the Significance of Touch in Our Social Relationships?
Harlow's Studies
Lack of Touching and Early Development
Functions of Touch
When Are We Likely to Touch?
Differences in Amount and Type of Touch

How Does Our Use of Space and Territory Affect Our Social Relationships?
Territoriality
Personal Space

Humans have a special system of communication called language. That system was discussed in the last chapter. Language is a powerful tool that enables us to share information, negotiate relationships, store information in the form of texts (which are records made permanent for succeeding generations), and develop new concepts, ideas, and technologies. However, language is not the only means by which we interact. Indeed, nonverbal behaviors such as facial expressions, body type, vocal qualities such as pitch, tone, and rate, the clothing we choose, and the environments we construct all carry important information about our moods, feelings, personalities, socioeconomic class, and so on.

ECOLOGICAL ANALYSIS

McArthur and Baron (1983, p. 219) have written: "According to the ecological position, we are sensitive to adaptively relevant information, as opposed to all possible information." That we are especially sensitive to nonverbal information suggests its fundamental role in our ability to adapt to our surroundings and the other individuals included in those surroundings.

> For example, emotions such as anger and fear should be most readily perceived because they are most essential to adaptive action on the part of the perceiver. Similarly, the stable attributes of domineeringness, aggressiveness, and strength should be perceived more readily than kindness, intelligence, or reliability because the former are more essential to adaptive action [survival]. (1983, p. 219).

They go on to argue that emotional expressions, which are largely communicated by nonverbal means, are likely to be most amenable to an ecological analysis. Many of our emotional expressions are found in all humans, regardless of culture, as well as in all primates. Indeed, some expressions, such as fear and anger, are found in all mammals, and their enactment is also similar (e.g., a direct, sustained gaze as a sign of threat). McArthur and Baron continue:

> Consistent with this evolutionary perspective, there is evidence of a close coordination between the social interaction opportunities available in a given ecological niche and the expressive potential of inhabitants of that niche. For example, [it has been] observed that animals whose niche required a high level of social coordination, such as the plain-dwelling baboon as opposed to the forest-dwelling mandrill baboon, have a more mobile facial musculature for expressing emotion. (1983, p. 226)

Thus, the ecology in which we evolved had a significant influence on the outcome of our anatomical, sensory, physiological, and neural development. Further, our behavior, especially our social behavior, reciprocally influenced the way we responded to and altered our ecology. In humans, and to varying degrees in other species (e.g., Bonner, 1980), our social connections developed into cultures, which exert considerable influence on our behaviors and perceptions. Moreover, cultural practices influence the ways in which we perceive, modify, and attempt to control our ecology.

Maybe because they are so fundamental and critical to our survival, nonverbal behaviors are frequently produced, processed, and analyzed at a low level of awareness. That is, we generally tend to focus attention on what is being said rather than explicitly attending to nonverbal behaviors and characteristics. Of course, some nonverbal behaviors are so striking, novel, or unexpected that we recognize them quite consciously. But generally, they are processed rather automatically. An exchange between Sam and Diane from an episode of TV's "Cheers" illustrates the point. A little background: Diane's mother has called Diane at the bar to report that a member of the family, Elizabeth Barrett Browning, has died. When the patrons of the bar learn that Elizabeth is "just" a cat, they return their attention to the Celtics game on the TV. Diane feels snubbed and betrayed, and later explains:

Diane (whimpering): "I need sympathy."

Sam (in disgust): "Well, why didn't you say so?"

Diane (indignant): "I did with the look in my eye, the knit of my brow, and the set of my stance."

Sam (exasperated): "Why didn't you use words?"

We can hear what we say, and thus have immediate feedback and opportunity to make corrections or modifications in vocabulary, grammar, and style. We don't see ourselves, however, and therefore feedback about our own facial expressions, gestures, and so on (**nonverbal feedback**) is limited. The reflection we see in the mirror is also not exactly like what other people see, and it is rather disconcerting to view ourselves on videotape for the first time. It is one of the few opportunities we get to see ourselves as others see us. It is also a useful device for helping teachers to improve their classroom style and helping speakers to improve their delivery. Political consultants use it to help their candidates appear more authoritative and credible. Since we typically don't see our own behavior, we are less aware of the messages we may be sending, and therefore less able to modify them if they are inaccurate or inappropriate to the situation.

Thus, overriding goals of this chapter are to (1) overview the anatomical, sensory, and neural underpinnings of nonverbal behavior, (2) help you become more aware of the ways in which nonverbal behaviors affect your perceptions and evaluations of others, and (3) help you understand how your nonverbal behaviors and characteristics may be affecting others' judgments of you.

TYPES OF NONVERBAL SIGNS

As you have already learned, there are three basic types of communication signs: *symptoms* are naturally occurring signs such as body type, hair color, and size, and signs that reveal particular emotional states such as fear, happiness, and anger. *Semblances* are signs that resemble their referents or the symptoms on which they are based. Thus, begging (holding out one's hand to request some desired object) is a semblance based on the symptom of reaching to grab something. The American Sign Language sign for *drink* is a semblance that mimics the act of drinking. A hologram is a three-dimensional representation that we also classify as a semblance. Semblances may be so abstract that they look very little like the original and thus are on the border between semblance and symbol. *Symbols* are arbitrary, and are learned through experience.

These various types of signs (symptoms, semblances, and symbols) occur in concert to create an overall image of a person at a particular moment, as well as over repeated observations and interactions. We all have typical patterns of nonverbal behavior that reflect or reveal our personalities, overall dispositions, attitudes, and emotional stability.

Some nonverbal behaviors are not unique to a single human group and are found among people of many cultures and among species of nonhuman animals (Chevalier-Skolnikoff, 1982; Ekman, 1973; Ekman & Friesen, 1971). For example, basic facial expressions such as threat grimaces and frowns, and some patterns of gaze are common in other human cultures and in monkeys and apes, and the meanings of those signs seem to be similar (Shively, 1985; Keating, 1985). In fact, a direct stare into the eyes of another is clearly interpreted as a threat by wolves, dogs, lions, monkeys, apes, and humans, to name only a few. These symptomatic signs are part of our genetic history as mammals and primates, and they are a natural consequence of our particular body design and brain.

OUR PRIMATE LINK: SENSORY AND NEURAL

All humans, monkeys, and apes depend on three primary senses: hearing, vision, and touch. People do not have the range of sound sensitivity possessed by other animals, such as elephant, dog, dolphin, and cat, but humans are particularly sensitive to the sounds made by other humans. Humans have well-developed day vision, and see in a wide range of **colors.** And it is thought that color can influence our moods (Mehrabian and Russell, 1974), preferences for environments, attributions of attractiveness, and so forth (Maslow and Mintz, 1956; Kitchens, Herron, Behnke, and Beatty, 1977).

Moreover, humans have well-developed hand-to-eye coordination and excellent depth perception. The **structure of our hands** enables us to manipulate objects, identify them by touch, and even modify them into tools. Of course, the fact that we **walk upright** helped considerably, for it freed our hands for carrying things, making tools, and playing games such as tennis and football. The mobility of our fingers also enables us to make the manual gestures that allow the hearing impaired to communicate in sign language.

The Human Brain

The portions of our brain devoted to vision, hearing, and motor control of the hands are enormous compared to those areas devoted to **smell** and taste, which are generally poorly developed in people and most other primates. There is some evidence that odors can stimulate memories for past experiences, and may affect our moods and feelings of well-being. And perfumes such as essential oils and incense have been widely used for centuries. However, our senses of smell and taste are inferior to our hearing, vision, and sense of touch.

The Brain's Hemispheres The human brain is also interesting in that it is divided into two halves (hemispheres), left and right, and each hemisphere appears to be responsible for different tasks related to communication (Sperry, 1974). The right hemisphere handles most nonverbal behavior while the left hemisphere is largely responsible for the task of producing, comprehending, and interpreting spoken language. The tasks of locating ourselves in space, tracking objects, understanding pantomime and music, interpreting vocalizations such as laughing, crying, and coughing, and producing and interpreting facial expressions seem to be handled in the right hemisphere.

Lancker (1991) found that the "right hemisphere has a special role in establishing, maintaining, and processing personally relevant aspects of the individual's world" (p. 64). Additionally, visuographic skills such as those associated with reading and writing, gestural ability, and memory for events and stories generally seem to be processed in the right hemisphere. It may be that symptoms and semblances are processed in the right hemisphere and symbols are processed in the left, although this proposition has not been tested experimentally (see: Liska, 1993; Donald, 1991; Chernigovskaya, 1989; Andersen, Garrison, & Andersen, 1979).

Effects of Brain Damage The research on how the brain produces and understands communication behavior is based largely on people who have had severe brain trauma, such as a brain tumor or a stroke, and who have lost the ability to do certain things they could do prior to the trauma. People who suffer trauma to the left hemisphere may as a result be unable to speak and/or understand spoken language. Damage to the right hemisphere may produce any, or some combination, of the following disabilities:

1. Difficulty in identifying a familiar object on the basis of touch.
2. Difficulty in locating an object in space.

3. Difficulty in getting dressed or in finding one's way to a familiar place.
4. The individual may be unable to copy simple geometric designs and may produce disjointed and disorganized drawings.
5. The individual may produce bizarre and inappropriate facial expressions and may have difficulty recognizing others on the basis of facial features.
6. The individual may be unable to read or write.
7. Generally, spatial skills such as recognizing and tracking oneself, other people, and objects may be impaired.

Ants communicate via chemical transmission of information, bats use echolocation, and dolphins use sonar. Elephants use a system of calls transmitted at a frequency too low for humans to detect, dogs can identify individuals on the basis of odor, and cats mark their territory by leaving a scent from a gland under their tails. Monkeys and apes communicate using a wide range of visual signs such as body position and orientation, eye gaze, and facial expressions, and a variety of vocalizations. Likewise humans communicate using visual and vocal signs.

FUNCTIONS AND OUTCOMES OF NONVERBAL BEHAVIOR

Nonverbal communication may be classified by codes, functions, and/or outcomes. Nonverbal codes include visual-auditory codes, such as body position, movement, and orientation (kinesics), physical appearance, and vocal characteristics (vocalics); contact codes involving touch (haptics) and territory (proxemics); and cultural codes including use of space, time, artifacts, and environments.

Nonverbal communication serves a number of important functions, including complementing, contradicting, repeating, regulating, substituting for, and/or accenting the verbal message (Ekman and Friesen, 1969 a, b).

1. In the movie *Dead Poet's Society*, Robin Williams' character emphasized the importance of seeing things from a different perspective by standing on his desk to get a different view of the room. His nonverbal behavior **complemented** the words he used.
2. A friend expresses interest in a story you are telling but, rather than looking at you, she is gazing around the room, shuffling papers, and checking her watch. Just how interested is she? This is an example of a nonverbal message that **contradicts** the verbal one.
3. Some nonverbal behaviors **reinforce** the verbal message, sometimes by **repetition.** Speakers are advised to repeat their major points several times

in a speech. This is frequently accomplished by saying "My first point is . . . " while at the same time holding up an index finger to indicate the number 1.

4. Nonverbal signs serve as a means for **regulating** and **coordinating** conversation. Speakers signal the ends of their speaking turns by leaning back and turning attention toward other members of the group. Listeners indicate when they want a speaking turn by leaning forward, gesturing, and/or opening their mouths in preparation for speaking. We attempt to override interruptions by looking away from the interruptor, talking louder, or holding up a hand in an attempt to silence them.

5. Nonverbal behaviors sometimes **substitute** for a verbal message. We may indicate anger with another by giving them the "silent treatment," and young children frequently indicate anger by sticking their tongues out.

6. Nonverbal behaviors can **accent,** or emphasize, a verbal message, as when a storyteller pauses at the proper point in a gripping story in order to accentuate a particularly suspenseful moment.

Burgoon, Buller, and Woodall (1989) offer another functional arrangement that suggests a more central role for nonverbal behavior in daily interaction. They note that nonverbal behavior is important in conveying emotional information; is central to impression formation and management of those impressions; facilitates identifying race, gender, personality, and culture; structures interaction; is important in defining our relationships with others; and can aid or inhibit our ability to process and comprehend information. Further, nonverbal behaviors provide important clues to **deception.** Finally, nonverbal behavior plays a significant part in our ability to **influence** others or be influenced by them. Thus, nonverbal behavior is important in structuring, regulating, and monitoring social relationships and social ecologies.

Summary Our repertoire of nonverbal behaviors includes symptomatic, semblamatic, and symbolic signs, some of which are shared by members of other cultures and species. Those signs include a number of facial expressions, some vocal characteristics, and signs associated with body type, position, and stance. These signs provide important information about the emotional states of others, one's status relative to the status of others, and one's personality. Moreover, these signs serve as a means for regulating interaction, for influencing others' opinions and behaviors, and for managing social relationships. Nonverbal communication is used to **influence** and **deceive** others, manage impressions, **identify** race, gender, cultural and/or ethnic background, reveal **emotions,** structure **conversations,** and **maintain roles** within various types of social relationships.

HOW DO ENVIRONMENTAL CHARACTERISTICS AFFECT OUR PERCEPTIONS?

Those of you who have camped for an extended period of time in a remote area away from the trappings of the modern world have tasted life as it was thousands of years ago. This is assuming, of course, that you didn't camp in a Winnebago fully equipped with a battery operated TV, a portable stereo, and a fully stocked wet-bar. If you "roughed it," you probably woke up with the sun, hiked and explored during the day, and stayed close to camp and the campfire after dark. You may have tried your hand at catching fish for dinner, which you cooked over a fire, and sought edible greens and mushrooms for a salad.

If you were in the right locale, you may have listened to the sounds of wolves, coyotes, or mountain lions as they hunted their own meals. You probably were very selective about the number and kinds of things you carried in your pack, choosing items that would serve only basic needs. Clothes would be selected for their appropriateness to the climate, rather than fashion, and you may have done laundry in the nearest stream. Your ears would have been treated to the sounds of birds, insects, and small animals rather than the din of phones, traffic, and people. Your experiences in the "wild" would depend upon understanding the signs of nature rather than the artificial environments humans have created in recent times.

Early vs. Contemporary Human Environments

Until relatively recently, at least in terms of geologic time, humans depended on their interpretation of environmental symptoms. Early humans did not build homes or office buildings, but camped by lakes or streams or in open areas. Very early in our evolution, humans probably still sought shelter in the trees at night, just as chimpanzees do now. Early humans wandered large areas of land, their movements tied to seasonal foods such as fruits and vegetables, and to the migrations of the animals they hunted. Possessions would have been few, for they were too difficult to carry over the distances they needed to travel. In fact, the accumulation of goods and personal belongings didn't occur to any great extent until humans developed agriculture some 12,000 years ago. It was at that point that humans built permanent dwellings, began to manufacture and accumulate goods such as clothing, tools, pottery and personal ornaments such as jewelry, and built civilizations based on trading manufactured goods, agricultural products, and skilled services.

For these early people, survival depended upon an intimate knowledge of an environment quite different from the one we inhabit. They found their way around by looking at natural landmarks rather than noting highway signs, street signs, or other landmarks, such as buildings (i.e., semblances and symbols). As far as we know, these people did not make maps of their territories, but used rock formations, streams, and other natural landmarks (i.e., symptoms) to find their way. Food was not piled into a cart at the local 24-hour grocery, but was gathered from various parts of their territory according to the season. They didn't go to their local butcher to buy a roast sealed in plastic. Instead, they learned the habits of the species they hunted, tracked them, and, if they were very lucky, made a kill. Unlike most contemporary humans, they found their own food and processed their own meat. Obtaining food was a full-time job, because they had no means of storing perishables. It was truly feast or famine, and their survival depended upon the whims of nature, their skills at locating and identifying edible plants, and their ability to interpret nonhuman animal behavior.

Most people living today have had few encounters with wild animals. Yet our early ancestors would have been preyed upon by many species, and their survival depended upon their knowing the habits and behaviors of these predators. Hunter-gatherers would have made camp at sundown, for many predators hunt at dusk and in the early hours of dawn. These people would have become quite skilled at reading the behavior of prey animals; such signs would provide clues to the presence of animals dangerous to humans.

Time was not noted by checking a digital watch or a grandfather clock, but would have been calculated by astrological events: sunrise and sunset, changes in the position of the sun, and variations in the cycle of the moon.

These people didn't have jobs, homes, or personal effects to signal their status in the group; instead, status and rank would probably depend on their skills as food gatherers and hunters. High status might also have been granted to those elders who were perceived as a source of great wisdom, which could benefit the survival of the whole group. The traditions and experiences accumulated by the elders of the group would be passed down in the form of oral stories, rituals, and ceremonies. A skilled storyteller was probably considered a person of great importance, one who commanded considerable respect.

The world we inhabit is quite different from that of our ancestors, and our daily lives are governed more by the semblances and symbols we have created than by environmental symptoms. We protect ourselves from predators, now largely other humans, by building homes with lockable doors and security alarms. Few of us hunt, gather, or raise our own food. Instead we buy food in cans and packages, frequently preseasoned and precooked, and our meats come in forms that give no hint as to what the whole animal looked like. Clocks and calendars govern our behavior; and stores, offices, and manufacturing plants run around the clock, thanks to electricity.

Whereas our ancestors traveled by foot, which certainly restricted the territory they could cover, we commute to work and to school, and travel long distances on vacations by some form of motorized vehicle, thus making our perceptions of distance radically different from those who went before us. Whereas our ancestors had very little knowledge of the world and other people outside of their own territory, we can be transported by plane to even the remotest of civilizations in a matter of hours. And television has brought the rest of the world into sharp focus by satellite transmission that brings far away places into our homes. Even environmental catastrophes such as hurricanes and snow storms can be predicted via modern meteorology, and then widely broadcast by radio and television. Indeed, many of us live well protected from the fits and spasms of the natural world.

The Modern Environment and Its Effects

The first homes were probably simply a means of protecting the inhabitants from the elements and from predators. Over the years, however, homes took on additional characteristics, and now they provide important clues to personality, rank and status in society. The structure of a house is a fixed feature, and includes the building materials and exterior and interior design.

Rustic Home vs. High-Rise Condo I live in a small village in the southern Rockies of Colorado where people frequently build homes out of native materials, because they are readily available, and so they blend in better with the environment. The homes sometimes reflect the Spanish and Native American influence on the area, and sometimes they are built to look like the ranch homes of the early west. These homes frequently have many large windows for taking in the view, and are, out of necessity, built to accommodate the contours of mountainous land. The people in my village tend to be outdoorsy, and large decks, patios, and lots of land surrounding their homes reflect this interest. People here value space and privacy, and their homes reflect these values.

Contrast this with people who live in condominium complexes where the dwellings are connected to one another, indistinguishable from each other. The land within the walls of the complex is not private; it's common land for all those who live there. Space and privacy are necessarily restricted by the proximity of neighbors, the design of the complex, and the limited amount of land.

Now, think about the glass-and-steel high-rise apartment buildings of modern cities, whose inhabitants have only their interior living space and the streets and city parks for their territory. Where I live, the amount of land people can call their own is a sign of status. For high-rise apartment dwellers, status goes up according to which floor they are on, with the top floor or penthouse reserved for those of highest rank—that is, to the extent that rank and status are a function of ability to pay high rent.

Furniture and Decor Fixed features such as the size and shape of rooms have considerable influence on our patterns of interaction. Our feelings of intimacy, formality, and willingness to engage in conversation may result, in part, from the size and type of room we are in. Both the arrangement of moveable features such as furniture and the objects that decorate the room influence conversational patterns. A small room filled with comfortable chairs arranged to face one another can facilitate feelings of coziness and congeniality, and increase interaction. On the other hand, a large office dominated by a big desk, straight-back chairs, and a formal arrangement may make us feel intimidated and therefore hesitant to communicate.

The choice of furniture and other items of decoration, including floor coverings, lighting, and color, reveal a great deal about the decorator. My house in Colorado contains rustic vine furniture, rocking chairs, an old oak icebox, and lots of books. The walls are covered with Native American prints, photos of the mountains, and artwork depicting animals, and many of the shelves display animal figurines. My two dogs and three cats always get the best seats in the house. The windows are covered only by lace curtains, to take advantage of our abundant sunlight, and the walls, where not paneled, are painted cream and pale yellow. A computer and printer, stacks of papers and books, and mugs filled with pens and pencils add considerable detail to the image of me you are probably forming. My backyard, front porch, and back deck have tables and chairs that are big, comfortable, and of rustic design. If you are guessing that I am rather informal, spend a lot of time outside, read a great deal, engage in writing of some kind, and like animals, you are right. Visitors tend to feel right at home in this setting and amongst these objects (sometimes more than I'd like).

Lighting Lighting appears to influence our work and social habits, with bright light facilitating task accomplishment and dimmer light more conducive to social interaction. Intimacy is probably facilitated by lower intensities of light. And more formal occasions, especially when associated with business and professional functions, are marked by brighter lights (Burgoon, Buller, and Woodall, 1989).

Use of Color Color has a significant effect on our moods and level of arousal (Acking and Kuller, 1972). Blues and greens appear to have a calming effect, yellows and oranges are energizing, grey, brown, and black may be associated with depression—a dark mood—and reds are arousing and sensual. I once lived in a garden-level apartment whose small bedroom with low ceiling had been painted the dark blue of a stormy sea. I spent one very restless and claustrophobic night in that room. The next day I painted it a pale yellow.

Temperature Temperature also affects our patterns of interaction, with cooler temperatures facilitating task accomplishment and warmer temperatures encouraging interaction—up to a point, of course (Holahan, 1982). We have all experienced hot, muggy days when even reaching to turn the fan up a notch was more effort than we could muster. Given that we live and work in largely climate-controlled buildings, temperatures can be set at will to facilitate or inhibit interaction.

Noise Noise—that is, any sound we don't want to hear—also affects communication (Holahan, 1982). Research indicates that intermittent noise is more distracting than consistent noise, which we habituate to eventually. Workers engaged in tasks requiring a high level of concentration are negatively affected by background noise, and their job performance may suffer. I have been to cocktail parties at professional conferences in which the noise level was so loud that I simply gave up talking with anyone and moved elsewhere. Certain types of background music may facilitate work but impede conversation. The level and type of noise, and our own sensitivity to it, influence our willingness and ability to communicate.

Time and Communication Behavior

Finally, time can also affect communication behavior. Time governs activities in our culture, far more than in other cultures (Hall, 1959). Americans seem to believe that time is money, and so can be bought and sold. Factory workers begin and quit work at the shriek of a whistle, whether the work is completed or not. Students pack up and leave classrooms, with the teacher sometimes in mid-sentence, at the sound of the bell or at the tolling of the classroom clock.

Americans never seem to have enough time. I frequently hear students wishing for more hours in the day, especially at the end of the semester. We have watches with alarms to tell us when to get up, take our medication, begin and end tasks, and so on. A glance at a watch may indicate that a conversation is over, it may signal that whoever looked at their watch is especially busy and thus important, or it may signal boredom with the task or conversation at hand. Time can be a sign of status. And who has not waited at length to see a physician, attorney, dean, or executive who always seems to be "running just a little behind." Yet, if we had been late for our appointment, no allowances would have been made. In this case, punctuality is a one-sided expectation.

Clocks The development of the clock in the 12th and 13th centuries by Benedictine monks apparently had a profound impact on the lives of those outside the monasteries (Postman, 1993), as well as on capitalistic cultures such as our own. The clock was originally designed to regulate prayer times during the course of the monks' day. By the 14th century it was regulating the daily routines of workers and merchants.

"The mechanical clock," as Lewis Mumford wrote, "made possible the idea of regular production, regular working hours and a standardized product." In short, without the clock, capitalism would have been quite impossible. The paradox, the surprise, and the wonder are that the clock was invented by men who wanted to devote themselves more rigorously to God; it ended as the technology of greatest use to men who wished to devote themselves to the accumulation of money. (Postman, 1993, p. 15)

Other cultures are not so bound by time, and this can cause considerable difficulty for Americans. Latino cultures are well known for their more relaxed and informal approach to keeping appointments and meeting deadlines (Hall, 1959). Many Native American cultures have no words for the future; for these people, appointments and deadlines may be irrelevant (Hall, 1959).

I spent some time in Kenya doing research with a colleague and found that we spent a great deal of our time waiting for things to happen. All of the advanced planning in the world didn't get results, and upon our arrival we found ourselves without the vehicle, supplies, and necessary papers we had arranged. It became increasingly clear that Kenyans moved to a rhythm quite different from that in the States. For Kenyans, plans for the future took a back seat to the demands of the present, and the future would be dealt with when and if it arrived. Nonetheless, though at first frustrated, I grew to like the system quite well.

Summary Overall, we perceive environmental attributes and characteristics in terms of their **formality-informality, warmth, privacy, familiarity, constraint** (how easily we think we can leave the environment), and distance (our physical or psychological **proximity** to other people involved in the interaction). The environments we create reveal a great deal about us as individuals, as well as about our culture. Moreover, environments are sometimes specifically designed to influence our perceptions in particular ways. Dentists and physicians now attempt to provide environments that induce feelings of warmth and relaxation. Some offices are designed to inhibit conversation, enhance privacy, and increase formality, while others are designed to facilitate warmth and informal interaction. In such cases, the structure and design of the environment depend upon the function it will serve and, to be realistic, on the resources available to make it serve those functions in the best way possible.

Robert Sommer (1965, 1974), a professor at the University of California at Davis, conducts research on the effects of environments on all kinds of behavior, but especially communication behavior. He studies airports, bars, office buildings, and classrooms. He designed some classrooms at UCD to study the effects of lighting, color, and style and arrangement of furniture on students' performance and perceptions of their class. As you might guess, he found that the standard classroom is not well designed for the exchange of ideas. He offered several suggestions for correcting the problem: comfortable furniture that can be moved at will, natural and incandescent lighting, which is easier on the eyes, larger rooms in which students can easily form groups, and soft colors that are a midpoint between those that energize and those that have a calming effect.

Judging from the classrooms I inhabit, his words went unnoticed. However, many universities are old, designed long before people became aware of the impact of environmental characteristics on human behavior. In these days of tight money, renovating buildings to serve better the purposes for which they were designed may be deemed too costly. In some cases, then, our only option is to be aware of the impact of these environments on our perceptions and behavior and attempt to adjust accordingly.

WHAT DO OUR BODIES, FACES, AND EYES SAY ABOUT US?

"She had a face that launched a thousand ships." "It was written all over her face." "If looks could kill, I would be dead and buried." "Their eyes spoke the language of love." "He walks as though he carried the weight of the world on his shoulders." What all of these commonplace sayings emphasize is the potentially powerful messages we send with our bodies, faces, and eyes. The point of this discussion is to highlight the ways in which our faces, bodies, and eyes reveal our feelings for others, our social standing relative to others, our general personality traits, and so on.

Body Type

Bodies are generally identified as one of three types: **ectomorphic,** characterized as slender and long limbed; **mesomorphic,** characterized as athletic and muscular; and **endomorphic,** characterized as a rounded and heavy build.

Body Type and Personality Research (Sheldon, 1942, 1954; Lester, 1982) indicates that specific personality traits are perceived to be associated with these different body types. The ectomorph is described as nervous, tense, detached, meticulous, and tactful. The mesomorph is described as confident, energetic, dominant, self-reliant, adventuresome, and hot-tempered. The endomorph is characterized as slow, sociable, relaxed, good-natured, and forgiving. Body characteristics such as height and weight are included in these overall body types. Status and power are associated with height, and tall people are generally perceived more positively than are short people, up to a point, especially for men. Heavy people are generally considered unattractive and are frequently shunned. These are, of course, merely typical associations made about personality on the basis of body type alone. This does not mean that mesomorphs are really adventuresome or that ectomorphs are really tactful or that tall people are more powerful.

How Advertising Exploits Body Type Associations   However, these associations are clearly exploited—by advertisers, for example. Think about the body types of the men used in commercials that feature products associated with the outdoors, sports, or vehicles that will take us on the road to adventure. The men in these commercials typically have a mesomorphic build. Women featured in commercials tend to be those with an ectomorphic build. Indeed, thinness, especially for women, is highly valued in this culture. Some blame the recent explosion in cases of bulimia and anorexia nervosa among women on this emphasis on being thin. The message that a woman must be long and lean in order to be considered attractive and that a man must be muscular and fit is repeatedly reinforced by the media.

Culturally Reinforced Body Type Images   It is easier to understand why the mesomorphic body type is preferred in males than it is to understand the current trend for thinness in women. Contrary to the adage that one can never be too rich or too thin, one can be too thin, and the body clearly compensates for this condition by going into "starvation" mode in an attempt to conserve energy. Women who drop below about 10 percent body fat cease menstruation. This confers a clear survival advantage because a pregnant or lactating woman needs a certain amount of body fat to sustain her life and the life of her child. Additionally, the starved body ultimately will begin to consume muscle and organ tissue in an attempt to generate the energy necessary for life to continue. Thus, striving to attain the ideal body image portrayed in fashion magazines and in advertising has a number of undesirable consequences, including dissatisfaction with one's physical image and the development of bizarre eating disorders.

Attractiveness Norms   But how important is attractiveness? Generally, women who are considered attractive receive higher grades in school (Murphy, Nelson, and Cheap, 1981; Singer, 1964; Singer and Lamb, 1966; Clifford and Walster, 1973), are more persuasive, are given lighter sentences for crimes, and are far more likely to marry than are unattractive women. Additionally, unattractive children receive less attention from their teachers. Teachers distance themselves from unattractive children by reducing eye contact, speaking to them less frequently, and maintaining greater physical distance during interaction. Widgery and Webster (1969) found that attractive people generally were rated as more credible than unattractive people.

Finally, perceptions of attractiveness as we age reveal a double standard when applied to men and women. Men become more distinguished and attractive with age, but women do not. Consider that ads for cosmetics that claim to fight the aging process are aimed almost exclusively at women. Consider also that women are more likely than men to have cosmetic surgery (face lifts and liposuction) designed to conceal the effects of aging. Ways to treat baldness, a typically male trait and one associated with age, have engaged men for generations. Otherwise, the changes in appearance that come with age seem to be more acceptable for men than for women.

Certainly, then, attractive people receive more social rewards, have more opportunities to engage in relationships, and have more opportunities to attain success due, in part, to their early experiences in school. Overall, attractive people are perceived to have more socially desirable characteristics (Bar-Tal and Saxe, 1976). Even young children show preferences for attractive over unattractive peers. Dion and Berscheid (1972), for example, found that nursery school children described attractive children as more likable, while unattractive children were described as mean and aggressive. Further, people with certain body characteristics may be expected to behave in particular ways: The mesomorph may be expected to be more dominant and therefore may behave in more dominant ways. The tendency to behave in ways consistent with the expectations of others is sometimes called the *self-fulfilling prophecy* or *Pygmalion effect*. McArthur and Baron (1983) describe the self-fulfilling prophecy as "(a) eliciting from others the behaviors we expect to perceive, and (b) perceiving in others the behaviors and traits we expect to perceive" (p. 233).

Attractiveness Norms Through History Standards of attractiveness have changed considerably over time. Those of you who have studied ancient Greek and Roman sculpture may have noticed that male body types were generally mesomophic while female body types were typically endomorphic. If art is a reflection of the standards of beauty for that time, then mesomorphic males and endomorphic females were the ideal body types.

That these body types were once considered ideals makes some sense from an evolutionary point of view. Early in our evolution as hunter-gatherers, muscular males may have been preferred mates because they were better able to hunt and protect the group, their mates, and their offspring. Females with large breasts and full hips and thighs may have been preferred by males, since these characteristics reflect reproductive potential. Nursing and caring for offspring drained the fat and energy reserves of females, especially during lean times. And the stores of fat on the breasts, hips, and thighs of females may have made them more able to withstand the stresses of a hunter-gatherer lifestyle and thus raise more children to adulthood. Over the course of time, these characteristics of survival became institutionalized as standards of beauty.

Endomorphic body types appear to be the standard for both males and females from the Middle Ages through the late 1900s. This body type may have suggested wealth and thus become associated with status. Heaviness was an indication that a person had access to steady sources of food and did not engage in manual labor. Both are signs of prosperity, and those who were prosperous were more desirable and thus more likely to mate and leave offspring. The endomorphic body type for both males and females was evidently a standard of attractiveness until recent times.

Culture and Climate Typical body types also differ across human cultures, and many anthropologists believe that these body type differences are originally the result of differences in climate (e.g., Campbell, 1988; Fagan, 1992). Tall, thin people tend to be found in hot, dry climates, while a more compact and round body type is characteristic of people who live in cold climates, where stores of body fat act as insulation from the cold. Tall, thin people have more skin surface and thus dispel heat more effectively. This would not be advantageous for those in a cold climate who need to conserve heat. Since we tend to mate with people who resemble ourselves, these body types would persist and eventually become formalized as standards of attractiveness.

Clothing and Personal Effects

Morris (1977) has emphasized the importance of clothing in transmitting social signals. He has proposed three functions of clothing: comfort/protection, modesty, and cultural display.

Comfort and Protection Clothing is certainly utilitarian, and protects us from the elements. And styles of clothing reflect the particular characteristics of the climate in which the wearers live. People from the Middle East who dress traditionally wear long, loose robes of thin cotton in light colors to protect themselves from the intense heat and sun of their desert climate. The lighter colors reflect heat, and the loose-fitting robes allow air to circulate, thus cooling the body. The Native Americans of the northern plains protected themselves from the cold and snow of winter by wearing leather suits and pants and buffalo hide moccasins and robes.

Modesty Clothing also serves to conceal parts of the body. Such modesty varies from individual to individual, from culture to culture, and over time. Traditional Muslim women are required to cover themselves completely except for their eyes. During the 1960s, some American women pushed the established norms of modesty to the limits by wearing miniskirts that barely covered their posteriors, and by going braless and topless. The Broadway musical *Hair* ended with a nude scene that caused quite a stir; I well remember the audience's reaction when I first saw the play in the early 1970s. Full body exposure and rather explicit sexual poses have been featured in magazines such as *Playboy* and *Penthouse* since the 1970s. The annual swimsuit edition of *Sports Illustrated* is their best-selling issue. And the rock videos featured on MTV reflect the more relaxed standards of modesty evident in the 1990s.

Not everyone adheres to these more relaxed standards of modesty in dress, and the garments we choose—their fit, cut, and style—provide important clues to our individual and cultural standards of modesty.

Cultural Display Clothes also signal our social standing, interests and lifestyle, occupation, group identity, political beliefs, and sexual orientation (Thourlby, 1978; Mathes and Kempher, 1976). Social movements are marked, in part, by the clothing and personal effects of those involved in them.

I was quite active politically in the '60s and early '70s, and my typical uniform was an army jacket or fringed suede jacket, bell bottom pants that looked like the American flag (the stars and stripes decorated my posterior), lots of silver rings, and, of course, many strands of beads. Such attire quickly identified me as a member of the antiwar movement to insiders and outsiders alike. However, while I no longer dress that way, my political beliefs have changed very little.

While I was at Indiana University, the punk movement hit, and members of the group were immediately recognizable from their black leather jackets, their hair styles (dyed blue, green, or purple, and spiked or assymetrical), and jewelry made of chains.

I once served as a research associate at a primate research facility and was required to wear a white lab coat even though I did my work in the outdoor field stations. Although the white coat was in part utilitarian, in that it kept my clothes clean, equally as important was that it identified me as a member of the group.

Initial Impressions Dress is most powerful in initial impressions, and those effects tend to diminish as we get to know a person. Interviews are an excellent illustration of the effects of dress on interviewers' initial perceptions of an interviewee's abilities (Watson and Smeltzer, 1982). The uniform for men is clearly the suit, so they have fewer problems than do women, who have no such standard uniform (Molloy, 1988).

Forsythe, Drake, and Cox (1985) conducted a study in which they dressed a woman in various outfits for a job interview. The same woman was rated more favorably when dressed in a skirted navy suit than when dressed in a light beige dress with a gathered skirt and round collar. The suit apparently made the woman look more professional, businesslike, and official. Students' perceptions of college professors are also influenced by dress. Professors dressed rather formally in a traditional dark suit were rated as organized, knowledgeable, and better prepared, while professors attired more informally (jeans, sport shirt, and sneakers) were judged as friendly, flexible, fair, and enthusiastic. Some sex differences emerged, in that male professors dressed formally were perceived as more knowledgeable than female professors dressed formally.

Personal Effects and Makeup Personal effects such as glasses (Levy and Poll, 1976; Hamid, 1968), briefcases (Korda, 1977), and jewelry (Molloy, 1988) and the use of cosmetics (McKeachie, 1952; Cox and Glick, 1986) have been shown to influence perceptions of competence and authority.

Sunglasses Sunglasses hide our eyes and act somewhat like a mask (Stengel, 1984). They also allow us to look at others at will. My eyes are very sensitive to fluorescent lighting, and I frequently wear rather lightly tinted sunglasses during class. My students have reported that they felt very uneasy at first because the sunglasses hid my eyes and thus concealed the direction and nature of my gaze.

Regular Glasses Regular glasses have typically been associated with bookishness and intelligence. Glasses worn only for reading are typically associated with age. An episode of TV's "Northern Exposure" focused on this very issue: Maggie discovered that she needed reading glasses. The eye doctor explained that it was not uncommon for people in their thirties to need reading glasses and that farsightedness was a normal result of aging. Maggie resisted getting glasses because others would then know she was getting older.

Glasses can also be used as a prop. For instance, putting your glasses away may signal the end of a meeting; playing with your glasses may indicate boredom with a conversation or nervousness and stress.

Briefcase The briefcase seems to be the status symbol of professional men and women, especially for women, who are still trying to fit into the largely male-dominated corporate world (Korda, 1977).

Cosmetics Cosmetics apparently enhance perceptions of femininity, sensuality, and attractiveness, but detract from perceptions of job-related competence (Cox and Glick, 1986).

How we dress may also affect how we feel about ourselves. The notion that we feel good when we believe that we look good probably has some truth to it, for looking good may enhance our feelings of confidence and self-esteem. And confidence and self-esteem are likely to improve our communication competence.

Other Influences It is important to remember that the effects of dress and personal artifacts are subject to the influence of the media, the economy, and time. Not too long ago pants were considered inappropriate for women, and jeans were worn only by cowboys and farmers. Now we can buy denim tuxedos and evening gowns. A briefcase may be a symbol of status for the moment but fall into disgrace a year from now. "Power ties" were first yellow, then red, and who knows what by the time you are finished reading this book. According to a recent *Time* (1991), the trend in the '90s will be a return to more basic American values such as family and home, and a move away from the materialistic values of the '80s. The claim advanced in this article is that Americans are adopting a lifestyle of minimalism, with emphasis on environmental issues, conservation of resources (natural and monetary), and fashions and home furnishings that are "politically correct." Therefore, fake furs are replacing the real thing as a result of the impact of the animal rights movement, and there is a trend toward clothing made of natural rather than petroleum-based synthetics, another reflection of changing attitudes toward the environment.

Body Position, Posture, and Orientation

Two people are engaged in conversation. One is seated in an upright posture, feet flat on the floor, while the other is lounging in a chair, one ankle balanced on the knee of the other leg. Who is the more dominant person in this interaction? The answer is that the person with the more relaxed, asymmetrical posture is probably the dominant one. Those of higher status and dominance tend to assume more relaxed postures, use more expansive gestures, and stand taller than those of lower rank (Goffman, 1961).

Monkeys and apes behave in similar ways, and these status-related body positions are thought to be deeply ingrained in our evolutionary history (Weisfeld and Beresford, 1982; Liska, 1990).

The extent to which members of a dyad or group maintain congruent body position is a reflection of their relative status (Burgoon, Buller, and Woodall, 1989). Those of equal status will have similar postures (congruence), while those of unequal status will have incongruent body positions. The task in which the group is engaged also influences the degree of congruence or incongruence. Groups engaged in competition with another group mirror one another's body position less than when all groups are in cooperation (LaFrance, 1985).

Body posture is also a reflection of immediacy (liking) and relaxation. Forward lean is one good indicator of liking, whereas backward lean, asymmetrical body position, and relaxed hands are associated with relaxation (Mehrabian, 1971). In general, body positions that improve visibility and reduce physical distance are associated with liking, relaxation, and an open, positive attitude.

There are some gender differences in body position, and they tend to be those associated with differences in status and dominance (see Hall, 1984). While men generally tend to adopt the postures associated with relaxation, women tend to use the body positions and orientations associated with lower status and dominance. Men walk in a way that demonstrates relaxation and confidence, while women walk with their legs close together and arms close to their bodies. The latter style is not indicative of a relaxed, confident style.

Gestures

Gestures have been categorized by Ekman and Friesen (1969a) as *emblems* (symbols); *illustrators,* such as pointing; *regulators,* such as turn-taking cues; *affect displays* that reveal our current emotional state; and *adaptors,* such as tapping a pencil or moving our feet.

Emblems Emblems are gestural symbols, such as the "OK" sign or raising an index finger to indicate the number 1. These gestures, like language, are learned and culture-specific. I was warned before attending a conference in Brazil that the gesture meaning "OK" in our culture means something quite different to Brazilians. For them our sign for OK is akin to "flipping the bird." I didn't realize at the time how frequently and unconsciously I use that gesture until I found myself using it with a Brazilian bus driver from whom I had asked directions. I signaled that I understood with the OK sign, only to have the doors of the bus slammed emphatically in my face.

Illustrators Illustrators are gestures that accompany speech by aiding in description, showing spatial relationships, emphasizing main points, and so on. The gestures used to indicate direction are illustrators.

Regulators Regulators are gestures that direct the flow of conversation, and include head nods, hand movements, and body lean and position. Regulators control the flow of conversation.

Affect Displays Emotional states such as happiness, sadness, and nervousness are revealed by body posture and stance, and by gestures such as crossing the arms or reaching out to touch another. Gestures combined with body posture reflect the intensity of emotion.

Adaptors Adaptors are signs that serve physical or psychological functions and help an individual release stress. Playing with your hair, fiddling with a pencil, or shaking your leg are all adaptors. Adaptors such as foot shuffling and fiddling with objects are generally unconscious behaviors, and as such may leak information about the goals and intentions of the individual, even when the individual is attempting to conceal that information. Ekman and Friesen (1969b) have discovered that clues to deception are most often revealed by the lower body and hands. In addition to other symptoms, such as increased eye blink rate and perspiration, foot shuffling and object manipulation are important indicators of anxiety, and anxiety is frequently associated with deceptive attempts. (See Table 10.1.)

Communication Gestures serve important communicative functions in that they help us construct and comprehend verbal messages. While there are individual differences in the amount of gesturing, most people gesture when they are trying to formulate a verbal message. The belief is that gesturing helps us find appropriate words and facilitates structuring messages. People tend to gesture more when they are describing a process, giving complex spatial directions, or making fine verbal discriminations (Baxter, Winters, and Hammer, 1968; Cohen, 1977). That people gesture while talking on the phone is some indication of the importance of gesture in producing oral messages. Gestures also help us understand oral messages better, especially when the content of those messages is detailed and complicated or when the message describes a spatial relationship such as giving directions (Cohen and Harrison, 1973).

One of the exercises I use to illustrate this point is to draw a rather complicated geometric figure and have someone describe the design to the class without the aid of any gestures. The rest of the class then attempts to reproduce the design based on the oral description. The next step is to describe the design with the aid of gestures and have the class draw the design again. As you might imagine, the figures drawn without the aid of the gestures are largely inaccurate. However, accuracy improves considerably with the addition of gestures. The discussion following this exercise generally centers on how frustrating it is to try to talk and listen without the benefit of gestures.

Faces and Facial Expressions

Evolution of the Face The evolution of the human face can be traced back approximately 350 million years to a fish called *Crossopterygia*, which migrated to land at about that time. This fish had both gills and lungs, and it is the gill muscles and gill arch bones that led to a muscular veil that eventually developed into the human face. Approximately 70 million years ago some mammals took to the trees and among their descendants are the living primates:

TABLE 10.1 Symptoms of Deception

Below is a list of clues a listener can use to detect deception in a speaker. They are *signals*—or better, *symptoms*—because they bear a natural, unchangeable relation to the physical states they represent. They are not *symbols*, because they are not arbitrary. Thus they do not constitute communication in and of themselves, by definition. To say that a speaker "communicates" the fact that he is attempting to deceive seems to be a silly use of the word. On the other hand, these symptoms of deception are *extremely* important to a listener trying to understand and evaluate a speaker's communication, as are many other symptoms of speakers' various psychological and biological states. They are like the context in which communication occurs, in that, while they do not themselves constitute communication, they are integrally involved in it, associated with it, and necessary to its interpretation. A person who claims to understand communication must understand and be sensitive to both the contexts in which it occurs and the symptoms associated with it.

Face	*Body*	*Voice*	*Language*
Micromomentary facial expressions	Pointless hand mannerisms (rings, pencils, drumming, nails)	Restricted pitch variety	Type-token ratio
Pupil dilation	Hair grooming	Pitch breaks and quavering (muscle tension)	Verbal ("Freudian") slips
Eye blink rate	Foot shuffling (vestigial)	Restricted pitch quality (absence of resonances)	
Perspiration	Posture shifts	Breathiness	
Eyebrow flashes	Leg crossing	Increased or decreased speaking frequency	
Muscle tension	Palsy		
Dry mouth			
Averted gaze			
Excessive frowning			
Excessive and inappropriate smiling			
Excessive and inappropriate laughing			
Lip biting			

humans, monkeys, and apes. As a result of their arboreal existence, these mammals developed acute color vision and depth perception, their hearing became highly tuned to the sounds of their compatriots, and, due to a diet of fruit, their teeth decreased in size. They developed grasping hands with sensitive finger pads, and their brains became increasingly larger. They lived in groups and developed close social bonds with their kin. Importantly, infants were born dependent on their mothers for survival and therefore enjoyed a long protected period in which they could explore their environment and play with their peers. These attributes played a key role in fostering interaction. These mammals and their successors probably lived in rather small territories and came into regular face-to-face contact with one another. Faces, then, would be important sources of information. Early on, infants spend most of their time with their mothers, and part of that time is spent in face-to-face interaction. Subtle changes in facial movements could be easily monitored by the mother, and her behavior could be adjusted accordingly.

Facial Expression   Over time, the muscles of the human face became highly specialized. The muscles of the face also came under voluntary control, and individuals could alter their expressions to suit social needs. The result was the highly mobile and expressive faces that surround us in our daily life. Further, faces became highly individualized, and many primates recognize one another largely on the basis of faces.

Facial recognition and expression are primary, or "primitive," traits, because the source of these capabilities is far back in the history of our species (Darwin, 1872). And we share a number of basic facial expressions with our primate relatives, including anger, fear, sadness, happiness, and surprise. An additional expression, disgust, is evident in all human cultures. All of these expressions develop early in childhood. Even congenitally blind infants exhibit the same facial expressions as their sighted counterparts. Faces are considered "preferred patterns," because we are predisposed to make sense out of the pattern. At approximately three weeks, infants demonstrate a preference for the image of the human face over all other images (see Landau, 1989).

Norms for Emotional Display   Along with the voice, faces are the best indicators of emotions and moods. Body position, stance, and coordination help us judge the intensity of emotion. We learn the norms (called *affect display rules*) for when, how long, and to what degree or intensity emotional displays are appropriate in various situations. These norms vary radically across cultures. When these norms are violated we tend to make negative evaluations of the individual. Depending on the nature of the norm violation, we may judge the person to be foreign, insensitive, emotionally overwrought, or emotionally unstable.

Facial Management   People don't learn how to smile; they learn when smiling is appropriate. Ekman, Friesen, and Ellsworth (1982) refer to this as facial management. They propose four ways in which we manage our facial expressions in social situations: intensify them, deintensify them, neutralize them, or mask them. Sometimes we enhance or exaggerate facial expressions to maintain positive social interactions. Imagine your response to your mother when she drops in for an unexpected visit on the very weekend you've planned to have an extended date with a person you've lusted after for a long time. This may be the time you choose to "grin and bear it," and you respond with exaggerated enthusiasm.

Sometimes we need to deintensify our facial responses. You may be really angry with a professor who chewed you out publicly, but if and when you confront him or her about it you are likely to try to act rational and composed.

Some situations call upon us to avoid emotional displays altogether. I recently went to a friend's wake, and all of us in attendance did our best to act as normal as possible.

Finally, sometimes we substitute a more socially appropriate emotion for the one we are actually feeling. Watch the losing team after a football game as they congratulate the members of the winning team. Though they must feel dejected, angry, or frustrated, most will put on a big smile and hug the winners.

As you already know, we have considerable control over our faces; as a result, we can modify, exaggerate, or substitute one expression for another. Our ability to do so is related to age, gender, individual differences, and training (Zivin, 1982). Control over the facial muscles begins at birth (Charlesworth and Kreutzer, 1973). Early on, smiling is induced by a face represented by two eyes, a nose, and a forehead (Wolff, 1963; Vine, 1973). By about age two to three months a human face is the best elicitor of smiling (Reynolds, 1981).

Overall, women are better at expressing emotions than men, although this difference may be the result of gender stereotyping (Hall, 1984). That is, because expressions of emotion are more acceptable for women than for men, women may be better at it because of all the practice they get.

Encoders There appear to be two types of encoders: externalizers and internalizers. **Externalizers,** which women tend to be, are particularly skilled at portraying emotion; **internalizers,** who tend to be men, are considerably less adept (Malandro, Barker, and Barker, 1989). These two types seem to be related to specific personality traits. Externalizers tend to be more social, extroverted, and higher in self-esteem than internalizers.

Decoding Emotions While we are reasonably good at identifying emotions based on facial expressions, we typically are unable to identify what cues led us to associate a behavior with a specific emotion. The social context provides important information about emotions. We know that people may cry when they are happy as well as when they are sad. Yet the two forms of crying may be indistinguishable. Thus, we use clues from the social situation to determine the emotional reasons for someone's tears. If the person who is crying has just received an acceptance to Harvard Law School, we can presume that happiness motivated the tears.

The accuracy of our judgments is influenced by the nature of the expression and by the gender of the decoder. Overall, pleasant emotions, particularly happiness, are the easiest expressions to identify (Feinman and Feldman, 1982). It should come as no surprise that posed facial expressions are easier to recognize than are spontaneous ones (Fujita, Harper, and Wiens, 1980). Finally, generally speaking, women are better than men at identifying facial expressions. Males, however, get better at identifying the facial expressions of others as they get to know the individual better (Hall, 1984; Wagner, MacDonald, and Manstead, 1986).

Types of Facial Displays There appear to be three main types of facial displays. Since there are no "pure" emotions (for example, anger and fear frequently go hand in hand), the first type of facial display is called the **affect blend.** The second type is called **affect partials,** which are expressions in which one part of the face shows the major emotion. Malandro, Barker, and Barker (1989) cite the example of a kidnap victim who tries to remain calm and to mask any expression of fear. However, the fact that the person is afraid may show in the eyes but not in any other part of the face.

The third type, **micromomentary facial expressions,** are fleeting expressions that cross the face so swiftly that they can only be identified when videotaped and then played back in slow motion. Videotapes of people talking demonstrate that micromomentary facial expressions are sometimes incompatible with overall facial expressions and the verbal message. Although these facial expressions occur below our visual threshold for explicit recognition, such expressions have been demonstrated to affect our judgments. Psychologists are particularly interested in micromomentary facial expressions, for they can be important in diagnosis and treatment.

Clearly there is a strong relationship between our ability to produce facial expressions and our ability to identify and understand facial expressions. Generally, women are better than men at producing and recognizing facial expressions, as are those with more extroverted personalities. Further, the ability to produce and recognize facial expressions improves with age (Mayo and LaFrance, 1978). Finally, while facial expressions are similar across cultures, the display rules for producing facial expressions differ considerably across cultures.

Eye Behavior and Gaze

Our language is filled with references to the power of our eyes. In ancient Greece a fixed stare was thought to have the power to bring physical harm; hence the phrase "the evil eye." Various eye movements are associated with a range of expression: (1) a downward glance indicates modesty; (2) wide eyes suggest frankness, wonder, or terror; and (3) eyes rolled upward may indicate fatigue or suggest that another's behavior is strange. Further, excessive blinking may be flirtatious or indicate anxiety and stress. **Eye blink rate** tends to decrease when we are focused on a task. And, though our pupils dilate and constrict in response to changing light conditions, **pupil dilation** is also associated with interest, arousal, and attentiveness (Hayes and Plax, 1971).

Importance of Gaze Gaze serves as a means for regulating conversation, monitoring feedback, and expressing emotion, and is important in communicating the nature of interpersonal relationships.

Regulating Conversation Gaze helps in regulating the flow of conversation in that it is a sign of when to begin and end conversations and is one factor in turn-taking cues (Kendon, 1967; Wiemann and Knapp, 1975). Suppose you are in the cafeteria and see someone you know casually but don't care for. The person's moving your way, and you fear they may try to initiate conversation. One way to forestall conversation is to avoid looking at the person. Now suppose you see someone at some distance you *do* want to talk to; you may look their way in hopes they will see you and come over to talk. I can generally tell if my students have done the reading for a class meeting on the basis of their eye behavior. If they stare at their desks when I begin asking questions about the reading, I generally assume they have not done the reading. Typically, we avert gaze when we feel uncomfortable or embarrassed. Further, eye contact is used in turn-taking in conversation. If we feel someone is going to interrupt, we tend to look away in order to keep our speaking turn.

Monitoring Feedback Gaze is also important in monitoring feedback. A direct gaze generally indicates attention. Note, however, that an uninterrupted gaze or stare is usually associated with aggression, assertiveness, or dominance, depending upon the situation. We tend to look away from conversational partners when we are trying to process difficult or complex information. We also tend to look away when we are asked questions that require reflection rather than factual responses. Finally, we watch others involved in a conversation to check their responses to what we have said, to check their attentiveness to and thus their interest in the topic of the conversation, and to monitor their feelings toward us.

Expressing Emotion Eyes and eyebrows work together to reveal emotional states. Picture someone whose eyes are squinted, with their brows knitted tightly together. What emotion is the person feeling? Surprise, anger, happiness? Probably the individual is revealing anger. Raised brows and wide eyes generally indicate surprise or terror, and our evaluation will depend upon the situation the other person is in, as well as the emotion revealed by the rest of the face and by body position and stance. All of these factors combine to give us an overall impression of the moods and feelings of another person.

Gaze signals the feelings, attitudes, level of liking, and degree of interest of conversational interactants. We tend to look at those with whom we are interpersonally involved, look longer at those objects and people we like or those events that are novel, and we look longer at objects and people that are rewarding. Positive relationships are characterized by high levels of mutual gaze, while negative relationships are characterized by less mutual gaze. There are some exceptions, however: Intense gaze and mutual gaze are evident in intimidation, insults, and open hostility and aggression. Of course, gaze is not the only indication of the nature of relationships; the level of intimacy is also indicated by physical proximity, amount of smiling, tone of voice, and so forth (Burgoon, Buller, and Woodall, 1989).

Gaze and Status   The relative status of interactants is signaled by patterns of gaze. Submissive primates watch dominant animals more closely than they watch those of lower status. This pattern is also characteristic of humans, and breaking eye contact is a reliable index of dominance/submissiveness. The individual who breaks the gaze first is the submissive individual in the pair. Those who are looked at more often and for a longer duration are assumed to be of higher status and more dominant. *Visual dominance behavior* (Exline, Ellyson, and Long, 1975), a characteristic of those in high positions, conforms to the following pattern: Low-status people are looked at less and receive less talk directed their way. High-status people look more at others when they are speaking than when they are listening. In a group, people of intermediate dominance are looked at the most, because both those of high and those of low status look in their direction. The high-status person receives eye contact characterized as intermittent. People who show visual dominance behavior are generally perceived as leaders. Further, higher-status people may even control the gaze of others. Lower-status people tend to follow the gaze of high-status people; that is, they look at what high-status people look at. Moreover, high-status people can keep attention focused on themselves.

Gaze and Personality   Personal and personality characteristics also influence amount of gaze. Those who are extroverted or high in need for affiliation and involvement tend to engage in gaze and mutual gaze more than those who are introverted or low in self-esteem. A person who is trying to be persuasive will look more at others, and perceptions of credibility are affected by patterns of gaze. Typically, more gaze is associated with sincerity, truthfulness, and friendliness.

Gender Differences   Finally, there are some gender differences in patterns of gaze; those tend to be the same patterns we see in interactants of differing status. Overall, females tend to look at all others more than do males. Females look more at others on almost all measures of gaze, including frequency and duration of gaze (Libby, 1970). Many argue that this pattern of gaze characteristic of women is the result of the fact that their status is lower relative to men (Hall, 1984).

Summary   Our faces and eyes are important sources of information about our relative status, emotional states, level of involvement in a conversation, and our feelings of liking or disliking for others. These clues combined with other nonverbal behaviors such as body type, stance, and orientation have important implications for how we are perceived and evaluated and how we perceive and judge others. Our voices are also significant in revealing emotional states, and they help us to identify individuals and regulate conversation.

WHAT DO OUR VOICES REVEAL ABOUT US?

Our voices are unique, and are another way in which we identify and differentiate among individuals. Voices also provide a basis on which we determine the sex, occupation, ethnic background, and personality of another (Burgoon, Buller, and Woodall, 1989). Vocal cues also contribute to our perceptions of the emotional states of others and their credibility, and they help us determine whether or not someone is attempting to deceive us. While we obviously have control over our voices in that we can produce the sounds of our language, vocal characteristics such as tone, pitch, rate, and accent are typically less under voluntary control. Thus, many of the vocal cues discussed here are symptoms of our physiological states of the moment; none of these vocal characteristics are symbols.

Judging Emotions from the Voice

We are reasonably accurate at judging emotions on the basis of vocal qualities such as rate, tone, and pitch. The most reliably rated emotions on the basis of voice alone are anger, nervousness, sadness, and happiness (Apple and Hecht, 1982). Further, decoding accuracy tends to increase as a relationship develops (Hornstein, 1967). When we are excited, our voices tend to get higher in pitch and louder, and the rate of speech increases. Vocal cues associated with sadness tend to be the opposite, so the voice sounds flat and lifeless, and the rate of speech tends to decrease. What vocal qualities do you typically associate with expressions of anger, love, and respect?

Vocal cues are important in initial impressions, and research has demonstrated that we are reasonably consistent in our guesses about someone's socioeconomic background (Harms, 1961), age, and sex on the basis of voice alone (Graddol and Swann, 1983). However, some of those judgments are clearly not necessarily accurate. According to a study by Williams (1970), for example, those who spoke a nonstandard form of English were labeled as culturally disadvantaged, and were rated lower on measures of success, ability, intelligence, and social awareness than were speakers of standard English. This does not, of course, necessarily mean that those attributions are well founded. Generally, we revise such attributions if given the opportunity to get to know a person.

Vocal Preferences

We appear to have preferences for some voices over others: A strong voice with a moderate rate of speech and a lot of vocal variety is associated with positive characteristics. A nasal voice is rated as highly unpleasant (Addington, 1968). Moderately-fast to fast speech rates are associated with communication competence and increased ratings of social attractiveness and credibility (Street and Brady, 1982). And increasing pitch variety yields perceptions of extroversion.

Interpreting Vocal Characteristics

Restricted pitch variety, pitch breaks and quavering resulting from muscle tension, restricted pitch quality, breathiness, increased or decreased speaking frequency, stammering or stuttering, and pauses may indicated anxiety or attempts at deception, depending upon the circumstances (Mahl, 1959). For most of us, attempting to deceive another produces some anxiety, since we are socialized to believe that deception and lying are inappropriate, if not sinful. A number of other factors may be considered when we are determining the extent to which another person is being truthful. These include an increase in eye blink rate, muscle tension in the face, dry mouth, an averted gaze, foot shuffling, and fidgeting with objects such as pencils and rings (Knapp and Comadena, 1979; deTurck and Miller; 1985; Ekman, 1985).

The situation is essential in our determination of the truthfulness of another. Some situations, such as public presentations, induce such behavior, which is probably nothing more than symptoms of nervousness and stress. However, experienced speakers (such as politicians) who exhibit some combination of these behaviors may lead us to suspect their motives, since we typically don't expect experienced speakers to be visibly nervous. It may be, however, that these persons are speaking to a "hostile" audience, that is, an audience in extreme disagreement with them. In such a situation even the most adept and assured speakers may evidence symptoms of tension.

How Voice Signals Status

Authority, expertise, dominance, and status are signaled by a "confident" voice, which is characterized by greater energy and loudness, faster tempo, fewer and shorter pauses, higher and more varied pitch, more expressiveness, and greater fluency. This type of voice is deemed businesslike, professional, and rather impersonal. It is also associated with higher ratings of credibility (Burgoon, Buller, and Woodall, 1989).

Meanings of Silence

Silence is a powerful indicator of respect, reverence, and authority, and can create interpersonal distance. Silence is frequently an indication of, and necessary to, cognitive planning; such silence is typical of reflective thinking, planning future messages, and the like. Silence is used to show respect for authority, and children learn quickly to be quiet in church, at funerals, and when someone of high status has the floor. Silence can also be used as a form of disapproval, as in the "silent treatment," or as a way to distance ourselves or withdraw from interaction with others. On the other hand, silence can reflect our feelings of comfort and security with a close friend or significant other. Sometimes there is simply no need to talk, and we feel no sense of anxiety over silence when in the company of those we know well.

Our voices identify us as individuals, reveal important clues to our emotional states, personality, age, and sex, and they play an important role in our perceptions of the credibility, competence, and honesty of others. Our voices reflect our feelings for others, and silence can serve to increase or decrease interpersonal and social distance.

WHAT IS THE SIGNIFICANCE OF TOUCH IN OUR SOCIAL RELATIONSHIPS?

Touch is critical to our physical health, mental well-being, and social development. Tactile sensitivity may be the first postnatal sensory process to become functional. The importance of touch is evident in studies of animal, as well as human, growth and development.

Harlow's Studies

In a series of famous studies, Harry Harlow, a primatologist, and his associates (e.g., Harlow and Harlow, 1962) investigated the effects of social deprivation on the physical and behavioral development of rhesus monkeys. He noted that monkeys deprived of the normal touching and grooming offered by the mother produced a host of abnormal behaviors. In addition to an increased number of physical ailments, slower physical maturation, and smaller size, those monkeys isolated from others were never able to develop normal social relationships. Indeed, when introduced to other monkeys, the isolated monkeys fled in terror. They acted as though they didn't even recognize themselves as similar to the others. They tried to hide in a corner, engaged in many self-mutilating behaviors such as tearing at their hair and picking at their flesh; and when other monkeys came near, they shrank away and screamed. Those of you who get to watch videotapes of these studies will undoubtedly find yourselves horrified by the results.

Lack of Touching and Early Development

Humans, too, require physical contact, as shown by orphans who grow up with little touching. In the 19th century, a disease once called *marasmus* (from the Greek meaning "wasting away"), or infantile atrophy, killed more than half of infants in their first year (Montagu, 1971; Burgoon, Buller, and Woodall, 1989). Death was attributed to lack of touch. In the early 1900s, the death rate of infants under one year of age at orphanages in the United States was between 90 percent and 100 percent. Youngsters who receive little physical contact during infancy may walk and talk later than normal and may have difficulties with reading and speech. Further, schizophrenic children are reported to have been deprived of physical contact early in life (Farb, 1978).

It is important to remember, however, that homes in which physical contact is minimal may be lacking in other important characteristics for promoting healthy physiological, psychological, and social development. Nevertheless, because touch is thought to be so important in human development, infants born prematurely and confined to an incubator now receive regular touching and handling by hospital personnel and by their parents, who are allowed to visit and touch for short periods of time throughout the day.

Another source of information regarding the importance of touch comes from research on the effects that the stroking of a dog or cat has on disturbed children, the elderly, and on others: The stroking of pets reduces blood pressure and provides a communication outlet for autistic children who withdraw from human contact. The mental outlook and physical health of elderly confined to nursing homes improves considerably when they have the opportunity to spend time with and touch pets. (See: Arkow, 1986; Delta Society, 1986.)

Functions of Touch

There are several functions of touch (Heslin and Alper, 1983). The first is **functional-professional**. We have all been touched by people whose job it is to examine various parts of our bodies. Physicians, dentists, nurses, and physical therapists need to touch our bodies in places and in ways that we wouldn't tolerate from most others. This type of touching is typically rather cold and impersonal. **Social-polite** touching comes in the form of handshakes, a touch on the arm, or a pat on the back. It is a form of acknowledgement or recognition and it is governed by cultural conventions.

The third function, **friendship-warmth,** follows cultural conventions, is gender-specific, but is also negotiated by those involved in the relationship. Two men walking hand-in-hand is considered quite acceptable in some parts of Europe. This is not the case in the United States. However, two women walking with their arms around each other is not frowned upon. Touching between friends of the opposite sex is sometimes misinterpreted as having a sexual connotation; this may be one source of misunderstanding in what is now referred to as *date rape.*

Touch between lovers, the **love-intimacy** dimension, and touch that accompanies **sexual arousal,** the last function, is private, and is negotiated by those involved in the relationship. It is the kind of touching associated with physical attraction and arousal.

When Are We Likely to Touch?

There are a number of conditions under which we are more likely to touch: (1) when giving information or advice rather than asking for it; (2) when giving an order rather than responding to one; (3) when asking for a favor rather than agreeing to one; (4) when trying to persuade rather than being persuaded; (5) when engaged in intimate rather than casual conversation; (6) when communicating excitement; and (7) when receiving messages of support and sympathy.

Differences in Amount and Type of Touch

There are also differences in the amount and type of touch we receive. The highest frequency and duration of touch is in mother-infant interactions, especially from birth to approximately two years of age. Female children receive more touch than do male children. Further, female children are weaned later than are male children. The amount and type of touch we receive appears to decrease from kindergarten on into adulthood. However, opposite-sex touching increases during adolescence. The least amount of touch occurs during adulthood (see: Jourard, 1966; Rosenfeld, Kartus, and Ray, 1976).

Avoidance of Touch Avoidance of touch occurs in rather predictable ways, and such avoidance is to some extent culturally determined. Mothers can caress their sons, but fathers are taught to avoid prolonged contact with their daughters. As already mentioned, there are sanctions against same-sex touching, especially under certain circumstances. Hugs and pats on the rear are common among football and basketball players when engaged in a game, but inappropriate in other circumstances. Males in this culture who touch one another frequently and in ways typically associated with intimacy will probably be perceived as homosexual. Males are not supposed to touch platonic female friends in ways that suggest sexual attraction and arousal. This is only a sampling of cultural conventions regarding touch avoidance; I am sure you can think of many others.

The Messages of Touch Touch transmits a number of messages about our attitudes, emotions, status, and sociability. Touch can be used as a reward, and many children report that they are hugged as a reward for good behavior. Touch can send emotional messages such as liking/disliking, affiliation, aggression, sexual interest, and dependence, and can be used to get attention and to manage interaction. Who touches whom during an interaction is a clue to the relative status of the participants. The person of higher status is generally the one who initiates touch. The person who initiates touch generally controls the interaction, but then this is characteristic of those of higher status generally.

There was a male graduate student at a university I once taught at who called female faculty "hon" and frequently put an arm around them. Needless to say, this behavior was met with considerable disapproval. This person is no longer a graduate student at that university, although I suspect there were other reasons for his leaving.

Summary Touch can bring us closer to others; yet touch may also be perceived as an intrusion on our private space. Spacing and territory as aspects of communication have to do with our desire to secure areas of our own; encroachments on areas we claim may result in considerable personal and interpersonal distress.

HOW DOES OUR USE OF SPACE AND TERRITORY AFFECT OUR SOCIAL RELATIONSHIPS?

Territoriality

All animals, including humans, are territorial, although some more than others. Dogs, cats, hyena, and wolves mark and defend their territories against the intrusion of outsiders. In fact, those and other animals' lives are largely spent engaged in defense of what they feel they own. Unlike humans, other animals do not tolerate outsiders in their territories.

Humans, however, make it a habit to invite others into their territory. Of course, the operative word here is *invite;* many of us are not especially fond of uninvited guests. While we don't engage in territorial defense to the extent other animals do, we certainly mark and protect our territories with fences, human guards, guard dogs, alarm systems, and "no trespassing" signs. The extent to which we require and guard territory varies across individuals (I know some ranch owners who meet intruders with the barrel end of a shotgun). The gangs we hear so much about lately appear highly territorial, and many a death has resulted from one gang trying to take over another gang's turf.

What Is a Territory? A territory need not be a large plot of land; it may be your side of your dorm room, or your closets, drawers, and work space at home, or a table at a restaurant or library. One of the interesting aspects of territoriality is that we mark our spaces; and in doing so, apparently dissuade others from using the space. Research on territorial behavior in libraries suggests that marking a space with books, papers, and a coat will reserve us that space (Krail and Leventhal, 1976). Imagine that you are going out by yourself for lunch or dinner. You are seated at a table that is yours for the whole meal, even if the table can accommodate several more people.

In Kenya, I discovered, if you are at a table by yourself that can seat more than just one person, others come and sit with you, uninvited. The first time it happened to me I was quite surprised and not especially happy about it. This was, after all, an invasion of my space. However, I ended up talking with some very interesting people. After that, meals by myself were considerably less interesting.

Personal Space

Personal space (proxemics) is sort of a bubble of space we carry around with us. In this culture, personal space is an area of about 12–18 inches surrounding our bodies (Hall, 1963). Personal space is highly variable across individuals, and some people react more negatively to violations of their space than do others. Women, for example, generally respond less negatively to violations of personal space than men. The situation is complicated, however, by the fact that, in some studies, women were less troubled by invasions from the side (Fisher and Byrne, 1975), while men were more troubled by invasions from the front (Pederson and Heaston, 1972). Generally speaking, our spatial needs increase over the course of our lifetimes (Hayduk, 1978).

Interpersonal Distance The distance between interactants is an indication of the nature of their relationship. In this culture, intimate distance is from 0 to about 18 inches, personal distance is from about 1 1/2 to 4 feet, social distance is from about 4 to 8 feet, and public distance is from about 8 feet to the limits of vision and hearing (Hall, 1963). Higher-status people are typically given more space by others, and their space is less frequently invaded than is that of low-status people (Dean, Willis, and Hewitt, 1975). We generally stand closer to those we like than to those we dislike (Mehrabian, 1969).

If we find ourselves in crowded situations in which we cannot physically distance ourselves from others, we can increase psychological distance by avoiding eye contact with others. On the other hand, consider the age-old story of two lovers across a crowded room who yearn to be together but are held captive by other conversational obligations. They decrease the distance between them by engaging in sustained eye contact.

Territory and space are defined by the individual as well as by the culture. While we may not engage in territorial defense to the extent other animals do, it is clear that we mark our territory in various ways in an attempt to keep others out. We tend to allow others into our space on the basis of our feelings for them, and we manage space using other nonverbal behaviors such as gaze and touch.

CONCLUSION

In this chapter we have sought to highlight and illustrate the ways in which nonverbal behavior affects our perceptions of others as well as others' perceptions of us. Our nonverbal behaviors are a potentially powerful source of information. Because we frequently are unaware of those behaviors, it is important that we consider their potential impact. We have attempted to provide a mirror into which we could peer and examine behaviors we rarely see.

KEY TERMS AND CONCEPTS

nonverbal feedback
awareness
nonverbal signs
nonverbal behaviors
   of animals
sensory sensitivity
   (color vision,
   upright walking,
   finger mobility)
odors
brain hemispheres
intercultural differences
emotional displays

personal space
kinesics
physical appearance
haptics
proxemics
space
time
artifacts
environments
complement
contradict
repetition
regulation

substitute
accenting
influence
deception
group identification
emotion
conversational
   structure
role maintenance
influence of
   environmental
   characteristics
formality

warmth
privacy
familiarity
constraint
proximity
body types
   ectomorphic
   endomorphic
attractiveness norms
culture and climate
clothing and
   personal effects

body position
   posture
   orientation
gestures
faces and
   facial expressions
types of encoders
   (Externalizers,
   Internalizers)
decoding emotions
types of facial displays
   (affect blend,

affect partials,
micromomentary)
patterns of gaze
   (eye blink rate,
   pupil dilation)
vocal characteristics
touch (functional professional, social-polite, friendship-warmth, love-intimacy)
space and territory

REFERENCES

Acking, C. A., and Kuller, R. (1972). The perception of an interior as a function of its color. *Ergonomics* 15: 645–654.

Addington, D. W. (1968). The relationship of selected vocal characteristics to personality perception. *Speech Monographs* 35: 492–503.

Andersen, P. A., Garrison, J. P. and Andersen, J. F. (1979). Implications of a neurophysiological approach for the study of nonverbal communication. *Human Communication Research* 6: 74–89.

Apple, W., and Hecht, K. (1982). Speaking emotionally: The relation between verbal and vocal communication of affect. *Journal of Personality and Social Psychology* 42: 864–875.

Arkow, P. S. (1986). *Pet Therapy: A Study and Resource Guide for the Use of Animals in Selected Therapies.* Colorado Springs, Colo.: Humane Society of the Pikes Peak Region.

Bar-Tal, D., and Saxe, L. (1976). Physical attractiveness and its relationships to sex-role stereotyping. *Sex Roles* 2: 123–133.

Baxter, J. C., Winters, E. P., and Hammer, R. E. (1968). Gestural behavior during a brief interview as a function of cognitive variables. *Journal of Personality and Social Psychology* 8: 303–307.

Bonner, J. T. (1980). *The Evolution of Culture in Animals.* Princeton, N.J.: Princeton University Press.

Burgoon, J. K., Buller, D. B., and Woodall, W. G. (1989). *Nonverbal Communication: The Unspoken Dialogue.* New York: Harper & Row.

Campbell, B. (1988). *Humankind Emerging,* 5th ed. Glenview, Ill.: Scott, Foresman and Co.

Castro, J. (1991). The simple life. *Time* 137 (April 8): 58–63.

Charlesworth, W. R., and Kreutzer, M. A. (1973). Facial expressions of infants and children. In *Darwin and Facial Expression: A Century of Research in Review*, edited by P. Ekman, pp. 91–168. New York: Academic Press.

Chernigovskaya, T. (1989). Modes of consciousness: Cultural, functional and neurophysiological dimensions. Paper presented at the annual meeting of the Language Origins Society, Amsterdam.

Chevalier-Skolnikoff, S. (1982). A cognitive analysis of facial behavior in old world monkeys, apes, and human beings. In *Primate Communication*, edited by C. T. Snowdon, C. H. Brown, and M. R. Petersen, pp. 303–368. Cambridge, England: Cambridge University Press.

Clifford, M. M., and Walster, E. H. (1973). The effect of physical attractiveness in teacher expectation. *Sociological Education* 46: 248–258.

Cohen, A. A. (1977). The communicative functions of hand illustrators. *Journal of Communication* 27: 54–63.

Cohen, A. A., and Harrison, R. P. (1973). Intentionality in the use of hand illustrators in face-to-face communication situations. *Journal of Personality and Social Psychology* 28: 276–279.

Cox, C. L., and Glick, W. H. (1986). Resume evaluations and cosmetic use: When more is not better. *Sex Roles* 14(1/2): 51–58.

Darwin, C. (1872). *The Expression of Emotions in Man and Animals.* London: John Murray.

Dean, L. M., Willis, F. N., and Hewitt, J. (1975). Initial interaction distance among individuals equal and unequal in military rank. *Journal of Personality and Social Psychology* 32: 294–299.

Delta Society. (1986). *Living Together: People, Animals, and the Environment.* Linda M. Hines, ed. Boston: Delta Society.

deTurck, M. A., and Miller, G. R. (1985). Deception and arousal: Isolating the behavioral correlates of deception. *Human Communication Research* 12: 181–201.

Dion, K. K., and Berscheid, E. (1972). Physical attractiveness and evaluation of children's transgressions. *Journal of Personality and Social Psychology* 30: 207–213.

Donald, M. (1991). *Origins of the Modern Mind.* Cambridge, Mass.: Harvard University Press.

Ekman, P. (1973). Cross-cultural studies of facial expression. In *Darwin and Facial Expression: A Century of Research in Review,* edited by P. Ekman, pp. 169–222. New York: Academic Press.

———. (1985). *Telling Lies: Clues to Deceit in the Marketplace, Politics, and Marriage.* New York: Norton.

Ekman, P., and Friesen, W. (1969a). The repertoire of nonverbal behavior: Categories, origins, usage, and coding. *Semiotica* 1: 49–98.

———. (1969b). Nonverbal leakage and clues to deception. *Psychiatry* 32: 88–106.

———. (1971). Constants across cultures in the face and emotion. *Personality and Social Psychology* 17(2): 124–129.

Ekman, P., Friesen, W. V., and Ellsworth, P. (1982). Conceptual ambiguities. In *Emotion in the Human Face,* 2nd ed., edited by P. Ekman, pp. 7–21. Cambridge, England: Cambridge University Press.

Exline, R. V., Ellyson, S. L., and Long, B. (1975). Visual behavior as an aspect of power role relationships. In *Nonverbal Communication of Aggression,* edited by P. Pliner, L. Krames, and T. Alloway, pp. 21–52. New York: Plenum.

Fagan, B. M. (1992). *People of the Earth.* New York: HarperCollins.

Farb, P. (1978). *Humankind.* New York: Bantam Books.

Feinman, J. A., and Feldman, R. S. (1982). Decoding children's expressions of affect. *Child Development* 53: 710–716.

Fisher, J. D., and Byrne, D. (1975). Too close for comfort: Sex differences in response to invasions of personal space. *Journal of Personality and Social Psychology* 32: 15–21.

Forsythe, S., Drake, M. F., and Cox, C. E. (1985). Influence of applicant's dress on interviewer's selection decisions. *Journal of Applied Psychology* 70(2): 374–378.

Fujita, B. N., Harper, R. G., and Wiens, A. N. (1980). Encoding-decoding of nonverbal emotional messages: Sex differences in spontaneous and enacted expressions. *Journal of Nonverbal Behavior* 4: 131–145.

Goffman, E. (1961). *Encounters: Two Studies in the Sociology of Interaction.* Indianapolis, Ind.: Bobbs-Merrill.

Graddol, D., and J. Swann. (1983). Speaking fundamental frequency: Some physical and social correlates. *Language and Speech* 26(4): 351–365.

Gudykunst, W. B. (1991). *Bridging Differences: Effective Intergroup Communication.* Newbury Park, Calif.: Sage.

Gudykunst, W. B., and Kim, Y. Y. (1984). *Communicating with Strangers: An Approach to Intercultural Communication.* Reading, Mass.: Addison-Wesley.

Hall, E. T. (1959). *The Silent Language.* Greenwich, Conn.: Fawcett.

———. (1963). A system for the notation of proxemic behavior. *American Anthropologist* 65: 1003–1026.

———. (1966). *The Hidden Dimension.* Garden City, N.Y.: Doubleday.

———. (1977). *Beyond Culture.* Garden City, N.Y.: Anchor/Doubleday.

Hall, J. A. (1984). *Nonverbal Sex Differences.* Baltimore and London: The Johns Hopkins University Press.

Hamid, P. N. (1968). Style of dress as a perceptual cue in impression formation. *Perceptual and Motor Skills* 26: 904–906.

Harlow, H. F., and Harlow, M. K. (1962). The effect of rearing conditions on behavior. *Bulletin of the Menninger Clinic* 26: 213–224.

Harms, L. S. (1961). Listener judgments of status cues in speech. *Quarterly Journal of Speech* 47: 164–168.

Hayduk, L. A. (1978). Personal space: An evaluative and orienting overview. *Psychological Bulletin* 85: 117–134.

Hayes, E. R., and Plax, T. G. (1971). Pupillary response to supportive and aversive verbal messages. *Speech Monographs* 38: 316–320.

Heslin, R. and Alper, T. (1983). Touch: A bonding gesture. In *Nonverbal Interaction,* edited by J. M. Wiemann and R. P. Harrison, pp. 47–75. Beverly Hills, Calif.: Sage.

Holahan, C. J. (1982). *Environmental Psychology.* New York: Random House.

Hornstein, M. G. (1967). Accuracy of emotional communication and interpersonal compatibility. *Journal of Personality* 35: 20–30.

Jourard, S. M. (1966). An exploratory study of body accessibility. *British Journal of Social and Clinical Psychology,* 5, 221–231.

Keating, C. F. (1985). Human dominance signals: The primate in us. In *Power, Dominance, and Nonverbal Behavior,* edited by S. L. Ellyson and J. F. Dovidio, pp. 89–108. New York: Springer-Verlag.

Kendon, A. (1967). Some functions of gaze-direction in social interaction. *Acta Psychologia* 26: 22–63.

Kitchens, J. T., Herron, T. P. Behnke, R. R., and Beatty, M. J. (1977). Environmental esthetics and interpersonal attraction. *Western Journal of Speech Communication* 41: 279–283.

Korda, M. (1977). *Success: How Every Man and Woman Can Achieve It.* New York: Random House.

Knapp, M. L. and Comadena, M. E. (1979). Telling it like it isn't: A review of theory and research on deceptive communications. *Human Communication Research* 5: 270–285.

Krail, K., and Leventhal, G. (1976). The sex variable in the intrusion of personal space. *Sociometry* 39: 170–173.

LaFrance, M. (1985). Postural mirroring and intergroup relations. *Personality and Social Psychology Bulletin* 11(2): 207–217.

Lancker, D. V. (1991). Personal relevance and the human right hemisphere. *Brain and Cognition* 17: 64–92.

Landau, T. (1989). *About Faces: The Evolution of the Human Face.* New York: Doubleday.

Lester, D. (1982). Ectomorphy and personality. *Psychological Reports* 51: 1182.

Levy, R., and Poll, A. P. (1976). Through a glass darkly. *Dun's Review* 77–78.

Libby, W. (1970). Eye contact and direction of looking as stable individual differences. *Journal of Experimental Research in Personality* 4: 303–312.

Liska, J. (1990). Dominance-seeking strategies in primates: An evolutionary perspective. *Human Evolution,* 5,(1), 75–90.

———. (1993). Bee dances, bird songs, monkey calls, and cetecean sonar: Is speech unique? *Western Journal of Communication* 57(1): 1–26.

Mahl, G. F. (1959). Disturbances in the patients' speech as a function of anxiety. Paper presented at the Eastern Psychological Association, Atlantic City. Reprinted in *Trends in Content Analysis*, edited by I. Pool. Urbana: University of Illinois Press, pp. 89–130.

Malandro, L. A., Barker, L., and Barker, D. A. (1989). *Nonverbal Communication,* 2nd ed. New York: Random House.

Maslow, A. H., and Mintz, N. L. (1956). Effects of esthetic surroundings: I. Initial effects of three esthetic conditions upon perceiving "energy" and "well-being" in faces. *Journal of Psychology* 41: 247–254.

Mathes, E., and Kempher, S. B. (1976). Clothing as a nonverbal communicator of sexual attitudes and behavior. *Perceptual and Motor Skills* 43: 495–498.

Mayo, C., and LaFrance, M. (1978). On the acquisition of nonverbal communication: A review. *Merrill Palmer Quarterly* 24: 213–228.

McArthur, L. Z., and Baron, R. M. (1983). Toward an ecological theory of social perception. *Psychological Review* 90(3): 215–238.

McKeachie, W. (1952). Lipstick as a determiner of first impressions on personality: An experiment for the general psychology course. *Journal of Social Psychology* 36: 241–244.

Mehrabian, A. (1969). Significance of posture and position in the communication of attitude and status relationships. *Psychological Bulletin* 71: 359–373.

———. (1971). *Silent Messages.* Belmont, Calif.: Wadsworth.

Mehrabian, A., and J. A. Russell. (1974). *An Approach to Environmental Psychology.* Cambridge, Mass.: MIT Press.

Molloy, J. T. (1988). *The New Dress for Success Book.* New York: Warner Books.

Montagu, A. (1971). *Touching: The Human Significance of the Skin.* New York: Columbia University Press.

Morris, D. (1977). *Manwatching: A Field Guide to Human Behavior.* New York: Harry N. Abrams.

Murphy, M. J., Nelson, D. A., and Cheap, T. L. (1981). Rated and actual performance of high school students as a function of sex and attractiveness. *Psychological Reports* 48: 103–106.

Pederson, D. M., and Heaston, A. B. (1972). The effects of sex of subject, of approaching person, and angle of approach upon personal space. *Journal of Psychology* 82: 277–286.

Postman, N. (1993). *Technopoly.* New York: Vintage Books.

Reynolds, P. C. (1981). *On the Evolution of Human Behavior.* Berkeley: University of California Press.

Rosenfeld, L. B., Kartics, S. and Ray, C. (1976). Body accessibility revisited. *Journal of Communication*, 26(3), 27–30.

Sheldon, W. H. (1942). *The Varieties of Temperament.* New York: Hafner.

———. (1954). *Atlas of Man: A Guide for Somatotyping the Adult Male at All Ages.* New York: Harper & Brothers.

Shively, C. (1985). The evolution of dominance hierarchies in nonhuman primate societies. In *Power, Dominance, and Nonverbal Behavior,* edited by S. L. Ellyson and J. F. Dovidio, pp. 67–88. New York: Springer-Verlag.

Singer, J. E. (1964). The use of manipulative strategies: Machiavellianism and attractiveness. *Sociometry* 27: 128–151.

Singer, J. E., and Lamb, P. F. (1966). Social concern, body size, and birth order. *Journal of Social Psychology* 68: 143–151.

Sommer, R. (1965). Further studies in small group ecology. *Sociometry* 28: 338–348.

———. (1974). *Tight Spaces: Hard Architecture and How to Humanize It.* Englewood Cliffs, N.J.: Prentice-Hall.

Sperry, R. W. (1974). Lateral specialization in the surgically separated hemispheres. In *The Neurosciences: Third Study Program,* edited by F. O. Schmitt and F. G. Worden, pp. 5–19. Cambridge, Mass.: MIT Press.

Stengel, R. (1984). Status in the shading game. *Time* (July 23): 87–88.

Street, R. L., Jr., and Brady, R. M. (1982). Speech rate acceptance ranges as a function of evaluative domain, listener speech rate, and communication content. *Communication Monographs* 49: 290–308.

Thourlby, W. (1978). *You Are What You Wear.* New York: New American Library.

Vine, I. (1973). The role of facial-visual signalling in early social development. In *Social Communication and Movement,* edited by M. van Cranach and O. Vine, pp. 195–298. New York: Academic Press.

Wagner, H. L., MacDonald, C. J., and Manstead, A. S. R. (1986). Communication of individual emotions by spontaneous facial expressions. *Journal of Personality and Social Psychology* 50: 737–743.

Watson, K. W., and Smeltzer, L. R. (1982). Perceptions of nonverbal communication during the selection interview. *The ABCA Bulletin* 19: 30–34.

Weisfeld, G. E., and Beresford, J. M. (1982). Erectness of posture as an indicator of dominance or success in humans. *Motivation and Emotion* 6(2): 113–131.

Wexner, L. B. (1954). The degree to which colors (hues) are associated with mood-tones. *Journal of Applied Psychology* 38: 432–435.

Widgery, R. N., and Webster, B. (1969). The effects of physical attractiveness upon perceived initial credibility. *Michigan Speech Journal* 4: 9–15.

Wiemann, J. M., and M. L. Knapp. (1975). Turn-taking in conversations. *Journal of Communication* 25(2): 75–92.

Williams, F. (1970). The psychological correlates of speech characteristics: On sounding disadvantaged. *Journal of Speech and Hearing Research* 13: 472–488.

Wolff, P. (1963). Observations on the early development of smiling. In *Determinants of Infant Behavior,* edited by B. M. Foss, Vol. 2, pp. 113–138. London: Methuen.

Zivin, G. (1982). Watching the sands shift: Conceptualizing development of nonverbal mastery. In *Development of Nonverbal Behavior in Children,* edited by R. S. Feldman, pp. 63–98. New York: Springer-Verlag.

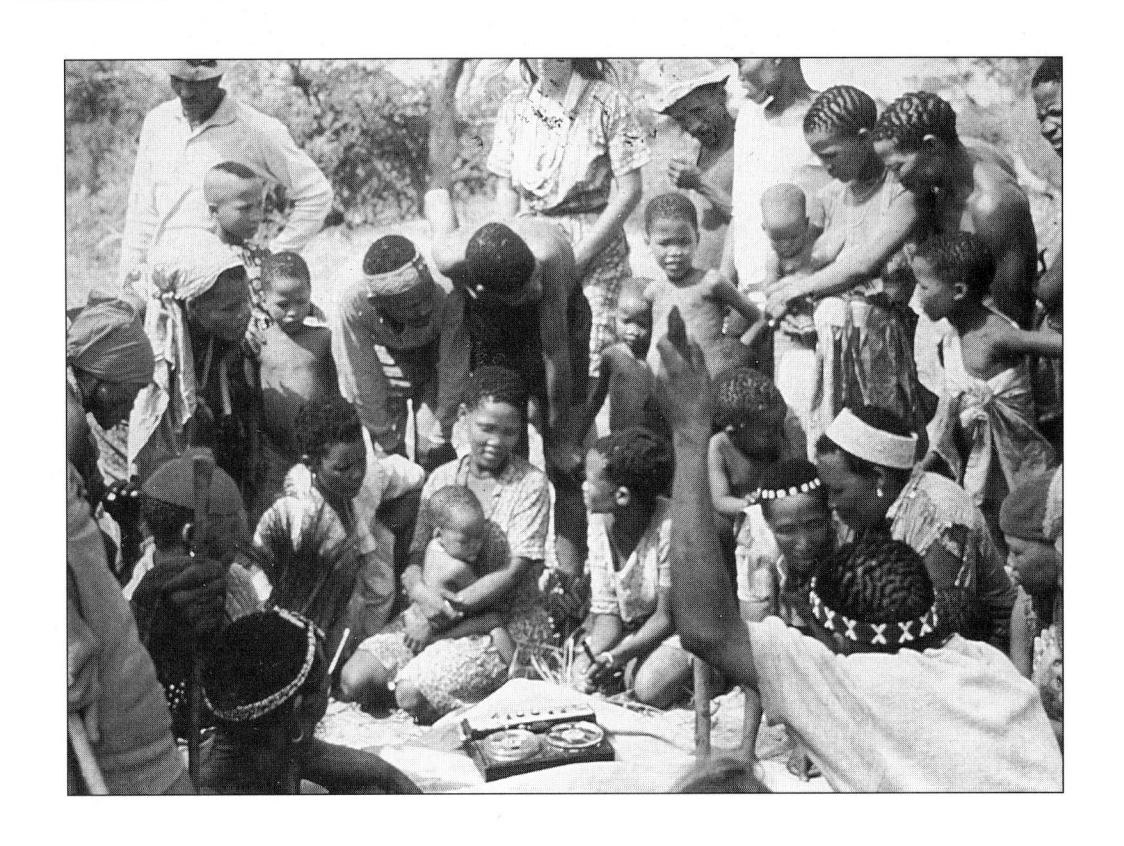

The easiest kind of relationship for me is with ten thousand people. The hardest is with one.

—*Joan Baez*

UNIT 4

Types of Communication Ecologies

While the principles and components of communication offered thus far apply to all communication ecologies, there are some special considerations, some particular constraints that operate in specific communication ecologies. The focus of this unit is on these particular contextual characteristics.

The language of personal relationships is likely to be less formal, more idiosyncratic, and more emotionally charged than that found in work groups and organizational settings. Further, interpersonal contact is generally more direct and face-to-face, and incorporates more intense nonverbal signs, such as touch, than is likely to be found in more structured settings such as that of the organization. The nature of the groups to which we belong is also a constraining factor, in that social groups may bear more similarity to our personal relationships than do task or work groups. Further, negotiation processes in division of labor become more complicated in groups and organizations, if for no other reason than because of the number of people involved.

Organizations pose special problems because of their hierarchical structure, the number of levels and people involved, and the fact that communication may involve less face-to-face interaction among those levels, and even between groups on the same level. Communication in organizations may include a great number of written messages, which, because they lack important nonverbal information, may be more easily misinterpreted.

Since we obtain considerable knowledge about the events in our world via the media, it is important to know where all the information comes from, how it is managed at various levels and points in the process, and who generated the information, including their biases, sources, and so forth. Because we rarely have direct access to the information processing, assessment of the quality of the information presented by the media is difficult. Again, these are special considerations that are analyzed here.

Finally, communication differs across cultures, which can put those of us unfamiliar with the communication practices of different cultures at a considerable disadvantage. Even if we never travel to another land, we are likely to meet those of other cultures in our own country, and those meetings can benefit from a mutual understanding of communication expectations. Moreover, analysis of the events occurring in other cultures will be facilitated by exposure to their cultural conventions. We may not become culturally literate, but we can at least learn to appreciate the differences.

A relationship is what happens between two people who are waiting for something better to come along.

—*Unknown*

Interpersonal Relationships 11

CHAPTER OUTLINE

First Impressions and Initial Interaction
  Self-Perception
  Perception of Potential Partners
  Social Exchange, Predicted Outcome Value, and Reinforcement

Relationship Development
  Perception of the Relationship
  Content and Relational Dimensions of Conversation

  Equity Negotiation
  Reciprocal Self-Concept Support
  Stages of Developing and Stable Relationships

Relational Equilibrium
  Relational Intricacies

Relationship Dissolution
  Phases of Relationship Dissolution

The term *interpersonal communication* is used differently at different schools and in different areas of the country. When the two of us taught in California, in both the University of California and the California State University systems, a professor said to be interested in **interpersonal** communication was one who studied **relational** communication. When we moved to the Midwest, we were surprised to find at one university that the divisions in the department were organizational communication, mass communication, and interpersonal communication, so that anyone not in organizational or mass communication was in interpersonal communication. At another university, the division was between mass communication and interpersonal communication. This was a use of the term with which we were not familiar. But this broad usage is not maintained consistently throughout the Midwest. At the university where I presently teach, only one professor teaches "interpersonal" courses, and those courses deal predominantly with dyadic relationships. This chapter will deal with relational communication.

FIRST IMPRESSIONS AND INITIAL INTERACTION

Sidney and Jake met at the library near the beginning of fall semester last year. They were introduced by a mutual friend. The three of them studied together for an hour before the friend had to leave. Then Sidney and Jake began talking. They were sitting at a table in an otherwise empty corner of the library. Neither had ever had a course in relational communication nor in general communication theory, but they had perceptions of themselves and began to develop perceptions of one another.

Self-Perception

Sidney recently spent a good deal of time thinking about who she was, probably because she had just transferred from a community college in her hometown, where she had spent two years, to this large state university, where she lived in a dormitory with two roommates. That created an unusual crisis of self-awareness, whereas at home she had not thought much about who she was, being content to know she *was,* protected by her parents and sisters. Jake, too, was in a sort of crisis of self-awareness, because his steady girlfriend from last year had just decided to transfer to another school this fall, after they had spent the summer together working at a camp. He had begun to ask himself why she had done that after all the plans they had made, and what it had to do with the sort of person he was. Thus both were in a high state of self-awareness. That was not a characteristic state for either of them, for both had spent most of the recent past just *being,* without any careful self-examination.

We might be able to help them at this stage, based on some of the theory we have discussed in previous chapters. Or not. Understanding oneself and understanding the others who are potential partners in relationships is the first step in forming relationships. We have already discussed those concerns in earlier chapters. Chapter 5 dealt in part with personality characteristics such as dogmatism, self-esteem, the need to manipulate others, and sex-role stereotyping. Understanding such characteristics is fundamental to understanding self as well as others, but there's no need to repeat what was said there.

I also described the sorts of attributes one infers regarding others. Now I want to add that we also infer such attributes regarding ourselves, on the basis of internal data such as our feelings in particular situations as well as how others react to us and what they tell us we are like. The attributes to which I refer are such characteristics as honesty, power, physical attractiveness, intentions, needs/goals, sexual preference, sexuality, warmth, politeness, compliance/persuasibility, responsibility, opinions on important issues, empathic ability, need for affiliation, need for intimacy, extroversion/introversion, bias, security, aggressiveness, educational level, and socioeconomic status.

We never finish understanding ourselves in terms of these attributes or the many others I have mentioned, in part because we are to some extent constantly changing. A person is always a work in progress. But the formation of relationships will not wait until we completely understand ourselves, let alone the others available to whom we may relate.

Multiple Selves   Of course, both Sidney and Jake had **multiple selves** available from which to choose. Sidney could be the naive little girl who just left home; she could be a sophisticated junior at the Big U, she could be an artist, since she planned to declare art as her major . . . the list goes on. Jake could be the tough guy who rode a motorcycle; he could be the caring environmentalist he had been at camp last summer; or he could be studious, which would be especially easy, considering he met Sidney in the library.

True Self vs. Enacted Self   Which of these were their **"true" selves?** Perhaps all of them; perhaps none of them. To Goffman (1959) the question is irrelevant, since he argued **self** is **enacted,** consisting of how one presents oneself, not something internal. Their material **possessions** constituted their "selves" to some extent, so Sidney's art supplies and Jake's motorcycle constituted their selves. So did their **religious** and **philosophical** beliefs, Sidney's small-town Protestantism and Jake's sometimes Catholicism, the latter being neglected more often than he would like to admit.

But much of their perceived selves had been developed in **communication interactions,** especially what others had told them they were like, and their comparisons of themselves to the significant others in their social circles. These **social selves** were undergoing some change, since Jake's exgirlfriend had recently tried to set him straight about who he was, and had made some unflattering comparisons. Sidney's new roommates had some opinions of her that differed drastically from those of her friends in her home town, and she had some new acquaintances with whom to compare herself.

Perception of Potential Partners

We are constantly **perceiving others** on the basis of those same characteristics. But others are also perceived in terms of their similarity to ourselves, especially their opinion and goal similarity, and in terms of their reward potential. (At this point it would probably be good to review the theories of person-perception described in Chapter 5, including George Kelly's Personal Construct Theory, the theories of Asch and the gestalt theorists, Goffman's self-presentation theory, the prototype theory of Cantor and Mischel, and the attribution theories of Howard Kelley and Jones and Davis.)

Uncertainty Reduction But why were Sidney and Jake engaging in this mutual exploration? Both were placing themselves at risk. Jake was risking another failed relationship, and Sidney was risking rejection by what appeared to be a university man who had been at the Big U for two years, whereas she was just a community-college transfer away from home for the first time.

Berger and Calabrese (1986) believe this sort of initial interaction is motivated by a need to reduce uncertainty. They describe three phases of such interactions: **entry, personal,** and **exit**. In each phase, communicators adopt different strategies for reducing uncertainty.

Entry Phase Conversation in the entry phase is likely to be awkward and sparse, since the mutual uncertainty of the communicators is high. But such conversation as occurs is likely to be of the **information-seeking** variety. "So how do you know Roger?" would be a likely initial gambit, since friendship with Roger was the one thing they knew they had in common. Each could also observe the books the other had taken from the shelves, and ask about them, which would lead to the inevitable question, "So what is your major?" Since Jake was wearing a t-shirt that said, "Liberal Arts Major—Will Think for Food," they could laugh about that, and test each other's sense of humor.

According to Berger and Calabrese, as uncertainty is reduced, the amount of obvious information seeking will decrease, although conversation may increase. If the two begin to perceive similarities between themselves, uncertainty is further reduced. For instance, you may recall from the movie *The Breakfast Club* that the strangers thrown together in Saturday afternoon detention became friends when they discovered they were similar in having unhappy home lives.

Personal Phase But information such as that must await the *personal* phase. Jake would not immediately disclose the recent end of a love affair, and Sidney would not disclose just how uncomfortable she was at the Big U because she had just left a sheltered home-life. Many relational textbooks describe **self-disclosure** in the glowing terms generally reserved for such cultural necessities as Velcro and Ziploc bags. But if either Jake or Sidney had begun excessive self-disclosure in the entry phase, the story would probably end here; they would have frightened the other away. (Of course, I would not allow them to do that, because I have further use for them, and I do control their destinies.) Self-disclosure is a strategy to be managed and used sparingly in the initial stages of a relationship. Sidney was especially suspicious of self-disclosure. The night before, she had been at a local bar with her roommates when a guy who had been drinking too much asked her what her sign was. She replied, "Do Not Disturb," which cracked up her roommates, who had not expected such repartee from her.

Exit Phase As the degree of perceived similarity increased during the personal phase, so did the amount of self-disclosure. They were attracted to one another enough so that, when the clock forced them into the exit phase of this initial encounter, they agreed to meet again.

The Uncertainty Reduction Theory of Berger and Calabrese is much more complicated than this brief description. It consists of seven "axioms" and twenty-one "theorems" that are just more complex than needed in this brief treatment. However, if you are interested, you can consult other sources [e.g., Infante, Rancer, and Womack (1993)] or ask your professor.

Social Exchange, Predicted Outcome Value, and Reinforcement

But how can we explain why Sidney and Jake were attracted to one another enough to make arrangements to pursue the relationship further? For that matter, how does anyone choose another with whom to form a relationship?

The Goals/Grasp Model Revisited My answer is bound to be in terms of the model my co-author and I devised for just such a purpose: The GOALS/GRASP Model, described in some detail in Chapter 5. We believe one chooses another on the basis of Goals Operant and Achievable in Light of the Situation (GOALS) and the Goal-Relevant Aspects of the Situation Perceived (GRASP). That is, the choice of the other is determined by the GOALS imposed by the situation and the aspects of the situation that impede and facilitate achievement of those GOALS. The intersection of these GOALS and GRASP produce criteria for an acceptable and desirable other.

In the movie *This Property Condemned*, Natalie Wood portrays an attractive young woman trapped in a small railroad town who dreams of escaping to an exciting life in a big city. Robert Redford plays the representative of the railroad sent to close down the railroad yard. Redford offers Wood the opportunity to follow him to New Orleans. Leaving aside the complications of the plot, Wood accepts his invitation, although what she does in the process ultimately dooms their relationship.

In this case it is rather easy to see what the young woman's GOALS were, what the GRASP were that constrained her achievement of those GOALS, and what the criteria were that emerged from the coincidence of these GOALS and GRASP. The GRASP were largely financial, although given that Wood was a naive young woman who knew little of the outside world, she was also constrained by her lack of worldly knowledge. Redford's character met the criteria for a desirable other, in that he was financially successful, sophisticated, and lived in New Orleans. This is not to deprecate Redford's physical attractiveness, which undoubtedly satisfied another of the young woman's GOALS, but it is clear from the unattractive men she approached before Redford that physical attractiveness was a desirable but not necessary criterion.

This sounds like a really cynical model, doesn't it, since it seems to imply we choose others with whom to form relationships on the basis of what they have to offer us? But I believe we do just that. In *This Property Condemned*, what the Redford character has to offer the Wood character is obvious and crass, and that is what makes it appear so cynical. The fact it is obvious is why I chose it as an illustration.

But even in the most romantic relationship, the two parties are fulfilling their GOALS; both parties are experiencing some satisfaction, or the relationship would not last. As I write this I am also listening with half my brain to an episode of "Designing Women" in which Mary Jo is dating a very attractive male model with what she describes as a most incredible body. The other women in the cast question whether Mary Jo can continue to satisfy her GOALS in a purely physical relationship. But one of them says, "For years men have had their bimbos; let Mary Jo have her dumbo." Eventually Mary Jo concludes her GOALS are not being satisfied, and resolves to end the relationship. Unfortunately—or fortunately, depending on your point of view—Dumbo decides he will end the relationship, and does so before Mary Jo has her chance. But what if Dumbo had been an intelligent male model, thus satisfying more of Mary Jo's GOALS? After all, there is nothing inherently stupid about attractive people, although that is a stereotype perpetuated by the media.

However, we have all encountered relationships in which one of the pair, and sometimes both, do not seem to be satisfying any apparent GOALS. Take it simply on faith that the relationship would not continue if this were true. We as observers cannot always make such judgments. After all, masochists need someone to abuse them, and sadists need someone to abuse.

Jake's GOALS in the situation I have described seem obvious because I have given some of his background. He needed to find a woman he could trust not to hurt him again. The GRASP is the fact that he was at a large university where it was difficult to meet women he knew could be trusted. His criteria included a woman for whom a friend would vouch, and one who appeared to be relatively unsophisticated, not actively on the make. *Propinquity*, or nearness and accessibility, was another important criterion, so he did not have to make obvious overtures that would commit him to either himself or others. By luck, Sidney met all those criteria. Her GOALS included finding a guy with whom she could discuss her uncertainty about life at the Big U without being ridiculed. Her GRASP was essentially the same as his, the difficulty of the social situation at the Big U, as were her criteria.

Predicted Outcome Value Theories The GOALS/GRASP model is very similar to other theories variously described as "Predicted Outcome Value" theories, "Social Exchange" theories, and "Reinforcement" theories. Predicted Outcome Value theory was developed by Sunnafrank (1986). The AESOP model described in Chapter 7 suggested that we choose among alternative Plans on the basis of the Consequences we expect to result from each.

There are a number of similar decision theories, including Fishbein's Theory of Reasoned Action. They have been termed *Subjective Expected Utility* (SEU) theories, and were first developed to explain decisions in the field of economics. *Predicted Outcome Value* is similar, but Sunnafrank has applied it to the choice of a partner in a relationship. Basically the assumption is the same as in other SEU theories, that one will choose that alternative, in this case that relationship, that appears to yield the most positive outcomes with the least negative outcomes. Sunnafrank predicts people will pursue those relationships they predict will produce the most positive outcomes, and will pursue those topics in initial interactions that seem likely to be most rewarding.

Social Exchange Theories Social Exchange theories were first advanced in psychology and sociology (Walster, Walster, and Berscheid, 1978), but have been applied to relational communication by Roloff (1981). The basic idea is that two people choose to enter into that relationship that maximizes rewards and minimizes costs; the relationship continues so long as that balance continues, and will be terminated when one or the other of the partners perceives themselves as being short-changed. However, the term **equity** is important in Social Exchange theory. The prediction is not that the two partners in a relationship must receive equal benefits and pay equal costs. That would be too easy, and probably wrong. Instead, the cost-benefit *ratio* for each partner must remain positive. One partner may receive fewer benefits at greater cost in comparison to the other, and may complain about the inequity, but will not abandon the relationship until it becomes more costly than it is rewarding.

There are some complications. One of these is the **matching hypothesis.** People will seek out those they feel are equal in attractiveness to themselves. But *attractiveness* must be carefully defined. It is not necessarily physical attractiveness. That would mean Loni Anderson would always be attracted to Burt Reynolds, and in fact that was a somewhat unusual pairing; further, they would not have divorced. People who are highly intelligent may be attracted to those who are physically attractive, and that may be reciprocated. Or those who are physically attractive may match themselves with those who are socially adept and fun to be with, or who have enough money to show them a good time. The marriage of Julia Roberts, the female lead of *Pretty Woman*, to Lyle Lovett, not exactly a male model, has puzzled many, and for good reason, but might be explained per this theory by the fact that Lovett is an extremely talented and intelligent musician. Consider the marriages of Billy Joel to Christie Brinkley and Cindy Crawford to Richard Gere. On the basis of this theory, how long do you think they will last? Hint: Joel and Brinkley just filed for divorce.

Another complication is that, while *equity* is easier to calculate in the beginning stages of a relationship, this becomes much more difficult in long-term relationships, first because the rewards and costs become less obvious over time and, second, because while a relationship may appear inequitable over a short period, the partners know the equity has been balanced in the past and is likely to balance out in the future.

Clearly, Social Exchange theory makes predictions well beyond initial interaction, extending into later relationship development. However, it does apply to the initial interaction of Jake and Sidney. They were both moderately physically attractive, so they were "matched" in that sense. Had one been clearly more physically attractive than the other, the matching hypothesis would predict that the other would have had to be highly intelligent or have a very pleasing personality or something else attractive to maintain the match.

Reinforcement Theories Reinforcement theory, initially advanced by Donn Byrne (see especially 1971, though much of this work was done in the 1960s), took the position that we are attracted to others who reward us and dislike those who punish us, not a particularly surprising prediction. Reward and punishment can be verbal, but may be physical as well. However, this general position soon turned into something more specific: that interpersonal *similarity* is especially rewarding.

Perceived Similarity–Attraction Hypothesis Subsequent research has determined it is **perceived similarity** that is important, not actual similarity. Of the various types of similarity, Byrne concluded from his own research that it is similarity in *attitudes* that produces the most attraction to another. This finding seems to have been confirmed by most other researchers, although similarity on any of the six dimensions listed by Berscheid & Walster (1978) (attitude, personality, physical characteristics, social characteristics, intelligence, and education) seems to produce greater attraction. Remember, similarity on these dimensions has generally been *perceived,* and is not necessarily actual.

One note of caution. Though the immediate temptation may be to conclude that similarity *causes* attraction, the relationship may actually not be that simple. Byrne used the "bogus stranger" technique in most of his work. That is, subjects saw a description of a hypothetical stranger that was designed to be either similar to them or different from them. Under those conditions it can be said the similarity "caused" the attraction. But the strangers were not real; they were only "paper-and-pencil people."

The coauthors of this book, with two graduate students, have recently demonstrated that subjects perceive others very differently depending on whether their descriptions are written or read aloud by the "others" themselves, and the differences vary depending on the target people and the person-perception scales on which they are rated. Moreover, it may be that in *actual* relationships over a period of time, those partners who are initially attracted to one another come, for some other reason, to exaggerate their similarities. This matter was debated in a 1992 issue of *Communication Monographs* and has not yet been settled.

RELATIONSHIP DEVELOPMENT

Perception of the Relationship

One of the most important issues in a **developing relationship** is how the two partners perceive that relationship. **Stewart's *my*⟶*you* Model** (1973) has described a model that seems useful for describing this process. In Stewart's model *my*⟶*me* represents my self-perception, and *my*⟶*you* represents my perception of you. *Your*⟶*you* is your self-perception, and *your*⟶*me* is your perception of me. You get the picture. But more complicated perceptions can be represented. *My*⟶*your*⟶*me* is my perception of your perception of me, *my*⟶*your*⟶*you* is my perception of what you think of yourself, and *your*⟶*my*⟶*me* and *your*⟶*my*⟶*you* must be becoming obvious by now.

But if we add some modifications to Stewart's basic model, we can represent perceptions of our relationship, thusly:

my⟶*us*

your⟶*us*

my⟶*your*⟶*us*

your⟶*my*⟶*us*

Finally, if we use parentheses to enclose messages we send to one another, we can represent my attempt to tell you about my perception of your perception of our relationship:

my (*my*⟶*your*⟶*us*) *you*

Obviously, it is possible to carry this beyond what is useful. But the diagrams do suggest just how complicated are the perceptions involved in a relationship, and how complicated is the communication about those perceptions. Wilmot (1987) does something similar with the use of the terms *perspective, metaperspective,* and *meta-meta-perspective.* One of his most interesting insights is that the partners in a relationship can come to believe they understand and agree with one another because, in fact, each misunderstands the other. For more detail, the interested reader can consult his book.

Content and Relational Dimensions of Conversation

Now suppose we return to Sidney and Jake for a moment. They may be able to do without us, but we can hardly do without them. As they return to their respective homes, each thinks about what just happened, beginning to build perceptions of their relationship. Since they spent no time during this initial meeting discussing their relationship, since all their exchanges were, on the surface, "content" messages, they have to search these content messages for hidden "relational" meaning.

As relationships develop, there usually are two dimensions of each interpersonal exchange, a dimension that represents the *content* of the utterance, and another that represents *relational meaning*. Sidney remembers Jake saying "I took a course in nature photography once. I didn't do well." Did that mean Jake thinks art is difficult, and respects me for majoring in it? Or did that mean he thinks it is boring and thinks I may be boring? The *content meaning* was clear: Jake took a photography course once and didn't do well. What Sidney was searching for was a clue to Jake's feelings about her, the *relational meaning*.

Over the next few weeks Jake and Sidney worked through fairly predictable processes as their relationship developed. One of those processes involved exchanging messages about their respective perceptions of their relationship. At first those messages were embedded in what appeared to be purely content statements, but as they came to trust one another more they began to exchange more direct messages about their relationship. At one point Jake openly asked, "What are we doing here? Is this relationship going anywhere?" This led to a two-hour discussion of their mutual perceptions.

Equity Negotiation

A second process in which they engaged was **equity negotiation,** in which they explored the possible costs and rewards of this relationship for each of them, to determine if their respective cost-benefit ratios were worth the continued investment.

Message Exchange Patterns   One way to think about both these processes is that suggested by Millar and Rogers (1987). They describe three types of message exchange patterns: **control, trust,** and **intimacy.** They view relational messages as being **one-up,** or dominance-seeking, **one-down,** or dominance-granting, or **one-across,** dominance-neutral, insofar as they relate to the *control* pattern. But they are quite explicit in arguing that single messages are not units of communication; they code *interacts,* which are sequences of messages involving a message followed by a response. Frequently—perhaps even usually—the messages coded appear to be content messages on the surface; but it is the relational dimension that actually is coded. The *trust* aspect has not been so well developed, but it measures the extent to which the partners admit their dependency on one another and expect the other not to take advantage of that dependency. The *intimacy* aspect concerns the extent to which the two partners use one another to confirm the solidarity of the relationship.

As Jake and Sidney sat at the table in the restaurant where they had their first "real" date after the library meeting, as they were studying the menu, Jake said, "I've had this special here before. It's great." Then when the waiter arrived he said, "We'll both have the special." That was a message that had a content dimension, certainly, since it told the waiter what to bring them; but it also had a relational dimension, because it was a one-up message to Sidney that Jake intended to assume dominance in their relationship, at least in matters such as ordering.

Sidney then had a choice to make. She could maintain silence and, as they say, "Silence gives consent," or she could say, "That sounds good to me." In either case she would be responding to a one-up message with a one-down message, granting dominance. Or she could say, "I'll wait; I'm not ready to order yet." That would be at least close to a one-across message, since it would neither challenge nor affirm Jake's bid for dominance. The third possibility would be to say, "Now wait a minute, man, I'd like to do my own ordering," which would be a one-up response to a one-up message, and would make it clear Jake's bid for dominance was being challenged. It is on the basis of such exchanges that dominance is established and equity negotiated. If Sidney granted dominance at that point, it would have been more difficult later to recall the incident and register explicitly her objection to it.

Reciprocal Self-Concept Support

Another process that was proceeding at this point was **reciprocal self-concept support,** as Cushman and Florence (1974) have put it. Partners in a relationship provide this service for one another to a greater or lesser degree. If Sidney had decided to adopt her role as artist for the purposes of this relationship, she would have expected Jake to support that self-concept rather than question it. If Jake had decided to adopt his role as a sensitive environmentalist, he would have been more attracted to Sidney if she had affirmed that role than if she had pointed out actions that were inconsistent with it. But Sidney and Jake decided to continue their relationship. *Decided* is a strange term, of course, since it implies that the decision was reached consciously, which was probably not the case. They simply came to perceive the relationship similarly, negotiated equity and dominance by means of the **relational messages** concealed in their **content** messages, and came to support one another's self-concepts satisfactorily.

Stages of Developing and Stable Relationships

Many theorists have described stages they believe relationships go through as they move toward relationship equilibrium, or stability. I prefer that of Knapp (1984), because it is more specific than many. The first three stages seem to be characteristic of relationship development, while the last two seem characteristic of equilibrium. The stages listed by Knapp are initiating, experimenting, intensifying, integrating, and bonding.

Initiation I have already described to some extent how Sidney and Jake moved through the early stages. The relationship was *initiated* in the library, where they exchanged small talk and relatively trivial information about one another, and assessed one another as potential partners.

Experimentation In the restaurant, once having committed themselves to spending at least a minimal amount of time together, they began the **experimenting** stage, as they engaged in further but more consequential small talk, trying to identify areas of similarity or complementarity that might form the basis for a longer-lasting relationship. In a sense this was also a mutually arranged audition for a future role. In this case both participants understood it as a safe arena within which there were no further commitments. That is not always the case. Sometimes one or the other of the participants will attach too much significance to this stage, and be hurt when it does not lead to the third stage. This stage was experimental in the sense that the two parties were testing one another.

In the case of Sidney and Jake the second stage ended when Jake took Sidney home (only because I do not have the space to follow them through a more involved relationship). But sometimes the experimenting stage will continue beyond a first date. At the door Sidney and Jake had a somewhat awkward moment, because that is the point at which arrangements are ordinarily made to move into the third phase, if both parties have been satisfied with the audition. Jake could have postponed making such arrangements by saying "I'll call you," or Sidney could have done the same by saying "I'm going home tomorrow for the weekend. Maybe I'll see you when I get back." She could say that as I just wrote it, or she could end with a questioning inflection: "Maybe I'll see you when I get back?"

The issue of a goodnight kiss or more intimate physical contact goes beyond the scope of this chapter. But Sidney could have invited Jake to come in, which would probably have accelerated the relationship, if she had felt satisfied with the audition and confident he was also satisfied. Fortunately, she was able to say truthfully—and ambiguously—"My roommates are home or I'd invite you in. Will I see you again?" Service. The ball was in Jake's court.

His answer set the stage for the next phase. "I'd like that. We're having a party at the house with a few couples next Tuesday night. Would you come with me?" The fact that he used the word *couples* implied that he wanted to test their viability as a couple. He could have said "a few *other* couples," which would have further implied he was beginning to think of them as a couple.

Sidney could have declined that invitation if she was not ready for the "couples" stage, and could have made an alternate suggestion. Instead she accepted.

Intensification At the party, at which they appeared as a couple, the experimenting stage began to slide into **intensifying.** Each was able to observe the other in a social situation, which had not been possible at the library or the restaurant, so experimenting was continuing. Jake had something of an advantage, since these were his friends, but Sidney had the opportunity to observe the sort of people he chose as friends. Sidney was especially interested in the words Jake used when introducing her, and had the opportunity to hear some of his disclosures to people he had known longer. After the party they had a great deal to discuss, and it was at this point that the intensification stage really began in earnest. They sat in the car for some time before Sidney went in, and self-disclosure was the order of the evening. They learned a great deal more about one another's personalities, fears, and dreams than they had heard before.

RELATIONAL EQUILIBRIUM

Integration In the **integration** phase Jake and Sidney began to think of themselves as a couple, and their friends began to think of them in those terms. When one was invited to an event, the other was also invited, if it was appropriate. They began to make some decisions jointly. No longer would Jake inquire, "Do you want to go to the play Friday night?" Instead he would ask, "Do *we* want to go to the play Friday night?" implying he would not go if she wanted to do something else.

Bonding The final phase Knapp describes is **bonding.** This is frequently marriage in our culture, but living together has become very common. Other public commitments might be characterized as *quasi-bonding.* When Sidney invited Jake to visit her family one weekend, it was a sort of public announcement of bonding. When they attended the wedding of one of Jake's friends who lived in another town, it constituted a sort of bonding.

Relational Intricacies

Wilmot (1987) describes in some detail what he terms *relational intricacies* that occur in the equilibrium stage. They are self-fulfilling prophecies, paradoxes, double binds, dyadic dialectics, and spirals.

Self-Fulfilling Prophecies No doubt you are familiar with the concept of **self-fulfilling prophecies.** Had Sidney predicted an early end to their relationship, she might have begun to prepare for it by withholding her affection and commitment, which would have contributed to the early end of their relationship.

Paradoxes A **paradox** is an internally contradictory communication. Translating into our scenario an example Wilmot provides, suppose Jake were to tell Sidney, "I want you to be more spontaneous." This would create a paradox for Sidney, because if she were spontaneous she would be complying with Jake's request, which would not be spontaneous at all.

Double Binds Suppose she were suddenly to leap on him while they were walking in the woods, trying to be spontaneous, they tumbled into the grass, and he said, "You have to let me know before you do things like that." This would have converted the paradox into a **double bind,** in that what she was being told to do before being spontaneous, forewarn him, would make it impossible for her to be spontaneous.

Dyadic Dialectics A **dyadic dialectic** would occur if Sidney were to say that seeing others would make them appreciate one another more, whereas Jake were to say seeing others might destroy their relationship. Both might be true; the couple must decide how to deal with the two poles. They may find a way to allow themselves to have time with others of the opposite sex with the understanding that those relationships are to be purely platonic. In this way both are granted some healthy freedom without threat to the relationship.

Spirals **Spirals** can be either progressive or regressive. According to Wilmot, "When participants serve each other's needs such that A's acts reinforce B and B's acts reinforce A, the synergy of the system makes the relationship progressively better." Suppose Jake unexpectedly brings Sidney a dozen roses for no particular reason, and Sidney later gives him a sheepskin seat for his motorcycle. This could produce a **progressive spiral.** It could also spiral them both into bankruptcy. A **regressive spiral** would occur if Jake were to see Sidney innocently at a bar with George, and instead of joining them he later met with an attractive lady from his psych class in a situation in which he knew one of Sidney's friends would see him, and Sidney, instead of asking him about it, made sure he saw her with another man, . . . and on and on, creating a regressive spiral.

RELATIONSHIP DISSOLUTION: I've Looked at Love from Both Sides Now

Phases of Relationship Dissolution

Duck (1982) lists five phases of relationship dissolution: breakdown, the intrapsychic phase, the dyadic phase, the social phase, and the grave dressing phase.

Now don't get nervous about Jake and Sidney. I am not going to put them through the torment of ending a relationship just for purposes of illustration. We are not dissecting frogs here. Jake and Sidney lived happily ever after.

Breakdown Now that we are through with that, let me clarify Duck's categories. In the **breakdown** phase, one or both partners become dissatisfied with the relationship, most likely because the cost-benefit ratio has become unsatisfying.

Intrapsychic Phase In the **intrapsychic phase,** the dissatisfied partner begins to focus on the other person's strengths and weaknesses and the costs of remaining in the relationship in comparison to the costs of getting out. The two may contrive tests of one another during this phase. This phase lasts as long as the doubts remain internal.

Dyadic Phase In the **dyadic phase,** the dissatisfied partner expresses the doubts to the other partner, generally expressing them in terms of the relationship rather than by attacking the other.

Social Phase In the **social phase,** the two parties begin to negotiate the conditions they will maintain after the dissolution. This is where the dissatisfied partner usually proposes "seeing other people" or a "temporary separation" because, they say, it would "do us good." They may confront the question of whether they can remain "just friends." Both partners will probably begin to talk to friends who might justify the decision, and will begin to put the blame on the other.

Grave Dressing Phase In the **grave dressing phase,** both parties will try to rationalize the dissolution decision, will try to make sense of the relationship in some way that will preserve some positive results, will construct a story as to what caused the dissolution, generally blaming the other, and will publicly disseminate that story.

Relationship dissolution has its costs and its rewards. To the extent the relationship served important needs, the costs at first are bound to be greater than the rewards. This sometimes causes the dissolution process to be very slow, and may be responsible for what Wilmot terms *oscillation*, a period during which the parties move apart and then back together. I know a couple in a small town where I have spent much time who have been divorced twice and remarried twice. At the moment they seem to be doing well together.

On the other hand, some take the advice of Paul Simon in his song "There Must Be 50 Ways to Leave Your Lover": "Just slip out the back, Jack; Make a new plan, Stan...." We must add, to avoid being sexist: "Find a new thrill, Jill; Give him the shoe, Sue; Just lose this pain, Jane; find a new squeeze, Louise ... and set yourself free." The implication is that relationships are best ended suddenly. But best for whom?

KEY TERMS AND CONCEPTS

- interpersonal/relational
- self-perception
- multiple selves
- "true" self
- enacted self
- social self
- self as possessions
- self as religious/philosophical beliefs
- self as reflected in communication interactions
- perception of others (per theories from Chapter 5)
- uncertainty reduction
- entry, personal, and exit phases of initial interaction
- information seeking
- self-disclosure
- interpersonal attraction as explained by the GOALS/GRASP Model
- Predicted Outcome Value theory, Social Exchange theory (including equity and matching hypothesis),
- Perceived Similarity-Attraction Hypothesis) relationship development
- Stewart's *my→you* Model
- perception of the relationship
- equity negotiation
- control-trust-intimacy interacts
- one-up, one-down, one-across messages
- reciprocal self-concept support
- relational and content dimensions of conversational exchanges
- stages of developing and stable relationships
- initiation
- experimentation
- intensification
- integration
- bonding
- self-fulfilling prophecies
- paradoxes
- double binds
- dyadic dialectics
- progressive and regressive spirals
- phases of relationship dissolution
- breakdown
- intrapsychic phase
- dyadic phase
- social phase
- grave dressing phase

REFERENCES

Berger, C. R., and Calabrese, R. J. (1986). Some explorations in initial interaction and beyond: Toward a developmental theory of interpersonal communication. *Human Communication Research* 1: 99–112.

Berscheid, E., and Walster, E. H. (1978). *Interpersonal Attraction,* 2nd ed. Reading, Mass.: Addison-Wesley.

Byrne, D. (1971). *The Attraction Paradigm.* New York: Academic Press.

Cushman, D. P., and Florence, T. (1974). Development of interpersonal communication theory. *Today's Speech* 22: 11–15.

Duck, S. (ed.). (1982). *Personal Relationships.* Vol. IV, *Dissolving personal relationships,* pp. 1–30. New York: Academic Press.

Goffman, E. (1959). *The Presentation of Self in Everyday Life.* Garden City, N.Y.: Doubleday/Anchor.

Infante, D. A., Rancer, A. S., and Womack, D. F. (1993). *Building Communication Theory,* 2nd ed. Prospect Heights, Ill.: Waveland.

Knapp, M. L. (1984). *Interpersonal Communication and Human Relationships.* Boston: Allyn & Bacon.

Millar, F. E., and Rogers, L. E. (1987). Relational dimensions of interpersonal dynamics. In *Interpersonal Processes: New Directions in Communication Research,* edited by M. E. Roloff and G. R. Miller, pp. 117–139. Newbury Park, Calif.: Sage.

Roloff, M. E. (1981). *Interpersonal Communication: The Social Exchange Approach.* Beverly Hills, Calif.: Sage.

Stewart, J. (ed.). (1973). *Bridges, Not Walls.* Editor's introduction. Reading, Mass.: Addison-Wesley.

Sunnafrank, M. (1986). Predicted outcome value during initial interactions: A reformulation of uncertainty reduction theory. *Human Communication Research* 13: 3–33.

Walster, E., Walster, G. W., and Berscheid, E. (1978). *Equity: Theory and Research.* Boston: Allyn & Bacon.

Wilmot, W. W. (1987). *Dyadic Communication,* 3rd ed. New York: Random House.

The committee is a cul-de-sac down which ideas are lured and then quietly strangled.
 —Sir Barnett Cocks, ca. 1907

Groups and Organizations

12

CHAPTER OUTLINE

Groups

What Constitutes a Group?
Why Do People Join Groups?
How Do Groups Stay Together?
How Are Groups Structured?
What Influences Group Interaction?
What Is the Best Way to Resolve Group Conflict?

How Do Groups and Organizations Differ?

How Is Communication in Organizations Structured?

Theory X vs. Theory Y
Networks
Formal Networks
Informal Networks
External Networks

Groups and organizations are ecologies that influence patterns of communication in particular ways. They are ecologies in that they control information, provide the mechanisms for selecting which information is important and which is not, and provide the means for organizing information. Postman (1993, p. 84) describes a **bureaucracy** as "simply a coordinated series of techniques for reducing the amount of information that requires processing." He explains the rise of bureaucracies and the "bureaucracy effect" thusly (p. 86): "Techniques for managing information became more necessary, extensive, and complex, the number of people and structures required to manage those techniques grew, and so did the amount of information *generated* by bureaucratic techniques." This situation has spiraled, resulting in more bureaucracies that coordinate other bureaucracies, creating still more information, and thus increased need for more bureaucratic structure in order to control that information. "Bureaucracy now not only solves problems but creates them" (p. 86).

Groups and organizations bear considerable similarity to one another in that they involve a collection of people striving to achieve mutually agreed-upon goals. The people and groups are linked by a network of information that constrains or facilitates goal achievement. The information networks may be formal, informal, or some combination of the two. Groups and organizations evolve norms and expectations for the behavior of their members, which norms and expectations undergo repeated evaluation and change. These and other aspects of group and organizational structure and process are the concern of this chapter.

GROUPS

For a class assignment, let us imagine you are asked to analyze the patterns of communication in a small group. You decide to analyze the Anthropology Club on campus because two of your friends, Jessica and Adam, have already come to you, a communication major, to discuss the problems confronting the club. Jessica and Adam are its president and secretary, respectively. The club holds annual events such as picnics to raise money for the club, arranges outings to visit local archaeological digs, and holds monthly meetings at which invited scholars speak. Club members are responsible for scheduling and hosting these events. The stories Jessica and Adam tell you about the group have a familiar ring: Not everyone pulls their weight, members make promises and then don't follow through, some people complain that "no one listens to them," and some members do all the talking while others remain silent. Jessica and Adam want to know how they can encourage more participation and commitment, as well as how to resolve some conflicts and problems facing the club. What do you tell them?

The situation we have just described is probably typical of groups in general, whether families, social groups, task groups, or interconnected groups couched within a larger organization. If you have ever done a group project for a class, been a member of a social or work group, or organized a fundraiser, you have probably encountered the same problems of which Jessica and Adam complain. The question is: What can be done about it? You decide that the best approach is to attend a couple of their meetings and observe their interaction. You also know that you must talk with individual members to get their perspective on the group. Before beginning, you decide to review the information on (1) what constitutes a group; (2) why people join groups; (3) how groups are formed and maintained; (4) the roles and norms characteristic of the group; and (5) how communication patterns are influenced in social structures such as groups.

What Constitutes a Group?

Small Groups vs. Aggregates In the previous chapter we discussed the communication patterns typical of dyads. Fundamentally, a group has evolved when a third person is added to a dyad. However, just adding a third person does not necessarily make a group. A group of people at an airport waiting at the gate for their flight is not a group; rather it's an **aggregate.** It's not a group because the people in it do not share a common purpose or a set of norms and procedures specifically worked out by the group. Nor do they share a common bond, a sense of group identity, or see themselves as interdependent. A **group,** then, is a collection of people who have come together because: (1) all involved share an interest in or value for the groups' activities (e.g., baseball card collecting, or needlework, or dog showing); (2) the members have common goals (e.g., working to change some policy on campus or working to get a specific candidate elected); (3) group members value their affiliation with one another for its own sake; and (4) group members seek specific external rewards that membership in the group can help them achieve (e.g., belonging to the Anthropology Club may help members get into graduate school or get a good job after graduation).

Types of Groups Some groups entail a long-term commitment; others, such as juries, come together for a short time to engage in a specific **task**. Some groups emphasize decision making, such as juries and personnel committees. Other groups may best be described as problem-solving groups; study commissions are an example. Some groups are largely **social** in nature (e.g., fraternities and sororities, sci-fi clubs, and the like). Therapy groups are largely concerned with treatment of personal or social problems and include groups such as sensitivity training, Alcoholics Anonymous, and Weight Watchers. Another type of group is a study group, in which members help one another learn a specific task, read and discuss books, or **study** some problem area. So called "think tanks" are an example. Many groups are **combinations**, in that they provide important social networks and alliances, as well as involve study of a problem or issue, and enact coordinated decisions that affect the groups' membership and functioning.

Why Do People Join Groups

Membership in groups and organizations is inescapable. We are born into a group—the family—and will spend the rest of our lives affiliated with groups and organizations of various types. We may not be able to avoid group participation, but we do have some control over the types of groups and organizations with which we affiliate.

Social Comparison Festinger (1954) argued that groups provide us with the means for social comparison, and that we join groups to gain information about ourselves. According to Festinger, the primary need groups fill is the need for **certainty** and **balance**.

Uniformity of Opinion Further, he suggested, groups provide for **uniformity of opinion**. Group members can exert pressure on other members to conform to the prevailing group opinion. To the extent that an individual member is attracted to a group and its goals, that individual will alter his or her opinions, beliefs, and behaviors to fall in line with group thinking. Thus, members of a group will share similar opinions.

However, generally we have access to more than one group, which affords a diversity of opinion across groups. Festinger (1954) wrote that "it may very well be that the segmentation into groups is what allows a society to maintain a variety of opinions within it and to accommodate persons with a wide range of abilities" (p. 136). Therefore, if one is not happy with the opinions held by one group, one is free to join another group, with a different set of norms, opinions, and expectations.

Another theorist, **Schutz** (1958, 1966, 1977), focused on three fundamental needs fulfilled by group membership: inclusion, control, and affection.

Inclusion Inclusion touches our sense of feeling important and worthwhile. Belonging to a group provides a sense of identity and belonging. In fact, members may in part define themselves in terms of their group membership. Members of sororities and fraternities frequently wear their greek letters to signify their membership and affiliation. The members of the Anthropology Club at the school at which I am currently a Visiting Professor are now deciding how their club t-shirts should read. And my coauthor has a favorite t-shirt signifying his membership in the Cognitive Sciences Program. Thus, the groups and organizations to which we belong provide us part of our identity.

Control As you might have already guessed, groups can also satisfy our needs to feel in **control**, to control others, and to maintain a position of power and esteem. Maintaining a leadership position in a group may make us feel important, competent, responsible, and effective. Jessica and Adam may find that members of their group who complain that "no one listens to them" are actually expressing dissatisfaction with their inability to control the group or to exercise leadership. Those who sit by silently and watch may actually desire little control or may be, in Schutz's terms, *undersocial.*

Affection We all need to feel that we are loved and appreciated by others and that we can maintain satisfactory relationships characterized by closeness and intimacy. Groups may provide this closeness and intimacy; in the process they make us feel like valued people.

Schutz claimed that different types of people seek different types of groups. And groups probably need to balance their members along those lines. Thus, a group with all leaders and no followers will probably disintegrate. Certainly a group with many members who are high in need for control will experience some power struggles that evidence themselves as open conflict and unpleasant conversations. Some people may use the group as a way to form close personal relationships, and may direct group discussion in those directions. Those members who prefer less personal relationships may become difficult or avoid interaction altogether. Thus, the needs of the members may have considerable impact on the communication that occurs within the group.

How Do Groups Stay Together?

Thus far I have focused on how groups serve individual needs. But groups are not static entities; they change as a result of new members, new information, and new situations. Group members, then, are constantly evaluating the performance of the group relative to their expectations. Likewise, the rest of the group is also evaluating the group. It is a reciprocal process of mutual evaluation.

Moreland and Levine (1982) identified three recurring phases in group interaction: evaluation, commitment, and role transitions. These three phases are interdependent, in that a change in one is likely to produce a change in the others. Let's use your observations of the hypothetical Anthropology Club as illustration.

Evaluation Phase At the first meeting you attended, the members were trying to decide what logo and saying would be most appropriate for the club t-shirt. This discussion had gone on at several meetings, and Jessica indicated that they needed to make a decision soon. Several people had ideas, but one person, Henry, was pushing his idea very forcefully. He interrupted others, spoke negatively of their ideas, and generally hogged the conversation. He kept pushing them to adopt his idea and get the decision made. Some people sat silently, but appeared disgruntled with the way things were going. Others were politely trying to provide a more open atmosphere for discussion. And Jessica, as the group leader, was trying to get Henry to settle down. But he persisted.

Finally, Henry was confronted by Adam and several others. They told Henry that at this point they were interested in a variety of ideas and would make a decision after carefully considering everyone's input. This is an example of the **evaluation** phase. That is, some of the members thought Henry was deviating from the group's norms, and their evaluation of him was clearly negative.

Commitment Phase Henry protested that he was tired of nothing but "talk, talk, talk" and wanted to get the decision made "*now.*" Henry called for a vote. The others emphatically voted against him. Henry expressed his displeasure, but his comments now appeared to fall on deaf ears. Henry began to complain that the group was becoming a real problem for him and that no one appreciated his efforts to "get things done." This is an example of the **commitment** phase, for Henry was indicating that his commitment to the group was waning. Henry sat silently while other members returned to discussing other t-shirt ideas.

Role Transition   A short time later Henry stood up, made a couple of derogatory remarks, and walked out in a huff. This illustrates a **role transition**: Henry apparently thought through his role in the group, concluded that he was unwilling to change to meet their standards, and instead chose to leave. You later learn that Henry dropped out of the club.

Types of Role Transitions   Moreland and Levine also described major role transitions (entry, acceptance, divergence, and exit) relative to group phases (investigation, socialization, maintenance, resocialization, and remembrance). To illustrate these transitions and phases, I will use Jessica's experiences with the Anthropology Club.

   Investigation   Groups typically seek out new members (**investigation**); similarly, individuals seek to join groups that will suit their needs. Jessica was a new anthropology major, a junior, and a transfer to the university. Consequently, Jessica was looking for new relationships. The club was kicking off the school year with active recruitment for new members, and Jessica met Adam in a class. Adam, a senior and club member for two years, felt that the club could use a member like Jessica, whom he perceived as smart, responsible, and especially interested in the major. Jessica thought the club would be a good way to get involved on campus and meet new people with similar interests. Adam invited her to a meeting, all the other members seemed to like her, she liked them, and she joined.

   Entry   Joining the group is the **entry** phase and it is likely to be marked with some sort of ceremony, reception, or the like. Recruitment for the Anthropology Club had gone pretty well, and they decided to have a party to welcome the new members. This is a difficult time for everyone because a new member is an unknown, so an initiation serves to establish a bond of commitment between the new member and the established group. Groups may hold a welcoming breakfast, office reception, or special lunch in which they show off their new member and reinforce the group choice.

   Socialization   **Socialization** is the process of teaching the new member how to fit in with the group. During this phase the group may hold orientation sessions, provide a mentor, who is likely to be an established and trusted member of the group, to serve as an individual role model for the new person, or a training program during which the new person is initiated into the inner workings of the group. Because Adam had recruited Jessica he took the role of "coach" and relayed information about who did what, what tasks and events they had planned for the year, and suggested things that Jessica could do to get involved. Jessica threw herself into the group's activities and soon became invaluable in her level of commitment and dedication to the group. She followed through on promises, attended all of the meetings, willingly took on jobs for the club, and had good ideas that she readily shared with the others.

Acceptance   Everyone agreed that Jessica fit in, and thus she was accepted into the fold. The **acceptance** transition accompanies successful socialization, and the new member is considered a full-fledged member of the group. This transition may be marked by inclusion in informal networks, increased trust and access to more personal information, and so forth. At this point the new member has moved from the periphery to the core of the group. The new member's loyalty and commitment to the group is reinforced and reciprocated. And this was true in Jessica's case. She was invited to informal gatherings outside of the group activities, was told several "secrets" about others, and was offered access to study materials and files maintained by the group.

Maintenance   The acceptance transition ushers in the **maintenance** phase, characterized by high levels of commitment and negotiation of roles. That is, the new member looks to fill a particular role in the group, and may even seek to evict a long-term member from that role. For example, the new member may seek to replace another as leader, which Jessica sought to do. Jessica felt the current leader was ineffectual; and after some months Jessica had taken a leadership position.

Divergence   If the others see this as acceptable, which they did in Jessica's case, all is well. If not, then a transition to **divergence** will occur. During this time the group will probably shunt the new person off to the sidelines, not include them in informal conversation, cut off access to in-group information, and probably devise ways to terminate the relationship. Of course, the new person may decide to divorce themselves from the group, and begin locating a new group to join.

Resocialization   If the new member is especially hard to replace, or the damage not too severe, the group may attempt **resocialization** before deciding to terminate the relationship.

Exit   If that fails, the final transition is *exit*. There are various ways the group may terminate the relationship. If the Anthropology Club came to dislike Jessica as a leader, they could vote her out of office and replace her with someone else. Universities that decide to not tenure one of their group generally provide a "grace year" to allow the person to find a new group. Early retirement is another way to terminate a member gracefully. Sometimes the termination is more personal, involving attempts to publicly humiliate the new member, attack them professionally or personally, or simply make their life so uncomfortable that the newcomer chooses to leave. The latter is especially likely if termination by the established group is not possible, as in the case of tenured faculty at a public school or university. It is also likely if the group is not in a position simply to get rid of a member. This would be the case with the Anthropology Club. They might be able to vote Jessica out of office; but since the club has an open membership, they could not simply throw her out. Instead they might ostracize her by not including her in activities, not choosing her for projects, and/or ignoring her.

Remembrance   After ties have been severed, both parties will go through a period of **remembrance** during which both the established group and the newcomer will attempt to gain perspective on the experience. This is the phase when both will decide whether they will maintain any degree of relationship or abandon the relationship altogether.

This model is especially useful in describing the interdependence of group members, the ways in which group associations can facilitate or constrain individual needs, and changes groups pass through over time.

How Are Groups Structured?

Groups develop **norms,** guidelines or expectations, about what behavior and opinions are acceptable. Group norms develop over time and tend to be rather stable even as membership changes. Groups develop norms regarding how decisions will be made (e.g., majority rule or consensus), setting the agenda for meetings, and the types and nature of interaction. Some groups are tolerant of conflict, while others attempt to avoid it. Some groups run their meetings according to the rules of Parliamentary Procedure, while others are more open and free-form. Some groups, but especially large decision-making groups and organizations, explicitly state the rules and norms for conducting business; more informal groups operate with norms that are understood but rarely written down. These norms guide the behavior of the group.

A group is a collection of individuals, and each individual adopts a different role within the group. Some people generate ideas easily; others are better at getting the group motivated. Some people are good at working out conflict; others are better at producing conflict. Some people are good at asking questions; others are better at seeking answers. The structure of the group is based on this differentiation among roles (Shaw, 1981).

Role Categories Benne and Sheats (1948) described three categories of roles group members adopt: group task roles, group building and maintenance roles, and individual roles.

Group Task Roles **Group task** roles are aimed at issues of problem solving. Some members of the group will adopt roles in this area, including seeking information, evaluating evidence, orienting (keeping the group focused on the task), stating opinions, and recording group opinions and decisions.

Group Building and Maintenance People who are concerned with **group building and maintenance** focus on the socioemotional aspects of the group process. These roles include encouraging others, reducing tension and negotiating conflict, promoting open channels of communication, compromising, and good listening.

Individual Roles The last category, **individual roles,** includes behavior that seeks to satisfy individual needs, sometimes at the expense of effective group process. Benne and Sheats described a person who is overly dominant and attacks others as the *aggressor*. They also described the *dominator*, who tries to control the discussion; the *blocker*, who is hostile and negative; and the *self-confessor*, who focuses on their personal problems even when inappropriate.

The Study of Leadership One of the most important roles in the group is that of leader. And identifying the characteristics of good leaders has generated considerable interest, and focused on four approaches to the study of leadership: trait, functional, style, and situational.

Trait Approach The **trait** approach focused on the characteristics that differentiated leaders from nonleaders. Stogdill (1974) summarized the traits possessed by leaders: physical characteristics, such as height, age, and weight; social characteristics, such as adaptability, attractiveness, and nurturance; social background attributes, such as education and social status; and a host of personality traits, including alertness, extroversion, originality, self-confidence, and aggressiveness. And, while many of these may be desirable leadership traits, they did not go very far in predicting who will be leaders or in explaining why people with few of these characteristics emerge as leaders.

Functional Approach The **functional** approach to leadership focused not on individual characteristics but on behaviors that facilitated group effectiveness. Cragan and Wright (1986) suggested that leaders serve several functions: (1) task behaviors, such as seeking and evaluating ideas; (2) procedural behaviors, such as setting goals, setting the agenda, and clarifying ideas; and (3) promoting interpersonal relations by regulating discussion so all get an opportunity to express their ideas, and by resolving conflict.

Style Approach White and Lippett (1968) studied the communication style of leaders and identified three types: authoritarian, democratic, and laissez-faire. The *authoritarian* leader exerts control over all aspects of the group process, which has been found effective in certain types of groups (e.g., groups in which decisions have to be made rapidly, such as in emergency situations or military maneuvers), although at the expense of member satisfaction. A leader with a *democratic* style encourages group participation in all aspects of the group process and frequently seeks consensus among group members on all decisions or decisions that are made by majority rule. The *laissez-faire* leader is one who provides minimal direction and could be characterized as "hands off" in their approach to leadership.

Situational Approach The **situational** approach seeks to understand the conditions under which some leadership styles are better than others. Fisher (1986) called this the "it depends" approach. That is, what are considered desirable traits, behaviors, and styles in a leader depend upon the particular group, its history, the personalities of the members, their goals, and so forth. Fisher (1986, pp. 211–213) went on to suggest several myths about leadership that result from his analysis of the existing research:

> (1) Leaders exert their leadership during discussion by using direct attempts to influence followers; (2) Leaders perform certain functions which are peculiar to leadership; (3) Leadership is similar to supervision or management; management is thus a special kind of leadership; (4) Leaders typically behave with a particular "style," typically described as democratic, autocratic, or laissez-faire; and (5) Many groups have two leaders—one who handles the social dimension of the group and one who handles the task dimension.

Melcher (1977, p. 94) wrote that "the study of leadership in the last seventy years has resulted in little accumulated knowledge that permits one to understand or predict the effects of leadership approaches or that provides a better understanding of how to be an effective leader." The point seems to be that what makes a good leader or what constitutes effective leadership is a complicated issue without any easy prescriptions.

What Influences Group Interaction?

Phases of Interaction Over time, groups go through a variety of phases in their interaction. Bales and Strodtbeck (1951) described three such phases: orientation, evaluation, and control. In the **orientation** phase, groups focus on getting organized, identifying the problem or issue to be considered, and seek information from individual members. In the **evaluation** phase, communication focuses on handling conflicting opinions, evaluating the quality and reliability of the information at their disposal, and offering possible solutions. **Communication** during the control phase is used to coordinate the activities of group members so as to implement effectively the chosen solution.

Other researchers (e.g., Tuckman, 1965; Ellis and Fisher, 1975) expanded on this analysis and described the following phases in group development: orientation, conflict, emergence, and reinforcement.

Orientation At one of the Anthropology Club meetings you attend, they are initiating discussion of what to do for the annual fundraiser. They need to decide what kind of event to host, what to sell, and so forth. The money they raise goes toward field trips, which are highly valued by the group members. Initially you observe that there is obvious uneasiness among the members as they begin discussing ideas. You decide this is because they do not know how their ideas and opinions will be received by the others. You find their conversation is especially polite and tentative, and is characterized by frequent periods of silence. This is the *orientation* phase.

Conflict As the meeting continues, you note that people seem to loosen up a great deal, ideas are offered with more strength of conviction, and occasional arguments break out. You notice small coalitions emerging, and you even see that there is some struggle for leadership of the discussion. While Jessica is the designated leader, she does not appear to be the only "leader" at this point. Adam appears to be leading the discussion, and you decide this is because he is a "senior" member of the group and ran a very successful fundraiser last year. You observe that ideas tend to be directed toward Adam, and he plays an important role in deciding who speaks and for how long. Further, Adam tends to speak more often and for longer periods than other members. Adam speaks to Jessica more frequently than to others, and solicits her opinions directly, which indicates that Jessica too is assuming a position of power. She and Adam form a "power hierarchy." Finally, you note that when others address Adam they tend to do so in a more deferential and approval-seeking manner. This also seems to characterize Jessica and Adam's interaction with each other. This is the **conflict** stage.

Emergence Later in the meeting you note that a single idea seems to be gaining support. Disagreements are minimal, coalitions are dissipating, and no one appears to be struggling for control over the discussion. This is the *emergence* stage in the group's decision making.

Reinforcement Finally a decision has been made, and everyone seems especially pleased with their efforts. The conversation is positive and supportive, and everyone is expressing opinions of support for the collective decision. They are all sure that this will be "*the* most successful fundraiser ever," and conversation focuses on the specific tasks for which various members will be responsible. This is the **reinforcement** phase.

What Is The Best Way to Resolve Group Conflict?

Jessica has talked with you at some length about the amount of conflict in the club, and she has sought your advice for coping with it. Jessica is worried that the level of conflict in the group is too high and may impede its effectiveness. More importantly, Jessica is worried that conflict will have a negative impact on the social relationships among the members. Since you have observed club meetings on several occasions, you feel you have sufficient data on which to base your response to Jessica's concerns.

Groupthink First, you assure Jessica that conflict is a normal part of all relationships, and that in groups it is an important component of problem solving and decision making. For example, Nemeth (1986) found that conflict served to improve the quality of group decision making. In fact, insufficient conflict in the form of open discussion of opinions can result in **groupthink,** which is known to produce less than competent decisions. Janis (1982) analyzed the decisions of high-level political groups (e.g., on the Bay of Pigs invasion, and on escalation of the Vietnam War) and concluded that these obviously bad decisions were due to a lack of diversity of opinion, a lack of open consideration of a variety of opinions, and insufficient critical assessment of the proposed solution.

Janis noted three symptoms of groupthink: First, the group tends to overestimate their own importance and to see themselves as "right" or "good," while opposing groups are "wrong" or "evil." Second, the group becomes insulated and closed to any information that might raise question with their course of action. Third, the group demands consensus of opinion at all costs. These factors can, and have, resulted in decisions with disastrous consequences. Generally the group fails to conduct a thorough and careful analysis of the information bearing on the problem, the proposed solutions, or the potential consequences of those proposed solutions. Further, the group may depend solely upon information from within the group, a closed system, meaning the information may be biased. And, due to the strong feelings of *cohesion* (a sense of team spirit) among group members, those who may be feeling uncertain about the group's decision are unlikely to challenge it.

Janis suggested several ways to avoid groupthink. Among others, he recommended that the leader encourage members to express any doubts or reservations they might have. He also suggested that the leader avoid expressing support for any particular solution, especially early on in the discussion. Members should seek information from sources outside the group. He even suggested assigning the role of devil's advocate to one of the members to ensure that ideas are openly challenged, carefully analyzed, and so forth. Since Jessica is the president and thus the designated leader of the club, she can play an important role in preventing the group from developing the symptoms of groupthink.

Hirokawa (1985) observed that groups that have a thorough understanding of the problem, that generate a wide range of reasonable potential solutions, that devise explicit criteria for making a choice among those solutions, and that carefully consider both the positive and the negative consequences for each possible solution are more likely to produce a quality decision. Like Janis, Gouran and Hirokawa (1986) found that encouraging argument, what they termed *counteractive influence*, resulted in better decisions and also in greater member satisfaction with the decision-making process.

But, Jessica protests, isn't some conflict destructive to decision making and likely to hurt interpersonal relations? Yes, you respond. Conflict that focuses on the personal characteristics of others can be very damaging. Disagreements that focus on members' self-concept or self-esteem are probably unrelated to the issues facing the group, and are likely to result in bad relationships, unwillingness to cooperate, and unwillingness to engage in discussion. This can only thwart effective group functioning. Self-centeredness, with little regard to what is best for the group, can also be damaging. Those who seek personal gain and glory at the expense of the group will contribute little to the quality of the group decision. The style in which one engages in conflict can also be damaging. Verbal aggressiveness will probably result in defensiveness, hostility, and bad feelings.

Public Compliance vs. Private Acceptance   Jessica goes on to tell you that she worries that some of the members of the club conform to group decisions even though they do not support the decision. These people tend to avoid engaging in the conflict phase of discussion, but later will privately complain to others that they didn't agree with the decision. She wonders what causes this. You reply that groups can act to pressure others to **conform,** or that some members may perceive pressure even if it isn't actually present. According to Kiesler and Kiesler (1969), some people will conform in public, called **public compliance.** That is, in the presence of other group members they may favorably support the decision, but privately they may feel otherwise. **Private acceptance,** according to Kiesler and Kiesler, is conformity with group norms, because the person has changed opinion due to information obtained from the group. Again, you suggest that creating an open atmosphere in which people feel free to disagree and to openly discuss information is the best remedy to prevent merely the appearance of agreement.

Summary Jessica is impressed with your analysis and the suggestions you have offered, and she asks you to come to a special meeting to discuss your findings. She argues that since we all must interact in groups, regardless of our major or career goals, your information would be beneficial to all members of the Anthropology Club. Your report to them should focus on your observations of their group process, and should also contain the following: (1) an explanation of how groups differ from dyads and aggregates; (2) a discussion of the reasons why people choose groups; (3) an overview of the "typical" phases of group development, maintenance, and decision making; (4) the development of group norms and individual roles; (5) influences on group discussion patterns; and (6) the role of conflict, consensus, and conformity in group discussion.

HOW DO GROUPS AND ORGANIZATIONS DIFFER?

Organizations are collections of individuals generally organized into various groups that are hierarchically arranged. Organizations, unlike dyads and groups, have formal patterns of information flow, a formal power structure and leadership hierarchy, and a formal decision-making structure. Unlike dyads and groups, the expectations for behavior (norms) and rules by which decisions are made are typically written down. Organizations also employ policies that are not explicit but that need to be understood if a person is to survive in the organization. (Of course, organizations include informal communication networks with behavioral expectations that may be in conflict with formal expectations.)

Further, the operation and communication patterns within any given organization are influenced by the geographic location of the organization, the physical structures that house the organization, the physical communication system (e.g., phones, computers), whether the organization deals in products or services, the size of the organization (e.g., number of employees), whether it is private or public, whether it is employee owned, the extent to which it is unionized, and whether it is a profit or nonprofit organization.

Contemporary organizational theorists view organizations as social units that strive for mutually derived specific goals (Etzonini, 1964), that realize cooperative action is important in goal attainment (Farace, Monge, and Russell, 1977), and that use information and shared meanings to attain agreed-upon goals (Wilson, Goodall, and Waagen, 1986). Organizations are viewed as cultures (Pacanowsky and O'Donnell-Trujillo, 1982, 1983) in which the members play many different interdependent roles; in doing so, the members create shared visions of meaning and reality via their process of interaction. Kreps (1984, cited in Goldhaber, 1993, p. 69) argued that organizational culture emerges from the development of "collectively held underlying logics and legends about organizational life and the organization's identity." Kreps continues:

> These logics and legends are imbedded in and transmitted through formal and informal channels of organizational communication. **Organizational** culture is communicated to organizational members and relevant others informally through interpersonal storytelling and gossiping using the organization's grapevine as a primary medium, and communicated formally through the use of advertising, slogans, **organizational** documents, group meetings, and public presentations. As an **organization's** identity emerges, organizational members interpret the **organization's** past and present, making sense of the phenomena of organiza- tional life and creating stories and legends about **organizational** activities. These stories and legends often provide a thematic base for the development of collective visions about the future development of the organization. Culturally derived explanations about what the organization is, what it does, how it goes about accomplishing its goals, where it has been, where it is going, and what role organization members play in these activities are essential elements in the development of an organizational identity. (Cited in Goldhaber, 1993, p. 69)

HOW IS COMMUNICATION IN ORGANIZATIONS STRUCTURED?

Theory X vs. Theory Y

The formal **flow of information** in organizations was described by McGregor (1960) as **Theory X** and **Theory Y.** A Theory X structure is like a pyramid in which information flows down from the top. Decisions are made by a few people in top management. Leaders assume that their employees should be regulated via a system of tangible rewards and punishments, and require explicit direction and careful control. This structure is typical of that found in the chain of command in the military. Theory Y organizations, on the other hand, believe that people receive intrinsic rewards from work, and are capable of self-direction and responsible decision making. The information flow in Theory Y organizations is more diffuse, and the input from those outside of managerial positions is regularly sought after. Decision making involves people throughout the organization, and feedback within and across departments and levels is encouraged. These types of organizational structure should not be perceived as distinct. Any given organization may be at some point between the two types, or may incorporate principles from both.

Networks

Another way to describe the pattern of communication in organizations is through network analysis (Bavelas, 1948). Network analysis is used to describe the flow of messages between and within organization levels, assesses the extent of influence of those messages, and identifies the relationships among individuals or groups within the organization.

Bavelas, (1948) described five networks: all-channel, "Y," chain, circle, and wheel (see Figure 12.1). As you can see, the *all-channel* network directly links all members of the group or all groups in the system. It affords the most information flow and potentially allows equal influence by all members or groups. The *wheel* emphasizes a central position or leader through which all information must flow. Because the leader plays a central position, and because the other positions (members or groups) cannot interact directly with one another, the leader has the greatest influence and can initiate or censor information at will.

You can now probably work through the other networks and assess their potential efficiency in transmitting information, as well as the potential influence of the various positions. Their efficiency depends upon the *distance* between members, defined as the number of links through which a message must flow. Those in a central position have more opportunity to exert influence over the flow of information. The person or group that occupies a central position has the most potential for leadership, greater potential for controlling the content of the information, and greater potential control over to whom the information is transmitted. Centralized networks have been found to be more efficient and to make faster decisions, especially when the problems to be solved are simple. Decentralized networks such as the all-channel are more efficient when the task is complex. These findings need to be qualified, because they were generated in a laboratory setting, which does not necessarily approximate the typical organizational setting. Further, Fisher (1980) argued that the differences in performance across networks tends to decrease over time, probably because the people involved grow accustomed to the network structure. Nevertheless, the structure of networks seems to have important implications for the efficiency of information processing and for the satisfaction with the task expressed by members of the various networks. I used to teach a course in group communication, and I used an exercise to illustrate network analysis and function. In most instances, those who belonged to the all-channel network liked the structure better than those in the other structures. And this was the case even if they didn't "win" by solving the problem first.

Formal Networks

The formal flow of communication in organizations can be described as *downward, upward,* or *lateral.* According to D. Fisher (1993, p. 37), "downward com-

FIGURE 12.1
Communication Networks.

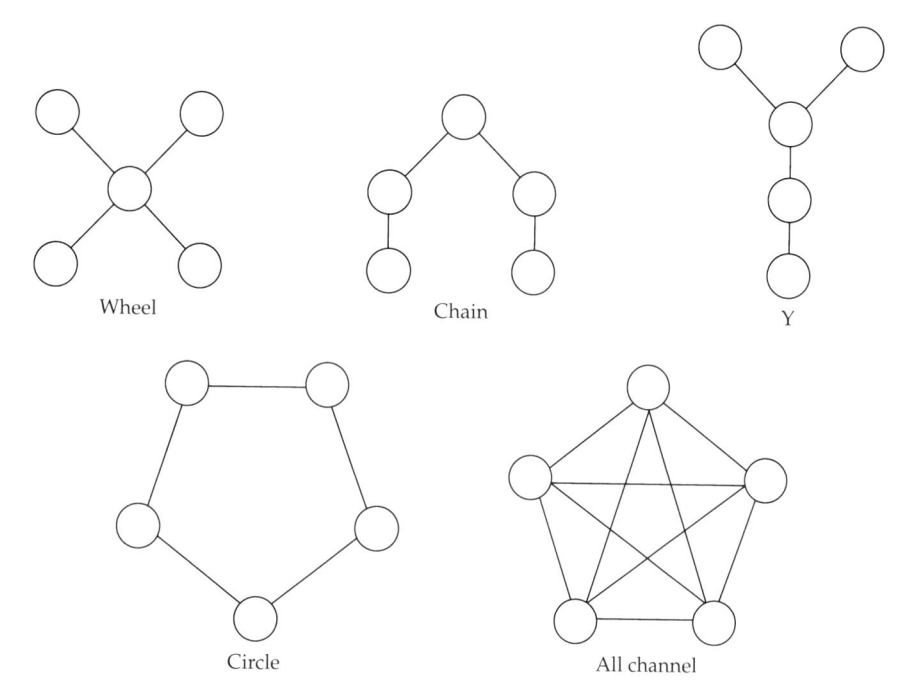

Wheel   Chain   Y

Circle   All channel

Source: Based on A. Bavelas, 1948. *Applied Anthropology 7*, pp. 16–30.

munication commands and instructs; upward communication informs; lateral communication coordinates." He goes on to note a number of problems with each type of communication flow.

Downward Communication Downward communication sometimes never reaches those on the bottom rungs, and what was sent may not resemble what was received. Frequently this information comes in the form of memos, which may stop at a supervisor's level and never get transmitted to those who work for that supervisor: The supervisors may not see the information as "relevant" to anyone other than themselves.

Upward Communication Upward communication may never reach the people for whom it was intended, for a number of reasons. If it involves complaints about an immediate supervisor, that person may censor the information in an attempt to protect his or her reputation or job. Or a secretary may not want to bother the head honcho with "trivial" information, may redirect the information to someone else, or simply file it. Physical distance may impede upward message flow, especially if the headquarters that house executives for whom the information is intended are some distance from the plant, other offices, or outlets. Rossen and Tesser (cited in D. Fisher, 1993) report that upward communication may also be restricted by *mum,* "minimize unpleasant messages."

Lateral Communication Lateral communication moves among those of equal rank in the organization. At a college or university, faculty talk laterally with faculty, although the rank of individual faculty does make some difference under some circumstances. Tenured faculty participate in some decisions and information exchange to which untenured faculty are not invited. Sometimes the outcome of those meetings is not passed "down" to the untenured faculty.

But faculty at all ranks from various departments still engage in a great deal of lateral communication. Some of this is informally transmitted information around the lunch table, in offices, and at social events. Much of the interaction is more formally organized, and occurs in committee meetings attended by representatives of the total faculty. This is probably especially true if the university has a large faculty. Smaller institutions may allow for greater lateral interaction among faculty. For instance, I once taught at a private liberal arts school with about 1,000 students and 80 faculty. The entire faculty met once a month to discuss and vote on issues that affected all departments. Informal interaction among the faculty was also enhanced by the small size of the faculty.

Lateral communication is far from perfect. Competition among departments, fear of offending peers, knowledge that upper management encourages vertical rather than lateral communication, and increasing specialization of knowledge can undermine the lateral movement of information necessary to coordinating the efforts of various subunits in the organization.

Informal Networks

Informal networks (sometimes called *the grapevine*) form among those who have frequent contact due to physical proximity, job similarity, and so on. "An organization's informal network operates whenever two accountants regularly join two members of the market research department for lunch; it emerges whenever one office borrows a box of computer paper from another office rather than going through the company's official (but slower) supply system" (D. Fisher, 1993, p. 109). These networks can be used to undermine the formal system, can be used to supplement it, and/or can further organizational goals by allowing access to information beyond the formal avenues.

Interestingly, while most of us believe that information gathered from the grapevine is only, at best, half right, some researchers have found that the grapevine is fast and accurate (Davis, 1977; Walton, 1961). As D. Fisher (1993, p. 111–112) wrote:

In most organizations, members can often predict how information will spread, who usually spreads it, and who always seems to "know what's going on."

By recognizing the nature of grapevines, organization members can best take advantage of these informal communication devices and make them as effective as possible. Those who develop good working relationships with informal leaders who play central roles in the grapevine will be well informed. The grapevine can help solve problems. To someone "thinking out loud" about a business or personal problem, the grapevine will often bring help or suggestions. Managers and others can use the grapevine's speed to rapidly disseminate information; by providing informal leaders with important and accurate information, supervisors can halt the spread of untrue rumors. New ideas can often be tested through the grapevine on a trial basis. Trying to abolish or suppress the grapevine is not a good idea. Most attempts to do so succeed only in strengthening it.

External Networks

Organizations interact with other groups outside of the organizational structure. Organizations are linked to others via advertising, news releases, public presentations by company representatives, public relations activities, and so forth. They are also connected to outside groups via informal contact. Members of an organization may be perceived as unofficial representatives or spokespeople for their company, and the physical facilities maintained by the organization provide additional information in creating a public image of organizations.

Marketing and public relations are critical in managing images of organizations. Marketing research allows organizations to obtain information about the public, while public relations enables them to provide information to the public. Organizations have also come to depend upon lobbying groups to represent their interests in national and state legislation. Finally, media form an important link between organizations and the public. A great deal of what we learn about an organization is reported by the media; thus, organizations are increasingly concerned with the extent to which they are presented accurately.

CONCLUSION

The study of organizational communication, including advertising and public relations, has become a popular area of study. Interest in organizational communication has undoubtedly expanded with the increase in the number of organizations; and with that increase, the need to understand how communication affected productivity, worker satisfaction, public image, and profits took on more significance. Most people in the United States will find themselves employed by an organization. Understanding how organizations function can facilitate their ability to survive and thrive in an organizational setting.

We have merely highlighted how communication in organizations differs from communication in other contexts. There are also a number of similarities. Like groups and cultures, organizations and their members are integrated by a complex web of communication. Also like groups and cultures, organizations use communication to generate shared meanings, negotiate activities and division of labor, maintain norms and standards for the behavior of their members, and coordinate visions of reality. Organizations develop traditions, construct images of themselves, and monitor and seek information from their environment. The structure of groups and organizations also introduces problems peculiar to them. Those peculiarities have been the focus of this discussion.

KEY TERMS AND CONCEPTS

bureaucracy
small groups vs. aggregates
types of groups (task, social, study, combinations)
needs (Festinger: certainty, balance, uniformity of opinion; Schutz: inclusion, control, affection)
phases of group interaction (Moreland and Levine: evaluation, commitment, role transitions)
role transitions (entry, acceptance, divergence, exit)
group phases (investigation, socialization, maintenance, resocialization, remembrance)
norms
roles (group task roles, group building and maintenance roles, individual roles)
leadership (trait, functional, situational)
developing communication patterns (orientation, evaluation, control)
conflict
groupthink (symptoms of and methods for combating it)
conformity (public compliance, private acceptance)
definitions of an organization
flow of information (Theory X, Theory Y)
networks (formal, informal, external)

REFERENCES

Bales, R. F., and Strodtbeck, F. L. (1951). Phases in group problem-solving. *Journal of Abnormal and Social Psychology* 46: 485–495.

Bavelas, A. (1948). A mathematical model for group structures. *Applied Anthropology* 7: 16–30.

Benne, K. D., and Sheats, P. (1948). Functional roles of group members. *Journal of Social Issues* 4: 41–49.

Cragen, J. F., and Wright, D. W. (1986). *Communication in Small Group Discussions,* 2nd ed. St. Paul, Minn.: West.

Davis, K. (1977). *Human Behavior at Work.* New York: McGraw-Hill.

Eisenberg, E. M., and Goodall, H. L., Jr. (1993). *Organizational Communication: Balancing Creativity and Constraint.* New York: St. Martin's Press.

Ellis, D. G., and Fisher, B. A. (1975). Phases of conflict in small group development: A markov analysis. *Human Communication Research* 1: 195–212.

Etzonini, A. (1964). *Modern Organizations.* Englewood Cliffs, N.J.: Prentice-Hall.

Farace, R., Monge, P., and Russell, H. (1977). *Communicating and Organizing.* Reading, Mass.: Addison-Wesley.

Festinger, L. (1954). A theory of social comparison processes. *Human Relations* 2: 117–140.

Fisher, B. A. (1980). *Small-Group Decision-Making,* 3rd ed. New York: McGraw-Hill.

———. (1986). Leadership: When does the difference make a difference? In *Communication and Group Decision-Making,* edited by R. Y. Hirokawa and M. S. Poole, pp. 197–215. Beverly Hills, Calif.: Sage.

Fisher, D. (1993). *Communication in Organizations,* 2nd ed. Minneapolis, Minn.: West.

Goldhaber, G. M. (1993). *Organizational Communication,* 6th ed. Madison, Wisc.: Brown & Benchmark.

Gouran, D. S., and Hirokawa, R. Y. (1986). Counteractive functions of communication in effective group decision making. In *Communication and Group Decision-Making,* edited by R. Y. Hirokawa and M. S. Poole, pp. 81–90. Beverly Hills, Calif.: Sage.

Hirokawa, R. Y. (1985). Discussion procedures and decision-making performance: A test of a functional perspective. *Human Communication Research* 12: 203–224.

Janis, I. L. (1982). *Groupthink: Psychological Studies of Policy Decisions and Fiascoes,* 2nd ed. Boston: Houghton Mifflin.

Kiesler, C. A., and Kiesler, S. B. (1969). *Conformity.* Reading, Mass.: Addison-Wesley.

Kreps, G. (1984). Organizational culture and organizational development: Promoting flexibility in an urban hospital. Paper presented at the annual meeting of the International Communication Association, San Francisco.

McGregor, D. (1960). *Human Side of Enterprise.* New York: McGraw-Hill.

Melcher, A. (1977). Leadership models and research approaches. In *Leadership: The Cutting Edge,* edited by J. Hunt and L. Larson, pp. 94–108. Carbondale, Ill.: Southern Illinois University Press.

Moreland, R. L., and Levine, J. M. (1982). Socialization in small groups: Temporal changes in individual-group relations. In *Advances in Experimental Social Relations,* Vol. 15, edited by L. Berkowitz, pp. 137–193. New York: Academic Press.

Nemeth, C. J. (1986). Differential contributions of majority and minority influence. *Psychological Review* 93: 23–32.

Pacanowsky, M. E., and O'Donnell-Trujillo, N. (1982). Communication and organizational cultures. *Western Journal of Speech Communication* 46: 115–130.

———. (1983). Organizational communication as cultural performance. *Communication Monographs* 50: 126–147.

Postman, N. (1993). *Technopoly.* New York: Vintage Books.

Putnam, L. L., and Pacanowsky, M. E., (eds.). (1983). *Communication and Organizations: An Interpretive Approach.* Newbury Park, Calif.: Sage.

Schockley-Zalabak, P. (1988). *Fundamentals of Organizational Communication.* New York: Longman.

Schutz, W. (1958). Firo: A Three-Dimensional Theory of Interpersonal Behavior. New York: Holt, Rinehart, & Winston.

———. (1966). *The Interpersonal Underworld.* Palo Alto, Calif.: Science and Behavior Books.

———. (1977). The postulate of interpersonal needs. In *A Reader in Human Communication,* 2nd ed., edited by J. M. Civikly, pp. 174–184. New York: Random House.

Shaw, M. E. (1981). *Group Dynamics: The Psychology of Small-Group Behavior,* 3rd ed. New York: McGraw-Hill.

Stogdill, R. M. (1974). *Handbook of Leadership: A Survey of Theory and Research.* New York: Free Press.

Tuckman, B. (1965). Developmental sequences in small groups. *Psychological Bulletin* 63: 384–399.

Walton, E. (1961). How efficient is the grapevine? *Personnel* March–April, 28, 45–49.

White, R. K., and Lippett, R. (1968). Leader behavior and member reaction in three social climates. In *Group Dynamics: Research and Theory*, 3rd ed., edited by D. Cathwright and A. Zander, pp. 318–335. New York: Harper & Row.

Wilson, G., Goodall, H., and Waagen, C. (1986). *Organizational Communication*. New York: Harper & Row.

Wilson, G. L., and Hanna, M. S. (1993). *Groups in Context*, 3rd ed. New York: McGraw-Hill.

*I read magazines. I watch television. I know
how people are supposed to treat one another.*
> —Shelly, "Northern Exposure"

One nation under television . . .
> —The Truth About Lies: Tube as Reality

Mediated Communication

13

CHAPTER OUTLINE

Functions of Media
- *Surveillance*
- *Selection and Interpretation of Information*
- *Cultural Transmission*
- *Social Roles*
- *Establishment of Personal Identity*
- *Entertainment*
- *Interpersonal Interaction*
- *Uses and Gratifications*

Media Effects
- *Diffusion of Innovations*
- *Media-Effects Models*
- *Televised Sex and Violence*

Media, Reality, and Censorship
- *Media Construction of Reality*
- *Media as an Economic Force*
- *Effects of Advertising*
- *News as Entertainment*

Earlier in this book we argued that relative to other species, humans were unusual in their ability to access information from distant times and remote places. It is the sciences of archaeology and geology that are largely responsible for providing us access to messages from our remote past and long-extinct ancestors. But it is the mass media that have allowed us to travel to distant places without leaving the comforts of our homes.

Moreover, without the media, most of us would remain unaware of the scientific explorations that have revealed the remains of our ancestors. Mass media have facilitated the forging of links with other nations and cultures, thus making possible the construction of global markets and economies. The media afford individuals the opportunity to voice their opinions around the nation and world, and it is not unusual for groups to gain recognition solely as a result of media exposure. Not only did the 1993 stand-off in Waco, Texas, between David Koresh's religious cult and federal agents attract considerable media attention, but Koresh insisted that he would not negotiate until the media aired a message he had for the world, which they did. Unfortunately, he did not live up to his end of the bargain.

The media structure our social reality to the extent that they tell us how we should live, dress, and interact with others, direct our attention to some events over others, and provide an image of the world and its inhabitants filtered through the beliefs, values, and biases of those who control the process, that is, the camera people, editors, publishers, and advertisers.

Given this power to shape our images of the world and our place in it, it is essential to critically examine the structure, functions, and effects of media on our perceptions, beliefs, values, and decisions. Thus, we will discuss (1) the functions of media in society; (2) the effects of the media; (3) censorship of media content; and (4) approaches to studying the effects of media on society.

FUNCTIONS OF MEDIA

Four functions of the media have been identified: surveillance, selection and interpretation of information, cultural transmission (Lasswell, 1948), and entertainment (Wright, 1959). Further, the media serve to establish and reinforce social roles and personal identity, and influence the content of our conversations and nature of our interpersonal relationships. The specific effects of these media functions will be described in greater detail later in the chapter.

Surveillance

The media monitor world events, such as pending natural weather extremes and potential military conflicts. Although there were many deaths and injuries resulting from 1992's Hurricane Andrew, most agree that it would have had a much greater impact on human life had it not been for the early warnings provided by weather forecasts aired by the media. Further, the media provide stock market information, traffic reports, economic reports, pending legislation, and so forth, information that may affect our daily lives.

While such reporting is frequently to our advantage, it has been suggested that the media may exaggerate situations and cause panic. Additionally, because the media tend to focus on negative information such as natural or human-made disasters and violence, people who consume a lot of media see the world as a more dangerous place than it actually is. On the other hand, exposure to extreme portrayals of violence may have an anesthetizing effect on viewers.

Selection and Interpretation of Information

The media instruct us on how to react to events, and act as a guide to determining what events are important and of concern. The media may alter or reinforce public opinion and thus perpetuate stereotypes, promote conformity at the expense of individual differences, exclude representation of minority opinion, and "preserve and extend power that may need to be checked" (Severin and Tankard, 1988, p. 218). On the other hand, the media can also act as a check on governmental excesses, as was illustrated by the famous case of Watergate, which ultimately resulted in the resignation of the late President Nixon.

Agenda Setting This function is sometimes referred to as **agenda setting**. What this means is that media, and especially news reports, can determine what issues are significant, relevant, and worth thinking and talking about. This can have positive effects in that we become aware of problems we otherwise might not have access to. For example, until recently colleges and universities were not required to report campus crimes, which resulted in campuses' being viewed as islands of safety in a crime-infested sea. So, for instance, women may have felt comfortable walking alone after dark on college campuses because they believed that it was safe. Unfortunately, many discovered the hard way that the safety of campuses was merely an illusion, and one with potentially life-threatening consequences. In 1990 the Student-Right-to-Know and Campus Security Act was passed requiring colleges and universities to report criminal activity. An examination of those reports suggests that campuses are far from safe refuges from crime. On the other hand, we may tend to be more suspicious of people than is actually warranted due to the images and stories offered in the news. Just because someone is dressed in black leather, wears chain belts, and sports multicolored hair does not necessarily make them a potential threat or a devotee of the attitudes suggested in some heavy metal music; yet, these are likely conclusions we might draw based on media portrayals.

Pseudo-Events This function includes the creation of **pseudo-events**, and the development of images and personalities for products and public figures. The Super Bowl, actually just another football game, has taken on the character of a national holiday thanks to the media coverage it receives. Advertisers and public relations firms have connected various brands of beer with images of young, tan, attractive people enjoying one another's company in the mountains or at the beach while conveniently avoiding showing the real effects of alcohol consumption on behavior, which is frequently not a pretty sight. Virginia Slims cigarette ads suggest that independence is correlated with smoking, and a recent Pepsi commercial suggested that senior citizens can recharge their batteries by drinking Pepsi.

Cultural Transmission

The media serve to promote cultural norms and introduce subcultural practices to mass society. Media participate in the socialization process and facilitate social cohesion via common experiences. Cultural values are reflected in and created by the media. That the media emphasize and promote standardization of beliefs and behavior is a point of critical concern.

Social Roles

As a part of this socialization function, media provide role models and prescriptions or expectations for behavior appropriate to those roles. Overall, male characters on TV outnumber female characters by a ratio of 3 to 1 (Signorielli, 1984). This ratio varies depending on the type of program: Males predominate in adventure programs by 6 to 1, while soap operas have roughly equal numbers of male and female characters (Barcus, 1983). Further, while some change has occurred in the past several years, female characters are still portrayed primarily as wives or mothers. Female characters center their concerns on family and interpersonal relationships, even in such programs as "L.A. Law," "Murphy Brown," "Designing Women," and "Northern Exposure."

Even in these trend-setting programs, work takes a backseat to more traditional concerns. Although Clare of "The Cosby Show" is an attorney, few, if any, episodes feature her professional life. I have, however, seen several episodes that focus on Cliff's professional life.

And traditional role relationships between men and women are likely to be stressed on TV. Men dominate women (Turow, 1974), and women characters are more emotional and more in need of the support from others than are men (Greenberg, Richards, and Henderson, 1980). These findings are consistent with those for children's programs as well (Barcus, 1978, 1983; Schechtman, 1978). Finally, women are frequently portrayed as sex objects, especially in advertising and music videos.

Establishment of Personal Identity

While our self-concept is learned via interaction with other people, its development is also influenced by the media. In their theory of mediated interpersonal communication, Cathcart and Gumpert (1986) emphasize the role of media in developing and reinforcing self-image. The media provide pictures of what is "standard," "normal," "acceptable," and "ideal." Consumers compare themselves to those images, and learn to value and aspire to them. And repeated exposure to those images intensifies the effect. I am reminded of a recent ad that begins: "Having a gold MasterCard with a $5000 limit doesn't make you a better person. Or does it?" Hey, I don't have one of those, so what kind of person am I? (Oh, not to worry. I have *the card*, the American Express Card. And I never leave home without it.)

Entertainment

This is a primary function of the media. Newspapers regularly offer critiques of restaurants, films, and plays; activity schedules; and articles devoted to hobbies and travel. Films and a great deal of television programming are designed to provide diversions and escape from the rigors of everyday life. It has been suggested that the media actually "encourage escapism, corrupt fine art, lower public taste, and prevent the growth of an appreciation for the arts" (Severin and Tankard, 1988, p. 219).

Interpersonal Interaction

You can examine your own conversations for evidence that the media frequently provide the substance of our conversations with others. Groups of people come together specifically to watch major media events such as the Super Bowl, Academy Awards, and Final Four basketball games. And discussion is likely to center on the event. I show documentaries in many of my courses as a means for providing a common stimulus for discussion. And my colleagues in animal behavior frequently focus discussion on nature programs offered on public access television and on the Discovery channel. I suspect that the constant coverage of the Persian Gulf War provided the topic of conversation at many dinner tables.

People can participate quite directly in the media and thus establish a more interpersonal relationship by calling telephone partylines or call-in radio shows. Avery and Ellis (1979) found that some people prefer this mode of interaction to "real" friends, and use it as a substitute for face-to-face interaction (Avery and McCain, 1982).

So far discussion has focused largely on what the media *do* to audiences, which is really only half the picture. The use of propaganda in WWI and WWII, the rise of Hitler, and the effects of Orson Welles' 1938 radio broadcast of *War of the Worlds* fed growing concern with the power of the media. "Under these conditions it is no surprise that the prevalent image of the mass media was that of a hypodermic needle or a bullet. This was a concept of the media with direct, immediate, and powerful effects on any individual they reached" (Severin and Tankard, 1988, p. 197).

Fundamental to the bullet or **hypodermic-needle theory of media influences** was the belief that audiences were passive agents, a view consistent with the psychological principle of stimulus-response contingencies that was then the foundation for explaining behavior. More contemporary theory views audiences as active participants in media consumption. This view has resulted in an examination of how audiences use media to satisfy their own needs and goals. This perspective is called *uses and gratifications.*

Uses and Gratifications

Researchers advocating this position presume that different people use the same message for different purposes. For example, people studied in the 1940s by Herzog (1944) used radio soap operas as a way to minimize their own problems, as an escape, or as a means for providing solutions potentially useful for solving their own problems.

Media may be used as a diversion, as a substitute for personal relationships, as a means for self-understanding and self-awareness, and for monitoring information (surveillance) (McQuail, Blumler, and Brown, 1972). Other typologies are fairly similar. Katz, Gurevitch, and Haas (1973) identify five categories of needs: seeking information (cognitive), affect, building confidence or status (personal integrative), enhancing contacts with family and friends (social integrative), and tension release. Rubin (1979) reports six reasons that children offer for watching television: learning, passing time, companionship, escape, excitement, and relaxation.

People may **select** certain types of programming in response to how they are feeling at the moment. Bryant and Zillman (1984) found that "stressed subjects watched nearly six times as much relaxing television as did bored subjects, bored subjects watched nearly twice as much exciting fare as did stressed subjects." (p. 12).

The uses and gratifications approach has been criticized for being atheoretical, for being vague in defining key concepts such as *needs,* and because it overemphasizes the use of self-report data, which has increasingly become suspect. However, it still remains an important contribution and alternative to conceptualizations of audiences as passive observers whose thoughts, beliefs, and values are dictated by the whims of media agents and agencies.

MEDIA EFFECTS

Clearly the media serve multiple roles and functions, and people use the media for a variety of purposes depending upon their specific needs at that time. The effects of the media on individual perceptions, beliefs, and decisions, as well as on the collective perceptions of society have received substantial investigation.

Early studies of voting behavior from the perspective of the bullet or hypodermic-needle theory found that personal contacts called "opinion leaders" play a significant role in individual decision making. *Opinion leaders* are those people of influence who pass on information from the media to others in their group. Opinion leaders were characterized as people who others wish to emulate, who are broadly exposed to and make use of a variety of media sources, who maintain contacts outside of the group, who are accessible, and who associate with other influential people. Thus, most people do not get their information directly from the media, but from others who do get their information directly from the media, a process called the **two-step flow** of communication.

This view turned out to be oversimplified and has since been replaced with the **multistep flow** model used in research on diffusion of innovations.

Diffusion of Innovations

The question of concern in this area is how innovations (new practices, ideas, or objects) are adopted or rejected by individuals and communities.

Stages of Innovation   Rogers (1983) describes five stages in the process: (1) exposure to and understanding of the innovation; (2) development of an attitude toward the innovation via persuasion; (3) the decision to accept or reject the innovation; (4) implementation of the innovation; and (5) maintenance or reversal of the decision. The decisions may result in a number of consequences, which may or may not have been anticipated, may be desirable or undesirable, and may be direct and immediate or indirect and delayed. Finally, some people or groups may readily adopt innovations while others tend to reject all change. Rogers describes **innovators** as people eager to experiment with new ideas, **early adopters** as people or groups with high influence, **early majority** as those who engage in frequent interaction but are rarely leaders, **late majority** as those who are skeptical but adopt as a result of pressure, and **laggards** as those who tend to cling to the past and are frequently on the fringes or isolated from the decision process.

Change Agents   Change agents play a critical role in the innovation process. A change agent is a professional person who attempts to influence the adopting or rejecting of innovations. A change agent might be a salesperson with a pesticide company pushing the adoption of a new, more powerful pesticide, a missionary trying to convince tribal leaders to provide birth control for the women of the tribe, or a nonprofit environmental organization arguing for the setting aside of a specific area as a wildlife preserve.

Gatekeepers   Like opinion leaders, change agents are **gatekeepers.**

Outside the Media   Gatekeepers get their information from the media and disseminate it to others with whom they interact. Gatekeepers are typically specialized in the type of information they transmit, although there are always exceptions. Further, gatekeepers form networks. So in evaluating the credibility of any gatekeeper it is important to know how many previous gatekeepers participated in the flow of information, where the information originated, and whether it has been confirmed by more than one report.

Within the Media   There are gatekeepers within the media as well. Camera operators, editors, and journalists are all examples of people with a gatekeeping function. In that role, they participate in selecting the information to be presented, and determine the manner in which it will be presented. Broadcast news directors and managing editors of newspapers decide where in the program or paper a story will appear and how much time or space will be devoted to it. Further, their decisions are influenced by other gatekeepers, such as the owners and the advertisers.

Apparently, key players who have access to information and can control its dissemination have the potential to bring about important changes in policy and to influence the adoption or rejection of innovative ideas and practices. The two-step and more recent multistep flow models were an attempt to explain the flow of information and the effects of that flow on the diffusion of ideas. Other models have been developed to explain or predict the potential and actual effects of the media.

Media-Effects Models

While the bullet theory emphasized the direct and immediate impact of media on audiences, some have argued that the effects are limited and mediated by processes such as selective exposure, selective perception, and selective retention, the influences of group norms, and variations in opinion leadership (Klapper, 1960).

Cultivation Model   Gerbner and his associates (1980) have offered the **cultivation model,** which is based on comparisons of heavy media consumers with light media consumers. Gerbner focuses on television viewing practices, and claims that television "is a key member of the family, the one who tells most of the stories most of the time" (p. 14).

The differences between light and heavy television viewers are rather interesting. First, heavy viewers tend to overestimate the number of people living in the United States, the percentage of people in the United States in law enforcement, and the likelihood they will be the victims of violence. This tendency to overestimate makes sense when one considers that most television characters are American, some 20 percent of television characters are in law enforcement, and television programs and news reports emphasize violence and crime.

Other factors such as income level and sex of the viewer tend to qualify these results. For example, light viewers from low-income groups tend to agree with heavy viewers that the world is a dangerous place, whereas light viewers from high-income groups do not appear to be so fearful. That women who are heavy viewers tend to agree that we need to be fearful of crime may be explained by the fact that they are portrayed on television as particularly vulnerable to crime.

McLuhan's Global Village McLuhan (1965) claimed that television would do away with individual nations and produce a **global village.** Television, he argued, is a visual, auditory, and tactile medium that alters the way we perceive and think. It was he who coined the phrase "The medium is the message." McLuhan argued that the emphasis on printed material produces a way of thinking that is linear, sequential, and logical. Television, he suggested, returns us to a more primitive state in that it emphasizes more sensory stimulation than does print, which is a purely visual medium. For McLuhan, print is the domain of the left hemisphere, with its proclivity for processing linear, sequential information, while television exercises the intuitive, gestaltic, and picture-oriented right hemisphere. Those who decry the deterioration of the writing skills of young people claim television as the cause.

McLuhan's ideas have had considerable impact and have been expanded upon by people like Neil Postman (1985).

Spiral of Silence Noelle-Neumann (1980) espouses a theory called the **spiral of silence,** which attributes more power to media influence on public opinion than do some other theories. Noelle-Neumann argues that media effects are cumulative and consonant, because various media sources adopt a unified view of the same events, and stories are generalized across all media sources (ubiquitous). In this view silence works to perpetuate the majority opinion because people who perceive their opinions to be in the minority remain silent. Further, they remain silent when they perceive that their opinions are not represented. Thus, their silence serves both as a statement of their isolation and as a means for keeping them isolated.

Media Hegemony The theory of **media hegemony** finds its source in Marxist ideology and critical theory. Put simply, this view holds that the ideas of the ruling class become the ruling ideas. Media agencies and content are controlled by the dominant or ruling class and facilitate control by this class over all others. Three specific hypotheses have been suggested (Altheide, 1984): (1) Journalists are trained to adopt the dominant ideology. (2) Media content reflects a conservative perspective and tends to support the status quo. (3) Reporting is slanted pro-America, and coverage of foreign countries is negative.

Attempts to demonstrate the tenability of these hypotheses have yielded mixed results. Based on a survey of those results, Severin and Tankard (1988) conclude that journalists adopt a variety of ideological positions, the status quo is not always supported by media reporting, and news reports do not necessarily reflect negative evaluations of other countries and their governments.

Televised Sex and Violence

The effects of violence have received considerable attention due to the pervasiveness of violence in television programming and films. On the basis of laboratory and survey research, we can conclude that exposure to televised violence results in an increase in aggressive behavior. Several hypotheses have been offered relevant to this finding. These results eliminated the *catharsis hypothesis,* which suggests that viewing violence will reduce acts of aggression. Another explanation suggests increases in violence will result because viewers will imitate the observed behavior. And third, viewers will feel less inhibited as a consequence of seeing violence on television. These latter two hypotheses have received considerable support.

The behaviors enacted on television provide a model for viewers, which can strengthen or weaken inhibitions. "In televised representations, physical and verbal aggression is often shown as a solution to interpersonal conflicts. Aggression is portrayed as socially acceptable, relatively successful; and it is socially sanctioned by 'superheros' triumphing over evil by violent means" (Linz and Donnerstein, 1989, p. 273). Thus, viewers may try to replicate the aggression because it appears to be legitimate and successful. If such actions work in real life, they are reinforced and will be used again.

Huesmann and Malamuth (1986) offer five conditions relevant to sustaining the relationship between television viewing and aggressive behavior in children: (1) intellectual achievement, (2) social popularity, (3) identification with television characters, (4) belief in the realism of the portrayed violence, and (5) amount of fantasizing about violence. Aggression is more common among children with poor academic skills than among those who perform better at school. Moreover, children with poor academic skills tend to watch a lot of television, especially programs with violent content, and report believing this represents reality. Aggressive children are less popular, and unpopular children are also more aggressive. Finally, the extent to which a child identifies with television characters influences the likelihood that they will adopt that character's behavior; and more aggressive children tend to identify with characters that behave aggressively. Note that this does not conform with the more one-sided view of the powerful effects of television. In this case, both the child and television work together to initiate and reinforce violent behavior.

Desensitization Repeated exposure to portrayals of violence may desensitize viewers. **Desensitization** has proven a successful treatment for people with particular phobias. Desensitization frequently produces a reduction in anxiety or arousal by merely exposing individuals to the objects or situations they fear. The same general principle has been tested by examining male reactions to films picturing violence against women. College-age men viewed these films over a five-day period. Their perceptions of the degree of violence and degradation decreased significantly over the five days. Further, their anxiety over the material decreased significantly and their enjoyment of the material increased.

Zillman, Weaver, Mundorf, and Aust (1986) interviewed preadolescents who watch "slasher films" at home with their friends. They suggested that this situation facilitates the desensitization process and serves a number of interpersonal goals as well. Young males can prove their courage and fearlessness in the face of blood and gore, which in fact grows easier with each exposure to the violent content. Young females can squeal and squirm, and they look to the fearless male for comfort and protection; indeed, their reasoning is supported by the data.

In another study using college students as subjects, Zillmann et al. (1986), discovered that reactions to portrayals of violence that conformed to traditional sex-role stereotypes and expectations enhanced perceptions of attractiveness.

Finally, how the victim of a rape is portrayed influences perceptions. Males who watched a film in which the victim of a rape was shown to be sexually aroused believed that a higher percentage of women would derive pleasure from sexual assaults than did those who saw the rape portrayed as a negative experience (Malamuth and Check, 1985). Zillman and Bryant (1982) found that four hours and forty-eight minutes of exposure to pornography over six weeks led viewers to recommend shorter prison terms for rapists and resulted in less support for the women's rights movement and in less concern for the victims of rape.

Finally, people who live in circumstances where real violence is a common experience and who watch a lot of television may get especially powerful reinforcement for engaging in violent behavior. According to Will (1993) results of research on children's exposure to crime in major U.S. cities show that among elementary-school-age children, 90 percent had witnessed violence, 70 percent had seen a weapon used, and 40 percent had seen a corpse. A study at Boston Children's Hospital reports that 10 percent of the children treated witnessed a stabbing or shooting by the age of six. And an estimated 10 to 20 percent of children living in Los Angeles have witnessed homicides.

If it holds that we teach as we are taught, then it is no surprise that violence has become commonplace. With all that real violence surrounding us, media might do well to deemphasize its occurrence and instead present alternative patterns of behavior.

MEDIA, REALITY, AND CENSORSHIP

Media Construction of Reality

McLuhan, Postman, and others argue that media do not just represent reality but **construct** it. If media can influence what issues are relevant, important, and worth thinking about, if media can forge specific beliefs, values, and cultural practices, if media can create and destroy events and personalities, then their influence is indeed potent and worthy of examination. Attempts to structure reality and our perceptions of it result from a network of decisions made by those who are in positions to control the media and its content, such as owners, advertisers, journalists and newscasters, and television programmers.

Media as an Economic Force

According to Jones and Anderson (1977), the newspaper industry is the third-largest employer in the United States. Twelve conglomerates control about half of the newspapers, as well as book and magazine publishing, radio, television, and cable. Yet local newspapers have been disappearing at a rapid rate, largely as a result of competition from electronic media such as network television and cable.

And cable has been growing at an unprecedented rate. Some project that by the mid-1990s, 500 channels will be available (Waters and Beachy, 1993). Commercial networks, on the other hand, are "already victims of shrinking audience shares and siphoned-off ad revenues" (Waters and Beachy, 1993, p. 75). Gerbner is reported to be skeptical of all this diversity in programming. In an interview with *Newsweek,* he said: "The TV audience has never clamored for diversity. Their attitude is: I know what I want and I want more of it" (p. 76). He goes on to speculate that the high cost of multicast TV will further widen the information gap between the rich and the poor.

With ownership of the media concentrated in the hands of the few, and with print media such as newspapers increasingly concentrated in a few major publications, the potential for control over what information is disseminated is enormous (see Barber, 1988; Postman, 1993).

Effects of Advertising

Further, since the media are dependent upon advertising as their primary source of revenue, advertisers and the companies they represent also have enormous opportunity to control the content of the media. Bagdikian (1977, p. 20) writes: "One wonders whether Harcourt Brace Jovanovich will now think twice before publishing an otherwise acceptable manuscript if it contains material displeasing to the advertisers who are now a source of the concern's revenue."

Reporting a case in which *Modern Medicine,* a publication of the *New York Times,* ran a series of articles on medical incompetence that resulted in the loss of 260 pages of advertising from medical companies, Bagdikian (1977, p. 20) wonders "if other newspaper conglomerates would have been as willing as the Times Company to get rid of such a property: it would strike many as simpler not to assign reporters to stories that might offend someone doing business with a subsidiary."

A recent video presentation titled *The Truth About Lies: Tube as Reality* stated that television is an advertising medium, and advertisers are solely interested in hawking their wares to the largest audience possible. Thus, a program with high ratings, and therefore a large market share, gets advertiser support regardless of program content. American TV, they charge, is a "system of censorship," and censorship is heavily influenced by advertiser needs. According to this view, television programming operates at the whim of capitalists interested only in turning a profit.

One consequence of this may be the push to present an idealized version of people that emphasizes similarities and conformity. If all people are the same, then they need and want the same products. And the characters on television tend to come from higher socioeconomic backgrounds, thus attracting a more upscale audience of people with more disposable income. Further:

> Reporters, editors, camera operators, and news anchors are also more frequently drawn from the upper middle class, or aspire to it, and identify with the officials they cover. It is often charged that this identification and these aspirations bias their perspective on the society they report, often unconsciously. . . .
>
> In a documentary dealing with press coverage of a presidential primary, a national television network followed a candidate and the working press. The following comments by working reporters at a soup kitchen for the destitute, where a presidential candidate was to appear, were broadcast [on "Frontline," 1984]:
>
> I'm just wondering whether they had to go out this morning and round up some winos to get in line.
>
> What wine are they serving for lunch?
>
> That's what this guy said, this big guy. He gets our producer aside and he says, "This is a shame, you people coming in here, the press, invading these people's privacy, these poor people," and so forth. (Severin and Tankard, 1988, pp. 220–221)

Moreover, members of the boards of directors of media conglomerates frequently are also members of the boards of directors of other corporations, many of which pay substantial sums in advertising to the media conglomerates. This incestuous relationship has the potential to influence media programming and news reporting in ways that result in censorship of ideas other than their own.

News as Entertainment

Postman (1985, pp. 87–88) writes:

> Entertainment is the supra-ideology of all discourse on television. No matter what is depicted or from what point of view, the overarching presumption is that it is there for our amusement and pleasure. That is why even on news shows which provide us daily with fragments of tragedy and barbarism, we are urged to "join them tomorrow." What for? One would think that several minutes of murder and mayhem would suffice as material for a month of sleepless nights. We accept the newscasters' invitation because we know that the "news" is not to be taken seriously, that it is all in fun, so to say. Everything about a news show tells us this—the good looks and amiability of the cast, their pleasant banter, the exciting music that opens and closes the show, the vivid film footage, the attractive commercials—all these and more suggest that what we have just seen is no cause for weeping. A news show, to put it plainly, is a format for entertainment, not for education, reflection or catharsis.

And the competition for market share and advertising dollars means that each network or cable station must provide more entertainment than the others. This seems to have resulted in increasingly sensationalized versions of reality, as illustrated in the new crop of tabloid shows (e.g., "Hard Copy"), which borrow the forms and authority of news but basically provide entertainment, or if we adopt Postman's characterization of the news, provide *more* entertainment.

In their effort to provide more sensationalistic versions of reality, news programs and reporting may cross the line and *create* situations that border on outright dishonesty. An article in *Newsweek* (Feb. 22, 1993) surveys several such instances, most notably the "Dateline NBC" story on older GM pickup trucks. It seems that an incendiary device in the form of toy rockets that spilled gasoline on impact (to ensure a fiery crash) were used to create the image that these trucks were especially dangerous. It was later discovered that these devices may not have been the cause of the fire (see *Newsweek*, Mar. 15, 1993). The point is that an attempt was made to support their view regardless of the actual facts. Less devious, but equally damaging, news reports of the *suspicion* that cellular phones may produce brain tumors had sweeping effects on the sale of cellular phones. Serious study of the possibility is probably in progress, but the fact remains that no one yet knows if cellular phones present a health hazard. Drawing this conclusion on the basis of a single untested incident is far from rational.

CONCLUSION

By way of summary we return again to the writing of Neil Postman:

> When Galileo remarked that the language of nature is written in mathematics, he meant it only as a metaphor. Nature itself does not speak. Neither do our minds or our bodies or, more to the point of this book, our bodies politic. Our conversations about nature and about ourselves are conducted in whatever "languages" we find it possible and convenient to employ. We do not see nature or intelligence or human motivation or ideology as "it" is but only as our languages are. And our languages are our media. Our media are our metaphors. Our metaphors create the content of our culture. (1985, p. 15)

If this is true, then the metaphors we live by, many of which are created and sustained by the media, deserve critical examination and reflection. Are they the metaphors that will facilitate our survival? Or will we find ourselves living out a fantasy while reality plots our demise?

KEY TERMS AND CONCEPTS

media functions
  surveillance, selection and interpretation, agenda setting, cultural transmission, establishment of personal identity entertainment, interpersonal interaction
hypodermic-needle theory of media influences
uses and gratifications

media selection
media effects
two-step flow, multi-step flow, diffusion of innovations
stages of diffusion
innovators
early adopters
early and late majorities
laggards
change agents
gatekeepers
cultivation model

of media effects
global village
spiral of silence
media hegemony
sex and violence desensitization
reality and censorship
media construction of reality
media as an economic force
effects of advertising

REFERENCES

Alter, J. (1993, 15 March). The incendiary aftershocks. *Newsweek*, 65.

Altheide, D. L. (1984). Media hegemony: A failure of perspective. *Public Opinion Quarterly* 48: 476–490.

Altschull, J. H. (1984). *Agents of Power: The Role of the News Media in Human Affairs.* White Plains, N.Y.: Longman.

Avery, R. K., and Ellis, D. G. (1979). Talk radio as an interpersonal phenomenon. In *Inter/Media: Interpersonal Communication in a Media World,* edited by G. Gumpert and R. Cathcart, pp. 108–115. New York: Oxford University Press.

Avery, R. K., and McCain, T. A. (1982). Interpersonal and mediated encounters: A reorientation to the mass communication process. In *Inter/Media: Interpersonal Communication in a Media World,* 2nd ed., edited by G. Gumpert and R. Cathcart, pp. 29–40. New York: Oxford University Press.

Bagdikian, B. (1977). Newspaper mergers: The final phase. *Columbia Journalism Review* (March–April): 17–22.

Barber, B. (1988). The second American revolution. In *Impact of Mass Media,* 2nd ed., edited by R. E. Hiebert and C. Reuss, pp. 500–509. New York: Longman.

Barcus, F. E. (1978). *Commercial Children's Television on Weekend and Weekday Afternoons.* Newtonville, Mass.: Action for Children's Television.

———. (1983). *Images of Life on Children's Television: Sex Roles, Minorities and Families.* New York: Praeger.

Biagi, S. (1990). *Media Impact.* Belmont, Calif.: Wadsworth.

Bryant, J., and Zillmann, D. (1984). Using television to alleviate boredom and stress: Selective exposure as a function of induced excitational states. *Journal of Broadcasting* 28: 1–20.

Cathcart, R., and Gumpert, G. (1986). I am a camera: The mediated self. *Communication Quarterly* 34: 89–102.

Christians, C. G., Rotzoll, K. B., and Fackler, M. (1987). *Media Ethics,* 2nd ed. New York: Longman.

DeFleur, M. L., and Ball-Rokeach, S. (1989). *Theories of Mass Communication,* 5th ed. New York: Longman.

Gerbner, G., Gross, L. P., Morgan, M., and Signorielli, N. (1980). The "mainstreaming" of America: Violence profile no. 11. *Journal of Communication* 30(3): 10–29.

Greenberg, B., Richards, M., and Henderson, L. (1980). Trends in sex-role portrayals on television. In *Life on Television: Content Analyses of U.S. TV Drama,* edited by B. Greenberg, Norwood, N.J.: Ablex.

Herzog, H. (1944). Motivations and gratifications of daily serial listeners. In *Radio Research 1942–1943,* edited by P. Lazarsfeld and F. Stranton, New York: Duell, Sloan and Pearce.

Huesmann, L. R., and Malamuth, N. (1986). Media violence and anti-social behavior: An overview. *Journal of Social Issues* 42: 1–6.

Jones, W., and Anderson, L. (1977). The newspaper business. (Madison, Wisc.) *Capital Times* 15 (August): p. 25.

Katz, E. M. Gurevitch, and Haas, H. (1973). On the use of the mass media for important things. *American Sociological Review* 38: 164–181.

Klapper, J. T. (1960). *The Effects of Mass Communication.* New York: Free Press.

Lasswell, H. (1948). The structure and function of communication in society. In *The Communication of Ideas,* edited by L. Bryson, pp. 37–51. New York: Institute for Religious and Social Studies.

Linz, D. G, and Donnerstein, E. (1989). The effects of violent messages in the mass media. In *Message Effects in Communication Science,* edited by J. J. Bradac, pp. 263–293. Newbury Park, Calif.: Sage.

Malamuth, N., and Check, J. V. P. (1985). The effects of aggressive pornography on beliefs in rape myths: Individual differences. *Journal of Research in Personality* 19: 299–320.

McLuhan, M. (1965). *Understanding Media: The Extensions of Man.* New York: McGraw-Hill.

McQuail, D., Blumler, J. G., and Brown, J. R. (1972). The television audience: A revised perspective. In *Sociology of Mass Communications,* edited by D. McQuail, Harmondsworth, England: Penguin.

Noelle-Neumann, E. (1980). Mass media and social change in developed societies. In *Mass Communication Review Yearbook,* Vol. 1, edited by G. C. Wilhoit and H. de Bock, pp. 657–678. Beverly Hills, Calif.: Sage.

Postman, N. (1985). *Amusing Ourselves to Death.* New York: Penguin.

———. (1993). *Technopoly.* New York: Vintage Books.

Rogers, E. (1983). *Diffusion of Innovations,* 3rd ed. New York: Free Press.

Rubin, A. M. (1979). Television use by children and adolescents. *Human Communication Research* 5: 109–120.

Schechtman, S. A. (1978). Occupational portrayal of men and women on the most frequently mentioned television shows of pre-school children. *Resource in Education* (Eric document reproduction service).

Schwartz, J., Washington, F., Fleming, C., and Hamilton, K. (1993, 22 February). No scandal, no story. *Newsweek,* 42–43.

Severin, W. J., and Tankard, J. W., Jr. (1988). *Communication Theories,* 2nd ed. White Plains, N.Y.: Longman.

Siebert, F. S., Peterson, T. B., and Schramm, W. (1956). *Four Theories of the Press.* Urbana: University of Illinois Press.

Signorielli, N. (1984). The demography of the television world. In *Cultural Indicators: An International Symposium,* edited by G. Melischeck, K. E. Rosengren, and J. Stappers. Vienna: Austrian Academy of Sciences.

Turow, J. (1974). Advising and ordering: Daytime, prime time. *Journal of Communication* 24(2): 138–141.

Waters, H. F., and Beachy, L. (1993, 1 March). Next year, 500 Channels. *Newsweek* 75–76.

Will, G. (1993). Editorial. *Newsweek* (March 22): p. 78.

Wright, C. (1959). *Mass Communication.* New York: Random House.

Zillmann, D., and Bryant, J. (1982). Pornography, sexual callousness and the trivialization of rape. *Journal of Communication* 32(4): 10–21.

Zillman, D., Weaver, J. B., Mundorf, N., and Aust, C. F. (1986). Effects of an opposite-gender companion's affect to horror on distress, delight, and attraction. *Journal of Personality and Social Psychology* 51: 586–594.

Travel is fatal to prejudice, bigotry, and narrow-mindedness.

—*Mark Twain*

Communication and Culture

14

CHAPTER OUTLINE

What Are Some Dimensions on Which Cultures Differ?
Individualism vs. Collectivism
High vs. Low Context

What Is the Relationship Between Culture and Language?
Language and Perception
Honorifics, Titles, and Status

How Do Language Styles Differ Across Cultures?
Restricted vs. Elaborated Codes
Direct vs. Indirect Communication Styles
Elaborate, Exacting, and Succinct Communication Styles
Personal vs. Contextual Communication Styles
Instrumental and Affective Styles

What Are Some Cultural Differences in Nonverbal Behavior?
Ritual Behaviors
Posture
Back-Channeling
Personal Space
Subgroup Differences

What Beliefs and Values Define American Culture?
Beliefs About the Physical World
Beliefs About Human Nature
Beliefs About the Supernatural
Values: Family, Friends, and Money

What Problems Might We Encounter in Cross-Cultural Exchanges?
Conflicting Beliefs or Values
Ethnocentrism
Conflicting Priorities
Conflicting Cultural Assumptions
Conflicting Behavioral Expectations

Cultures also differ with respect to the types of information important to them. Kenyans who lead traditional rural lives use natural rather than artificial landmarks for finding their way around. While we Americans depend upon maps, street signs, billboards, and buildings for our daily travels, many Kenyans depend upon rock formations, landscapes, trees, rivers, and watering holes as their guides. For many Kenyans, time is measured by the ebb and flow of daylight, while we measure time on the basis of watches, clocks, buzzers, and bells. The overall pace of life in Kenya is rhythmic and slow, while the pace of life in industrialized countries tends to be staccato and fast.

Basic **beliefs** and **values** held in common by members of the culture, and the shared **norms** and **expectations** about appropriate and effective social interaction also differ across cultures. For example, people in the United States value directness in conversation. People in the United States also tend to evaluate others on the basis of what they do. It is common for us to ask questions such as "What do you do?" when first introduced to another person. In Asian cultures people are evaluated by what group they belong to rather than what they do for a living. People in Western industrialized nations tend to think in linear rather than holistic terms, are more interested in facts than in ideas, and believe in mastery over nature. Asian and African people perceive the world more holistically, view ideas as more important than facts, and believe in harmony with nature. Studies of predominant values shared by members of various cultures point up other differences. In the United States, for example, self-confidence, individual progress and achievement, good adjustment, and status are considered important. In Greece, on the other hand, affiliation, societal well-being, and conformity to the norms of the culture are highly valued.

So these are some ways in which cultures differ. But *what is culture?* Basically, **culture** is "what is learned from the cumulative experience of past generations, shared among contemporaries, and preserved beyond the individual life span of a society's members" (Farb, 1978, p. 331). Gudykunst (1991) defines culture as a shared "system of knowledge." And this knowledge is passed down in the form of oral and written laws, histories, stories, and myths. Cultures are not **static**, however, and one has only to read the history of white American culture in the United States to note the immense changes that have occurred over time. For example, witch hunts and slavery are now deemed illegal as well as immoral. There is also considerable diversity within a culture, meaning that not all members of a single culture support mainstream cultural beliefs and values. People differ with respect to level of education, socioeconomic standing, gender, geographic location (e.g., urban versus rural), dialect, religion, and political affiliation. These differences are the source of cultural **changes.** Some women living in the late 1800s did not accept the dominant cultural belief that politics was exclusively the domain of men. Those women banded together and fought for the right of all women in the United States to vote. Their efforts resulted in a law granting women that right.

With these ideas in mind, let's explore some specific ways in which cultures differ and the implications of those differences for communication across cultures.

WHAT ARE SOME DIMENSIONS ON WHICH CULTURES DIFFER?

In 1985 I went to Kenya for an extended period of time to study elephant tool use. In the process, I was introduced to a culture vastly different from my own. I researched in a game reserve called Samburu-Buffalo Springs, which is about 100 miles from the capital city of Nairobi. The tribe native to and living in the area are the Samburu, cousins to the Masai who inhabit the southern portion of Kenya. Their language is Samburu, a Maa language. While English is one of the two "legal" or "official" languages of Kenya, a result of the fact that Kenya was colonized and governed by the British, not all rural people learn English. My knowledge of Swahili was limited, so gesture and pantomime formed the foundation for many of my conversations. Swahili, a Bantu language that is the other legal or official language of Kenya, is widely spoken in east Africa.

The Samburu are predominantly pastoralists, that is herders of cattle and goats, and cattle are still the major criterion of wealth. The elders are the ruling body, and the status of related families determines a person's position in the society. "It is a social world in which privilege is given to seniority, as is common throughout Africa" (Karp, 1986, p. 207). Power and status are largely conferred on the basis of family position, age, and ability. Women are circumcised at about age fifteen and are married immediately thereafter. They marry one of the elders but are allowed affairs with unmarried men. Polygamy is still practiced.

Territories traditionally belong (not in the sense of ownership but of use) to family lineages rather than to individuals. And most African societies are not consumption oriented. In fact, "Africans seem to have preferred to invest their resources in personal relations. . . . A wealthy person obtained more satisfaction out of loaning or giving his wealth to others in return for personal support and obedience than in using it to buy goods" (Schneider, 1986, p. 193).

My colleague and I rented a small, thatched hut from the smaller of the two lodges in the reserve. Samburu River Lodge, my temporary home, hosted small groups of tourists who visited the preserve. Most groups were *Wazunga* (white people) from Europe, Canada, and the United States, and they typically arrived late one afternoon and left the following noon. We shared our hut with a variety of lizards, a toad that lived in the shower, and a multitude of insects. Our hut consisted of a room with two beds, each covered by mosquito netting, a desk we requested, which took the lodge manager considerable effort and time to find, and a nightstand. An archway led to an area with a rod for hanging clothes and a sink. A second archway led to an area with a drain in the center, a shower nozzle on one wall, and a stool on the other. There were no newspapers, phones, TVs, or radios, and electricity was generated for only a couple of hours each evening. Mail was supposed to get picked up every Friday in Isiolo, a small collection of huts, tin-roofed shacks, and an open market, but that schedule turned out to be overly optimistic. One avoided venturing out on foot after dark due to the risk of encountering a lion or leopard out hunting, and the lodge had an armed guard posted at night to keep a watchful eye on our wild neighbors. Other than the news offered by the tourists, we were isolated from the events of the world outside our game reserve.

The Samburu are largely unaware of the world outside their domain, and their days are consumed with finding sufficient water and food for their livestock and with protecting them from the predators that are a constant threat. Their survival depends upon the whims of nature, and they are, out of necessity, experts on the potential food sources in their territory. They obtain the bulk of their food by hunting, gathering, and trading with agriculturalists. Their possessions are few, and fall in the category of necessities such as clothing, cooking pots, and spears.

They were quite curious about the car we were driving in our daily travels with the elephants in the area, but especially fascinated with the mirrors on the car. Some of them had never seen their reflection in a mirror, and they seemed astonished and puzzled by it. They also thought it strange that two white women would spend time following and watching elephants, *Ndovu* in Swahili. They offered to tell us all about elephants so we wouldn't have to waste our time. For them, elephants are just a normal part of life and nothing to get overly excited about.

Kenyans, and indeed most Africans, provide an interesting contrast to U.S. culture. The two cultures differ with respect to two important cultural dimensions: (1) the extent to which the culture is individualistic or collectivistic, and (2) the extent to which the culture is high or low context. Kenya is a collectivistic and high-context culture, while the United States is an individualistic and low-context culture.

Individualism vs. Collectivism

In an **individualistic** culture such as that of the United States, emphasis is on achievement of individual needs and goals. Self-actualization of the individual's unique talents and potential is more important than the achievement of group goals and needs. A **collectivistic** culture is one in which individual goals are considered less important than group goals. China is an example of a collectivistic culture, and one of their proverbs describes this view quite well: "Tall trees are cut down." Chinese society is one in which "bending is a virtue, resistance or determination a crime" (Schaller, 1993, p. 60). "Confucian tradition stresses respect for hierarchy and the common good rather than prizing individual desires and a free spirit" (1993, p. 77). As Gudykunst and Ting-Toomey write, "The 'I' identity has precedence in individualistic cultures over the 'we' identity, which takes precedence in collectivistic cultures" (1988, p. 40). Asian and African cultures are generally considered collectivistic, while German, Scandinavian, and British cultures are called individualistic.

> In Kenyan tribes nobody is an isolated individual. Rather his uniqueness is a secondary fact.... First, and foremost, he is several people's contemporary. His life is founded on these facts economically, socially and physically. In this system group activities are dominant, responsibility is shared and accountability is collective.... Because of the emphasis on collectivity, harmony and cooperation among the group tend to be emphasized more than individual function and responsibility. (Saleh and Gufwoli, 1982, p. 327)

The Samburu tend to stay within a prescribed territory belonging to their family, travel infrequently beyond territorial boundaries, live in closely connected family units, and maintain lifetime friendships. Contrast this with American society, which is "characterized by a high rate of social and spatial mobility, by relatively unimportant kinship relations, and by the expectation that many friendships will not last" (Karp, 1986, p. 209).

High vs. Low Context

Hall (1977) argued that the typical pattern of communication practiced in a specific culture differs with respect to the level of context required to understand messages. The communication found in **high-context** cultures is typically less direct and more ambiguous than that found in **low-context** cultures. In a low-context culture, what is said is taken more literally than a high-context culture. "The dominant American temper calls for clear and direct communication. It expresses itself in such common injunctions as 'Say what you mean,' 'Don't beat around the bush,' and 'Get to the point' " (Levine, 1985, p. 28).

Asian and African cultures are high-context cultures, and careful attention must be paid to situational features as well as to the nonverbal behaviors of the speaker.

> In other words, they pay more attention to context than in individualistic cultures. To save face sometimes they let the context speak for itself. For example, in Indonesia a young man courted an upper-class woman, and sent his mother to visit the woman's mother to arrange a marriage. The woman's mother served his mother tea and bananas. Since tea is

never served with banana that was the signal that the answer is "no." This way the woman's mother did not have to insult his mother by openly saying "no." The objects spoke for her. (Gudykunst, 1991, p. 50)

I quickly learned that Kenyans were reluctant to say no to any of my questions. Some of the "roads" I traveled were little more than elephant paths, unmarked, and available maps frequently showed only the major roads. Therefore, I sometimes had to depend upon directions from people walking along the road. On a couple of occasions I asked those whom I passed if I was still headed towards Meru. Of course, I was told that I was. I later discovered that I was not on the right road. I felt quite put out by what I considered to be flagrant dishonesty. But the lodge cook, Adam, told me that it would have been rude for them to correct me. Thereafter, I asked questions such as "Which way is Meru?" that did not allow for a simple yes-or-no answer.

Responsibility for the actions of self and others differs depending upon cultural orientation.

> Also in HC [high context] systems, people in place of authority are personally and truly (not just in theory) responsible for the actions of subordinates down to the lowest man. In LC [low context] systems, responsibility is diffused throughout the system and difficult to pin down—a point that President Nixon exploited in his Watergate defense. Paradoxically, when something happens to a low-context system, everyone runs for cover and "the system" is supposed to protect its members. If a scapegoat is needed, the most plausible low-ranking scapegoat is chosen. In the My Lai incident, a lieutenant took the rap. (Hall, 1977, p. 113)

American culture is toward the low end of the context scale, but somewhat above German, Swiss, and Scandinavian cultures. China, Japan, Native American, and African cultures are at the high end of the context dimension.

It is important to remember that these dimensions on which cultures differ are not either/or categories. That is, while U.S. culture is best described as individualistic, this does not mean that conformity to group norms and expectations is unimportant. Indeed, laws are created to prescribe punishment for those who do not conform. People who "blow the whistle" on companies that violate moral codes or laws may suffer severe consequences. Remember, for example, Karen Silkwood, who blew the whistle on the nuclear plant she worked for, was fired for her act, harassed by persons unknown but thought to be associated with the nuclear industry, and later died under highly suspicious circumstances. Her story was told in the movie *Silkwood*.

And, while individuals are generally held accountable for their behavior, there are circumstances in which we blame an individual's behavior on the norms of the group to which they belong. Patty Hearst claimed that the political group that kidnapped her forced her to carry a gun and help them rob a California bank. People who do not conform to the norms of our culture are generally ostracized and labeled as deviant. Further, while North Americans emphasize directness in conversation, directness is not always the most appropriate or effective means for achieving goals. Political rhetoric is frequently vague and ambiguous, an approach in part designed to offend as few voters as possible.

Some situations require considerable politeness and diplomacy. When we speak with those of higher status, such as bosses and teachers, we tend to be more indirect. And while the United States is best characterized as a low-context culture, people are still aware of and respond to contextual cues. One may avoid political discussions with people who hold differing opinions, one may attempt to talk "smart" when in the company of highly educated people, and one is likely to speak more softly in formal than in informal situations. Context is also more important in some situations than in others.

> In an American court of law, the attorneys, the judge, and the jury are impelled by custom and legal practice to pay attention only to what is legally part of the record. Context, by design, carries very little weight. Contrast this with a situation in which an employee is trying to decipher the boss's behavior—whether he is pleased or not, and if he is going to grant a raise. Every little clue is a story in itself, as is the employee's knowledge of behavior in the past. (Hall, 1977, p. 89)

The point is that these cultural tendencies are broad generalizations that do not apply in all situations or to all people. It is just that North Americans *generally* favor directness over indirectness, and consider individual goals to be more important than those of the group.

These two cultural characteristics are highly related to one another, in that collectivistic cultures are also high-context cultures, while individualistic cultures are typically low-context cultures.

WHAT IS THE RELATIONSHIP BETWEEN CULTURE AND LANGUAGE?

Language is one of the defining characteristics of culture. And the language we speak appears to influence the way we categorize the people, objects, and events we encounter daily.

Language and Perception

The degree to which the specific language we use influences our perceptions has received considerable attention. Benjamin Lee Whorf studied the Hopi language as a means of demonstrating that language did not merely express ideas, but *molds* ideas. He discovered, for example, that the grammar of the Hopi language does not include verb tenses, that is, indicators of past, present, or future. And Hopi do not see time as linear and sequential as do most Americans and Europeans. For Hopi, time is perceived as holistic, circular, and diffuse (Whorf, 1956). Hopi treat every "thing" as an event, but distinguish between short-term and long-term events. A storm is a short-term event; a Hopi dwelling is also an event, but one considered as long-term.

While Whorf focused his analysis on the differences of grammatical structures among languages, some have looked to vocabulary as clues to the way different languages structure perceptions. Boas (1911) examined two languages: Eskimo and English. He noted that Eskimos had more than twenty words for *snow,* with each word describing a different type of snow. Given the environment Eskimos inhabit, identifying various types of snow would be useful. More importantly, they then perceive these different types of snow more efficiently and accurately because they have the language necessary to guide their perceptions. Thus, language and perception intertwine to create one another.

Honorifics, Titles, and Status

Japanese people are very status oriented and must decide before they begin to speak which of six possible levels of status to attribute to their conversational partner, and then they must maintain that level throughout the conversation. In American English we tend to use **titles** that, for women at least, indicate marital **status.** A woman may be *Miss, Ms,* or *Mrs.,* but a man is always a *Mr.* Ours tends to be an informal society, and we also attempt to keep up the illusion of equality, so titles such as *Doctor, Professor, Honorable Judge,* and *Mr. President* are generally used by convention, by those of lesser status, or in formal situations such as a business meeting or conference.

Japanese, who emphasize status, use **honorific markers** when addressing others: *-sama* is very polite, *-san* is neutral, *-chian* is the diminutive, *-kun* is used only for men, and *-sensei* is "now used to refer to someone whose capabilities are respected, especially a teacher or politician" (Crystal, 1987, p. 99).

One of the ways we can identify events, objects, and beliefs that are significant to a culture is by examining its language. There are many different words in Arabic to describe various types of camels, words that describe their function, breed, size, and condition. A camel is not just a camel as it would undoubtedly be to a speaker of American English.

It seems, then, that the language we use has some influence on the way we organize, think about, and express the relationships among significant features of our environment. We learn to look for certain features, discriminate among objects and events, and categorize those objects and events in part based on the structure (grammar) and vocabulary of our particular language. Thus, North Americans may not be able to tell one camel from another, but Arabs are likely to find it difficult to identify all the different types, sizes, and uses of vehicles that are readily recognizable to most of us. English speakers can easily identify a car, lorry, bus, taxi, moped, motorcycle, truck, rig, eighteen-wheeler, and so on (Crystal, 1987, p. 15).

HOW DO LANGUAGE STYLES DIFFER ACROSS CULTURES?

Restricted vs. Elaborated Codes

Basil Bernstein (1966) noted that groups differ with respect to the patterns of interaction typically used by their members. He noted that some groups use an elaborated code, while others use a restricted code. An **elaborated code** has a greater variety in vocabulary and more complex grammar than does a restricted code. A **restricted code** depends upon a lot of shared knowledge on the part of the users, and is somewhat akin to the structure of language used in a telegram. Bernstein argued initially that members of lower socioeconomic classes tend to use restricted codes, while members of middle and upper socioeconomic classes use elaborated codes.

Gudykunst and Kim (1984) suggested that Bernstein's categories closely parallel communication patterns in high- and low-context cultures. That is, high-context cultures tend to use restricted codes, so a significant portion of the meaning lies in the context (interpersonal relationships, physical environment, gesture, intonation, and so on). Low-context cultures tend to use elaborated codes, so most of the meaning resides in the verbal message. Gudykunst and Kim write that "speakers using elaborated codes employ verbal amplification to communicate, placing relatively little reliance on nonverbal and other contextual cues" (1984, p. 138).

Recall the story of the man who wanted to marry out of his social class. His mother's visit to the mother of the woman he wanted to marry is an excellent illustration of a restricted code employed by a high-context culture. Neither mother broached the subject of marriage; instead, the fact that tea and bananas were never served together was sufficient to indicate that the marriage would not happen.

As an American, imagine your frustration at trying to decode the meaning of this message. Minimally, you would need to know that tea and bananas were not served together, that discussing your son's wishes was not appropriate, and that an up-front "no" would be considered quite rude. Further, you would have to implicitly understand that serving tea and bananas in this particular circumstance meant "no." Those of us who come from cultures that make meanings explicit through words would undoubtedly be thoroughly confused. Bernstein writes:

> The speech is played out against a backdrop of assumptions common to the speakers, against a set of closely shared interests and identifications, against a system of shared expectations; in short, it presupposes a local cultural identity which reduces the need for the speakers to elaborate their intent verbally and to make it explicit. (1966, pp. 433–434)

This is not to suggest that words are unimportant in high-context cultures. In Asian cultures, for example, words are important to the maintenance of social unity and harmony. While Western cultures have great faith in the power of words, Asian cultures recognize the biases and limitations of language, a recognition that borders on mistrust of words (Gudykunst and Kim, 1984). Oratory and rhetoric have long and respected traditions in Western cultures and are powerful tools of influence. "A primary function of speech [and writing] . . . is to express one's ideas and thoughts as clearly, logically, and persuasively as possible, so the speaker can be fully recognized for his or her individuality in influencing others" (Gudykunst and Kim, 1984, p. 140). I would add that Western education is largely devoted to teaching elaborated codes of expression, and has been since the teaching of oratory in ancient Greece and Rome. For Westerners, words can divide and conquer; for Easterners, words provide the means for preserving unity and harmony.

Silence, or the lack of words, is perceived differently by different cultures. White North Americans generally find silence uncomfortable, while the Pueblo Indians associate silence with power: "Indians feel that silence is part of the concentration that compels results. Speech, therefore, is restricted or taboo in certain ritual circumstances. The Pueblos have a profound conviction about the reasonableness of secretiveness. As long as one remains silent 'his power is still in him' " (Dutton, 1983, p. 14).

Direct vs. Indirect Communication Styles

A **direct style** is particularly prevalent in Western cultures. North Americans tend to express their feelings, desires, opinions, and intentions openly, although this tendency is modified by contextual constraints. North Americans live by the norm of "say what you mean and mean what you say." Open debate and argument are generally accepted and even encouraged in the United States. An **indirect** (polite) **style** is characteristic of Asian and African cultures. An Asian is more likely to provide "an agreeable and pleasant answer to a question when a literal, factual answer might be unpleasant or embarrassing" (Gudykunst and Kim, 1984, p. 142). Truthfulness is less important than cordiality in many Asian cultures.

Saving Face Politeness is important to unity and harmony, which are in turn dependent upon respect for the "face" of others.[1] **Face** generally refers to public self-image, and saving others face is considered especially important in Asian cultures.

> "Face" is a very powerful concept to Asian peoples. "Face" is fundamentally a code of honor similar to the Western notion of a man's word. This code is based on reverence for the family over individuality. In China the ancestor cult is extremely ancient and emphasizes continuity of familial lines. Reverence for elders was strongly supported by the teachings of Confucius. "Face" developed over time to be a rigid code of behavior that has preserved the family line and promoted family solidarity. Saving face means living up to the standards set by the family. Losing face suggests that one has failed to live up to the family standards, and this has grave consequences for all concerned. (Landau, 1989, p. 208)

Refusal Strategies In Korean culture, for example, one does not openly disagree or flatly reject a request, because that would threaten the face of the other person. Inook Lyuh (1992) conducted an investigation of the differences between the **refusal strategies** used by North Americans and those used by Koreans. Overall she found that rejections used by Koreans contain more regrets and are less specific and less elaborated than the refusal strategies used by North Americans. When confronted by people of higher status, both Koreans and North Americans adopted more polite forms of refusal.

Face-saving for self and others is also important in Western cultures, but apparently not to the extent found among Asians, or for the same reasons. Westerners attempt to maintain consistency between their private self-conception and their public image. That is, they attempt to be "authentic" in all situations. Asians see the "self" as relationally and situationally created, and they strive to save the face of others and in doing so avoid bringing shame to self. The individualistic tendencies of North Americans result in a view of individuals as free agents, and preserving face preserves "one's autonomy, own territory, and own space, while simultaneously respecting the other person's need for space and privacy" (Gudykunst and Ting-Toomey, 1988, p. 86).

Among the Pueblo Indians of North America, ridicule, gossip, and open criticism are the primary **means of social control** and keep individuals from deviating from cultural norms and expectations. "Indians are keenly sensitive to being singled out for public disapproval, laughter, or ostracism. They refrain from wrongdoing on the basis of such censure" (Dutton, 1983, p. 13). The Pueblo people still believe that if a person does wrong, "illness may befall his village or family group, a disastrous flood may destroy his property and crops, or severe drought may lay waste his season's efforts. It is much safer to observe the rules" (Dutton, 1983, p. 14). Thus, people save face by conforming to expectations.

Elaborate, Exacting, and Succinct Communication Styles

Elaborate Style   An **elaborate** style is one rich in metaphor, proverbs, highly expressive language, and hyperbole. Middle Eastern people characteristically use an elaborate style in speaking. By contrast to the speech and writing of North Americans, Middle Eastern style is exaggerated, frequently poetic, and even overbearing. Middle Eastern people also gesture vigorously and communicate at a close distance, which intensifies the effects of their verbal style. (More about that when we discuss cultural differences in nonverbal behavior later in this chapter).

Exacting Style   North Americans and many northern Europeans typically use an **exacting** style, characterized as economical and precise. Gudykunst and Ting-Toomey (1988) note that an exacting style is one in which "one's contribution in language interaction ought to be neither more nor less information than is required" (p. 105). A typical compliment might be: "Your child is attractive (or cute, sweet, and so on)." An exacting style might be characterized as providing "just the facts."

Succinct Style   A **succinct style** is characterized by understatement, pauses, and silences. As you might already be guessing, this style is associated with high-context cultures such as Japanese and Chinese.

Arabs in particular consider intense and emphatic expression of opinion to be important. While a simple "no" will be taken literally by a North American who has offered more wine to a guest, Arabs are compelled to repeat "no" several times and interject oaths such as "by God." To do otherwise might indicate that the "no" meant just the opposite (Almaney and Alwan, 1982). Japanese guests might simply avert their gaze and remain silent as indication that they were not interested in more wine.

I encountered just such a situation while staying at the Norfolk Hotel in Nairobi, Kenya. I was sipping tea one evening on the hotel terrace and working on notes for a presentation I was to give the next day. I was at a table by myself. However, in Kenya, unlike the United States, one doesn't "own" a table, so others will sit at the table without an invitation. Any available seat is fair game. When an Arab man in his thirties joined me, I acknowledged his arrival and then returned to my work. He interrupted me to ask if I would like a drink. I said no. He continued to insist and, although I continued to say no, moments later a Tusker beer appeared in front of me. I told the waiter to take it back. Next the man asked if I would like to join him elsewhere for dinner.

I said no. He was persistent and soon I was being invited to his flat. Outwardly I was trying to maintain my cool throughout this exchange, but in actuality I was seething and indignant. I thought to myself, what about the word *no* does this guy not understand? When I could no longer contain myself, I told him off and began to stalk off. He stopped me and said: "Oh, I didn't understand that you wanted to be alone." I never saw him again.

Personal vs. Contextual Communication Styles

A **personal style** emphasizes *I* and is generally found in low-context cultures; a **contextual style** emphasizes one's status and role and is typically found in high-context cultures. In English, *I* necessarily comes at the beginning of a sentence and thus stands as emphasis for the speaker's individuality. In many Asian languages, people do not call attention to themselves, so sentences frequently make only indirect reference to the speaker, or the reference to the speaker comes late in the sentence. A person-oriented style emphasizes **informality** and equality of social relationships, while a contextual style stresses **formality** and differences in social standing of the conversational participants.

> Americans tend to treat other people with informality and directness. They shun the formal codes of conduct, titles, honorifics, and ritualistic manners in the interaction with others. They instead prefer a first-name basis and direct address. They also strive to equalize the language style between the sexes. In sharp contrast, the Japanese are likely to assume that formality is essential in their human relations. They are apt to feel uncomfortable in some informal situations. The value of formality in the language style and in the protocol allows for a smooth and predictable interaction for the Japanese. (Okabe, 1983, p. 27)

I have advised and directed the studies of several Asian doctoral students over the past several years. I encourage all of my graduate students to call me by my first name, in part because we work together closely and generally become friends in the course of our long-term relationship. My American graduate students usually call me by my first name after I suggest that they do so. This is not the case with my Asian students, however. One former student, who hails from Hong Kong and with whom I am friends, insists on calling me Dr. Liska, which I find uncomfortable. She too now has the Ph.D., yet I would not call her by her title except under specific professional circumstances. She explains that even with a Ph.D., she will never be my equal because I was her teacher/mentor. Only those she perceives as peers are called by their first names.

There are some differences among Asian cultures. Inook Lyuh explained to me that in Korea, power and status are derived from one's family's standing, while in Japan status and power are largely determined by the standing of the company for whom one works. This helps to explain why Japanese "introduce themselves saying things like 'I belong to Mitsubishi Bank'" (Gudykunst, 1991, p. 97). Status for Americans is generally based on the ranking of their profession (e.g., physician, teacher, attorney) and by how much money they make. Family lineage and the company for whom they work is of lesser importance than in Asian cultures.

Instrumental and Affective Styles

An **instrumental** style is characteristic of low-context, individualistic cultures and is **sender-oriented.** That is, the sender is expected to provide all of the information in the verbal message; the receiver is expected to provide little information. This style is highly related to the elaborated code we discussed earlier, in that very little is assumed because the meaning is made explicit in the verbal message. Thus, the receiver is not required to analyze the context to any great degree.

On the other hand, an affective style is **listener-oriented,** and since the verbal message may only provide hints as to the speaker's opinions, feelings, and so forth, the listener must interpret contextual cues in order to come to some understanding of the speaker's meaning. This style is most often found in high-context, collectivistic cultures such as Asian and African. An affective style probably employs a restricted code.

Intuition and Nunchi Intuition, which is important in high-context societies but tends to be downplayed in low-context societies, is essential to understanding the messages of others. Koreans talk about **nunchi,** which is described as "interpretation of others' facial expressions or what they say" plus what is "hidden in their hearts" (Kim, 1975, p. 7). Low-context cultures apparently take little for granted, and expect the verbal message to reveal explicitly the sender's motives and intentions.

Instrumental language is goal-directed, whereas affective language is relationally oriented. Instrumental language also tends to be direct, exact, and personal/individual. Affective language tends to be succinct, indirect, and contextual.

Again, I want to emphasize that these linguistic and stylistic differences among cultures do not apply universally; that is, they are generalizations that may not describe the verbal behavior of all members of a culture. Burgoon (1985, p. 360) writes:

> There is also considerable within-culture variability as a function of subgroup and contextual norms. In particular, such "people" factors as gender, age, socioeconomic status, race, and personality make a difference. So do contextual factors as the type of occupation in work settings and environmental constraints.

However, to the extent these tendencies appear in the verbal behavior of the members of a culture, interaction across cultural lines may be difficult.

WHAT ARE SOME CULTURAL DIFFERENCES IN NONVERBAL BEHAVIOR?

People differ in terms of their build, skin color, facial structure, and so on. Some of those differences are indicators of cultural, racial, and ethnic identity. Typically, we are not adept at recognizing individual differences in races other than our own. Thus, all Asians may look so similar to our eyes that we have difficulty remembering them as individuals. Familiarity with a race or an ethnic group improves our ability to identify them as individuals.

However, we are good at recognizing facial expressions, regardless of race, subgroup, or culture. Expressions of anger, happiness, sadness, and so on are universal to all people, and recognition of such expressions of emotion appears to be a part of our biological heritage. This is also true of patterns of eye contact and gaze.

Still, the intensity of those expressions, and the norms governing when they are appropriate, differ considerably across cultures. Asians tend not to reveal their emotions openly, while Arabs are expected to show their emotions openly and intensely. Courtesy and social discipline are highly valued by Asians and expression of especially negative emotions is discouraged. Indeed, Asians are more likely to smile, giggle, or laugh nervously if someone in their company behaves inappropriately. Americans are more likely to indicate mild displeasure or attempt to remain neutral.

The recent encounter between blacks and Koreans during the 1992 riots in Los Angeles following the Rodney King verdict point up differences in norms of expression between the two groups. Blacks complained that Koreans were unfriendly and rude, while Koreans saw blacks as overbearing and loud. These perceptions are in part based on differences in nonverbal style. Korean culture does not emphasize expressiveness; black culture does. For Koreans, "people who smile a lot are airheads" (Inook Lyuh, personal communication).

In a lecture on cultural differences between Japan and the United States, a Japanese graduate student explained that Japanese see Americans as "big, loud, and hairy" (Mayumi Kubota, lecture at Indiana University, 1990). After spending some time with Asians, I can well understand how they might come to see us this way. Their approach to interaction when compared to ours is quiet, controlled, and polite (indirect). This is not to suggest that Americans are more emotional than Japanese; we simply express our feelings more freely.

Overall, North Americans are more expressive, touch one another more, sit closer, and maintain more eye contact than people of Asian cultures, but do so less than people of Latino, Mediterranean, and Middle Eastern cultures. One of my graduate students, a Greek national, told me that he first found talking to Americans very difficult because they were such inexpressive listeners. He complained that he never knew what we were thinking because we sat passively and listened, only nodding or muttering "hmmm" occasionally. He explained that people in Greece actively participate in a conversation even when they are the listener. The listener is expected to exclaim, nod, gesture, and so on. In the United States such behavior may indicate that the listener is trying to take the speaker's turn, is insensitive to the conventions of conversational exchange, or is hyperactive. Kubota (1991) found that Japanese use far more expressive back-channeling than do Americans.

Ritual Behaviors

Greeting Behavior Ritual behaviors such as greetings also vary across cultures. In France men embrace and kiss in greeting; this behavior is rare among British and American men. In the United States men greet with a handshake and a slap on the back or shoulder. My Hungarian friends greet me and one another with a kiss on each facial cheek. One of my former graduate students who is from mainland China bows as a form of greeting. In fact, initially she bowed every time she encountered me. I had some difficulty in knowing quite how to respond. I found the same behavior in South Korea, and learned that the depth of the bow correlated to the perceived distance in status between those who bowed and those who were the object of the bow. After a few days I found myself bowing in return and finding the gesture quite natural.

A student I know, Steve, who is native to the United States, met his wife, a native of Zimbabwe, while he was working there as a missionary. During a visit to her home he was introduced to a friend of hers. Steve immediately offered his hand in greeting, but the friend put his wrist up to Steve's wrist instead of shaking his hand. Completely confused by this gesture, Steve attempted to follow suit. It was then the friend's turn to look confused. Steve's wife later explained that the friend had been out working in the garden and his hands were dirty, so it would have been rude for him to touch Steve's hand directly.

Head Nods A head nod meaning "no" in Greece, Southern Italy, Bulgaria, or Turkey is easily mistaken for "yes" among those of us from cultures where a similar head nod is a sign of affirmation (Burgoon, Buller, and Woodall, 1989).

"OK" Sign Symbolic gestures such as the "OK" sign have vastly different meanings in different cultures. Former President Nixon committed a faux pas during a visit to Latin America by using that sign, for there it refers to female genitalia. While in Brazil I inadvertently used the "OK" gesture to indicate that I understood the directions I had just been given by a bus driver. He turned quite red, because in Brazil that gesture means what "flipping the bird" does here.

Posture

Postures differ across cultures. Whereas American students may adopt a relaxed pose when sitting in front of a person of higher status, this is a sign of disrespect in many Asian and African nations. In Thailand it is offensive to sit with one's foot or feet pointing toward another person. Apparently, feet are considered to be "the most objectionable and lowest body component" (Gudykunst and Kim, 1984, p. 157).

Vocal Characteristics

Of all vocal characteristics, volume appears to have the most culturally dissimilar meaning. Arabs believe that loudness connotes strength and sincerity, whereas a softer tone is perceived as weak or devious. Britons, like most other Europeans, use a softer voice than do Americans. And in contrast to Asians, Americans are boisterous.

Back-Channeling

Britons use little back-channeling in conversation (head nods and vocalizations such as "hmmm") but maintain steady and direct eye contact in close attention to the speaker's eyes. Americans also direct their gaze toward the speaker, but they do not sustain eye contact and may even look away from the speaker for long periods of time. In Greece staring into the face of another while conversing is normal. "Greeks often feel that they are being ignored, while the English speakers feel as if they are being stared at" (Landau, 1989, p. 176). Blacks living in the United States typically interpret sustained eye contact as a sign of hostility rather than attention. For blacks, looking directly at another, especially a person of higher status, is a sign of disrespect. It means quite the opposite in white American culture. Asian women are discouraged from looking directly at others, especially men, and Asian men do not look directly at their superiors; to do so might be interpreted as defiance or disrespect.

Personal Space

Americans generally do not like to have their personal space violated, and our behavior in close quarters stands as illustration of this norm. Consider your behavior in a crowded elevator. How do you distance yourself from others? One way is to avoid eye contact with them, which is one way we try to maintain personal space. Another way in such situations is to avoid touching others. In fact, Americans, along with Germans, British, Japanese, and Chinese, are classified as nontactile cultures. Apparently the Chinese especially dislike being touched and avoid even handshakes in greeting. Bowing in greeting obviates the need to touch another. Upper-class British avoid tactile exchanges even with their own children (Montagu, 1971).

An episode of TV's "Family Ties" plays on this norm. In this episode, Alex has an opportunity to study at Oxford University in England. His roommate is from British royalty and is quite taken by a picture of Alex hugging his father. In one scene, we see Alex and his British roommate at the roommate's estate. They are leaving for a trip. The British fellow requests a hug from his father, who looks appalled and calls on one of the servants to hug his son, which the servant does. Alex looks on incredulously. It seems that even Americans are more touch-oriented than the British; but, of course, individual and social-class differences within members of the same culture are also important. On the other hand, Arabs, Latinos, Russians, and those of Jewish descent are very tactile, and their social relationships involve lots of touching, even in public situations (Watson and Graves, 1966; Shuter, 1977).

Subgroup Differences

These differences are relative and a matter of degree. Subgroups and individual differences are also important. For example, American men are generally taught to control and hide their emotions, while women are allowed to express themselves more openly. In contrast, Arab men may weep in public and Iranian men are expected to be openly emotional and shed tears freely. Women of both cultures, however, are expected to exhibit control and remain passive (Landau, 1989).

The United States has frequently been referred to as a "melting pot," that is, a blend of many different cultures, so we are more likely to run into communication differences than do people who live in a "purer" culture. White Americans living in close proximity to Puerto Ricans may encounter interaction difficulties simply on the basis of differences in eye contact behavior. Whites are taught to look directly at those of authority, while Puerto Ricans learn to show respect by looking away. Puerto Ricans are more similar to blacks in this respect than to whites. Native Americans value silence and concealment of emotions in contrast to white Europeans, and these differences led whites to believe that Indians did not feel the same emotions as the whites. Conversely, Native Americans found white people boorish and brutish: "Perhaps it never occurred to you that the white man puzzled the Indian. To his way of thinking, the white man was rude and lacking in good manners. He was selfish and refused to share food, clothing, etc., even when he had an abundance" (Wissler, 1966, p. 304).

Wissler describes a visit with an Indian family:

> I found them in a teepee, raised the door flap, entered and took a seat in the place reserved for guests. No one looked up or said a word. A child was present, but it too kept quiet. I took out my notebook and began to write. After an interval of ten minutes or more, my host took up a pipe, filled it and, after lighting it, passed it to me. After a few circuits of the pipe my host began a monologue, expressing his pleasure that I should have seen fit to honor him with a visit. When sure that he had finished, I made a similar talk, not as good as his because it was far less natural. (p. 303)

He further illustrates the differences between white and Native American cultures:

> It was a different world the Indians lived in. We spend our time on paved roads and cross streams on bridges. We have cleared away the forests, dried up the swamps and destroyed much of the interesting wildlife of the country. Much of the native flora has been swept away to make room for crops, meadows and golf courses. Surrounding ourselves by all sorts of mechanical aids, we have forgotten nature as the Indian knew it. He was at home in the forest; we are afraid. So much of our world is man-made that we think in terms of mechanics, a world which we manipulate and control. With the Indian it was different. He saw living creatures on every hand; he spied upon them until he knew their ways; he marveled at their skill in eluding him, their humanlike ways and his inability to communicate with them. He felt the forest as a living thing; the trees were to him almost as persons, and the winds were the breath of some great unseen supernatural. When the storm clouds rolled, the thunder pealed, the tornado crashed through the trees, he felt the presence of powers upon the highest level of creative and destructive force. As he walked abroad, he felt himself in the presence of living things conscious of his existence, who could speak to him, if they chose, and at any time change his fortunes for good or ill. To them he turned for guidance and wisdom. (p. 305)

The lifestyle of Native Americans described by Wissler and others is largely a thing of the past. Yet many native peoples continue to cling to the views of their ancestors and engage in traditional occupations, arts, and lifestyles. These people are our neighbors, yet they are as foreign to many of us as are those who live on the other side of the earth. We may share a continent, but we are vastly different in ideology, history, and behavior. The consequences of the clash of white immigrant cultures with Native American cultures is poignant testimony to the problems inherent in understanding and negotiating cross-cultural harmony.

WHAT BELIEFS AND VALUES DEFINE AMERICAN CULTURE?

All cultures have a set of assumptions or truisms that are generally accepted without question and that guide thought and judgment. These assumptions are viewed as facts about the world. You as an individual may not actively hold or agree with these assumptions. But to the extent that they are held by the majority in the culture, they will influence the way people in your own and other cultures perceive you. They may form the stereotype of the "typical American" held by those of other cultures. If you visit another country, this stereotype may determine how you are treated, because the residents of that country *expect* you to conform to the stereotype they maintain. And, in unconscious defense of your own cultural beliefs and values, you may actually come to behave in accordance with the stereotype. Or you may think, "But I am not a *typical* American—I don't believe all those things," and so you may be confused by the way people treat you. Awareness of your cultural assumptions can improve communication within and across cultures, just as awareness of the assumptions made by other cultures enables you to understand your own culture better and therefore understand yourself better.

We can divide basic beliefs into three categories: beliefs about the *physical world*, beliefs about *human nature*, and beliefs about *the supernatural*.

Beliefs About the Physical World

Postman (1993) writes that "in cultures that have a democratic ethos, relatively weak traditions, and a high receptivity to new technologies, everyone is inclined to be enthusiastic about technological changes . . . especially in the United States, where the lust for what is new has no bounds, do we find this childlike conviction most widely held" (p. 11). American culture promotes the belief that progress achieved through science and technology will enable us to dominate nature. Therefore we strive to control the forces of nature by developing earthquake-proof buildings, by developing surgical techniques to retain the appearance of youth, and by changing the course of rivers to build towns and golf courses. Genetic engineering is touted as the way to thwart genetic afflictions such as Down's Syndrome. We are attempting to conserve rare species of animals through selective breeding in zoos. We exterminate animals we see as pests, and "manage" species of wildlife we find appealing, which means we isolate certain species in parks and reserves and sometimes maintain their populations by hunting or systematic "culling," a euphemism for killing.

Humans are the center of the universe, and their needs are ranked above all others. This view of the place of humans in the natural world has become highly controversial, and some Americans no longer see science and technology as *the* solutions to environmental problems. Nevertheless, this is still a dominant theme in American politics and education. Change may be fundamental to all cultures, but it is frequently slow in coming.

Beliefs About Human Nature

In part as a consequence of our fascination with the dependence upon science and technology, Americans tend to believe that all aspects of reality, including human intelligence and emotions, are best expressed numerically. Postman (1993, p. 13) writes: "Our psychologists, sociologists, and educators find it quite impossible to do their work without numbers. They believe that without numbers they cannot acquire or express authentic knowledge." You are probably aware of the importance attached to your scores on IQ tests, SATs, and (for those interested in graduate school) GREs (Graduate Record Exams). Of course, your potential is not really reflected in a single score such as that on an IQ test. Intelligence is a multidimensional construct, not a single entity. One of the most rigorous attacks on IQ tests is offered by Gould (1981). Earlier, Thorndike (1975), a psychologist, made this observation about IQ tests: "Just what they measure is not known; how far it is proper to add, subtract, multiply, divide, and compute ratios with the measures obtained is not known; just what the measures signify concerning intellect is not known" (cited in Postman, 1993, p. 131). Nevertheless, these tests are used to determine what school we will get into, the quality of that institution, and so forth. The point is: We Americans appear to be especially susceptible to believing that numbers reflect reality (e.g., Postman, 1993).

Americans seem to believe that people are basically rational and are able to make decisions on the basis of "the facts." We believe that justice is blind to color, creed, and gender, and expect that juries of our peers are able to disregard those characteristics and make fair decisions based on the evidence. Our history is littered with examples of the fallibility of this assumption. People are frequently not rational, being swayed by irrelevancies produced by bias and prejudice, and the resulting decisions are therefore sometimes unfair and unjust. For some, the verdict in the Rodney King case is an example of the bias and prejudice inherent in people's decisions. In fact, civil rights laws were instituted as a way of controlling these human tendencies toward irrationality.

Beliefs About the Supernatural

American views of the supernatural appear paradoxical. We believe that people can better themselves via hard work and ingenuity, that humans are somehow special—the pinnacle of evolution—and the center of an orderly universe. Yet most Americans believe in an all-powerful being who controls their destinies and that *this* being occupies the pinnacle and central position. We might reconcile this seeming paradox thusly: (1) God *rewards* hard work, ingenuity, and good behavior, and (2) the apparent order of the universe is evidence that it was created by a supreme being, since such order would not occur by chance. Even evolution can be reconciled with this logic by assuming that "God at some point created the universe and continues to preside over its development" (Cronkhite, 1976, p. 380).

Values: Family, Friends, and Money

Dominant American values follow rather directly from these beliefs. Americans place a high value on individuality because they believe that an individual is capable of overcoming adversity through hard work, native ability, and creativity. Youth is associated with progress and is therefore valued over age. And "doing" is valued because it is the substance of progress and change.

Americans prefer an individualistic, democratic, open, and mobile orientation toward the family. Family lineage is not as important among Americans as it is in other cultures. Rights and responsibilities are not strongly associated with birth order and age, and children are almost expected to move away from the family home. Care for the infirm and the elderly becomes the responsibility of the state, and social services and institutions have been created to provide care and support for such people.

Americans are free to choose their own friends and mates rather than have such relationships arranged by their families or social groups. While titles and lineage are of little concern, *property* (including money, cars, land, and homes) is jealously guarded, and if loaned or given away it is at the whim of the individual owner. Money may not make the *world* go round, but it certainly spins the United States. This emphasis on material goods is even evident in our conception of time. In this culture "time is money," and time can be bought, sold, and borrowed. We "spend time" in a fashion similar to the way we spend money. Time, then, like money and land, is a valuable commodity, a material *thing*.

WHAT PROBLEMS MIGHT WE ENCOUNTER IN CROSS-CULTURAL EXCHANGES?

Conflicting Beliefs or Values

First, and most obviously, *people are uncomfortable in cultures with beliefs and values that differ from those of their own culture or subgroup.* Imagine that two groups of people have been assembled to play a game. One group is told that the object of the game is to compete to win; the other group is told that the object is to engage in cooperative social interaction. When these two groups get together, they will essentially be playing a different game.

In fact, this is exactly the way in which a game of cross-cultural awareness is set up, and the results are fascinating. After only a short while, each group so thoroughly identifies with its own goals and expectations that it rejects those of the other group. Now, imagine a *lifetime* of acculturation to a particular way of believing, valuing, and behaving. The potential for problems and conflicts among cultures and subgroups is enormous.

Ethnocentrism

Second, *there is a strong tendency to describe another culture in terms of our own culture.* This is generally called *ethnocentrism,* which means that people tend to view their group or culture as superior to all others, and to see their group's beliefs and values as universal. Robin Lakoff (1990) offers this description:

> We see all behavior from our own internal perspective: what would that mean if I did it? And, of course, if I, as a member of my own group, did what that person did in the presence of other members of my group, it would be strange or bad. . . . [W]e don't usually extrapolate, we don't say "Yes, but in his frame of reference, what would it mean?" We assume the possibility of direct transfer of meaning, that a gesture or act in Culture A can be understood in the same way by members of Culture C. Often this is true: there are universals of behavior, but as often that is a dangerous assumption; and by cavalierly ignoring the need for translation, we make misunderstanding inevitable.
> (pp. 165–66)

This stance is likely to develop because we have been so thoroughly indoctrinated to the norms and expectations of our own culture that it is difficult to conceive of another way of doing and believing. It is difficult for us even to imagine that there is any alternative to the way our own culture functions. Of course, there are numerous alternatives, and none of them are necessarily or inherently right or wrong, they are just different.

Conflicting Priorities

Third, *travelers generally fail to notice what is relevant and valuable in another culture.* In my encounter with the Arab man in Kenya, I didn't realize that "no" meant something dramatically different to him than to me. I didn't know that I was expected to indicate, emphatically, loudly, and repeatedly, that I merely wanted to be left alone. To my mind, such behavior would have been rude, insensitive, and inappropriate. To his way of thinking I was undoubtedly being coy and insincere. Schaller's experiences living in China (1993, p. 23) provide another illustration:

> I was exotic and probably bizarre; I certainly needed to be broken of some barbaric habits. I said "Thank you" when someone helped or showed kindness. Such casual thanking was a cheap payoff; one does not express gratitude with words but with later deeds. I greeted others in the morning and said "Good night," behavior quite "ridiculous," as one expressed it. Why was I so infernally formal? Not for months did I learn that these were mistakes.

Conflicting Cultural Assumptions

Fourth, *travelers tend to misinterpret the actions of the members of other cultures because of their own cultural assumptions.* Imagine, for example, the problems faced by people from cultures that perceive time differently. An episode of TV's "L.A. Law" illustrates the potential conflicts. In this episode, the featured law firm of McKinsey and Brackman was representing a Honduran farm worker in a suit against an American chemical manufacturing firm. Some 400 farm workers had become sterile as a result of exposure to high levels of a pesticide produced by that firm. Moreover, this pesticide had invaded the water system of the village, with the potential of causing long-term health problems. The Honduran representative wanted to settle immediately, but the American lawyers wanted to make sure that the chemical firm provided a large sum of money to be set aside to cover future health problems, which the chemical company didn't want to do. The negotiations weren't going well and the American attorneys discovered why: The Honduran had been bought off by the chemical company to the tune of $1 million. When the American attorneys confronted him, he explained that his people needed the money *now*, that they couldn't be concerned about possible future health problems. In this case, differing views about time were the critical point of conflict. The American attorneys looked to the future, while the Honduran was solely concerned with the present.

An American professor describes his first day as a visiting lecturer in Brazil:

> My class was scheduled from 10 until noon. Many students came late, some very late. Several arrived after 10:30. A few showed up closer to 11. Two came after that. All of the latecomers wore the relaxed smile that I came, later, to enjoy. Each one said hello, and although a few apologized briefly, none seemed terribly concerned about lateness. They assumed that I understood. (Levine and Wolff, 1985, p. 30)

Such lateness would not be tolerated in the United States, whereas it is the norm in Brazil. The behavior is not intended to offend guests, it is simply the way things are done.

Conflicting Behavioral Expectations

Finally, *travelers are likely to violate specific behavioral expectations that they don't know about.* An American may interpret the intense eye contact of a Greek as aggressive and hostile, when, in fact, the person is merely showing interest in the American's conversation. Such misunderstandings can result in more than just ruffled feelings on the part of both parties; they can become the "stuff" of serious intercultural conflicts.

CONCLUSION

A television ad for Taco Bell claims that "cultures are merging," something of which most of us are aware. Technological developments such as the telephone, computer, television, satellites, and air travel have brought people of many cultures into closer contact, and we now have a world market and a global economy. European nations are adopting a common monetary system, and the former Soviet Union has opened its doors to Western companies and ideas. The lifestyles of tribal peoples have forever changed due to the influx of foreign business, money, and ideas. Likewise, Westerners have incorporated many of the arts, crafts, and ideas of other peoples into their own cultures. Immigrants bring with them a set of cultural baggage that influences their new culture in irreversible ways. The points at which cultures intersect inevitably bring about conflicts as people attempt to negotiate their respective beliefs, values, and behavioral expectations.

While problems will necessarily arise, they can be minimized by *awareness* of cultural differences. Further, respect for cultural differences is essential to cross-cultural understanding. This means that we need to maintain a tolerant and open point of view in which we recognize that cultural differences result from the fact that different people have solved problems in the best way they can, given the circumstances of their history and the environment in which they live. Learning the language of another culture is only one step toward understanding. Learning the beliefs and values that define another culture is essential to global cooperation and unity. As Gudykunst (1991) so aptly observed:

> Linguistic knowledge alone, however, is not enough to ensure that our communication with people from other cultures or ethnic groups will progress smoothly and/or be effective. Confucius said that "human beings are drawn close to one another by their common nature, but habits and customs keep them apart." Misunderstandings in intercultural and interethnic encounters often stem from not knowing the norms and rules guiding the communication of people from different cultures and/or ethnic groups. If we understand others' languages, but not their cultures, we can make fluent fools of ourselves. (p. 2)

KEY TERMS AND CONCEPTS

cultures and their environments
beliefs, values, norms, and expectations
culture
static vs. changing nature of cultures
dimensions of cultural differences
individualism
collectivism
high context
low context, language and perception, honorifics, titles, and status
language styles across cultures
restricted and elaborated codes
direct vs. indirect communication
face
styles
refusal strategies
means of social control
elaborate, exacting, and succinct communication styles
personal vs. contextual styles
formality-informality
listener-oriented vs. sender-oriented styles
intuition and *nunchi*
nonverbal symbols
vocal characteristics
back-channeling
physical world, human nature, supernatural
family, friends, and money

NOTES

1. For theoretical discussions of politeness see: R. Brown and S. Levinson, Universals in Linguistic Usage: Politeness Phenomena, in *Questions and Politeness,* ed. E. Goody (Cambridge, England: Cambridge University Press, 1978) pp. 56–289; T. S. Lim, A New Model of Politeness in Discourse, paper presented at the annual meeting of the Speech Communication Association (New Orleans, Nov. 1988); T. S. Lim and J. W. Bowers, Facework: Solidarity, approbation, and tact, *Human Communication Research* 17 (1991): 415–450.

REFERENCES

Almaney, A., and Alwan, A. (1982). *Communicating with Arabs.* Prospect Heights, Ill: Waveland Press.

Bernstein, B. (1966). Elaborated and restricted codes. In *Communication and Culture,* edited by A. Smith, pp. 126–133. New York: Holt, Rinehart, and Winston.

Boas, F. (1911). Introduction. In *Handbook of American Indian Languages,* Vol. 40. Washington, D.C.: Smithsonian Institution.

Burgoon, J. (1985). Nonverbal signals. In *Handbook of Interpersonal Communication*, edited by M. Knapp and G. Miller, pp. 344–390. Beverly Hills, Calif.: Sage.

Burgoon, J. K., Buller, D. B., and Woodall, W. G. (1989). *Nonverbal Communication: The Unspoken Dialogue.* New York: Harper & Row.

Cronkhite, G. (1976). *Communication and Awareness.* Menlo Park, Calif.: Benjamin Cummings.

Crystal, D. (1987). *The Cambridge Encyclopedia of Language.* Cambridge, England: Cambridge University Press.

Dutton, B. P. (1983). *American Indians of the Southwest.* Albuquerque: University of New Mexico Press.

Farb, P. (1978). *Humankind.* New York: Bantam.

Gould, S. J. (1981). *The Mismeasure of Man.* New York: Norton.

Gudykunst, W. B. (1991). *Bridging Differences: Effective Intergroup Communication.* Newbury Park, Calif.: Sage.

Gudykunst, W. B., and Kim, Y. Y. (1984). *Communicating with Strangers: An Approach to Intercultural Communication.* Reading, Mass.: Addison-Wesley.

Gudykunst, W. B., and Ting-Toomey, S. (1988). *Culture and Interpersonal Communication.* Newbury Park, Calif.: Sage.

Hall, E. T. (1977). *Beyond Culture.* Garden City, N.Y.: Anchor.

Karp, I. (1986). African systems of thought. In *Africa,* 2nd ed., edited by P. M. Martin and P. O'Meara, pp. 199–211. Bloomington: Indiana University Press.

Kim, K. (1975). Cross-cultural differences between Americans and Koreans in nonverbal behavior. In *The Korean Language: Its Structure and Social Projection,* edited by H-M Sohn, pp. 5–18. Honolulu: University of Hawaii Press.

Kubota, M. (1990). Class Lecture at Indiana University, Bloomington.

Kubota, M. (1991). The use of back channel behaviors by Japanese and American bilingual persons. Dissertation, Indiana University.

Lakoff, R. T. (1990). *Talking Power: The Politics of Language.* New York: Basic Books.

Landau, T. (1989). *About Faces.* New York: Doubleday.

Levine, D. (1985). *The Flight from Ambiguity.* Chicago: University of Chicago Press.

Levine, R., and Wolff, E. (1985). Social time: The heartbeat of culture. *Psychology Today* (March): 28–30.

Lyuh, I. (1992). A Comparison of Korean and American Refusal Strategies. Paper presented at the Sixth International Conference on Pragmatics and Language Learning, Urbana, Illinois.

Montagu, A. (1971). *Touching: The Human Significance of Skin.* New York: Columbia University Press.

Okabe, R. (1983). Cultural assumptions of East and West: Japan and the United States. In *International Communication Theory,* edited by W. Gudykunst, pp. 21–44. Beverly Hills, Calif.: Sage.

Postman, N. (1993). *Technopoly.* New York: Vintage.

Saleh, S., and Gufwoli, P. (1982). The transfer of management techniques and practices: The Kenya case. In *Diversity and Unity in Cross-Cultural Psychology,* edited by R. Rath, H. Asthana, D. Sinha, and J. Sinha, Lisse, Netherlands: Swets and Zeitlinger.

Schaller, G. (1993). *The Last Panda.* Chicago: University of Chicago Press.

Schneider, H. K. (1986). Traditional african economies. In *Africa,* 2nd ed., edited by P. M. Martin and P. O'Meara, Bloomington: Indiana University Press.

Shuter, R. (1977). A field study of nonverbal communication in Germany, Italy, and the United States. *Communication Monographs* 44: 298–305.

Thorndike, E. L. (1975 March/April). *The National Elementary Principle.* (Cited in Postman, N. (1993). *Technopoly.* New York: Vintage.

Watson, O. M., and Graves, T. D. (1966). Quantitative research in proxemic behavior. *American Anthropologist* 68: 971–985.

Whorf, B. L. (1956). *Language, Thought, and Reality.* New York: Wiley.

Wissler, C. (1966). *Indians of the United States,* rev. ed. New York: Doubleday.

If all the beasts were gone,
man would die from loneliness of spirit,
for whatever happens to the beast,
happens to the man.
All things are connected.
Whatever befalls the earth,
befalls the sons of earth.

—Chief Seathl

Some Final Thoughts

15

CHAPTER OUTLINE

Role of Communication in Forging Human Communities

The Natural World vs. the World of Symbols

Cross-Cultural Differences

Intracultural Differences

Problems and Solutions

Ethics

Our concern has been with describing the role of communication in forging human communities at many different levels (e.g., species, individual, group, and culture) and from various perspectives (e.g., evolutionary-biological, historical, linguistic, and psychological). As grounding for this view we have taken the position that we are inextricably intertwined with all facets of our world and all of its inhabitants. We are merely one species in a massive and complex network of beings, all interconnected in their quest for survival, and all dependent upon the ecological forces that shape their habitat.

ROLE OF COMMUNICATION IN FORGING HUMAN COMMUNITIES

Communication is a pervasive phenomenon in that it is a characteristic of all known species. All animals use some form and level of communication in interacting with other members of their own and other species. All animals use a system comprised of symptoms; some species have added semblances to their repertoire. What appears to set humans apart from other species is their ability to create and use symbols, and thus to forge relationships based on visions of reality that do not exist in the natural world.

THE NATURAL WORLD VS. THE WORLD OF SYMBOLS

For humans, the natural world—characterized by astronomical, geologic, and genetic forces—has been supplemented by a world of ideas—a world of symbols. Human groups may be defined on the basis of genetic and geographic characteristics. However, groups are also distinguished on the basis of their ideas. And those ideas may differ considerably from group to group. Groups of people are organized and governed by symbolic decree, and that in turn influences how members of the group use symbols with one another. Moreover, these ideas will influence how environments are created, modified, and manipulated.

CROSS-CULTURAL DIFFERENCES

Eames (1993, p. 54), an anthropologist, provides some insights into how vastly ideas may differ. Eames studies Nigerian culture and reports that unlike American conceptions of justice as fair and equal treatment for all, Nigerians live by the aphorism "It's not what you know, it's who you know." The Nigerian "social system [is based on] status, relationships, and rights [are] fundamentally negotiable and justice [was] never impartial." In Nigeria immigration officials, for example, sign your form only if they can put you in their debt. "For those unlucky enough to be without connections, . . . the only other option is bribery—where the supplicant initiates a personal relationship of sorts and the ensuing favor evens matters up." Indeed, she notes that "all legitimate authority derives from being in a position to grant favors and not the other way around." Of course, bribing an official of the U.S. government is likely to land both parties in jail. Although it may occur occasionally, it is not just frowned upon; there are laws against it.

I observed an incident in Kenya that gave me considerable pause. A child of about eleven or twelve ran down the street followed by a police officer and by a shopkeeper who was yelling that the boy had stolen from him. When the police officer caught the boy, he beat him resoundingly. I was appalled and astonished, and it took great self-control not to intercede and scream, "police brutality!" I looked around at the small crowd that had gathered, and was equally appalled and astonished to discover that none of them seemed in the least disturbed by the police officer's behavior. The events surrounding Rodney King's beating by a group of police officers, two of whom were ultimately found guilty, clearly indicates the degree to which many Americans find this behavior unacceptable.

According to the United Nations Human Rights Center, "at least half the world's population is deprived of basic human rights and subject to violations ranging from torture and executions to slavery and starvation" (*Chicago Tribune*, 1993). The loss of human rights and dignity include arbitrary arrests, restrictions on expression of opinion, corrupt judicial systems, and violent assaults, including torture, rape, and mass executions. Many of these situations result from political and economic instability. Clearly, all is not well with the world.

It is important to note that all cultures have words for *justice, equality,* and so forth, but we cannot assume that they mean the same things as our words or are implemented similarly. And while we might find their meanings strange or even repugnant, those ideas and their implementation seem as reasonable to them as ours do to us.

INTRACULTURAL DIFFERENCES

Different **ideas** are also found among groups within cultures. The 1993 standoff in Waco, Texas, between the Branch Davidians and FBI agents ended in an inferno, thus validating the name of their headquarters: "Ranch Apocalypse." Although we are guaranteed religious freedom in this country, the Branch Davidians were viewed largely as an undesirable and possibly even dangerous cult. And while their lifestyle may have touched few people who lived beyond their fence, the fifty-one days they stood fast against the FBI brought them into all of our homes via the media. And what did we learn about them in those fifty-one days of headlines?

> Even after 51 days facing each other across the wind-swept plains of central Texas, the FBI and Branch Davidians were still aliens to each other—viewing reality through very different prisms. Outside the barbed wire encircling Ranch Apocalypse, the imperative was clear: uphold the law. Inside, the Branch Davidians believed they answered to a higher authority. It was a recipe for disaster. (*Newsweek,* 1993, p. 22).

This conflict lasted a mere fifty-one days. The ethnic conflicts in Bosnia and in Northern Ireland have been going on for centuries, interspersed with brief periods of uneasy peace. On a happier note, a preliminary peace accord between Israel and Palestine has been signed. Although this does not guarantee that all parties involved in the conflict will shake hands and invite one another over for dinner, it is a step in the right direction. The symbolic gesture of signing a treaty legitimizes the efforts of all to cooperate with their neighbors and to grant them their rights as individuals and as humans. If the word *peace* is uttered often enough, it may come to be so in actions and deeds.

PROBLEMS AND SOLUTIONS

The media provide a daily litany of the woes confronting our world: war, famine, conflicts over religion, sexual preference, individual rights, limited resources, and ancestral homelands, burgeoning human populations straining planetary resources, decaying neighborhoods fraught with violence, increasing racial tensions, wanton environmental destruction, and so forth. Of these, some risks may be more overpowering than others. Diamond (1992, p. 350) writes:

> The risks of a nuclear holocaust and of an environmental holocaust constitute the two really pressing questions facing the human race today. Compared to these two clouds, our usual obsessions with cancer, AIDS, and diet pale into insignificance, because those problems don't threaten the survival of the human species. If the nuclear and environmental risks should not materialize, we'll have plenty of leisure time to solve bagatelles like cancer. If we fail to avert those two risks, solving cancer won't have helped us anyway.

Resolutions to these two **problems** rest in part on our ability to learn from the mistakes of those who went before, as well as to disseminate relevant information to those who follow. These lessons from the past are widely available, but Diamond (1992) points to one that occurred on our own soil:

> The American Southwest has over 100,000 square miles of pinyon-juniper woodland that we are exploiting more and more for firewood. Unfortunately, the U.S. Forest Service has little data available to help it calculate sustainable yields and recovery rates in that woodland. Yet the Anasazi already tried the experiment and miscalculated, with the result that the woodland still hasn't recovered in Chaco Canyon after over eight hundred years. (p. 336)
>
> From this point of view it's beyond understanding to see modern societies repeating the past's suicidal ecological mismanagement, with much more powerful tools of destruction in the hands of far more people. (p. 337)

Yet on a global scale we continue to repeat the mistakes made by thousands of generations. And we do so, or so we say, in our own best interests. Yet, if we truly had our best interests in mind, we would face the fact that we are not just a globally interconnected network of cultures and political-economic systems, but a complex interconnection of species for which the survival of one is connected to the survival of all. Now, it is the case that species come and go, their arisings and departures governed by climatic changes, the habits of other species, and so forth. However, the present rate of extinctions far exceeds "normal" levels, thanks to the overwhelming efforts of a single species—humans (Wilson, 1993). Second, we might ask—So what? What should we care about spotted owls, wolves, and beetles?

Diamond responds: "Like all species, we depend on other species for our existence, in many ways. Some of the most obvious ways are that other species produce the oxygen we breathe, absorb the carbon dioxide we exhale, decompose our sewage, provide our food, maintain the fertility of our soil, and provide our wood and paper" (1992, p. 361).

Remedies to these problems require the cooperation of many nations, and will come at a substantial price to be shouldered by all. We cannot isolate ourselves, determined to clean up our own small nest without cleaning up the vast nest we call earth. Solutions, compromises, negotiations, and sacrifices can only result from global cooperative efforts, and those efforts will proceed largely via a process of sharing and negotiating symbolic realities.

Yet even small steps at a local level initiated by the efforts of a few willing to speak out with firm yet reasoned tones can ripple throughout the world. Consider that a handful of eloquent voices spawned legislation that guaranteed equal rights under the law for all regardless of race. This is not to suggest that racial problems are a thing of the past, because they are not. But it stands as illustration of the potential of communication to bring problems to the forefront, to offer solutions, and at least to bring about some change for the better. There are many other examples of small groups of people bringing about important changes, but the point is to highlight how reality can be altered by the efforts of a few. Of course, the outcome may not always be for the better. History is littered with examples of how the eloquence of a single voice or a few voices brought changes disastrous to the humans whose lives they touched.

Unsuccessful communication may result in anything, ranging from minor misunderstandings to massive conflicts. However, even "successful" communication may result in problems. Wars, traffic jams, deforestation, colonialism, and apartheid would not be possible without carefully orchestrated communication.

ETHICS

This brings us squarely to the issue of **ethics.** Ethical systems change through time and vary across and within cultures. Moreover, standards of ethics vary from individual to individual. Finally, we suspect that all of us have found ourselves in situations in which we compromised our personal ethics. Fudging on taxes, telling white lies to save face, to be polite, or to avoid punishment, withholding information because we "don't want to get involved" or think it "none of our business," blaming others for our own shortcomings, and so forth are probably common ethical infractions we all commit at some time or other.

Rather than sermonize on what constitutes ethical communication behavior, we instead wish to make you aware and wary of the fact that communication can be used to enlighten and inform. It can also be used to mislead and manipulate. How you choose to use it is probably your own business, although we hope that most of you choose the former most of the time. But the reality of life is that one cannot assume that what one reads and hears is accurate, objective, or constructed with any thought as to the best interests of those who will consume it. Even the most reputable of sources may mislead, although not deliberately, because they were misinformed, biased, ego-involved, or the like. Others may deliberately attempt to misrepresent because they have some personal stake in manipulating the "facts." It is up to you to be skilled at sifting through information, to be concerned with seeking out inconsistencies, to be careful in evaluating sources, to be aware of situations in which information may be incomplete, biased, and/or based on skimpy data. Thus an overriding goal in writing this book has been to facilitate your skills at "crap-detection."

We are concerned that you may have now concluded that all the problems of the world are the result of or can be resolved via communication. We do *not* believe this is the case. While communication may be integral to confronting many of the problems currently facing us, not all problems arise from or can be redressed by communication. As one illustration, let us examine the famine in Somalia. The famine largely results from a desert environment in which sufficient food cannot be grown. All the talk in the world will not change those environmental conditions and consequences. And the people cannot move to more amenable environments, because those are already occupied, and the carrying capacity of those neighboring environments appear to be stretched to the limit. Like the elephants who find their territories increasingly occupied by other species, especially humans, fighting for their own survival, the Somalies have no place to go.

Cronkhite (1976, p. 398) offers another example.

> As a simple illustration, imagine two starving cavemen fighting over a piece of meat. The problem is not a lack of communication. They probably understand each other perfectly. They *may* be able to use communication to solve the problem—by devising cooperative strategies for hunting, for example—but if one succeeds in killing the other, it would be strange to say that poor communication was the cause.

As a way of summarizing the point, we turn to the words of Kursh (1971, p. 189):

> In this day and age one of the most popular forms of piety has to do with communication, somewhat narrowly defined. An ailment called "lack of communication" has taken the place of original sin as an expla-

nation for the ills of the world, while "better communication" is trotted out on every occasion as a universal panacea.

Communication seems to be as essential to our lives as eating, breathing, and slaking thirst. It is a central medium by which we experience and come to know our world and its inhabitants. It is the glue that binds us into communities, and it is the substance of our best and worst achievements. With communication we can emphasize with others, create and destroy relationships, make decisions, move emotions, and facilitate and inhibit awareness. As Cronkhite (1976, p. 400) said: "It is a social disease for which there is no known cure." For better or worse, we are stuck with it. Our hope is that we have helped you better understand the ways in which communication structures your world, your relationships, and yourself.

KEY TERMS AND CONCEPTS

role of communication in forging human communities

natural world
world of symbols
cross-cultural differences

ideas
problems and solutions
ethics

REFERENCES

Chicago Tribune. (1993, April 19).

Cronkhite, G. (1976). *Communication and Awareness.* Menlo Park, Calif.: Benjamin Cummings.

Diamond, J. (1992). *The Third Chimpanzee: The Evolution and Future of the Human Animal.* New York: HarperPerennial.

Eames, E. A. (1993). Navigating Nigerian bureaucracies; or "Why can't you beg?" she demanded. In *Anthropology 93/94,* edited by E. Angelino, pp. 53–56. Guilford, Colo.: Dushkin.

Kantrowitz, B., Carroll, G., Amin, P., Barrett, T., Cohn, B., and Liu, M. (1993, 3 May). Day of Judgment. *Newsweek,* 22–27.

Kursh, C. O. (1971). The benefits of poor communication. *Psychoanalytic Review* 58: 189–208.

Wilson, E. O. (1993). Is humanity suicidal? *New York Times Magazine* (May 30): 24–29.

Student Activities and Discussion Topics

DEAR STUDENTS

Your professor will have specific assignments for you to complete throughout the semester or quarter. You may be asked to write a paper, present a report, or construct a project on one or more of the topics covered in the text. We offer the following project descriptions, questions, readings, and videos and films to help you in developing ideas for these types of assignments. In the event you decide to adopt one of these ideas for a class assignment, we encourage you to discuss it with your professor to make sure you are meeting the specific requirements of the assignment. In many cases, you may be able to modify our ideas to fit the particular assignment. We hope these suggestions help you in developing your own questions about and approaches to the study of communication.

GENERAL

Write a research paper answering a research question or supporting a thesis. The basic assignment is to analyze a communication event occurring in one of the contexts discussed in this book. Analyze a public speech, an interpersonal encounter, a small-group meeting, a meeting within an organization, communication within an organization, an intercultural encounter, a newscast or documentary, an advertising campaign, a protest movement, an instance of what is popularly called "brainwashing," or a political or religious campaign. You might choose to analyze a less obviously purposeful form of persuasion such as TV or film dramas or comedies; docudramas; novels or short stories; magazine feature articles; some form of print journalism, including newspaper reporting or editorials; or some form of art, especially including music such as albums and rock videos or strictly visual art. However, in these latter cases especially remember to focus on the *rhetorical* functions, not the aesthetics.

You are free to use quantitative research methods such as content analysis and public opinion surveys to supplement your critical analysis. In fact, your professors might encourage you to do so. They might encourage you to conduct an experiment testing some hypothesis if you wish, but remember that the basic assignment is a rhetorical analysis.

One thing *not* covered in this activity is a paper that consists entirely of library research, reporting what others have written on some topic. You should conduct original research and supplement it with library research.

Please discuss your thesis or research question and your procedure with your professor before you begin. The thesis or research question is to be *generic*. That is, the paper is to illustrate a thesis or answer a question regarding a *principle of communication theory;* it is not to be a thesis or question regarding the specific communication event you have chosen to analyze. See the explanation of theses and research questions at the end of this manual.

Organize your research report into sections in which you state the thesis or research question, justify your studying it, justify your choice of a communication event to analyze, report a few other articles in which writers have studied your thesis or question or have studied your communication event, analyze the event, and close with a brief discussion of the implications of your findings.

CHAPTER 1: A RATIONALE FOR AN ECOLOGICAL PERSPECTIVE ON COMMUNICATION

1. On your way from Manaus to Brasilia, Brazil, your small plane develops engine trouble. You have no choice but to parachute into unfamiliar territory. The pilot will jump after you, and so you will be on your own. You know you are somewhere over the rain forest in the heart of Brazil, a place you have never visited. You've heard stories of cannibal tribes, venomous snakes, frogs whose poison kills upon touch, and swamps that swallow the unwary. Until now you have dismissed those stories as tall tales. But as you survey the scene below, you begin to worry about your fate in the event they are true. You close your eyes, hold your breath, and jump. You touch the ground, look about you, and realize that most of your supplies are in the doomed plane. Panic sets in. You do have your backpack with you, and you dump the contents on the ground: a bottle of water, some granola bars, some trail mix, a compass, a knife, a small first aid kit, a camping cook set, a change of clothes, and a mosquito net. You

know that people live in the rain forest and must therefore have access to the necessities of life. But, you wonder, what do they eat? How do they know what water is safe to drink? How do they distinguish poisonous from edible plants? How do they know which animals are harmless and which pose a threat? You know that the answers must be out there but you don't have a clue as to how to use the available information.

Gather together a group of your friends or classmates and devise a survival plan for your predicament. Attempt to identify the specific environmental signs that might help you survive in the rain forest. Consider also how you might use the tools in your pack to provide shelter, obtain food and water, find your way out of the rain forest, and so forth. How will you feel about not having the company of other people?

To return to your predicament: While suspended in the air over the rain forest, you surveyed the scene below you and saw what you thought was a small village. You know that the people in this area would still live a hunter-gatherer style and speak a language with which you are unfamiliar. You decide to find that small village. How will you approach the villagers? How will you cross the language barrier? By what means will you communicate with them so you can learn how to survive in their environment?

2. Spend a day away from technology and people. Go to an isolated place—the woods, the mountains, or the desert—and spend the day watching the behavior of the animals you encounter. Leave your watch at home and instead attempt to tell the time by observing the movement of the sun. Carefully examine the terrain, the plants and trees, and the interplay of light and shadow cast by the sun. Close your eyes and touch your surroundings. Attempt to identify the various plants and trees merely by touching their stalks, leaves, and flowers. Get close enough to smell the various distinctive odors. Write down your thoughts and observations as you move slowly through the area.

When you return to civilization, make notes of your reactions. Turn on the television, log on to your computer, go to the mall, and make note of the kinds of information now available to you. How is it different from the information available in the woods, mountains, or beach?

Now read Bill McKibbean's book *The Age of Missing Information* (1993, Plume) in which he reports what he learned from spending a week in the woods compared to what he learned from television. Were your experiences, thoughts, and observations similar to his? Which environment did you prefer? Why?

3. Discuss your views of nature with a group of friends or classmates. Is nature something to be feared and conquered, or is nature something to be respected and enjoyed? Should "wildness" be preserved, or tamed? Do other species have "rights" similar to those humans should have? Are all species and ecologies equally significant?

    If you are interested in pursuing this subject for a paper, we recommend the following resources:

    a. Cavalieri, P. and Singer, P. (Eds.). (1993). *The Great Ape Project: Equality Beyond Humanity.* New York: St. Martin's Press.
    b. Hoage, R. J. (Ed.). (1989). *Perceptions of Animals in American Culture.* Washington, D.C.: Smithsonian Institution Press.
    c. Mason, J. (1993). *An Unnatural Order: Uncovering the Roots of Our Domination of Nature and Each Other.* New York: Simon & Schuster.
    d. Morris, D. (1990). *The Animal Contract: An Impassioned and Rational Guide to Sharing the Planet and Saving Our Common World.* New York: Warner.
    e. Serpell, J. (1986). *In the Company of Animals: A Study of Human-Animal Relationships.* Oxford, England: Basil Blackwell.

4. Conduct your own survey of attitudes toward nature. You might want to use the following items for your survey. We have included several items designed to see whether watching television and reading about nature are important influences on people's attitudes toward nature. You might add additional items that you feel are relevant and important. We think this could be the foundation for a paper or project.

    Where there is a range of answers, indicate your choice with a checkmark.

    1. I am from the (1) Northeast (2) Southeast (3) Midwest (4) Southwest (5) West Coast (6) Northwest (7) Central Plains States (8) outside U.S.A.
    2. Religious preference:
       (1) Catholic (2) Protestant (3) Jewish (4) other (5) not religious
    3. I belong to at least one environmental organization. (1) yes (2) no
    4. I camp frequently__:__:__:__:__:__:__never.
    5. It is__:__:__:__:__:__:__is not important to preserve as many animals as possible.
    6. I do__:__:__:__:__:__:__do not approve of hunting for food.
    7. I do__:__:__:__:__:__:__do not approve of hunting for sport.
    8. I go to the zoo often__:__:__:__:__:__:__rarely.

9. I watch nature programs on television often__:__:__:__:__:__:__rarely.
10. I do__:__:__:__:__:__:__do not think that all animals should have rights similar to those people have.
11. I eat meat regularly__:__:__:__:__:__:__rarely.
12. My training/experience with nondomestic or wild animals is extensive__:__:__:__:__:__:__none.
13. My experience with companion animals (e.g., cats, dogs, birds) is extensive__:__:__:__:__:__:__none.
14. I read books and magazines about nature often__:__:__:__:__:__:__rarely.
15. I frequently__:__:__:__:__:__:__rarely have discussions about animals with friends or family.
16. I watch television often__:__:__:__:__:__:__rarely.
17. For me, environmental issues are of major__:__:__:__:__:__:__minor concern.
18. In general I do__:__:__:__:__:__:__do not approve of using animals for research.
19. It is__:__:__:__:__:__:__is not acceptable to use animals for research if it helps to understand or prevent human disease.
20. I do__:__:__:__:__:__:__do not approve of using monkeys and apes such as chimpanzees and baboons as organ donors for humans.
21. I do__:__:__:__:__:__:__do not agree with the following statement: Humans are the only species to use advanced forms of communication (e.g., language and speech).
22. I do__:__:__:__:__:__:__do not agree with the following statement: Human needs are more important than the needs of other animals.
23. I do__:__:__:__:__:__:__do not agree with the following statement: Environmental preservation is more important than economic development.
24. I read newspapers often__:__:__:__:__:__:__rarely.
25. I read for pleasure often__:__:__:__:__:__:__rarely.

Source: Questionnaire developed by Jo Liska. See Liska, J. (1994). *Sapiens, Simians, Spiders, and Snakes: The Role of Media in Developing Attitudes toward Biodiversity.* Paper presented at Cornell University, Ithaca, New York.

5. View *The Gods Must Be Crazy* (parts I and II), and compare the lives of the Bushmen living in the Kalahari Desert with those people who reside in the city. What happens when they must switch environments? What must they learn in order to survive? What signs are significant in each environment? In what ways are those signs different?

6. This is an exercise I have developed as a means for identifying how people feel about a variety of nonhuman animals. It is a variation on the "Who shall survive?" game. Write up brief descriptions of ten nonhuman animals (e.g., tiger, mountain gorilla, wolf, spotted owl, salmon, dust mites, coral snake) and include also a general description of a human. If you can, include a photo representing each species you choose. Now, gather a group of about six of your friends and classmates (from other classes) and tell them that they are the Committee for the Preservation of Endangered and Threatened Species. Further instruct them that only five of the ten species can be saved, and their job is to select the five species. Have them independently choose and list the five species they would save. Give them fifteen minutes to make their selections. Then put them into the group and ask them to discuss their selections and the reasons for their selections. As a group, they must come to *consensus* regarding the final list of species to save. Give the group thirty minutes to come to their joint decision.

    Their discussion should be quite revealing of their attitudes toward the various species, as well as of their attitudes toward the relationship between human and nonhuman species. Do they always include humans as one of the species they would save? What reasons do they give for eliminating some of the species? What reasons do they give for saving the species they choose? Be sure to compare their individual decisions with those made by the group. You might interview them individually to find out what influenced any changes they made.

    This could be an interesting study for a paper or project. I suggest that you run the exercise with several groups and compare the outcomes of their decisions. To what extent are their selections similar? To what extent are their reasons similar? What tentative general conclusions about attitudes toward nonhuman animals can you draw based on the total set of selections and reasons?

    Note: You might want to read *The Final Forest* by William Dietrich (1992, New York: Simon & Schuster). It is an analysis of the various perspectives taken by loggers, environmentalists, biologists, and government officials on the battle to save old-growth forests and the spotted owl. It is an excellent illustration of detailed analysis of the parties and perspectives involved in influencing opinions and policies.

CHAPTER 2: COMMUNICATION AND SURVIVAL

1. By analyzing television programs describe how our views of censorship have changed over the past thirty years. For example, you might examine the changes in how intimate relationships are portrayed

on early programs such as "I Love Lucy" and "The Donna Reed Show" with more recent similar programs such as "Love and War," "Married . . . With Children," and "Mad About You." One change is in the explicitness with which sexual relationships are portrayed. Another change is in the openness with which sexual relationships are discussed. You might want to speculate on the potential impact of these portrayals of intimate relationships on our expectations about our "real" relationships.

2. Using television programming as your barometer, analyze how views of the family have changed over the past thirty or so years. Cable channels such as Nickelodeon are a good resource for early television programs. You might use "The Donna Reed Show" and "Leave It to Beaver" as representative of early views, and compare them to current shows such as "The Nanny," "Evening Shade," "Roseanne," and "Dave's World." "The Brady Bunch" and "Family Ties" would be useful because they fall between early and current programs. What impact do you suppose these programs have had on our conceptions of family life? How realistic are they?

3. Again using television as your vehicle for analysis, compare the changing roles of women as reflected in television programs such as "The Mary Tyler Moore Show" and "Murphy Brown." Is MTM a "liberated woman" just because she is a single professional woman? In what ways is she similar to Murphy? In what respects is she different from Murphy? To your mind, who makes a better role model? Is either of them a realistic portrayal of women?

4. Analyze a half-hour television program by classifying all the signs you observe into the three categories of signs we discuss: symptoms, semblances, and symbols. Can you identify any signs that don't appear to fit into these categories or that fall on the borders between categories? To what extent is context important in deciding to what category a particular sign belongs?

5. Analyze views of nature by examining them either historically or cross-culturally. You might (1) compare the views of nature as expressed in the Bible with those expressed in the writings of the Hindu or Buddhist religion; (2) analyze rock and cave images of animals produced by early humans, and compare those to contemporary art focusing on animal subjects; (3) look at the literature produced by a long-lived environmental organization such as the Audubon Society, and note how their representation of nature has changed over time; or (4) examine environmental legislation as it has been developing since the formation of the United States. Examine the messages about nature as an illustration of the evolution of ideas.

6. For a week, keep a journal of all your interactions with others. Classify your interactions in accordance with the functions of communication described in this chapter. Do you find that your interactions fall mainly into one category, or are they widely distributed across categories? Do some of your interactions fall into more than one of the functions? What kind of overall pattern emerges?

CHAPTER 3: THE GHOSTS OF OUR ANCESTORS

1. Go outside, to a zoo, or to an animal park and spend some time observing the behavior of another species. Take notes focusing on their "view" of the world. What kind of ecology do they inhabit? How do they interact with other members of their species? What kinds of communication signs and channels do they use? What kinds of information are relevant to them?

2. Go to the zoo and choose a primate species to observe. What similarities do you note between that species and your own? What are your reactions to them? What appear to be their reactions to you? Describe in detail the environment in which they live, and then speculate on how that environment influences their behavior. How would you feel if you had to live in that environment?

3. Since some of you may not have easy access to a zoo, go to the library video/film section and find a tape or film to watch about some species of primate. What kinds of communication behaviors do you see? In what ways are they similar to our own?

4. Speculate about and try to describe the "typical day" in the life of early humans like *Homo erectus*. What do you suppose they communicated about? What would their family life be like? What activities constituted their day? What important things did children have to learn? What did males do? What did females do? What do you suppose they did on rainy days?

5. Speculate about the likely impact virtual reality will have on our lives. If, for example, you could travel to another country without ever leaving your own home, would you prefer that to an actual visit? Do you think people will avoid "real" social relationships and instead become involved with those offered in virtual reality? Will we need to have "wild" places in nature when we can instead create them with virtual reality? Will virtual reality take over as a primary form of entertainment? What effects might it have on the ways we teach and learn in schools?

6. Keep a diary of your time spent (1) reading, (2) writing letters, (3) talking on the phone, (4) working on the computer, (5) watching television, and (6) listening to the radio. Other than required readings for courses, what kinds of things do you read? Do you write letters? If so, to whom? How much time do you spend on the phone compared to other communication activities? Do you use the computer for games, word processing, electronic mail, and so forth? Do you belong to any computer networks? What kinds of programs do you watch on television? When do you watch television? Which (radio, television, or newspaper) do you depend upon for news about the world? Could you live without any of these communication technologies? Why or why not?

7. We briefly described "information superhighways" and raised some of the concerns about how these information highways will affect our lives. We noted Neil Postman's concern that we are putting a new technology into place before we understand its effects on our ecology, personal lives, and social structure. Provide your own speculation about those potential effects. If you are especially interested in the topic, you might explore some of the popular news magazines and literature (e.g., Postman's *Technopoly*) and write a paper about the potential impact of this new technology. You might also interview some experts in communication technology for their views of the potential effects of this massive data network. You might also interview some nonexperts to gather their opinions on the subject. How familiar are they with this new technology? To what extent do they feel that they will have inexpensive and easy access to it? How do they think it will change the way we do business?

8. Included in Wendell Berry's collection of essays *What Are People For?* (San Francisco: North Point Press, 1990) are two essays explaining why he refuses to buy and use a computer: "Why I Am not Going to Buy a Computer" and "Feminism, the Body, and the Machine." Read those two essays and evaluate his arguments. To what extent do you agree with them? Did he persuade you to throw your computer out the window? What arguments would you offer in favor of computers?

9. Those especially interested in new communication technologies might want to look at a new publication called *Wired*. If you are familiar with Internet, you can access the text of *Wired* (by typing: gopher wired.com) and you can then scan the contents. Since there are variations in gopher commands from one institution to the next, you will probably want to check with your computer center for specific commands to access gopher.

10. If you don't belong to a computer network, you might want to join one to see what it is like. One communication network is called CRTNET, and the address to join is: t3b@psuvm.bitnet. Another communication network is called COMSERVE and you may join it by typing the following address: comserve@rpitsvm.bitnet. Send the command JOIN your name. This should cause a computer to enroll you. If it does not work, you can send a message to real people at: support@rpitsvm.bitnet.

    For those of you interested in environmental issues, a new paperless journal is available. To gain access on Internet use the following command greendisk@igc.apc.org. (If you are on compuserve, type 70760,2721. The snail mail address is Greendisk, P.O. Box 32224, Washington, DC 20007. Phone: 1-800-484-7616.

CHAPTER 4: ORIGINS OF CONTEMPORARY COMMUNICATION THEORY

1. You probably have your own personal theory of communication. It may include some of the following generalizations: (1) If I am organized and clear I will be understood by others. (2) If I choose language that is adapted to the education, age, and socioeconomic levels of my listener, I will be perceived as similar to them. (3) If I am polite and deferent to those in positions of authority, my behavior will be seen as appropriate. (4) If I use communication to raise the self-esteem of another, they will like me. Continue adding to this list until you have developed a general theory of communication. Be sure to consider various influences on the process, such as personality variables, status differences, the potential influence of various contexts (e.g., group, dyads, public). Compare your personal theory of communication to those produced by your classmates. In fact, this could be a group endeavor.

2. What theory of communication do you think television news producers have? How do you suppose they would characterize their audiences?

3. Ask other communication professors about their training in communication. What approaches did they learn? What approaches do they use now? What major changes in approaches to the study of communication do they report? What new directions do they predict for the future of the study of communication?

CHAPTER 5: COMMUNICATION AND THE SOCIAL ENVIRONMENT

1. How are men and women presented in magazine and television advertisements? What roles do they play? How do they behave? In what ways is their behavior, their physical characteristics, dress, and so forth consistent with sex role stereotypes? What does the choice of actors and actions say about advertisers' conceptions of their audiences? You might want to examine ads on television, for example, and note changes in the types of actors and their actions at various time periods throughout the day. Do you see distinct changes in the ads from daytime to prime time? Do you see differences in ads on network versus cable channels?

2. When you face a major decision such as choice of college or career, or are about to make a major purchase, whom do you consult for advice? Do you seek the opinions of your friends, family, experts, media, and so forth? Which sources do you seek most frequently? Do you check multiple sources?

3. How do you react to learning that your family, friends, co-workers, bosses, or instructors have beliefs and values different from yours? Do you attempt to change their opinions? Do you attempt to examine your own opinions and change them? Do you find yourself questioning your own judgments? Do you ridicule their opinions?

4. If you were going to try to teach someone to be more empathic, how would you go about it?

5. What communication characteristics do you associate with an "ideal" communicator? Ask your friends to provide their conceptions, and compare them. Does your conception of the "ideal" communicator vary depending upon situational variables? You might consider, for example, what type of person you choose when you need advice or support, compared to who you choose simply to socialize with. What kinds of communication behaviors do you believe make the "ideal" professor? Does the content of the course alter your conception?

6. How dogmatic or open-minded do you think you are, given the description of Dogmatism in this textbook? Check your self-perceptions with your friends' perceptions of you.

7. Repeat Exercise #1 with Machiavellianism. Remember, communication majors are especially likely to be Machiavellian. Does being Machiavellian necessarily mean you are unethical?

8. Using the movie *Twelve Angry Men*, describe each of the twelve characters in terms of the personality characteristics described in this

chapter. Who is dogmatic? Machiavellian? Low in self-esteem? High in internal or external locus of control? Who is most open-minded? Who is most empathic and observant? Discuss these characterizations in class.

9. Below we have reproduced a series of scenarios depicting behavior on the part of one person directed toward another, with a scale following each scenario on which you are asked to indicate the extent to which you believe the behavior to constitute sexual harassment. These scenarios and the scales were constructed by two of our students who were undergraduates at the time, Donna Potter and D. Michele Hoover. We have reproduced them with the students' permission. Complete the scales and then discuss the scenarios with the other members of your class. Does it matter if the actor is male and the person toward whom the behavior is directed is female, or vice versa? Are there differences between the perceptions of the men and the women in your class? Ms. Potter and Ms. Hoover concluded that for their sample of undergraduate students at Indiana University, "Although males and females ranked the questions similarly, it is clear that men attributed less sexual harassment to the scenarios in general." Is that true in your class?

MALE_____   FEMALE_____

Please rate the following situations on a scale of 0–6. –0– is definitely not sexual harassment, –6– is definitely sexual harassment, the scales in the middle are variations.

1. You are in a class and the professor tells an obscene joke.

    0 1 2 3 4 5 6

2. The boss tells their assistant that he/she looks particularly nice in the color he/she is wearing.

    0 1 2 3 4 5 6

3. You are in a class where every day when you arrive the instructor says: "Here's the hot, sexy thing we've all been waiting for!"

    0 1 2 3 4 5 6

4. The manager taps one of his/her employees on the butt after he/she makes a sale.

    0 1 2 3 4 5 6

5. After class you go up to the professor to have him/her clarify a point and they say, "Wow! You're looking **good**!"

    0 1 2 3 4 5 6

6. The head of the media planning department becomes attracted to the head of the promotions department and begins sending notes signed your secret admirer to the person.

0 1 2 3 4 5 6

7. The same person (#6) begins sending pornographic pictures with explicit handwritten messages scrawled across the bottom of the pictures.
(Never revealing their true identity, but using made up sexual names.)

0 1 2 3 4 5 6

8. You are in an instructor's office just talking and joking around when they suggest, "Hey, why don't we go grab a beer?"

0 1 2 3 4 5 6

9. The executive director tells his/her assistant that if he/she needs an ear to listen about their broken love relationship, they will be there for them.

0 1 2 3 4 5 6

10. The interviewer asks the interviewee if they are dating anyone.

0 1 2 3 4 5 6

11. You go to a professor to ask them for a recommendation (which is very important to your future career). They say in an inviting tone: "You know it would help me write a better recommendation if I knew you better. Why don't we go back to my office to discuss ways I can get to know you better?"

0 1 2 3 4 5 6

12. The CEO calls his/her assistants his/her boys or girls. For example, when talking to a client the CEO often says things like: I'll have my boys/girls look into that for you, OR, I'll have my boy/girl get us some coffee and donuts.

0 1 2 3 4 5 6

13. A sales person walks into the office of his/her manager for his/her weekly visit and is confronted with the following situation. (The manager has already asked the sales person out and been turned down.) The manager unbuttons the first 4 buttons on his/her blouse/shirt and claims to be hot . . . .

0 1 2 3 4 5 6

14. You go to an instructor's office hours. They close and lock the door behind you. While you are discussing an issue they walk be-

hind you and place their hands on your shoulders and then begin to massage them. They say, "Relax."

0 1 2 3 4 5 6

15. An aspiring assistant and his/her boss are checking the final details at the site for the Annual Christmas Party. No one else has arrived for the party and no one is expected to arrive for at least an hour. The assistant traps his/her boss under the mistletoe and passionately kisses the unsuspecting boss.

0 1 2 3 4 5 6

16. In the deserted building, the Vice President and an executive assistant step into an elevator after working late into the wee hours of the morning. Once in the elevator, the Vice President hits the stop button and uses his/her key to lock the elevator control panel. The V.P. then pins the assistant against the wall and begins to kiss, caress, and fondle the body of the assistant.

0 1 2 3 4 5 6

17. The professor alludes to sexually oriented jokes and always seems to smile at the same student.

0 1 2 3 4 5 6

18. The professor then asks this student to be his/her personal research assistant even though the professor knows that the student has a very enjoyable job already.

0 1 2 3 4 5 6

19. The interviewer obviously gives the interviewee a once-over upon the interviewee's entrance into the room, paying close attention to very private, intimate body parts.

0 1 2 3 4 5 6

20. You are at the office hours of a professor to see what you can do to improve your grade. After a few academic suggestions, they suggest you continue this conversation with them at their house.

0 1 2 3 4 5 6

21. An interviewee walks into an interviewing situation and is confronted by 5 interviewers of the opposite sex. All of these interviewers are hostile toward the sex of the interviewee and openly express that they think people of the interviewee's sex do not do well in the organization.

0 1 2 3 4 5 6

22. The CEO calls his/her assistant into his/her office and while the assistant is taking notes, the CEO walks behind the assistant and

begins breathing and speaking into the assistant's ear and neck. The CEO then begins kissing the neck of the assistant.

0 1 2 3 4 5 6

23. You go to a professor's office to discuss a problem you are having in that class. They suggest that you go to dinner with them and you can discuss the problem then.

    0 1 2 3 4 5 6

24. A professor confesses to a student that he/she is attracted to the student after the professor realizes that the anonymous notes he/she has been receiving are from the student. The professor leans over and begins to kiss the student. (Keep in mind the professor believes it is a mutual romantic attraction.)

    0 1 2 3 4 5 6

25. During an interview, the interviewer reaches across the desk and gently brushes your hand with theirs.

    0 1 2 3 4 5 6

10. Imagine that you are a member of a student/faculty committee charged with writing a Code of Ethics for your school. Part of that Code is to include a section describing what constitutes sexual harassment, forbidding it, and specifying penalties. The Code will apply to both students and faculty, although the definitions and penalties may differ. Write your proposal for that section of the Code and discuss it with the rest of your class.

CHAPTER 6: THE ECOLOGY OF IDEAS: OPINION FORMATION AND CHANGE

1. Using the movie *The Breakfast Club* (available at video stores) as your stimulus, try to identify all the ego-defense mechanisms you observe the various characters using.
2. You have chosen to pursue a college career and you have chosen to attend a specific college. Not attending college immediately has some advantages and attending college immediately has some disadvantages, probably financial, that cause you to feel dissonant about the choice you have made. The school you chose has some disadvantages and others have advantages, both of which make you feel dissonant. You have made your choice, but you still have to deal with that dissonance. What are the sources of that dissonance, specif-

ically, and how are you dealing with it? As a reality check, discuss this with your friends and classmates to see if they also perceive you to be doing what you think you are doing.

3. According to Rokeach, each of us has certain "values" that define who we are, without which we would not be the same people. See if you can list those central values that define who you are. How difficult would it be to get you to change those values? If you feel comfortable doing it, share your list with other students in your class or with your friends.

4. Choose some opinions you presently hold, important or just matters of taste, and try to remember how you may have learned those opinions by either classical or operant conditioning. Share your recollections with your class.

5. Watch some TV commercials or find advertisements in magazines and try to find examples of those that are using either classical or vicarious operant conditioning to influence you.

6. Listen for examples of others using wishful thinking in decision-making, and see if you can catch yourself doing it. Share these with your class. Do not use names.

7. Try to find instances in which you and others seem to be using their opinions to express the kinds of people you or they believe they are or would like to be. Ask your friends to help you with your self-analysis. Do you believe opinions serving this value-expressive function are necessarily insincere? That is, are they "real" opinions?

CHAPTER 7: THE ECOLOGY OF IDEAS: COGNITIVE PROCESSING, CRITICAL THINKING, AND SOCIAL INFLUENCES

1. "Artificial intelligence" is the study of how computer programs can be written to mimic human mental activity. What would a computer program have to be capable of to perform the cognitive activities described in the AESOP Model of cognitive processing of messages? Make your description in terms specific enough that a computer programmer could write it as an algorithm (a series of very specific program instructions). Do you believe a computer program could perform these functions? That is, could it "learn" to process and evaluate persuasive messages? What would be the problems?

2. Develop your own list of rules for critical thinking and decision making. Ask others to contribute their own rules.

3. One summer we saw two bumper stickers on a pickup truck in Lincoln, Nebraska. One said "I'll forgive Jane Fonda when the Jews forgive Hitler." Discuss with your class the cultural (historical) knowledge you would have to know to understand the message of this bumper sticker. What is its message? What might be the political beliefs of the owner of the pickup be?

   The second bumper sticker read "Ted Kennedy's car has killed more people than my gun." Repeat the exercise and discussion with this bumper sticker. Do the two bumper stickers create a consistent impression of the political views of the owner of the pickup? How so?

4. James Thurber wrote a short story—a fantasy—titled "If Grant Had Been Drinking at Appomattox." Discuss with your class the cultural (historical) knowledge you would need to have to understand this title. Then read the short story to see if your inferences were correct. How would you explain the title to an intelligent person from another culture, who is fluent in English?

5. Search for examples of Kahane's types of fallacies in speeches, TV commercials, and magazine ads.

6. Analyze a persuasive speech or speeches looking for the organizational characteristics described in this chapter. Consider especially whether the speakers tell in their introductions whether they intend to persuade. What is your reaction to these organizational characteristics?

7. When you try to gain compliance from others, which of the compliance-gaining strategies are you most likely to use? In what situations? What strategies have others tried to use on you? Have you resisted their attempts? How? You might want to keep a diary or list of the strategies you use or observe during a day or two.

8. Think about what you consider to be the most and least socially acceptable compliance-gaining strategies from the following list. Do you agree with the judgments of Ng's subjects? How would you rank-order them differently?

Compliance-gaining Tactics

Extremely Prosocial Tactics

Male	Female	Tactic	Grand Mean
1.06	1.09	1. Be straightforward when I ask for compliance.	1.08
1.63	0.86	2. Simply ask for compliance.	1.18
1.51	1.10	3. Explain why they should comply.	1.27

Compliance-gaining Tactics (continued)

Extremely Prosocial Tactics

Male	Female	Tactic	Grand Mean
1.56	1.12	4. Provide reasons to support my request.	1.30
1.60	1.29	5. Negotiate something agreeable to both of us.	1.42
1.40	1.47	6. Be nice and polite to him/her before asking for compliance.	1.46
1.75	1.36	7. Attempt a compromise.	1.55
1.80	1.38	8. Tell him/her that it was very thoughtful to comply.	1.55
1.84	1.40	9. Tell them how important their compliance is.	1.58
1.99	1.45	10. Be tactful when I ask for compliance.	1.68
1.86	1.51	11. Reason with them.	1.69
1.89	1.81	12. Argue logically.	1.84

Moderately Prosocial Tactics

Male	Female	Tactic	Grand Mean
2.22	2.06	13. Make suggestions to gain compliance.	2.21
2.50	2.24	14. Tell the person that his/her compliance would help me.	2.36
2.66	2.83	15. Use humor to make him/her comply.	2.76
2.85	2.79	16. Tell the person that his/her compliance would make me happy.	2.81
3.00	3.04	17. Drop subtle hints.	3.02
3.28	2.93	18. Persuade the person to comply.	3.15
3.29	3.32	19. Ask him/her to comply simply because I asked.	3.31
3.23	3.39	20. Tell the person that he/she would feel good about themselves.	3.33
3.12	3.53	21. Try to persuade him/her that my way is right.	3.35
3.54	3.66	22. Hint at what I want.	3.62
3.38	3.94	23. Be sweet, charming, helpful and pleasant before bringing up the topic of disagreement.	3.71
3.51.	3.89	24. Tell the person that his/her compliance would eventually help himself/herself.	3.73
3.79	3.95	25. Promise to do a favor in return for compliance.	3.88
3.73	3.99	26. Bargain for compliance.	3.88
3.89	4.39	27. Appeal to the person's affection for me.	4.18
3.97	4.63	28. Ask a third party to talk to the other person.	4.35
4.01	4.70	29. Use flattery.	4.41
4.28	4.59	30. Tell them I like them before requesting their compliance.	4.47

Moderately Antisocial Tactics

Male	Female	Tactic	Grand Mean
4.22	4.70	31. Appeal to the person's ego.	4.51
4.35	4.64	32. Put my arm around the person before requesting compliance.	4.53
4.35	4.79	33. Tell them I love them before requesting compliance.	4.61
4.40	4.85	34. Tell the person that I need his/her compliance very badly.	4.66
4.38	4.87	35. Act cute when I ask for compliance.	4.67
4.54	4.92	36. Make the person believe that he/she is doing me a favor.	4.76
4.57	5.01	37. Reward the person before requesting compliance.	4.83

Compliance-gaining Tactics (continued)

Moderately Antisocial Tactics

Male	Female	Tactic	Grand Mean
4.56	5.15	38. Promise future favors.	4.90
4.61	5.11	39. Tell the person I would reward him/her if he/she complied.	4.91
4.70	5.10	40. Recall past favors I've done and ask for him/her to comply.	4.94
4.78	5.45	41. Call in past favors.	5.17
4.82	5.43	42. Promise to be more friendly in the future.	5.18
5.02	5.47	43. Ask a third party to help me get what I want.	5.28
4.87	5.61	44. Act so nice that he/she later cannot refuse when I ask him/her for my own way.	5.30
5.42	5.35	45. Tell the person that his/her noncompliance would make me feel very unhappy.	5.38
5.16	5.76	46. Tell the person that if he/she complied, he/she would be rewarded because good things come to good people.	5.50
5.15	5.89	47. Tell the person that a person with "good" qualities would comply.	5.58
5.03	6.11	48. Give gifts in order to gain compliance.	5.66
5.43	6.06	49. Use the power of one's position.	5.79
5.48	6.05	50. Appear helpless.	5.81
5.77	5.84	51. Do anything and everything I can to make him/her comply.	5.82
5.63	6.02	52. Repeatedly remind him/her of what I want until he/she gives in.	5.86
5.49	6.23	53. Tell the person that people he/she values would think better of him/her if he/she complied.	5.90
5.80	6.00	54. Compliment the person before asking for compliance.	5.92
5.73	6.24	55. Keep repeating my point until the other person gives in.	6.01
5.72	6.31	56. Argue until this person changes his/her mind.	6.06
5.68	6.44	57. Tell them that "good" people would comply.	6.10
5.88	6.70	58. Warn him/her that noncompliance would produce negative consequences.	6.34
6.00	6.60	59. Tell him/her that it would be very inconsiderate for him/her not to comply.	6.35
6.31	6.38	60. Beg for compliance.	6.35
6.11	6.89	61. Tell the person that his/her noncompliance would be a selfish act.	6.54
6.21	7.07	62. Offer the person money in order to make him/her comply.	6.71
6.27	7.08	63. Get the other's friends to put pressure on them.	6.73
6.44	6.96	64. Grovel for their compliance.	6.75
6.49	6.99	65. Make him/her feel guilty.	6.78
6.34	7.10	66. Tell the person that he/she would feel ashamed of himself/herself if he/she failed to comply.	6.79

Extremely Antisocial Tactics

Male	Female	Tactic	Grand Mean
6.63	7.34	67. Tell the person that people he/she values would think worse of him/her if he/she failed to comply.	7.03
6.62	7.38	68. Act irritated toward him/her until he/she complied.	7.07

Compliance-gaining Tactics (continued)

Extremely Antisocial Tactics

Male	Female	Tactic	Grand Mean
6.79	7.30	69. Use the "silent treatment."	7.09
6.84	7.30	70. Intimidate them into compliance.	7.10
6.91	7.39	71. Withdraw my affection until he/she complies.	7.18
6.99	7.58	72. Not talk to the person until he/she complies.	7.33
6.90	7.65	73. Tell them that if they don't comply I'll never do anything for them in the future.	7.34
6.84	7.69	74. Tell the person that only a person with "bad" qualities would not comply.	7.34
7.29	7.40	75. Pout or cry until I get my way.	7.35
7.04	7.68	76. Suggest that our friendship is dependent upon their compliance.	7.40
6.95	7.74	77. Tell them only "bad" people would not comply.	7.41
7.13	7.70	78. Demand that they comply.	7.46
7.09	7.85	79. Tell them that only "hateful" people would not comply.	7.51
7.31	7.88	80. Order the person to comply.	7.62
7.39	7.87	81. Tell the person that if he/she fails to comply, he/she would be punished because bad things happen to uncooperative people.	7.67
7.44	8.02	82. Tell the person that I would punish them if they don't comply.	7.78
7.38	8.08	83. Tell the person that he/she would not be my friend anymore if they do not comply.	7.79
7.55	8.12	84. Get angry and demand that he/she gives in.	7.88
7.71	8.11	85. Force the person to comply.	7.92
7.66	8.19	86. Use verbal threats in order to make him/her comply.	7.94
7.56	8.37	87. Tell the person that I would hate him/her if he/she did not comply.	8.03
7.76	8.23	88. Tell them that if they don't comply I'll never speak to them again.	8.03
7.93	8.28	89. Punish them until they comply.	8.11
7.82	8.36	90. Stamp my feet and scream.	8.13
7.81	8.45	91. Tell them that if they don't comply the secret they have shared will be made public.	8.18
7.92	8.48	92. Throw things.	8.25
8.21	8.51	93. Threaten to harm them if they don't comply.	8.36
8.25	8.46	94. Hit them until they comply.	8.38
8.21	8.65	95. Threaten to destroy something they value if they don't comply.	8.47
8.24	8.63	96. Threaten to harm a third party unrelated to the dispute if they don't comply.	8.47
8.38	8.66	97. Use physical force in order to make him/her comply.	8.51
8.49	8.68	98. Threaten to harm someone close to them if they don't comply.	8.60
8.50	8.75	99. Hit them in the mouth.	8.65
8.50	8.77	100. Take hostages.	8.66

Source: Ng. R., Liska, J., and Cronkhite, G. (1992). A social acceptability scale for compliance-gaining strategies and its application to competence research. Paper presented at the annual meeting of the Speech Communication Association, Chicago, Illinois.

CHAPTER 8: THEORIES OF LANGUAGE MEANING

1. Construct concrete examples for what you mean by *love, hate, justice, fairness,* and *communication competence.* What difficulties did you have in finding concrete examples? Ask your friends or classmates to provide concrete examples for those words. What difficulties do they report? Were the examples similar across the people who participated?

2. Look up the dictionary (semantic) meanings of the words listed in #1 above. How concrete are those definitions? Are those the definitions you think of when you hear those words?

3. Keep track of the times when you ask someone what they mean by something they have said, or times when someone has asked you to explain what you mean. What kinds of meaning were you (they) seeking? How did you go about explaining yourself? How did they go about explaining themselves? Were their answers more or less abstract than the original word?

4. Ask your parents how they taught you to talk. Did they use the referential theory, pointing to objects and naming them, or the behavioral/reinforcement theory, praising you and giving you treats when you made sounds such as "Ma" or "Da" that seemed appropriate in the context in which they were uttered, or some rule-governed theory in which they taught you the conditions under which certain sounds and utterances were appropriate, or some combination of those three? Did they use different teaching methods at different learning stages? If you have a child of your own, or a niece or nephew, or a child of a friend, or a younger sibling who is at an early stage of learning language, you might spend some time observing how that child is being taught meaning.

CHAPTER 9: RESEARCH ON LANGUAGE EFFECTS

1. Choose any episode of "Designing Women" and analyze the language style of the main female characters (Charlene, Julia, Mary Jo, and Suzanne). Does the language style of any of these characters conform to the stereotype of "women's language"? Now compare their styles with those of either the male characters on the same program or the male characters in "Frasier" or "Home Improvement." Are their styles consistent with "male language"?

2. Interview your friends and classmates on their opinions about "politically correct" language. Do they agree or disagree with it? Do they see it as a form of censorship? Do they attempt to speak in a PC manner? What are your views on the subject?

3. You might develop a survey to assess the extent to which college students are familiar with "politically correct" language. Put together a list of politically correct terms (see *The Official Politically Correct Dictionary and Handbook* by Beard and Cerf, 1992, cited in this chapter) and ask your friends and classmates to define those terms. How accurate and familiar are they with those terms? You might then ask them to choose which term they prefer: the politically correct one or the more common one.

4. Some argue that if we change the language, people's attitudes and opinions will change to fit the language. For instance, if people learn to call those with inherited intellectual deficiencies *mentally challenged* rather than *mentally retarded* their attitudes and opinions about that group will change. Do you agree? Why or why not? What support from research can you apply to support your position?

5. Think about the language you use regularly around your friends and in the dorm. Do you use that same language at home with your family? If not, why not? What are the pragmatic rules that apply in these instances?

6. Every language and every culture has its own norms by which one decides how to address another person. Those norms usually have to do with the age, the status, and the social closeness of the other person. In Japanese, for example, you would probably follow the first name of one of your classmates with *-san,* but addressing your professors you would follow their last names with *-sensei,* reserved for a teacher or person of higher status or age. To show his humility, because a person's family is a major source of one's prestige in Japan, a Japanese man is expected to introduce his son as *gu-soku* and his wife as *gu-sai,* meaning, respectively, *my stupid son* and *my stupid wife.* The wife, however, might reasonably introduce her husband as *my lazy husband.* These are not insults to the son, wife, or husband; they are expected norms of humility. In German, *Sie* and *du* are words for *you,* the first being reserved for someone who is unfamiliar to you, and the second being used with a peer of your own age and status with whom you are well acquainted. When we taught in the University of California system it was quite acceptable to address other professors by their first names and for students to address their professors by their first names. It was something of a culture shock when we taught

in the East and Midwest to discover professors were generally addressed as "Dr." or "Professor," even by one another. What are the norms of address at your school, in the town where your school is located, in your hometown, and in your family? Compare your perceptions of those norms with those of your classmates.

7. Should apes in American zoos be referred to as Simian-Americans? Why or why not? What sort of person would say yes, and what sort would say no?

8. Reproduced below in its original form with the permission of Todd and Marie Thomas is a letter written by Cleve Thomas in 1906 to his intended and the woman who did in fact become his wife. He was working at the time in Texas and she had remained behind in Kentucky. The letter is rife with similes, which are similar to metaphors except that they contain the word "like," whereas a metaphor does not. Analyze this letter and discuss with your classmates whether you believe it was written totally seriously, as a humorous effort (what we would now call "camp"), or somewhere in between humorous and serious. What clues can you find in the letter itself? What do you know about social customs around the turn of the century that might help you decide? What effect would the letter have today? What sort of letter would a young man write to his significant other today? Would he write a letter at all, or would he use some other medium?

DENISON COTTON MILL CO.

MANUFACTURERS OF COTTON YARNS

FLAT AND STANDARD DUCKS

DENISON, TEXAS, Oct. 17, 1906.

My Dearest Sweetheart:-
    Every time I think of you, my heart flops up and down like a churn dasher; sensations of joy caper over it like young goats over a stable roof, and thrill through it like Spanish needles through old linen trousers. As a goslin swimmeth through a mud puddle, so swim I in a sea of glory. Visions of ecstatic rapure, thicker than the hair on a blacking brush, and brighter than the hues of a humming-

bird's pinions visit me in my slumbers, and, borne on their invisible wings your image stands before me and I reach out to grasp it like a pointer snapping at a blue-bottle fly.

When I first beheld your angelic perfections I was bewildered, and my brain whirled around like a bumble bee under a glass tumbler, my eyes stood open like cellar doors in a country town, and I lifted up my ears to catch the silvery accents of your voice. My tongue refused to wag, and in silent adoration I drank the sweet affection of love, as a thirsty man swalloweth a tumbler of hot whiskey punch.

Since the light of your face first fell upon my life, I sometimes feel as If I could lift myself up by my suspenders to the top of the church steeple and pull the bell rope for Sunday School. Day and night you are in my thoughts.

When Ourora, blushing like a bride, arises from her saffron-colored clouds; when the jay birds pipe their tuneful lay in the apple tree down by the spring-house; when the crow's shrill clarion heralds the coming of morn; when the awakening pig arises from his bed and grunteth and goeth forth for his refreshments; when the drowsy beetle wheels his droning flight at noontime; when the lowing herd comes home at miling time I think of thee, and like a piece of gum elastic, my heart seem stretched clear across my bosom.

Your hair is like the mane of my sorrell horse powdered with gold, a and the brass pins skewered through your waterfall fill me with unuterable awe. Your forehead is smoother than the elbow of an old coat. Your eyes are glorious to contemplate; and in their liquid depths I behold legions of little cupids bathing like a consort of ants in an old army cracker. When thy head lays pressed against my manly breast, the fire of your eyes penetrates my whole anatomy like a load of buck shot goes through an old rotten apple. Your nose is as perfect as if carved from a hunk of Parsian marble, and your mouth is puckered with sweetness. Nectar lingers on your lips like honey on a bear's paw, and myriads of kisses are there ready to fly out and light somewhere like young bluebirds, out of their parents nest. Your laugh rings in my ears like the music of harp strings, or the bleat of a stray lamb on a bleak hillside. The dimples in your cheeks are like flowers in a bed of roses, or the hollows in cakes of home made sugar. I an dying to fly to thy presence and pour out the burnings eloquence of my love as a thrifty housewife pours out hot coffee. Away from you I am as melancholy as a sick cat. Sometimes I can hear the Junebugs of despondency buzzing in my ears, and I feel the cold lizards of despair crawling down my back. Uncouth fears, like a thousand minnows nibble at my spirits, and my soul is pierced with doubth like an old cheese bored with skippers. My love for you is stronger than the smell of patent butter, or the kick of a young cow; and more selfish than kittn's first catawaul. As a song bird hankers for trap; as a weaned pup lings for new milk, so I long for thee. You are fairer than a speckled pullet, than a Yankee doughnut fried in sorghum molasses; brighter than the topnot plumage on the head of a Muscovy duck. You are candy, kisses, reisins, pound cake and sweetened toddy altogether. And if these few lines will enable you to see the inside of my soul, and assist me in winning your affections, I shall be as happy as a woodpecker on a cherry tree, or a stage horse in a green pasture. If you cannot reciprocate my soul-mastering passion, I will pine away like a poisoned bed bug and fall away form the flourishing vine like an untimely branch. And, in the coming years, when the shadows grow from the hills, and the philosophical frog sings his cheerful evening hymns you, happy in anothers love, can come and shed a tear and catch cold upon the last resting-place of,

Yours with a heart as big as a ham,

CHAPTER 10: FUNCTIONS OF NONVERBAL COMMUNICATION IN SOCIAL RELATIONSHIPS

1. Look at your living space through the eyes of someone seeing it for the first time. Analyze it in detail. What does it say about you? Now

show it to someone who has not seen it before. Ask them to describe the type of person who lives there. To what extent does their description match you?

2. Sketch your view of the ideal classroom for a seminar of eight to twenty people or for a small auditorium suited to a group of not more than 100. Be sure to consider a design that facilitates class discussion, is well-suited to multimedia presentations, allows for comfort, and so forth. Presume that, for once, money is no object—unrealistic, but more fun.

3. Analyze home furnishing ads from a variety of magazines and describe the intended audience. What clues did you use in identifying the intended audience? Ask some of your friends to engage in the same process. Are their judgments similar to yours?

4. Videotape yourself interacting with (a) another person and (b) a group of about four to six people. Then watch and analyze your nonverbal communication behavior. Are you surprised by what you see?

5. Choose any episode of "Designing Women" and analyze the different nonverbal communication styles of each of the main characters (Julia, Charlene, Mary Jo, and Suzanne). Do any of them exemplify stereotypical female communication behavior?

6. Choose any episode of "Frasier" and analyze the nonverbal communication styles of the male characters (Frasier, Niles, and the father). Do any of them portray stereotypical male behavior? Do any of them behave more in line with what is described as typically a feminine style of nonverbal communication?

7. I frequently go to a local eatery to write. I take my computer, diskettes, a pile of books, and notes. I set up shop in a corner booth, drink numerous cups of coffee, and generally get a lot of work accomplished. I stay about 3-1/2 hours, which is the battery life of my laptop computer. I go to that environment because it has sufficient stimulation, but not so much that it interferes with my work. Describe the environment in which you do your best studying and writing. Be specific, and provide details. Compare your descriptions with those of your friends and classmates.

8. Tape a television program while you are not watching it and then watch the tape with the sound turned off. Make notes about how the various characters felt about one another, based solely on facial expressions, eye contact and gaze, environmental cues, gestures, and so forth. Now play the tape with the sound on. How accurate were your perceptions? What kinds of information did the talk provide? How did it differ from the information provided by nonverbal cues?

9. Do you agree with the statement that "a picture is worth a thousand words"? Why or why not? Are there circumstances in which a picture would not be as informative as a thousand words? Provide examples of those circumstances.

CHAPTER 11: INTERPERSONAL RELATIONSHIPS

1. We think the film *The Breakfast Club* is an excellent resource for analyzing interpersonal relationships. You might focus your analysis on how the characters' perceptions of one another change over the course of their time together in detention. Speculate as to whether or not their friendships will persist after detention. What stereotypes do they attribute to one another? In what ways do their nonverbal and verbal behaviors reinforce those stereotypes? Who changes the most over the course of the movie? Do you identify with any character in particular? Do any of those characters remind you of people you know? How did you get along with those people? How might others stereotype you? How do you think that stereotyping affected your relationship with others?

2. Find a film (big screen or small) that you think illustrates the stages of relational development, equilibrium, and dissolution. What kinds of communication behaviors characterize those stages? Some good films for this purpose with which we are familiar, for example, are *When Harry Met Sally, Annie Hall, John and Mary, The Big Chill, Diner, St. Elmo's Fire, Sleepless in Seattle, Pretty Woman, Waiter, There's a Girl In My Soup, The Way We Were,* and *The Sterile Cuckoo.*

3. I developed a close friendship with a person whom I intensely disliked at first meeting. Because this person was a friend of another dear friend of mine, I was forced to spend some time with this person. Over time I realized that I had misjudged them. Have you ever experienced a similar situation? What do you think accounted for your initial impression? What do you think prompted you to change that impression?

CHAPTER 12: GROUPS AND ORGANIZATIONS

1. Watch any episode of "Star Trek: The Next Generation" on TV and analyze the leadership style of Jean Luc Picard, the Captain of the

Starship Enterprise. How would you categorize his style? How close is his style to your conception of the "ideal" leader? Now describe the leadership styles of Captain Kirk on the original "Star Trek" and the Captain on "Star Trek: Deep Space Nine." How would you classify their styles? How do their styles differ from that of Picard's? Which leadership style is closer to your ideal?

2. Ask some of your friends and classmates to describe their vision of the communication style of the ideal leader. Compare the answers provided by males with those offered by females. Are there any differences?

3. Ted and one of his co-workers do not get along. Ted has a tendency to be cocky, and to think his ideas deserve more attention than he perceives they receive. As a result, Ted has had some conflict with his boss. His co-worker appears to be one of the boss's favorites. Actually, Ted thinks his co-worker "sucks up" to the boss and is therefore treated with favoritism. Ted thinks his boss is down on him because he doesn't play that game. Ted also believes that his co-worker is trying to "steal" one of his clients. One day he happens upon his co-worker having lunch with the client, who just happens to be a woman. Hoping to thwart his co-worker's attempt to steal his client, Ted goes back to the office and tells the "office gossip" that his co-worker is having an affair with one of the clients, a company "no no." Ted reasons that his boss will fire his co-worker for the infraction, and Ted will keep his client. His boss hears about the rumor and Ted's role in starting it, and pays Ted a visit.

   Pretend you are the boss. How would you handle this situation? (*Hint:* The client has heard the rumor and has threatened to withdraw her business entirely. Further, Ted's co-worker and the client went to school together and have maintained a long-term friendship, which includes occasional lunches.) Now put yourself in Ted's position. How might Ted have handled this situation more effectively?

4. Ask your friends and classmates to describe a positive group experience and a negative group experience. Ask them to explain why one group worked well while the other did not. Do you find similarities in their descriptions? Now ask them to identify problems typical of groups, and their suggestions for remedying those problems.

5. Interview one or more of your professors about their perceptions of the way information flows within your school. How are decisions made at your school? Do they feel that they are well informed? Do they participate directly in decision making? If so, at what level and to what extent? Is there a grapevine? If so, to what extent do they feel it is sufficient and accurate? Do they feel that they have direct access

to university administrators? What problems do they see with the organizational structure of the university? What solutions do they recommend?

6. Return to the project #6 outlined for Chapter 1. This could be a useful study of group decision making and conflict. You might want to consider this for a project on those aspects of the group process.

CHAPTER 13: MEDIATED COMMUNICATION

1. Keep a diary of your media use. When and what do you watch on television? Why did you watch what you did and when you did? Were you bored or procrastinating? Were you feeling stressed? Or were you actually interested in the particular program? When do you listen to the radio? Is your choice of music dependent upon the activity it will accompany? Are you a regular reader of newspapers? What section do you read first? Why? Do you discuss what you read/watch/hear with your friends? If other members of your class are keeping media diaries, exchange them and discuss the differences and similarities. How does your media use compare with that found by researchers and reported in this chapter?

2. How do you feel about violence on television, in films, and in video games? Are you a patron of such videos and films? Why? Which ones or types?

3. Compare newspaper and television news coverage of the same stories. In what respects do those reports differ? Which report did you believe? How did you decide?

4. Euphemisms are common in political speeches and news reports. Remember that a *euphemism* is the substitution of a pleasant word for an unpleasant one. The following examples are euphemisms: *collateral damage* means *dead civilians; aversion therapy* means *beatings in prison; downsizing* means *firing employees.*

    Choose newspaper accounts of a variety of stories, and find the euphemisms. Discuss how they bias the story and influence your feelings about the event. Then substitute the "real" meanings in place of the euphemisms. How does this change the impact of the story on the public?

5. You may be familiar with the old party game of rumor transmission: One person creates a story and whispers it to another person, and that person repeats the story to the next, and so forth. The last person to hear the story tells the group what they heard. Try this game,

and discuss how the message gets distorted as it moves from person to person. Then consider how this phenomenon can affect your ability to make a good decision. For example, how reliable is information you get from news sources? Consider that a news item travels through several human filters before it reaches you.

CHAPTER 14: COMMUNICATION AND CULTURE

1. Conduct your own survey of interracial and intercultural stereotypes. Ask some of your friends, family, and classmates to write short descriptions or list characteristics they attribute to those of other races and cultures. Are the descriptions similar across the people who participated? Can you detect whether they feel favorably or unfavorably toward the other races and cultures by examining the language they used in their descriptions? How accurate do you believe those descriptions to be?

2. Review the list of U.S. cultural norms. Do you personally subscribe to those norms? Interview other members of your class or your friends to find out if they agree with those norms.

3. Analyze television advertisements by applying the beliefs and values typical of American culture. For example, in what ways do ads appeal to our need for new and improved products? In what ways do ads appeal to our belief that progress will be achieved through the application of science and technology? In what ways do ads appeal to our sense of individuality?

4. Interview someone from another culture. Ask them what they believed about Americans before they arrived, how accurate those impressions turned out to be, and what communication problems and differences they encountered. Ask them to describe their own culture and to detail the expectations about communication behavior typical of their culture.

5. If you have been to another culture, describe it. In what ways was it different from the United States? In what ways were the people different? In what ways was their environment different? What communication difficulties did you encounter? How did you attempt to deal with those difficulties? With what degree of success?

6. Analyze cultural differences as presented in *The Gods Must Be Crazy* (parts I and II). Write down as many differences as you can. Can you place the cultures represented along the cultural dimensions discussed in the chapter?

7. Visit a museum and explore the displays of artifacts from other cultures and other periods in history. What image do they provide of that culture and of what that culture considered significant and important? What information do those artifacts reveal about that culture's beliefs, values, and lifestyle? Based on those artifacts, can you develop a story of the kind of lives those people lived?

8. We export American television throughout the world. For those who come to know Americans solely via television, what image do you suppose those of other cultures are building of us? What kind of people are we? What is important and significant to us? How do we spend our time? What styles of communication are appropriate, effective, and desirable? How realistic are these television portrayals?

THESES AND RESEARCH QUESTIONS

Research papers must contain a generic *thesis* or a generic *research question*. A thesis is not a research question, nor vice versa; they are alternative forms of expressing the central idea of a paper. A generic thesis is a single-sentence statement of whatever you intend to prove, demonstrate, or illustrate in the paper. It is the *point* of your paper. It is not a statement of purpose, unless the statement of purpose *contains* the thesis, as in the following form: "My purpose is to demonstrate the following thesis: . . . ". There is nothing wrong with having a statement of purpose, but it does not substitute for a thesis. A statement of purpose does not necessarily force one to focus the way a thesis does. One can write "My purpose is to discuss . . .", or "My purpose is to examine . . .," or "My purpose is to explore . . . ". We have had students wander off discussing, examining, and exploring, never to be heard from again.

A *generic* thesis is not a statement about the event being analyzed, if the paper uses some descriptive (e.g., critical analysis, content analysis, survey) methodology. Rather it is a statement of some alleged rhetorical/communication principle that your paper will prove, demonstrate, or illustrate by examining that particular event.

You can substitute a generic *research question* for the thesis. If you choose this option, the research question must be a sentence, in the form of a question, that makes specific what you want to find out about some suspected rhetorical/communication principle by doing the paper. Again, it will not be a question about the specific event being analyzed; it will be a question in which the specific event is never mentioned, but a question that can be answered, at least in part, by studying the specific event you have chosen.

A *series* of research questions is not satisfactory, either. The function of the thesis or research question is to prevent you from jumping on your horse, like the proverbial general, and riding off in all directions. A *series* of research questions still allows you to ride off in *several* directions, and that is not acceptable. Once you have stated a single central research question, however, it might be a good organizational device to ask several questions that are logically subservient to it that will, perhaps, serve as your major divisions.

We are so insistent about this approach because a thesis or research question performs at least three important functions for you and your professor(s). First, in a research proposal, it assures the professor(s) that you know in advance the point you are going to try to make or the question you are going to try to answer. It prevents them from approving a "fishing expedition," or at least it describes rather specifically the nature of the fish for which you will be searching.

Second, it forces you to clarify *for yourself* the point you want to make or the question you want to answer, and thus renders irrelevant, or at least tangential, a great deal of information and a great many sources that might otherwise clutter up your life. It becomes the touchstone by which to apply the relevance criterion, a beacon toward which to direct your struggles when you are otherwise drowning in a sea of facts, statistics, quotations, and references. Less metaphorically, it may save you a great deal of time.

Third, when you submit the finished product, the thesis or research question gives your professor(s) something against which to judge it, and a standard you will be aware of from the start. Your professor(s) will be asking: "Does this paper provide adequate proof, demonstration, or illustration of the thesis, or does it adequately answer the research question?"

The following examples are intended to illustrate the differences among generic theses, generic research questions, nongeneric theses and research questions, and statements of purpose. The original generic thesis is drawn from one of the better papers we have received:

Generic Thesis

"It is possible to analyze the cultural assumptions of a political public address in order to determine 'who' the politician feels his audience is."

Generic Research Question

"Is it possible to analyze the cultural assumptions of a political public address in order to determine 'who' the politician feels his audience is?"

Non-Generic Thesis

"The 'Checkers' speech of Richard Nixon reveals he had the following conception of the cultural assumptions of his audience: . . . ".

Non-Generic Research Question

"What does Richard Nixon's 'Checkers' speech reveal his conception of the cultural assumptions of his audience to have been?"

[The non-generic versions might interest historians, Nixon-lovers, and Nixon-haters, but, without further elaboration, the nongeneric versions are not of much interest to those trying to construct rhetorical/communication theories.]

Statement of Purpose

"It is the purpose of this paper to explore the relation between the cultural assumptions of audiences and those expressed in political public addresses delivered to those audiences."

[This statement of purpose could keep a researcher busy "exploring" for months. In fact, it is more likely that the researchers will do very shallow, disorganized, but expensive and time-consuming jobs of "exploring" and will return home very frustrated with little more than damaged egos to show for their trouble, or they will return to their professor(s) some time later and speak thusly: "What I really want to do is. . . ".

Copyrights and Acknowledgments

Gregory Bateson, Excerpts from *Steps to an Ecology of Mind* © 1972 Lippincott/Crowell. Published by Chandler Publishing Company.

D. Michele Hoover and Donna Potter, Sexual harassment scales used with permission of students.

I.L. Janis and L. Mann, A Schematic Balance Sheet Grid for Conceptualizing Decisional Conflict from *Decision Making: A Psychological Analysis of Conflict, Choice, and Commitment* © 1977. Published by Free Press, a division of Macmillan Publishing Company, Inc.

G. Marwell and D. Schmitt, Sixteen Compliance-Gaining Strategies from "Dimensions of Compliance-gaining Behavior: An Empirical Analysis" © 1967. Published by *Sociometry,* 30: 350–364. Public domain.

Neil Postman, Excerpts from *Amusing Ourselves to Death* © 1985 Neil Postman. Published by Viking Penguin, a division of Penguin Books USA, Inc.

Neil Postman, Excerpts from *Technopoly* © 1992 Neil Postman. Reprinted by permission of Alfred A. Knopf, Inc.

Todd Thomas, Letter from Cleve Thomas to Mary Fiest used with permission of Todd Thomas.

Index

A

Accents, nature of, 245
Accommodation, and dialects, 246
Adaptation, and environments, 5–6
Adaptors, gestures, 285–286
Ad hominem argument, 195
Advertising
 and body type associations, 279
 commercials and conditioning, 145–146
 image making in, 82–83
 relationship with media, 364–365
 and sex, 150–151
Advertising industry, beginning of, 60
AESOP model
 consequences in, 178–183
 entities in, 176–178
 plans in, 179, 183–185
 relationships in, 176–178
Affect blend, facial expression, 290
Affect displays, 285
Affective and Epistemological Schema of Perception. *See* AESOP model
Affect partials, facial expression, 290
Africans
 collectivist culture of, 377
 greeting behavior, 388

high-context culture of, 375–376
posture, meaning of, 389
Agenda setting, and media, 355
Aggression, and television viewing, 362
Alphabet, 57–58
 importance of, 57–58
 invention of, 57
Ambiguity, 194
Androgyny
 examples of, 128–129
 meaning of, 127
Animal communication
 elephants, 6
 genetic factors in, 48–49
 insects, 45–46
 nonverbal, 268
 primates, 27, 33, 46, 49–50
 symptomatic signs in, 23
 whales, 33–34
 wolves, 34
Apes, communication of, 33
Argument, Toulmin's model, 184
Aristotle, 80–81
Assertive language, 244
Associations, 230
Attitudes
 compared to beliefs, 167–168
 definition of, 154
 formation and ego-defense, 153–154
Attractiveness

changing norms, 280–281
 effects of, 279–280
 and relationship formation, 317
Attribution theory, 113–115
 and augmentation, 114
 and correspondence inference theory, 113
 and covariation, 114
 and discounting, 113–114
Augmentation, 114
Austin, Gilbert, 86
Authoritarianism, 120
Authoritarian leader, 338

B

Back-channeling, cultural differences, 389
Bacon, Francis, 85
Balance theory, 159–160
Behavioral theories,
 of language meaning, 226–227
Beliefs, 154–155
 American beliefs, 392–393
 compared to attitudes, 167–168
 classification of, 155
 cultural conflict about, 394–395
 definition of, 154
Bell, Alexander Graham, 65
Bem Sex-Role Inventory, 129–130
Berger, P. L., 91
Bias

types of linguistic bias, 241–242
 See also Sexist language
Black English, 247–248
 attitudes of white listeners toward, 247–248
 and education of black children, 248
Bleek, Wilhelm, 55
Blinking, 291
Body position
 gender differences, 285
 as nonverbal communication, 284–285
Body posture, 284–285
 cultural differences, 389
 and liking, 284–285
 and status, 284
Body type, 278–281
 and advertising, 279
 and climate, 281
 ectomorphic, 278
 endomorphic, 278, 281
 mesomorphic, 278
 and personality, 278–279
 thinness as ideal image, 279
Bormann, Ernest, 90
Bowers, John Waite, 89–90
Brain
 damage, effects of, 269–270
 hemispheres of, 269
Briefcase, 283
Bulwer, William Henry, 86
Bureaucracy, 329
Burke, Kenneth, 89

C

Campbell, George, 86
Causal schemata, 113
Cave drawings, 52–54
    African versus European, 54–55
    execution of, 53
    significance of, 53–54
    and writing, 54
Central processing, 187
Champollion, Jean Francois, 56
Change agents, 359
Chimpanzees, communication of, 27, 46, 50
Chinese
    collectivist culture of, 376–377
    greeting behavior, 388
Chomsky, Noam, 35, 88
Cicero, 81
Clarity, of language, 255–256
Classical conditioning, 144–145
    Pavlovian experiments, 145
    and TV commercials, 145
Classical era, rhetorical theory, 78–84
    Aristotle, 80–81
    Cicero, 81
    Corax, 78
    Isocrates, 82
    Plato, 79–80
    St. Augustine, 83–84
    Sophists, 82
Climate, and body type, 281
Closed-mindedness. *See* Dogmatism
Clothing, 281–283
    as cultural display, 282
    and first impressions, 282–283
    functions of, 281–282
    personal effects, types of, 283
    and trends, 284
Cognition
    and communication, 10–12
    definition of, 9
    and television viewing, 9–10
Cognitive dissonance theory, 162–165
    example of, 163–164
    and opinions, 165
Cognitive ecologies, 8–12
Cognitive theories, of language meaning, 227–231
Collectivist culture, 376–377
Color, effects of, 275
Comedy, as barrier to critical thinking, 188
Commercials, and conditioning, 145–146
Communication
    and cognition, 10–12
    and evolution of ideas, 35–38
    and gestures, 285
    and human communities, 403
    and human survival, 33–35
    messages, 22–26
    and self-image, 149–150
    signs in, 22
    stages of, 26
Communication anxiety
    causes of, 125
    measurement of, 125, 126
    and self-esteem, 125
    treatment of, 126
Communication behavior, and time, 276
Communication functions
    facilitation of cooperation, 29–31
    information gathering, 27–29
    reduction of conflict, 30–31
    self-actualization, 31–33
Communication styles
    contextual, 385–386
    direct and indirect, 382–384
    elaborated and restricted, 381–382
    exacting, 384
    listener-oriented, 386
    personal, 385
    sender-oriented, 386
    succinct, 384–385
Communication theory
    classical era, 78–84
    contemporary theory, 87–93
    developmental approaches, 95–97
    human interaction view, 94–95
    information theory, 92–93
    mechanistic view, 94
    Middle Ages, 84–85
    Renaissance, 85
    scientific perspective, 85–86
    semiotics, 95
    systems approach, 95
    Yale Studies, 92
    See also specific eras
Compliance, compliance-gaining strategies, 202–205
Computers, 61–63
    and information superhighways, 62–63
    uses of, 63
Conflict
    cultural, 394–397
    group, 339, 340
Conformity, and group decision making, 341
Consequences
    in AESOP model, 178–183
    Decisional Balance Sheet, 180–183
Consistency, 158–159
Constructivism, 95
Contemporary communication theory, 87–93
    rhetoric as knowledge, 90–91
    rhetoric as meaning, 88
    rhetoric as motive, 89–90
    rhetoric as value, 88–89
Contextual communication style, 385–386
Conversion phenomenon, opinions, 156–157
Cooperation, and communication, 29–31
Coordinated management of meaning, 95
Corax, 64, 78
Correspondence inference theory, 113
Cosmetics, 283
Covariation, 114
Credibility, 132–135
    as barrier to critical thinking, 187–188
    and dialects, 246
    factor-analytic approach, 132–134
    functional approach to, 134–135
    of reference person, 135–136
    study of, 86
    tests of testimony, 135
Critical decisions, basis of, 29
Critical thinking
    barriers to, 185–192
    and cultural literacy, 192–194
    importance of, 28–29
Critical thinking fallacies, 194–197
    ad hominem argument, 195
    ambiguity, 194
    appeal to authority, 194
    fallacious even if valid, 196
    hasty conclusion, 195
    irrelevant reason, 194
    provincialism, 194
    questionable analogy, 196

questionable cause, 195
questionable classification, 195
questionable premise, 196
slippery slope, 194
statistical fallacies, 197
suppressed evidence, 196
tokenism, 195
two wrongs making right, 195
Crystal, David, 245
Cultivation model, media, 360
Cultural conflict, 394–397
  about beliefs/values, 394–395
  and behavioral expectations, 397
  and cultural assumptions, 396
  ethnocentrism, 395
  priority conflicts, 395–396
Cultural evolution, 15
Cultural literacy
  and critical thinking, 192–194
  meaning of, 192
Cultural transmission, and media, 355–356
Culture
  beliefs/values of American culture, 392–394
  collectivist culture, 376–377
  concept of time, 276–277, 396
  cultural changes, 374
  definition of, 8, 374
  dimensions of cultural differences, 375–379
  high-context culture, 377–378
  and human rights, 404–405
  and ideas, 405
  individualistic culture, 376, 377

low-context culture, 377, 378
Culture and language
  communication styles, elaborate, 384
  contextual communication style, 385–386
  direct and indirect communication styles, 382–384
  elaborate communication style, 384
  elaborated and restricted codes, 381–382
  exacting communication style, 384
  and high-context cultures, 382, 386
  honorifics/titles/status, use of, 380–381
  instrumental communication style, 386
  intuition, use of, 386
  language and perception relationship, 379–380
  listener-oriented communication style, 386
  and low-context cultures, 381–382, 386
  personal communication style, 385
  sender-oriented communication style, 386
  succinct communication style, 384–385
Culture and nonverbal behavior, 387–392
  back-channeling, 389
  greeting behavior, 388
  head nods, 388
  OK gestures, 388–389
  personal space, 389–390
  subgroup differences, 390–391
  vocal characteristics, 389
Cuneiform, 56

D
Date rape, 297
Deception
  indicators of, 287, 294
  and nonverbal behavior, 271
  and speech, 294
Decisional Balance Sheet, 180–183
Decision making
  cognitive dissonance theory, 162–165
  critical decisions, 179–180, 185
  critical thinking barriers, 185–192
  group, 340–341
  and logical thinking, 165–167
Deductive knowledge, 86
Defense mechanisms, 151–152
  and attitude formation, 153–154
  functions of, 151
  types of, 151–152
Deferential language, 244
Democratic leader, 338
Denial, defense mechanism, 151
Desensitization, of phobias, 362
Developmental approaches, communication theory, 95–97
Dialects, 244–249
  and accommodation, 246
  Black English, 247–248
  effects of, 245–247
  geographic, effects of, 245–246
  Hispanic dialect, 249
  compared to language difference, 245
Dieter, 64
Direct communication style, 382, 383
Discounting, 113–114
Displacement, defense mechanism, 152

Dogmatism, 120–123, 158
  characteristics of dogmatic persons, 120–123
Dominance
  and assertive language, 244
  determination of, 47
  and gaze, 292
Double bind, and relationships, 324
Doublespeak, 237
  nature of, 236
Downward communication, organizations, 345
Drama, as barrier to critical thinking, 188
Dyadic dialectic, 324
Dyadic dialectics, and relationships, 324

E
Early humans
  cave drawings, 52–54
  fire, use of, 52
  interaction with environment, 272–273
  toolmaking of, 51–52
  upright walking of, 50–51, 268
  writing, 54, 55
Ecology
  cognitive ecologies, 8–12
  human effects on ecologies, 12–15
  nature of study, 3–4, 105
  physical ecologies, 4–6
  sociocultural ecologies, 6–8
Ectomorphic body type, 278
Ego-defense, 153–154
Ego-maintenance, 148–157
  defense mechanisms, 151–152
  ego-defense, 153–154
  ego-involvement, 154–158

Index 447

and self-image, 149–151
and value-expression, 149
Elaborate communication style, 384
Elaborated code, in language, 381
Elements of Rhetoric (Whately), 86
Elephants, communication of, 6
Emblems, gestures, 285
Emotional expressions, ecological analysis of, 266–267
Emotions
    affect displays, 285
    decoding of, 289–290
    expression of, gender differences, 289
    externalizers/internalizers, 289
    and eye behavior, 290–292
    and facial expression, 288, 289–290
    and voice, 293–294
Empathy
    and communication, 32
    meaning of, 116
    versus projection, 117–119
    and self-disclosure, 116–117, 118
Enacted self, 313
Endomorphic body type, 278, 281
Entertainment
    and media, 357
    news as, 366
    social interaction as, 33
Entities, in AESOP model, 176–178
Entropy, 93
Environment
    and adaptation, 5–6
    characteristics of, 4
    and early humans, 272–273

See also Modern environment
Eskimo language, 251, 380
Ethics, 407–408
    and communication behavior, 408
Ethnocentrism, 395
Euphemisms, nature of, 238
Evolution
    cultural, 15
    of humans, 50–52
    of ideas, 35–38, 173–175
    of primates, 45
Exacting communication style, 384
Externalizers, 289
Eye behavior
    blinking, 291
    and emotions, 290–292
    gaze, 290–293
Eye contact. *See* Gaze
Eyeglasses, 283

F
Face, saving face, 383
Facial expression, 286–293
    and emotions, 288, 289–290
    evolution of, 286–288
    gaze, 290–293
    management of, 288–289
    norms for, 288
    types of facial displays, 290
Factor-analysis, of credibility, 132–134
Faculties, 85–86
Fallacies. *See* Critical thinking fallacies
Fantasy themes, in communication, 90
Feelings of Inadequacy Scale, 124
Figurative language, 256–259
    metaphors, 257
Fire, and early humans, 52
First impressions, and clothing, 282–283

Formal networks, 344–346
Friendship, and touch, 297
Functional approach, leadership, 337
Furniture, effects of, 274–275

G
Gatekeepers, media-related, 359–360
Gaze, 290–293
    cultural differences, 389, 390
    functions of, 291–292
    gender differences, 293
    and personality, 292
    and status, 292
Gender differences
    body position, 285
    expression of emotion, 289
    gaze patterns, 293
    personal space, 299
General Semantics, 253–255
    indexing system, 253
    language and reality, 254–255
Gestalt theory, of person perception, 112
Gestures, 285–286
    categories of, 285
    communication function of, 285
Global village, 361
GOALS/GRASP Model, 106–109, 115
    relationship development, 315–316
Goffman, Erving, 91–92, 112, 118, 313
Grapevine, 346–347
Greeks, rhetorical theory, 78–82
Greeting behaviors, cultural differences, 388
Group decision making
    and conformity, 341
    groupthink, 340–341
    and private acceptance, 341

and public compliance, 341
Groups
    body position of members, 284
    composition of, 330–331
    conflict, 339, 340
    functions of, 137
    influences on group interaction, 338–340
    leadership, 337–338
    membership, reasons for, 331–333
    membership groups, 136–137
    needs fulfilled by, 332–333
    compared to organizations, 342
    phases in group interaction, 333–334
    reference groups, 136–137
    role categories, 337
    role transitions in, 334–336
    structure of, 336
    types of, 331
Groupthink, 340–341
Gutenberg press, 59

H
Hall, E. T., 92
Hard-wired behaviors, 48–49
Harlow, Harry, 31–32, 295
Head nods, cultural differences, 388
Hearst, William Randolph, 60
Hemispheres of brain, 269
Hieroglyphics, 56
High-context cultures, 376, 377–378
    and intuition, 386
    language in, 382, 386
Hispanics
    dialect, 249
    eye contact, 390

448 Index

Homes, rustic versus high-rise, 274
Homo erectus, 50, 51, 52
Homo habilis, 50, 51
Homo sapiens, 50, 51, 52
Honorific markers, in language, 380
Hopi language, 252–253, 379–380
Hovland, Carl, 92
Human interaction view, communication theory, 94–95
Human nature, American beliefs about, 393
Human rights, and culture, 405
Humans, evolution of, 50–52. *See* Early humans
Hypodermic-need theory, of media influence, 357

I

Ideas
 evolution of, 35–38, 173–175
 intracultural differences, 405
Identification with the aggressor, defense mechanism, 151
Illocutionary acts, 224–225
Illustrators, gestures, 285
Image making, in advertising, 82–83
Indexing system, General Semantics, 253
Indirect communication style, 382–383
Individualistic culture, 376, 377
Individual roles, in groups, 337
Inferred attributes, and person perception, 109–112
Informal networks, 346–347
Information gathering, 27–29

Information superhighway, 62–63
Information theory, 92–93
Innovation, 359
 stages in process, 359
Innovators
 change agents, 359
 types of, 359
Insects, communication of, 45–46
Instrumental communication style, 386
Intensity, of language, 259
Intention, and communication, 25–26
Interaction rituals, 118
Internal-External Locus of Control Scale, 126–127
Internalizers, 289
Internal mediating responses
 and language meaning, 230
 and opinion formation, 147
Intuition, and interpretation of others, 386
Intuitive knowledge, 86
Irrelevant reason, 194
Isocrates, 82

J

Janis, Irving, 92
Japanese
 honorifics in language, 380
 and status, 386

K

Kelley, Harold, 92
Kelley, Howard, 113
Kelly, George, 111
Knowledge
 forms of, 86
 rhetoric as knowing, 90–91
Koreans
 expressiveness of, 387
 nunchi, 386
 refusal methods of, 383

L

Laissez-faire leader, 338
Lakoff, Robin, 242–244, 395
Language
 clarity of, 255–256
 and culture. *See* Culture and language
 figurative, 256–257
 intensity of, 259
 morphemes, 218
 norms in, 214–215
 and perception, 251–253, 379–380
 phonemes, 217–218
 phonemic level, 217
 pragmatic level, 219–220
 principles of, 215–216
 rules of, 214, 216–217
 semantic level, 219–220
 sensory, 257–259
 syntactic rules, 218–219
 and thought, 251–255
Language Acquisition Device (LAD), 35
Language development, stages of, 26–27
Language meaning
 behavioral theories, 226–227
 cognitive theories, 227–231
 referential theories, 220–222
 rule-governed theories, 222–226
 triangle of meaning, 221
Lateral communication, organizations, 346
Lazersfeld, Paul, 91
Leadership, 337–338
 functional approach, 337
 situational approach, 338
 style approach, 338
 styles of, 338
 trait approach, 337
Learning

 classical conditioning, 144–145
 operant conditioning, 145–146
 of opinions, 146–148
Letter writing, 85
Lighting, effects of, 275
Linguistic relativity hypothesis, 251–253
Linotype, historical view, 59–60
Listener-oriented communication style, 386
Locus of control, 126–127
 and communication, 127
 meaning of, 126
 measurement of, 126–127
Logical thinking, and decision making, 165–167
Love, and touch, 297
Low-context cultures, 377, 378
 language in, 381–382, 386
Luckman, T., 91
Lying. *See* Deception

M

Machiavellianism, 123–124
 measurement of, 123
 types of, 123–124
McLuhan, Marshall, 88, 361
Magazines, historical view, 60
Maps, functions of, 77
Masochistic reactions, as defense mechanism, 152
Matching hypothesis, relationships, 317–318
Meaning, rhetoric as, 88
Mechanistic view, communication theory, 94
Media
 and communication flow, 359
 construction of reality, 363–364
 cultivation model, 360

Index

as economic force, 364
and entertainment, 366
functions of, 354–358
gatekeepers, 359–360
hypodermic-need theory, 357, 358
and innovation process, 359
media hegemony theory, 361
relationship with advertising, 364–365
spiral of silence theory, 361
See also Television
Membership groups, 136–137
Mesomorphic body type, 278
Messages, 22–26
intention versus nonintention, 25–26
semblances, 24–25
symbols, 25
symptoms, 22–23
Metaphors, 257
Micromomentary facial expressions, 290
Middle Ages, rhetorical theory in, 84–85
Middle Easterners, communication style, 384
Models, functions of, 77
Modern environment
color, 275
furniture/decor, 274–275
lighting, 275
noise, 276
rustic home versus high-rise, 274
temperature, 275–276
Modern rhetorical theory, 85–87
Morphemes, 218
Motive, rhetoric as, 89–90
Multiple selves, 313

N
National Association of Academic Teachers of Public Speaking, 87
Natural forces, influences of, 13–14
Naturalistic study, of communication, 96
Networks, organizational, 344–347
Newspapers, 59–60
historical view, 59–60
News reporting, media, 354
Noise, effects of, 276
Noncausal reasoning, as barrier to critical thinking, 185–187
Nonverbal behavior
and animals, 268
body posture, 284–285
and brain, 269
and culture. *See* Culture and nonverbal behavior
deception, indicators of, 287
facial expression, 286–293
functions of, 270–271
gestures, 285–286
and level of awareness, 267
nonverbal codes, types of, 270
personal effects, 283
personal space, 299–300
physical appearance, 279–283
territoriality, 298–299
touch, 295–298
voice, 293–295
See also Physical appearance
Nonverbal feedback, 267
Norms, and language, 214–215
Nuemann, John von, 61
Nunchi, 386

O
Obscenity, 259–261
Ochs, Donovan, 89–90
Official languages, political aspects, 249–250
On Christian Doctrine (St. Augustine), 84
Open-mindedness, 120, 122
Operant conditioning
process of, 145–146
and TV commercials, 146
vicarious conditioning, 146
Opinions
balance theory, 159–160
cognitive dissonance theory, 165
conformity and groups, 137
conversion phenomenon, 156–157
and latitudes of acceptance/noncommitment/rejection, 157
learning of, 146–148
Oral discourse, technologies related to, 64–65
Organizational communication
communication channels in, 343
downward communication, 345
external networks, 347
formal networks, 344–346
informal networks, 346–347
lateral communication, 346
networks, 344–345
Theory X and Theory Y, 343
upward communication, 345–346
Organizations
compared to groups, 342
nature of, 342
Osgood, Charles, 146–147

P
Paper, development of, 58
Paradox, and relationships, 324
Paranoid reactions, as defense mechanism, 152
Pavlov, Ivan, 145
Pentad, 89
Perceived similarity-attraction hypothesis, 318–319
Perception
and language, 251–253, 379–380
person perception, 109–116
of relationship, 313, 319–320
social perception, 106–116
Perelman, Chaim, 90
Peripheral processing, 187
Perlocutionary acts, 225
Personal communication style, 385
Personal construct theory, 95
and person perception, 111
Personal effects, 283
Personality
as barrier to critical thinking, 188
and body type, 278–279
and gaze, 292
Personality characteristics, 119–132
androgyny, 127–129
dogmatism, 120–123
locus of control, 126–127
Machiavellianism, 123–124
self-esteem, 124–126
Personal Report of Communication Anxiety, 125, 126
Personal space, 299–300
cultural differences, 389–390

gender differences, 299
interpersonal distance,
  299–300
Person perception
  attribution theory,
    113–115
  cyclical reassessment
    in, 115–116
  Gestalt theory of, 112
  GOALS/GRASP
    Model, 106–109, 115
  inferred attributes in,
    109–112
  and personal constructs, 111
  and personality characteristics, 119–132
  and prototypes,
    112–113
  and self-disclosure, 116
  self-presentation
    in, 112
Perspective, meaning
  of, 93
Persuasion, 197–201
  compliance-gaining
    strategies, 202–205
  and speeches, 198–201
Phenomenology, 91
Phonemes, 217–218
Phonemic level,
  language, 217
Photography, 65–66
  development, 66
Physical appearance
  attractiveness, importance of, 279–280
  body type, 278–281
  clothing, 281–283
  personal effects, 283
Physical ecologies, 4–6
Physical world,
  American beliefs
    about, 392–393
Pictographs, 52
Plato, 79–80
Politics, and language,
  249–250
Pony Express, 60
Pragmatic level, language,
  219–220

Preaching, 85
Prejudice, as defense
  mechanism, 153–154
Presuppositions, 228
Primates
  body position of, 284
  characteristics of, 45
  communication of, 27,
    33, 46, 49–50
  evolution of, 45
Principles, of language,
  215–216
Printing press, 58–59
Private acceptance,
  and group decision
    making, 341
Probabilities, logical thinking in, 165–167
Procedures, 229–230
Projection
  defense mechanism, 151
  versus empathy,
    117–119
Pronouns, sexist, 239–240
Propositions, cognitive approach to, 228
Prototypes, and person
  perception, 112–113
Provincialism, 194
Proxemics. See Personal
  space
Pseudo-events, and
  media, 355
Public compliance,
  and group decision
    making, 341
Publishing
  newspapers, 59–60
  and printing press, 59
Pueblo Indians, language
  use, 382, 383
Pulitzer, Joseph, 60

Q
Quintillian, 82

R
Radio
  functions of, 64
  short-wave radio, 64

Reaction formation, defense mechanism, 151
Redundancy, 93
Reference groups, 136–137
  versus membership
    groups, 136–137
Reference persons,
  characteristics of,
    135–136
Referential theories, 88
  of language meaning,
    220–222
  limitations of, 222
  triangle of meaning
    theory, 221
Refusal strategies, in
  language, 383
Regulators, gestures, 285
Relationships
  in AESOP model,
    176–178
  developmental stages,
    322–323
  dissolution of, 325–326
  equilibrium in, 323–324
  GOALS/GRASP
    Model, 315–316
  initial interactions,
    313–315
  interpersonal attraction, 315–319
  intricacies in, 324
  matching hypothesis,
    317–318
  perceived similarity-attraction hypothesis,
    318–319
  perception of relationship, 319–320
  reasons for development of, 320–321
  and self-perception,
    312–313
  social exchange theory,
    317–318
  uncertainty reduction
    theory, 314–315
Renaissance, rhetorical
  theory in, 85
Repression, defense mechanism, 151

Restricted code, in language, 382, 383
Rhetorical depiction, as
  barrier to critical
    thinking, 189–192
Rhetor Stone, 64
Richards, I. A., 88, 221
Rock drawings, 52–55
  See also Cave drawings
Roles
  of group members, 337
  role transitions and
    groups, 334–336
Romans, rhetorical
  theory, 81
Rosetta Stone, 56
Rule-governed theories
  of language meaning,
    222–226
  rule-use theory,
    223–224
  speech acts, rules of,
    224–225
Rules, of language, 214,
  216–217

S
St. Augustine, 83–84
Sapir-Whorf hypothesis,
  251–253
Saving face, 383
Scapegoating, defense
  mechanism, 152
Schemata
  causal schemata, 113
  nature of, 113
Scientific perspective, of
  rhetorical theory, 85–86
Selective exposure, 29
Selective perception, 29
Self-actualization
  and communication,
    31–33
  and self-image, 150
Self-concept, media influences on, 356–357
Self-disclosure, 116
  and empathy,
    116–117, 118
  and relationship development, 314

Self-esteem, 124–126
  and communication anxiety, 125
  measurement of, 124
Self-fulfilling prophesy, 280
  and relationships, 324
Self-image, 149–151
  and communication, 149–150
  ideal self-image, 149
  multiple selves, 313
  perceived self-image, 149
  true versus enacted self, 313
  and values, 155
Self-perception, and relationships, 312–313
Semantic anomalies, 220
Semantic level, language, 219–220
Semantic redeployment, nature of, 236–238
Semblances, 11, 24–25
  nature of, 11, 24–25, 268
  ritual semblances, 26
Semiotics, nature of study, 95
Sender-oriented communication style, 386
Sensory language, 257–259
Sexist language, 239–244
  and pronoun use, 239–240
  and word endings, 240–241
  and word *man*, 240
Sex-role stereotyping, 128–132
  examples of, 128–129
  measurement of, 129–132
  and media, 356
Sexual Equality eXam, 130–132
Shannon, Claude, 92
Sheridan, Thomas, 86
Sholes, Christopher Latham, 61

Signs, forms of, 22
Silence, meanings of, 295, 382, 390
Situational approach, leadership, 338
Skinner, B. F., 88, 94, 145, 226
Slippery slope, 194
Social Construction of Reality, The (Luckman), 91
Social control, and language, 383
Social exchange theory, relationship development, 317–318
Social groups, 331
Social isolation
  effects of, 31–32
  Harlow's experiments, 31–32, 295–296
Sociality, and communication, 45–48
Socialization process, 334–335
Social perception, 106–116
  inferred attributes about others, 109–116
  situational criteria for, 106–109
  See also Person perception
Social reality, and groups, 137
Social self, 313
Social structure, alterations of, 7–8
Social support, and groups, 137
Sociocultural ecologies, 6–8
Socrates, 79, 90
Songs, images of lyrics, 227–228
Sophists, 82, 86
Sour-grapes theory, 160–161
Speech acts, 224–225
  illocutionary acts, 224–225
  perlocutionary acts, 225
Speech Association of America, 87

Speech Communication Association, 87
Speeches
  introduction and conclusion of, 199–200
  organization of, 199, 200–201
  and persuasion, 198–201
Spirals
  progressive and regressive, 324–325
  and relationships, 324
Spiral of silence theory, media, 361
Stasis, 81
Statistical fallacies, 197
Status
  and body posture, 284
  cultural differences, 386
  and gaze, 292
  indicators in language, 380
  and voice, 295
Stereotyping, sex-roles, 128–132
Street talk, 238
Study groups, 331
Style approach, leadership, 338
Succinct communication style, 384–385
Sunglasses, 283
Supernatural, American beliefs about, 393
Syllabic writing, 57
Symbols, 11–12, 25
  functions of, 11–12, 25, 268
Symptoms, 11, 22–23
  nature of, 11, 22–23, 267–268
Syntactic rules, 218–219
System, nature of, 95
Systems approach, communication theory, 95

T
Tabloid shows, 366
Tag question, 242

Task-oriented groups, 331
  task roles in, 337
Telegraph, 60–61
Telephone, impact of, 65
Television
  and aggression, 362
  commercials and conditioning, 145–146
  conformity of characters portrayed, 365
  development of, 66–67
  and global village, 361
  impact on cognition, 9–10
  impact of, 67–69
  tabloid shows, 366
  televised speeches, 198–199
  and violence, 361–363
Temperature, effects of, 275–276
Territoriality, 298–299
  of humans, 12–13, 298–299
  territory, nature of, 299
Tests of testimony, 135
Theory, 77–78
  nature of, 77–78
Theory X organization, 343
Theory Y organization, 343
Thought and language
  General Semantics, 253–255
  linguistic relativity hypothesis, 251–253
Time
  and communication behavior, 276
  cross-cultural view, 276–277, 396
  development of clocks, 276
Titles, in language, 380
Tokenism, 195
Tools, and early humans, 51–52
Topics, 228
Touch, 295–298
  avoidance of, 297–298

conditions for touching, 297
cultural differences, 390
friendship-warmth touch, 297
functional-professional touch, 296–297
functions of, 296–297
lack of, and early development, 296
love-intimacy touch, 297
messages conveyed by, 298
social-polite touch, 297
Toulmin, Stephen, 90
Trait approach, leadership, 337
Typesetting, historical view, 59–60
Typewriter, invention of, 61

U
Uncertainty reduction theory, relationship development, 314–315
Unconscious, 152–153
Upright walking, of humans, 50–51, 268
Upward communication, organizations, 345–346

V
Value-expression, and self-identity, 149
Values
 of Americans, 394
 definition of, 154
 rhetoric as, 88–89
 and self-image, 155
Vicarious conditioning, 146
Violence, and television viewing, 361–363
Voice, 293–295
 cultural differences, 389
 and emotions, 293–294
 silence, use of, 295
 and status, 295
 vocal characteristics, interpretation of, 294
 vocal preferences, 294

W
Weaver, Warren, 92
Whales, communication of, 33–34
Whately, Richard, 86
Whistling languages, 6
Whorf, Benjamin Lee, 379–380
Willing suspension of critical analysis, 188–189
Wishful thinking, 166
Wolves, communication of, 34
Women's language, 242–244
 characteristics of, 242–243
 research on, 243–244
Writing
 alphabet, 57–58
 cuneiform, 56
 early humans, 54, 55
 hieroglyphics, 56
 newspapers/magazines, 59–60
 paper, development of, 58
 and printing press, 58–59
 syllabic writing, 57
 telegraph, 60–61
 and typewriter, 61

Y
Yale Studies, 92
Young, Thomas, 56

Z
Zworykin, Vladimir, 66